Springer Polar Sciences

Series Editor
James D. Ford, Priestley International Centre for Climate, University of Leeds, Leeds, West Yorkshire, UK

Editorial Board Members
Sean Desjardins, Groningen Institute of Archaeology, University of Groningen, Groningen, The Netherlands
Hajo Eicken, International Arctic Research Center, University of Alaska, Fairbanks, AK, USA
Marianne Falardeau-Cote, Université Laval, Québec, QC, Canada
Jen Jackson, British Antarctic Survey, Cambridge, UK
Tero Mustonen, University of Eastern Finland, Joensuu, Finland
Marina Nenasheva, Department of Philosophy and Sociology,
Northern Arctic Federal University, Arkhangelsk, The Arkhangelsk Area, Russia
Julia Olsen, Faculty of Social Sciences, Nord University, Bodø, Norway

This Series is now being indexed by SCOPUS.

Springer Polar Sciences is an interdisciplinary book series that is dedicated to research in the Arctic, sub-Arctic regions, and the Antarctic. In recent years, the polar regions have received increased scientific and public interest. Both the Arctic and Antarctic have been recognized as key regions in the regulation of the global climate, and polar ecosystems have been identified to be particularly susceptible to the ongoing environmental changes. These changes are having widespread implications for human communities, businesses, and governance systems and are interacting with demographic shifts, globalisation, resource development, cultural change, territorial disputes, and growing calls for self-determination in some regions. Consequently, the international efforts in polar research have been enhanced considerably, and a wealth of new findings is being produced at a growing rate by the international community of polar researchers and those who live in the region.

Springer Polar Sciences aims to present a broad platform that will include state-of-the-art research, bringing together both science, humanities, and perspectives rooted in indigenous and local knowledge to facilitate an exchange of knowledge between the various polar science communities. The series offers an outlet to publish contributions, monographs, edited works, conference proceedings, etc. Topics and perspectives will be broad and will include, but not be limited to, climate change impacts, climate change policy, environmental change, polar ecology, governance, health, economics, indigenous populations, tourism, resource extraction activities, and research design in polar regions. Books published in the series will appeal to scientists, students, polar researchers, community leaders, and policy makers.

Spencer Acadia
Editor

Library and Information Sciences in Arctic and Northern Studies

 Springer

Editor
Spencer Acadia 🆔
Research Methods and Information Science
University of Denver
Denver, CO, USA

ISSN 2510-0475   ISSN 2510-0483   (electronic)
Springer Polar Sciences
ISBN 978-3-031-54714-0   ISBN 978-3-031-54715-7   (eBook)
https://doi.org/10.1007/978-3-031-54715-7

This work was supported by Yosef Wosk Libraries, Museums, and Archives Fund (Canada).

© The Editor(s) (if applicable) and The Author(s), under exclusive license to Springer Nature Switzerland AG 2024
This work is subject to copyright. All rights are solely and exclusively licensed by the Publisher, whether the whole or part of the material is concerned, specifically the rights of translation, reprinting, reuse of illustrations, recitation, broadcasting, reproduction on microfilms or in any other physical way, and transmission or information storage and retrieval, electronic adaptation, computer software, or by similar or dissimilar methodology now known or hereafter developed.
The use of general descriptive names, registered names, trademarks, service marks, etc. in this publication does not imply, even in the absence of a specific statement, that such names are exempt from the relevant protective laws and regulations and therefore free for general use.
The publisher, the authors, and the editors are safe to assume that the advice and information in this book are believed to be true and accurate at the date of publication. Neither the publisher nor the authors or the editors give a warranty, expressed or implied, with respect to the material contained herein or for any errors or omissions that may have been made. The publisher remains neutral with regard to jurisdictional claims in published maps and institutional affiliations.

This Springer imprint is published by the registered company Springer Nature Switzerland AG
The registered company address is: Gewerbestrasse 11, 6330 Cham, Switzerland

If disposing of this product, please recycle the paper.

For the Arctic

Acknowledgments

Thank you to my dear friend and fellow scholar Marthe Tolnes Fjellestad who continues to support and inspire me. Much gratitude is given to Professor Yosef Wosk whose generous grant contribution encouraging this book helped it become a reality. In addition, thanks to all copyright holders, both individuals and institutions, granting permissions for their images to be included with this work.

Many thanks are due to all authors who contributed a chapter to this book. Without the dedicated effort and patience of all contributors, this book could not have happened.

Denver, Colorado, USA   Spencer Acadia

Contents

1 Introduction: Connecting LIS to Arctic and Northern Studies 1
Spencer Acadia

2 The Polar Libraries Colloquy 9
Sandra M. Campbell, Cecilie Tang Møldrup, and Susanna Parikka

3 The Decolonization of Arctic Library and Archives Metadata (DALAM) Thematic Network at the University of the Arctic 25
Sharon Farnel, Sandra M. Campbell, David Cox II, Lars Iselid, Peter Lund, Susanna Parikka, Sharon Rankin, Ivar Stokkeland, and Päivi Wendelius

4 Polar Correspondence in an English City: The Scott Polar Research Institute Library 41
Katie Hill, Peter Lund, and Naomi Boneham

5 A Review of the Culturally Responsive Guidelines of Alaska Public Libraries 67
Erin Hollingsworth and Tyson Rinio

6 The Liquid Arctic and Digitalization 85
Spencer Acadia

7 The Limits of Everyday Digitalization in the Arctic: A Digital Security Perspective 151
Mirva Salminen and Laurence Morris

8 Polar Research Data Management: Understanding Technical Implementation and Policy Decisions in the Era of FAIR Data 175
Gregory Vey, Wesley Van Wychen, Chantelle Verhey, Peter Pulsifer, and Ellsworth LeDrew

9 **Tracking and Unlocking the Past: Documentation of Arctic Indigenous Languages** 191
Lenore A. Grenoble and Vanda B. Ignatieva

10 **Enhancing Digital Libraries through Digital Storytelling: The Case of the Inuvialuit Digital Library**..................... 209
Sharon Farnel, Ali Shiri, Ethel-Jean Gruben, Beverly Siliuyaq Amos, and Lena Kotokak

11 **Digital Humanities of the North: Open Access to Research Data for Multiple User Groups**.................... 227
Erich Kasten

12 **Selected Sources of Information about the History of Exploration of the Arctic Region from the Collection of the Siberian Federal University Scientific Library**............. 241
Elena N. Kasyanchuk, Valentina A. Koreshkova, Olga I. Babina, Irina A. Tsvetichkina, and Ruslan A. Baryshev

13 **A Descriptive Review of Research Studies by the Central Libraries of the Far Northern Regions of the Northwestern, Ural, and Siberian Federal Districts and the Far Eastern Federal District During 2017–2020** 259
Alesia G. Kuznetsova

14 **The Irish Impact: Charting a Course for the Development of Historical Arctic and Northern Studies on the Island of Ireland** 277
Sarah Milne and Chelsi Slotten

15 **Part I: Library and Archives Engagement and Outreach Programs Using Sources from the Arctic and Northern Regions**..................................... 319
Christena McKillop, Nadine Hoffman, and Regina Landwehr

16 **Part II: Using Arctic and Northern Sources for Information and Archival Literacy and Research**............. 343
Nadine Hoffman, Christena McKillop, and Regina Landwehr

About the Contributors

Spencer Acadia holds a PhD in sociology, an MA in psychology, and an MLS. Currently, Spencer is an Assistant Professor in the LIS program for the Research Methods and Information Science department at the University of Denver. Spencer teaches courses in social sciences research methods, academic librarianship, collection development and management, and global LIS research and practice. Previously, Spencer spent ten years as an academic librarian. Spencer is co-editor of the book *Library and Information Studies for Arctic Social Sciences and Humanities* published by Routledge in 2020. From 2012 to 2022, Spencer was active in the International Federation of Library Associations (IFLA), serving in a variety of leadership positions, and also organized a conference session at the 2017 International Arctic Social Science Association conference in Umeå (ICASS-IX). One of Spencer's research interests is LIS in, for, and about Arctic and Northern studies. Learn more about Spencer's work at: https://www.spenceracadia.com/.

Beverly Siliuyaq Amos is an Inuvialuk from the Inuvialuit Region who was raised in Sachs Harbour, Banks Island, Canada, the most northerly and isolated village in the Western Arctic. She speaks the ancient coastal dialect of Sallirmiutun which she acquired from her parents and elders. She has been an Inuvialuktun translator and advocate for over 30 years keeping language and cultural issues at the forefront so that they are not forgotten. She is involved with initiatives that document, revitalize, promote, and celebrate Inuvialuktun. Her upbringing which included the old ways of thinking, doing, and believing has paved a pathway of lifelong passion and commitment to promote and share Inuvialuit knowledge with the next generation as the ancestors have done for generations before us.

Olga I. Babina is Assistant Vice-Rector for Research, Siberian Federal University in Krasnoyarsk. Author of more than 70 educational and scientific works, Olga's research interests include library and information sciences, information technology, informatization of education, and personnel management.

Ruslan A. Baryshev holds a PhD in philosophy (Candidate of Science in Philosophy) and is the current Vice-Rector for Research, Siberian Federal University in Krasnoyarsk. With over 100 published educational and scientific works, Ruslan's research interests are in library and information sciences, information technology, informatization of education, and intellectual property.

Naomi Boneham is an Archivist at the Scott Polar Research Institute (SPRI). Naomi was project manager for the JISC-funded *Freeze Frame – Historic Polar Images* project and has overseen the transfer of the archives catalogues from various paper records to a digital collections management system. The SPRI Archives provides an opportunity to combine her interest in cataloguing theory with the ability to remain in daily contact with researchers. Naomi worked in County Record Offices on a variety of projects before joining SPRI in 2006.

Sandra M. (Sandy) Campbell is Emerita Librarian at the University of Alberta Library in Edmonton, Canada. Most recently, Sandy was a public services librarian at the John W. Scott Health Sciences Library. Sandy is a member of the Polar Libraries Colloquy (PLC), serving as the PLC liaison to the University of the Arctic (UArctic). She is also the Secretary of the UArctic thematic network Decolonization of Arctic Library and Archives Metadata (DALAM). Sandy has published and presented nationally and internationally on polar information, information literacy, health librarianship, and systematic reviewing.

David Cox II is an Associate Professor and Technical Services Librarian at the William A. Egan Library at the University of Alaska Southeast in Juneau. Much of his time is spent working with the library's Cyril George Indigenous Knowledge Collection, including enhancing it with grants and university initiative funds. His recent work involves adapting the Brian Deer Classification System for the Egan Library and leading review of the materials to reclassify them. He is a member of the Alaska Native Subject Headings Grant Project team.

Sharon Farnel (MLIS, PhD) is a settler born and raised in the land now known as Canada. She lives, works, and studies in Amiskwacîwâskahikan (Beaver Hills House), also known as Edmonton, located in Treaty 6 and Metis Territory. She is currently Head, Metadata Strategies at the University of Alberta Library and co-lead of the University of the Arctic thematic network on Decolonization of Arctic Library and Archives Metadata (DALAM). She is an active participant in the library's decolonizing description initiatives, and, since 2014, has been working with community collaborators in the Inuvialuit Settlement Region in the northwest Arctic region in Canada on community-driven, culturally responsive knowledge organization and resource description for their digital library. Current efforts are focused on the development and implementation of real-time digital storytelling functionality for the digital library through the *Inuvialuit Voices* project. She is passionate about working with communities to understand how we can unsettle our practices and find better ways forward together.

About the Contributors

Lenore A. Grenoble is the John Matthews Manly Distinguished Service Professor in the Department of Linguistics at the University of Chicago and Director of the Arctic Linguistic Ecology Lab at the M. K. Ammosov North-Eastern Federal University in Yakutsk, Russia, specializing in Slavic and Arctic Indigenous languages. Her research focuses on language contact and shift, vitality and sustainability, documentation, and revitalization. Her primary fieldwork engages with speakers in far Northeastern Russia, Siberia, and Greenland. She is currently engaged in a major project that brings together linguistic, sociolinguistic, and psycholinguistic factors in contact-induced morphosyntactic change and shift, together with a study of the relationship of climate change, urbanization, language vitality, and well-being in Arctic Indigenous communities.

Ethel-Jean Gruben is Manager of Inuvialuit Cultural Centre Pitquhiit-Pitqusiit in Inuvik, Northwest Territories, Canada.

Katie Hill has researched human-environment relationships in relation to aesthetics and epistemology in the sub-Arctic since 2009. Her research is enhanced by her library work.

Nadine Hoffman holds a BA from the University of Calgary and an MLIS from the University of Alberta. A librarian at the University of Calgary since 2002, Nadine is the Natural Resources, Energy, & Environmental Law and History Librarian with responsibility for area studies including Northern Studies. Her chapter "Controlled Vocabulary and Indigenous Terminology in Canadian Arctic Legal Research" from the book *Library and Information Studies for Arctic Social Sciences and Humanities* was awarded the Michael Silverstein Prize from the Canadian Association of Law Libraries in June 2020, as well as the University of Calgary Teaching Award for Libraries and Cultural Resources in June 2021. Nadine's research interests include legal research, embedded librarianship, search terminology, teaching with primary sources, interdisciplinary library services, and legislative research.

Erin Hollingsworth holds an MLIS, First Nations concentration from the iSchool at the University of British Columbia, and an MEd from the University of Montana. She has experience working in tribal, academic, public, and K–12 libraries in Montana, Canada, and Alaska. Her research interests include the cross-cultural exchange of information, especially in the formal settings of schools and libraries. Currently, she is District Librarian for the North Slope Borough School District, the northernmost and largest school district in the United States, where she is responsible for overseeing the operation of the 11 libraries spread across eight Arctic Alaskan Bush villages. She is also active with the Alaska Library Association as a past president, as well as the American Indian Library Association where she has served as a member of the American Indian Youth Literature Award jury. She is a past ALA Emerging Leader and participant of the Pacific Northwest Library Association LEADS initiative.

xiv

Vanda B. Ignatieva is a leading researcher at the Institute of Humanitarian Research and the Problems of Small Peoples of the North, Yakutsk Research Center of the Siberian Branch of the Russian Academy of Sciences, and at the Arctic Linguistic Ecology Laboratory, M. K. Ammosov North-Eastern Federal University in Yakutsk. She deals with the identity and lifestyles of Indigenous peoples and the transformation of local and spatial cultures in the process of modernization. Her current research concerns the evolution of climate, economy, and culture of the Republic of Sakha (Yakutia), as well as study of its intellectual landscape and the biographies of Sakha intellectuals of the early twentieth century.

Lars Iselid is a librarian at the Umeå University Library in Sweden. He works with discovery systems, metadata, and cataloguing of books with special references to romance languages, preferably French. He also has a long experience of the library industry as a speaker, teacher, consultant, and writer, and worked both for private industry and as self-employed. He also teaches, since more than 20 years ago, at the Library and Information Science Programme at Umeå University.

Erich Kasten (Dr. Phil.) studied social and cultural anthropology and taught at the Free University of Berlin. He has conducted extensive field research in the Canadian Pacific Northwest and Kamchatka and has curated international museum exhibitions. As the first coordinator of the Siberian research group at the Max Planck Institute for Social Anthropology in Halle, he studied transformations in post-Soviet Siberia. In ensuing projects for UNESCO and the National Science Foundation, he documented and analyzed Indigenous knowledge. Since 2010, Erich has been the director of Kulturstiftung Sibirien gGmbH [Foundation for Siberian Cultures] in Fürstenberg/Havel (Germany) and of its publishing house, where he is the co-editor with Igor Krupnik and Gail Fondahl of the newly established series *A Fractured North*. He is an associated researcher and partner of various academic institutions such as the Cultures, Environment, Arctic, Representations, and Climate (CEARC) research center at the University of Versailles-St. Quentin and the Hokkaido Museum of Northern Peoples. Since 2019, he has launched several websites: dh-north.org, ek-north.org, and mu-north.org (in preparation) with the purpose of encouraging discourses with local communities on Indigenous knowledge for sustaining the cultural heritage of the peoples of the North. Currently, he is developing interactive websites on museum collections in collaboration with museums and Indigenous communities in the North. More about Erich can be found at https://dh-north.org/dossiers/erich-kasten/en.

Elena N. Kasyanchuk holds a PhD in cultural studies (Candidate of Culturology) and is current Director, Siberian Federal University Scientific Library in Krasnoyarsk. Elena's research interests are in library and information sciences and cultural studies, publishing more than 25 scientific works to date.

Valentina A. Koreshkova is Head of the Methodical Sector, Scientific Library, Siberian Federal University in Krasnoyarsk, Russia.

Lena Kotokak is a Regional Language Coordinator with the Inuvialuit Cultural Centre Pitquhiit-Pitqusiit in Inuvik, Northwest Territories, Canada.

Alesia G. Kuznetsova received a master's degree in 2017 from the St. Petersburg State Institute of Culture. Currently, Alesia is a researcher at the National Library of Russia, Department of Science and Methodology, Sector of Library Management, specializing in central libraries of Russian regions.

Regina Landwehr is Archivist Emerita and retired Director of Archival Operations for Archives and Special Collections at the University of Calgary, a position held from 2020 to 2022. While at the University of Calgary since 2005, she fostered the development of teaching and research opportunities using archival collections. Previously, she was a professional archivist in several municipal and community archives in western Canada and the records management analyst for the University of Victoria in British Columbia. She holds a BSc (Honors) in archaeology from the University of Calgary, a MAS from the University of British Columbia, and a Practicing NAAB Appraiser (PNA) Certificate from the Canadian National Archival Appraisal Board (NAAB). Regina received the 2023 Alan D. Ridge Award of Merit from the Alberta Society of Archivists for her chapter "An archival Odyssey: The CBC Records in the John P. L. Roberts Fonds," as well as several grants including a Killam Research and Scholarship Leave Fellowship grant and a Social Sciences and Humanities Research Council (SSHRC) grant.

Ellsworth LeDrew is a Professor in the Department of Geography and Environmental Management at the University of Waterloo. He was appointed University Professor in 2009 and Distinguished Professor Emeritus in 2018. He is a Fellow of the Institute of Electrical and Electronic Engineers, Fellow of the Canadian Aeronautics and Space Institute, and Fellow of the Royal Canadian Geographical Society. In 2005, he was awarded the Gold Medal by the Canadian Remote Sensing Society. He has served on the NSERC Earth-Sciences grant selection committee from 1988 to 1991, chairing the committee from 1990 to 1991, and was a member of the NSERC Committee for Special Initiatives and Programs from 1994 to 1998. He has also served as Vice-President of the Canadian Remote Sensing Society from 1997 to 1998, and President from 1999 to 2001.

Peter Lund leads the Polar Library and Archives service at the Scott Polar Research Institute, University of Cambridge. Since taking up this position in 2015, he has managed *By Endurance we Conquer – the Shackleton Project*, which was awarded funding from the UK's National Lottery Heritage Fund, and a project to migrate the library's catalogue into the University of Cambridge's library management system. Peter is currently working to decolonize the library's subject headings and other metadata. In previous academic liaison and research support roles at the University of Canterbury in Christchurch, New Zealand, Peter led teams of subject librarians in the aftermath of the 2010–2011 Christchurch earthquakes.

Christena McKillop is a librarian at the University of Calgary. She is the librarian for the Department of English. In 2020, she took on the Interim Associate University Librarian role for Archives and Special Collections until 2022. From 2018 to 2020, she was the learning, engagement, and outreach librarian in the Archives and Special Collections. Previously, she was the director of the Education Library at the Faculty of Education at Western University from 2002–2017. Throughout her career, she has worked closely with faculty and students to provide library and research support. Her research interests include student learning, information literacy, and primary source literacy. She holds a BA from University of Toronto and an MLIS from Western University.

Sarah Milne is a Senior Maritime Researcher at the Halpin Centre for Research and Innovation at the National Maritime College of Ireland, which is part of the Munster Technology University campus. As of 2020, she holds a PhD in Arctic politics and regional security from the University of Limerick, Ireland, and received an MA in Russian and East European studies from the University of Birmingham in 2010. Her current role as a researcher at the Halpin Centre involves working full-time on the Horizon Europe-funded project *Artificial Intelligence-Based Virtual Control Room for the Arctic* (www.ai-arc.eu). Sarah currently is Chair of the Humanities and Social Science Working Group for the Network of Arctic Researchers Ireland and has a broad range of research interests including but not limited to Arctic safety and security, Arctic politics and governance, science and technology studies, international relations, cultural diplomacy, and Irish heritage studies.

Cecilie Tang Møldrup is the librarian at the Polar Library, University of Copenhagen. She has a master's degree in history, as well as Greenlandic and Arctic studies, from the University of Copenhagen. She is a co-host of the popular festival, *Arctic Days*, in Copenhagen. In addition, she is a member of the Steering Committee of the Polar Libraries Colloquy and co-editor of the *Polar Libraries Bulletin*.

Laurence Morris is Academic Skills Development Manager with Leeds Beckett University in the UK, a Senior Fellow of Advance HE, Fellow of the UK's Royal Geographical Society, and an Associate of Leeds Beckett's Centre for Learning and Teaching. He is also a published poet and experienced mountaineer.

Susanna Parikka works as Library Director at Lapland University Consortium (LUC) Library in Rovaniemi, Finland since 2010. Susanna has a master's degree in library and information science from Åbo Akademi University, the only Swedish-language multidisciplinary university in Finland. She is active in Nordic library co-operation as a founding member of the Nordic Association of University Administrators (NUAS) Library Group. She is also the chair of Polar Libraries Colloquy Steering Committee and co-editor of the *Polar Libraries Bulletin*.

About the Contributors

Peter Pulsifer is an Associate Professor with the Department of Geography and Environmental Studies at Carleton University. As a specialist in geomatics and cartography, Peter's research addresses questions related to the use of geographic information with a particular focus on supporting interoperability; that is, the ability of (geographic) information systems to readily share information and operations. Since 2006, Peter's research has focused on partnering to address priority issues of Inuit and other Indigenous Peoples of the Arctic (i.e., Gwich'in, Yup'ik, and Saami). Currently, Peter is the co-lead of the Canadian Consortium for Arctic Data Interoperability and outgoing Chair of the IASC-SAON Arctic Data Committee.

Sharon Rankin is an academic librarian at McGill University Library in Montréal, with research interest in periodicals published by or about Inuit communities across Canada.

Tyson Rinio is Associate Professor of Library Science and Off-Campus Services Librarian at the University of Alaska Fairbanks. He was born and raised in Fairbanks and received his library degree from the University of Arizona, Knowledge River Program in 2003. His research interests are in Indigenous libraries and librarianship and library collection preservation.

Mirva Salminen is Assistant Professor of Societal Security at UiT – the Arctic University of Norway, as well as Project Specialist at Aalto University in Finland and Visiting Senior Researcher at the Arctic Centre, University of Lapland. Her research focuses on the different aspects of cyber security.

Ali Shiri is a Professor in the School of Library and Information Studies at the University of Alberta and currently serving as Vice Dean of the Faculty of Graduate Studies and Research. He received his PhD in information science from the University of Strathclyde, Department of Computer and Information Sciences in Glasgow, Scotland in 2004. Over the past two decades, Ali has taught, researched, and wrote about digital libraries and digital information interaction, knowledge organization, and data and learning analytics. In his current research, funded by the Social Sciences and Humanities Research Council of Canada, he is developing cultural heritage digital libraries and digital storytelling systems for the Inuvialuit communities in the Northwest Territories in Canada's Western Arctic.

Chelsi Slotten is a Product Manager at Sage Publications. She holds a PhD in anthropology from American University. Her PhD work focuses on how gender impacts lived experiences and identity formation during the Viking Age. She also holds an MSc in Palaeopathology from Durham University. Chelsi is a member of the Humanities and Social Science Working Group for the Network of Arctic Researchers Ireland (NARI) and previously worked at the Arctic Studies Center at the Smithsonian National Museum of Natural History in Washington, DC. She is dedicated to increasing public scholarship through her work as cohost on the *Women in Archaeology* podcast.

Ivar Stokkeland is head of the Polar Library at the Norwegian Polar Institute in Tromsø where he has been working for more than 20 years.

Irina A. Tsvetichkina holds a PhD in history (Candidate of Sciences in History) and is currently Associate Professor, Institute of Business Process Management, Siberian Federal University in Krasnoyarsk. Authoring more than 30 scientific works to date, Irina's research interests are in library and information sciences, personnel management, and digital technologies in education.

Wesley Van Wychen is an Assistant Professor in the Department of Geography and Environmental Management at the University of Waterloo. His research interests include remote sensing, glaciology, Arctic climate, and polar data management and data rescue. Prior to becoming a faculty member, he was Associate Director of the Canadian Cryospheric Information Network and Polar Data Catalogue at the University of Waterloo.

Chantelle Verhey is both a Data Specialist at the Polar Data Catalogue and a Research Associate for the World Data System-International Technology Office hosted at Ocean Networks Canada. She has a Master of Science degree in environmental management from the University of Reading in the UK and is currently enrolled as a PhD student at Carleton University. Chantelle is presently combining her research and work experience to enhance data interoperability within the polar scientific community through the use of semantic technologies.

Gregory Vey is Director of Research Data Strategy for the Waterloo Climate Institute, as well as Adjunct Assistant Professor in the Department of Geography and Environmental Management at the University of Waterloo. His role involves the strategic planning of data architecture and infrastructure with particular attention to data discovery and interoperability. He also oversees operations for the Canadian Cryospheric Information Network and Polar Data Catalogue.

Päivi Wendelius is a cataloguing librarian at the Oulu University Library in Finland. She works in the Information Resource Services department with a particular focus on the Saami collection.

List of Figures

Fig. 4.1 The Scott Polar Research Institute at the University
of Cambridge. (Photo credit: SPRI) 45

Fig. 4.2 A table of meteorological data from the Terra Nova
Expedition of 1910–1913 as published
in *Meteorological Journal*. (Photo credit: SPRI) 47

Fig. 4.3 First-floor interior of the original SPRI building, 1948.
(Photo credit: SPRI) 49

Fig. 4.4 Rotunda staircase connecting SPRI's three floors.
(Photo credit: SPRI) 52

Fig. 5.1 Map of Alaska showing the location of the North Slope
Borough. (Map credit: M. T. Fjellestad via openstreetmap.org,
2023. CC BY-SA 2.0) 75

Fig. 5.2 Map of North Slope Borough showing the location
of the seven remote villages where the school libraries
serve as community public libraries, as well as the borough
seat of Utqiaġvik. (Map credit: M. T. Fjellestad via
openstreetmap.org, 2023. CC BY-SA 2.0) 75

Fig. 5.3 *Arctic Odyssey* mural at Tuzzy Consortium Library.
(Mural created by Annie Patterson. Photo credit:
E. Hollingsworth) 76

Fig. 8.1 Example of an entity-relationship (ER) diagram modelled
from metadata tables at the Polar Data Catalogue.
(Screenshot credit: G. Vey) 181

Fig. 8.2 Example of JSON-LD metadata topology using
a metadata record at the Polar Data Catalogue.
(Screenshot credit: G. Vey) 185

Fig. 9.1	*Russko-jakutsko-tungusskij slovar'* [The Russian-Sakha-Tungus Dictionary] written by P. V. Sleptsov in 1908. Figure credit: Manuscript Department of the Institute for Humanities Research and Indigenous Studies of the North, Siberian Branch of Russian Academy of Sciences. Funds No. 5, inventory 3, matter 298, sheet 29	201
Fig. 9.2	*Aiyyhyt algyha* [Good Wishes of Aiyyhyt] recorded by A. A. Savvin in 1938. Figure credit: Manuscript Department of the Institute for Humanities Research and Indigenous Studies of the North, Siberian Branch of Russian Academy of Sciences. Funds No. 5, inventory 3, matter 101, sheet 6	202
Fig. 9.3	*Tanceval'nye vozglasy kolymskix evenov* [Dancing Shouts of the Kolyma Even] recorded by G. N. Tretyakov in 1940. Figure credit: Manuscript Department of the Institute for Humanities Research and Indigenous Studies of the North, Siberian Branch of Russian Academy of Sciences. Funds No. 5, inventory 3, matter 442, sheet 4	203
Fig. 9.4	(**a**) Word sample in Russian from the Russko-Ustinsky region. The word *veret'e* was recorded by G. A. Shub, N. A. Gabyshev, et al. in 1946. Figure credit: Manuscript Department of the Institute for Humanities Research and Indigenous Studies of the North, Siberian Branch of Russian Academy of Sciences. Fund No. 5, inventory 3, matter 7668, sheet 400. (**b**) Word sample in Russian from the Russko-Ustinsky region. The word *jakša* was recorded by G. A. Shub, N. A. Gabyshev, et al. in 1946. Figure credit: Manuscript Department of the Institute for Humanities Research and Indigenous Studies of the North, Siberian Branch of Russian Academy of Sciences. Fund No. 5, inventory 3, matter 7668, sheet 407	205
Fig. 10.1	Map of the Inuvialuit Settlement Region (ISR), Canada. (Map credit: Joint Secretariat)	211
Fig. 10.2	Photograph of the Inuvialuit Cultural Centre Pitquhiit-Pitqusiit (ICRC) in Inuvik. (Photo credit: A. Shiri)	213
Fig. 10.3	Screenshot of the Inuvialuit Digital Library (IDL) homepage, 2021. (Screenshot credit: A. Shiri)	214
Fig. 10.4	The *Inuvialuit Voices* team at lunch in Edmonton, Alberta, Canada. (Photo credit: A. Shiri)	216
Fig. 11.1	Use of the FSC's digital learning tools during a school class in Lesnaya, Kamchatka, Russia in 2012. (Photo credit: E. Kasten)	229
Fig. 11.2	Map with documented languages presented on or in preparation for the Digital Humanities of the North website. (Map credit: Kulturstiftung Sibirien)	231

List of Figures xxi

Fig. 11.3 Video seminar in Kazym, Western Siberia with,
from left to right, Stephan Dudeck, Tat'iana Liubavina,
and Anastasiia Brusnitsina, 2021. (Photo credit:
E. Fedotova and S. Dudeck)... 232

Fig. 11.4 Alyona Khabarovskaia comments on an Even old garment
during a seminar in Yakutsk, Russia in 2019.
(Video still credit: E. Kasten)... 236

Fig. 11.5 Lydiia Chechulina comments on a Koryak festive garment
from 1900 during a workshop at the FSC, 2020.
(Video still credit: E. Kasten)... 237

Fig. 11.6 Koryak fur coat made and worn by Tamara Khupkhi
in Tilichiki, Kamchatka, Russia in 2002.
(Photo credit: E. Kasten)... 237

Fig. 12.1 Map of Russia showing Krasnoyarsk Territory
and the cities of Krasnoyarsk and Norlisk in Russia.
(Map credit: Yu. Afanas'eva and SibFU Scientific Library) 243

Fig. 12.2 Book cover of *Narody Sibiri* [Peoples of Siberia], 1956 edition,
edited by M. G. Levin and L. P. Potapov, published
by the Publishing House of the USSR Academy of Sciences.
(Image credit: SibFU Scientific Library) 248

Fig. 12.3 Page 22 of *Narody Sibiri* [Peoples of Siberia] (1956).
The four images depict leather processing, including
scraping the mezdra with nails, scraping the mezdra
with a hook, kneading the leather, and cutting out the skin
on the ground. Published by the Archive of the Museum
of Anthropology and Ethnography of the USSR Academy
of Sciences. (Image credit: SibFU Scientific Library)..................... 249

Fig. 12.4 Title page of the book *Uraangkhai Sakhalar: Ocherki drevnej
istorii yakutov* [Uraangkhai – Sakhalar: Essays on the Ancient
History of the Yakuts] (1937) by G. V. Ksenofontov,
published by East Siberian Regional Publishing House.
(Image credit: SibFU Scientific Library) 251

Fig. 12.5 Journal cover of *Sibirskaja Zhivaja Starina*
[Siberian Living Starina] (1929), published by the Russian
Geographical Society, East Siberian Department.
(Image credit: SibFU Scientific Library) 252

Fig. 12.6 Page 25 of *Narody Sibiri* [Peoples of Siberia] (1956).
The two images depict an illustration of reconstruction
of a palaeolithic dwelling Buret' and an archaeological site.
Top image by V. Zaporozhskaja. Bottom image
by N. Tyumentcev. Published by the Archive of the Museum
of Anthropology and Ethnography of the USSR Academy
of Sciences. (Image credit: SibFU Scientific Library)..................... 253

xxii   List of Figures

Fig. 12.7 Title page of the book *Turukhanskij kraj: ekonomicheskoe obozrenie s istoricheskoj spravkoj* [Turukhansk Territory: An Economic Review with a Historical Outline] (1930) by G. N. Tarasenkov, published by Turukhansk RIK. (Image credit: SibFU Scientific Library) 255

Fig. 12.8 Map of Turukhansk Territory published in the book *Turukhanskij kraj: ekonomicheskoe obozrenie s istoricheskoj spravkoj* [Turukhansk Territory: An Economic Review with a Historical Outline] (1930). (Image credit: V. Konstantinovskij) 256

Fig. 13.1 Map of the Russian Extreme North. (Map credit: Hellerick. CC BY-SA 3.0 DEED. https://commons.wikimedia.org/wiki/File: Map_of_the_Russian_Extreme_North.svg).................................... 261

Fig. 13.2 Pie chart of themes and corresponding percentages for studies conducted by central libraries in the Far North of Russia, 2017–2019. (Chart credit: A. G. Kuznetsova using data from the Tsentral'nyye biblioteki sub"yektov Rossiyskoy Federatsii [Central Libraries of Russian Regions] database) 266

Fig. 14.1 Map of landmarks in the Faroe Islands with Irish connections. (Map credit: G. Taylor)... 291

Fig. 14.2 Map of locations in Iceland with Irish connections. (Map credit: G. Taylor) 293

Fig. 14.3 Map of stage one of Tim Severin's journey to recreate the St. Brendan's voyage across the North Atlantic, beginning in Brandon Creek, Co. Kerry, Ireland. (Map credit: G. Taylor) 296

Fig. 14.4 Map of potential longphuirt locations in Ireland. (Map credit: G. Taylor) 299

Fig. 15.1 *General map of part of the North-West Territories including the province of Manitoba shewing Dominion land surveys to 31 December 1882.* Map created by J. Johnston (1883). (Figure credit: LCR Digital Collections, University of Calgary. https://bit.ly/3PkyPgx) 324

Fig. 15.2 Handwritten letter with red seal from Sir John Franklin to William Pryce Cumby dated 1 August 1832. (Figure credit: LCR Digital Collections, University of Calgary. https://bit.ly/3uB3le8)................................... 333

Fig. 15.3 Four men on the expedition to Hudson Bay and Cumberland Gulf in the Steamship *Diana* in 1897 under the command of William Wakeham (shown here as the second person from the right). Photographer unknown. (Figure credit: LCR Digital Collections, University of Calgary. Arctic Institute of North America Collection. http://bit.ly/3ODBm6j)..................... 334

List of Figures   xxiii

Fig. 15.4 *H.M.S. Hecla in Winter Harbour.* Pencil and crayon drawing by Rear-Admiral Frederick William Beechey from the 1819–1820 Parry Expedition. (Figure credit: LCR Digital Collections, University of Calgary. https://bit.ly/3Rrb9sO) 334

Fig. 15.5 *Septentrionalium Terrarum descriptio*, the first known map of the North Pole by cartographer Gerardus Mercator. This version is a hand-coloured eighteenth-century reprint of the original 1595 map. (Figure credit: LCR Digital Collections, University of Calgary. https://bit.ly/3yRpxmO) 335

Fig. 16.1 Undergraduate students learn about the rare and unique materials in the University of Calgary's Archives and Special Collections through in-person opportunities to examine selected items. (Photo credit: D. Brown, University of Calgary) 353

Fig. 16.2 Students in the Archives and Special Collections classroom examine a selection of items from the University of Calgary's Archives and Special Collections. (Photo credit: D. Brown, University of Calgary) 357

Fig. 16.3 The steamship *Diana* under the command of William Wakeham in 1897. The ship was used in the expedition to Hudson Bay and Cumberland Gulf in northern Canada. (Photo credit: AINA collection, 32.85.M34, Archives and Special Collections, University of Calgary) 358

List of Tables

Table 2.1	List of Polar Libraries Colloquy meetings	12
Table 2.2	Results of 2020–2021 Polar Libraries Colloquy members survey (N = 38) regarding benefits of membership	17
Table 6.1	Number of airports located in the Arctic	97
Table 6.2	List of medium (M) and large (L) shopping centres in the Nordic Arctic	103
Table 6.3	Number of fast-food locations from six top global fast-food chains (GFFCs) in 16 Alaskan cities/towns	108
Table 6.4	Number of accommodations establishments (AEs) from six top accommodations companies/brands (ACBs) in the most populous municipalities in northern Sweden	110
Table 6.5	List of selected official key readings on digitalization in Arctic countries, territories, and regions	117
Table 6.6	Data showing mobile subscriptions, internet users, and 4G coverage in Arctic countries and territories	121
Table 13.1	Number of libraries in the Far North, 2017–2019	263
Table 13.2	Number of research studies published by central libraries of the Far North, 2017–2020	265
Table 14.1	Suggested research topics and sub-groupings within the Network of Arctic Researchers Ireland, Humanities and Social Science Working Group	286
Table 16.1	Document analysis worksheet used when teaching primary source and archival literacy	354
Table 16.2	Example study questions used when teaching primary source and archival literacy	355

Chapter 1
Introduction: Connecting LIS to Arctic and Northern Studies

Spencer Acadia ⓘ

Abstract This brief chapter outlines the other 15 chapters of the book *Library and Information Sciences in Arctic and Northern Studies*, as well as provides the purpose and rationale for the book. The chapters and book, as a whole, situate library and information sciences/studies (LIS) as an indispensable companion for Arctic and Northern research and projects and aims to inspire collaboration between LIS and Arctic and Northern studies.

Keywords Arctic archives · Arctic libraries · Arctic library and information sciences (LIS) · Arctic library and information studies (LIS)

1.1 Purpose of This Book

This book is a follow-up to Acadia and Fjellestad's (2020b) title *Library and Information Studies for Arctic Social Sciences and Humanities*. That book contains 18 chapters, including a foreword by well-known Arctic anthropologist and curator Igor Krupnik, featuring a wide range of themes and issues situated at the juncture of library and information studies/sciences (LIS) and Arctic humanities and social sciences. The overall point of that book, and of the current one as well, is to begin a concerted and deliberate effort to integrate LIS into Arctic and Northern studies. Arctic and Northern research tends to focus on natural sciences with little—albeit emerging—attention to social sciences and humanities. Moreover, within Arctic natural sciences, social sciences, and humanities scholarship, LIS as a discipline and practice is largely absent compared to other academic fields. Thus, this book continues the aim of demonstrating how LIS is and can be an important—but often overlooked—contributor in the advancement of studies and sciences situated within Northern and Arctic contexts, in addition to presenting LIS professionals and

---

S. Acadia (✉)
University of Denver, Denver, CO, USA

© The Author(s), under exclusive license to Springer Nature
Switzerland AG 2024
S. Acadia (ed.), *Library and Information Sciences in Arctic and Northern Studies*, Springer Polar Sciences, https://doi.org/10.1007/978-3-031-54715-7_1

scholars worldwide with some understanding of topics and challenges, as well as historical and current activities and advancements, that are important to Arctic and Northern studies.

1.2 Inside This Book

Featuring an international cadre of authors from Canada, Denmark, Finland, Germany, Ireland, Norway, Russia, Sweden, the United Kingdom, and the United States, including Alaska, this book contains 16 chapters, this one and 15 others, at the intersection of Arctic and Northern studies and LIS. Each chapter is briefly outlined below.

In Chap. 2, Sandra M. Campbell, Cecilie Tang Møldrup, and Susanna Parikka provide a history of the Polar Libraries Colloquy (PLC), a professional association dedicated to LIS and LIS-related matters pertaining to the polar regions, including its administrative structure, goals, and activities. In addition, the chapter discusses the results of a recent PLC member survey and offers a glimpse at the future of the association. Chapter 3 by Sharon Farnel, Sandra M. Campbell, David Cox II, Lars Iselid, Peter Lund, Susanna Parikka, Sharon Rankin, Ivar Stokkeland, and Päivi Wendelius introduces the purpose, development, and ongoing work of the Decolonization of Arctic Library and Archives Metadata (DALAM) thematic group, part of the University of the Arctic and in which PLC is active. Concerning Arctic and Northern Indigenous peoples and communities, the chapter includes international discussion of the need to decolonize metadata, subject headings, and descriptions of library collections and their items. These chapters draw attention to the two much-needed conduits—PLC and DALAM—for ongoing professional engagement in Arctic and Northern LIS.

Chapter 4 by Katie Hill, Peter Lund, and Naomi Boneham serves as an introduction to the University of Cambridge's Scott Polar Research Institute (SPRI), as well as its library, and considers the important role of correspondence in the sense of anthropologist Tim Ingold. The chapter uses Ingold's notion of knowledge generation as correspondence, along with interviews of SPRI researchers and employees, to lay out a history of SPRI and position the SPRI Library as a hub of knowledge co-creation. Particular attention is paid to SPRI's Russian collection, and the ongoing difficulties of Arctic communication brought on by Russia's invasion of Ukraine. The SPRI and materials held by its library and archives are invaluable to Arctic and Northern studies and this chapter expertly tells the origin story of the SPRI, its development across the decades since its creation, and the role of the SPRI as a centre of co-created knowledge via correspondence.

In Chap. 5, Erin Hollingsworth and Tyson Rinio offer a review of the *Culturally Responsive Guidelines for Alaska Public Libraries*, a document designed to improve and support libraries serving Native Alaskans. Via personal communication, the authors provide insight from one of the original creators of the Guidelines, David Ongley, to explain its origin, history, and revisions. In addition, the chapter

1 Introduction: Connecting LIS to Arctic and Northern Studies

considers the Guidelines within the larger contexts of Alaska education, the American Library Association, and the Society of American Archivists. Concluding the chapter is consideration of the Guidelines in shaping public libraries with specific examples from the North Slope, Fairbanks, Juneau, and other locations across Alaska. This chapter is fundamental for understanding LIS in the Alaskan instance specifically and is relevant for Indigenous LIS generally.

As mentioned earlier, in 2020b Acadia and Fjellestad published the edited volume *Library and Information Studies for Arctic Social Sciences and Humanities*. In the introductory chapter of that book (Acadia & Fjellestad, 2020a), 'the Arctic' is examined by way of critical sociological concepts such as globalization, migration, place, southern theory, urbanization, and more. In Chap. 6 of the current book, Acadia continues this work by introducing the concept of Liquid Arctic. Using sociologist Zygmunt Bauman's liquid metaphor, Acadia argues that positioning the Arctic as liquid is needed to better understand and describe Arctic change. As an interdisciplinary chapter, and to illustrate the Liquid Arctic, Acadia draws on multiple literatures, including discussion of various global problems; decline of the nation-state; human migration and movement of people; sense of accelerated time; rise of non-places such as airports and hotels; consumer consumption by way of fast-food restaurants and shopping malls; and tourism. The rise of digitalization in, for, and about the Arctic and North is included as an aspect of the Liquid Arctic with consideration given especially to digital cultural heritage and research data management as examples. One key contribution of this chapter is the argument that the concept of Liquid Arctic is a necessary extension of the more common Global Arctic concept toward more fully understanding the nature of current and future Arctic change.

Chapter 7 by Salminen and Morris also take digitalization as a topic of interest, emphasizing the importance and limitations of it in Arctic contexts. Following Salminen's (2019, 2021, 2022) prior work (see also Salminen & Hossain, 2018; Salminen et al., 2020), the authors discuss digitalization alongside related topics such as sociotechnical change, infrastructural development, connectivity, security, and more, concluding that Arctic digitalization introduces vulnerabilities to which little attention has been given. Along with the many opportunities and benefits possible with Arctic digitalization also come detriments (e.g., cybercrime, information breaches, lack of privacy, etc.). The chapter ends with consideration of the roles that libraries can and do play in Arctic digitalization, thus indicating that LIS professionals and scholars can be—and should be—more active in the study and development of Arctic digitalization and its projects.

In Chap. 8, Gregory Vey, Wesley Van Wychen, Chantelle Verhey, Peter Pulsifer, and Ellsworth LeDrew examine research data management (RDM) in the polar context. The authors use the *Polar Data Catalogue* (PDC) as an example of a polar RDM solution, including its history and development, while focusing on five technical topics of interest: (1) metadata standards, (2) data architecture, (3) semantics and interoperability, (4) dissemination and knowledge mobilization, and (5) organizational policy. The chapter also includes consideration of FAIR data principles, APIs, and more. Challenges for and the future of the PDC, and RDM more generally, are discussed. Given the longstanding need for concentrated management of Arctic research data, this chapter is an important addition to the literature on the organization and accessibility of polar data.

The next three chapters turn to several Indigenous topics of interest to LIS. First, Chap. 9 is part of the ongoing work by Grenoble related to Arctic Indigenous cultures, especially languages (e.g., Grenoble, 2018, 2020, 2022; Grenoble et al., 2023). In the chapter, Grenoble and Ignatieva discuss the challenges of locating and accessing Indigenous language materials and include brief overviews of some existing language archives and repositories containing materials in and related to Arctic and Northern Indigenous languages. The authors use the Institute of Humanitarian Research and the Problems of Indigenous Minorities of the North in Yakutsk, Russia as a case study, showcasing their various Indigenous language holdings. Importantly, this chapter draws attention to the vulnerabilities of Arctic and Northern Indigenous languages. Many of these languages are endangered and LIS academics and professionals can collaborate with Indigenous communities, anthropologists, linguists, and other language scholars to develop methods of Indigenous language preservation and continuity.

In Chap. 10, and building off the earlier *Digital Library North* project, Sharon Farnel, Ali Shiri, Ethel-Jean Gruben, Beverly Siliuyaq Amos, and Lena Kotokak profile the Inuvialuit Digital Library and the role of digital storytelling via the *Inuvialuit Voices* project. Continuing the work of both Farnel and Shiri (e.g., Farnel, 2021; Farnel & Shiri, 2019, 2020; Farnel et al., 2017; Shiri, 2017; Shiri & Stobbs, 2018; Shiri et al., 2017, 2022), the authors show via *Inuvialuit Voices* and examples of other Indigenous storytelling projects that digital storytelling can be used as a technique to capture Indigenous heritage, including language. Details of a storytelling event in 2019 featuring Inuvialuit Elders are provided, as is inclusion of the ways in which LIS professionals can be, and have been, key constituents in digital storytelling processes.

Chapter 11 continues the work of Kasten (2020) by providing an overview of both the *Digital Humanities of the North* and *Environmental Knowledge of the North* websites. The sites are operated by the Kulturstiftung Sibirien [Foundation for Siberian Cultures] (FSC), founded by Kasten in 2010. Both sites offer extensive materials related to the Indigenous communities of Siberia and the Russian Far East. Via these websites and other collections available through the FSC, Indigenous heritage is digitally preserved, and the use of its materials encouraged. The chapter includes consideration of future prospects such as continued emphasis of various research themes, facilitating connections between Arctic and Northern sciences and humanities, and continued co-production of knowledge with Indigenous stakeholders. This chapter is effective at detailing some of the ongoing work of the FSC in terms of providing a digital platform dedicated to the preservation of and access to Indigenous materials.

Building upon the previous work of Kasyanchuk et al. (2018), Chap. 12 by Elena N. Kasyanchuk, Valentina A. Koreshkova, Olga I. Babina, Irina A. Tsvetochkina, and Ruslan A. Baryshev centres the Siberian Federal University (SibFU) Scientific Library as a case study, taking as its emphasis resources about Arctic exploration. The chapter provides a background on SibFU, as well as its Institute of the North and the Arctic, and describes the research work of the Scientific Library. The chapter describes the SibFU Library's rare fonds, including several noteworthy, rare materials relating to Arctic expeditions. This chapter underscores the crucial task of libraries and archives to preserve materials for multidisciplinary Arctic and Northern studies, as well as the fact that rare Arctic materials can become objects of study in and of themselves.

Author Alesia G. Kuznetsova in Chap. 13 extends Kuznetsova's (2020) previous analysis of research studies conducted by the Central Libraries of Russia (CLR) located in the country's Far North, Far East, and Siberia. This chapter includes an update with newer data along with descriptions of various CLR studies, concentrating on those that examine library services and issues in the Buryatia Republic of the Russian Far East. This chapter is valuable because, as the author points out, CLR studies are not easy to locate, are not always publicly available, and may not be published at all. Thus, any available information about these studies are welcome additions to the LIS literature.

In Chap. 14, Milne and Slotten extensively lay out a case for Ireland's Arctic interests, providing historical and contemporary confirmation of Irish-Arctic connections, including evidence of Viking heritage in Ireland. The chapter also analyses two key Irish documents—*A Strategy for the Nordic Regions* and *Global Ireland: Ireland's Strategy for the Nordic Region to 2025*—and introduces the Network of Arctic Researchers in Ireland. The chapter concludes with four practical recommendations for the continuing development of Irish-Arctic relations, including alliance with LIS scholars and professionals in all related information and digital projects. This chapter leads to a greater understanding of Ireland's ambitions in the Arctic and their relationship to the North while proposing that Irish-Arctic studies can benefit from partnership with LIS.

The final two chapters of the book demonstrate real-world use of Arctic and Northern library and archives resources in higher education via case studies from the University of Calgary in Canada. First, Chap. 15 by Christena McKillop, Nadine Hoffman, and Regina Landwehr detail several examples of library, archives, and special collections outreach to and engagement with students and faculty. The chapter highlights use of the Arctic Institute of North America collections and Glenbow Library and Archives collections and discusses impacts of the COVID-19 pandemic on accessibility through digitization. Then, Chap. 16 by the same Hoffman, McKillop, and Landwehr describes specific instances where Arctic, Northern, and Canadian resources are used to engage learning and research, especially in the promotion of archival and library literacies. These two chapters are exemplary in revealing how Arctic and Northern collections can be used in teaching, learning, and research within higher education.

1.3 Conclusion

Although this book is a follow-up to Acadia and Fjellestad's (2020b) previous one, it also stands alone as an anthology of contributions in the purposeful endeavour to recognize and acknowledge LIS as a disciplinary collaborator for enhancing Arctic and Northern studies. In addition, it is my hope that this volume of work will, first, urge Arctic researchers, scientists, academics, and Indigenous community members to include LIS professionals and scholars in their activities and projects, and second, encourage LIS scholars and professionals working in Arctic and Northern topics and contexts to publish their valuable work.

References

Acadia, S., & Fjellestad, M. T. (2020a). Introduction: Why this book and why the Arctic? In S. Acadia & M. T. Fjellestad (Eds.), *Library and information studies for Arctic social sciences and humanities* (pp. 1–65). Routledge.

Acadia, S., & Fjellestad, M. T. (Eds.). (2020b). *Library and information studies for Arctic social sciences and humanities*. Routledge.

Farnel, S. (2021, June 7–10). "Northern relations": Collaborating "in a good way" to develop the Inuvialuit Digital Library metadata framework [Conference paper]. *Proceedings of the Annual Conference of CAIS/Actes Du congrès Annuel De l'ACSI*, 1–6. Calgary, Alberta, Canada. https://doi.org/mcj8

Farnel, S., & Shiri, A. (2019). Community-driven knowledge organization for cultural heritage digital libraries: The case of the Inuvialuit settlement region. *Advances in Classification Research online*, 29th ASIS SIG/CR classification research workshop, 9–12. https://doi.org/mckb

Farnel, S., & Shiri, A. (2020). Indigenous community driven knowledge organization at the interface: The case of the Inuvialuit digital library [Conference paper]. In M. Lykke, T. Svarre, M. Skov, & D. Martínez-Ávila (Eds.), *Proceedings of the 16th international ISKO conference* (pp. 123–132). Ergon.

Farnel, S., Shiri, A., Campbell, S., Cockney, C., Rathi, D., & Stobbs, R. (2017). A community-driven metadata framework for describing cultural resources: The digital library north project. *Cataloging and Classification Quarterly, 55*(5), 289–306. https://doi.org/gmbv6p

Grenoble, L. A. (2018). Arctic indigenous languages: Vitality and revitalization. In L. Hinton, L. Huss, & G. Roche (Eds.), *Routledge handbook of language revitalization* (pp. 345–354). Routledge.

Grenoble, L. A. (2020). Urbanization, language vitality, and multilingualism in Russian Eurasia. In J. F. Hacking, J. S. Hardy, & M. P. Romaniello (Eds.), *Russia in Asia: Imaginations, interactions, and realities* (pp. 183–202). Routledge.

Grenoble, L. A. (2022). Contact and shift: Colonization and urbanization in the Arctic. In S. Mufwene & A. M. Escobar (Eds.), *Cambridge handbook of language contact* (Vol. 2, pp. 473–501). Cambridge University Press.

Grenoble, L. A., Vinokurova, A. A., & Nesterova, E. V. (2023). Language vitality and sustainability: Minority indigenous languages in the Sakha Republic. In J. P. Ziker, J. Ferguson, & V. Davydov (Eds.), *The Siberian world* (pp. 31–46). Routledge.

Kasten, E. (2020). Fieldwork on Kamchatka peninsula and the creation of the Foundation for Siberian Cultures: Towards an open-access database of indigenous languages and knowledge from the Russian Far East. In S. Acadia & M. T. Fjellestad (Eds.), *Library and information studies for Arctic social sciences and humanities* (pp. 329–352). Routledge.

1 Introduction: Connecting LIS to Arctic and Northern Studies

Kasyanchuk, E. N., Kazantseva, V. P., & Baryshev, R. A. (2018). Nauchnaya biblioteka Sibirskogo federal'nogo universiteta: Itogi raboty, zadachi, oriyentiry [Scientific library of the Siberian Federal University: Results of work, tasks, guidelines]. *Scientific and Technical Libraries, 4*, 23–32. https://doi.org/h6ns

Kuznetsova, A. G. (2020, November 26–27). *O nauchnykh issledovaniyakh, provodimykh tsentral'nymi bibliotekami regionov Rossiyskoy Federatsii* [On scientific studies carried out by central libraries of Russian Federation regions] [Conference paper]. Scientific and practical conference of young specialists to the 225th anniversary of the founding of the Russian National Library: Traditions and innovations. St. Petersburg, Russia. Russian National Library.

Salminen, M. (2019). Refocusing and redefining cybersecurity: Individual security in the digitalising European high north. *Yearbook of Polar Law Online, 10*(1), 321–356. https://doi.org/jppm

Salminen, M. (2021). Arkipäivän digitaalinen turvallisuus Euroopan pohjoisilla alueilla: Tapaustutkimus Tunturi-Lapista [Everyday digital security in the northern regions of Europe: A case study from Finnish Lapland]. *Media ja viestintä* [Media and Communication], *44*(1), 158–180. https://doi.org/jppn

Salminen, M. (2022). "Et nää on näitä meiän kyberhyökkäyksiä nämä" ["you don't see these are our cyberattacks"]: The government of one and all in everyday digital security in Finnish Lapland. [Doctoral dissertation, University of Lapland]. https://bit.ly/3Y1VuU3. Accessed 9 Dec 2023.

Salminen, M., & Hossain, K. (2018). Digitalisation and human security dimensions in cybersecurity: An appraisal for the European high north. *Polar Record, 54*(2), 108–118. https://doi.org/gd3p39

Salminen, M., Zojer, G., & Hossain, K. (2020). Comprehensive cybersecurity and human rights in the digitalising European high north. In M. Salminen, G. Zojer, & K. Hossain (Eds.), *Digitalisation and human security. A multi-disciplinary approach to cybersecurity in the European high North* (pp. 21–55). Palgrave Macmillan. https://doi.org/jppq

Shiri, A. (2017, 8–12 June). Digital library development to support sustainable information services: A case study of the *Inuvialuit settlement region in Canada's North* [Conference presentation]. ICASS IX: The 9th international congress on Arctic social sciences. Umeå, Sweden.

Shiri, A., & Stobbs, R. (2018, November 10–14). Community-driven user evaluation of the Inuvialuit Cultural Heritage Digital Library [Conference paper]. *Proceedings of ASIS&T 2018: Association for Information Science and Technology*, 55, 440–449. Vancouver, British Columbia, Canada. https://doi.org/g8fq

Shiri, A., Cockney, C., Farnel, S., Rathi, D., Stobbs, R., & Campbell, S. (2017, June 8–12). Methodological considerations in developing digital libraries for the Arctic communities: The case of Canada's north [Conference presentation]. ICASS IX: The 9th international congress on Arctic social sciences. Umeå, Sweden.

Shiri, A., Howard, D., & Farnel, S. (2022). Indigenous digital storytelling: Digital interfaces supporting cultural heritage preservation and access. *International Information and Library Review, 54*(2), 93–144. https://doi.org/gnqr25

Chapter 2
The Polar Libraries Colloquy

Sandra M. Campbell ⓘ**, Cecilie Tang Møldrup, and Susanna Parikka** ⓘ

Abstract The Polar Libraries Colloquy (PLC) is a voluntary professional membership organization for archivists, librarians, and others with an interest in Arctic and Antarctic collections and information. The PLC first met in 1971 and over its 50 years there has been, and is now, much large-scale global change, especially in the world of information. Even though the PLC is a small and geographically dispersed organization, it has successfully existed for half a century and remains a vibrant and active community. This chapter presents a brief history of the PLC along with discussion of the PLC's goals and successes. The chapter also describes the PLC's operations and activities, and, based on a 2020–2021 PLC member survey, suggests where the organization may be headed in the future.

Keywords Antarctic information · Arctic information · Information science associations · Library associations · Polar Libraries

2.1 Background

The Polar Libraries Colloquy (PLC) first met in 1971 in response to the need for improved communication about and control of information throughout and related to the Circumpolar North. By the 1960s there were well-established collections of

---

S. M. Campbell (✉)
University of Alberta, Edmonton, AB, Canada
e-mail: scampbel@ualberta.ca

C. T. Møldrup
University of Copenhagen, Copenhagen, Denmark
e-mail: cqw916@hum.ku.dk

S. Parikka
University of Lapland, Rovaniemi, Finland
e-mail: susanna.parikka@ulapland.fi

© The Author(s), under exclusive license to Springer Nature
Switzerland AG 2024
S. Acadia (ed.), *Library and Information Sciences in Arctic and Northern Studies*, Springer Polar Sciences, https://doi.org/10.1007/978-3-031-54715-7_2

polar materials across various institutions throughout Canada, Scandinavia, the United Kingdom, the United States, and other countries (Corley Murchison, 2000–2001). While librarians and archivists working in the North often knew each other or knew about each other through publications and correspondence or attendance at regional and national conferences, there was little coordinated information available about what their collections held, what materials were being acquired, and what events in polar information were occurring (Colloquy on Northern Library Resources, 1971). Moreover, there was little opportunity to share information among polar archivists and librarians due to the lack of a professional library and information sciences (LIS) organization dedicated to and specialized in Arctic and Antarctic matters.

In the late 1960s and early 1970s, there was a strong interest in the future of and possibilities in the Circumpolar North. This increased interest became evident due to a rise in demand for Arctic and Northern information. In Scandinavia, the North Calotte Council (LobbyFacts, n.d.) was created to promote cross-border cooperation between the northernmost counties of Finland, Sweden, and Norway. The Sámi people were working towards greater recognition and Greenland was pushing for self-government (Broderstad, 2011; Dahl, 1986). In Finland, large northern rivers were harnessed for waterpower (Myllyntaus, 1983) and the search for oil and minerals expanded across the northernmost parts of North America, fueling demand for mining- and petroleum-related information. In 1968, large oil reserves were discovered at Prudhoe Bay, Alaska and proposals were developed to build pipelines from Alaska through the Mackenzie Valley to Alberta, Canada (Berger, 1977). Much like what was happening in Greenland, northern Canadian Indigenous peoples were also working towards self-government (Inuit Nunangat, 1978). Libraries and archives responded to new information needs as best they could with the resources they had. Information about the availability of materials held in specific archives and libraries was often gained through telephone conversations, telex messages, or letters sent by mail (Colloquy on Northern Library Resources, 1971). Copies of articles and loaned materials were sent to requestors by mail as computing in libraries and archives was just beginning (Booth, 1965; Colloquy on Northern Library Resources, 1971). The unique knowledge of individual librarians, archivists, and other information professionals remained researchers' best resource for discovering the existence of specific materials. Against this backdrop, the PLC was created as the Colloquy on Northern Library Resources.

G. A. (Nita) Cooke (1974, p. 10), a then-librarian at the Boreal Institute for Northern Studies (BINS) in Edmonton and writing after the 5th Colloquy, described the PLC's early development: Two Canadian librarians, Garth Graham of the Yukon Territory Library Services Branch and Nora Corley Murchison of the Arctic Institute of North America (AINA) (https://arctic.ucalgary.ca/) "thought it would be a good idea for librarians whose libraries were oriented towards northern regions to get together to exchange ideas and information about each other's collections and needs." From that idea came the first official meeting of the Colloquy in 1971. The meeting was attended by 25 librarians, 24 from North American institutions and one from the Scott Polar Research Institute (SPRI) (https://www.spri.cam.ac.uk/) in Cambridge, England. Colloquy meetings were held annually in the four following years: Hanover, New Hampshire in 1972; Cambridge in 1973; Montréal in 1974; and Rovaniemi in 1975. By the third meeting in Cambridge, the Colloquy's name had changed to Northern Libraries Colloquy and European participation had expanded to include archivists and librarians from Denmark, England, Finland, France, Germany, and Norway. In addition, several enduring characteristics of the Colloquy were established: First, the use of the term *colloquy*, defined as a conversational exchange or dialogue, was chosen because it represented the intended purpose of the meetings to foster conversations and information exchange. Second, publication of the proceedings of each Colloquy was established as the responsibility of the host institution. Third, one of the overall aims of the rotating meeting was to increase knowledge among information professionals of the resources held by the host institution (Northern Libraries Colloquy, 1973).

2.2 Has PLC Been Successful in Achieving Its Goals?

Success of the PLC and the reasons why it has been a vibrant organization across five decades can be better understood by examining its stated goals, organizational structure and stability, value to the larger community, and the value that individuals derive from membership.

2.2.1 Stated Goals

In 1976, the Colloquy described its three main goals: (1) convening biannually, (2) publishing a bulletin at least three times a year, and (3) encouraging the production of publications useful to member libraries and their users (*Northern Libraries Bulletin*, 1976). The following three sections enumerate how the PLC has succeeded in accomplishing these goals.

2.2.1.1 Biannual Colloquy Meetings

As shown in Table 2.1, the Colloquy has met 28 times from 1971 to 2022. In 2020, the meeting was postponed due to the global COVID-19 pandemic. The meetings normally alternate between Europe and North America, with some countries hosting several times. In July 2004, a mid-term meeting was held in Hobart, Australia jointly with the International Association of Aquatic and Marine Science Library and Information Centres who also co-sponsored the PLC's 1998 meeting in Iceland (Carle, 2005).

12 S. M. Campbell et al.

Table 2.1 List of Polar Libraries Colloquy meetings

Colloquy & theme	Date held	Location
29th Colloquy *Arctic connections*	9–14 June 2024	Tromsø, Norway
28th Colloquy *Sharing polar cultures and knowledge:* *Perspectives from libraries and archives*	5–11 June 2022	Québec City, Québec
27th Colloquy *Developing polar networks: Ideas and* *possibilities for the future*	10–16 June 2018	Rovaniemi, Finland
26th Colloquy *Mapping change, chitduug gha nen' ch'etnetl'edz*	10–15 July 2016	Fairbanks, Alaska
25th Colloquy *Connecting communities: Collaborating, creating,* *and communicating*	29 June–3 July 2014	Cambridge, UK
24th Colloquy *Cold regions: Pivot points, focal points*	11–14 June 2012	Boulder, Colorado
23rd Colloquy *Cool libraries in a melting world*	13–18 June 2010	Bremerhaven, Germany
22nd Colloquy *Currents of change: The future of polar* *information*	2–6 June 2008	Edmonton, Alberta
21st Colloquy *Building polar networks: A strategy for the future*	8–12 May 2006	Rome, Italy
20th Colloquy *Polar research: Let us share –Amiqqaaluta*	7–11 June 2004	Ottawa, Ontario
19th Colloquy *Poles apart – Poles online*	17–21 June 2002	Copenhagen, Denmark
18th Colloquy *Gateways, archives, and libraries into the next* *millennium*	12–17 June 2000	Winnipeg, Manitoba
17th Colloquy *Electronic information and publications: Looking* *to the electronic future, let's not forget the archival* *past*	20–25 September 1998	Reykjavik, Iceland
16th Colloquy *Creativity lighting the poles: Collaborative* *solutions to common problems*	17–22 June 1996	Anchorage, Alaska
15th Colloquy *Bipolar information initiatives: The needs of polar* *research*	3–8 July 1994	Cambridge, UK
14th Colloquy *International sharing of polar information* *resources*	3–7 May 1992	Columbus, Ohio
13th Colloquy *Man's future in Arctic areas*	10–14 June 1990	Rovaniemi, Finland
12th Colloquy	5–9 June 1988	Boulder, Colorado

(continued)

2 The Polar Libraries Colloquy

Table 2.1 (continued)

Colloquy & theme	Date held	Location
11th Colloquy	9–12 June 1986	Luleå, Sweden
10th Colloquy	12–16 August 1984	St. John's, Newfoundland
9th Colloquy	2–6 June 1982	Tromsø, Norway
8th Colloquy	1–6 June 1980	Edmonton, Alberta & Whitehorse, Yukon
7th Colloquy	19–23 September 1978	Paris, France
6th Colloquy	12–15 July 1976	Fairbanks, Alaska
5th Colloquy	26–30 May 1975	Rovaniemi, Finland
4th Colloquy	2–6 June 1974	Montréal, Québec
3rd Colloquy	25–29 June 1973	Cambridge, UK
2nd Colloquy	31 May–2 June 1972	Hanover, New Hampshire
1st Colloquy	16–17 June 1971	Edmonton, Alberta

Table credit: S. Campbell and Polar Libraries Colloquy
Note: Colloquies 1 through 12 did not have a dedicated theme

Rotating the meeting location allows people living and working in varied geographies to attend the Colloquy who otherwise may not have the opportunity. Indeed, most meetings are attended by large contingents of local participants. The 8th Colloquy in 1980 was an experiment in holding the meeting in two Canadian cities: the first part in Edmonton, and the second in Whitehorse. Cooke (1990, p. 12), as one of the organizers, comments that "logistically, this proved to be somewhat of a nightmare and the idea has not been repeated by subsequent organizers." The Colloquy is usually a weeklong immersive experience, giving participants time to become acquainted, explore local collections, and enjoy the hosting city and region.

2.2.1.2 Northern Libraries Bulletin/Polar Libraries Bulletin

Although the Bulletin has not met the goal of publishing 2–3 times per year as set out in the Colloquy's 1976 goals, 85 issues were published as of Spring 2022. The first 36 issues were published as *Northern Libraries Bulletin*, while the latter remaining ones as *Polar Libraries Bulletin* (https://polarlibraries.org/polar-libraries-bulletin/). Publication of the Bulletin remains active with a pattern of one or two issues annually, though there was a gap between Autumn 1997 and Winter 2000.

The Bulletin was initially published as a photocopied and stapled document mailed via post to Colloquy members, but eventually became available in both print and electronic formats. In 2009, the Bulletin transitioned to a digital-only publication available online. Since its beginning, the Bulletin serves the dual purpose of being a record of the Colloquy's activities and a communication device for the Colloquy's membership. The early issues are largely dedicated to describing upcoming Colloquy plans and reporting on past Colloquies, but other content includes descriptions of collections held by libraries and archives, new book and journal announcements, articles about government and industrial actions that impact polar information, and notices about personnel changes and individual librarian life events. With the development of electronic communication, the focus of the Bulletin shifted somewhat, now being less newsy and more focused on Colloquy business.

2.2.1.3 Encouraging Other Publications

In the Colloquy's early years, there was an explosion in polar publishing and many projects were undertaken by organizations to make information about Arctic and Antarctic collections accessible as PLC members collaborated on the creation of bibliographic resources and finding tools. For example, in the first Bulletin, Harry King at the SPRI reports that there was "a good chance that the SPRI card catalog [would] be published" and Cooke describes the development of two experimental *Key Word in Context* indexes at the Boreal Institute Library, one a monthly index to journals received at the library, and the other—*Northern Titles Index*—"a useful tool to bridge the gap between receipt of journals, indexing pertinent articles in the catalogue, and full abstracting in Arctic Bibliography" (Northern Libraries Bulletin, 1971, pp. 1, 3). By the late 1970s, the PLC provided a more scholarly publication venue via its conference proceedings beginning with the *Proceedings of the Seventh Northern Libraries Colloquy*; that year, the Colloquy was held in Paris. The Proceedings included papers presented at the Colloquy, some of which are full bibliographies, as well as the full text of the *Polar and Cold Regions Resources: A Directory* which describes the collections of 115 libraries along with a full catalogue of 143 museum collections in 16 countries and a list of more than 500 films (Corley, 1982). Later, in 1990, the PolarPac database was created by combining records for the holdings of multiple libraries. By its third iteration, PolarPac3 contained records for 50 libraries with items in 77 different languages and 65% percent of the titles listed were unique with only one location (West & McCarthy, 1994). PolarPac3 contained records from five citation databases: Bibliography of Alaska and Polar Regions, National Snow and Ice Data Center database, Oil Spill Public Information Center newspaper database, ANCESTORS database, and Lapponica (Polar Pac Release Information: The Polar Pac Database, 1992). PolarPac's fifth and final edition was released in 1997. In 2012, Heather Lane (p. 168) reports that "further development [of PolarPac] to a web-based service has been hampered by the lack of funding for a suitable technological solution that can be readily shared by all PLC member organisations."

The *Proceedings of the 13th Colloquy* in 1990 provides a snapshot of the state of polar database development at that time. In addition to PolarPac discussions, the Proceedings document the struggles of participants who were building both broad and subject specific databases. For instance, a paper by Ron Inouye (1990) of University of Alaska Fairbanks (UAF) discusses the impact of the volume of documents related to the 1989 Exxon Valdez oil spill on the Bibliography of Alaskana database, while Sauli Laitinen (1990) of the Technical Research Centre of Finland describes more than 400 Scandinavian databases located across Denmark, Finland, Norway, and Sweden. Despite growth in quantity and quality of polar databases, volatility in their development, delivery, and accessibility remains.

2.3 Administrative Simplicity and Stability

A part of the Colloquy's success stems from its adherence to its original mission of providing a network for conversation among and exchange of information between its members. Since its beginnings, the PLC strives to be a simple, practical, and flexible organization. For the first few years, the Colloquy was not a formal organization, but rather an annual meeting of people who were interested in the same kinds of information and trying to solve the same kinds of problems. For the first Colloquy in June 1971, all sessions were chaired by different members and notes were taken by volunteer rapporteurs. The Colloquy saw its first business meeting in 1974 chaired by Irene Coutinho of the AINA and a main topic of discussion was the structure of the Colloquy where Arthur Looker of the Canada Defense Research Board presented a resolution:

> While we have managed to operate quite successfully for four years without any formal organization, it is becoming apparent that if we intend to continue our meetings it would be desirable to have some organizational structure. There are several reasons for this: a) Although the hosts of the last four years have done a marvellous job and have not complained, there is a great deal of evidence to suggest that the load was considerable and that there are details that could be handled by a formal organization; b) We have looked at the possibilities of obtaining grants from governments to assist in bringing foreign nationals and to defray other expenses. This is much easier to do with a formal organization; c) The onus of establishing the theme of the Colloquy each year and the obtaining of speakers has devolved on the host. An organization could help to spread this responsibility. (Northern Libraries Colloquy, 1974, p. 43)

The minutes read that "a lively discussion followed. It was decided to keep the Colloquy informal with suggestions that the President and Secretary should be from the host country and the Treasurer from elsewhere" (p. 43). However, the PLC varied from this formula over time, particularly in not rotating the secretary and treasurer roles to maintain consistency and easier maintenance of records and accounts, but the president—now called the chair of the steering committee—routinely rotates.

In 1976, the Colloquy published its formal purpose:

> To enable all librarians, archivists and bibliographers from the North (North defined as per map in volume fifteen of the Arctic Bibliography plus Iceland) and from all libraries with significant polar collections to have the opportunity to get together to promote cooperation, to learn of available resources, and to discuss mutual problems. (Northern Libraries Bulletin, 1976, p. 1)

Yet, nearly 10 years later in 1988 at the 12th Northern Libraries Colloquy, a further motion to formalize the organization itself failed. The motion cites the advantages to formalization, including continuity of projects, lending of political clout, and heightened status to fundraise and secure grants. Some disadvantages mentioned include loss of independence and flexibility, the need for continued annual dues, and requirement of formal membership. Also, at this meeting was approved a name change to Polar Libraries Colloquy. Rather than launching a separate group, the name change was proposed to incorporate the Antarctic into the continuing emphasis on the Arctic (Brennan & Andrews, 1988, p. 25). Six years later in 1994, the *Constitution of the Polar Libraries Colloquy* was approved, formally defining the PLC's organization and structure (Polar Libraries Colloquy, n.d.-a). The Constitution does not place any requirements on the PLC's steering committee in terms of ongoing expenditures or assumption of risk.

The PLC's standing committee members are elected, and its chairperson changes every two years. A list of past steering committee chairs is available on the PLC website (Polar Libraries Colloquy, n.d.-b). For practical reasons, the secretary and treasurer often serve multiple terms. Many other functions are managed voluntarily by members internationally, often over long periods of time. For example, the PLC's listserv has been managed by the AINA since 1994. In addition, the PLC's website was managed for many years at the University of Lapland in Rovaniemi but management of it switched over to the AINA in 2016 (Christoffersen Vossepoel, 2016). Over the history of the Bulletin, several different teams managed its editorial and publishing activities, mostly at the UAF. Additionally, the PLC's archives are held as part of the Elmer E. Rasmuson Library's Alaska and Polar Regions Collections and Archives at the UAF (https://library.uaf.edu/aprca). The PLC gains stability from having its functions internationally dispersed because when political environments or budgetary restrictions in one country impacts the ability of one member to contribute, the strengths and stability of members in other countries buoy the organization's operations.

2.4 Value of Membership: A Survey

While there exists theoretical work on membership in voluntary professional organizations, for example, on incentives, commitment, and detachment (Knoke, 1988), as well as engagement motivations (Hager, 2014), much of it assumes that the professional association is structured for the purpose of professional certification and advocacy for professional members. However, the purposes for which the PLC was created do not include professional certification nor member-level advocacy. Knoke (1988) describes three areas of incentive that attract members to voluntary organizations: (1) utilitarian (i.e., benefit to the member); (2) social (i.e., coordinated social and recreational activities); and (3) normative (i.e., public goods that require collective efforts to influence governmental policy makers). In a 2020–2021 survey, PLC members were asked to respond to questions about their reasons for joining and maintaining membership. Responses were analysed using Knoke's framework.

In the survey, members were asked to rank via close-ended question the benefits that they derived from PLC membership. A total of 38 completed surveys were returned. The two most frequently cited benefits were "learning about new polar resources" (92.1%) and "building a network of colleagues who do the same work" (89.5%) (Campbell et al., 2020–2021). Complete rankings are provided in Table 2.2. The combination of an academic and professional conference, as well as opportunities for socializing and networking (i.e., the utilitarian and social incentives of Knoke), create strong motivation for members to join the PLC and continue membership. The PLC is an essential hub through which polar archivists, librarians, and others meet both remotely and in person to exchange information, receive education, present scholarly works, and stay current in their field, as well as build friendships, travel, and socialize.

Part of the PLC's success is that it fills a niche in the landscape of organizations for information professionals; it is the only international network designed with polar archivists, librarians, and others in the LIS field in mind. While the PLC welcomes anyone with an interest in polar information, members tend to work within institutions that have some Arctic or Antarctic significance (e.g., academic institutions, government or quasi-government agencies, research organizations, etc.). Sometimes, institutions are specific to polar activities, such as the British Antarctic Survey, but more often the library or archives is a subunit of a larger institution with Arctic or Antarctic interests. As a result, these librarians and archivists may be the

Table 2.2 Results of 2020–2021 Polar Libraries Colloquy members survey (N = 38) regarding benefits of membership

Response	Percent of respondents[a]
Learning about new polar resources	92.1%
Building a network of colleagues who do the same work	89.5%
Being inspired by polar colleagues	86.8%
Learning about new research in polar information	86.8%
Socializing with friends and colleagues	78.9%
Travel to different polar areas and learning	65.8%
Opportunity to present scholarly works	63.2%
Opportunity to serve on PLC committees	52.6%

Table credit: S. Campbell
[a]Respondents could select multiple responses

only ones who work with polar information within their libraries and archives. Thus, these workers may be isolated from other information professionals sharing polar interests and that isolation is often the impetus to seek out and join the PLC.

In the early years of the Northern Libraries Colloquy, there existed a clear need to share information among information professionals and across institutions and geographies as polar collections were being established. In the first Bulletin, Ted Ryberg of the University of Alaska Library reports the appointment of an Arctic bibliographer, and there was an announcement about the expansion of space at the Yukon Regional Headquarters (*Northern Libraries Bulletin*, 1971). Librarians and archivists alike launched new polar information services and identified materials to add to their expanding collections. Also mentioned in the first issue of the Bulletin, the AINA offered "starter sets" of "Arctic and technical papers and other special publications ... in order to assist northern libraries, educational and other institutions in building up their information, and stimulate the distribution of certain of its publications" (*Northern Libraries Bulletin*, 1971, p. 1). By reading the Bulletin, PLC members could keep up-to-date with their polar colleagues' work in developing finding aids for unique and rare collections, including large library databases, and experimenting with new technologies and search techniques. Moreover, the Northern Libraries Colloquy provided an emerging professional platform where members could share ideas about how to build shared information systems for the polar world.

Since 1976, PLC members could attend the Colloquy every two years to present the advances in their work and learn about colleagues' challenges and achievements. In addition, each Colloquy meeting often features an afternoon excursion to showcase the local environment. For example, at one meeting in Fairbanks, participants took a paddle wheeler cruise down the Chena River and were entertained by a small float plane's acrobatics, along with a stop for a sled-dog demonstration and visit to a living history museum (Campbell & Lund, 2016). At a meeting in Boulder, Colorado, participants visited the United States Geological Survey Ice Core Lab and took photos with ice cores from their own countries (Campbell, 2012). In addition to the afternoon excursion, there is often a pre- or post-Colloquy tour, giving participants more in-depth experience of notable local sites. In Reykjavík, for instance, attendees took a day-long Golden Circle tour to visit the Gullfoss waterfall, Geysir geothermal area, and Thingvellir National Park (Hedinsdottir et al., 1999). While in Bremerhaven, Germany, attendees travelled further north to visit the German island of Neuwerk by crossing the northern seabed by horse-drawn watt wagon (Campbell & Maloney, 2011). Another popular social event includes a banquet of local cuisine that is often held at a noteworthy location. For example, at one meeting in Finland, the banquet was held east of Helsinki on historic Vartiosaari Island. Also known as Watch Island, Vartiosaari was used by the Finnish Defence Forces during the Second World War (Mäntylä, 2018).

2.5 Value to the Broader Community

Knoke's (1988, p. 315) third incentive for attracting members to voluntary organizations is normative aspects having to do with "public goods that require collective efforts to influence governmental policy makers." Although this incentive is not and never has been an explicit focus within the PLC's mandate, the Colloquy sometimes provides external advice, encouragement, and support on behalf of members via strategic assignment of PLC delegates to work with other institutions. For instance, since 2015 a delegate serves as a participating member of the International Arctic Science Committee (https://iasc.info/). Also, the Colloquy joined the University of the Arctic (UArctic) (https://www.uarctic.org/) in May 2005 as a member in their international organization category. By joining UArctic, the PLC was granted a delegate seat in the UArctic Council, later known as the UArctic Assembly (Campbell, 2005). In 2022, the PLC led the creation of a new UArctic Thematic Network called Decolonization of Arctic Library and Archives Metadata (DALAM) (https://www.uarctic.org/activities/thematic-networks/decolonization-of-arctic-library-and-archives-metadata-dalam/) to be an international forum for librarians, archivists, and others to work together on the decolonization of metadata.

Finally, via the William Mills Prize awarded biennially since 2006, the PLC draws attention to polar nonfiction publications. Created in memory of the late William Mills (1951–2004), librarian and keeper of collections at the SPRI, the prize is awarded every 2 years by the Colloquy. Lists of nominated titles and prize recipients are published on the PLC website (Polar Libraries Colloquy, n.d.-c). Winning titles are announced to the community through the pollib-L listserv, in the Bulletin, and social media.

2.6 Looking to the Future

In the 2020–2021 Colloquy survey, members were asked to comment on what actions, if any, the PLC should take to maintain its effectiveness and relevance in the future. Most responses centred around staying the course, placing value on the PLC's position as an international home for polar librarians, archivists, and other information professionals. Two general areas for improvements mentioned by members include: (1) broadening membership, and (2) increased use of technology to engage membership. Concerning membership issues, respondents noted that membership fees should be kept low, and the Colloquy should include in its roster more workers from smaller northern libraries and archives. Members supported creating a stronger social media presence, providing occasional webinars between Colloquies, improving content of the Bulletin, and finding ways to engage members in PLC activities (Campbell et al., 2020–2021).

The PLC is and always has been a network of archivists, librarians, and other LIS practitioners working within the polar information environment. Subject matter addressed in Colloquy meetings and other communication arises organically from the interests of members and polar information is now in demand more than ever. In the Arctic particularly, massive environmental change driven by rising temperatures impacts all aspects of the environment and human life (Council of Canadian Academies, 2019; Hanssen-Bauer et al., 2019; Moon et al., 2021; Rantanen et al., 2022). As Arctic and Northern residents cope, adapt, and take advantage of changing conditions, there is demand for data and information on sea ice change, natural resource exploration, permafrost melt and its impact on built and natural environments, geopolitical changes, health, tourism, and more. Because the impact of climate change disproportionately affects residents at high latitudes (Council of Canadian Academies, 2019; Furgal & Prowse, 2008; Jaakkola et al., 2018), there is also need for information about social justice issues, particularly related to northern Indigenous peoples which, in turn, drives demand for both current and historical information produced by and about Indigenous communities. Because the PLC fills a unique niche, is member-defined and member-driven, and is responsive to changes in members interests and needs, members believe it has a long-lasting future.

2.7 Conclusion

The PLC's longevity and success are rooted in the simplicity of its mandate, its administrative effectiveness, positioning in the community, and focus on the needs of its membership, including information exchange and social interaction. In addition, continuity of the PLC is due to decisions of the Colloquy's founders, especially that the organization is and should always be viewed in the framework of a conversation among members. The Colloquy itself does not engage in expensive or risky projects, allowing it to maintain low membership fees, and the organization and costs of hosting biennial meetings are wholly the responsibility of the hosting institution—they must absorb any losses, but also get to keep any profit. Administratively, the PLC is small and agile. For sake of stability, steering committee members often serve for extended periods.

The PLC's attraction for members is due in part to it filling a unique but much needed niche in the LIS field as there are no other organizations specifically for librarians, archivists, and other information professionals working in Arctic and Antarctic environments or with polar materials and information. A part of the enduring success of the Colloquy is that its week-long biennial meeting encompasses many opportunities for members to network, socialize, and build working relationships and friendships. To be sure, the engaging and memorable shared experiences of Colloquy meetings has kept the Colloquy stable and operational for 50 years on.

References

Berger, T. R. (1977). Northern frontier, northern homeland: The report of the Mackenzie Valley pipeline inquiry: Vol. 1. Minister of Supply and Services Canada. https://bit.ly/482Kaer. Accessed 7 Dec 2023.

Booth, A. D. (1965). *Digital computers in action*. Pergamon.

Brennan, A. M., & Andrews, M. (Eds.). (1988, June 5–9). *Twelfth Northern Libraries Colloquy*, Boulder, Colorado, United States. World Data Center for Glaciology (Snow and Ice). https://bit.ly/3WaDoh8. Accessed 7 Dec 2023.

Broderstad, E. G. (2011). The promises and challenges of Indigenous self-determination: The Sámi case. *International Journal, 66*(4), 893–907. https://bit.ly/3xyf9yp. Accessed 7 Dec 2023

Campbell, S. (2005, Summer). Polar Libraries Colloquy joins University of the Arctic: Report from the 8th University of the Arctic Council Meeting. *Polar Libraries Bulletin, 57*, 1, 4. https://bit.ly/3OnWfRz. Accessed 7 Dec 2023.

Campbell, S. (2012, Fall). Social highlights from PLC 2012. *Polar Libraries Bulletin, 69*, 1–3. https://bit.ly/3y0hUK6. Accessed 7 Dec 2023.

Campbell, S., & Lund, P. (2016, Fall). PLC 2016: Day-by-day. *Polar Libraries Bulletin, 77*, 2, 14–16. https://bit.ly/39CqZj5. Accessed 7 Dec 2023.

Campbell, S., & Maloney, E. (2011). A tale of adventure from 2010 PLC in Bremerhaven: The Wadden Sea: To Neuwerk by wattwagen. *Polar Libraries Bulletin, 66*, 1–2, 12–16. https://bit.ly/3xZMuUg. Accessed 7 Dec 2023.

Campbell, S., Parikka, S., & Tang-Møldrup, C. (2020, Fall–2021, spring). Join for the knowledge, stay for the fun: Preliminary PLC survey results. *Polar Libraries Bulletin, 83*, 3–4. https://bit.ly/3QtChGX. Accessed 7 Dec 2023.

Carle, D. O. (2005, Summer). Tasmanian travels: IAMSLIC 2004 in Hobart. *Polar Libraries Bulletin, 57*, 5–6. https://bit.ly/3OnWfRz. Accessed 7 Dec 2023.

Christoffersen Vossepoel, S. (2016, Fall). PLC launches new website. *Polar Libraries Bulletin, 77*, 19. https://bit.ly/39CqZj5. Accessed 7 Dec 2023.

Colloquy on Northern Library Resources [Conference session notes]. (1971, June 16–17). Edmonton, Alberta, Canada. Arctic Institute of North America and Boreal Institute for Northern Studies. https://doi.org/jqxx

Cooke, G. A. (1974, April). The Northern Libraries Colloquy: A brief history. *Library Association of Alberta Bulletin, 5*(2), 101–103. https://doi.org/jqxz

Cooke, G. A. (1990, June 10–14). A brief history of the Polar Libraries Colloquy [Conference paper]. In R. Kivilahti, L. Kurppa, & M. Pretes (Eds.), *Man's future in Arctic areas: Proceedings of the 13th Polar Libraries Colloquy* (pp. 10–13), University of Lapland. https://doi.org/hz8n

Corley, N. T. (1982). Les bibliothèques arctiques [Arctic libraries]. In J. Malaurie & S. Devers (Eds.), *Arctica 1978: VIIe Congrès international des bibliothèques Nordiques* [Arctica 1978: 7th Northern Libraries Colloquy] (pp. 381–511), Paris, France, 19–23 September 1978. Colloques internationaux du Centre national de la recherche scientifique [International Conferences of the National Centre for Scientific Research]. https://doi.org/jqzb

Corley Murchison, N. T. (2000, Fall–2001, Spring). Northern/Polar Libraries Colloquy: A brief history. *Polar Libraries Bulletin, 48/49*, 7–8. https://bit.ly/3OjZZnd

Council of Canadian Academies/Conseil des académies canadiennes. (2019). *Canada's top climate change risks: The expert panel on climate change risks and adaptation potential*. https://bit.ly/3WQ6tP5. Accessed 7 Dec 2023.

Dahl, J. (1986). Greenland: Political structure of self-government. *Arctic Anthropology, 23*(1/2), 315–324. https://bit.ly/3I9oILh. Accessed 7 Dec 2023

Furgal, C., & Prowse, T. D. (2008). Northern Canada. In D. S. Lemmen, F. J. Warren, J. Lacroix, & E. Bush (Eds.), *From impacts to adaptation: Canada in a changing climate 2007* (pp. 57–118). Government of Canada/Gouvernement du Canada. https://bit.ly/3G7nJcQ. Accessed 7 Dec 2023

Hager, M. A. (2014). Engagement motivations in professional associations. *Nonprofit and Voluntary Sector Quarterly, 43*(Suppl 2), 39S–60S. https://doi.org/f54r6v.

Hanssen-Bauer, I., Førland, E. J., Hisdal, H., Mayer, S., Sandø, A. B., & Sorteberg, A. (Eds.). (2019). *Climate in Svalbard 2100: A knowledge base for climate adaptation.* Norwegian Centre for Climate Services. https://bit.ly/3WzFneU. Accessed 7 Dec 2023

Hedinsdottir, P., Einarsson, E., Palsdottir, G., Ingolfsdottir, S., & Magnusdottir, S. (1999). Introduction and acknowledgement. In J. W. Markham, A. L. Duda, & M. Andrews (Eds.), *Electronic information and publications: Looking to the future, let's not forget the archival past: Proceedings of the 24th annual conference of the International Association of Aquatic and Marine Science Libraries and Information Centers (IAMSLIC) and the 17th Polar Libraries Colloquy (PLC)* (pp. 3–6), Reykjavík, Iceland, 20–25 September 1998. IAMSLIC. https://bit.ly/3hFS34S. Accessed 7 Dec 2023.

Inouye, R. K. (1990, June 10–14). Bibliography of Alaskana and the 1989 Prince William Sound oil spill [Conference paper]. In R. Kivilahti, L. Kurppa, & M. Pretes (Eds.), *Man's future in Arctic areas: Proceedings of the 13th Polar Libraries Colloquy* (pp. 78–82), University of Lapland. https://doi.org/hz8n

Inuit Nunangat. (1978). *The people's land: A struggle for survival.* Northwest Territories Inuit Land Claims Commission.

Jaakkola, J. J. K., Juntunen, S. & Näkkäläjärvi, K. (2018). The holistic effects of climate change on the culture, well-being, and health of the Saami, the only Indigenous people in the European Union. *Current Environmental Health Reports, 5,* 401–417. https://doi.org/gh2s3r

Knoke, D. (1988). Incentives in collective action organizations. *American Sociological Review, 53*(3), 311–329. https://doi.org/b4qcs6

Laitinen, S. (1990, June 10–14). Scandinavian databases as a source of information about the Arctic region [Conference paper]. In R. Kivilahti, L. Kurppa, & M. Pretes (Eds.), *Man's future in Arctic areas: Proceedings of the 13th Polar Libraries Colloquy* (pp. 150–154), University of Lapland. https://doi.org/hz8n

Lane, H. (2012, June 11–14). Models for the EU Arctic information Centre: Engaging the Polar Libraries Colloquy [Conference paper]. *Cold regions: Pivot points, focal points: Proceedings of the 24th Polar Libraries Colloquy* (pp. 163–173), Boulder, Colorado, United States. https://bit.ly/3N0afjl. Accessed 7 Dec 2023.

LobbyFacts.eu. (n.d.). *North Calotte Council* (NCC). https://bit.ly/3OqxPHh. Accessed 7 Dec 2023.

Mäntylä, R. (2018, Fall). A few Colloquy impressions. *Polar Libraries Bulletin, 80,* 14. https://bit.ly/3mYLcmo. Accessed 7 Dec 2023.

Moon, T. A., Druckenmiller, M. L., & Thoman, R. L. (Eds.). (2021). Executive summary. In *Arctic report card 2021: Rapid and pronounced warming continues to drive the evolution of the Arctic environment* (pp. 4–7). U.S. National Oceanic and Atmospheric Administration. https://doi.org/hpbs

Myllyntaus, T. (1983). Hydro- and thermal power in Finnish industry in the nineteenth and twentieth centuries. *Scandinavian Journal of History, 8*(1/4), 109–118. https://doi.org/dqg27g

Northern Libraries Bulletin. (1971, October). 1, 1–4. https://bit.ly/3PGzSIQ. Accessed 7 Dec 2023.

Northern Libraries Bulletin. (1976, January). 13, 1–14. https://bit.ly/3P7jU9r. Accessed 7 Dec 2023.

Northern Libraries Colloquy. (1973, June 25–29). *Third Northern Libraries Colloquy, Cambridge, England.* Scott Polar Research Institute.

Northern Libraries Colloquy. (1974, June 3–6). Business meeting. In I. Coutinho (Ed.), *Proceedings of the fourth Northern Libraries Colloquy* (p. 42), Arctic Institute of North America.

Polar Libraries Colloquy (PLC). (n.d.-a). *Constitution of the Polar Libraries Colloquy.* https://bit.ly/3AxxHSi. Accessed 7 Dec 2023.

Polar Libraries Colloquy (PLC). (n.d.-b). *Past PLC chairs.* https://bit.ly/3R7Orpe. Accessed 7 Dec 2023.

2 The Polar Libraries Colloquy

Polar Libraries Colloquy (PLC). (n.d.-c). *William Mills Prize*. https://bit.ly/3IbnmgO. Accessed 7 Dec 2023.

Polar Pac Release Information: The Polar Pac Database [Insert]. (1992). *LaserCat user's manual* (2nd Rev. Ed.). Western Libraries Network.

Rantanen, M., Karpechko, A. Y., Lipponen, A., Nordling, K., Hyvärinen, O., Ruosteenoja, K., Vihma, T., & Laaksonen, A. (2022). The Arctic has warmed nearly four times faster than the globe since 1979. *Communications Earth and Environment, 3*, Article 168, 1–10. https://doi.org/h8qd

West, S. M., & McCarthy, P. H. (1994). Polar infromation [sic]: An international approach. *Electronic Green Journal, 1*, 1–8. https://doi.org/h35c

Chapter 3
The Decolonization of Arctic Library and Archives Metadata (DALAM) Thematic Network at the University of the Arctic

Sharon Farnel ⓘ, Sandra M. Campbell ⓘ, David Cox II ⓘ, Lars Iselid, Peter Lund ⓘ, Susanna Parikka ⓘ, Sharon Rankin ⓘ, Ivar Stokkeland, and Päivi Wendelius

Abstract In 2022, the Polar Libraries Colloquy created a thematic network within the University of the Arctic thematic network's structure to address the decolonization of metadata. Metadata, including archival description, subject headings, and other descriptive terminology, sometimes includes terms that are offensive to Indigenous peoples, incorrect, or too general to be useful. The purpose of the Decolonization of Arctic Library and Archives Metadata (DALAM) thematic network is to create an alliance of librarians, archivists, and other information professionals working in metadata decolonization. The network, provisionally approved in 2022, focuses on member education and information as well as resource sharing with the goal of improving efficiencies in circumpolar metadata decolonization efforts. This chapter details the creation of DALAM, its purpose, and its future activities.

Keywords Archival description · Arctic Indigenous peoples · Decolonization · Metadata · Polar Libraries Colloquy · Subject headings · University of the Arctic

---

S. Farnel (✉) · S. M. Campbell
University of Alberta, Edmonton, AB, Canada
e-mail: sharon.farnel@ualberta.ca; scampbel@ualberta.ca

D. Cox II
University of Alaska Southeast, Juneau, AK, USA
e-mail: dbcoxii@alaska.edu

L. Iselid
Umeå University, Umeå, Sweden
e-mail: lars.iselid@umu.se

P. Lund
Scott Polar Research Institute Library, University of Cambridge, Cambridge, UK
e-mail: opl21@cam.ac.uk

© The Author(s), under exclusive license to Springer Nature
Switzerland AG 2024
S. Acadia (ed.), *Library and Information Sciences in Arctic and Northern Studies*, Springer Polar Sciences, https://doi.org/10.1007/978-3-031-54715-7_3

3.1 Introduction

In 2022, a new University of the Arctic (UArctic) (https://www.uarctic.org/) thematic network was created to focus on the decolonization of Arctic library and archives metadata. As an international effort, the Decolonization of Arctic Library and Archives Metadata, or DALAM (UArctic, n.d.-c), aims to address the incorrect, inappropriate, insufficiently specific, colonially-focused, and sometimes derogatory terminology in metadata, subject headings, and materials descriptions of Arctic collections held in libraries, archives, data repositories, and other information repositories around the world.

3.1.1 Polar Libraries Colloquy and the University of the Arctic

The Polar Libraries Colloquy (PLC) (https://polarlibraries.org/) is an international organization of librarians, archivists, and information professionals working in polar regions or working with polar-related collections held outside polar regions. Many PLC members work in University of the Arctic (UArctic) (n.d.-a) member institutions. The PLC joined UArctic as an institutional member in 2005, bringing the perspective of library and archival services to the organization (Campbell, 2007).

The UArctic (2014) was created in 2001 as a

> cooperative network of universities, colleges, research institutes, and other organizations concerned with education and research in and about the North. UArctic builds and strengthens collective resources and collaborative infrastructure that enables member institutions to better serve their constituents and their regions. Through cooperation in education, research, and outreach we enhance human capacity in the North, promote viable communities and sustainable economies, and forge global partnerships.

UArctic is a visionary organization grounded in the knowledge that the geography and setting of the Circumpolar North create educational issues, challenges, and needs that are common to the peoples of that region. In fact, residents of the Arctic and North have more in common with each other than with those located in the

S. Parikka
University of Lapland, Rovaniemi, Finland
e-mail: susanna.parikka@ulapland.fi

S. Rankin
McGill University, Montréal, QC, Canada
e-mail: sharon.rankin@mcgill.ca

I. Stokkeland
Norwegian Polar Institute, Tromsø, Norway
e-mail: ivar.stokkeland@npolar.no

P. Wendelius
University of Oulu, Oulu, Finland
e-mail: paivi.wendelius@oulu.fi

south, even within the same countries (Arctic Centre, n.d.). Initially, UArctic was designed to increase students' knowledge of and engagement with the North, but over time, developed additional services to enable students' learning. For example, to encourage student exchanges among UArctic institutions, a northern content course catalogue was created to show which universities across the UArctic system offer courses learners could attend as international students. Also, the north2north mobility program (UArctic, n.d.-b) helps students travel to UArctic institutions to study. A series of courses taught remotely and onsite at various member institutions results in the Bachelor of Circumpolar Studies degree, representing formal education with a thorough grounding in Northern studies. A system of thematic networks was also developed to assist researchers at worldwide organizations to come together around areas of common interest (UArctic, n.d.-d), and it is within this structure that the DALAM thematic network was created.

3.2 Decolonization of Metadata, Subject Headings, and Description

Libraries and archives in many countries, including UArctic member countries, hold collections of materials by, for, and about Indigenous peoples. The standards most often used to organize and classify most of these collections come from a Western tradition and, therefore, reflect a colonial worldview. These standards include controlled vocabularies such as the Library of Congress Subject Headings (LCSH) and the National Library of Medicine's Medical Subject Headings (MeSH), as well as classification systems such as Library of Congress Classification (LCC), Dewey Decimal Classification (DDC), and Universal Decimal Classification (UDC). Furthermore, descriptive records are usually created in the language of the colonial power rather than the languages of Indigenous peoples. The result is that the language used to describe these collections is often incorrect, culturally inappropriate, or derogatory. The problematic and harmful impacts of these standards and practices are well documented and generally acknowledged within the library and archives professions (Berman, 1995, 2000; Bosom & Dunne, 2017; Bullard et al., 2022; Duarte & Belarde-Lewis, 2015; Farnel, 2021; Hoffman, 2022; Littletree & Metoyer, 2015; Olson, 1999; Rigby, 2022; Sandy & Bossaller, 2017).

Recent movements in many countries to acknowledge and redress past wrongs have given new urgency in revisiting and revising problematic standards and practices. As Perera (2022, pp. 356–357) notes, efforts in this area are known by names such as "critical cataloguing," "inclusive description," "ethical description/cataloguing," "radical cataloguing," "conscientious cataloguing/editing," "reparative description," and "anti-racist description." When focused specifically on materials by, for, and about Indigenous peoples, this work is often referred to as *decolonizing*, aimed at centring Indigenous terminology, culture, and knowledge in descriptive standards and practices. *Decolonization* is defined as the process of deconstructing colonial ideologies of the superiority and privilege of Western thought and approaches. It involves dismantling structures that perpetuate the status quo, addressing unbalanced power dynamics, valuing, and revitalizing Indigenous knowledge and approaches, and weeding out settler biases or assumption. (Cull et al., 2018, p. 7)

In the context of resource description, this work most commonly involves working around subject headings and classification numbers assigned to resources. This resource description often explores the terminology that exists within formal knowledge organization systems such as LCSH, LCC, or DDC and replacing terminology with local alternatives and proposing changes such as enhancing descriptions with keywords, improving content taken from the resources themselves, adding creator affiliations, or creating descriptions in local languages. Within the archival context, where subject headings and classification are less commonly used, efforts focus on revising descriptions to surface the often-unmentioned Indigenous voices and stories.

Why is decolonization work necessary in libraries and archives? A key reason that may seem obvious but deserves repeating is the problematic nature of language itself. As Styres (2019, p. 25) reminds us, "language is never neutral – it can teach us, inform us, entertain us, persuade us, and manipulate us – it can misguide and misdirect truths, thereby perpetuating colonial myths and stereotypical representations." In addition, both Mai (2016) and Bowker and Star (2000) emphasize that all classifications are arbitrary and contextual and cannot nor should not be applied universally. Certainly, libraries and archives have long been complicit in "perpetuating colonial approaches to knowledge by replacing traditional knowledge with Western knowledge, especially in physical libraries established under colonial regimes" (Burgess, 2015, slide 3).

Further necessity for change comes from both moral and professional imperatives. According to the United Nations' (2008) *Declaration on the Rights of Indigenous Peoples*, Indigenous peoples have the right to "maintain, protect and develop the past, present, and future manifestations of their cultures" (Article 11, p. 6) and to "revitalize, use, develop, and transmit to future generations their histories, languages, oral traditions, philosophies, writing systems and literatures, and to designate and retain their own names for communities, places, and persons" (Article 13, p. 7). The ability to access information in your own language is a powerful cultural affirmation.

The archival and library professions are beginning to acknowledge the biases inherent in standards and practices, calling upon its members for action. For example, the Cataloging Ethics Steering Committee (2022, p. 2), a joint group formed from members of the Canadian, American, and British cataloguing communities, notes:

Cataloguing standards and practices are currently and historically characterised by racism, white supremacy, colonialism, othering, and oppression. We recognise that neither cataloguing nor cataloguers are neutral, and we endorse critical cataloguing as an approach to our shared work with the goal of making metadata inclusive and resources accessible.

In the Canadian context, the Steering Committee on Canada's Archives (2022, p. 48) reiterates that

> mainstream archival arrangement and description standards and practices are based on a Eurocentric worldview. Such standards and practices actively marginalize and disenfranchise First Nations, Inuit, and Métis peoples; decontextualize First Nations, Inuit, and Métis histories; and hinder meaningful access to archival materials by and about First Nations, Inuit, and Métis peoples. Canada's archival communities must continue to collaborate with First Nations, Inuit, and Métis governments, communities, and organizations to enrich arrangement and description processes with taxonomies and vocabularies that reflect the varied cultures, languages, histories, and knowledge systems of the governments and communities represented in the archives' collections.

This work involves collaborating with Indigenous peoples to revise standards and practices so that subject headings, descriptive terminology, and metadata appropriately reflect the worldviews, languages, and preferences of the Indigenous populations to whom records are related. Such collaboration requires commitment, resources, and collective action across and among communities, organizations, and individuals.

3.3 Library- and Archives-Related Decolonization Activities in Different Countries

Individual colonial powers colonized various parts of the world, including the Arctic. In colonized countries, governments and other institutions reinforce and perpetuate colonial structures. In countries with colonized Indigenous populations, including much of the Arctic, these Indigenous peoples have worked, and are working, on decolonization efforts. Decolonization of cultural institutions such as libraries, archives, and museums are a part of these broader decolonization efforts. Decolonization of metadata, and specifically Arctic-related metadata, is a small part of a global decolonization effort emerging out of social justice, recognizing that archives and libraries must do more to represent marginalized voices in existing and future collections accurately, respectfully, and inclusively. Peoples, regions, and countries of the Arctic take various approaches to decolonizing metadata and are at different stages in the process.

3.3.1 Alaska

In the United States, efforts towards decolonization have been ongoing for many years. In 2021, in Alaska, members from the Alaska Library Network (ALN) received a State of Alaska Interlibrary Cooperation Grant from the Alaska State Library to investigate the development and creation of a controlled vocabulary for Alaska Native subject headings. A committee was created (ALN, 2023) and, while the initial work plan was to present proposed changes to the Library of Congress, the Program for Cooperative Cataloging (PCC) recommendation to pursue the use or creation of separate thesauri led committee efforts in that direction first, with Library of Congress petitions to follow afterwards (Baxmeyer, 2022).

3.3.2 Canada

In the 1970s, in Canada, Brian Deer created the Brian Deer Classification System (University of British Columbia Library, 2023) to reflect local Indigenous peoples and cultures. After the Truth and Reconciliation Commission of Canada issued its *Calls to Action* in 2015, other Canadian librarians, archivists, and information professionals began working on decolonization efforts. While much of this activity is concentrated in southern Canada, considerable work is being done in Nunavut to incorporate Inuit language into catalogues and create catalogue records using syllabics (Rigby, 2020, 2022).

3.3.3 The Nordic View

The Sámi are the only officially recognized Indigenous people of the European Union (Fáktalávvu, 2023). The Sámi people have traditionally lived, and still live, in areas that extend over the four countries of Norway, Sweden, Finland, and Russia, a cultural region referred to as Sápmi, including the northern parts of Fennoscandia. Sámi Giellagáldu (https://www.giella.org/) is a pan-Nordic language authority and the highest decision-making establishment for the Sámi languages—of which there are nine—that was established in 2022 after several language-related projects between 2013 and 2021 (Institute for the Languages of Finland, 2022). The rise of the American Indian Movement (http://aimovement.org/) since the 1950s and 1960s, expansion of solidarity among Indigenous peoples, and strengthening of Sámi identity after the controversial construction of the hydroelectric power plant in northern Norway—known as the Alta conflict—in the 1980s all led to the revitalization of culture throughout Sápmi (Frandy, 2015). The four neighbouring countries all participate in a common, digitally available *Sami Bibliography* that has a common interface (https://bibsys-almaprimo.hosted.exlibrisgroup.com/primo-explore/search?vid=SAPMI). The Nordic Sámi bibliographies can also be reached via a common search. The *Sami Bibliography* is a joint project between the National Library of Norway, the Sámi Special Library at the Rovaniemi City Library in Finland, the Murmansk State Regional Universal Scientific Library, and Ájtte, the Swedish Mountain and Sámi Museum. Every country accumulates its own

3 The Decolonization of Arctic Library and Archives Metadata (DALAM) Thematic... 31

bibliography, and the records/files are harvested to the common *Sami Bibliography* which is on the server of the National Library of Norway. These Sámi bibliographies cover literature published in Finland, Sweden, and Norway about the Sámi and their culture, as well as materials written by Sámi and in Sámi languages, including books, articles, recordings, videos, and more.

3.3.3.1 Finland

In Finland, the Finnish Sámi bibliography is part of the national Finna search service operated by the Kansalliskirjasto [National Library of Finland] (https://www.kansalliskirjasto.fi/). Most of Finnish libraries', museums', and archives' contents are findable via Finna (https://www.finna.fi/). The General Finnish Ontology [Yleinen suomalainen ontologia], YSO, (https://finto.fi/yso/fi/) is a modern ontology with linked data that is generally used in Finland and new terms and other changes to YSO are made by suggesting them to the National Library. The National Library is currently involved in a two-year project aiming to support Sámi languages within digital systems. One of the aims of the project is to translate YSO into Sámi languages (National Library of Finland, n.d.). In addition, there exists a thesaurus, *Lapponica* (https://finto.fi/lapponica/en/), that is used in Finland at the Rovaniemi City Library's Sámi Special Library which cooperates with the National Library. Overall, many efforts have been made to improve the presence of Sámi languages in libraries, but more work is needed, and the improved findability and visibility of Sámi materials in Finnish cultural institutions is an important goal for the future.

3.3.3.2 Norway

In Norway since the early 1980s, a Sámi bibliographic database (https://samisk.oria.no) was created at the university library in Trondheim. The National Library of Norway [Nasjonalbiblioteket] (https://www.nb.no/) have operated the database since 1993. In addition to DDC, the bibliography uses a classification scheme, also used by the library at the Sámi Parliament [Sámediggi—Sametinget] (https://sametinget.no) in Norway, developed by the Sámi scholar Anders Lööv (1943–2006). Lööv's classification scheme is also use in other Sámi bibliographies in all four neighbouring countries: Norway, Russia, Finland, and Sweden. In general, the decolonization and modernization of subject headings in Norwegian library systems first took place in the 1980s and is an evolving practice as terminologies change. However, and worth noting, very few Norwegian libraries add subject headings and other metadata in Sámi languages.

3.3.3.3 Sweden

DDC was introduced to Swedish research libraries from 2010 and in some Swedish public libraries from 2012. As with any classification system, DDC has its drawbacks regarding the visibility of some subjects, and some of DDC's problems are addressed by Cocq (2021) using Sámi studies as an example. Since 2000, there is a national thesaurus in Sweden, *Svenska ämnesord* [Swedish Subject Words] (National Library of Sweden, n.d.), that takes inspiration from LCSH. The thesaurus is continuously updated and revised with new subject headings that follow corresponding changes in modern vocabulary but has not led to any projects specific to decolonization of subject terms. Spot-checking the thesaurus has not given any indication that decolonization is a significant issue in this matter currently, though there is a need to develop subject headings with suggestions of new terms and find more granularity in existing ones. In Sweden, the responsibility for the Sámi bibliography lies with the Ájtte Museum (https://www.ajtte.com/) in Jokkmokk whose library registers materials into the national Libris database.

3.3.3.4 United Kingdom

In the UK, there has recently been more awareness of the need for decolonization in libraries and archives, and cultural and heritage organizations are examining their subject indexing terminology to remove inappropriate terminology. The National Library of Scotland [Leabharlann Nàiseanta na h-Alba], for instance, adopted a systematic approach to the removal of harmful and disrespectful colonial subject indexing in 2021 (Campsie, 2021). As part of this work Carissa Chew, working in an internship at the National Library, created the *Inclusive Terminology Glossary* (https://culturalheritageterminology.co.uk/glossary) which has since been republished as a live collaborative project (Chew, 2023). A section of the glossary lists terminology covering Indigenous peoples of Canada, Greenland, Siberia, and the Russian Far East. While the glossary provides a useful reference for those seeking to decolonize their subject index terms, and as the website acknowledges, "heritage professionals are encouraged to use their best judgement and consult relevant communities and/or additional resources when the information contained within the Glossary is not sufficient" (para. 1).

In the 1960s, Brian Roberts of the Scott Polar Research Institute Library (SPRI) which holds one of the primary Arctic research collections in the UK, adapted the Universal Decimal Classification (UDC) system to polar regions, creating Polar UDC (Gilbert & Lane, 2008); it is still used at the SPRI and, to some extent, at two Norwegian libraries. While this adaptation was not developed with decolonization in mind, it was an important step in making a classification system that recognized the unique aspects of the polar regions. While revisions have been made over time, more work is required to improve the accuracy and respectfulness of the scheme to make it truly responsive to Arctic Indigenous peoples and their environment. In

2020, SPRI, now a member of DALAM, began working on a metadata decolonization program for the SPRI Library (Peers et al., 2020).

3.4 Creation of the Decolonization of Arctic Library and Archives Metadata (DALAM) Thematic Network

3.4.1 History and Development

Working within UArctic and decolonization contexts, the PLC created the new UArctic thematic network, Decolonization of Arctic Library and Archives Metadata (DALAM), in June 2022. The impetus for creating this group was recognition from PLC members that this topic needed action in many of the members' own libraries and archives. The idea for creating this organization specifically as a UArctic thematic network arose from the fact that UArctic is the only circumpolar organization devoted to Arctic education; its membership covers the entire geography of the Arctic, and its structure provides mechanisms for pan-Arctic communications. The creation of DALAM was the culmination of a year-long effort by a group of PLC members. Much of the development work occurred in 2021 during the second year of the COVID-19 pandemic. Because of pandemic restrictions and the internationally dispersed nature of the group, development meetings were virtual, and the group met monthly to create the proposal for DALAM. The monthly meetings also allowed members to commiserate and begin building a mutual sense of the barriers and needs of members struggling with metadata issues surrounding decolonization.

3.4.2 Purposes and Goals

The primary objective of DALAM involves collaborating with Indigenous peoples to revise standards and practices so that subject headings, descriptive terminology, and metadata are the most accurate in reflecting Indigenous cultures and peoples. Within this broad objective, DALAM (UArctic, n.d.-c, para. 2) has several specific goals: (1) "to help libraries and archives correct the culturally inappropriate, incorrect, and colonially centred metadata, subject headings, and descriptive records which currently exist in Arctic collections"; (2) "to support Indigenous peoples in defining the ways in which they and their environments are described in this domain"; (3) "to make Arctic Indigenous languages more present in metadata, subject headings, and descriptive records"; and (4) "to build infrastructure, practices, tools, and relationships among thematic network partners to promote sustainability going forward." By leveraging the combined strengths of UArctic and the PLC, DALAM aims to help members work together to develop relevant processes, protocols, and standards, as well as share individual libraries' and archives' advances in this area so that decolonization of metadata can be hastened across the circumpolar region.

3.4.3 Administrative Structure

Because the PLC is the lead organization for DALAM, the chair of the PLC Steering Committee is also the DALAM lead. The PLC chairperson is elected every two years; thus, the formal lead of DALAM will change biennially. Throughout the development process and at the time of DALAM's launch, Peter Lund of the SPRI held the chair/lead position, but as of 7 June 2022, one of the current authors (Susanna Parikka at the University of Lapland) took over the position. DALAM also has two continuing vice-leads, currently as of this writing Shannon Christoffersen at the University of Calgary and one of the current authors (Sharon Farnel at the University of Alberta). DALAM members recognize that a network so focused on Indigenous issues should have at minimum an Indigenous vice-lead and efforts to identify such a candidate to fill that role are ongoing.

3.4.4 Membership

Membership in DALAM is open to any librarian, archivist, or information professional who is a PLC member or member of a UArctic institution. The group started small but is growing. Communications inviting new members were sent through both UArctic and PLC communication channels including various email lists, social media, and the *Polar Libraries Bulletin* (https://polarlibraries.org/polar-libraries-bulletin/). As of January 2023, DALAM had 25 members from 20 institutions across the nine countries of Canada, Denmark, Finland, Germany, Greenland, Norway, Sweden, the United Kingdom, and the United States. While most DALAM members are from academic institutions, there is some member diversity (e.g., a school board and a national library and archives). Diversity is also evident by the involvement of the Inuit Tapiriit Kanatami (https://www.itk.ca/), a Canadian Inuit organization helping members understand and advocate for Canadian Inuit human rights and interests. The Nordic countries are also strongly represented in DALAM, bringing connections to and diversity from the Sámi people. Additionally, multiple Alaskan members lead DALAM's membership from the United States. Several Canadian universities are also represented in DALAM, both French and English speaking. Heterogeneity among DALAM members is not restricted to geography, but also includes diversity in libraries' and archives' collections content and metadata. Some of these institutions acquire catalogue records from international suppliers (e.g., Library of Congress) and national libraries, while others use in-house, 'home grown' sources such as the Répertoire de vedettes-matière in Québec.

3.4.5 Accomplishments

DALAM's first major accomplishment was its creation. After a year of development, and with the support and guidance of UArctic's Vice-President Networks, UArctic Indigenous Issues Committee, and Vice-President Indigenous, DALAM was provisionally endorsed in early June 2022 at the UArctic Assembly, held in Portland, Maine. DALAM is working towards final UArctic approval in 2023. The second major accomplishment was delivery of a workshop offered several days after UArctic's initial approval of DALAM. Workshop attendees indicated various levels of knowledge about decolonization, but many issues related to the decolonization of Arctic metadata were still identified nonetheless, including the need to develop plans and processes for beginning widespread metadata decolonization. The workshop was held in-person at the 2022 Polar Libraries Colloquy in Québec City and led by one of the current authors (Sharon Farnel), a lead researcher and practitioner in the field.

The workshop provided an overview of various issues and challenges related to the decolonization of metadata, including strategies for identifying subject headings and descriptive terms that are inappropriate, as well as issues involved in identifying culturally appropriate terminology. The complexities of working with a variety of organizations and institutions, including Indigenous organizations, to make the changes was also highlighted. In particular, the workshop underscored the need to ensure that community organizations are consulted, as well as the importance of having enough time to reflect upon and discuss potential changes. Participants in the workshop also had the opportunity to discuss decolonization in their own libraries and archives, and to learn from each other's experiences. Participants exited the workshop with a list of resources related to decolonizing metadata and a better understanding of the varied processes and time commitments needed, as well as a new supportive network of colleagues who are working on the same challenges. Indeed, the main outcome of the workshop was the solidification of a new network of colleagues dedicated to working on the decolonization of metadata.

3.4.6 Challenges

As with all international organizations, DALAM faces the challenges of operating across many time zones, languages, national and institutional cultures, and governmental environments. DALAM plans to address these challenges by conducting most of its work online, providing asynchronous resources, and holding in-person meetings at different locations. Regional working groups may also mitigate some of these challenges. Some DALAM members also are resident in the traditional lands of many different Indigenous groups whose concerns, attitudes, and approaches to decolonization vary widely and may be, at times, contradictory; words and terminology derogatory to some groups may be desirable to others. DALAM aims to provide a platform where discussions about these differences can be had and solutions to these problems developed.

While Indigenous librarians and archivists exist, few of them work in Arctic institutions. As such, DALAM has yet to identify an Indigenous co-lead. However, several Indigenous members are already part of DALAM, and the group is committed to both increasing Indigenous membership and leadership. DALAM is aware that some countries neither recognize colonialism nor Indigenous populations, preferring instead to identify 'ethnic minorities.' Consequently, some Arctic regions are underrepresented in DALAM, but the network will continue to seek and engage with librarians and archivists in these areas.

3.4.7 Future Activities

Despite the short timeframe over which DALAM has existed, its members have identified several areas requiring additional work. First, while decolonization is an issue that impacts all colonized peoples around the world, many individuals are not aware of the myriad harms caused by culturally inappropriate metadata. DALAM members must continue highlighting the importance of improving metadata to the broader library and information science community and, specifically, to Arctic and Northern librarians and archivists. Second, while work is ongoing in many areas of metadata decolonization, standards are only beginning to develop. DALAM members must work together to create standards that provide guidance to librarians and archivists for dealing with all aspects of decolonization and indigenization of metadata. Third, because many member organizations are only beginning the decolonization process, DALAM will identify or offer continuing education and technical training for members, and early plans for this include collating and making available existing online educational resources and hosting a biennial in-person workshop at the annual Polar Libraries Colloquy. Fourth, to ensure efficient sharing of information, DALAM will create an online space for shared resources, including a list of resources that document culturally appropriate terms identified through consultation with Arctic communities. Fifth, and finally, a great deal remains unknown or misunderstood about decolonization of Arctic metadata. Thus, DALAM will encourage the creation and sharing of research across various venues, including publications in scholarly journals and presentations at the annual Polar Libraries Colloquy and other conferences.

3.5 Conclusion

Much harm caused by the presence of colonialism in metadata occurs at the local and personal levels. For example, individuals are harmed by having to use a pejorative term to search for themselves in library catalogues or archival records. Many organizations (e.g., the Library of Congress, Universal Decimal Classification Consortium, etc.) that create and maintain harmful classification systems and terminologies have international reach, daily exporting their descriptive records to libraries across the globe. Recently, Jody Wilson-Raybould, a member of the We Wai Kai Nation on Vancouver Island, and former Minister of Justice and Attorney General of Canada, defined the concept of the *inbetweeners* as people and communities who "create the space for Indigenous nations and communities to rebuild and create understanding between Indigenous and non-Indigenous communities" (Portman, 2022, p. B6). Indeed, DALAM is an inbetweener organization; it seeks to build structures, processes, and communication channels to close gaps between Indigenous peoples and local and international metadata organizations, as well as aims to better understand the impacts of colonialism in metadata and ensure metadata is respectful and culturally appropriate.

References

Alaska Library Network (ALN). (2023). *Alaska native subject headings grant project.* https://bit.ly/40iY5tc. Accessed 8 Dec 2023.

Arctic Centre, University of Lapland. (n.d.). *Arctic Indigenous peoples.* http://bit.ly/3ZnfD6i. Accessed 8 Dec 2023.

Baxmeyer, J. W. (2022, June 1). *Statement regarding the replacement of "Illegal aliens" in LCSH* [Electronic mailing list message]. https://bit.ly/3JEdr4A. Accessed 8 Dec 2023.

Berman, S. (1995). When the subject is Indians. *American Indian Libraries Newsletter, 18*(2). http://bit.ly/3LPjEgD. Accessed 8 Dec 2023.

Berman, S. (2000, June). Finding material on "those people" (and their concerns) in library catalogs. *MultiCultural Review*, 26–52. https://bit.ly/40jqQWL. Accessed 8 Dec 2023.

Bosom, A., & Dunne, A. (2017). Implementing the Brian Deer Classification Scheme for Aanischaaukamikw Cree Cultural Institute. *Collection Management, 42*(3/4), 280–293. https://doi.org/j34m

Bowker, G. C., & Star, S. L. (2000). *Sorting things out: Classification and its consequences.* MIT Press.

Bullard, J., Watson, B., & Purdome, C. (2022). Misrepresentation in the surrogate: Author critiques of "Indians of North America" subject headings. *Cataloging and Classification Quarterly, 60*(6/7), 599–619. https://doi.org/j34n

Burgess, J. T. F. (2015, March 4). *Cognitive justice and the LIS curriculum* [Webinar]. ALISEXChange.

Campbell, S. (2007, Fall). Report to the polar libraries colloquy on the University of the Arctic Council meeting held at Arkhangelsk, Russia, June 4–9, 2007. *Polar Libraries Bulletin, 59*, 7–8. https://bit.ly/3JGjJRc. Accessed 8 Dec 2023.

Campsie, A. (2021, October 18). Leading historian speaks out as National Library of Scotland rewrites 'harmful' colonial language. *The Scotsman.* https://bit.ly/3TOYj95. Accessed 8 Dec 2023.

Cataloging Ethics Steering Committee. (2022). *Cataloguing code of ethics.* http://bit.ly/3KjMlS1. Accessed 8 Dec 2023.

Cocq, C. (2021). Revisiting the digital humanities through the lens of Indigenous studies—or how to question the cultural blindness of our technologies and practices. *Journal of the Association for Information Science and Technology, 73*(2), 333–344. https://doi.org/gmkj9m

Chew, C. (2023). Inclusive Terminology Glossary. https://bit.ly/3U0hRt3. Accessed 8 Dec 2023.

Cull, I., Hancock, R. L. A., McKeown, S., Pidgeon, M., & Vedan, A. (2018). *Pulling together: A guide for indigenization of post-secondary institutions*. BC Campus. http://bit.ly/3K9PFPi. Accessed 8 Dec 2023.

Duarte, M. E., & Belarde-Lewis, M. (2015). Imagining: Creating spaces for Indigenous ontologies. *Cataloging and Classification Quarterly, 53*(5/6), 677–702. https://doi.org/gghn2c

Fáktalávvu: Faktoja saamelaisista [Facts about the Sámi]. (2023). *UKK* [FAQ]. http://bit.ly/40k9cSN. Accessed 8 Dec 2023.

Farnel, S. (2021, September 14–15). *Local, regional, national: Revising subject headings to respectfully represent Indigenous peoples in Canada* [Conference paper]. Tarik Akan meetings 3: International language and meaning symposium, Istanbul, Türkiye.

Frandy, T. (2015). Suden kaikki nimet: Sudet ja dekolonisaatio Saamenmaassa [All the names of the wolf: Wolves and decolonization in Saami]. In J. Hiedanpää & O. Ratamäki (Eds.), *Suden kanssa* [Within the Wolf] (pp. 42–65). Lapland University Press. http://bit.ly/3nh1NVD. Accessed 8 Dec 2023.

Gilbert, M., & Lane, H. (2008). Forty-five numbers for snow: A brief introduction to the UDC for polar libraries. *Extensions and Corrections to the UDC, 30*, 23–25. http://bit.ly/3JO0dCe. Accessed 8 Dec 2023.

Hoffman, N. (2022). Controlled vocabulary and Indigenous terminology in Canadian Arctic legal research. In S. Acadia & M. T. Fjellestad (Eds.), *Library and information studies for Arctic social sciences and humanities* (pp. 110–132). Routledge.

Institute for the Languages of Finland/Kotimaisten kielten keskus. (2022). *Saamen kielille pysyvä kielenhuoltoelin* [A permanent language maintenance body for the Sámi languages]. http://bit.ly/40jCh0D. Accessed 8 Dec 2023.

Littletree, S., & Metoyer, C. A. (2015). Knowledge organization from an Indigenous perspective: The Mashantucket Pequot Thesaurus of American Indian Terminology Project. *Cataloging and Classification Quarterly, 53*(5/6), 640–657. https://doi.org/gf2d7j

Mai, J.-E. (2016). Marginalization and exclusion: Unraveling systemic bias in classification. *Knowledge Organization, 43*(5), 324–330.

National Library of Finland/Kansalliskirjasto. (n.d.). *Saamelaiskielten tuki digitaalisissa palveluissa* [Support for Sámi languages in digital services]. http://bit.ly/3Zh454v. Accessed 8 Dec 2023.

National Library of Sweden/Kungliga biblioteket. (n.d.). *Svenska ämnesord* [Swedish subject words]. http://bit.ly/3FVAtD4. Accessed 8 Dec 2023.

Olson, H. A. (1999). Cultural discourses of classification: Indigenous alternatives to the tradition of Aristotle, Durkheim, and Foucault. *Advances in Classification Research Online, 10*(1), 107–124. http://bit.ly/3KaHOkI. Accessed 8 Dec 2023.

Peers, E., Marsh, F., & Lund, P. (2020). *Decolonising the SPRI library: Position paper*. https://doi.org/j34t

Perera, T. (2022). Description specialists and inclusive description work and/or initiatives: An exploratory study. *Cataloging and Classification Quarterly, 60*(5), 355–386. https://doi.org/j34v

Portman, J. (2022, November 12). Messy past informs messy present: True reconciliation presents an inspiring blueprint for change. *Edmonton Journal*, B6.

Rigby, C. (2020, January 29–February 1). *Promoting Indigenous language through descriptive cataloguing: Ten years+ of Nunavut experience*. Ontario Library Association Super Conference, Toronto, ON, Canada. https://bit.ly/3FUQkBP. Accessed 8 Dec 2023.

Rigby, C. (2022). ᓄᓇᕗᒻᒥ ᐅᖃᓕᒫᒐᖃᕐᕕᒻᒥᑦ ᑎᑭᓴᒃᓴᐃᑦ = Nunavummi Uqalimaagaqarvimmit Tikisaaksait = Nunavut's library catalogues and the preservation and promotion of Inuit language materials. In S. Acadia & M. T. Fjellestad (Eds.), *Library and information studies for Arctic social sciences and humanities* (pp. 389–407). Routledge.

Sandy, H. M., & Bossaller, J. (2017). Providing cognitively just subject access to Indigenous knowledge through knowledge organization systems. *Cataloging and Classification Quarterly, 55*(3), 129–152. https://doi.org/grfrxt

3 The Decolonization of Arctic Library and Archives Metadata (DALAM) Thematic... 39

Steering Committee on Canada's Archives/Comité directeur sur les archives canadiennes. (2022). *Reconciliation framework: The response to the report of the Truth and Reconciliation Commission Taskforce.* https://bit.ly/3ZcrvYM. Accessed 8 Dec 2023.

Styres, S. (2019). Literacies of land: Decolonizing narratives, storying, and literature. In L. T. Smith, E. Tuck, & K. W. Yang (Eds.), *Indigenous and decolonizing studies in education: Mapping the long view* (pp. 24–37). Routledge. https://doi.org/j34w

Truth and Reconciliation Commission of Canada/Commission de vérité et réconciliation du Canada. (2015). *Calls to action.* https://bit.ly/3nOLc8D. Accessed 8 Dec 2023.

United Nations. (2008). *Declaration on the rights of Indigenous peoples.* https://bit.ly/3FSZ639. Accessed 8 Dec 2023.

University of British Columbia Library. (2023). *Indigenous librarianship: Brian Deer Classification System.* http://bit.ly/3JNXxoa. Accessed 8 Dec 2023.

University of the Arctic (UArctic). (2014, January 28). *News: About UArctic.* https://bit.ly/3Rcj79S. Accessed 8 Dec 2023.

University of the Arctic (UArctic). (n.d.-a). *Members.* http://bit.ly/3TSx8dK. Accessed 8 Dec 2023.

University of the Arctic (UArctic). (n.d.-b). *north2north.* https://bit.ly/46SoxMV. Accessed 8 Dec 2023.

University of the Arctic (UArctic). (n.d.-c). *Thematic network on decolonization of Arctic library and archives metadata.* https://bit.ly/3FZDKBw. Accessed 8 Dec 2023.

University of the Arctic (UArctic). (n.d.-d). *Thematic networks and institutes.* http://bit.ly/3FUZ0rL. Accessed 8 Dec 2023.

Chapter 4
Polar Correspondence in an English City: The Scott Polar Research Institute Library

Katie Hill, Peter Lund ⓘ, and Naomi Boneham

Abstract The Scott Polar Research Institute (SPRI) Library at the University of Cambridge holds a unique collection of polar literature. This chapter incorporates Tim Ingold's account of knowledge generation as correspondence into a history of the SPRI Library. Ingold suggests that knowledge arises within the ontogenetic engagement of beings in correspondence; knowledge is thus dialogic and processual rather than a fixed entity. This chapter shows how SPRI, and especially the library, became a key point of contact between people, places, and artefacts across time and space by fostering a correspondence—an ongoing co-creation of beings and knowledge—crystallizing into the library's collection of books, maps, pamphlets and grey literature, creating as it did so possibilities for future correspondence. The chapter demonstrates how this correspondence changed over the twentieth and twenty-first centuries thus far through the advent of the digital era. The SPRI Library is a hub within a loose network connected by the internet, a network that now includes members of Arctic Indigenous communities as equal collaborators. The chapter suggests that a correspondence mediated by digital technology can complement but not replace the direct engagement of people and material.

Keywords Arctic Indigenous peoples · Decolonization · Polar archives · Polar libraries · Polar regions · Scott Polar Research Institute (SPRI) · Tim Ingold

---

K. Hill (✉)
Independent Scholar, London, UK
e-mail: library@spri.cam.ac.uk

P. Lund · N. Boneham
Scott Polar Research Institute Library, University of Cambridge, Cambridge, UK

© The Author(s), under exclusive license to Springer Nature
Switzerland AG 2024
S. Acadia (ed.), *Library and Information Sciences in Arctic and Northern Studies*, Springer Polar Sciences, https://doi.org/10.1007/978-3-031-54715-7_4

4.1 Introduction

The Scott Polar Research Institute (SPRI) (https://www.spri.cam.ac.uk/) is a unique concatenation of personal initiative, historical circumstance, and the characteristics of the polar regions. The SPRI's spatial and temporal attributes are both easy to pinpoint, and impossible to define. It occupies a single building in the English city of Cambridge; this building is part of the University of Cambridge's estate, as the SPRI is part of this University's geography department. However, SPRI's activities are focused on two vast, distant spaces which themselves are historically contingent in their definition, scope, and nature (cf. Bravo, 2019). The SPRI can claim 1920 as its exact year of foundation, even if its future is unknown, dependent as it is on the changing context of global polar research. In fact, SPRI's most consistent and influential quality is its capacity to facilitate encounters and engagement across time and space. The subject of this chapter affords this capacity: the SPRI Library (https://www.spri.cam.ac.uk/library/).

The idea of founding a polar institute famously emerged during Robert Scott's (1868–1912) ill-fated Antarctic expedition of 1910–1913, during which Scott perished. The account of Frank Debenham (1883–1965), SPRI's founder and first director, confirms how this idea was embedded in the physical experience of the polar exploration of the time, the close personal relationships polar exploration both engendered and required, and the consequent desire to help present and future comrades in the shared project of polar research (Debenham, 1945; cf. Debenham, 1921, 1926, 1933). Debenham and Raymond Priestly (1886–1974) were making a geological survey of Mount Erebus; Priestley had visited Erebus a couple of years earlier. As they worked, they reflected on the need for a central repository of polar field records to save future polar explorers from unnecessary repetitions of previous investigation. Later, Debenham and Charles Wright (1887–1975) discussed the necessity of passing on the adaptations in equipment they had made because of their fieldwork experience to help their future colleagues. A few weeks passed and Debenham found himself sheltering from an Antarctic blizzard in Ernest Shackleton's (1874–1922) old hut. As Debenham was investigating the supplies abandoned by Shackleton's group, he found some writing paper. This paper was "so heavy in quality and smooth of surface that it positively invited one to write" (Debenham, 1945, p. 223). Debenham, using the beautiful, thick paper left by his predecessor, wrote out a plan for a polar institute to act as a repository of field records, research reports, and equipment. This institute would enable future polar explorers to build on their predecessors' efforts and accomplishments.

Debenham's written plan is an instance of correspondence, in the sense recently proposed by Tim Ingold (2021). Ingold's account of correspondence arises out of questioning historically contingent understandings of humanity, knowledge, and environment so prominent in social anthropology for the last three decades (cf. Kohn, 2015; Scott, 2013; Viveiros De Castro, 1998), a discussion emerging from the post-colonialist critique of the discipline. Post-colonialist scholars stated that anthropology's conventional categories were inadequate to engage with the lived experience of anthropologists in their field settings; these categories encouraged anthropologists to misrepresent their consultants' testimony in texts that themselves were acts of colonialist appropriation (cf. Holbraad & Pedersen, 2017). Twentieth century social anthropology could not but reflect an influence from the widespread assumptions of post-Enlightenment Euro-America, positing a separated-out and essentialized humanity, natural world, and knowledge. Anthropologists found, however, that their status as self-sufficient human beings creating externalized bodies of knowledge was impossible to sustain given the huge variety of epistemology and action that exists across space and time. Their work feeds into the realization among information professionals that libraries are organized according to historically contingent perceptions of knowledge generation, ignoring other epistemological traditions such as the knowledge of Indigenous Arctic communities (e.g., Acadia & Fjellestad, 2021; Duarte & Belarde-Lewis, 2015). The current chapter links the post-colonialist reflections on epistemology and ontology in social anthropology to library and information studies (LIS) through the use of Ingold's work. In so doing, the chapter adds to the discussion and practice of decolonization in LIS by setting the history of the SPRI Library within paradigms that already incorporate a critique of the post-Enlightenment tradition (cf. Duarte & Belarde-Lewis, 2015).

Ingold recommends a focus on ontogeny rather than ontology (i.e., a recognition that any kind of being is a process of active formation juxtaposed against and therefore in relation with other processual beings) (Ingold, 2021, p. 8). People do not exist in isolation from each other or their environments, as Indigenous collaborators from around the world have been telling anthropologists for decades (cf. Ingold, 2000; Viveiros de Castro, 1998). *Correspondence*, as Ingold suggests, is the open-ended process whereby beings move along together, and, in doing so, differentiate themselves in relation to each other as emergent entities (Ingold, 2021, p. 8). Further, Ingold contends that knowledge arises within the mutual becoming of beings in correspondence; it is essentially dialogical, as all social life is dialogical (Ingold, 2021, p. 11). Knowledge is given and shared through the open communion of beings in formation as it feeds into and nourishes this ongoing communion; it is thus an open-ended and constantly changing process rather than a fixed and self-sufficient entity that can be collected and stored, as existence itself is open-ended and processual.

Debenham was becoming himself in tandem with Shackleton's old hut, the wind and ice of the Antarctic blizzard, and the slope of Mount Erebus while also moving along with his companion polar explorers' past, present, and future, ruminating on his experiences of Antarctic land, sea, and climate, and the people who would face the Antarctic after him. Debenham's attention to the Antarctic, and his openness to its action on him and his companions, brought forth a new existence planned out on foolscap: the organization that would become the SPRI. Debenham's correspondence, in Ingold's sense, was engendering knowledge; it was an acceptance of the possibilities afforded by the intersection of people, land, weather, paper, and ink to create new entities and their stories. Thus, the SPRI began within a correspondence between Debenham and his human and non-human companions. At first, this correspondence took the physical form of a hand-written plan to develop into a building with a library. This institute, and especially the library at its heart, became a key point of contact between people, places, and artefacts across time and space, fostering a correspondence—an ongoing co-creation of beings and knowledge—which crystallized into the library's collection of books, maps, pamphlets, and grey literature, creating as it did so possibilities for future correspondence.

This chapter presents a brief history of the SPRI Library using historical accounts, archives, and interviews as source materials. Some of these interviews were conducted during SPRI's (2023) own effort to document its history during the 1990s and early 2000s, while 10 others were conducted more recently by the current authors for the purposes of this chapter during November 2021–November 2022 (see Appendix for interviewee alphanumeric pseudonyms and dates of interview). This chapter shows how the quality of the library's correspondence has changed through SPRI's success in generating the scientific data Debenham and colleagues sought to obtain, while also describing SPRI's transformation into a loose network connected by the internet, a network that now includes members of Arctic Indigenous communities as equal collaborators. The internet age refigured SPRI's correspondence into a proliferation of electronic messages rather than personal contact, while facilitating the inclusion of Arctic communities. A great deal of the knowledge that SPRI's network generates now takes the form of data (i.e., fixed measurements and codes that can be both manipulated and incorporated into communication). Finally, the chapter suggests that the fragility of digital correspondence is demonstrated by the consequences of Russia's full-scale invasion of Ukraine in 2022; a correspondence mediated by digital technology cannot replace the direct engagement of people, material, and organisms. Fruitful knowledge generation rests in a correspondence close enough to afford mutual co-formation, as Ingold suggests.

This chapter's first section shows that correspondence was key to both Debenham's research and SPRI's early formation, even if the intentions, methods, and forms of communication of Debenham and colleagues fell firmly within the remit of post-Enlightenment colonialist science. The SPRI began as a close-knit community of people who had committed themselves to the pursuit of polar science, co-creating themselves and one another in their devotion to their shared project alongside both the colonialist paradigms and polar environments that also shaped the project. The storing and manipulation of data began to drive the library's activities over the second half of the twentieth century, as the second section of this chapter describes. Technologies, methodologies, and communicative conventions emerged that changed the practice of polar science and its information management along with the polar regions themselves. This technological development eventually introduced the internet as the key technology of polar research, library management, and communication in general; it emptied the library's physical space of researchers by enabling the collection to be searched from around the world. This chapter's third section uses as an example the SPRI Library's Russian collection to illustrate how the expansion of transport and digital infrastructures, the twists and turns of international politics, and the efforts of particular individuals finally brought Arctic Indigenous communities into a direct conversation with the SPRI. As this chapter was being written, the Russian Federation launched the SPRI into a new phase of its polar research via Vladimir Putin's invasion of Ukraine on 24 February 2022.

The power of data to unite communities of researchers has been undermined, as have the emergent collaborations and correspondences between members of Russian Indigenous communities and the rest of the world. The SPRI Library is left with an imperative to regenerate this correspondence as an intertwined process of contact, knowledge, and life.

4.2 The Scott Polar Research Institution's (SPRI) Foundation in Correspondence

The SPRI (Fig. 4.1) and its collections received their first impetus from the age of heroic exploration, a project of knowledge generation that was undoubtedly colonialist in that it sought to define and measure territories regarded as 'unexplored,' but the individuals who committed themselves to the SPRI firmly understood that it would lead to the betterment of humanity (cf. Debenham, 1921, 1945; Speak, 2008). As the following paragraphs describe, the SPRI and its collections came into existence through the efforts of people, both paid and unpaid, who believed that polar research had an intrinsic moral value and their sense of shared purpose created longstanding personal relationships with each other and like-minded individuals across the world, shaping each other within a correspondence that continued Debenham's engagements during the Terra Nova—or, more formally, the British Antarctic Expedition of 1910–1913. As a result, a unique and eclectic collection of books and papers was amassed, often through donations and bequests.

The personal relationships behind SPRI's inception reflected the skills and activities constituting the knowledge generation of the time, in addition to the physical,

Fig. 4.1 The Scott Polar Research Institute at the University of Cambridge. (Photo credit: SPRI)

moral, and psychological traits required by polar research. Early twentieth-century polar research demanded physical and mental stamina as much as it required technical capability and, perhaps most of all, the powerful motivation of attaining either personal fame, knowledge for the benefit of humankind, or both (Breitfuss, 1928; Mirsky, 1970; Worsley, 1927). Polar research was regarded as a heroic enterprise in early twentieth-century England to the extent that the SPRI was able to rely on voluntary labour during its early years (Debenham, 1945). The SPRI had no paid librarian until 1946; instead, volunteers catalogued equipment, maps, and books. The senior academic staff were also willing to do their share of unpaid "scrubbing" when necessary (Debenham, 1945, p. 234).

Thus, the SPRI and its library fostered knowledge production out of collaborations founded in the twin contemporary imaginaries of heroism and the pursuit of scientific understanding (Wilson, 2003; cf. Debenham, 1921; Firth Scott, 1906). The aim was to map and measure the polar regions largely according to the quantitative techniques and paradigms of the 'hard' sciences as part of the effort to understand how the entire world and its systems worked (Breitfuss, 1928; Debenham, 1921, 1926; Levere, 1993; Mirsky, 1970). Polar researchers understood that they, as self-sufficient human beings, needed to measure and record the polar regions, creating sets of reliable data. These data were, and are, seen as fixed entities to be stored once gathered; they converted the power and unpredictability of the polar regions into numbers and tables and, in doing so, both distanced and tamed polar environments within an often-unwitting act of colonialist appropriation. Figure 4.2 demonstrates this phenomenon via a table presenting meteorological data from the Terra Nova Expedition. Data simultaneously formed the basis of the international conversation about the polar regions known as polar research.

However, the technical capabilities of early twentieth-century Euro-American researchers in the polar regions were limited as they had to rely on shared experience while attempting, firstly, to reach the polar regions and, secondly, to record their cartographic, meteorological, geological, botanical, zoological, and occasionally ethnographic observations. Knowledge formation occurred out of enthusiasm rather than professionalized technical specialization or sustained government funding and its participants combined the assumptions and objectives of empiricist science with an earnest desire to try out new tricks in polar exploration, while learning from each other, as Debenham's, Priestly's, and Wright's conversations in Antarctica demonstrate. Polar research was rooted in a correspondence of human beings and environments, even if the knowledge it aimed to generate tended to fix the polar regions in bodies of abstracted data.

The activities of Winifred Drake, the first director's assistant, show how the contributions of well-wishers shaped the SPRI and its future. Drake not only worked unpaid for the SPRI until 1930, but also took the lead in organizing SPRI's "social life," establishing a pattern whereby assistant staff would also act as hosts (Debenham, 1945, p. 232). Debenham states that Drake and subsequent successors "did much to create the friendly atmosphere which has been a marked characteristic of the Institute" (Debenham, 1945, p. 232). The SPRI became a kind of social club

TABLE 63. METEOROLOGICAL JOURNAL.

JULY, 1911.

CAPE ADARE.

Day.	Hour.	Cloud.				Visibility of Glacier.	Rain or Snow.	Sunshine Hours (since last observation).	Aurora.	Drift.	Remarks.
		Amount.	Kind.	Direction from							
				Upper.	Lower.						
JULY, 1911.											
4	2	7	Haze, Nb.	---	—	Obs.	S. spic.	—	NW to SE	0	Haze.
,,	4	7	Haze, Nb.	—	—	Obs.	S. spic.	—	None	0	Stars shining.
,,	6	10	Nb.	—	—	Obs.	S. spic.	—	None	0	
,,	8	10	Nb.	—	—	Obs.	S. spic.	—	None	0	
,,	10	10	Nb.	—	—	Obs.	S. spic.	—	None	0	Just a light snow falling.
,,	12	10	Nb.	—	—	Obs.	S. spic.	—	—	0	
,,	14	6	Haze, Nb.	—	—	Obs.	0	—	—	0	Moon just rising behind Cape Adare.
,,	16	4	Ci.-Cu., St.	—	—	Obs.	0	—	—	0	Clearing.
,,	18	8	Ci.-Cu., St.	—	—	Obs.	0	—	None	0	Moon just showing through clouds, whitish close halo.
,,	20	9	Nb., haze	—	—	Obs.	S. spic.	—	None	0	22° halo round moon.
,,	22	5	Nb., haze, St.	—	—	Obs.	S. spic.	—	None	0	Moon just showing through haze.
,,	24	10	Nb.	—	—	Obs.	S. gran.	—	None	0	Moon invisible.
5	2	10	Nb.	—	—	Obs.	0	—	None	0	
,,	4	5	Haze, Nb.	—	—	Obs.	S. slt. spic.	—	N to NE	0	
,,	6	10	Nb.	—	—	Obs.	S. spic.	—	None	0	Too much snow falling for aurora to be seen.
,,	8	9½	Nb.	—	—	Obs.	S. slt. gran.	—	None	0	Long streaks of yellow light along the northern horizon.
,,	10	9½	Haze, Nb.	—	—	Obs.	0	—	None	0	Long streaks of yellow light along the northern horizon tinged with red.
,,	12	9½	Haze, Nb.	—	—	Obs.	S. slt. gran.	—	None	0	Fine red sky to N.
,,	14	9½	Haze, Nb.	—	—	Obs.	0	—	None	0	Long streak of white light from N to W horizon.
,,	16	10	Nb.	—	—	Obs.	0	—	None	0	
,,	18	10	Nb.	—	—	Obs.	0	—	None	0	
,,	20	10	Nb.	—	—	Obs.	0	—	None	0	
,,	22	10	Nb.	—	—	Obs.	S. slt. spic.	—	None	0	
,,	24	10	Nb.	—	—	Obs.	S. slt. spic.	—	None	0	Very light, with diffused moonlight.
6	2	9	Nb.	—	—	Obs.	0	—	None	0	Clearing to W.
,,	4	10	Nb.	—	—	Obs.	0	—	None	0	
,,	6	10	Nb.	—	—	Obs.	0	—	None	Low	Low drift.
,,	8	10	Nb.	—	—	Obs.	0	—	None	0	

Fig. 4.2 A table of meteorological data from the Terra Nova Expedition of 1910–1913 as published in *Meteorological Journal*. (Photo credit: SPRI)

for enthusiasts of polar research while affording women an active role in the general enterprise even if it was limited to clerical work (Debenham, 1945; Speak, 2008).

The ethos of the SPRI and its library was set from the beginning: The SPRI would be a convivial gathering place that facilitates collaboration. The international family of *Polaires* would have a place to gather and exchange information (Debenham, 1945, p. 231; Speak, 2008, p. 62). Debenham and colleagues may not have realized that this multinational collaboration was in fact limited to Europeans, North Americans, and Australians. The *Polaires* may have met members of Indigenous Arctic communities on their expeditions, and even adopted their practices as did the explorer Vilhjalmur Stefansson (1879–1962), but they could hardly have imagined them as colleagues because the physical and cultural barriers were too great and intensified by the prevailing tendency to regard Indigenous communities as 'primitive.'

In accordance with Debenham's plan, the SPRI Library began as a multidisciplinary research collection for practical use; it was designed to enable successive generations of polar researchers to learn from their forbears and act as a repository of all the available information in any format related to polar research in the similar way that the SPRI Museum (https://www.spri.cam.ac.uk/museum/) was initially intended to preserve examples of research equipment (Speak, 2008, p. 68). Thus, the SPRI would become a hub for polar researchers across the world, generating a network of collaboration across space and time. As Debenham (1945, p. 228) described, in the early years, the SPRI did indeed act as a "clearing house" for information about the polar regions: He would receive piles of letters, all inquiring about various aspects of polar research. Even if Debenham and other institute members were unable to answer all the questions they received, they were able to direct people to the right sources of information, whether these were texts or individual people. Debenham (1945, p. 228) wrote that "being in touch with a wide circle of polar men, we were rarely at a loss to say who was the particular expert to consult on any matter." Hence, the first institute researchers were effectively also the information professionals of their time: Academic research and librarianship had not yet developed the technical and professional specializations that emerged over the twentieth century (cf. Cox & Corrall, 2013).

Library collecting policies were broad from the start, corresponding to SPRI's status as a clearinghouse for polar research. This breadth of remit allowed the collections to be shaped by several individuals in SPRI's broader network, whether they were staff members, external donors, or both. Formats included maps, monographs, newspapers, theses, periodicals, reports, conference proceedings, and fictional publications. The published work was complemented by original manuscript material, such as exploration journals, scientific notes, and a wealth of correspondence; this material is now kept in SPRI's Archive (Holland, 1982). While the working documents of the Terra Nova Expedition were the first papers to be deposited, the archive collection quickly expanded to embrace the North. This move brought in large manuscript collections and published accounts relating to the nineteenth-century European exploration of the Canadian Arctic, thus creating the first indirect and highly colonialist contacts between the SPRI and peoples who called the Arctic home. As the collections expanded, the SPRI Archive's Anglo-centric collecting policy led to a stronger representation of UK and European perspectives, in contrast to those of Indigenous Arctic communities. However, the library's wider remit affords it a better mix of perspectives. New material arrived through purchases, exchanges, and often bequests from private individuals such as Väinö Tanner (1881–1948), a former professor of geography at the University of Helsinki and Charles Swithinbank (1926–2014), a polar explorer and glaciologist. SPRI's acquisitions could not have happened without the existence of personal connections and the good will they generated.

The SPRI quickly outgrew its first physical accommodation, initially only a few rooms in the Sedgwick Museum at the University of Cambridge. In 1927, the SPRI moved to Lensfield House, later replaced by a purpose-built building on the same site in 1934. This building remains the core of the SPRI with two significant extensions. The oldest part of the library takes up the first floor of the original building (Fig. 4.3); for many years morning coffee would be served in these rooms, sometimes with Chelsea buns as a treat. The library was indeed regarded as the 'heart' of the SPRI for many decades (Interviewee R2; R3; King, 2000). The personal engagement that took place amidst the library's books, pamphlets, tables, and chairs was central to SPRI's research.

Fig. 4.3 First-floor interior of the original SPRI building, 1948. (Photo credit: SPRI)

The enthusiasm for polar research that united SPRI's community generated a culture of longstanding commitment which lasted throughout the twentieth century (Speak, 2008, p. 111). A staff member who replaced the assistant librarian, Anne Savours (1927–2022) while on sabbatical during the 1950s, remembers lodging with the Debenhams: The SPRI was like a family, and she loved it so much that she had to be gently "pushed out" when Savours returned to work (Interviewee LS3). Examples of long-serving staff include Debenham himself, who effectively dedicated his life to the SPRI and geography department; Harry King (1921–2013), librarian from 1955 to 1983; Brian Roberts (1912–1978), a researcher at the SPRI from 1937 to 1975; and Terence Armstrong (1920–1996), SPRI's Russian specialist from 1946 to 1983. As described below, both Roberts and Armstrong contributed a great deal to the library even though they were research staff. Their work demonstrates the porous boundaries between research and library work which persisted at the SPRI until the second half of the twentieth century. The length of time research and library staff devoted to the SPRI also enabled long-term personal relationships to develop among its members and the broader polar research community.

Traces left by the passion and camaraderie that powered SPRI's foundation and early years are still seen in the library and archive, and in their collections. In particular, the habit of donating relevant material has continued as friendly researchers from around the world have sent the SPRI research reports, books published in the Arctic, and grey literature in various forms. Thus, the network of dedicated *Polaires*, in collaboration with numerous librarians and volunteers created a collection of extremely rare material and this collection is one manifestation of the knowledge generation pursued during the age of heroic exploration. Knowledge, even in the form of scientific data, emerged from personal engagements that shaped lives and intentions within an ongoing correspondence. The Indigenous peoples of the Arctic, however, have an ambivalent presence within the knowledge generation of the heroic era. The rapid transformations in technology and communication after the Second World War, described in the next section, finally brought members of Indigenous communities into SPRI's orbit.

4.3 The Cold War and Expansion of Technology

Knowledge generation at the SPRI and its library changed in form, format, and scope as the twentieth century progressed. If the family of *Polaires* was international from its inception, the intensity and reach of SPRI's international collaborations were given additional impetus during the Cold War; the network of relationships grew wider as knowledge generation was channelled into a proliferation of specialized academic disciplines and the profession of information management. The romance and camaraderie of heroic exploration was replaced by the development of increasingly elaborate methods of data gathering, analysis, and retrieval even though personal connections between librarians and researchers remained important. Finally, the digital era brought its own revolution to the SPRI Library and the

4 Polar Correspondence in an English City: The Scott Polar Research Institute Library   51

knowledge generation it facilitates. To be sure, SPRI's correspondence has been reconfigured, along with its library.

Polar science formed part of the wider growth of professionalized science and technological development over the second half of the twentieth century which led the world into the digital era (Ichikawa, 2019; Roberts, 2014; Van der Watt et al., 2019). A cluster of motivations, often connected to military activity, encouraged governments to sponsor scientific research over the twentieth century as an engine of technological development (cf. Eckener, 1958). The generation of technical knowledge through research in engineering and the 'hard' sciences created new possibilities for polar research as polar regions were transformed. The national administrations of Arctic regions all used changing technologies to modernize Arctic territories, replacing earlier settlements with networks of towns and villages; in many cases this modernization aimed to reach and extract the Arctic's natural resources (Armstrong et al., 1978; Fogelson, 1992; James Tester & Kulchyski, 1994; SPRI Archive Folder MS160; MS170/10; MS170/12). Hence, infrastructures for travel, communication, and satellite observation made polar regions more accessible to researchers than ever before, facilitating interaction between researchers across the world. This spiralling interchange of scientific research and technological development is a clear demonstration of Bruno Latour's (1993) claim that empirical science creates its own object. The SPRI and its library were incorporated into a project of knowledge generation that was transforming quickly in interaction with its object of study: the polar regions.

The Cold War (1947–1991) was a key driver of government investment into scientific research and technological development, and the SPRI was closely integrated into this relationship. In fact, Roberts combined a post at the Foreign and Commonwealth Office with his work at the SPRI (Interviewee R3; King & Savours, 1995; Roberts & Heavens, 2020). During the Second World War (1939–1945), the SPRI became an information centre for the Admiralty, much to Debenham's displeasure, and SPRI's close connection with the UK Government continued (Roberts & Heavens, 2020; Speak, 2008). Hence, SPRI's trajectory after the war was part of the twin expansions of polar research in the Soviet Union and the West as the US and Canada sought to catch up with, and then overtake, what they perceived to be the Soviet Union's pre-eminence in Arctic science (Roberts, 2014; Van der Watt et al., 2019). As Roberts (2014) describes, Arctic science was for all sides both a source of key information for resource exploitation and military strategy, as well as a foreign policy instrument.

Accordingly, the SPRI expanded during the Cold War. Gordon Robin (1921–2004), the SPRI director at the time, secured a grant from the Ford Foundation, enabling expansion of the SPRI building; this extension was finished in 1968 (Bicknell, 1968; Interviewee R2). Additional space was provided for the information collections, including a purpose-built archive store. Further additions to the building were made later in the twentieth century and, in 1998, the Antarctic Collection was moved into the newly built Shackleton Memorial Library (https://www.spri.cam.ac.uk/library/building/), consisting of a rotunda staircase between SPRI's three floors (Fig. 4.4). William Mills (1951–2004) was librarian at the time

Fig. 4.4 Rotunda staircase connecting SPRI's three floors. (Photo credit: SPRI)

and the project was also overseen by Captain Joe Wubbold and received financial support from researcher and explorer Thomas Manning (1911–1998). The network of polar enthusiasts remained important to SPRI's fortunes, existing alongside the political and military incentives to support polar research. The number of research staff and students also increased over the second half of the twentieth century.

The SPRI Library continued its initial intention to amass and collate all the polar literature it could possibly find, remaining a kind of clearinghouse of polar information. In interviews, one former archivist emphasizes that the SPRI Library aims to be the best polar library in the world, although not necessarily the best Arctic library (Interviewee LS2). The SPRI Library's bibliographic work increased, as did its contributions to the International Polar Years from 1957, including its work as a World Data Centre (WDC) (Macqueen & Mills, 1995). The International Council of Science created the WDC system to archive and distribute data collected from the observational programs of the 1957–1958 International Geophysical Year. The WDC for glaciology was based at the SPRI Library as the primary bibliographic centre for glaciology (Macqueen & Mills, 1995). The quantity and nature of this data generated a new, specialized role: data centre manager. At its peak, the WDC received 2000 enquiries a year (SPRI, 2012). The WDC also facilitated the growth of SPRI's collection, including its rare and valuable grey literature.

The expansion of scientific research in general fostered an increasing specialization of discipline and theme, and clearer recognition of contrasting professional identities among researchers. Librarians were no exception; as research outputs proliferated, so did the different activities involved in managing these data and the corresponding variation in specializations incorporated into the new profession of information management (cf. Cox & Corrall, 2013). The work of SPRI's collection managers had increasingly become distinguished from the work of SPRI's researchers. The library team gradually changed from the pre-war gathering of volunteers and researchers to a professional team of area bibliographers, archivists, and library assistants. SPRI's largest library team consisted of two full-time and six part-time staff.

The library produced the print publication *Recent Polar and Glaciological Literature*, later *Polar and Glaciological Abstracts* (PGA), from 1934 to 2015 in its capacity as information centre for global polar research. PGA provided up-to-date listings of polar literature to libraries across the world and, in 1988, had over 300 subscribers (Porter & Galpin, 1988). This publication, alongside SPRI's academic journal the *Polar Record*, enabled the SPRI to enter reciprocal exchanges with libraries across the world. The SPRI Library team were able systematically to collect polar literature from around the world, as they collated this literature into PGA. The SPRI also produced volumes such as *Keyguide to Information Sources on the Polar and Cold Regions* (Mills & Speak, 1998). This book contains both bibliographies on polar research in the arts and sciences, as well as lists of relevant institutions and specialists. Before the digital era, the SPRI Library was indeed the place to find out which polar researchers were doing what, and where (Interviewee LS2; R2). SPRI librarians developed their relationships with colleagues in the Americas, Australasia, and Western Europe while, at the same time, Terence Armstrong worked on SPRI's relationships with Soviet librarians and academics. As travel became easier, SPRI librarians and archivists—notably William Mills, Harry King, Shirley Sawtell, and Robert Headland—visited their colleagues across the world and received international visits in turn. Moreover, SPRI staff members began slowly to develop direct contacts with members of Arctic Indigenous communities from 1954.

The transition to professionalized post-war science and data management entailed a corresponding development in the construction of metadata. During SPRI's early decades, handwritten accession registers were split to cover the three distinct collecting areas: archive, library, and museum. For the former two, this information was then transferred into paper and card catalogues, covering author name and then expedition or subject, respectively. The SPRI experimented with a variety of classification systems through the 1930s and early 1940s. As King (2000) remembers, much confusion was created by the fact that each of the many volunteer cataloguers had their own system. Eventually, Roberts adopted the Universal Decimal Classification (UDC) scheme for the library, rewriting sections of it to suit the needs of polar collections. Initially, Polar UDC was compiled from the general English, German, French, and Dutch UDC schedules and translated where appropriate. The work was published and enlarged with eight subsequent supplements between 1950 and 1956 (Roberts, 1956). The British Glaciological Society and a variety of experts helped adapt and expand the UDC schedule following the first edition, and the second edition became known as UDC for Use in Polar Libraries.

As this expansion indicates, other polar libraries were interested in adopting Roberts' cataloguing system and the Norwegian Polar Institute continues to use it. As one former archivist explains in an interview, a universal system based on numbers rather than the alphabet enabled libraries to sidestep the variations in polar place names caused by international politics and the ongoing discovery of Antarctica (Interviewee LS2). Thus, Polar UDC allowed an exchange of ideas across huge political and geographic divides. The schedule, still used in spreadsheet form, retains many features of standard UDC, namely its hierarchical structure, controlled vocabulary, and many of its standard codes (cf. Gilbert & Lane, 2008).

Technologically, the SPRI Library was ahead of its time, at least until the 1990s. Martin Porter developed an electronic catalogue called SPRILIB during the early 1980s based on Muscat software (Porter & Galpin, 1988). Much of the card catalogue was replaced by this bibliographic database in 1985 even if the card catalogue remained in use, and as of 2023, the library began the process of card catalogue digitization. The Muscat catalogue contains just over 200,000 analytical records—a legacy of the days when SPRI's bibliographers wrote abstracts of journal articles and book chapters for inclusion in PGA—as well as 50,000 records of monographs. The catalogue enabled users to search the database on computer terminals installed near the library's entrance, allowing for detailed searching across subject and author fields (Porter & Galpin, 1988). The system was developed further to facilitate a current awareness service called SPRILIST, extracting material for inclusion in PGA while allowing reformatted entries to be added to the Cambridge University Union Catalogue. In 1996, the SPRI website was launched and included a link to the SPRILIB catalogue. Users could search SPRILIB via the internet from 1997, though it would not have been the most up-to-date version of the catalogue because it had to be manually updated at regular intervals. For much of the period of SPRILIB's existence, the technical structure of the catalogue was maintained and improved by Rick Frohlich. The current SPRI webmaster, Martin Lucas-Smith, revamped the interface in 2010 and SPRILIB remained in use until 2019 when it was migrated into iDiscover, the University of Cambridge's online catalogue.

The SPRI Library and its users had opportunities to engage with the internet and its possibilities comparatively early, however the transformation in research practice brought on by the digital era did not make itself apparent until the twenty-first century. Researchers continued to depend on the expertise of library staff as they navigated the collection, often seeking consults as they searched the SPRILIB database and card catalogues. One current researcher interviewed for this chapter remembers the SPRI during the 1980s: The combination of the card catalogue with journal offprints and the librarians' bibliographic expertise worked well, although SPRILIB was a "step in the right direction" (Interviewee R4). Researchers did not necessarily enjoy using SPRILIB (Interviewee LS5; R2; R4; R5) and SPRI Library staff and researchers relied on their personal knowledge of important polar research institutions, publications, and people, as well as the information that was becoming increasingly available via the internet. Thus, the library staff were still critical to the research process and librarians' personalities could significantly influence research projects (Interviewee LS5; R2; R4; R5).

4 Polar Correspondence in an English City: The Scott Polar Research Institute Library 55

Technology might have changed the practice of polar research, but personal engagement remained crucial. The SPRI, therefore, continued to function as a sort of scientific social club. Researchers anticipated regular coffee breaks to find out who was visiting the SPRI that day (Interviewee R3). This social club continued to revolve around the library: Both a SPRI researcher and a former bibliographer interviewed remember that a key purpose of the library was to facilitate meetings between researchers (Interviewee LS5; R3). Current SPRI staff along with retired associates remember streams of visitors to the library from overseas, joining SPRI graduate students and local researchers in what was a calm and convivial intellectual space. One retired archivist said that it was unusual not to have at least one overseas visitor. SPRI graduate students were given desks in the library until the Wubbold Room became available (Interviewee LS2; LS4; R3; R5). Undergraduate users, however, were rare and visitors generally had a longstanding interest in the polar regions if they were not postgraduate students (Interviewee LS4).

In an interview, a current SPRI researcher remembers the SPRI Library of the 1980s as quite a formal, serious space with its own gravitas, yet the atmosphere was also friendly, and the staff kind and helpful (Interviewee R3). Conversation within the library was allowed, but it had to be tactful (Interviewee R3). SPRI's roots in the traditions of heroic exploration and Cold War science were also palpable; to this interviewee, the SPRI felt like a Naval college. In another interview, one retired researcher who moved to the SPRI from the Navy corroborates this atmosphere, immediately feeling at home at the SPRI (Interviewee R5). Yet another retired researcher remembers enjoying the "feel" of the library—the scent of the books, for example—in addition to its courteous, helpful staff (Interviewee R2). Conversely, one library staff member remarks that visitors were often awed by the library, hearing so much about it that they were amazed finally to be viewing the library collection at last (Interviewee LS4). This member of staff found it quite difficult to deal with these visitors because of the hard work needed to put them at their ease; the constant round of social events could become tiring (Interviewee LS4). This person's comments indicate the extent to which library staff members continued to act as hosts, as well as information professionals, whose courtesy was reciprocated both by the hundreds of Christmas cards they received every year, and the volume of rare material donated by visitors, students, and SPRI staff (Interviewee LS5; R4; R5). This material often included a huge variety of ephemera and grey literature, thus affording a rich and unique variety of sources (Interviewee LS2).

The experience of one retired glaciologist captured via interview encapsulates the transformation the advent of internet access wrought at the end of the 1990s (Interviewee R2). The interviewee first entered the SPRI as an undergraduate in 1978 and worked sporadically there during the 1980s and early 1990s. Upon returning to the SPRI in 2001, the interviewee found that the library had emptied; for glaciologists, the print collection had become almost obsolete (Interviewee R2). This participant along with former colleagues had become accustomed to finding and sharing their data and articles using the internet, rather than the library's combination of staff, bibliographies, and catalogues. In addition, they began to collaborate remotely, navigating their way through the constantly expanding volume of global polar science literature and data (Interviewee R4; R5); this created new activities for library staff, including the facilitation of open data management. Thus, the technologies generated by Cold War science—most obviously, the internet—have transformed the SPRI Library's processes, especially surrounding the new preoccupation of polar science: climate change. Scientific knowledge continues to shape its object, while the work of its information professionals shifts in tandem.

However, as all researchers and librarians interviewed for this chapter emphasize, the print collection in its variety of formats retains a critical importance for both humanities researchers and 'hard' scientists because it reveals histories of polar exploration, the emergence of science—especially of climate change—and, crucially, of Arctic Indigenous communities. The collection also contains historical data and methodologies, which are occasionally necessary for empirical polar scientists. One retired researcher notes during interview that the burgeoning volume of material available via the internet can be unreliable as it may be incomplete and can disappear altogether (Interviewee R5). The SPRI print collection continues to offer access to material that is otherwise unavailable.

The SPRI Library of the twenty-first century receives fewer visitors even though its international reputation remains. Humanities researchers worldwide continue to use the library and are joined by an increasing number of undergraduate students who may simply be using its study space. In fact, the internet has established new connections and collaborations by reducing the library's importance as a space for meeting and contact. Indeed, the family of *Polaires* has extended; while connections may be looser, their reach has expanded. Personal encounters over a cup of morning coffee remain significant, but the bulk of engagement now consists of electronic messages. Much research at the SPRI focuses on modelling datasets about the changing climate because the direct physical experience of the polar regions is important, yet not essential to all polar research. The correspondence between people and the polar regions, as well as the research it incorporates, has become digitally mediated. Simultaneously, the digital age has finally brought the Arctic's Indigenous communities into direct and equal contact with the SPRI, as the next section of this chapter explains.

4.4 The Russian Collection

The history of the SPRI Library's Russian collection demonstrates clearly the intersection of international politics, individual initiative, and acquaintance network that generated the collection as a whole. An openness to personal engagement is a crucial part of this story because SPRI's Russian collection could not have come into being without the willingness of individuals in the UK and the Arctic to move along in concert with each other via correspondence. This history also shows how changing communication technologies, Indigenous lifeways, and international politics transformed polar research into a mutually acknowledged collaboration between Indigenous scholars, community members, and researchers from outside the Arctic.

If the Indigenous peoples of Arctic Russia featured in the SPRI Library initially only as the subjects of ethnographic research, they were to become close colleagues, easily reached thanks to social media.

The SPRI was founded in the same year as the expedition that was to become the Soviet Union's own specialist institute for polar research: the Arkticheskiy i Antarkticheskiy Nauchno-Issledovatel'skiy Institut [Arctic and Antarctic Research Institute] (https://www.aari.ru/) (AARI) in Leningrad, now Saint Petersburg (SPRI Archive Folder MS170/10; MS170/12). The later Tsarist Government had been unwilling to invest significant resources into researching its Arctic territories (McCannon, 1998, p. 17), however the early Soviet administration saw the hitherto untapped resources of the Russian Arctic as key to the Soviet state's survival (Breitfuss, 1928; Hirsch, 2005; McCannon, 1998; Slezkine, 1994; SPRI Archive Folder MS159; MS160; MS170/10; MS170/12). The Soviet Government were to create an enormous network of research institutes and infrastructures across the Soviet Arctic intended to identify and exploit its resources while drawing its peoples into the fabric of the Soviet State (cf. Hirsch, 2005; McCannon, 1998; Slezkine, 1994; SPRI Archive Folder MS170/10; MS170/12). This Soviet policy resembled the modernizing policies of other Arctic states over the second half of the twentieth century (Armstrong et al., 1978; James Tester & Kulchyski, 1994). These institutions generated both a huge body of multidisciplinary research on the polar regions and the Soviet-era industries and policies that transformed the Russian Arctic. Indeed, Soviet polar research was instrumental in creating its object. Researchers and librarians at the SPRI were aware of the Soviet Union's burgeoning polar research establishment and sought to connect it to researchers in the West, succeeding in amassing a collection of Tsarist and early Soviet material that is extremely hard to find outside of Russia.

Debenham was in contact with the AARI in 1927 as letters in the SPRI Archive show, arranging various exchanges of material and corresponding with figures such as the Soviet glaciologist Vladimir Wiese (1886–1954) (SPRI Archive Folder WF001.1). During the early 1930s, Otto Schmidt (1891–1956), the then AARI director, visited the SPRI, initiating further exchanges (Warren, 1995, p. 101). In 1933, Debenham published an article about the SPRI in *Arctica*, a journal started by the AARI with the explicit intention of generating discussions between Soviet and non-Soviet polar researchers. Debenham's interactions with the AARI indicate that the political atmosphere of the early 1930s afforded a relatively free and friendly interaction between Soviet and Western academics (cf. Vitebsky & Alekseyev, 2015). Soviet polar researchers in the 1930s seem to have been a distant branch of the *Polaires*, but part of the family, nonetheless.

The Russian-German polar scientist Leonid Breitfuss (1864–1950) provided a key link between Soviet and European polar research, having close familiarity with both the German and Russian research establishments, and making it his business to keep track of the international polar research community and its publications. The SPRI Archive show that Breitfuss and Debenham were corresponding in 1927 (SPRI Archive Folder WF069.41) and, shortly after Breitfuss' death in 1950, the SPRI Library bought his collection of over a thousand books, pamphlets, and maps, much of which was from Tsarist Russia and the Soviet Union. SPRI's connections with the Soviet Union and the possibilities they offered were inflected by the international political situation. For example, the SPRI was able to purchase Breitfuss' collection largely because the relevant German institutions were financially crippled in the immediate aftermath of World War II (cf. Lüdecke, 2001). The twists and turns of international politics also shaped the library's dealings with the few booksellers that offered Soviet material. Supplies from Russia ceased during the 1940s because of the Second World War and Stalinist repressions of the late 1940s and early 1950s, during which supplying Soviet academic material to foreigners became dangerous (cf. Roberts, 2014, p. 129).

Another person who has profoundly enriched the SPRI Library's collection is the anthropologist Ethel Lindgren (1905–1988) who conducted fieldwork in east Siberia and Manchuria during the 1930s, later bequeathing her book collection to the SPRI. Lindgren lived and worked in Cambridge and was a well-known visitor to the library during the second half of the twentieth century (King, 2000). Lindgren's collection juxtaposes Tsarist and early Soviet ethnographies of Siberian communities against Bolshevik discussions of the policies needed to turn these Indigenous peoples into 'good Soviet citizens' (e.g., in editions of the journal *Sovietskaya Aziya* [Soviet Asia] from the late 1920s). The Soviet Administration was to launch a massive project of social engineering—often known now as the Soviet Nationalities Policy (SNP)—that aimed to purge the Soviet Union's non-Russian populations of all the attitudes and practices regarded by the Bolsheviks as 'primitive' (cf. Hirsch, 2005; Slezkine, 1994). The SNP was, and can still be, framed as the gift of modernist education, biomedicine, cultural production, and infrastructure to Indigenous populations; the loss of Indigenous knowledges, languages, and arts, however, was as profound as in the western Arctic. During the first half of the twentieth century, Indigenous Siberians were beyond the horizon of SPRI's communications, separated from SPRI's researchers by vast distances, mutual ignorance, and persistent assumptions about the 'primitive' nature of Indigenous Arctic societies. As an ethnographer who worked closely with Evenk and Sámi communities, Lindgren was one of very few points of contact.

The event that was to bring Indigenous Arctic communities directly into SPRI's orbit, as it massively expanded the library's Russian collection, was the appointment of Terence Armstrong as a research fellow in 1946 (Heap, 1996). Armstrong, having studied Russian at Cambridge University, was employed specifically to increase the SPRI's Russian collection. Over Armstrong's (1993) first decade at the SPRI, he effectively restarted SPRI's relationship with Soviet researchers after contact had been lost during the 1940s. Armstrong achieved this reconnection through an exchange visit between the SPRI and AARI over 1956–1957, the first of many trips to Soviet Russia (Armstrong, 1993; SPRI Archive Folder WF001.1; Warren, 1995). This visit established several regular exchanges, some of which were to last into the twenty-first century, between the SPRI and research institutions and libraries in Russia. Armstrong was also able to secure exchanges with Russian libraries further east, notably the Gosudarstvennaya publichnaya nauchno-tekhnicheskaya biblioteka Sibirskogo otdeleniya Rossiyskoy akademii nauk [State Public Scientific and Technical Library of the Siberian Branch of the Russian Academy of Sciences] (http://www.spsl.nsc.ru/) in Novosibirsk, even visiting parts of the Soviet Arctic during the 1960s and 1970s. Armstrong's first visit to Yakutsk was in 1967.

As states on either side of the Cold War divide stepped up their production of polar research, Armstrong secured and sometimes translated any sources he could find from the Soviet Union, including work by Indigenous scholars, while publishing his own research as an Arctic geographer. British geopolitical advisor Richard Bridge described Armstrong collecting "jigsaw pieces of information that built up into an impressively detailed overall picture of what was going on" (Heap, 1996, p. 266). Soviet books and journals flowed into the SPRI via exchanges, specialist booksellers, and as gifts from friendly contacts, generating the SPRI's unique collection of Soviet-era polar research. As suggested by this collection building, Armstrong's success was due to his willingness and ability to forge enduring and trusting relationships with Soviet colleagues, successfully weathering various political storms. Armstrong (1993) was sensitive to the difficulties his Soviet colleagues faced and offered help where possible (e.g., by carrying messages between cousins separated by the Iron Curtain). Soviet researchers could pass books on to the SPRI Library for safe keeping in case these books became politically undesirable and liable to be destroyed (Interviewee LS5). Armstrong conducted a correspondence through relationships with colleagues, as Breitfuss and Lindgren had also worked in correspondence with others; these engagements were attentive and transformative, often resulting in a creative generation of knowledge.

A 1954 voyage to Labrador, Canada to observe sea ice brought about Armstrong's first direct contact with an Arctic Indigenous community. The ship gave a lift to an Inuit family before 'dumping' Armstrong (1993) on a beach in Alaska at his request. Frank Darnell (1925–2018) once stated that this meeting began Armstrong's lifelong appreciation of Indigenous Arctic culture (Heap, 1996, p. 269). Via this trip, Armstrong encountered Inuit villages before they were radically changed over the second half of the twentieth century (Heap, 1996). This appreciation of Indigenous Arctic culture perhaps motivated Armstrong to consider the position of Siberia's Indigenous peoples in his research on the Russian expansion into the Arctic. Armstrong's book, *Russians in the Arctic: Aspects of Soviet Exploration and Exploitation of the Far North, 1937–57*, shows that during the 1950s he shared the conventional assumption that Indigenous Arctic peoples retained an ancient way of life and would benefit from a Euro-American education (Armstrong, 1958/1972, p. 115). However, Armstrong also criticized Soviet policy for its wholesale Russianization of Indigenous Siberian culture. Fearing that Indigenous lifeways were about to disappear, Armstrong (1958/1972, p. 132) wrote that "such a prospect may sadden only the sentimentalist; but the loss will be deeper than that. A national culture—the way of life of a people, evolved through the centuries—is a contribution to the world of infinite value, for when it has disappeared nothing can replace it."

Armstrong was to continue contacts with Arctic Indigenous communities in Alaska and, where possible, the Soviet Union. Although Armstrong (1993) believed that what he called the 'westernization' of Arctic Indigenous peoples of Canada, the United States, and Europe was inevitable, he realized and acknowledged that contact with Indigenous communities via this phenomenon was causing terrible problems (Heap, 1996). In the mid-1970s, Darnell and a group representing Indigenous communities from the western Arctic asked Armstrong to help organize a series of international seminars on "cross-cultural education in the Circumpolar North" (Heap, 1996, p. 269). As Darnell describes, these seminars were "designed by and for the people for whom the subject matter was a concern, that is, by and for the Indigenous people themselves" (Heap, 1996, p. 269; see Darnell, 1975). From 1975 onwards, these seminars aimed to provide a means for members of Indigenous Arctic communities to meet each other and develop their own education programs (Darnell, 1975). Armstrong (1993) believed that his contribution to these seminars was to speak up for Soviet Indigenous communities, as Soviet-era travel restrictions prevented them from attending; Armstrong stepped down from this role as these restrictions disappeared. Thanks to Armstrong's willingness to engage, the SPRI acquired the potential to become a hub of connection not just for Euro-American polar researchers but also Arctic Indigenous communities. Armstrong's collaborations were facilitated by transport and communication infrastructures that were spreading across the entire Arctic; modernization was creating possibilities for Indigenous political intervention as it, at the same time, undermined Indigenous lifeways.

Social anthropologist Piers Vitebsky joined the SPRI in 1986 to become the head of anthropology and Russian Northern studies. Vitebsky built on Armstrong's tradition of collaborating with Arctic Indigenous communities to revolutionize SPRI's relationship with Indigenous Siberians in particular. Vitebsky's career at the SPRI began just as the Soviet Administration was starting to crumble, affording new possibilities for foreign researchers to visit the Russian Arctic. Vitebsky was one of a vanguard of social anthropologists who were the first to reach the Siberian and Arctic hinterlands during the late 1980s and 1990s, and who laid the basis for a flurry of research into Siberia and the Russian Arctic during the 2000s and 2010s (Vitebsky & Alekseyev, 2015). Among Vitebsky's doctoral students were members of Indigenous communities from Siberia and Greenland. Arctic Indigenous peoples were finally becoming SPRI members and the distinction between researchers and their Indigenous 'others' could no longer exist. These new possibilities were fostered not only by the break-up of the Soviet Union, but also by the development of electronic communication as the use of email became widespread throughout Russia from the mid-2000s. Researchers from Europe and the Russian Arctic were able not only to meet in person, but also foster their collaborations and friendships through email exchanges.

Vitebsky and his students could not have pursued their research without the work of Isabella Warren, Russian bibliographer from 1990 to 2016. Warren worked closely with Vitebsky and SPRI's other researchers, in addition to her colleagues in Russian libraries. Warren was keen to foster the personal connections Armstrong had initiated and emphasized that personal connections were key to collecting material from the Russian Arctic, not "the icing on the cake" (Warren, 1995, p. 101; Warren, 1996). Like Armstrong, Warren visited Russia whenever possible, partly to develop personal relationships with Russian colleagues. During the 1990s

4 Polar Correspondence in an English City: The Scott Polar Research Institute Library 61

especially, obtaining material from Russia was highly complicated, if not chaotic. The specialist booksellers on which Armstrong relied went out of business, while the breakdown of the Russian state and economy prevented libraries from fulfilling their exchange promises (Warren, 2002). Warren and colleagues, both Indigenous and non-Indigenous, overcame these difficulties via close engagements with each other and their correspondence.

A wealth of valuable material to collect became available because Indigenous intellectuals—a product of the SNP's education programs—were finally able to write freely about their peoples' Soviet and pre-Soviet history. The end of the Soviet Union was accompanied by a wave of Indigenous cultural revitalization, producing an extensive literature on Indigenous tradition and practice (Vitebsky & Alekseyev, 2015). These books were, and still can be, produced very cheaply, on very small print runs, are fragile, and quickly become unobtainable. Vitebsky, his students, and colleagues, both Indigenous and non-Indigenous, made concerted efforts to transport material back to the SPRI Library. Researchers were occasionally able to organize new exchanges with Russian Arctic institutions, such as the Komi nauchnyy tsentr Ural'skogo otdeleniya Rossiyskoy akademii nauk [The Komi Academic Centre of the Ural Department of the Russian Academy of Sciences] (Warren, 2002, p. 19). In fact, Warren oversaw a further expansion of the Russian collection, as the Russian Federation clambered out of the chaos and disaster of the 1990s into the economic recovery of Vladimir Putin's earlier presidential terms.

Vitebsky, Warren, and their students and collaborators were enjoying a phase of unusual freedom of expression in Russia during the 1990s and 2000s despite Putin's early assertion of control over Russia's main mass media organs (cf. Zassourskiy, 2001). Vitebsky's students witnessed the slow increase of pressure on dissenting points of view in Russia over the 2000s and 2010s, including the careful management and suppression of Indigenous perspectives. Meanwhile the UK's funding for humanities research in Russia contracted rapidly after the economic crisis of 2008. The emergence of social media made it possible, however, for researchers and librarians in the UK to maintain contact with friends and collaborators in Russia and the wider Arctic into the 2020s. Engagements initiated through direct personal encounters would continue through exchanges of text messages, photographs, and YouTube links on social media. The Coronavirus pandemic, in fact, facilitated this process for librarians through the proliferation of virtual meetings it generated. Librarians from Europe, Russia, Canada, and the United States compared their pandemic experiences in Zoom meetings, further developing these relationships via WhatsApp. The emergence of the internet out of Cold War science created new forms of correspondence as the war itself dissipated. Members of Arctic Indigenous communities were, and are, engaging in these correspondences as equal members. Hence, the then senior library assistant Frances Marsh and Arctic information specialist Eleanor Peers launched in 2021 an online guide on decolonizing Arctic research, inviting digital and non-digital resource suggestions from Indigenous communities across the Arctic (Peers & Marsh, n.d.).

As of February 2022, correspondence with Russian Arctic Indigenous communities in particular is stalled by Putin's full-scale invasion of Ukraine. The Putin

Administration's aggression in Ukraine is mirrored by its growing abuse of Russia's mass communication, indicated above. The war and its propaganda create a breach between the community of Indigenous and non-Indigenous researchers and librarians inside and outside Russia that is difficult to overcome via digital communication. Individuals outside of Russia discover that their colleagues, friends, and family within Russia have an entirely contradictory understanding of the war; the website *Kovcheg* [The Ark] (https://kovcheg.live/), an organization for Russians who have emigrated because of the war, demonstrates this discrepancy in understanding. These differences in perception are so profound that they cannot be explained and settled through digitally mediated communication, especially when both sides are traumatized. A WhatsApp chat, or even a Zoom meeting, cannot replace the long, slow tea-drinking sessions that previously constituted research encounters in the Russian Arctic.

Further, the circulation of deliberate lies and distortions within Russia and beyond has reached the point where the authority of data itself is undermined. For example, Russia's leading independent polling organization, Levada-Tsentr [Levada Centre] (https://www.levada.ru/), is designated as an *inostrannyy agent* [foreign agent] by the Russian Government; its statistics cannot be used in Russia without the risk of legal action, while researchers outside of Russia must be careful to defend their use of its data (cf. Lussier, 2023). Academic researchers now find it difficult to make authoritative claims about Russian public opinion. Thus, data are revealed as an agreement on an authoritative communication process between researchers rather than the crystallization of self-sufficient knowledge (cf. Latour, 1993). Finally, the fragility of online resources noted in the previous section has become all too clear in the Russian case: Online material can simply disappear, even on sites that are not blocked for Russian citizens. This phenomenon was discussed recently at two virtual meetings organized by Akademicheskie Mosti [Academic Bridges] (2023), a group of scholars from the new Russian diaspora.

The SPRI Library retains responsibility towards Arctic Indigenous communities in general. The SPRI and its research are products of the colonialist effort to map the polar regions and their peoples as explained in this chapter and ignoring the need to redress the damage SPRI's colonialist heritage has caused re-instantiates this colonialist attack, especially for Russian Arctic Indigenous peoples under the Putin Administration. Accounts of Indigenous life, language, and practice that precede the full implementation of the SNP are valuable to cultural revitalization in the Russian Arctic. The SPRI Library's ethnographic holdings are both an important conduit of information about Indigenous Arctic communities for those outside of Russia, and a resource for the Russian Indigenous peoples themselves, as Russian Government propaganda attempts to falsify their history. SPRI researchers and librarians cannot ignore the value of SPRI's Russian collection to Indigenous communities living in an explicitly racist, colonial, and violent state. A correspondence with Russia must be maintained despite breakdown in digital communication.

4.5 Conclusion

The history of the SPRI Library shows how its collection and activities emerged at an intersection of historical event, environmental conditions, and individual action in common with twentieth and twenty-first century polar research. Knowledge generation at the SPRI continues to develop and change, and with it the SPRI Library itself. This knowledge generation is fundamentally a process of interconnection across space and time that changes in quality and form. This chapter shows how the correspondence at SPRI's heart—the library—overlaps with new forms of correspondence created by Cold War science and the digital revolution. The direct commingling of human beings passionate about the polar regions and their research now coexists with digitally mediated communication, creating networks that include the peoples of the Arctic. The books and papers on SPRI's shelves coincide with clouds of electronic articles, books, and datasets. To assume that digital formats and methodologies constitute the only relevant forms of polar research, however, is to replicate the colonialist research paradigms that exclude Indigenous knowledge, especially when the vulnerability of digital communication and data is made obvious by Russia's invasion of Ukraine.

The SPRI Library is committed to its work with the Indigenous communities of the Arctic: Efforts are being made to remove colonialist language from Polar UDC, and as part of this endeavour, SPRI Library staff are now contributing to the University of the Arctic's (n.d.) (https://www.uarctic.org/) Decolonization of Arctic Library and Archives Metadata (DALAM) network. SPRI's *Decolonising the SPRI: Position Paper*, finalized in 2020, makes clear the library's intention to continue both its collection of work by Indigenous Arctic writers and its communication with Indigenous Arctic communities about the valuable historical resources it preserves (Peers et al., 2020). Most of all, SPRI librarians aim to continue and cherish the long tradition of direct, personal correspondence; that is, SPRI's ongoing co-creation of people, books, papers, and environments. SPRI's rich collection of books, grey literature, unpublished manuscripts, and ephemera simultaneously emerges from this correspondence, forming the basis of its continuation. Within this collection, Russian books, pamphlets, and journals are both a reminder of SPRI's fruitful correspondence with the Russian Arctic and the hope and means of its resurrection.

Acknowledgements The authors wish to acknowledge and thank all 10 anonymous SPRI participants interviewed for this chapter, as well as Frances Marsh, Sandy Campbell, Ann Keith, Jeremy Wong, John Ash, Julian Dowdeswell, Martin Lucas-Smith, and Laura Ibbett. The authors also acknowledge the crucial work and insight of Frances Marsh to the SPRI Library's recent decolonizing efforts. Finally, the authors thank the Committee on Library and Information Resources at the Association for Slavic, East European, and Eurasian Studies (https://www.aseees.org/), for their organization of meetings throughout the ongoing COVID-19 global pandemic.

Appendix: List of Alphanumeric Pseudonyms of Interviewees as Cited in the Chapter and Dates the Interviews Took Place

Interviewee pseudonym	Date of interview
Library staff interviewee	
LS1	10 November 2022
LS2	22 February 2022
LS3	16 March 2022
LS4	16 December 2021
LS5	29 November 2021
Researcher interviewee	
R1	20 October 2021
R2	17 February 2022
R3	1 February 2022
R4	9 February 2022
R5	4 February 2022

Table credit: K. Hill, P. Lund, & N. Boneham

References

Acadia, S., & Fjellestad, M. T. (Eds.). (2021). *Library and information studies for Arctic social sciences and humanities*. Routledge.

Akademicheskie Mosti/Academic Bridges. (2023). *Kruglyy stol «Ot fevralya do fevralya: chto izmenilos' i chto budet dal'she?»* [Round table "From February to February: What has changed and what will happen next?"] [Event page]. https://bit.ly/3Ri6Xfk. Accessed 8 Dec 2023.

Armstrong, T. (1972). *The Russians in the Arctic: Aspects of Soviet exploration and exploitation of the Far North, 1937–1957*. Greenwood. (Original work published 1958).

Armstrong, T. (1993). *AV 03: Terence Armstrong oral history summary* [Oral history]. Interviewed by H. King. SPRI, University of Cambridge. https://bit.ly/3GAwdc4. Accessed 8 Dec 2023.

Armstrong, T., Rogers, G., & Rowley, G. (1978). *The Circumpolar North*. Methuen & Ltd.

Bicknell, P. (1968). The new building of the Scott Polar Research Institute. *Polar Record, 14*(90), 323–326. https://doi.org/ds44pz

Bravo, M. (2019). *North Pole*. Reaktion.

Breitfuss, L. L. (Ed.). (1928). *Arkticheskaya Oblast': Ee priroda, zadachi i tseli izucheniya. S risunkami, kartoyu i tablitseyu glavneishikh etapov zavoevaniyu Arktiki* [The Arctic region: Its nature, objectives and aims of study. With drawings, maps and a table of the main stages of the conquering of the Arctic]. Aeroarktik.

Cox, A. M., & Corrall, S. (2013). Advances in information science: Evolving academic library specialties. *Journal of the American Society for Information Science and Technology, 64*(8), 1526–1542. https://doi.org/f443cq

Darnell, F. (1975). *The second international conference on cross-cultural education in the circumpolar nations: Purpose and preliminary plan*. University of Alaska.

Debenham, F. (1921). The future of polar exploration. *Geographical Journal, 57*(1), 182–204. https://doi.org/fqp26h

Debenham, F. (1926). The Captain Scott Polar Research Institute. *Geographical Journal, 68*(1), 43–48. https://doi.org/bgxr6p

4 Polar Correspondence in an English City: The Scott Polar Research Institute Library 65

Debenham, F. (1933). The Scott Polar Research Institute, Cambridge, England, its history and aims. *Arctica, 1*, 67–71.

Debenham, F. (1945). Retrospect: The Scott Polar Research Institute 1920–45. *Polar Record,* 223–235. https://doi.org/b27jkw

Duarte, M. E., & Belarde-Lewis, M. (2015). Imagining: Creating spaces for Indigenous ontologies. *Cataloging and Classification Quarterly, 53*(5/6), 677–702. https://doi.org/gghn2c

Eckener, H. (1958). *My zeppelins* (D. Robinson, Trans.). Putnam.

Firth Scott, G. (1906). The romance of polar exploration: Interesting descriptions of Arctic and Antarctic adventure from the earliest time to the voyage of the "discovery". *C. Arthur Pearson.* https://bit.ly/3RmRpY6. Accessed 8 Dec 2023.

Fogelson, N. (1992). *Arctic exploration and international relations 1900–1932: A period of expanding national interests.* University of Alaska Press.

Gilbert, M., & Lane, H. (2008). Forty-five numbers for snow: A brief introduction to the UDC for polar libraries. *Extensions and Corrections to the UDC, 30*, 23–25. https://bit.ly/480DqOo. Accessed 8 Dec 2023.

Heap, J. (Ed.). (1996). Polar profile: Terence Edward Armstrong. *Polar Record*, 32(182), 265–271. https://doi.org/bm6z57

Hirsch, F. (2005). *Empire of nations: Ethnographic knowledge and the making of the Soviet Union.* Cornell University Press.

Holbraad, M., & Pedersen, M. A. (2017). *The ontological turn: An anthropological exposition.* Cambridge University Press.

Holland, C. (1982). *Manuscripts in the Scott Polar Research Institute, Cambridge, England: A catalogue.* Garland.

Ichikawa, H. (2019). *Soviet science and engineering in the shadow of the cold war.* Routledge.

Ingold, T. (2000). *The perception of the environment: Essays on livelihood, dwelling, and skill.* Routledge.

Ingold, T. (2021). *Correspondences.* Polity.

James Tester, F., & Kulchyski, P. (1994). *Tammarniit (mistakes): Inuit relocation in the eastern Arctic, 1939–63.* UBC Press.

King, H. (2000, October 12). *AV 16: Harry King oral history summary* [Oral history]. Interviewed by J. Heap. SPRI, University of Cambridge. https://bit.ly/475Oitr. Accessed 8 Dec 2023.

King, H. G. R., & Savours, A. M. (1995). *Polar pundit: Reminiscences about Brian Birley Roberts.* Polar Publications.

Kohn, E. (2015). Anthropology of ontologies. *Annual Review of Anthropology, 44*, 311–327. https://doi.org/gfkrkx

Latour, B. (1993). *We have never been modern* (C. Porter, Trans.). Harvard University Press.

Levere, T. H. (1993). *Science and the Canadian Arctic: A century of exploration 1818–1918.* Cambridge University Press.

Lüdecke, C. (2001). Leonid Ludwig Breitfuß (1864–1950) in Deutschland: Chronist der Polarforschung und die Umstände des Verkaufs seiner Bibliothek nach England. [Leonid Ludwig Breitfuß (1864–1950) in Germany: Chronicler of polar research and the circumstances of the sale of his library to England.]. *Polarforschung, 71*(3), 109–119. https://bit.ly/47QAxzO. Accessed 8 Dec 2023.

Lussier, D. (2023, February 13). *Trust, political participation, and the stability of Russia's regime* [Lecture paper]. Russian and Eurasian Studies Centre, St. Antony's College.

Macqueen, A., & Mills, W. (1995). World Data Centre. *Science International, 59*, 19–20.

McCannon, J. (1998). *Red Arctic: Polar exploration and the myth of the North in the Soviet Union, 1932–1939.* Oxford University Press.

Mills, W., & Speak, P. (1998). *Keyguide to information sources on the polar and cold regions.* Mansell.

Mirsky, J. (1970). *To the Arctic: The story of northern exploration from earliest times to the present.* University of Chicago Press. (Original work published 1934).

Peers, E., & Marsh, F. (n.d.). *Decolonising Arctic resources* [Research guide]. https://bit.ly/3tfUxN5. Accessed 8 Dec 2023.

Peers, E., Marsh, F., & Lund, P. (2020). *Decolonising the SPRI library: Position paper*. https://doi.org/j34t

Porter, M., & Galpin, V. (1988). Relevance feedback in a public access catalogue for a research library: Muscat at the Scott Polar Research Institute. *Program, 22*(1), 1–20. https://doi.org/bcq8qn

Roberts, B. B. (1956). *Abstract of the universal decimal classification for use in polar libraries*. SPRI, University of Cambridge.

Roberts, P. (2014). Scientists and sea ice under surveillance in the early Cold War. In S. Turchetti & P. Roberts (Eds.), *The surveillance imperative: Geosciences during the Cold War and beyond* (pp. 125–144). Palgrave Macmillan.

Roberts, J., & Heavens, S. (2020). *Penguin diplomacy: Brian Roberts, polar explorer, treaty maker, and conservationist*. Mereo.

Scott, M. W. (2013). The anthropology of ontology (religious science?). *Journal of the Royal Anthropological Institute, 19*(4), 859–872. https://bit.ly/4a65Rw5. Accessed 8 Dec 2023.

Scott Polar Research Institute (SPRI). (2012). *Scott Polar Research Institute review 2012: 86th annual report of the Scott Polar Research Institute, University of Cambridge, UK*. https://bit.ly/3TocbsC. Accessed 8 Dec 2023.

Scott Polar Research Institute (SPRI). (2023). *Oral history collection*. https://bit.ly/3uQUjg2. Accessed 8 Dec 2023.

Scott Polar Research Institute (SPRI) Archive Folders. Various dates. MS159; MS160; MS107/10; MS170/12; WF069.41; WF001.1.

Slezkine, Y. (1994). *Arctic mirrors: Russia and the small peoples of the north*. Cornell University Press.

Speak, P. (2008). *Deb: Geographer, scientist, Antarctic explorer*. Polar Publishing.

University of the Arctic. (n.d.). *Thematic network on decolonization of Arctic library and archives metadata (DALAM)*. https://bit.ly/3FZDKBw. Accessed 8 Dec 2023.

Van der Watt, L. M., Roberts, P., & Lajus, J. (2019). Institutions and the changing nature of Arctic research during the early Cold War. In S. Bocking & D. Heidt (Eds.), *Cold science: Environmental knowledge in the North American Arctic during the Cold War* (pp. 197–216). Routledge.

Vitebsky, P., & Alekseyev, A. (2015). Siberia. *Annual Review of Anthropology, 44*, 439–455. https://doi.org/gfkrk4

Viveiros de Castro, E. (1998). Cosmological deixis and Amerindian perspectivism. *Journal of the Royal Anthropological Institute, 4*(3), 469–488. https://doi.org/bbwbzt

Warren, I. (1995). The trials and tribulations of acquiring Russian material: The experience of the Scott Polar Research Institute Library [Conference paper]. In D. W. H. Walton, W. Mills, & C. M. Phillips (Eds.), *Bipolar information initiatives: The needs of polar research. Proceedings of the 15th Polar Libraries Colloquy* (pp. 101–103), Cambridge, UK, 3–8 July 1994. Bluntisham. https://doi.org/k742

Warren, I. (1996, June 17–22). Needs of Russian polar scientists and possibilities of organizing mutually beneficial exchanges [Conference paper]. In J. Braund-Allen & C. Innes-Taynor, (Eds.), *Creativity, lighting the poles: Collaborative solutions to common problems: Proceedings of the 16th Polar Libraries Colloquy* (pp. 62–66), Anchorage, Alaska, USA. Consortium Library, University of Alaska Anchorage. https://doi.org/k743

Warren, I. (2002). Building a regional collection: The case of the library of the Scott Polar Research Institute, University of Cambridge [Conference paper]. In H. Leich (Ed.), *Libraries in open societies: Proceedings of the fifth international Slavic librarians' conference* (pp. 13–20). Haworth.

Wilson, G. (2003). *The spiritual history of ice: Romanticism, science, and the imagination*. Palgrave Macmillan.

Worsley, F. A. (1927). *Under sail in the frozen north*. Stanley Paul & Co.

Zassourskiy, I. (2001). *Rekonstruktsiya Rossii: Mass-media i politika v 1990-e* [Reconstruction of Russia: Mass media and politics in the 1990s]. Moscow State University Publishers.

Chapter 5
A Review of the Culturally Responsive Guidelines of Alaska Public Libraries

Erin Hollingsworth and Tyson Rinio

Abstract By exploring its origin, history, and revisions, this chapter discusses the *Culturally Responsive Guidelines for Alaska Public Libraries*, a 2006 document sponsored by the Alaska State Library. The Guidelines are unique in that they were passed and accepted by the Alaskan library community at a time when similar culturally responsive guidelines were voted down by both the American Library Association and the Society of American Archivists. However, Alaskans approved the *Standards for Culturally Responsive Schools* more than a decade prior to the public library guidelines. The processes of the initial development and subsequent 2010 and 2018 revisions of the Guidelines are examined, as are the larger library, archival, and educational implications of them. Anecdotal evidence of the Guidelines being utilized to guide library actions in the state of Alaska is also discussed. The four areas of the Guidelines—Library Environment, Services and Programs, Collections, and Library Staff—are each examined with regards to libraries that serve Alaska Native communities. The history of culturally responsive library, archival, and educational policy work in Alaska is trailblazing: Information professionals in Alaska were ahead of their time, creating professional guidelines around the topics of diversity, equity, and inclusion, all while national organizations in the United States were pushing back against this shift.

Keywords Alaska libraries · Alaska Native · Arctic Indigenous peoples · Professional practice · Indigenous librarianship · Library history

---

E. Hollingsworth (✉)
North Slope Borough School District, Utqiaġvik, AK, USA
e-mail: erin.hollingsworth@nsbsd.org

T. Rinio
University of Alaska Fairbanks, Fairbanks, AK, USA
e-mail: tsrinio@alaska.edu

© The Author(s), under exclusive license to Springer Nature
Switzerland AG 2024
S. Acadia (ed.), *Library and Information Sciences in Arctic and Northern Studies*, Springer Polar Sciences, https://doi.org/10.1007/978-3-031-54715-7_5

5.1 Introduction

The *Culturally Responsive Guidelines for Alaska Public Libraries* (CRG) were created in response to the needs of Alaska's diverse populations. The history of the creation and ongoing improvements and additions to the Guidelines is provided in the current chapter. In addition, the authors engaged in participant research and interviews to document and record the events surrounding the creation of the CRG by working directly with library directors who developed the Guidelines and were participants in its subsequent revisions. The authors also interviewed professionals involved in efforts to pass similar guidelines at national library and archival organizations. Included in this chapter is also a discussion of the impact and connectedness the Guidelines have with regards to other library, archival, museum, and educational policies and guidance. Finally, the implementation of the Guidelines in Alaska public libraries is explored.

5.2 The *Culturally Responsive Guidelines for Alaska Public Libraries* (CRG) and their History

The *Culturally Responsive Guidelines for Alaska Public Libraries* (CRG) as they were first published in 2006 are replicated in Appendix 1.

5.2.1 Origin of the CRG

Each year, directors of the 20 largest public libraries in the state of Alaska, as determined by those communities with the largest populations using US Census data, convene for the annual Director's Leadership (DirLeads) retreat. This retreat is facilitated by the Alaska State Library (ASL) to discuss and share common issues, challenges, and solutions facing Alaskan public libraries. DirLead libraries can, and do, change as populations of communities fluctuate. The 20 libraries involved in the year of the CRG's creation were Anchorage, Barrow, Bethel, Fairbanks, Haines, Homer, Juneau, Kenai, Ketchikan, Kodiak, Kotzebue, Nome, Palmer, Petersburg, Seward, Sitka, Soldotna, Unalaska, Wasilla, Wrangell, and the ASL.

Prior to 2006, at the annual meeting in 1996, David Ongley, Director of the Tuzzy Consortium Library at Iḷisaġvik College in Utqiaġvik (formerly Barrow), introduced the topic of providing services specifically for Alaska Native communities across the state. After several years working as a library director in Alaska without having the issue of library services specifically for Alaska Native communities addressed, Ongley brought the concern to the DirLeads group. Ongley was met with director replies of "we have no Natives in our community" (D. Ongley, personal communication, 29 October 2020). Ongley knew that the directors were incorrect even if they, themselves, believed it to be true. Thus, Ongley obtained support from most of the other library directors in DirLeads to create a framework meant to address Indigenous library service needs.

In 2000, Ongley contacted Lotsee Patterson at the University of Oklahoma's School of Library and Information Services to request assistance with the process of facilitating a discussion among Alaska public library directors about what exactly a culturally responsive library should include. Ongley met with Patterson at the International Indigenous Librarian's Conference in Aoteoroa, New Zealand, developing the idea to create the Guidelines. Ongley, Patterson, and library directors from all regions of Alaska met that same year during the 2000 annual DirLeads meeting, but this time with a shared goal. Rather than the annual self-help meeting, the group deviated from their usual format and, with the support of Karen Crane, the Alaska state librarian at the time, they worked to draft the original Guidelines (D. Ongley, personal communication, 29 October 2020).

Although there were library directors who opposed the effort, they agreed to go along with the group to maintain consensus. During the October 2000 DirLeads meeting, the directors divided into different committees, each focusing on a different topic of the Guidelines. Patterson attended the meeting to help guide the conversations. The meeting was the basis for the document that would eventually become the *Culturally Responsive Guidelines for Alaska Public Libraries* (D. Ongley, personal communication, 29 October 2020). Ongley acknowledged that the *Alaska Standards for Culturally Responsive Schools* (Alaska Native Knowledge Network, 1998) significantly influenced the work of the library directors (D. Ongley, personal communication, 29 October 2020). The Standards were adopted by the Assembly of Alaska Native Educators in 1998 and endorsed by a wide range of Alaska Native and educational organizations around the state. The publications of Angayuqaq Oscar Kawagley and Ray Barnhardt, both preeminent scholars in the field of Alaska Native education, were also highly influential in shaping the Guidelines. Ongley was introduced to their work at the University of Alaska Fairbanks and believed it resonated with the movement towards improved cultural understandings in Alaskan libraries (D. Ongley, personal communication, 29 October 2020).

Given that a vast majority of professional librarians who are members of the American Library Association (ALA) (2012) identify as Caucasian, Alaskan library directors believed providing a tool to help the cultural diversity of the state would be beneficial. Ongley stated the expectations of the Guidelines were to provide a "starting place for people who didn't know where else to start in servicing their Native communities" (D. Ongley, personal communication, 29 October 2020). One thing important to keep in mind is that Ongley drafted the Guidelines with other Alaska librarians who did not acknowledge the presence of diversity in their library spaces. From the time of their conception, the larger plan for the Guidelines was to develop protocols and standards that could be implemented industry-wide beyond Alaska. However, this turned out not to be the case as many library and information sciences (LIS) professionals expressed that, while they believed the Guidelines were a good idea, no one was willing to follow through with actions to continue advancing their cause. Notwithstanding, the adaptation of the Guidelines gained ground within Alaska. Committee work with the DirLeads group to draft the Guidelines ended in 2006 and the Alaska Library Association (AkLA) formally adopted them in 2010.

Patterson and Ongley shared the Guidelines with their professional peers at the second International Conference of Indigenous Archives, Libraries, and Museums, sponsored by the Association of Tribal Archives, Libraries, and Museums (https://www.atalm.org/) in Tulsa, Oklahoma in June 2012. Ongley also shared the CRG with the Tribal College Librarians Institute (https://www.lib.montana.edu/tcli/), an annual meeting of tribal college library professionals held each summer at Montana State University in Bozeman. Both Patterson and Ongley planned to promote the Guidelines at the seventh International Indigenous Librarians' Forum in Karasjok, Norway in 2011, however Patterson attended alone because the runway lights were broken at the airport in Barrow and Ongley was unable to leave in time to catch connecting flights to Norway (D. Ongley, personal communication, 29 October 2020).

The AkLA adopted the Guidelines, and the ASL published them, but application has always been voluntary. From conversations with Ongley, it is apparent that the Guidelines were intended to be a living document that evolves to continue reflecting the Alaskan communities which they were created to serve and several revisions to the original document have occurred.

5.2.2 Revision of the CRG, 2010

The first round of revisions to the CRG occurred in 2010. Unfortunately, none of the official communications surrounding that process have been recovered, except for the memories of conversation about specifically adding a section to the Guidelines to address budgets; however, that never came to fruition (D. Ongley, personal communication, 29 October 2020). Ongley envisioned the development of a tool that could be used to help tribal libraries receive increased funding. When this idea was disseminated to tribes, librarians working on the revisions found that the discussion of budgets and potential policy around funding was met with suspicion and reserve. The revision committee did not receive any buy-in for the inclusion of the budget section from the Indigenous communities, disappointing some who saw the Guidelines as a tool to help guide the work of Alaskan libraries, while at the same time, being aware of the trends in national library and museum federal grant funding sources.

5.2.3 Revision of the CRG, 2018

In 2018, at the Alaska Native Issues Roundtable (ANIR) of the AkLA, the CRG was reviewed; it had not been formally reviewed since 2010. A small, volunteer group of reviewers assembled, initially from those attending the 2018 ANIR meeting.

Discussions among the roundtable attendees led to the invitation of other persons not in attendance but who were considered stakeholders and whose professional expertise would assist the review. The final list of participants settled at seven and included three rural public librarians serving predominantly Alaska Native communities and three librarians working in each of the campuses of the University of Alaska: Juneau, Anchorage, and Fairbanks. Finally, a representative of the Alaska Humanities Forum (AHF) (https://www.akhf.org/) was asked to join. The AHF (2022, para. 1) is "a non-profit organization that designs and facilitates experiences to bridge distance and difference—programming that shares and preserves the stories of people and places across our vast state and explores what it means to be Alaskan." The committee was formed in March 2018, holding its first meeting on 10 May 2018. As is common in committee meetings, the first gathering established scope and work methods. With volunteers working from a variety of locations around Alaska, virtual work was determined to be the best course, utilizing Google Documents, Zoom, and email. Each member of the committee reviewed the 2010 version of the guidelines independently prior to the next meeting. In addition, a session at the 2019 AkLA annual conference was necessary to reintroduce the updated Guidelines to the larger Alaska library community to elicit feedback.

The next step for the committee was data collection. A survey was circulated in late September 2018 by email through the AkLA state-wide mailing list. The survey (Appendix 2) was short, consisting of three open-ended questions enquiring about current library use and knowledge of the Guidelines. The survey was open for several weeks. Results (N = 50) indicated that while libraries were aware of the Guidelines, they were not using them. As had happened years before when Ongley was first investigating the issue, many libraries did not feel they served multicultural communities. As important as drafting and reviewing the Guidelines were, promoting them and seeking library buy-in needed increased attention. Furthermore, the survey indicated that there were many questions about how to apply the Guidelines. A reoccurring question was: "What does a culturally responsive library do on a daily basis?" Other common questions included: "How does a librarian know what is considered offensive to a community and what isn't?"; "Does this impact self-censorship?"; "Are you hiring Alaska Native people?"; "How far down the hierarchy do you need to go until you find an Alaska Native person in the library?" To the committee, these questions could be answered via community engagement. To serve communities in meaningful ways, individual libraries must know who their communities are and what their communities value and need. This philosophy is at the heart of the Guidelines.

The CRG review continued, leading to minor changes of wording and a slight shift away from the Alaska Native focus to a more generic consideration for all cultures. The original document was well crafted and after 9 years, only needed a few adjustments. The committee was fortunate to include Rayette Sterling from the AHF to help facilitate an AkLA conference session about the newly updated Guidelines. The initial listening and introduction session at the conference was set for 1 March 2019. Earlier that year in January, the updated Guidelines were circulated along with an invitation to join the session in March through the AkLA mailing list. Initial survey results were gathered with the intention of sharing them with conference session attendees. Sterling's strategy was to employ a 'heard, seen, respected' discussion theme as a springboard into the importance of the updated CRG (Liberating Structures, 2021). Small groups were formed in break-out sessions to discuss specific points. The planned session included sending attendees home with postcards to write down something they had done to make their library more culturally relevant to their communities to be mailed back a few weeks following the conference.

Sterling and one of the current authors (Tyson Rinio, chair of the ANIR), held the conference session in Spring 2019. The ensuing discussion was lively, leading to some interesting anecdotes of how foreboding and sometimes exclusive libraries seem. The librarians in attendance seemed genuinely interested in making culturally relevant changes in their libraries, but there were continued questions of exactly what this meant on a day-to-day basis. Throughout the discussion, the committee also recognized that while public library directors had been largely responsible for the CRG's creation, no one had been assigned custodian of the CRG; that is, who was responsible for the stewardship of the Guidelines? After thorough discussion, the decision was made that the ANIR would be tasked with a regular Guidelines review. Moreover, the Guidelines were added to the Alaska Native Knowledge Network (ANKN) website hosted by the University of Alaska Fairbanks. However, the ANKN site (http://www.ankn.uaf.edu/) has not been updated since 2011 at the time of this writing and the link to the CRG is non-functional. Given the continued questions of what cultural relevance looks like on a day-to-day basis, the committee surmised that a book of anecdotes would be a useful supplement to the CRG, though its creation was beyond the scope of the committee.

Finally, planning began for the 2020 AkLA conference. A follow-up listening session was intended for the conference to determine how people were implementing the Guidelines in their libraries. The COVID-19 pandemic, however, necessitated a substantial reworking of the conference to take place online and without the traditional conference proposal submission process. The follow-up conference session later in 2020 as initially planned was not possible and did not happen. Further work on the Guidelines is suspended temporarily but may be revisited in the future.

5.3 Larger Libraries, Archives, and Museums and Educational Implications

5.3.1 Alaska Education

Around the same time as the development of the CRG, the Assembly of Alaska Native Educators adopted the *Alaska Standards for Culturally Responsive Schools*. The Standards "provide a way for schools and communities to examine the extent to which they are attending to the educational and cultural well-being of the students in their care" (ANKN, 1998, p. 2) and are endorsed by several Alaska Native educators' unions, research organizations, the Alaska State Board of Education, and Alaska Federation of Natives, the state's largest Native organization. The Standards address the five areas of students, educators, schools, curriculum, and communities. Similar in intent, Alaskan librarians and educators sought to create professionals, spaces, and services that were culturally responsive, reflective, and inclusive for Alaska Natives. Much of the momentum in the state in the late 1990s and early 2000s was in the direction of working to create institutions that were responsive to the needs of Alaska Natives.

5.3.2 The American Library Association and Traditional Cultural Expressions

The ALA began working on guidelines regarding traditional cultural expressions around the same time Alaskan librarians were working on the CRG. Alaska librarian Sue Sherif was active within AkLA, ALA, and the American Indian Library Association, working diligently to communicate progress between groups and foster this work. Although documentation of early ALA committee work surrounding traditional cultural expression is unavailable online, a later draft, *Librarianship and Traditional Cultural Expressions: Nurturing Understanding and Respect 7.0*, is published on the ALA (2022) website. The draft was adopted in 2010 by the AkLA, the only US organization to do so.

Plans by the ALA to continue working on traditional cultural expression are long abandoned as there were early objections to it (e.g., opposition to language used in the document, concern that it promoted censorship through the call to restrict access to certain materials held in collections, and the belief that it did not accomplish what it set out to do regarding protection of materials related to traditional cultural expression). The AkLA experienced similar setbacks when working to formally recognize their own traditional cultural expressions document, the CRG. Attempts were made to introduce a formal document based on the AkLA adoption of the ALA's traditional cultural expressions document, but many of the same issues that were presented nationally were also problematic within Alaska.

5.3.3 The Society of American Archivists (SAA) and the Protocols for Native American Archival Materials

The *Protocols for Native American Archival Materials* were developed in 2006 by a working group of professionals known as the First Archivist Circle (2007). The Protocols were submitted to professional organizations, including the SAA, for endorsement in 2007. A proposal introducing the Protocols was developed by the Native American Archives Roundtable of the SAA and the SAA president established a task force that presented the Protocols and their findings to the SAA Council in 2008. While the Protocols failed to receive endorsement, a forum of three sessions was established at each of the SAA annual meetings from 2009 to 2011 (O'Neal, 2012).

Many of the same issues encountered in Alaska when considering the culturally responsive management of information were also discussed by archivists in SAA. One of the issues was the ongoing education of and about the Protocols highlighting the need for continually educating library and archival professionals about Indigenous issues (O'Neal, 2012). Although many other organizations endorsed the original 2006 Protocols, the SAA (2018) endorsed them formally after 12 years of work. Resources regarding the Protocols are available via the SAA (2022) website.

5.4 Implementation of the CRG in Alaska

As with all guidelines discussed in this chapter, acceptance of the CRG are entirely voluntary. Although implementation of the Guidelines is not forced, acceptance of them is considered best practice in Alaska.

5.4.1 Library Environment

The school libraries located in the seven remote villages of the North Slope of Alaska (as shown by Figs. 5.1 and 5.2) also serve as community public libraries. These libraries are part of the North Slope Borough School District public schools that operate public library hours in the evenings, weekends, and summertime when school is not in session. Many of the seven remote villages have populations under 500 people and the communities do not have the capacity to support a public library. The tribal entities designate the pre-K-12 school library as the official tribal library for the community and the Native American Library Services Basic Grant from the Institute of Museum and Library Services (IMLS) is awarded to fund the operations. The grants are awarded to Iḷisaġvik College (https://www.ilisagvik.edu/) and this arrangement is made possible through a memorandum of understanding with Tuzzy Consortium Library (TCL) (https://www.tuzzy.org/) overseen by the college. The physical library space has signage in English and Iñupiaq and many also include local art and science installations. For example, the library at Aḷak School in Wainwright has an articulated ring seal skeleton on display under glass. The library at Kali School in Point Lay has a skeleton of a beluga whale mounted on plexiglass and suspended from the ceiling over the public computers along with display cases of taxidermized local birds. Each school library in the North Slope has locally created Iñupiaq posters, student artwork, and local photographs on display.

5 A Review of the Culturally Responsive Guidelines of Alaska Public Libraries

Fig. 5.1 Map of Alaska showing the location of the North Slope Borough. (Map credit: M. T. Fjellestad via openstreetmap.org, 2023. CC BY-SA 2.0)

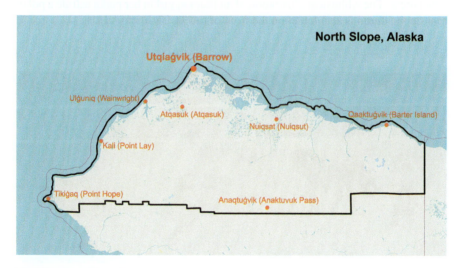

Fig. 5.2 Map of North Slope Borough showing the location of the seven remote villages where the school libraries serve as community public libraries, as well as the borough seat of Utqiaġvik. (Map credit: M. T. Fjellestad via openstreetmap.org, 2023. CC BY-SA 2.0)

The TCL, located in Utqiaġvik, has physical space full of reminders that it is located in an Iñupiaq community. This connection is reinforced by the fact that the TCL is housed in the same building as the North Slope Borough Iñupiat Heritage

Center (https://www.north-slope.org/departments/inupiat-history-language-culture/inupiat-heritage-center/). At the entrance of the library through the front doors that have bowhead whale handles is a large mixed media art installation created by Lawrence Ulaaq R. Ahvakana, a local Iñupiaq artist. The installation features a series of backlit stained-glass panels that depict Arctic surroundings throughout the course of a year. The two far ends of the panel depict the 24 h of polar Arctic night presented in deep blues with white ice, polar bears, and programmed multicoloured LEDs that mimic northern lights dancing in the sky. The next panels on each end and working towards the centre depict the local whaling culture with boats featured in the ornate glass. The middle panel is made up of bold orange and red colours, with emphasis on the midnight sun and illustrating the blanket toss that happens during Nalukataq summer celebrations. As described by Robinson (2016), the blanket toss requires 30 or more 'pullers' who stretch a large, reinforced skin, usually that of bearded seal. A 'jumper' then goes to the centre of the skin to be sent 20–40 ft. (6–9 m) into the air.

Once inside the library, individuals can view rotational displays of local artists' works (e.g., the frame-encased ceremonial baleen that was carried by the library's namesake, Evelyn Tuzroyluk Higbee, at the TCL's grand opening, and a beautiful mural behind the circulation desk titled *Arctic Odyssey* as shown in Fig. 5.3). The mural was created by Annie Patterson, commissioned by the local Rotary Club of Barrow Nuvuk. The art depicts the circumpolar peoples of the world in their traditional dress. The whimsical illustration of an Iñupiaq girl in her parka astride a polar bear on the mural is also found on the front of the TCL's library cards.

Fig. 5.3 *Arctic Odyssey* mural at Tuzzy Consortium Library. (Mural created by Annie Patterson. Photo credit: E. Hollingsworth)

5.4.2 Services and Programs

While working on this chapter, the authors reached out to several Alaskan public libraries to ask how the Guidelines have influenced policy and programming. Overwhelmingly, respondents discussed how the COVID-19 pandemic has changed library practice. Nonetheless, a variety of programs and outreach opportunities continue to strive towards putting the CRG into practice.

Bethel is a town of approximately 6000 persons on the Alaskan west coast (US Census Bureau, n.d.-a) and about 65% of them are Alaska Native. The Bethel Public Library's YouTube channel features tutorials about beadwork and fish cutting, and library staff assist with summer culture camps. The camps include ethnobotany in their summer reading program where an ethnobotanist works with local children to gather and identify plants while learning their uses. The library works with the local University of Alaska Cooperative Extension Service to provide canners for checkout and partners with Alaska Public Media for programming around *Molly of Denali*, a children's television show featuring an Alaska Native lead character. As COVID-19 changed library practices across Alaska, the library saw an opportunity to purchase a vehicle and start a book delivery service to make resources available to patrons that could not access them. This new mobile service is praised by village Elders (T. Quiner, personal communication, 25 February 2021).

The Martin Monson Regional Public Library in Naknek also partners with community members, most recently exhibiting artworks of nine Alaska Native Elders, including the city mayor, painted by a local artist. The library also hosted a visit by an author writing an ethnohistory about the local area, giving community members familiar with the area and Indigenous culture an opportunity to review the author's drafts and make suggestions and corrections. In addition, the library showcased two short format films created by a community member from the local youth and partnered with the Katmai Conservancy to advise and guide decisions that affect local subsistence practice.

In Fairbanks, the second largest community in Alaska with a regional population within the Fairbanks North Star Borough of over 95,000 people (US Census Bureau, n.d.-b), the public library serves diverse cultural groups from around the world. The library holds cross-cultural communication trainings, most recently focused on the Indigenous culture local to the Interior of Alaska where Fairbanks is located. The library also holds summer reading programs on local Indigenous topics. For the summer of 2020, the library planned a series of Native story times, encouraging Native language learning for young children. In addition, the library partnered with the local Native Corporation, shifting their original plan from reading books—of which there are few—to oral presentations of storytelling. Unfortunately, the project was suspended with the rise of COVID-19 (M. Harter, personal communication, 25 February 2021).

The Juneau-Douglas City Museum (https://juneau.org/library/museum) is in Juneau, Alaska's capital city. Although not a library, the museum does represent the cultural responsiveness toward which the Guidelines strive. The museum was designed to represent Juneau's diverse population and its purpose is "to collect, preserve, interpret, and exhibit those materials that document the cultures and history of the Juneau and Douglas area" (B. Weigel, personal communication, 26 February 2021). The museum seeks local Indigenous expertise when selecting new, and updating old, exhibits. One example of such an installation is an award-winning exhibit on the Unangax̂ internment (1942–1945) during World War II where the museum worked closely with local tribal government to ensure the story was told in the way they desired. The museum worked with these tribal governments to host a panel discussion about the exhibit, a video of which is available on the museum's YouTube channel. A recent collection acquired by the museum includes several artworks by Indigenous artists and the museum works with them to develop protocols around the handling, use, and education of the exhibited works.

5.4.3 Collections

To the best of the current authors' knowledge, there are no published collection policies that prioritize the collection of culturally responsive materials within public libraries in Alaska. However, there are ongoing efforts by the AkLA, ASL, and Alaska Center for the Book (https://www.alaskacenterforthebook.org/) to conduct diversity inventories, acquire locally created materials, and collaborate with members of local communities to work towards providing varied collection offerings. These organizations also support the publication of diverse materials authored by Alaskans.

Alaska Best Beginnings: Alaska's Early Childhood Investment (2012), an organization dedicated to preparing children in the state for academic success when they start school, supports Alaskan creators in the publication of multiple works, including *Babies on Track*, an early education set consisting of two board books, a DVD video, and other educational resources. The board books contain photographs of diverse babies' faces and images of common things found in Alaska, all without words. The intent behind these photographic collections is to encourage people engaging in media literacy with babies to do so in the language of their choice. Importance is placed upon the interaction with the language and the pages. To disseminate the sets into the hands of caregivers, Best Beginnings distributed them to public libraries, hospitals, and childcare centres. The resource was such a huge success that the organization published follow-up board books using the same formula of beautiful photography highlighting unique aspects of Alaskan life but free of any specific language or wording.

Another local organization promoting diversity in publication is the Sealaska Heritage Institute (https://www.sealaskaheritage.org/). A book they published, *Shanyaak'utlaax: Salmon Boy* (Marks et al., 2017), was the 2018 winner of the American Indian Library Association's American Indian Youth Literature Award for best picture book. Michaela Goade, the book's award-winning Alaska Native illustrator, became the first woman of colour ever to be awarded the prestigious Caldecott

Award in 2021 for illustrations in another picture book, *We Are Water Protectors* (Lindstrom, 2020). Goade credits the recognition of her Alaska Native culturally responsive work for putting this book and other works featuring Indigenous children's literature into the national limelight.

5.4.4 Library Staff

There is no ALA-accredited LIS education program within the state of Alaska. Thus, the ASL received funding in 2011 from the IMLS to provide extensive LIS training that grew out of the identified need expressed by the library directors who participated in the committee work to draft the CRG. The Alaska Native Libraries, Archives, and Museums Summit (ANLAMS) was:

> convened at the University of Alaska Consortium Library in April 2011. It was intended for professional and paraprofessional staff members working in Alaska libraries, museums, archives, and cultural centers that serve a significant Alaska Native population or who work with Alaska Native cultural materials. This summit was the result of a focus group of Alaska Native librarians, archivists, and cultural center staff. The Summit offered professional development and training at the paraprofessional and professional levels and was a launching point for a plan to make training in our fields more accessible for cultural heritage agencies throughout Alaska. (ASL, 2021, para. 1)

The summit offered multiple opportunities to meet with Indigenous scholars and leaders working in cultural institutions and provided the time and space for practitioners working in remote geographies of Alaska to network and build professional relationships. Following the initial summit, follow-up trainings occurred through 2013.

Based on the positive feedback and success of the initial ANLAMS, a follow-up grant project was proposed to continue library education with a focus on rural and Indigenous communities. An IMLS Laura Bush Twenty-First Century Librarian Program grant was subsequently received by the Alaska Library Network (ALN) (https://www.aklib.net/) in late 2017. Development of the grant was shared between the ALN and the AkLA's ANIR. The grant planned to improve the workforce for community and tribal libraries, with the secondary goal of disseminating course materials and project-produced webinars to national and regional library organizations. The result of this grant effort was a weeklong conference in October 2018. While there were additional plans for onsite projects in several rural communities, these were ultimately abandoned with the travel restrictions brought on by the COVID-19 pandemic in the spring of 2020. Instead, 21 professional development video modules were produced using Zoom as a presentation platform. This continuing education series is titled *Alaska Native Libraries, Archives, and Museums: Honoring Alaska Native Heritage* and hosted by the ASL (2022).

5.5 Conclusion

The *Culturally Responsive Guidelines for Alaska Public Libraries* is a document of library best practices that grew out of the need to be inclusive in institutions of information. Education professionals in Alaska were at the forefront of this movement, and library professionals in the state soon followed. Alaskan librarians and archivists worked to help encourage similar policies at national organizations with varying degrees of success. The Guidelines are a reminder to librarians to be mindful in their practice; they are a tool to provide a starting point for building community in the facilitation of relationships. Cross-cultural exchanges of information are nuanced and the Guidelines were developed with the intent to serve as a guide from which to begin culturally inclusive practice. The Guidelines are not forced upon libraries, but rather offer a voluntary path crafted by knowledgeable professionals who understand the need to prevent cultural missteps while cultivating positive experiences.

Acknowledgements *Quyanaqpak* to the professionals who worked to draft the CRG. *Quyanaqpak* also to those who took the time to remember, reflect, and share their experiences from the process. The authors express their sincerest gratitude and thanks.

Appendix 1: The *Culturally Responsive Guidelines for Alaska Public Libraries* (CRG) (AkLA, 2006)

Preface

The *Culturally Responsive Guidelines for Alaska Public Libraries* were developed by a group of Alaskan library directors at a workshop facilitated by Dr. Lotsee Patterson and sponsored by the Alaska State Library. (Some of these directors have retired or moved onto new positions). The goal of the workshop was to develop guidelines to help public librarians examine how they respond to the specific informational, educational, and cultural needs of their Alaska Native users and communities.

These Guidelines are predicated on the belief that culturally appropriate service to Indigenous peoples is a fundamental principle of Alaska public libraries, and that the best professional practices in this regard are associated with culturally responsive services, collections, programs, staff, and overall library environment.

While the impetus for developing the Guidelines was service to the Alaska Native community, as the library directors worked on the Guidelines it became clear that they could be applied other cultural groups resident in Alaska. The Guidelines are presented as basic statements in four broad areas. The statements are not intended to be inclusive, exclusive, or conclusive, and thus, should be carefully discussed, considered, and adapted to accommodate local circumstances and needs.

The Guidelines may be used to:

- Review mission and vision statements, goals, objectives, and policies to assure the integration of culturally appropriate practice.

- Examine the library environment and atmosphere provided for all library users.
- Review staff performance as it relates to practicing culturally specific behavior.
- Strengthen the commitment to facilitating and fostering the involvement of members of the Indigenous community.
- Adapt strategies and procedures to include culturally sensitive library practices.
- Guide preparation, training, and orientation of library staff to help them address the culturally specific needs of their Indigenous patrons.
- Serve as a benchmark against which to evaluate library programs, services, and collections.

Library Environment

- A culturally responsive library is open and inviting to all members of the community.
- A culturally responsive library utilizes local expertise to provide culturally appropriate displays of arts, crafts, and other forms of decoration and space design.
- A culturally responsive library makes use of facilities throughout the community to extend the library's mission beyond the walls of the library.
- A culturally responsive library sponsors ongoing activities and events that observe cultural traditions and provide opportunities to display and exchange knowledge of these traditions.
- A culturally responsive library involves local cultural representatives in deliberations and decision making for policies and programs.

Services and Programs

- A culturally responsive library holds regular formal and informal events to foster and to celebrate local culture.
- Culturally responsive programming involves members from local cultural groups in the planning and presentation of library programs.
- Culturally responsive programming and services are based on the expressed needs of the community.
- Culturally responsive programming recognizes and communicates the cultural heritage of the local area.
- Culturally responsive services reach out and adapt delivery to meet local needs.

Collections

- A culturally sensitive library provides assistance and leadership in teaching users how to evaluate material about cultural groups represented in its collections and programs.
- A culturally responsive library purchases and maintains collections that are sensitive to and accurately reflect Native cultures.
- A culturally responsive library seeks out sources of materials that may be outside the mainstream publishing and reviewing journals. A culturally responsive library seeks local community input and suggestions for purchase.
- A culturally responsive library incorporates unique elements of contemporary life in Native communities in Alaska, such as food gathering activities and the *Alaska Native Claims Settlement Act* (ANCSA), into its collection.

- A culturally responsive library encourages the development and preservation of materials that document and transmit local cultural knowledge.
- A culturally responsive library makes appropriate use of diverse formats and technologies to gather and make available traditional cultural knowledge.
- A culturally responsive library develops policies for appropriate handling of culturally sensitive materials.
- A culturally responsive library reviews its collections regularly to insure that existing materials are relevant and appropriate.
- A culturally responsive library collects materials in the languages used in its community when they are available.

Library Staff

- The culturally responsive library reflects the ethnic diversity of the local community in recruitment of library boards, administrators, staff, and volunteers
- A culturally responsive staff recognizes the validity and integrity of traditional knowledge systems.
- Culturally responsive staff is aware of local knowledge and cultural practices and incorporates it into their work. For example, hunting seasons and funeral practices that may require Native staff and patrons to be elsewhere, or eye contact with strangers, talkativeness, or the discipline of children.
- A culturally responsive staff is knowledgeable in areas of local history and cultural tradition.
- A culturally responsive staff provides opportunities for patrons to learn in a setting where local cultural knowledge and skills are naturally relevant.
- A culturally responsive staff utilizes the expertise of elders and culturally knowledgeable leaders in multiple ways.
- A culturally responsive staff will respect the cultural and intellectual property rights that pertain to aspects of local knowledge. Culturally responsive library staff members participate in local and regional events and activities in appropriate and supportive ways.

Appendix 2: Survey Questions Distributed Online by the 2018 CRG Revision Committee via the AkLA Mailing List

Survey questions
1. Have you heard of the guidelines?
2. Are you using them? How?
3. If not, what would a culturally responsive library look like to you?
Survey credit: ANIR

References

Alaska Humanities Forum (AHF). (2022). *About us*. https://bit.ly/3OecWyk. Accessed 8 Dec 2023.

Alaska Library Association (AkLA). (2006). *Culturally responsive guidelines for Alaska public libraries*. https://bit.ly/3RzrzRT. Accessed 8 Dec 2023.

Alaska Native Knowledge Network (ANKN). (1998). *Alaska standards for culturally responsive schools*. https://bit.ly/3PvSCtt. Accessed 8 Dec 2023.

Alaska State Library (ASL). (2021). *(ANLAMS) Alaska Native libraries, archives, and museums summit*. https://bit.ly/3PrYyDW. Accessed 8 Dec 2023.

Alaska State Library (ASL). (2022). *Alaska Native libraries, archives, and museums: Honoring Alaska Native heritage*. https://bit.ly/3yM5Knw. Accessed 8 Dec 2023.

American Library Association (ALA). (2012). *Diversity counts 2012 tables*. https://bit.ly/3o60rdL. Accessed 8 Dec 2023.

American Library Association (ALA). (2022). *Librarianship and traditional cultural expressions: Nurturing understanding and respect 7.0*. https://bit.ly/3RJZvZV. Accessed 8 Dec 2023.

Best Beginnings: Alaska's Early Childhood Investment. (2012, November 9). *Babies on track premieres huge success*. https://bit.ly/3yMvmR7. Accessed 8 Dec 2023.

First Archivist Circle. (2007). *Protocols for Native American archival materials*. https://bit.ly/3PBKN5g. Accessed 8 Dec 2023.

Liberating Structures. (2021). *Heard, seen, respected (HSR)*. SessionLab. https://bit.ly/3OdNEAv. Accessed 8 Dec 2023.

Lindstrom, C. (2020). *We are water protectors*. Roaring Brook.

Marks, J., Chester, H., Katzeek, D., Dauenhauer, N., & Dauenhauer, R. (2017). *Shanyaak'utlaax̱: Salmon boy*. Sealaska Heritage Institute.

O'Neal, J. R. (2012). *Final report: Native American protocols forum working group*. Society of American Archivists. https://bit.ly/3yHy6PI. Accessed 8 Dec 2023.

Robinson, E. (2016, April 14–16). Dancing in the air, standing out at sea: An analysis of Nalukataq, the blanket toss [Conference paper]. *Wellness and healing: Indigenous innovations and Alaska native research: Proceedings from the Alaska Native Studies Conference 2016*, Anchorage, AK, USA. Alaska Native Studies Council. https://bit.ly/3RgtDwF. Accessed 8 Dec 2023.

Society of American Archivists (SAA). (2018) *SAA council endorsement of protocols for Native American archival materials*. https://bit.ly/3PyleCf. Accessed 8 Dec 2023.

Society of American Archivists (SAA). (2022). *Protocols for Native American archival materials: Information and resources page*. https://bit.ly/3yLp58b. Accessed 8 Dec 2023.

US Census Bureau. (n.d.-a). *Quick facts: Bethel city, Alaska*. https://bit.ly/3Pdx8BD. Accessed 8 Dec 2023.

US Census Bureau. (n.d.-b). *Quick facts: Fairbanks North Star Borough, Alaska*. https://bit.ly/41dyByO. Accessed 8 Dec 2023.

Chapter 6
The Liquid Arctic and Digitalization

Spencer Acadia ⓘ

Abstract Following Zygmunt Bauman's concept of 'liquid modernity,' this inter-disciplinary chapter introduces Liquid Arctic as an extension of the Global Arctic discourse. Part I of the chapter discusses in basic terms what is meant by Liquid Arctic, including various global problems; decline of the nation-state; human migration and movement of people; sense of accelerated time; rise of non-places such as airports and hotels; consumer consumption by way of fast-food restaurants and shopping malls; and tourism. Part II provides an overview of the digitalization phenomenon as a characteristic of Liquid Arctic and explores digitalization in and of the Arctic by way of digital cultural heritage, specifically via discussion of the Arctic digital collections of libraries, archives, and museums, as well as research data management of Arctic digital datasets.

Keywords Arctic cultural heritage · Digital archives · Digital libraries · Digital museums · Digitalization · Global Arctic · Globalization · Liquid modernity · Research data management · Zygmunt Bauman

6.1 Introduction

In the true nature of Arctic and Northern studies, this chapter is interdisciplinary; it is not rooted exclusively in library and information science (LIS), though it should be of broad relevance to LIS professionals, researchers, and scholars interested in the wider discourses of complex issues regarding Arctic societal change, Arctic digital transformation, and Arctic cultural heritage. As such, this chapter is pertinent to varied readers with diverse interests in Arctic and Northern studies. The purpose

---

S. Acadia (✉)
University of Denver, Denver, CO, USA

© The Author(s), under exclusive license to Springer Nature
Switzerland AG 2024
S. Acadia (ed.), *Library and Information Sciences in Arctic and Northern Studies*, Springer Polar Sciences, https://doi.org/10.1007/978-3-031-54715-7_6

of this chapter is twofold: First, the concept of Liquid Arctic is proposed as an extension of and a descriptor alongside the more common and popular Global Arctic term. While true that the Arctic of today is indeed global, the current chapter argues that the Global Arctic framework, although not an incorrect depiction, is an insufficient one. Instead, the Arctic must be viewed as liquid—in Zygmunt Bauman's sense—to better grasp the unique state in which the contemporary, and future, Global Arctic exists. Second, and within the Liquid Arctic context, the chapter explores the concept of digitalization, which is of direct appeal to the discipline and practice of LIS. Digitalization is then discussed by way of digital cultural heritage using two examples: (1) Arctic digital collections of libraries, archives, and museums (LAMs), and (2) Arctic digital datasets and research data management. The chapter is intentionally painted with broad strokes of critical theory and concept as it aims both to describe the Arctic in its liquid modern condition and argue why LIS and LAMs with Arctic interests should find useful the conceptualization of the Circumpolar North as liquid.

Definitions of 'Arctic' are provided elsewhere (e.g., Dodds & Nuttall, 2019; Dodds & Woodward, 2021), but, in general, *Arctic* and *Circumpolar North* as used synonymously in this chapter refer to the collective northern geographic and geopolitical region of Alaska, Faroe Islands, Greenland, Iceland, northern Canada, northern Finland, northern Norway, both northern and far eastern Russia, and northern Sweden. The Arctic of today's late-modern and globalized world is a multinational collection of these regions and the nation-states of which they are a part, including Denmark and the United States. At further distance and through large international bodies such as the Arctic Council (https://arctic-council.org/), other world countries within Europe (e.g., Italy, Poland, Spain, etc.) and across Asia (e.g., China, India, Japan, etc.) stake their own circumpolar claims via right to occupy Arctic land, sea, ice, and air for research and science, freight shipping and transport, and entertainment and tourism. Although conceptualizing 'the' Arctic in terms of its similarities as one vast, unified geographic region does have some analytical value (see Acadia & Fjellestad, 2020), the Circumpolar North is a mosaic of many varied entities who wish to be independent and sovereign while simultaneously being part of a global Arctic, asserting their rights to belong to it. Within Bauman's liquid modernity is the "twin social processes of globalisation and individualisation" (Davis, 2016, p. 2); that is, doubly experiencing a reality as part of something larger in scope while simultaneously retaining individualistic characteristics. For the Liquid Arctic, this twin contradiction means that countries, corporations, non-governmental organizations, and other groups with their own individualistic autonomies are eager to be involved in the affairs of an interconnected and global Arctic.

In 2009, Vannini and colleagues passively mention liquid modernity in an article about the re-continentalization of Canada's northern archipelago, but those authors do not explore the idea of liquid modernity with any depth. Over 10 years later, in 2020, and although they did not use the Liquid Arctic term at the time, Acadia and Fjellestad (2020) previously describes the contemporary Arctic in its state of liquid modernity through examination of critical sociological concepts such as globalization, glocalization, migration, place, southern theory, urbanization, and more. The present chapter continues Acadia and Fjellestad's work by naming and introducing Liquid Arctic via sociologist Zygmunt Bauman's (1925–2017) idea of liquid modernity.

PART I

6.2 The Liquid Arctic: Uncertainty and Risk in the Circumpolar North

In this chapter, the term Liquid Arctic is not used exclusively to describe the melting of Arctic ice due to climate change, though such use would also be appropriate. Instead, Liquid Arctic as a framework is introduced to characterize the overall condition of late modernity in the Circumpolar North by invoking Bauman's notion of liquid modernity and applying it to the Arctic context. The Arctic has become a container within and through which the currents of global change, both old and new, ebb and flow. Change has always occurred across human existence in the Arctic as elsewhere, but liquid modernity refers to the unprecedented nature of this change and the profound worldwide transformation it brings. For Bauman, all aspects of human life in the contemporary globalized world—society, culture, economics, politics, and so on—are now in a condition of continuous fluidity, always fluctuating and shifting much like flowing water, the destination of which is unknown and unknowable. As said by Bauman (2011, p. 11), "what makes modernity 'liquid' … is its self-propelling, self-intensifying, compulsive and obsessive 'modernization,' as a result of which, like liquid, none of the consecutive forms of social life is able to maintain its shape for long."

Already and for a while now, the Arctic has been described as *Global* (Dodds, 2018; Finger & Heininen, 2019; Finger & Rekvig, 2022a; Shadian, 2018), *Interconnected* (Latola & Savela, 2017), *New* (Evengård et al., 2015), and *Evolving* (Lavengood, 2021). Moreover, accounts of Arctic *crashes* (Krupnik & Crowell, 2020), *futures* (Arbo et al., 2013; Avango et al., 2013; Brigham, 2007; Foundation for Environmental Strategic Research, 2012; Larsen & Hemmersam, 2018), and *megatrends* (Hansen et al., 2012; Rasmussen, 2011), all signalling Arctic transformation, have been and continue to be published. Via this published research, globalization of the Arctic is plentifully discussed (see also Heininen & Southcott, 2010; Keskitalo, 2008; Keskitalo & Southcott, 2014) and a full exposition of it cannot be provided here. However, what can be said is that the evidence is clear that the Arctic has become increasingly enmeshed in global affairs and risen as an emerging world region facing intense change. Of note is the ongoing Global Arctic project (https://globalarctic.org/) that rightly describes the Arctic in terms of large-scale change that affects, and is affected by, the rest of the world. To be sure, the Arctic of today is indeed global and globalized, but to classify it only as such—as Global Arctic—is insufficient; it certainly is global, but it is also more than that. Missing from both the overall Global Arctic discourse in general, as well as the Global Arctic project in particular, is an overarching theoretical framework upon which ideas and topics within these can be scrutinized. Two of the main architects of Global Arctic (Finger & Rekvig, 2022b, p. 16) write in the introduction to the second edition of their handbook that the Arctic is:

> losing the ability to govern itself, not just the Arctic's Indigenous peoples, but most of the Arctic states, driven as it is by different global forces, be they economic, ecological, or geopolitical. While this overall picture of the direction of the Arctic emerges relatively clearly, the question of the future of our Global Arctic project needs to be posed explicitly.

Thus, the current chapter aims to pose Liquid Arctic as a sensible and explicit extension of Global Arctic discourse generally, and the Global Arctic project specifically, via Bauman's liquid modernity. The current chapter, therefore, joins the ever-expanding library of Arctic literature by proposing Liquid Arctic as a conceptual and analytical device to envision, interpret, and explain the circumpolar change of today and the future, along with the abounding uncertainty, insecurity, risk, and anxiety this change generates.

The liquid aspect of Bauman's *liquid modernity* is meant to be used as a macro-, large-scale metaphor to help conceptualize the fluid, ever-changing, and impermanence of the times in which humanity now lives. In 2000, Bauman coined the term to describe the late-modern world as one where "change is *the only* permanence, and uncertainty *the only* certainty ... everything could happen, yet nothing can be done with confidence and certainty" [emphasis in original] (Bauman, 2000/2012, pp. viii, xiv). Indeed, according to Bauman (1997, 2007b), living in liquid modern times means coming to terms with the fact that change is a mainstay, bringing with it profound uncertainty of the future, global insecurity, high-profile risk, and foreboding anxiety. Bryant (2007, p. 129) takes Bauman a bit further by proclaiming that "we are all in a state of turbulence. Bauman's liquid modernity is not simply one characterized by flow, it encompasses turbulence, and this has become the norm." Uncertainty, insecurity, risk, anxiety, and turbulence in the liquid modern world is exemplified by the many growing late-modern problems and hazards that are global in their reach, including, for example, the effects of endemic and pandemic health emergencies and outbreaks, climate change, natural and human-made disaster, poverty and unequal distribution of wealth and resources, national exceptionalism, widespread circulation of mis- and dis-information, exploitative capitalism, financial crises, undue surveillance of everyday citizens by governments and corporations, and political turmoil and war.

Sociologist Ulrich Beck (1944–2015) opens the English edition of the book *World at Risk* with a declaration that encapsulates the threat of unending risk in today's world: "The anticipation of catastrophe is changing the world" (2009, p. 1). In the late 1980s, Beck developed the term *risk society* (1992), then later *world risk society* (1999, 2009), to explain the current era as one that is replete with these new kinds of widescale threats that are recognized as such and require preventative measures to mitigate. Sørensen and Christiansen (2014, p. 10) use air pollution as a striking example:

6 The Liquid Arctic and Digitalization

> The fact that massive air pollution exists … is not enough to call a given society—even though it may experience and suffer from massive air pollution—a risk society. The risk society emerges only once the pollution comes to be, and is perceived as, a problem in and by itself; risk society arises once people start to question whether a particular kind of product or production method can be seen as beneficial and whether the product is *worth* the pollution it causes [emphasis in original].

Threats to life have always existed and the presence of threats alone do not make a risk society; rather, it is marked by the presence of threats in conjunction with the growing recognition of them as larger, pervasive, and imminent problems. Such risks are often self-inflicted (i.e., human-made), resulting as undesired by-products from late-modern ways of living (e.g., industrialization, globalization, and technologization) (Hantrais & Lenihan, 2021; Sørensen & Christiansen, 2014); that is, over many generations, humans have strived to improve their ways of life via developments in technology and science. Yet, paradoxically, the side effects of those improvements to human living have created the many perils of societies at risk. As explained by Mythen and Walkate (2016, pp. 140–141): "the risk society is characterized by volatile threats that are global, universal in nature, and evade established systems of regulation. Within the risk society, hazards are not so much visited upon society by nature as generated as unplanned 'side effects' of economic, scientific, and technological development."

On science specifically, Smith (1999, p. 9) is aware that "science is just as likely to produce bad outcomes as good outcomes" and, as Sørensen and Christiansen (2014, p. 84) declare, this is a feature of risk society:

> On the one hand, there is a growing awareness that science plays a fairly big part in the production of new risks—and this awareness leads to a heightened criticism and scepticism toward science. On the other hand, we are utterly and undeniably dependent on science and its ability to inform us about the new and lurking hazards we are unable to see. It is no longer possible to count on our own senses to reveal hazards and dangers for us.

Global advances in science, medicine, technology, and information have, generally speaking, made the planet—especially 'developed' countries, but also 'developing' ones even if to a lesser degree—more comfortable and survivable for human life, yet in seeming contradiction, these efforts have also introduced severe negative repercussions, and while creating and enhancing new risks, these innovations also help identify and mitigate those same risks (Bauman, 2006).

In addition, science is a well-known vehicle of power and control in the Arctic as elsewhere. The construction of the Arctic as a venerated location of science, for example, happens when stakeholders such as research institutions, national governments, and corporations occupy Arctic place in the name of scientific exploration toward developing new knowledge. This scientific occupation of the Arctic leads to a sense of belonging; that is, these institutions believe through their scientific activity they have some claim to the Arctic. In this way via science, research institutions, researchers, and national governments perceive themselves as belonging to the Arctic. Roberts and Paglia (2016) explore how researchers in Svalbard conducting research on behalf of their institutions and governments use science—unwittingly or not—to stake a claim in 'belonging' to the far northern archipelago specifically and the Arctic generally. Even though Norway asserts sovereignty over Svalbard via the *Spitsbergen Treaty* of 1920 (Royal Ministry of Justice [Norway], 1988; see also Grydehøj et al., 2012) effective from 1925, other countries operate and engage in scientific activity on the islands. Thus, countries such as the Czech Republic, China, France, Germany, India, the Netherlands, Türkiye, and others (Pedersen, 2021; Strouk, 2021) use the power of science to politically articulate a rightful position in the Arctic without challenging Norway's sovereign power.

Instead of risk, sociologist Nico Stehr (1942–) prefers the terms 'fragile' and 'vulnerable' (Adolf & Stehr, 2017; Stehr, 2001a, b). Bauman also remarks on the vulnerable nature of late-modern human life by noting that the world is shadowed by the "spectre of vulnerability" where "we are all in danger, and we are all dangers to each other … The most technologically equipped generation in human history is the generation most haunted by feelings of insecurity and helplessness" (Bauman, 2006, pp. 98, 101). Bauman (2000/2012, p. xiv) continues: "Living under liquid modern conditions can be compared to walking in a minefield: everyone knows an explosion might happen at any moment and in any place, but no one knows when the moment will come and where the place will be." Bauman never explicitly mentions the Arctic or uses it as an example when writing about liquid modernity, nor does Beck describe the Arctic as a risk society, nor does Stehr label the Arctic as vulnerable or fragile. As such, the current chapter is unique in describing the Arctic using the liquid modernity concept, or said another way, thinking of the Arctic in liquid terms—as Liquid Arctic. Bauman (2000/2012, p. 114) does, however, speak of *blank spots* that are "islands and archipelagos as yet unheard of and un-adumbrated, landmasses waiting to be discovered and colonized, the untrodden and unclaimed interiors of continents…" The Arctic, therefore, might be thought of—certainly in the historical sense of Bauman—as a blank spot.

Several features of liquid modernity (Bauman, 2000/2012, 2006, 2007b, 2011; see also Smith's, 1999 treatment of Bauman and postmodernity, as well as Bauman's, 1998 examination of globalization) are divided into three subsections below, explicated both in general and Arctic-specific conditions.

6.2.1 Global Problems and Zombie Nations

Late-modern global problems such as those mentioned earlier cannot be solved exclusively within the jurisdiction of single nation-states and are not isolated to lone countries. Rather, the uncertainty, insecurity, risk, and anxiety brought on by these problems spill across nation-state borders—and entire continents—even while individual countries cling dearly to their assertions of authority over land, sea, ice, and air space. While various global problems deleteriously ravage all nations, no sovereign country feels compelled to yield its power to global partnerships by forfeiting its own confidence to resolve these problems on its own. Yet, even when allied toward a common cause, coalitions of countries together have not stymied the far-reaching impacts of liquid modern's global problems.

The notion of a nation-state, with its artificially constructed borders, might be considered what Beck calls a *zombie category* (Beck & Willms, 2004; see also Acadia & Fjellestad, 2020; Sørensen & Christiansen, 2014), an organized tradition, convention, institution, or classification that is simultaneously both dead and alive. A few other examples of zombie categories from sociology include concepts such as household, family, social class, and employment. For Beck, these terms have a zombie-like quality because they are no longer as relevant or useful in their definition and application as they once were due to immense social change (i.e., they are dead) yet continue to be used orthodoxically as if they are still meaningful as social containers (i.e., they are alive). The configurations of what is meant by 'employment,' 'family,' and so on are now so varied from what they once were in the past to the point where they now approach irrelevancy; what exactly constitutes employment or family is no longer as clear-cut for as many people. Beck's conception of zombie categories is not without criticism (e.g., Atkinson, 2007), but the essence conveyed in the idea is useful to understand the change of liquid modernity. In the case of the nation-state as a zombie category, it is dead because it cannot exist independently in a globalized world, but rather must rely on other countries—which, themselves, are also zombies—to survive. At the same time, the nation-state is alive because their presence and influence is so ingrained into the ways in which the globe is dissected and categorized. Indeed, people still reside in and move around within and across countries; live under country rule, politics, and laws, while also acknowledging and (mostly) respecting those of others; depend on government(s) to provide services, infrastructure, and protection; and adhere to a sense of reverence for and patriotism toward their own homeland.

Dodds (2018, p. 193), when commenting about Arctic and non-Arctic borders, warns that no assumptions should be made that "'Global Arctic' elides let alone erases historical and contemporary border-work," and, in that same spirit, Liquid Arctic neither implies eradication of borders and the relevance they have on the Arctic condition. After all, even though their "sovereignty is called into question," "legitimacy is undermined," and power and credibility are weakened, nation-states have not disappeared (Castells, 2000, p. 14; see also Urry, 2000b). Thus, while any one Arctic country does indeed have a role to play in the Arctic, they alone do not and cannot control the Arctic in total. Moreover, even if 'the Arctic' is conceptualized as a coalition of Arctic countries and Arctic peoples, it has now become a global entity where non-Arctic actors want to be, and are, a part of it.

In attempts to maintain their status on the global stage, nation-states and other entities now cultivate new relationships and alliances (i.e., networks) across borders, entering into new multinational and multi-institutional coalitions, professional associations, and research centre partnerships. Castells (2000) and Stalder (2006) mention the European Union, World Bank, United Nations, and World Trade Organization, among others, as examples of these formations, but Arctic-specific ones include, for instance, the Barents-Euro Arctic Council (https://barents-council.org/), European Polar Board (https://www.europeanpolarboard.org/), GRID-Arendal Polar and Climate Program (https://www.grida.no/activities/10), International Arctic Science Committee (https://iasc.info/), International Arctic Social Sciences Association (https://iassa.org/), Inuit Circumpolar Council (https://www.inuitcircumpolar.com/), Nordic Council (https://www.norden.org/en/nordic-council), Northern Forum (https://www.northernforum.org), Saami Council (https://www.saamicouncil.net/), and University of the Arctic (https://www.uarctic.org/), as well as the Arctic Council mentioned earlier and still others not mentioned here. These partnerships create cohesion—real and illusory—across nation-states via agreed-upon missions and shared visions. Arctic problems, much like their global counterparts, cannot be solved unilaterally by standalone nation-states, yet these nation-states via their Arctic policies and strategies give much attention to Arctic problems, in particular as a way to help facilitate research, support, and action for ameliorating Arctic threats.

A few examples of major ongoing Arctic problems are: (1) climate change, (2) population and economic uncertainty, and (3) geopolitical conflict. Arctic countries and other entities recognize these problems as salient, ongoing issues across the Circumpolar North as evidenced from the following 12 official Arctic documents, listed alphabetically by title: (1) *Arctic Connections: Scotland's Arctic Policy Framework* (Scottish Government, 2019); (2) *Canada's Arctic and Northern Policy Framework* (Government of Canada, 2019); (3) *The Faroe Islands in the Arctic* (Ministry of Foreign Affairs [Faroe Islands], 2022); (4) *Finland's Strategy for Arctic Policy* (Finnish Government, 2021); (5) *Foundations of the Russian Federation State Policy in the Arctic for the Period up to 2035* (Office of the President of the Russian Federation, 2020); (6) *Iceland's Policy on Matters Concerning the Arctic Region* (Ministry of Foreign Affairs [Iceland], 2021); (7) *Inuit Arctic Policy* (Inuit Circumpolar Council, 2010); (8) *Kingdom of Denmark: Strategy for the Arctic, 2011–2020* (Ministry of Foreign Affairs [Denmark] et al., 2011); (9) *National Strategy for the Arctic Region* (The White House [United States], 2022); (10) *Norway's Arctic Policy* (Ministry of Foreign Affairs [Norway], 2014); 11) *A Stronger EU Engagement for a Peaceful, Sustainable, and Prosperous Arctic* (European Commission, 2021a); 12) *Sweden's Strategy for the Arctic Region* (Government Offices of Sweden, 2020). Scotland is included here as its "northernmost islands are closer to the Arctic Circle than they are to London [and] were part of the Norwegian-Danish Kingdom until the end of the 15th century" (Scottish Government, 2019, p. 5). Plus, both of the Scottish archipelagos, Shetland and Orkney, have at different times expressed interest in independence by exiting the United Kingdom, or becoming a protectorate of it, as various movements on the islands called for a mix of autonomy and reunification with its Scandinavian neighbours of Denmark or Norway; most recently, Orkney has articulated this desire (Amery, 2023; Sanderson, 2023). The European Union is included here because three Arctic countries—Denmark, Finland, and Sweden—belong to it, though the Faroe Islands, Greenland, and Åland Islands are exempt from membership. The Inuit Circumpolar Council is included here because the Arctic is both an ancestral and contemporary home to Inuit peoples where they "have jurisdiction over half the entire Arctic, stretching over half of the world's circumference" (2010, p. 9). Also, a note about Denmark's Arctic policy: It covers the entire Danish Realm, including the country of Denmark, Greenland, and the Faroe Islands. The latter of these, however, also issued their own standalone policy in 2022.

Although full treatments of the aforementioned three major issues cannot be provided here, a few comments can be made within the context of these Arctic policies and strategies as representative of the most pressing instabilities underway across the globe generally but also in the Arctic specifically. All 12 of these documents mention, in various ways and to varying extents, the ongoing importance of Arctic transformation regarding climate, economies, and geopolitics. First, on climate change, existing literature has for some time now documented that climate change is occurring throughout the Arctic and demonstrated its ill-effects on land, sea, air, ice, animals, plants, and people (e.g., Arctic Monitoring and Assessment Programme, 2021; Hovelsrud et al., 2011, 2020; Keskitalo, 2008). These documents rightly mention climate change as a significant and dire concern, underscoring that its effects are not isolated to the Arctic but rather global in scale and require coordinated attention.

Second, regarding uncertainty in economic development and population, precarious boom-and-bust economies, often dependent on resources exploitation by large corporations and seasonal tourism, as well as stagnant human capital development and capacity building, are common in the Russian Arctic and other regions such as Greenland and Arctic Canada, leading to heightened unpredictability and unsustainability (Kekkonen et al., 2017; Larsen & Huskey, 2015; Orttung et al., 2021). In Arctic Russia in particular, volatile urbanization and industrialization are developmental problems. Emelyanova (2019, p. 738) refers to monotowns that are "more prone to crisis than other municipalities. All the monotowns of the [Russian] North and Arctic ... are either already in a difficult socioeconomic situation or face significant economic risk." Arctic populations also rise and fall over time depending on the specific countries, regions, and municipalities examined. For instance, the total populations of both the territory of Greenland and country of Russia in each's entirety have fluctuated since year 1950, and, of all Arctic states, are also the only two projected to have a future population decline in total. Yet, the particulars of specific areas within Arctic states provide more nuance as different growth scenarios—for example, within particular boroughs and census areas in Alaska, communes in Greenland, and northern regions of Sweden and Finland—suggest future population decline even if the larger areas of which they are a part expect overall increases (Heleniak, 2020, 2021). In addition to population retreat, an aging Arctic workforce and unemployment create challenges for sustained economic development (Gassen & Heleniak, 2019; Jungsberg et al., 2019). Notable, too, in terms of development is that eight of the 12 Arctic documents mention the importance of growth in technology, including digitalization, as a part of Arctic development and infrastructure. The digitalization component is especially visible in the Arctic documents of the European Union, the Nordics, and Scotland.

Third, though not impossible, major military conflict in the Arctic is unlikely (Arbo et al., 2013), and some scholars advise that the imminent threat and prediction of such is blown out of proportion (Heininen, 2019; Käpylä & Mikkola, 2019; Koivurova, 2016; Medby, 2023; Tunsjø, 2020). Nonetheless, at the end of 2023, the Arctic Council was comprised of eight Arctic nation-states, six permanent participants, and 38 observers, 13 of which are non-Arctic countries. To be sure, many other countries such as China, Japan, and South Korea (Delaunay & Landriault, 2020), various members of the North Atlantic Treaty Organization (NATO) alliance (Lavengood, 2021), and others wish to insert themselves into the Arctic so as to command presence on an increasingly crowded Arctic stage. Therefore, given that an increasing number of world players are expressing their own interests in Arctic capitalization, so too does the challenge of viable governance become more complex. Most of the 12 Arctic documents discuss the risk of conflict in the Circumpolar North, judging it to be overall unlikely, but possible enough to maintain strategic alliances and actively engage in planning for Arctic defence—and potential offence—against aggression. In addition, conflict as a concern for the Arctic need not be specific to the Arctic as demonstrated by, for example, both Finland's and Sweden's recent desire to join NATO due to Russia's war on Ukraine, though recent concerns began earlier with Russia's seizure of Crimea (Alberque & Schreer, 2022; Heininen, 2019; Käpylä & Mikkola, 2019), two actions by the Russian Government that are criticized by much of the global community. Both countries officially applied to join on the same day—18 May 2022—but only Finland successfully gained membership about a year later; Sweden's accession remains held up after failing to receive 100% of the required votes as both Hungary and Türkiye are reluctant to ratify. Although Sweden's and Finland's membership in NATO is unrelated to Arctic conflict specifically, their joining has implications for future Arctic activity and their relationships with Russia.

The important takeaway here is that these fundamental issues are not isolated to one Arctic country or territory, but rather are shared experiences throughout the Circumpolar North as demonstrated via Arctic policies and strategies. Nation-states serve their own purposes for Arctic peoples, but they have yet in isolation to design and deploy economic development initiatives that are sustainable long-term, quell the damaging effects of climate change, assuage the unfavourable impacts of population trends, or promise geopolitical peace and security. In this way, Arctic countries may be thought of collectively as constituting a Zombie Arctic because they are dead insofar as they are largely inefficient at—and insufficient for—solving Arctic problems on their own, problems which themselves spill outside of their borders across the Circumpolar North requiring multilateral alliances involving other Arctic and non-Arctic actors, yet at the same time they remain alive through standard territorialization processes such as border enforcement, government theatre, military manoeuvres, and national exceptionalism.

6.2.2 Non-places, Movement, and the Network Society

Places of meaning are increasingly re-placed with meaningless non-places. Bauman (2000/2012, p. 102; see also Augé, 2008 and Urry, 2000b) defines a *non-place* as "a space devoid of the symbolic expressions of identity, relations, and history: examples include airports, motorways, anonymous hotel rooms, public transport ... Never before in the history of the world have non-places occupied so much space."

Non-places are also referred to as "empty meeting grounds" (Urry, 2000a, p. 194) and are necessary to facilitate and oblige the mass movement of people and possessions, as well as the mass consumption of goods, services, and experiences. Moreover, non-places play an infrastructural role in the facilitation of networks within the global network society of Manuel Castells (1942–), even though Castells does not directly state this. Castells (2010) suggests that networks—that is, connectivity via information and communication technologies (ICTs)—between people, institutions, and their sociocultural environments are the drivers of change. Following Castells, Stalder (2006, p. 183) defines a *network* as "an enduring pattern of large-scale interaction among heterogenous social actors coordinating themselves through electronic information flows." These networks, as imagined by Castells, are made possible by the advancement of technologies, broadening of internet bandwidth, multiplication of computing power, and expansion of digital storage space and options (Adolf & Stehr, 2017; Webster, 2014).

Although Castells does not invoke non-place status, the online spaces that make possible network-building are antiseptic, pointless in and of themselves, and serve only as vessels through which networks flow, much like the flow of things and people in monotonous airports, public transit, and the like in the physical world. Moreover, Castells appears to sit nicely alongside Bauman and Beck because "the network society simultaneously heightens divisions while increasing integration of global affairs" (Webster, 2014, p. 110), two key seemingly contradictory features of both liquid modernity and risk society. Indeed, Castell's network society where individuals, organizations, companies, and governments may be perpetually interconnected is not inherently a good thing as globalization sometimes implies because interdependency, where actions of people and entities worldwide—whether known or not—has the potential to affect others in divisive ways (Bauman, 2006). Moreover, because networks are mobile and liquid, unlike structures which are fixed and solid, a society that is networked plays an "uninterrupted game of connecting to and disconnecting from those networks and the never-ending sequence of connections and disconnections replace determination, allegiance, and belonging" (Bauman, 2011, p. 14; see also Elliot & Urry, 2010). Thus, non-places through networks allow global integration that in turn contrarily creates division, partly experienced as dissonance in time and meaning where life is now lived at high-speed, and no one has any real commitment to anything or anyone beyond what can be consumed.

Related to the ease of networks thanks to non-places, modern existence is marked by the transient and never-still flow of individuals, of "the unstoppably rising volume of 'uprooted people'—migrants, refugees, exiles, asylum seekers: people on the move and without permanent abode" (Bauman, 2000/2012, p. xv; see also Webster, 2014). Add to this list international students and workers, business and leisure travellers, military members, evacuees from disasters, criminals as well as their victims, and the list goes on (Urry, 2007; see also Urry, 2000b). In the same year Bauman published the seminal book *Liquid Modernity*, John Urry (1946–2016) also wrote of mobility in a liquid sense, saying that *global fluids* are the "heterogenous, uneven, and unpredictable mobilities of people, information, objects, money, images, and risks that move chaotically across regions in strikingly faster and unpredictable shapes" (2000a, p. 194). About five years before Bauman and Urry, anthropologist Arjun Appadurai (1949–) wrote in 1996 (p. 33) of *ethnoscape*, a "fluid [and] irregular ... landscape of persons who constitute the shifting world in which we live: tourists, immigrants, refugees, exiles, guest workers, and other moving groups and individuals." The movement of people, however, is not merely physical, though it does indeed include them physically moving their bodies and possessions from here to there. This movement is also social and cultural because people bring with them their beliefs, customs, ideas, languages, preferences, emotions, and all the cultural and social aspects of being human that influence, on the one hand, the experiences that they, themselves, have as they move between new places, as well as, on the other hand, the makeup of the latest environments into which they move (Borja et al., 1997). Thus, the local and regional spaces of today become socially and culturally mixed—hybridized and creolized—as people shuffle in and out of places around the world. This meshing of cultures and societies is best observed in cities, though it can also be observed in smaller towns and rural regions, especially where costs of living may be lower, or where ample opportunities for employment exists. Moreover, the transitory nature of late-modern living is inevitable:

> We are all—to one extent or another, in body or thought, here and now or in the anticipated future, willingly or unwillingly—on the move; none of us can be certain that he or she has gained the right to any place once and for all and no one thinks that his or her staying in one place forever is a likely prospect. (Bauman, 1997, p. 93)

People have always been on the move throughout human history, but what makes mobility different now is the quickened pace at which people move about the globe, as well as the many options for movement available to them. The movement of people coming to, moving within, and exiting from the Arctic is no different. Extant literature explores Arctic migration, including the Arctic's growing number of immigrants and refugees (Heleniak & Jokinen, 2020, 2022; Jungsberg et al., 2019; Yeasmin et al., 2022). As a result of migration, some Arctic cities and towns are urbanized and diverse as evidenced by their bi- and multi-lingualism; multiculturalism; presence of international business; abundance of large buildings and mixed-use spaces; and proliferation of industrialization, and more recently, trade and knowledge-based economies (Huskey & Southcott, 2010; Nyseth, 2017). Now, the majority of Arctic residents live in cities and towns of at least 10,000 people across the Circumpolar North, and this is partly due to ongoing population change where individuals move away from smaller, rural settlements into larger, urban ones (Jungsberg et al., 2019). Even as early as 2010, half of the Arctic population was already living in urban areas (Weber et al., 2017). Thanks to the movement of people in and out of the Arctic, especially to and from cities and towns, non-places have become increasingly common.

The circumpolar spread of non-places and their facilitation of networks and movement becomes apparent when considering the distribution of airports across the Arctic. Data from the OurAirports database (https://ourairports.com/) indicates a total of almost 1400 airports dispersed across the Arctic, only about a hundred less than France and Germany combined using the same criteria as outlined in Table 6.1. About 700 of these airports are in Alaska alone, suggesting that it is by far the most air-connected region in the Arctic, followed by Russia with about 225 and Arctic Canada with 175. As a whole, the Nordic Arctic has 208 airports, with 82 of them (40%) in Iceland alone, pushing that country to the top of the Nordics in terms of airport distribution. The four largest Arctic airports—the Fairbanks International Airport (IATA: FAI), Ted Stevens Anchorage International Airport (IATA: ANC), Keflavik International Airport (IATA: KEF), and Tromsø Airport (IATA: TOS)—saw a combined total of 10.3 million passengers arrive and depart their facilities via air travel in 2022 (Statistics Iceland, n.d.-a; Statistics Norway, n.d.; US Bureau of Transportation Statistics, n.d.-b, n.d.-c). At the other end of the spectrum, the least connected airport-equipped Arctic area by air to the rest of the world—at least when simply comparing number of airports shown in the table—is the Faroe Islands (2022 total population: 53,954) (Statistics Faroe Islands, n.d.), serviced by a single airport, the Vágar Airport (IATA: FAE), in its capital of Tórshavn.

Table 6.1 Number of airports[a] located in the Arctic[b]

Geographic Location[c]	Number of Airports by Size[d]		
	Small	Medium	Large
United States			
Alaska	605	89	2
Canada			
Yukon	24	12	–
Northwest Territories	26	21	–
Nunavut	13	25	–
North[e] Québec	11	22	–
Labrador	13	7	–
Greenland	18	7	–
Iceland	73	8	1
Faroe Islands	–	1	–
Norway			
Jan Mayen	1	–	–
Nordland	7	10	–
Troms og Finnmark	11	12	1
Svalbard	2	1	–
Sweden			
Norrbotten	12	5	–
Västerbotten	4	6	–
Finland			
Lapland	6	6	–
North Ostrobothnia	10	3	–
Kainuu	2	1	–

(continued)

Table 6.1 (continued)

Geographic Location[c]	Number of Airports by Size[d]		
	Small	Medium	Large
Russia			
Murmansk Oblast	14	4	–
North[f]Karelia Republic	2	1	–
North[f]Arkhangelsk Oblast, including Novaya Zemlya and Franz Josef Land	14	4	–
Nenets Autonomous Okrug	8	2	–
North[f] Komi Republic	3	9	–
North[f] Khanty-Mansi Autonomous Okrug	2	2	–
Yamalo-Nenets Autonomous Okrug	9	7	–
North[f] Krasnoyarsk Krai, including Severnaya Zemlya	15	7	–
North[f] Sakha (Yakutia) Republic, including Anzhu Islands	50	17	–
Magadan Oblast	3	6	–
Chukotka Autonomous Okrug	15	4	–
Kamchatka Krai	22	3	–
Total =	995	335	4

Table credit: S. Acadia

[a]Airport data retrieved September and October 2023 from the OurAirports database (https://ourairports.com/). Numbers presented in the table exclude heliports, seaplane bases, and closed airports

[b]For current purposes, *Arctic* is defined as the geographic areas listed in the table. Because definitions of Arctic vary, the number of airports could vary depending on how the term is defined. For example, a map produced by Turunen (2019) at Nordregio takes a broader geographic perspective of the Arctic to include northern Manitoba and northern Ontario in Canada, as well as all of Arkhangelsk Oblast, all of Komi Republic, all of Khanty-Mansi Autonomous Okrug, all of Krasnoyarsk Krai, and all of Sakha (Yakutia) Republic, but none of Karelia Republic, in Russia

[c]Countries and territories are listed moving east from the International Date Line

[d]OurAirports (n.d.) defines *large airport* as a "land airport with scheduled major airline service with millions of passengers [per] year, or major military base," *medium airport* as a "land airport with scheduled regional airline service, or regular general aviation or military traffic," and *small airport* as a "land airport with little or no scheduled service, light general aviation traffic"

[e]'North' here is roughly from the 50th Parallel northward

[f]'North' here is roughly from the 63rd Parallel northward

Even some locations in the extreme Arctic have a public-use airport. In Arctic Canada, for instance, the Tanquary Fiord Airport (ICAO: CJQ6) is situated in the Quttinirpaaq National Park on Ellesmere Island, just above the Arctic Circle where the nearest town of Resolute, with its population of under 200 people in 2021 (Statistics Canada, 2023), is nearly 600 miles, or over 950 kilometres, to the south and has an airport servicing Quttinirpaaq. A chartered return flight from Quttinirpaaq back to Resolute is about $70,000 Canadian dollars (Parks Canada, 2023). Elsewhere in the North American Arctic, the three remote Alaskan islands of Adak (275 mi^2 / 712 km^2), St. George (35 mi^2 / 91 km^2), and St. Paul (296 mi^2 / 767 km^2) each have public airports; however, only one—Adak Airport (IATA: ADK)—is serviced by the major air carrier Alaska Airlines, and for all of 2022, close to 5000 total arrivals and departures were recorded (US Bureau of Transportation Statistics, n.d.-a), an average of over 400 travellers per month. In the Nordic Arctic, the archipelago of

Svalbard extends into the Arctic Ocean just past the 80th Parallel north and its commercial airport is serviced by two major airlines, Norwegian Airlines and Scandinavian Airlines. For the entire year of 2022, over 170,000 air passengers flew in and out of the Svalbard Airport (IATA: LYR) (Statistics Norway, n.d.). Military, research, and other private airports are also dotted across remote areas of Arctic Russia, Arctic North America, and the Nordic Arctic, including those in Eureka and Alert (Nunavut), Nord (Greenland), Olonkinbyen (Jan Mayen), Ny-Ålesund (Svalbard), Rogachevo (Novaya Zemlya), Nagurskoye (Franz Josef Land), Sredniy Ostrov (Severnaya Zemlya), and Temp (Anzhu Islands).

The purpose of the above details regarding Arctic airports is to point out the airport as a prime example of a non-place in the Arctic, of which there are many, that, in turn, is a feature of liquid modernity due to its ability to facilitate networks and bring about change. With such a large number and wide coverage of Arctic airports in operation, the internal flow of people (e.g., laborers, tourists, immigrants, soldiers, researchers, etc.), goods (e.g., food, clothing, household items, machinery, raw materials, etc.), and services (e.g., banks, holiday tours, retail shops, restaurants, hotels, etc.) within the Arctic, as well as external flow across northern and southern boundaries, is enabled. These flows of networks allow for the building of consumption and tourism throughout the Circumpolar North.

6.2.3 Accelerated Time, Consumption, and Tourism

On the topic of consumption, modern life is always moving and on the go; time is compressed, whizzing by at seemingly unprecedented speeds. The world is "permanently on fast forward" (Smith, 1999, p. 6) and the stop button shows no sign of being pressed. The concept of accelerated time as an experience of living in liquid modernity is explained by Rosa (2005/2013) as *social acceleration* along the three dimensions of technology, social change, and the pace of life. As described by Davis (2013, p. 16): "Liquid life is lived at incessant speed, a curiously 'hurried life' in which hyper-busyness has become normalized for many" (see also Campbell, 2013). Part and parcel of unrestrained consumption are both "capitalist expansion [and] technological innovations" (Lee, 2006, p. 362). Thus, these three components of liquid modernity—capitalism, technology, and consumption—in unimpeded form as they are now result in a life of rapidity measured by accelerated time. Life passes by quickly toward nothing in particular yet on a quest for everything all the while surrounded by crises brought on by the risks, uncertainties, insecurities, and anxieties of liquid modernity. As put by Bauman in a published 2017 interview by Tabet (p. 140): "we are now living under the tyranny of time [where] crises replace each other very quickly: before resolving the last one, you already fall into a new one." Unchecked consumption cultivates, and is cultivated by, a quickened life where time is punctuated (Bauman, 2007a) and perceived to move faster than it should as days, weeks, months, years, and decades—*lives*—accelerate further away from those living in them.

Not only does time seem to pass more quickly, but it does so always toward something—*anything*—new. People living in this condensed sense of time are dissatisfied with the *now*, perpetually looking forward to the *next*. Bauman (2000/2012, p. xii) describes this endless pursuit as "an unstoppable hunt for novelty." Yet, even though individuals remain on this never-ending quest for novelty, while at the same time seeking—and claiming—individuality and uniqueness, human behaviour has never been more uninteresting, vacuous, routine, and predictable as people go about their daily lives, thinking about and doing things similar to the day before (e.g., travelling to work, answering emails, eating the same meals at the same time of day, buying products from the same websites, spending time in the same social circles, streaming the same genres of music and films, etc.). Excitement in life is attained not in what individuals do now in the present but what they anticipate doing in the future as they move about in-person and online, planning their lives around a forecast of desired imminent activities (e.g., escaping on yearly holidays; arranging dinner dates with significant others, friends, and business partners; saving funds to buy a new house in the hopefully-not-too-distant future, etc.). This paradox of continual questing without ever reaching an end is equally true for organizations as it is for individuals. For example, companies promote illusory senses that their brands or products are different from and better than their competitors when, in reality, there is nothing all that special or superior about them because they, too, are stuck in the same novelty-seeking cycles as everyone else, having in common the very same anticipation for hot, new must-have items, experiences, and services.

Never finding satiety and continuously on the hunt for newness, human living is now marked by runaway consumption throughout one's lifetime. Long gone are any pretences of contentment, and the pursuit of instantaneous satisfaction is a road without end. A consumerist culture is at play here (Bauman, 2007a; Urry, 2000b), where people expect and are expected to make meaning of their lives by consuming and living to consume wherein there is unconstrained utilization and absorption of services (e.g., detailed and personalized attention from concierge, chef-prepared gourmet meals without imperfection, recommendations for trendy products by social media influencers, etc.); goods (e.g., designer clothing and jewellery, the latest and most-up-to-date electronics, premium wines and liquors, etc.); and experiences (e.g., luxury travel to near and far must-see destinations, gallery visits to catch sight of priceless and renowned art collections, visits to extravagant spa houses and salons to enjoy relaxation and VIP treatment, etc.), all comprising subjects and objects that are to be persistently devoured yet never offering fulfilment. The cycle of the pursuit of things and events—and, importantly, the (temporary) excitement they bring—endures when the obsession for consumption persists. This persistence lasts not because experiences, services, and goods are nowadays made to satisfy, but exactly the opposite: they are made *not* to satisfy so that consumers will continue wanting more, becoming the commodities they consume (Bauman, 2007a). The drive to consume may be more about performance of the act itself rather than the specificities of what is being consumed as people "have needs that can never be satisfied because they do not always know what they need," and—make no mistake—this is indeed a need because "consuming has today become an obligation

6 The Liquid Arctic and Digitalization

rather than simply a choice" (Blackshaw, 2005, pp. 92, 113). The late-modern world is made of shoppers seeking escalated gratification, remaining adamant about consumer choice while browsing the shelves of the world supermarket. Consumption and tourism brought on by, and a product of, accelerated time occurs now in the Arctic as it does elsewhere globally. That accelerated time has reached the Arctic is tellingly revealed in a 2002 book title by Krupnik and Jolly: *The Earth is Faster Now: Indigenous Observations of Arctic Environmental Change*. While the book's focus is on environmental and climate changes occurring across the Arctic, the basic principle of an accelerated Arctic can also be seen now by way of Arctic consumption and Arctic tourism.

Shopping as consumption is a worldwide performance, and the Arctic is not exempt. For both local citizens and travellers, shopping centres are spread out across the Circumpolar North, bringing international and global name brands to many Arctic cities. In Arkhangelsk and its neighbouring city of Severodvinsk are two TRTS Maksi [Maxi] malls. Of the two, Maxi in Arkhangelsk is massive with its three floors at over 65,500 m^2 (700,000 ft^2) on the Northern Dvina River and is but one of a handful of shopping centres in the city. The centre is not only for shopping international brands such as NewYorker, Terranova, and Yves Rocher but also consuming entertainment:

> The Maxi shopping centre is a sociocultural platform for residents of Arkhangelsk. Various events for the whole family are regularly held here: creative master classes, contests, shows, large-scale holidays, as well as educational leisure for children and much more. Auto festivals, performances at the dolphinarium, performances of traveling circuses, and attractions are held in the parking lot of the shopping centre. (Maxi Development Company, 2023, para. 13)

Nearly 600 km (400 mi) to the northwest of Arkhangelsk, in the city of Murmansk and near the coast of the Barents Sea, is the Murmansk Moll [Murmansk Mall], marketed as the "largest shopping and entertainment in the Arctic" (Nikoliers, 2023). The centre features close to 200 shops, as well as a movie cinema with total seating for 700 moviegoers. The centre even includes a loyalty program, incentivizing customers to spend their money at the mall while earning points for 'free' gifts.

In the Canadian Arctic, large commercial centres for entertainment and shopping typical in large cities are absent. Though the Centre Square Mall in Yellowknife opened in 1990, it was met with controversy and struggled to stay operational over the years, eventually being put up for sale in 2023 (Last, 2019; Williams, 2023). Nonetheless, and according to StoreLocate (https://www.storelocate.ca/), leading international retailer Wal-Mart maintains a small presence in Arctic Canada, with stores in Labrador City, Whitehorse, and Yellowknife, and, in addition, well-recognized national retail chain Canadian Tire operates in those same cities. Although Walmart and Canadian Tire are not themselves shopping centres, they are key examples of well-established stores known for their wide variety of available goods much like mall offerings. In Alaska, shopping malls are much more abundant even if concentrated in and around Fairbanks and Anchorage. Perhaps the grandest-in-scale Alaskan shopping centre is the Fifth Avenue Mall in Anchorage; it has five storeys and boasts over 100 stores, including numerous global and international brands such as Apple, Coach, and more (Simon Media Properties, 2023). The US state also has nine Walmart locations and five Costco warehouses, mostly clustered around the largest city areas of Anchorage, Juneau, and Fairbanks.

Medium- and large-sized shopping malls, along with the abundant opportunities they bring to purchase international and global products, are ever-present in the Nordic Arctic (see Table 6.2). Many Nordic shopping centres such as those in the table offer similar shopping experiences, at least in terms of their portfolios of usual European retailers such as Flying Tiger, H&M, Lindex, and others. Nuuk Center in Greenland is an exception here as its standardized European offerings are more limited, featuring mostly Scandinavian stores (e.g., Elgiganten, Kop & Kande, Lysbutikken, Synoptik, etc.) and Greenlandic ones such as those owned by the Pisiffik company. The most northern mainland Nordic Arctic shopping malls in Table 6.2 are AMFI Alta, Jekta, and K1, all three in Norway. In addition, Norway—specifically, Svalbard—has the northernmost shopping centre in the world: Lompensenteret, with 15 shops clustered in a space of about 2000 m^2 (20,000 ft^2). The quintessential Scandinavian giant IKEA has three Arctic store locations—one in Umeå and another in Haparanda, Sweden and one in Garðabær, Iceland—while smaller design studios and 'click and collect' collection points can be found across northern Finland, Norway, and Sweden. Indeed, consumer consumption is alive and well in the Nordic Arctic.

Various Arctic travel information and advertisement websites, even official ones with government backing, tout shopping as a must-do activity and its lure is enhanced by promises of both global and local selections. For instance, Visit Faroe Islands (n.d., para. 8) entices shoppers by juxtaposing local, unique Faroese offerings with the familiarity of a sprawling shopping mall experience to which many international travellers are accustomed:

> With shops spread out across Tórshavn's city center—many fitted into small, old wooden houses—the capital city is a great location for shopping. There is a wide range of shops featuring high-end fashion, local designers selling Faroese design, music shops, bookstores, and Faroese glassware and pottery. There is also a range of shops that sell Faroese designs and souvenirs from the Faroe Islands. All the shops are located in close proximity, making it easy to get around from one to another. Tórshavn is home to the country's largest shopping mall, called SMS. It includes clothing stores, a bookstore, a toy store, a pharmacy, a large grocery store, and an electronics store, among others.

Meanwhile, in Greenland, consumers are given a guide to souvenir shopping, featuring Greenlandic skincare products; home décor, textiles, and pottery; handmade jewellery and handicrafts; and more (Woodall, n.d.). Arctic Canada offers unique shopping experiences, too, as the Government of Yukon's Department of Tourism and Culture (n.d.-a, n.d.-b, paras. 1–2), for example, promotes shopping not only in the Yukon capital of Whitehorse and in Carcross in the Southern Lakes region, but also in Dawson where travellers are advertised a Klondike experience:

> The creeks in the Klondike still yield gold, and Dawson City's expert jewellers produce gorgeous gold nugget pieces. Browse the charming gift shops and galleries for other treasures like fine First Nations crafts, inspired art, and local souvenirs. Other expertly handcrafted items include delicious Yukon food products like wildberry jams, birch syrup, teas, coffee, craft beer, and spirits.

6 The Liquid Arctic and Digitalization

Table 6.2 List of medium (M) and large (L) shopping centres[a] in the Nordic Arctic

Location[b] & Name[c]	Square Meters (m²)[d]	Size	Number of Businesses[e]
Greenland			
Nuuk Center (Nuuk)	25,000	M	28
Iceland			
Smáralind (Reykjavík)	63,000	L	88
Kringlan (Reykjavík)	52,000	L	140
Glerártorg (Akureyri)	21,000	M	39
North[f] Norway			
City Nord (Bodø)	66,000	L	110
Jekta (Tromsø)	65,000	L	125
K1 (Tromsø)	45,000	L	16
Sjøkanten (Harstad)	42,000	L	17
AMFI Alta (Alta)	20,000	M	67
North[f] Sweden			
Avion (Umeå)	70,000	L	75
Solbacken (Skellefteå)	35,000	M	26
North[f] Finland			
Zepplin (Kempele)	31,000	M	78
Rajalla På Gränsen (Tornio)	26,000	M	41
Valkea (Oulu)	25,000	M	60
Ideapark (Oulu)	24,000	M	48
Revontuli (Rovaniemi)	21,000	M	27

Table credit: S. Acadia

[a]For current purposes, *shopping centre* is any general establishment of multiple retail stores and restaurants that are either inward- or outward-facing. Inward-facing centres are enclosed and connected via common walkways, while outward-facing centres are open-air. Centres may also include a mix of office, residential, financial, community, and other spaces. *Size* is defined as follows: *Medium* (20,000–39,999 m²) and *Large* (40,000–79,999 m²). These definitional criteria are based on European shopping centre classification and characteristics from the International Council of Shopping Centers (n.d.). Note that this list is not exhaustive of all possible medium and large shopping centres in the Nordics; rather, it is a curated list of some of the most popular establishments that also have their own websites to market the stores, restaurants, and other services and amenities offered

[b]Locations are listed by most western to most eastern in geography

[c] Names of shopping centres are listed from largest to smallest in square meters when more than one exists in the same geographic location

[d] Size of shopping centres in square miles was determined from a variety of sources, including centre websites, news articles, reports, and promotional material in October 2023. When stated size differed across multiple resources, the highest value was used

[e] The total number of businesses (e.g., stores, restaurants, cafés, etc.) for each shopping centre was determined by counting the actual number of businesses listed in each's respective online directory in October 2023

[f] North Norway includes Jan Mayen, Nordland, Troms og Finnmark, and Svalbard. North Sweden includes Norrbotten and Västerbotten. North Finland includes Lapland, North Ostrobothnia, and Kainuu

The point of the above discussion is not to serve as an advertisement or endorsement of any of the aforementioned centres and the stores they contain, but rather to underscore with concrete examples, using the presence of medium and large shopping malls as one point of data, that the Arctic has not escaped the lure—and demand—of consumer consumption. In fact, demand appears to be rising as, for example, Amazon recently opened a new facility in Anchorage that will aid in distribution of consumer goods throughout Alaska (DeMarban, 2022); new shopping districts in Iceland continue to pop up, such as the Selfoss Centre in 2021 (Visit South Iceland, 2022) and the Hafnartorg Gallery in Reykjavík in 2022 (Kyzer, 2022), both offering unique products and cuisine; and, also in 2022, Kiruna C, a collection of three distinct blocks with 43 businesses, opened in the recently relocated Swedish town of Kiruna.

Consumption manifests not only in the sale and purchase of goods from business to consumer through shopping, but also by way of tourism where, taken literally, "hundreds of thousands of itinerant consumers travel the world to seek new sights and experiences without the need to know or understand traditions. Hence, dead traditions are revived, or new traditions invented, as a form of entertainment for global tourists" (Lee, 2006, p. 362). Tourism of this sort offers excursions not to common places but rather locations that are considered exotic and adventurous (e.g., cruises to Antarctica, safaris across the African continent, hikes on the Great Wall of China, etc.), coupled with offerings of specialized experiences and themes (e.g., Disney vacation packages, overnight accommodation in ice hotels, local food and drink tours in both popular and out-of-the-way dwellings, etc.) (Elliott & Urry, 2010). Plus, a part of consuming tourism is the conspicuous display of it for others to witness and this is made much easier now via social media (e.g., see Varnajot, 2020 for an example of Instagram use by tourists to display their Arctic experiences in Rovaniemi). Thus, tourism and consumption go hand-in-hand. With Arctic tourism, tourists are mostly sold services and experiences, though goods such as souvenirs are mainstays, too.

Although there remains a lack of standardized and consistent statistical reporting across Arctic countries and territories making it difficult to compare travel and tourism data, especially at city/town, municipality, county, and regional levels, there is general consensus that Arctic tourism is trending upward (Fay & Karlsdóttir, 2011; Hall & Saarinen, 2010b, c). Using myriad data sources, Maher et al. (2021, p. 83) presents a table of the estimated number of pre-COVID-19 Arctic tourists broken down by country, region, or province where appropriate, approximating that over 12.5 million tourists, roughly the total population of Moscow, have visited the Arctic across varied years. Also using a variety of data sources, Bystrowska and Dawson (2017) provide a table of the estimated number of cruises and cruise passengers in years 2000 and 2010–2015 to Arctic Russia, Greenland, Svalbard, and Canada's Northwest Passage. Although data are spotty, the table shows that Svalbard is by far the most visited by cruise ships, with nearly 50,000 passengers annually in the five years from 2011–2015. Unsurprisingly, then, the biggest source of income for Svalbard residents is the provision of travel-related products and services as the tourism industry is largest employer on the archipelago (Kugiejko, 2021; Middleton, 2023; Saville, 2022).

Despite the lack of consistent and directly comparable cross-country data, "the general trend in the Arctic, as elsewhere when it comes to tourism, is that through the democratization of travel, transport technology developments, and increasing accessibility, some parts of the Arctic are witnessing increasing inbound tourism" (Huijbens, 2022, p. 13). Arctic tourism is often marketed for attracting the attention of tourists seeking specific interests, most commonly as adventure tourism; wildlife and nature tourism; ecotourism; rural tourism; island, coastal, marine, and water-borne tourism; Indigenous tourism; wintertime, winter sports, Christmas, and Santa Claus tourism, and 'last chance' tourism (Baldacchino, 2006; Bystrowska & Dawson, 2017; Demiroglu et al., 2020; Fay & Karlsdóttir, 2011; Fredman & Margaryan, 2020; Hall & Saarinen, 2010a, 2010c; Herva et al., 2020; Hovelsrud et al., 2020; Huijbens, 2022; Johnston et al., 2011; Lemelin et al., 2013; Maher, 2017; Müller, 2015; Müller et al., 2020; Ren et al., 2021; Saarinen & Varnajot, 2019; Veijola & Strauss-Mazzullo, 2019). In a review of earlier Arctic tourism literature published during 1980–2015, Stewart et al. (2017) found that out of 262 total publications nearly 40% were related to tourism involving cruising, wildlife, nature, adventuring, airborne opportunities, and 'last chance' experiences. This literature demonstrates that various forms of focused tourism across the Arctic are popular now and have been for quite some time. In particular and understandably so, water and ice play a key role in Arctic tourism as can be seen, for example, in the popularity of tourism by cruise ship to observe glaciers, icebergs, icefloes, and fjords; lagoon experiences, especially in Iceland (e.g., the Blue Lagoon complex on the Reykjanes Peninsula and the Glacier Lagoon of Jökulsárlón); excursions to archipelagos such as Svalbard and Lofoten; and snow and ski tourism, especially in northern Sweden and Finland. The vulnerability of water and ice (e.g., water toxicity, polluted rain, melting ice, etc.) and its environmental effects enhance the optics of last chance tourism. Last chance Arctic tourism in particular is characteristic of a Liquid Arctic because it implicitly suggests that the continued preservation of the Circumpolar North as it now exists is so rife with uncertainty and risk, mostly because of climate change and perception of accelerated time, that now—*right now*—is the time to visit the Arctic and it is a gamble not to do so because the Arctic will not—*cannot*—last much longer. The sense of urgency is intentional, even if used cleverly as a marketing tactic.

Not all forms of Arctic tourism involve themes as in the cases of, for instance, adventure, wildlife, or Santa Claus tourism. Sometimes, Arctic tourism, especially in cities, occurs simply by doing 'normal,' everyday activities. Using the Katuaq Cultural Centre in Nuuk, a case study by Cooper (2020) examines the idea that cultural centres can be a site of interaction between tourists and local residents. In doing so, Cooper invokes terminology such as third places, informal spaces, and community spaces to posit that a growing form of tourism is day-to-day tourism or tourism of the everyday, though Cooper does not use these terms. This type of tourism puts tourists in places of leisure to experience and witness everyday life as it passes by while interacting causally with local peoples and environments. Examples of this urban form of day-to-day, leisure, and observation tourism might be lounging in a café while enjoying a coffee and pastry; perusing bookshelves at a local library or bookstore; enjoying a beer or glass of wine in a local pub; or people-watching at a local park, city centre, or waterfront boulevard where the point of these experiences is to engage in daily activities that any given local resident might also engage while taking in the rather ordinary surroundings, observing—*being in*—that moment in time. In addition, some urban areas within the Arctic (e.g., Reykjavík, Rovaniemi, Tromsø, and Vadsø) intentionally market themselves as Arctic cities or hubs, offering everyday sites and services where visitors enjoy leisurely, casual activities such as those mentioned above (Müller et al., 2020). This tourism is not without criticism, however, as third-place, informal, and urban community spaces such as these may themselves be purposely Westernized so as to intentionally create a sense of familiarity and comfort to tourists and, moreover, may not be regular places visited by locals (Cooper, 2020). The point to mention here is that these everyday locations take on aspects of non-places where the pub, library, café, park, cultural centre, and so on—(non-) places where locals and tourists intermingle—become no different than airports or hotels insofar as they all become pinpoints on a tourism network to temporarily appease the masses in transit, stopping points along a journey where the tourist—not any distinct, meaningful location—becomes the centre of the experience.

Arctic Russia is one of the least visited regions of the Circumpolar North by tourists when considering its vast area. Citing a 2014 dissertation on tourism potential of the Russian Arctic, Maher et al. (2021) shows an estimated 500,000 tourist visits to Arctic Russia, quite a small number considering the region measures about 5 million km^2 (2 million mi^2) with over half of the Arctic Ocean's coastline (Arctic Council, 2023; Ministry for the Development of the Russian Far East and Arctic, n.d.). The regions of Arkhangelsk and Murmansk in the Russian Arctic, as well as Krasnoyarsk in Siberian Russia, see the most tourism activity. The rest of the Far North and Far East of Russia are not popular destinations for tourists; however, the Russian Government and a cadre of Russian billionaires seek to change this as part of ongoing tourism development strategies (Fedorinova, 2021; Kuchumov et al., 2023). As such, northern Russia is expected to become an Arctic tourist destination with various projects there finished or underway to attract 15 million international visitors by 2030 (Kubny, 2021). For instance, the recently expanded Natsional'nyy park «Russkaya Arktika» [Russian Arctic National Park] features a 'southern' area on Novaya Zemlya, and a northern area on the Franz Josef Land, both archipelagos in the Arctic Ocean (Arctic Russia: Tourism, n.d.-c). The village of Kimzha in the Arkhangelsk region has received increased attention since it was deemed in 2017 as Russia's 'most beautiful village in the country' (Arctic Russia: Tourism, n.d.-b). In the Far East, a new aerial cable system will connect the cities of Anadyr and Ugolnye Kopu (2023 populations: 12,993 and 3654, respectively) year-round, facilitating increased tourism traffic in that region of the Chukotka Autonomous Okrug (Arctic Russia: Tourism, n.d.-a; Federal State Statistics Service, 2023). These examples are just a few signalling Russia's desire to be a sought-after location for Arctic tourism. Notwithstanding Russia's wish to entice tourism consumers worldwide to the country, the spectre of war looms over Russia's ambitions as evident within the following larger discussion of both fast-food restaurants and hotels, where major global companies have completely ceased or temporarily paused operations.

6 The Liquid Arctic and Digitalization

In addition to tourism, the fast-food restaurant offers another window into consumer consumption; it is an example of a non-place that serves as a site of consumption for locals and travellers. Fast-food restaurants, also known as quick serve restaurants, are an example of non-places because their meaning lies only in their functionality and the infrastructural purpose they serve, namely, to provide sustenance to masses on the move as quickly, efficiently, and homogenously as possible. Fast food is an indicator of consumption, both literally (i.e., the eating of food) and symbolically (i.e., as a normalized representation of both global and fast-paced living). In the Arctic context, the example of fast food is useful for illustrating symbolic consumption as quick and convenient places to dine.

Eager to serve tourists and locals alike, there are around 500 total fast-food restaurant locations across Alaska; of these, over 300 are in the Anchorage municipality alone (Barnes Reports, 2023; IBISWorld, 2022). As shown in Table 6.3, six of the top global fast-food chains have a combined 125 locations in the 16 cities and towns in Alaska with a population of at least 2000. Arctic Canada is much sparser in its fast-food availability: The two most populated Canadian Arctic cities, Whitehorse (2021 population: 28,201) and Yellowknife (2021 population: 20,340) (Statistics Canada, 2023), have restaurants by KFC, McDonald's, Pizza Hut, Starbucks, and Subway, but no Burger King. Meanwhile, both KFC and Subway are found in Happy Valley-Goose Bay and Labrador City, but Nunavut only has KFCs, two in Iqualuit and one in Baker Lake. Starbucks competitor Tim Hortons is vastly more popular in Arctic Canada in terms of net locations as determined by its store locator: There are nearly 20 Tim Hortons compared to only two Starbucks.

In Nuuk, fast food and chain restaurant options do exist, but they are Danish establishments such as Sunset Boulevard and Bone's. The SMS shopping centre in Tórshavn also has a Sunset Boulevard, as well as Burger King. Of the six top chains from Table 6.3, only Subway and KFC have made their way to Iceland, but two other chains can be found in malls: the fast-pizza chain Sbarro at Kringlan in Reykjavík and other locations on the country's west coast, and causal dine-in chain TGI Friday's at Smáralind in Kópavogur. In addition, 23 Domino's Pizza restaurants are operating in Iceland, as well as two Taco Bell restaurants.

In 2018, Cint conducted a survey on fast-food establishments frequented by persons in Finland (n = 83,149), Norway (n = 22,656), and Sweden (n = 229,003) (Statista, 2023f, g, h). When comparing restaurants within and across each country, the survey found that McDonald's is the most popular fast-food establishment in all three. Notwithstanding Cint's results, McDonald's does not have big presence in the Finnish, Norwegian, or Swedish Arctic. In fact, Rovaniemi, Oulu, and Umeå are the only three cities in the region that have five or more locations of the six chains from Table 6.3; among these, both Subway and Burger King are popular, especially in shopping centres. Instead, national and regional chains are more common. For instance, using store locators of corresponding restaurants, the chains Frasses (18 locations), Max (12 locations), and Sibylla (7 locations) are plentifully found in Arctic Sweden, while both Kotipizza and Hesburger are common in Arctic Finland with nearly 80 locations combined.

Table 6.3 Number of fast-food locations from six top global fast-food chains[a] (GFFCs) in 16 Alaskan cities/towns

Geographic Location[b]	Population[c]	Number of Locations from Six Top GFFCs[d]					
		Burger King	KFC	McDonald's	Pizza Hut	Starbucks	Subway
Alaska, United States							
Anchorage	291,247	5	4	5	3	24	18
Fairbanks	32,515	1	2	3	1	6	3
Juneau	32,255	–	–	–	–	2	1
Wasilla	9054	1	1	1	1	4	3
Sitka	8458	–	–	–	–	–	1
Ketchikan	8192	–	–	–	–	1	1
Kenai	7424	–	–	1	–	1	2
Sterling	5918	–	–	1	–	–	–
Palmer	5888	–	–	1	–	2	2
Kodiak	5581	–	1	1	–	1	2
Homer	5522	–	–	1	–	1	1
Soldotna	4342	–	–	1	1	3	2
Valdez	3985	–	–	–	–	–	1
Nome	3699	–	–	–	–	–	1
Seward	2717	–	–	–	–	1	1
North Pole	2243	–	–	1	1	1	1
	Total =	7	8	16	7	47	40

Table credit: S. Acadia

[a]Top global fast-food chains were determined from Statista (2023e). For current purposes, *global fast-food chain* (GFFC) refers to a generally recognized brand of quick-service restaurants owned by a restaurant or hospitality company. Individual locations may be owned locally via franchise, but the brand itself remains owned by a parent company in the global restaurant and hospitality industry

[b]Geographic locations are listed by from most populated to least populated

[c]All Alaska population data is from the US Census (2020)

[d]GFFC data were determined by directly searching each website's store locator as follows: Burger King (https://www.bk.com/), KFC (https://www.kfc.com/), McDonald's (https://www.mcdonalds.com/), Pizza Hut (https://www.pizzahut.com/), Starbucks (https://www.starbucks.com/), and Subway (https://www.subway.com/)

No discussion of fast-food restaurants in Russia will be had here due to that country's war on Ukraine, still ongoing as of this writing. Because of Russia's actions, numerous global fast-food brands (e.g., Domino's, KFC, Pizza Hut, and others) have ceased operations (Creswell, 2022)—or, in the case of McDonald's and Starbucks, completely rebranded (Gershkovich, 2022; Jackson, 2022)—drastically altering the landscape of global fast-food enterprises not only in Russia as a whole but also in cities within the Russian Arctic, the lasting effects of which cannot yet be fully known.

Another example of the non-place encounter that dually serves as a location of both tourism and consumption is the hotel chain. While some hotels do offer interesting and unique experiences, those operated by global and international hotel chains seek to offer a mostly standardized and practical experience. Much like fast-food chains, hotel chains meet the functional and infrastructural purpose of temporary housing accommodations in an efficient and consistent manner. Hotel chains are a crucial part of the global tourism complex as they are quick to find, conveniently located, and affordable relative to their more exclusive luxury counterparts.

Global hotel chains do indeed have properties in the Arctic found mostly—but not exclusively—in the most populated cities. For instance, the two most populous Norwegian Arctic urban settlements are Bodø and Tromsø, both with populations over 40,000 in 2022 (Statistics Norway, 2022). In Norway, Choice, Radisson, Scandic, Strawberry, and Thon are five of the top companies operating in the country (MarketLine, 2023c; Statista, 2020a). According to property locators on each businesses' respective website, Tromsø has 15 total locations represented by these companies. Bodø has only a few less at 11 total from the same companies. Even Svalbard has one hotel each from Radisson, Strawberry, and Thon. In Iceland, Reykjavík has a 2023 population of 138,693 (Statistics Iceland, n.d.-b) and nearly 30 properties from several major hotel chains; however, this is not likely due as much to its larger population, but rather Iceland's—and Reykjavík's—global positioning as a popular tourist destination. As seen elsewhere in the Arctic, larger populations do not translate to more global hotel chain establishments: Although one of the most populous Arctic cities, Oulu in Finland (2021 population: 210,271) (Statistics Finland, n.d.) only has seven total properties from six of the top hotel companies there: Best Western, Finlandia, Lapland, Radisson, Scandic, and Sokos (MarketLine, 2023b). In Arctic Sweden, five of the top six hotel chains in that country are well represented with nearly 40 properties (see Table 6.4); this number is higher than the respective top chains in neighbouring Finland (16 total properties) and Norway (33 total properties).

In Canada, six of the top global hotel companies are Best Western, Choice, Hilton, InterContinental, Marriott, and Wyndham (Fitch Solutions Group, 2022a; MarketLine, 2023a). Of these, Best Western, Choice, and Wyndam do have a few properties in the two larger cities of Yellowknife and Whitehorse, but Iqualuit, with its smaller 2021 population of 7429 (Statistics Canada, 2023), does not have any hotels branded and owned by any of the six global companies. Iqualuit is not without accommodations options, however, as searches on Airbnb using a variety of date ranges shows a handful of results, mostly homestays and apartments. Other common booking sites (e.g., Agoda, Expedia, and Booking.com) indicate that mid-sized localities such as Akureyri, Nuuk, and Tórshavn in the Nordic Arctic—with their populations of 15,000 to 20,000 (Statistics Faroe Islands, n.d.; Statistics Greenland, 2023; Statistics Iceland, n.d.-b)—have a mix of some well-recognized hotel businesses, such as the global company Hilton in Tórshavn and the regional brand SØMA in Nuuk, along with private residences. Thus, even though some Arctic towns and cities may have few or no well-known global or regional hotel chain

Table 6.4 Number of accommodations establishments[a] (AEs) from six top accommodations companies/brands[b] (ACBs) in the most populous municipalities in northern Sweden

Geographic Location	Population[c]	Number of AEs from Six Top ACBs[d]					
		BWH	Choice	Elite	First	Scandic	Strawberry
Västerbotten							
Umeå	132,235	3	4	1	1	2	4
Skellefteå	74,402	1	1	1	–	1	1
Norrbotten							
Luleå	79,244	1	4	1	–	1	3
Piteå	42,362	–	–	1	–	–	–
Boden	28,048	–	1	–	–	–	1
Kiruna	22,423	1	–	2	–	1	1
Gällivare	17,420	–	–	–	–	1	–
Total =		6	10	6	1	6	10

Table credit: S. Acadia

[a]For current purposes, *accommodations establishment* (AE) refers to multi-unit commercial properties designed to provide lodging and other hospitality services to travellers. Hotels, lodges, motels, and resorts are examples of common commercial multi-unit establishments

[b]Accommodations companies/brands were determined using the following sources: Fitch Solutions Group (2022c), MarketLine (2023d), and Statista (2020b). For current purposes, *accommodations company/brand* (ACB) refers to large hospitality and investment companies who own accommodations establishments and whose brands and hotel chains are generally recognizable globally or regionally

[c]All Sweden population data is from Statistics Sweden (n.d.)

[d]AE data per ACB were determined by searching directly each ACB hotel booking website as follows: BWH (https://www.bestwestern.com/), Choice (https://www.choicehotels.com/sweden), Elite (https://elite.se/), First (https://www.firsthotels.com/), Scandic (https://www.scandichotels.com/), and Strawberry (https://www.strawberryhotels.com/)

properties, the market for accommodations—including lesser-known hotel, motel, and hostel brands, as well as private apartments, guesthouses, and homes—cannot be denied as people, goods, and services travel throughout the Arctic.

The market for accommodations in the Arctic is growing as evidenced by calls for new hotels and new hotel construction. In the Nordic Arctic, new hotels are opening in an attempt to keep up with high demand, especially in Iceland where "although hotel room supply has grown by approximately 6% in Reykjavík annually since 2008, its growth has been far outstripped by that of demand" (Collins, 2017, p. 9), and high-end developers have recently set their sights on Iceland. A boutique hotel company out of the United Arab Emirates, Edition, opened its new 253-room 5-star hotel in 2021 on the north side of Reykjavík, entertaining guests with a restaurant, café, three bars, and rooftop lounge, as well as meals prepared by a Michelin star chef. In downtown Reykjavík is Hilton's Iceland Parliament Hotel, opened in 2022. Outside of the capital, new startup Legendary Hotels and Resorts recently opened a family resort in Þykkvibær on the south coast of Iceland and a hotel in the small town of Hella, both 4-star rated establishments. Soon, the company will open another retreat in southern Iceland—this one described as a 5-star ultra-luxury property—with private guest transfers via Rolls Royce or helicopter.

6 The Liquid Arctic and Digitalization

These examples are just several in the recent explosion of luxury accommodation options appearing in the country as of late. Other examples of Arctic growth in accommodations are seen in Alaska. DeMarban (2023a, b) reports on a forthcoming ski resort to be built in Valdez, as well as a new 150-room lodge in Girdwood, southeast of Anchorage. Also in Alaska, Orr (2022) informs that several new hotels are planned for Anchorage proper, including two by global chain InterContinental Hotel Group and one by Marriott, and Hilton is building a 107-room hotel north of Anchorage in Wasilla. The 3000 ft^2 (280 m^2) 146-room Marriott property mentioned by Orr—called Aloft—is now open.

In addition, over the recent years, older hotels have been updated and refurbished such as the Arctic Oilfield Hotel in Alaska's North Slope town of Prudhoe Bay (Harrington, 2016) and the Anchorage Sheraton, a property with almost 25,000 ft^2 (2400 m^2) and a ballroom with 650-person maximum capacity (Swann, 2015). In the popular tourist destination of Carcross, Yukon south of Whitehorse on the Klondike Highway, the small—and allegedly haunted—Caribou Hotel, originally built in 1898, is undergoing complete rehabilitation (Kenter, 2019). Originally opened in the 1970s, Sorrisniva outside of Alta, Norway was updated in 2000 to offer the country's very first ice hotel and still stands as the world's northernmost one. Later in 2021, Sorrisniva modernized its offerings again with year-round accommodations.

Noteworthy, too, is that accommodations, ranging from modest residences to lavish resorts and lodges, are tucked away in secluded locations outside of cities and often capitalize on their 'far north,' Arctic location. For instance, on the shores of the Arctic Ocean in Utqiaġvik, Alaska—the northernmost city in the United States—is located the Top of the World Hotel. Elsewhere in Alaska, luxury mountain lodges and resorts are big business: Orr (2019) writes about one place in particular costing around $36,000 US dollars per person for a four-day package and another priced at $25,000 US dollars for a three-day stay, while Newman (2022) covers the adult-only 50,000 ft^2 (4700 m^2) Alyeska Resort with its well-advertised Nordic spa experience. To the east, the company Weber Arctic operates the 16-cabin Arctic Watch Wilderness Lodge on the north shore of Somerset Island in Nunavut, about 800 km (500 mi) above the Arctic Circle with nine-day stays priced as high as $25,500 Canadian dollars. Two examples from southern Iceland are the Ion Adventure Hotel and Torfhús Retreat. The former of these is a 45-room boutique establishment near Þjóðgarðurinn á Þingvöllum [Thingvellir National Park], an UNESCO World Heritage Site, while the latter is a collection of 25 small houses each complete with its own basalt stone hot pool. In northern Iceland, the experimental travel company Eleven operates Deplar Farm on the Tröllaskagi Peninsula, featuring 13 rooms each priced at about €3300 Euros per night. Northwest from Luleå, Sweden in the small town of Harads is the Arctic Bath Hotel with only 12 total cabins on and around River Lule. South of Finland's Lake Inari and adjacent to the Urho Kekkosen kansallispuisto [Urho Kekkonen National Park] is the Kakslauttanen Arctic Resort with a variety of accommodations offerings, including heated glass igloos. In Norway's far north town of Kirkenes is the Snowhotel, marketed as the world's only hotel constructed exclusively with ice and snow.

Also, as with the unfolding situation for fast-food chains in Russia, the same is true with global hotel chains: Russia's war on Ukraine has changed the business landscape. Hotel conglomerates such as Accor, InterContinental Group, Marriott, Hilton, and others have stopped planning new properties as well as suspended or shuttered operations entirely (*Companies are getting out of Russia*, 2022; Fitch Solutions Group, 2022b; Hancock, 2022; Nguyen, 2022; Statista, 2023d). As such, the inclusion of Russian Arctic hotel examples here is not practical because of the swift and ongoing change in business operations now happening across the country.

The specific examples of fast-food and accommodations provided above serve as a brief snapshot of evidence that people are indeed travelling within and into the Arctic, requiring places to eat and stay. Although the Circumpolar North remains remote compared to much of the rest of the world, it has become a site of consumption in a growing land of non-places in accelerated time. Also, the literal interpretation of consumption and tourism is but only one way to understand Arctic impact as these may also be understood as metaphorical and a way of living. Global tourism in the figurative, imaginative sense suggests that, thanks to consumption via technology, everyone has become, or has the potential to become, a tourist in life—a tourist *of* life *for* life—where many, if not all, aspects of living involve roaming from one place to another, both physically and online, with innumerable choices and decisions while aiming to minimize discomfort, maximize satisfaction, and experience a sense of belonging to communities and events at a distance (Franklin, 2003; Urry, 2000b). Thus, metaphorical tourism and consumption of the Arctic is enabled through modern technologies that put the Arctic online and on screens in front of consumers. The potential of and opportunities for this digital Arctic to reach wide global audiences is now a reality. With explanation of Liquid Arctic in mind, the next part of this chapter provides evidence and discussion of the Arctic's digital landscape that facilitates both the dissemination of the Arctic via digital availability and the interaction with the digital Arctic by interested online users.

PART II

6.3 Digitalization and the Liquid Arctic

Curiously and conspicuous by its absence, the primary books mentioned earlier regarding the themes of the *Global* Arctic, *New* Arctic, and *Interconnected* Arctic mostly overlook digital topics and issues in their chapters. Moreover, even though Heininen and Southcott (2010) acknowledge in the introduction to their now seminal book on Arctic globalization that "globalization refers to phenomena and systems that are truly worldwide in scale, such as information and communication systems and technologies of the World Wide Web" (p. 5), none of the subsequent eight chapters in their book are about ICTs, the internet, or any related digital topics in, for, or about Arctic and Northern contexts. The deficiency of digital discussion in these books is perplexing given that technology, internet connectivity, digitalization, computing, and the like have been included in the Arctic strategies and policies of Arctic nation-states and territories, and in the lives of Arctic citizens to varying degrees, for quite some time. Accepting that digitalization is a major component of liquid modernity and the Liquid Arctic, Part II of this chapter explores the digitalization phenomenon both in general and Arctic-specific settings. Indeed, Liquid Arctic as previously described above supports, and is supported by, technology. Whether the risky, uncertain, and fragile problems of liquid modernity (e.g., uncontrolled climate change, runaway capitalism, repeating financial crises, unpredictable migrations of people, etc.) or other descriptive features of it (e.g., expanding transnational coalitions; increasing quantity of and reliance on non-places; living in accelerated time; constant consuming of goods, services, and experiences, etc.), technology—both the quantitative increases and qualitative uses of it—has created new victories and dilemmas for human life. Like globalization, ICTs and increasing digital saturation is often regarded as something purely functional and positive, but—as also seen with globalization and its de-territorialization of human experience—is not always so (Dufva & Dufva, 2019; Floridi, 2014). In fact, digitalization is marked by unpredictability (Levin & Mamlok, 2021) much like Bauman's liquid modernity.

In 2021, Lee (pp. 70–71) notes that Bauman's liquid modernity "does not deal with digitization"—or digitalization, for that matter—and thus suggests that "liquid modernity *is now being replaced* by a digital form," that of digital modernity [emphasis added]. For current purposes, distinction between the terms digitization and digitalization is unimportant, but Lee makes the mistake here of assuming that replacement is inevitable in the first place, that both forms—liquid and digital—cannot coexist but instead 'the digital' must supersede 'the liquid.' A more accurate way to envision this relationship, perhaps, is to consider that digitalization is part of liquid modernity, not a replacement for it. Such a perspective makes more sense given Bauman's liquid metaphor that the conditions of the late-modern world are fluid, wrapping and contouring around itself and its surroundings. Seen this way, and much like the behaviour of water flowing around an object, digitalization—as it is so infused with late-modern life—is enveloped by liquid modernity, washing over it like ocean waves, becoming a part of it. Thus, technology and its digital promises do not supplant liquid modernity; rather, liquid modernity and digital life (re) enforce each other reciprocally. Technology is one element in the sea of liquid modernity that sustains its ecosystem, and liquid modernity is one attribute of technology that ensures its continued advancement, suggesting that digital does not replace liquid, rather they both complement each other.

The Organization for Economic Co-operation and Development (OECD) (2019a, p. 18) defines *digitalization* broadly as "the use of digital technologies and data as well as interconnection that results in new or changes to existing activities." As a large-scale, megatrend process and umbrella term, digitalization is the deep and widespread acceptance and utilization of the technological and digital means of *doing* and *being*; it is a state wherein that which is digital, and that which can be made digital, becomes an infrastructural, connective, and transformative part of day-to-day living (Dufva & Dufva, 2019; Levin & Mamlok, 2021; Randall &

Berlina, 2019; Valtysson et al., 2023). When speaking of globalization, Urry (2000b, p. 33) describes technology as *"infrastructural* developments routed literally or symbolically across societal borders" [emphasis added] and proceeds to provide a non-exhaustive list:

> fibre-optic cables, jet planes, audiovisual transmissions, digital televisions, computer networks including the internet, satellites, credit cards, faxes, electronic point-of-sale terminals, portable phones, electronic stock exchanges, high speed trains, and virtual reality … These technologies carry people, information, money, images, and risks. They flow within and across national societies in increasingly brief moments of time.

Nearly 25 years on from Urry's description, these and newer technologies—especially the internet—are now indispensable components of life for many around the world. Nearly 70% of the world's population, or 5.3 billion people, are now online, with the highest proportions of internet users in Europe (89%); the Commonwealth of Independent States (84%), which includes Russia; and the Americas (83%) (International Telecommunication Union, 2022). Since Urry, not only have technologies themselves expanded their impact, but also their capability to digitalize life in the name of convenience, security, consumption, and mobility. Experiencing life digitally and succumbing to digitalization is for many individuals and institutions not only expected but preferred as:

> we have widely embraced new communication technologies because of their basic promise to do things more swiftly for us, and by allowing us to circumnavigate the allegedly tedious, awkward, and time-consuming business of having to encounter other human beings in their physical proximity … By seeming to prefer 'online' instead of 'offline' life … we are increasingly devoid of any meaningful face-to-face contact in the course of our daily lives, preferring the multifarious screens that seem to dominate our every waking moment, including televisions, mobile phones, internet forums, emails, blog posts, comments threads, and those large digital screens that have ever so quietly taken up residence in our shared public spaces." (Davis, 2016, p. 3)

Living in liquid modernity means technology and its digital properties are now, first, infrastructural; that is, an integral part of how people live, work, travel, communicate, transact, and interact. Second, technology and its digital affordances are mobile as evidenced by smartphones, tablets, laptops, wi-fi, internet hotspots, satellites, and more. Thus, digitalization is both an antecedent and consequence of *digital mobility*, the condition where digital experiences are not anchored to stationary computers, rather they move along with individuals and as a seemingly inseparable part of individuals.

Mobile phones are just about everywhere. In 2019 when the total global population was 7.7 billion (United Nations, 2019), the total number of mobile phone subscriptions on the planet exceeded 8 billion, meaning that there were more active mobile phone subscriptions than people alive on Earth (Taylor, 2023). Data from the International Telecommunication Union (ITU) (2021, p. 17) indicate that "in almost half of the countries for which data are available for the 2018–2020 timeframe, more than 90% of the population own a mobile phone," and in 2022, 93% of Europe and 91% of the Commonwealth of Independent States owned a mobile phone, with the Americas falling shortly behind at 88% (ITU, 2022). Regarding smartphones,

6 The Liquid Arctic and Digitalization

which is a type of mobile phone, more than one-third of individuals globally—nearly 3 billion people—carry one (OECD, 2019a). In addition, digital mobility is improved by the commonplace use of applications or apps as a way to navigate and use the internet, especially mobile internet.

Moreover, although Sheller (2014) and colleagues (Büscher et al., 2016) do not subscribe to all of the ideas presented in this chapter, they do recognize that "the worldwide mobility system is arguably moving people and things differently, in more dynamic, complex, and trackable ways than ever before" and has facilitated "the movement of unpredictable risks" (Sheller, 2014, p. 795). The modern mobile age is one where individuals must constantly ask themselves where they are and where they are going, not only in the obvious physical sense, but also in the digital (Elliott & Urry, 2010; Halegoua, 2019). In liquid modernity, people are elsewhere, everywhere, and nowhere all at the same time, and their locations in those places are not only where they are now, but also where they have been in the past and where they will be in the future. Yet, with their task-filled lives spread across compressed space and accelerated time on digital devices, especially mobile ones, the destination of meaning and purpose is rarely reached for very long. Once a person completes a task, finishes a meeting, returns from a trip, or clicks 'buy now' or 'send'—that is, once they experience completion and satisfaction—they move on to the next action to be accomplished, propelled by mobile addiction throughout the now accelerated journey that is their lives.

In liquid modernity, "information flow[s] through global networks at unprecedented speeds" (Redshaw, 2020, p. 425), creating a type of digital society. Appadurai (1996, pp. 34–35) does not use the phrase digital society, preferring instead to use the terms *technoscape* to describe the "global configuration, also ever fluid, of technology and the fact that technology … now moves at high speeds across various kinds of previously impervious boundaries" and *mediascape* as "the distribution of the electronic capabilities to produce and disseminate information." Although a full excursus into digital society, and its allied information society and knowledge society, is beyond the scope of this chapter, worth noting is that while the saturation of ICTs is pivotal in various ways to all three society types, the widespread propagation of ICTs, the internet, computing power, and mass media means more than simply having quantitatively faster and progressively abundant online communication; it also means that these technologies qualitatively alter the ways in which life itself is organized and experienced (Webster, 2014). Some of these qualitative digital characteristics are mentioned by Floridi (2010, pp. 4–5) where "information-based, intangible assets; information-intensive services (especially business and property services, communications, finance and insurance, and entertainment); and information-oriented public sectors (especially education, public administration, and health care)" transform how people live, how businesses operate, how governments function, how media influences, and how society behaves. On media, Adolf and Stehr (2017, pp. 178–179, 184) use the term *mediatization* as a concept that:

> account[s] for the significance and the mechanisms by which the media, especially ICTs, (re)shape social processes such as everyday interaction, communication patterns, education, social conflicts, the political landscape, and social organization, but also the economy of modern societies ... We are dealing with a *societal* development that is beyond individual adaptation, and thus tantamount to a *structural* change ... It must be stressed that this is not merely a technological development [emphasis added].

Previous formats of communication media such as newspapers, radios, televisions, and so on, as well as the basic technology that allowed them to exist, have surely impacted how people think, behave, and interact. Yet, while analogue media brought about its own change in society over many long decades and generations, they have not created societal transformation at quite the same pace and extent as digital media. As put by Adolf and Stehr (2017, p. 180): "Digital media that sweep across modern life are not merely variations or more efficient extensions of traditional modes of communication."

Digitalization-related policies in Arctic countries (Table 6.5) inform the development of and lay out details and directions for digital strategies, policies, goals, programs, and agendas at the national level to address ongoing digital transformation of the Arctic. At the international regional level, the Nordic Council of Ministers and Nordregio regularly produce material on digital life in the Nordics and nearby Baltics. In 2020a, the Nordic Council of Ministers released the *Digital North 2.0* declaration, making firm a coalition comprised of Denmark, Estonia, Faroe Islands, Finland, Iceland, Greenland, Latvia, Lithuania, Norway, Sweden, and Åland Islands with specific digital transformation goals in mind. In 2014, the Digital Nations network (https://www.leadingdigitalgovs.org/) was created to collectively explore varied emerging technologies and digitalization topics such as digital governance, artificial intelligence, and more in their sustainable applications for and best practices in society. Of the ten current member nations, Canada and Denmark represent the Arctic. In 2017, the Arctic Council created the Task Force on Improved Connectivity in the Arctic, recognizing that "existing and emerging connectivity technologies are expected to become more widely available" across the Arctic where a "digital economy is taking shape" (2019, p. 12) Indeed, since 2018, the Arctic Economic Council (https://arcticeconomiccouncil.com/), via its Connectivity Working Group (2021), has brought attention to Arctic telecommunications and infrastructure issues, particularly with regard toward growing business opportunities, e-commerce, and economic development. Also, flurries of articles on digitalization development and outcomes have also recently appeared from Russia (e.g., Bannykh & Kostina, 2022; Ermolovskaya et al., 2020; Orzkhanova et al., 2021), signalling that country's commitment toward embracing digital society much like their Nordic and Baltic neighbours.

In a historical sense, mobilization of culture, knowledge, and information—much like the movement of people—has occurred throughout the Arctic for quite some time. For instance, Arctic Indigenous peoples have for centuries created, learned, and shared new intelligence via communication of information and knowledge (e.g., how to navigate long distances of snow and ice; how to hunt, fish, and gather land resources; how to participate in trade and bartering with other

Table 6.5 List of selected official key readings on digitalization in Arctic countries, territories, and regions

Country/Territory/Region[a]	Publication Year	Author	Selected Key Readings[b]
Country/Territory			
United States	2020	U.S. Agency for International Development (USAID)	Digital strategy 2020–2024
	2018	U.S. 115th Congress	Twenty-first Century Integrated Digital Experience Act
	2018	The White House	National cyber strategy of the United States of America
Canada	2023	Treasury Board of Canada Secretariat	The Government of Canada's digital ambition
	2022	Treasury Board of Canada Secretariat	Canada's digital ambition 2022
	2021	Treasury Board of Canada Secretariat	Canada's digital government strategy
	2019	Innovation, Science, and Economic Development Canada	Canada's digital charter in action
Greenland	2018	Danish Agency for Digitalisation & Government of Greenland	Det digitale samfund: National digitaliseringsstrategi 2018–2021 [The digital society: National digitalisation strategy 2018–2021]
Iceland	2021	Government of Iceland	Digital Iceland's digital policy
Faroe Islands	2015	Ministry of Foreign Affairs & Ministry of Finance	National digitalisation programme of the Faroe Islands
Norway	2021	Ministry of Local Government and Modernisation	Our new digital world
	2019	Ministry of Local Government and Modernisation	One digital public sector
	2017	Organisation for Economic Co-operation and Development	OECD digital government studies: Digital government review of Norway
	2017	Ministry of Foreign Affairs	International cyber strategy for Norway
	2016	Ministry of Local Government and Modernisation	Digital agenda for Norway in brief

(continued)

Table 6.5 (continued)

Country/ Territory/ Region[a]	Publication Year	Author	Selected Key Readings[b]
Denmark	2022	Ministry of Finance	*National strategy for digitalisation: Together in the digital development*
	2021	Danish Agency for Digitalisation	*Visions and recommendations for Denmark as a digital pioneer*
Sweden	2021	Ministry of Finance	*Data—en underutnyttjad resurs för Sverige: En strategi för ökad tillgång av data* [Data—An underutilized resource for Sweden: A strategy for increased access to data]
	2019b	Organisation for Economic Co-operation and Development	*OECD digital government studies: Digital government review of Sweden*
	2018	Organisation for Economic Co-operation and Development	*OECD reviews of digital transformation: Going digital in Sweden*
	2017	Ministry of Finance	*För ett hållbart digitaliserat Sverige—en digitaliseringsstrategi* [For a sustainable digitized Sweden—A digitization strategy]
Åland Islands	2012	Åland Regional Government	*Digital agenda för landskapet Åland* [Digital agenda for the Åland region]
Finland	2022	Finnish Government	*Finland's digital compass*
	2021	Ministry of Finance	*Suomen teknologiapolitiikka 2020-luvulla: Teknologialla ja tiedolla maailman kärkeen* [Finland's technology policy in the 2020s: Leading the world with technology and knowledge]
	2019	Ministry of Transport and Communications	*Turning Finland into the world leader in communications networks: Digital infrastructure strategy 2025*

6 The Liquid Arctic and Digitalization

Region/Country	Year	Source	Reading
Russia	2019	Ministry of Digital Development, Communications, and Mass Communications of the Russian Federation	*Prikaz No. 22 ot 30.01.2019: «Ob utverzhdenii plana deyatel'nosti rasshireniy razvitiya, svyazi i massovykh kommunikatsiy Rossiyskoy Federatsii na period 2019–2024 godov»* [Order No. 22 of January 30, 2019: On approval of the activity plan for expansion of development, communications, and mass communications of the Russian Federation for the period 2019–2024]
	2017	Administration, President of Russia	*Ukaz Prezidenta Rossiyskoy Federatsii ot 09.05.2017 g. No. 203: «O strategii razvitiya informatsionnogo obshchestva v Rossiyskoy Federatsii na 2017–2030 gody»* [Decree of the President of the Russian Federation dated 05/09/2017, No. 203: The strategy for the development of the information society in the Russian Federation for 2017–2030]
International Region			
European	2021b	European Commission	*2030 digital compass: The European way for the digital decade*
	2020	European Commission	*Shaping Europe's digital future*
Nordic	2022	Nordic Council of Ministers	*Monitoring digital inclusion in the Nordic-Baltic region*
	2020a	Nordic Council of Ministers	*Ministerial declaration: Digital North 2.0*
	2020b	Nordic Council of Ministers	*The Nordic region—Towards being the most sustainable and integrated region in the world: Action plan for 2021 to 2024*
	2020	Randall, Vestergård, & Meijer	*Rural perspectives on digital innovation*
	2019	Randall & Berlina	*Governing the digital transition in Nordic regions: The human element*

Table credit: S. Acadia

[a]Countries and territories are listed moving east from the International Date Line. Regions are listed alphabetically

[b]All selected key readings are official publications from national governments and intergovernmental cooperatives. References for each reading are provided in the References section of the chapter

communities; etc.). However, what is different now in liquid modernity is that mobility is systematized (Urry, 2007), meaning that human life is interconnected, lived, and organized around mobility via ICTs; it is no longer only that individuals and their possessions move around but now everything moves and has been given the ability to do so through ICTs: money, ideas, information, text, images, sound, science, data, culture, love, risk, democracy, knowledge, etc. (Selwyn, 2019; Urry, 2000a). In the Liquid Arctic, the growing role of mobility in living one's life is apparent, resulting in the emergence of a *mobility complex* that "involves a number of interdependent components that, in their totality, have the effect of remaking consumption, pleasure, work, friendship, and family life" (Elliott & Urry, 2010, p. 9).

Even in 2010, Castells (p. xxv–xxvi) remarks that "wireless communication … has been the fastest diffusing technology in the history of communication," estimating that more than 60% of the world's population had access to wireless ICTs in 2009. The ubiquity of mobile technology and the mobile complex cannot be overstated and, according to Donner (2015), the reach of mobile ICTs may be estimated by examining, among other things, connections, devices, users, and coverage. As usual, digitalization data across the Arctic are not easy to come by and are not standardized. Thus, a variety of resources must be used to paint a picture of Arctic digitalization. First, country-level data from North America, Russia, and Nordic Europe can be used as a reasonable starting point to understand the larger digital and technological contexts within which Arctic regions are situated, even if such data are not fully representative of Arctic urban and rural areas that are part of those countries. Second, nation-state data collected at the smaller regional areas (e.g., counties, administrative districts, municipalities, etc.), when available, are preferable as they are much more indicative of local and regional penetration of digitalization within countries and territories. What follows is an account of selected, non-exhaustive internet and device data as evidence of an increasingly connected and mobile Arctic, a necessary condition for Arctic digitalization.

Regarding internet connection and users, the majority of Nordic Europe enjoys fixed or mobile broadband, including rural areas (European Commission, 2022a, b, c, d, 2023a, b, c). As shown in Table 6.6, Arctic states where ≥95% of the total population use the internet are all part of Nordic Europe: Iceland, Faroe Islands, Norway, Denmark, and Sweden. Where <95% of the population use the internet are the United States, Canada, Finland, Russia, and Greenland. Notably, Greenland scores much lower than all others at about 70%. In the Nordics in 2022, Sweden had the greatest number of mobile internet users at nearly 9.2 million, or 85% of its total population, while Denmark, Finland, and Norway each hovered between 5 and 5.5 million (Statista, 2023b). In the same year in North America, the United States had just over 330 million mobile internet users, or 98.5% of its total population, compared to Canada at nearly 36 million, or 90% of its total population (Statista, 2022, 2023a). Similar data in the Russian instance show close to three-fourths of its population as mobile internet users (Statista, 2023c). Table 6.6 also shows that 4G coverage exists for ≥99% of all Arctic states' total population, except for Russia. Now, next generation 5G technology is rolling out in areas such as Alaska, the Faroe Islands, and Greenland (Barbour, 2020, 2022; Ericsson, 2022, 2023).

6 The Liquid Arctic and Digitalization

Table 6.6 Data[a] showing mobile subscriptions, internet users, and 4G coverage in Arctic countries and territories[b]

Country/ Territory	Total Population	Mobile Phone Subscriptions (Total #)	Total Internet Users (% of Pop.)	4G Coverage[c] (% of Pop.)
United States	338 million 2022	373 million 2022	91.8% 2021	99.9% 2021
Canada	38.5 million 2022	35.1 million 2022	92.8% 2021	99.4% 2022
Greenland	56,500 2022	66,600 2021	69.5% 2017	100% 2021
Iceland	373,000 2022	457,000 2022	99.7% 2021	100% 2022
Faroe Islands	53,100 2022	59,200 2021	97.6% 2017	100% 2021
Norway	5.43 million 2022	6.01 million 2022	99% 2022	99.9% 2022
Denmark	5.88 million 2022	7.44 million 2022	97.9% 2022	100% 2022
Sweden	10.5 million 2022	13.2 million 2022	95% 2022	100% 2022
Finland	5.54 million 2022	7.13 million 2022	93% 2022	100% 2022
Russia	146 million 2021	245 million 2022	90.4% 2022	92.6% 2022

Table credit: S. Acadia

[a]All data are found in the respective country or territory profile from the International Telecommunication Union (ITU) (https://www.itu.int/)

[b]Countries and territories are listed moving east from the International Date Line

[c]4G refers to the fourth generation of broadband cellular network technology; it debuted in December 2009

By proportions of households, Arctic broadband access is lowest in Magadan Oblast (31%), the autonomous okrugs of Chukotka (51%) and Nenets (56%), and Sakha (Yakutia) Republic (55%), all in Russia (Jungsburg et al., 2019). In Alaska, while 80% of residents have internet availability, the same proportion does not have access to internet that is affordable, and, for over 20% of residents, available internet is not high-speed (Alaska Broadband Office, 2023). Similarly in Greenland, internet access, while widely available, is often prohibitively expensive, reaching as high as 1000 Danish krone per month for 4Mbps service in remote locations (Abildgaard et al., 2022). Thus, in the Arctic, it is important to not only look at percent of coverage, but also other factors such as affordability of access, speed, and data limits. Writing in the 2018 *State of the Nordic Region* report, Johnsen et al. (2018) affirm that at least 65% of all households in all Arctic regions of Finland, Iceland, Norway, and Sweden have internet speeds reaching 30Mbps (megabits per second). Yet, at the local level, compared to regional, the percentage of households with 30Mbps+ vary considerably, especially between municipalities as in local rural areas of Arctic Finland, Norway, and Sweden, for example, the percentage of households can frequently drop below 50%. However, 10Gbps+ internet is on its way to the Arctic as, for instance, Nokia (2023) and CGI (2021) have committed to improve the fibre network infrastructure in Iceland and Alaska, respectively. Even if internet access is available and delivered with reasonable speed, data caps create significant barriers as Pasch and Kuhlke (2022) illustrate in the example of 4G service in Arviat, Nunavut.

Mobile subscriptions in Finland reached 9.2 million in 2021 (European Commission, 2022b), greatly exceeding the country's total 2021 population of about 5.6 million (Statistics Finland, n.d.), meaning there were nearly 4 million more mobile phone subscriptions in Finland than there were people living there. In Russia, over 80% of households are connected to the internet via handheld devices, followed by laptops at 40% (Statista, 2023c), indicating that Russian internet users are highly mobile. Using 2022 data from the ITU, Table 6.6 shows that Russia has 99 million more mobile phone subscriptions than people. Indeed, the pattern of having more mobile subscriptions than there are people in the total country population occurs in all Arctic nation-states and territories except one: Canada is the only Arctic country with more people—3.5 million more—than mobile phone subscriptions. In Canada in 2022, the most popular devices for accessing the internet among adult users were desktop and laptop computers (86%) with mobile phones coming in second at 75% and tablets third (44%) (Statista, 2023a). Of all Arctic regions, Iceland is the most mobile as "mobile phone penetration in Iceland surpassed fixed-line penetration as early as 1999, long before any other country … [and] … is among the highest in the world" (Lancaster, 2022, p. 46).

Not all of the Arctic is connected to the internet, fixed or mobile; as such, it may be said that a so-called digital divide aptly portrays the Arctic experience of internet access and connectivity (Ahmmed et al., 2022; Alaska Broadband Office, 2023; Delaunay & Landriault, 2020; Gladkova et al., 2020; Randall et al., 2020; see also Saunavaara et al., 2021 for an insightful Arctic history of telecommunication infrastructure and its challenges since the telegraph). The term *Arctic digital divide* is proposed by Kuersten (2018, p. 93), defined as a gap "between the average quality and price of telecommunications services in Arctic communities and those more southerly, with the former paying more for slower and less reliable connectivity…". The term is useful for understanding that when landline, wi-fi, or satellite internet is present, it may be more costly, throttled with slower speeds, limited with download caps, and require cumbersome contracts, particularly in relation to more populated southern areas within the same Arctic countries (e.g., southern Canada vs. Arctic Canada, the US vs. Alaska), as well as compared with developed non-Arctic countries. Although global organizations such as the World Bank (2023, para. 7) contend that the digital divide remains a key issue because "billions of people have still never used the internet," some scholars take a critical stance, reporting that the term is not well defined, not well measured, or simply outdated (e.g., Carlson & Isaacs, 2018; Gunkel, 2003; Tsatsou, 2011). Notwithstanding contestation, parts of the Arctic, particularly some rural areas, still struggle with internet accessibility and lack fast, reliable internet as is the case, for example, in the eastern parts of Iceland

and Westfjords and areas of Lofoten (Randall et al., 2020). At the same time, internet in other rural and remote Arctic areas performs just fine. For example, according to Randall et al. (2020, p. 18), "in the Faroe Islands the majority of the population (92%) have access to the internet from home and, even in the outlying islands, the connection is generally good."

In any case, internet access throughout the Circumpolar North has begun, and will continue, to improve in reliability and total number of new connections. Not long ago, Finnish company Cinia and Russian company MegaFon planned to connect Europe and Asia through Russia, but that project was scrapped and replaced with a new project between Cinia, Japanese company Arteria, and Alaskan company Far North Digital to accomplish the same goal but by re-routing cables the opposite direction (Bousquette, 2023). If fully realized, the proposed system, Far North Fiber (https://www.farnorthfiber.com/), will run from the Finnish-Norwegian border into the Atlantic Ocean, splitting back east to Ireland and continuing west through Canada's Northwest Passage and the Bering Strait to Japan, at a length of 15,000 km (9400 mi) and an estimated cost of more than $1 billion US dollars. Several pan-ocean cable systems like these have been proposed over the years to connect countries separated by vast distances by way of the Arctic while also connecting to the Arctic itself but failed to come to fruition (Delaunay & Landriault, 2020). Meanwhile, at the end of 2023 and as shown on TeleGeography's interactive Submarine Cable Map (https://www.submarinecablemap.com/), there are 35 distinctly named undersea cables and cable systems successfully connected, at minimum, to one Arctic land point. Of these sea cables, Polar Express (https://xn%2D%2De1ahdckegffejda6k5a1a.xn%2D%2Dp1ai/en/) is the longest, wrapping around northern and eastern Russia from the Barents Sea in the west to the Sea of Japan (East Sea) in the east at a length of 12,650 km (7861 mi) with nine total landing points; it is expected to be completed in 2026. Because of expansive projects such as these, some speculate that the Circumpolar North may become an inevitable centralized hub connecting internet and data traffic flow between the East (i.e., Asia-Pacific) and West (i.e., the Americas and Europe) (Christensen et al., 2018).

Not all Arctic cable projects are as large in scope compared to Polar Express and Far North Fiber. The Greenland Connect system (https://www.tusass.gl/en/infrastructure/submarine-cable/), for instance, connects Greenland from two international points—Newfoundland, Canada and Iceland—with 4600 km (nearly 3000 mi) of cable across the Atlantic. Svalbard is connected to mainland Norway via its 2800 km (1750 mi)-long cable thanks to Space Norway (https://spacenorway.no/en/what-we-do/operational-infrastructure/the-svalbard-fibre-optic-cable-connection/). Northern and western Alaska is connected via almost 2000 km (1250 mi) of cable at six landing points from Kotzebue to Wainwright by the Quintillion Subsea Cable Network (https://www.quintillionglobal.com/system/in-alaska/). The Ísland ljóstengt [Rural Fibre Project] in Iceland aims to "bring ≥100 Mb/s wired internet to 99.9% of households and businesses nationwide" (Ministry of Infrastructure [Iceland], n.d., para. 2). In addition, even smaller regional and local fibre pre- and completed developments continue to bring increased access and speed to Arctic areas. For example, the Alaska Fiberoptic Project (https://www.akfiberopticproject.

com/) intends to bring high-speed internet to 23 communities north of Fairbanks along the Yukon and Kuskokwim Rivers in 2026. According to Infrastructure Canada's interactive map in 2023 (https://www.infrastructure.gc.ca/gmap-gcarte/index-eng.html), Arctic broadband projects are underway in Northwest Territories, Nunavut, and Yukon, and investments have been made in North Québec and Labrador to bring rural and Indigenous residents high-speed internet (Innovation, Science, and Economic Development Canada, 2022a, b). These cable systems are highlighted here to demonstrate that the Arctic is ever more connected, both intra- and inter-nationally, and with increasing down/up speeds.

Undersea cables are not the only method of internet access in the Arctic as the reach of satellite internet is also prominent. The fleet of low-Earth orbit (LEO) satellites by Eutelsat OneWeb (https://oneweb.net/) is being used to bring Greenland, Iceland, and Arctic Canada online via satellite internet, and new satellite network portals are being built, such as the one in northern Sweden's city of Piteå by Arctic Space Technologies (https://arcticspace.com/) (Ahmmed et al., 2022; Eutelsat OneWeb, 2021, 2023a, b; Lipscomb, 2022). In addition, collaboration between Space Norway and Viasat will use highly elliptical orbit (HEO) satellites above the North Pole to bring continuous internet to the Arctic Circle (Edvardsen, 2022). Satellites, however, have their own difficulties as they "are inherently costlier, less reliable, and provide slower service than fixed, land-based systems like fiber optic cables … [and] … serve fewer customers" (Kuersten, 2018, p. 98).

Arctic life today has been, and will continue to be, swiftly altered to varying intensities, but circumpolar, nonetheless. Far-reaching technology and digital connectivity within the Arctic, as well as between the Arctic and 'outside' non-Arctic interests, allows individuals, communities, institutions, cities, and governments to become digital actors. Major fibre, mobile, and satellite internet infrastructure projects such as these just mentioned will also increase opportunities for Arctic Indigenous peoples throughout coastal, inlet, and interior Russia, Canada, Alaska, and Sápmi to become part of the larger online digital world if they so choose. Emerging evidence from northern circumpolar geographies demonstrate Arctic digitalization as seen by, for instance, the deployment of Apple iPads as a new tool for teaching and learning in Vardø schools (Wøien & Randall, 2019); creation of the Rafræn þjónustumiðstöð [Electronic Centre] in Reykjavík for assisting citizens, especially by way of technology, to receive quality of life welfare services (Randall & Sigurjónsdóttir, 2019); and execution of the *Digital Västerbotten* project that brought together 15 local administrations to promote cooperation around digitalization, resulting in 50 new e-services (Löfving et al., 2022).

Although the Arctic as a circumpolar region has now, and likely will continue to have, its own varied and uneven levels of scientific, political, social, cultural, and economic development compared with the countries of which it is a part as well as the rest of the world, the entire region will continue to be pushed towards digitalization even if Arctic residents are uncertain about its effects. For example, interview research on e-government in the Faroe Islands indicates that, while there is some scepticism about the potential success of e-government, a common sentiment expressed by residents is that "digitalization of the Faroe Islands is not optional but something that is a necessity to ensure the future of the Faroese people and attract people to come (back) to the Faroe Islands" (McBride, 2019, p. 210). Digitalization, therefore, is seen as a way to stay relevant and 'modern' as well as bridge disparities for residents who live in remote or rural areas that may not have much brick-and-mortar infrastructure related to government, business, healthcare, and other sought-after services (Löfving et al., 2022). Thus, even when outcomes are unpredictable and doubt is common, there seems to exist an overarching sense that digitalization is now a part of everyday life, even if some individuals remain unconnected, because 'the digital' is everywhere. To be sure, the Arctic in its late-modern, liquid form is increasingly digital via the process of digitalization, denoting a type of sociocultural change from which it, like much of the present-day world, cannot and will not escape, and the proliferation of ICTs along with increased calls toward digitalization by Arctic nation-state governments represents a new sociocultural shift unseen in the Circumpolar North until recently.

It is true that ICTs and digitalization provide the networks through which information and knowledge flows occur, but they are not the main drivers; that is, Arctic change has less to do with digitalization and ICTs in and of themselves and more to do with the ongoing social and cultural change they bring, as Webster (2014, p. 51) explains: "Technologies are undoubtedly important in making social changes, but they do not spring out of the ether." Said another way, and as put by Randall and Berlina (2019, pp. 8, 61): "digitalisation is more a human process than a technical one." The point is that Arctic digitalization is not alone caused by increases in quantity of knowledge, information, or technology, but is instead predicated on transformative cultural and social undercurrents that favour a globally integrated, digitally connected, and mobile Arctic. Therefore, the Liquid Arctic manifests itself through ICTs and digitalization due not exclusively to their presence and quantity but also via pressures external and internal to the Arctic for the Circumpolar North to become global—whether it wants to or not—often by way of these same technologies.

To conclude this part of the chapter, digitalization as described above is important for Arctic LIS as an area-focused profession and field of study, as well as LAMs both within the Circumpolar North and those outside of it holding Arctic collections, because it is indicative of not only a Liquid Arctic reality via large-scale social, cultural, economic, and political change but also of how that Arctic change is codified, preserved, accessed, and transmitted by way of information, data, culture, and knowledge; that is, heritage. Up to this point, the current chapter is purposefully designed to illuminate the constructs of and provide evidence for liquid modernity and digitalization, as well as introduce an understanding of the Liquid Arctic perspective, to archivists, curators, and librarians both in and outside of the Arctic who work with Arctic materials and collections. As mentioned earlier, Elliott and Urry (2010, p. 8) ask "where are our lives supposed to be going," concluding that—thanks to mobility—human lives remain unfulfilled as people are always chasing something, always moving here and there, always mobile physically and digitally. Although the focus here for Elliot and Urry is individual mobility where people, their activities, and their identities are transported in person, but especially online, effortlessly across the world in many cases, it is possible, too, to apply the same idea at a larger scale. In doing so, mobility becomes a characteristic not only of people but also heritage. Finally, then, the chapter now turns to Arctic digital cultural heritage to demonstrate real-life, practical roles and influences of digitalization on and in the Circumpolar North.

6.4 Arctic Digital Cultural Heritage

Liquid modernity is described, though not directly by Bauman, as a "new condition, characterized by the flow of (electronically conducted) information" (Gane, 2001, p. 268), and this portrayal is particularly important for LAMs because their conservatorship over digital data, information, knowledge, and culture is institutionalized as part of the education, practice, profession, and purpose of LIS—these are the enterprise of archives, museums, and libraries, as well as the people who work in them and the profession that advocates for them. The responsibility to collect, preserve, and make accessible analogue collections (e.g., print books, paper manuscripts, physical artifacts, etc.), and digital ones by extension, falls under the remit of LAMs; they have taken up the charge and are doing exactly this, even if digital uptake has not always been swift. As proclaimed by Hylland (2022, p. 813), "cultural production is to an increasing degree characterized by digitalization, mediatization, and the use of social media, sometimes described as platformization." A part of this production includes the work put in by archivists, librarians, and curators to digitalize analogue materials and curate born-digital files, as well as digitally manage and promote digital collections. To be sure, in the same way that governments, banks, universities, retail stores, entertainment platforms, etc. have a digital presence and provide electronic services nowadays, so too do most LAMs. By offering a bevy of convenient and now-expected e-services and e-formats, LAMs in Arctic countries are already participating in digitalization (e.g., Kim & Maltceva, 2022; Larsen, 2018; van Kempen et al., 2021; Valtysson, 2017), providing basic embedded e-services such as access to online public access catalogues, databases for finding periodicals and streaming music and films, and virtual assistance from library employees via email or online chat. In one European study, Vårheim et al. (2020) found that, out of over 3000 survey respondents from Denmark (n = 1004), Norway (n = 1021), and Sweden (n = 1005), more than half from each country used digital resources from either a public library, museum, or archives collectively. Moreover, specific cities in the Arctic countries of Canada, Finland, Sweden, and the United States consistently appear on ranked lists of informational cities, knowledge cities, creative cities, digital cities, and smart cities with consideration of the public library services offered (Audunson et al., 2019; Born et al., 2018; Mainka et al., 2013), though none of the cities themselves are located in the Circumpolar North.

Apart from standard services, however, is cultural production; that is, specialized digital cultural heritage content curated and managed by LAMs. *Digital cultural heritage* (DCH) as defined by Cameron (2021, p. 3) is "*all digital data* that a society sees as important to retain and keep as a source of knowledge for future generations.

6 The Liquid Arctic and Digitalization

Digital data therefore is the new cultural heritage of life, one that is increasingly threatened and therefore valued" [emphasis added]. While not directly invoking the digitalization term, Cameron (2021, p. 3) alludes to it:

> the interpenetration of the digital into everyday life alongside the replacement of traditional forms of heritage such as books, paper records, correspondence, photographs, film, sound recordings, and artefacts, in digital format, has led to a burgeoning of digital data, much of which has the potential to become heritage of the contemporary world.

Here, Cameron makes two key observations: first, interaction with 'the digital' is becoming, and has become, familiar for many people in their day-to-day lives; and second, digital data in all its various forms and displays may be constituted as heritage. Cameron also calls upon Bauman and liquid modernity in the 2015 book chapter "The Liquid Museum." In the chapter, Cameron says that museums, which once operated in the realm of certainty with their authoritative reconstructions of history, now are forced to function with growing uncertainty given the risk and unpredictability of late modernity, including confronting public scepticism, critique, and the questioning of histories that museums construct. Indeed, according to Cameron (2021, pp. 72, 76), DCH "emerges out of a perception of impending *crises*, either real or imagined, and the resultant *uncertainty* these conditions create for us ... [as well as] ... late modernity's obsession with digital data, digital media, novelty, desire, and obsolescence" [emphasis added]. Museums, and by association archives and libraries, in liquid modernity "are no longer hierarchical, closed, or fixed to a physical location" (Cameron, 2015, p. 355); rather, they have become distributed, open, mobile, and participatory via ICTs. Echoing Cameron's description of crisis and uncertainty, Rydbeck et al. (2023, p. 235) comment that "much of the utopian attitude that prevailed a decade or two ago has today been replaced by a somewhat dystopian attitude when faced with difficulties connected to digitalization." Whereas once LIS and LAMs looked opportunistically upon digitalization with hope of using it to improve their position as an authority on culture, knowledge, and information, it is no longer realistic for them to do so; the clean and neat utopia of LIS/LAMs as central authority figures has been replaced with a dystopia of decentralized risk and uncertainty, not unlike that which is found in Bauman's liquid modernity.

Nonetheless, both traditional LAMs offering online access to collections as well as born-digital LAMs are now common globally. Digital materials held by LAMs worldwide may be combinations of both born-digital items and digital surrogates (i.e., reproductions) (Cameron, 2021). While recognition of this burgeoning digital responsibility by LAMs has been slow to materialize, there now exists plenty of projects, websites, databases, institutions, and governments housing digital cultural heritage content such as, for example, the World Heritage List by UNESCO's World Heritage Centre; (https://whc.unesco.org); the many virtual collections of the United States' Smithsonian Institution (https://www.si.edu/) and the European Union's Europeana network (https://www.europeana.eu); the DigitaltMuseum in Norway (https://digitaltmuseum.no/); Kringla in Sweden (https://www.kringla.nu/), and many others. Via the Google Arts and Culture app (https://artsandculture.google.com/), mobile users have at their fingertips collections from participating museums, which, at the time of this writing, include the Nordnorsk Kunstmuseum [North Norwegian Art Museum] of Tromsø, Tækniminjasafn Austurlands [Technical Museum of East Iceland] of Seyðisfjörður, five different museums in the Russian city of Yakutsk, and Alaska's Anchorage Museum, in addition to numerous more southerly institutions within Arctic countries. In addition, some LAMs and heritage sites (HSs) offer dedicated apps for mobile users. For example, in Norway, the award-winning Kunstporten app (https://kunstapp.wordpress.com/about/) is used to instruct kids about Norwegian cultural heritage (Iranowska, 2020). Also, apps are developed and used for specific projects: For example, in Ireland, who formally applied for admittance into the Arctic Council as an observer (Government of Ireland, 2020), one heritage organization aims to create a new app for a specific heritage trail (Basaraba et al., 2019).

Earlier in the current chapter was presented a discussion of consumption and tourism as literal and metaphorical. Another aspect of metaphorical tourism is worldwide online digital travel. The digital collections available through the above and other online sources are prime locations for virtual tourism of the cultural, informational, and educational sort. LAMs, HSs, and other heritage entities take analogue collections and bring them to life online by way of digital collection accessibility via online platforms and databases, resulting in a compression of culture where artifacts, locations, and people are distilled into bits and bytes for consumption by virtual tourists. Global travel no longer occurs exclusively via airplanes, trains, and automobiles, but also by way of ICTs and the internet. Metaphorical travel via digital devices—or virtual travel (see Urry, 2007)—allows users of those devices to see the world on their screens. With access to the internet and a connectable device, online users can now remotely peruse the digital collections offered by LAMs and HSs. Consideration of LAMs and HSs as tourist spots is already noted in the existing academic and popular literature generally (e.g., Herreman, 1998; Kirshenblatt-Gimblett, 1998; Krueger, 2019), and within Arctic and Northern contexts specifically (Kugiejko, 2021; Pettersson & Müller, 2023; Roura, 2009), where tourists encounter a wide range of cultural artefacts and historical narratives that impart knowledge about local and regional humanities. However, not all Arctic materials are held in the Arctic, nor does all Arctic exposure take place within the Arctic.

Acadia and Fjellestad (2020) review the 'Arctic as place' concept, so that will not be replicated in full here. One key aspect of this concept, though, is that place is not merely geographic, and it is not always a static location. This notion is best illustrated when considering the scatter of 'Arctic deposits' distributed around the world when DCH is accessed from a computer or other digital device. In that moment, 'the Arctic' is transported from the North into faraway digital places for consumption by online users, sometime far removed from any static or geographic Arctic location. Thus, the Arctic in its various forms and as dispersed by digital LAMs is on access, available to anyone with a device and internet connection. A few examples of Arctic digital projects are the digital photo archives from the Perspektivet Museum (https://perspektivet.no/) in Tromsø; Arctic Indigenous digital storytelling across Canada (Shiri et al., 2022; Willox et al., 2012); and Alaska's vast digital archive (https://

vilda.alaska.edu/). Examples of online digital Arctic collections curated outside of the Circumpolar North include, for instance in the UK, the digital picture library and museum catalogue of the Scott Polar Research Institute (https://www.spri.cam.ac.uk/); in Germany, the digital publications, collections, and ethnographies presented by Digital Humanities of the North (https://dh-north.org/) (Kasten, 2020); and in the United States, The Ohio State University's Byrd Polar and Climate Research Center Archival Program (https://library.osu.edu/polararchives) and Stefansson Collection on Polar Exploration at Dartmouth University (https://www.dartmouth.edu/library/rauner/manuscripts/stefansson_guide.html).

Digital Arctic collections such as these and others worldwide are made up of various texts, images, and other media created by LAMs mostly designed for public use and consumption, whether by tourists, hobbyists, or researchers. Such collections may pertain to the Circumpolar North generally or relate to specific Arctic places and peoples. As these collections are available online, digital travellers around the world have access to them wherever they connect to the internet. If the marketing for the collections is done properly (Mason et al., 2018), they become digital attractions for users eager to engage in digital cultural tourism by way of visiting these virtual spaces while consuming, and at times participating in, these digital collections. While not always phrasing this phenomenon in terms of consumption and digital cultural tourism, several recent scholars (e.g., Edquist et al., 2023; Huvila et al., 2023; Massi et al., 2021; Roued-Cunliffe et al., 2023) remark that modern users do indeed seek active and participative engagement with LAMs and the cultural sector, often digitally. As put by Edquist et al. (2023, p. 76):

> In the past, users visited institutions and were passively presented with collections that experts had created and/or curated for exhibition. However, with new technology and new conceptions of the societal missions of LAM institutions, this older paradigm is being transformed, often summarized in catchphrases such as 'from collection to connection' … Digitalization has loosened the boundaries between library publications, museum artifacts, and archival records, as well as enabling new opportunities for user involvement and mediation.

To be sure, Arctic LAMs and HSs are already online: Both LAMs and HSs are using websites and digital platforms to promote their buildings, collections, and delivery of unique learning experiences, while at the same time, visitors to HSs and LAMs are using online spaces to interact with, post reviews and share photos of, tell stories about, add details on, and make decisions concerning their visits (Aldao & Mihalic, 2020; Andresen et al., 2020; Edelheim & Lee, 2017; Falk & Hagsten, 2022; Ianioglo & Rissanen, 2020; Skare, 2020) in the same way they do for other entertainment and cultural attractions, accommodations, and dining.

Arctic digital cultural heritage, however, is not limited to digital texts, photographs, and other artefacts. Following Cameron's (2021, p. 3) assertion that "all digital data" can be considered cultural heritage, this chapter proposes that Arctic datasets, too, are a form of Arctic DCH. Notwithstanding the swell of online collections featuring Arctic DCH, one specific type—that of digital datasets—receives much less attention than other forms such as texts, photographs, and audiovisual recordings. Arctic digital datasets are those sets of digital data created in, for, and about the Arctic that are rooted in scientific, social scientific, and humanistic disciplines such as anthropology, atmospheric science, biology, business, chemistry, climate science, history, physics, political science, psychology, sociology, and so on. These Arctic digital datasets are part of the Arctic's larger cultural heritage, not separate from it, and, therefore, the digital preservation of and online access to these datasets is just as paramount as it is for other artefacts. Despite growth in the sheer amount of Arctic digital datasets, there remains a lack of widespread concerted attention to them in the same way as other artefacts.

Although some entities are making headway to ensure the preservation and accessibility of Arctic datasets, this activity remains piecemeal at best as data management, data repositories, and other data services have blossomed, mostly in academic libraries, university research centres, and government agencies. One early repository is the Finnish Social Science Data Archive (2014) (https://www.fsd.tuni.fi/) created in 1999 with full online dataset availability added in 2014. Over the years, other online repositories specializing in Arctic data have emerged: The Polar Data Catalogue (https://polardata.ca/) was launched in Canada in 2007 though did not begin adding complete data files until 2011 (Canadian Cryospheric Information Network, 2023; Church et al., 2016) and Arctic Data Center (https://arcticdata.io/) was created in 2016, containing datasets and software downloads from NSF-funded projects. In 2019, the Arctic University of Norway rolled out TROLLing (https://dataverse.no/dataverse/trolling), a new language and linguistics open repository (Conzett, 2019). What remains unclear is whether these dataset collections and databases of data are securely managed for preservation and accessibility as part of larger and longer-term Arctic heritage. Arctic-related websites sometimes disappear overnight due to, among other things, a lack of long-term project stability or commitment from a sponsoring institution. Plus, some Arctic organizations and scholars mention the unreliable state of Arctic research data management, including lack of knowledge about and skills pertaining to data management plans, metadata, version control, and data citation, as well as difficulties with international and interdisciplinary data coordination and sharing (International Arctic Science Committee (IASC), 2021, 2022, 2023; Palsdottir, 2021). The Arctic research community would benefit from reassurance that Arctic datasets in perpetuity are treated both as important digital contributions to Arctic study and digital artefacts of Arctic heritage under the responsibility of LAMs with proper data infrastructure and LIS professionals well-trained in ethical data curation.

That more concerted direction and standardization is needed for polar (i.e., Arctic and Antarctic) dataset management internationally was expressed at the International Polar Year (IPY) 2007–2008 by way of a data policy it created in 2006 in advance of the IPY campaign (Hovelsrud & Krupnik, 2006; Krupnik et al., 2005). Realizing that preservation, accessibility, and sharing of datasets needed to be addressed, and recognizing its own lack of data procedure, the IASC, too, published a 2013 document containing principles and practices of data management to guide Arctic researchers. Since then, calls to unify Arctic data management, in policy and practice, have multiplied. The ongoing challenge is well put by EU-PolarNet (2023, para. 18):

6 The Liquid Arctic and Digitalization

> The data produced by European polar research is difficult and expensive to collect and needs to be effectively managed, served, and archived for a wide range of users. However, polar data management has lacked central co-ordination at the European level, and as a result is fragmented and the data often very difficult to access and use or be supplied in a timely manner. There is also a need to link with data sets held by other polar nations, particularly those in North America, with a similarly long record of polar research.

EU-PolarNet's observation led to their development in 2017 of data management recommendations that include discussion of issues related to technical systems interoperability and sustainability, data sharing policy, and more. In the *Arctic Horizons* report (Anderson et al., 2018, p. 3), Recommendation #9 states the need to "invest in data management, maintenance, and services for sharing, discoverability, and access; and seek to balance issues of confidentiality and information sovereignty with the open data movement," while Research Priority #9 calls for "innovations in data curation, management, sharing, discoverability, and access." The annual report of the Nordic e-Infrastructure Collaboration (2018, p. 11) includes, as a part of their *2020+ Strategy*, a "stronger focus on open science, open data, and equitable access" to data, including data management as a key competency. In 2021, the Interagency Arctic Research Policy Committee of the United States released the *Arctic Research Plan 2022–2026* wherein they included data management as a foundational activity, noting that "Arctic data … are irreplaceable … [and] … data management is critical to basic research, monitoring, and applied research in the Arctic" (p. 25). That same year, ArcticNet (2021) in Canada also released an extensive data management policy.

The central thread here is the importance of data and the growing need for all facets of data management, yet nearly 20 years now following IPY's data policy, the Arctic dataset landscape globally remains uneven in practice, sometimes fractured along nation-state lines, even if there is consensus on what is needed in principle. A quite practical question, for example, is: How are Arctic researchers ensuring that their datasets are properly assigned relevant metadata for optimized discoverability by other researchers? Such a question is not trivial given that:

> diversity in data and information types, formats, and needs makes it difficult to curate, discover, and access these data and information on a technical and social level. Existing metadata standards that can deal with this diversity in data types are often not detailed enough to be helpful. More research is needed to develop best practices in this arena that would allow for improved capacity to research linked databases for more robust syntheses. (Anderson et al., 2018, p. 23).

Some additional related questions might be: To which data repositories are Arctic researchers submitting their datasets and why? Are Arctic researchers publishing their datasets as part of journal article, book chapter, and book submissions? How is the concept of open data influencing researchers' decisions about data collection, discovery, access, and archiving? What roles are LAMs playing in Arctic research dataset management? This last question is especially poignant, too, because the functions of LIS and LAMs pertaining to Arctic datasets have yet to be fully realized by the broader Arctic research community despite the fact that data, knowledge, and information management are constitutive of specialities within LIS education and scholarship. LIS, especially those sub-disciplines dealing with data architecture, digital and data archiving, ICTs, and data and knowledge management, has a ripe opportunity to become involved with and help establish itself as an active Arctic research partner with conventional Arctic researchers and in concert with local Indigenous peoples. Research data management guides created by LAMs are a step in the right direction, but alone do not signal to Arctic researchers that LIS professionals and scholars truly can be partners in research lifecycles.

While it is important for LAMs to expertly, and ethically, preserve Arctic heritage, DCH is not immune from bias. When writing about museums and galleries, Mason et al. (2018, p. 13), state that these not only "serve as ambassadors for their nations by promoting them to other countries, they also provide unifying symbols for nations at home." Although those authors do not include libraries, archives, or heritage sites in their assertion, these may serve the same purpose by way of specialized collections; carefully curated exhibits; pristine upkeep; organized tour visits; and status designation as, for example, an UNESCO World Heritage Site. As said by Urry (2000b, p. 149):

> Since the mid-19th century, travel to see the key sites, texts, exhibitions, buildings landscapes, and achievements of a society has singularly developed that cultural sense of a national imagined presence. Particularly important in the genealogy of nationalism in most societies has been the founding of national museums, the development of national artists, architects, musicians, playwrights, novelists, historians, and archaeologists and the location of the nation's achievements in world exhibitions.

In the Arctic context, LAMs and HSs serve as sites of ambassadorship on the global stage both as representatives of their constituent countries as well as the Circumpolar North as a unique and culturally rich region. However, as institutions, LAMs and HSs have served in the past, and can still be used today, as sociopolitical vehicles for advancing national, cultural, and heritage agendas (e.g., oppression, colonization, propaganda, etc.). LAMs and HSs as tools of soft power, therefore, are not neutral spaces, neither physically nor virtually in the Arctic or elsewhere.

Important to keep in mind, too, is that the concept of DCH is a Eurocentric one (Cameron, 2021, p. 50) and, therefore, may not always be recognized by non-Western actors and Indigenous peoples—including those who call the North their home—as a legitimate strategy to protect knowledge and culture for the future. The *Arctic Horizons* report notes that a key shift in Arctic research is occurring that involves "the transition to understanding knowledge co-production as a central epistemological paradigm [that] refers to a joint process between academics and other knowledge holders in planning, carrying out, and disseminating research" (Anderson et al., 2018, p. 20). Accordingly, the co-production of knowledge where Indigenous and non-Indigenous persons and institutions work side-by-side to create new knowledge via synthesis of social sciences, humanities, and biophysical sciences along with local, traditional knowledge must reflect an integrated, participatory, and community-based paradigm. Given this trend, LAMs and related institutions where Arctic Indigenous culture and knowledge are involved, too, must establish a community-based participatory approach that directly involve Arctic Indigenous individuals and communities in all aspects of working with both analogue and digital cultural heritage. Such an approach demands, in its most fundamental sense, that Arctic Indigenous peoples become equal co-creators, co-researchers, and co-managers in all cultural and knowledge-based projects so that creative, administrative, and decision-making powers can be shared between Indigenous community members and non-Indigenous librarians, archivists, curators, and other LIS professionals and scholars. A few evident areas within LIS where co-production must take place is in the creation and application of metadata and controlled vocabulary, as well as awareness of and initiatives regarding long-term digital archiving, discovery, accessibility, sharing, and transfer, along with intellectual property and sovereignty, all of which invariably involve social and symbolic power.

The notion of power in LIS, especially regarding Indigenous issues, is not entirely new, though not much has been published on power and LIS specifically in Arctic contexts. In general terms, LAMs, HSs, and digitalization itself play important roles—unwittingly or not—in cultural, heritage, memory, and knowledge construction, production, legitimization, and maintenance through symbolic power embodied in these institutions, upheld by national governments and professional organizations, as authorities of culture and knowledge even at the expense of others (Čeginskas et al., 2021; Nyhlén & Gidlund, 2019). Evidence of this continued and reproduced colonization in the Arctic context is seen in common LIS activities such as creation and assignment of controlled vocabulary (Hoffman, 2020; Rigby, 2020), as well as hegemonic decisions such as what materials matter most, how they should be digitized, and who is responsible for the continued 'ownership' of cultural artefacts and skeletal remains (Joy, 2019; Lemelin & Baikie, 2011; Wråkberg & Granqvist, 2014). In the conduct of research, similar questions like these have led to the 'giving back' discourse in research as explained by Herman (2018, p. 2):

> The days of 'parachute' scholars, who descend into communities with their research agendas in hand and expect to get the data they want before they disappear—perhaps never to return, and with no intent of bestowing any benefits on the community—are becoming a thing of the past. Not only has the advent of feminist and postcolonial theories illuminated the exploitative nature of that approach, but Native communities themselves are increasingly demanding more say over or about the nature of research projects in their communities and on their lands and are willing to say no to projects that do not clearly serve their interests. Meanwhile, a number of guidelines for conducting research in Indigenous communities have proliferated, and they call for a much more inclusive and reciprocal approach to such work.

Historically, the power of LAMs has not been challenged much by Indigenous peoples, partly because Indigenous knowledge has a deeply entrenched oral and visual (i.e., not written) tradition, and due to long histories of colonization and imbalanced social power structures that favour the desires of explorer-settlers over native inhabitants. However, the importance of reciprocity and the dialogue of giving back has made its way into the Arctic Indigenous heritage, knowledge, and memory sector as seen, for example, in the work of the Exchange for Local Observations and Knowledge of the Arctic (https://eloka-arctic.org/) that includes the "establishment of protocols and methods that use digital technologies to share and preserve documented forms of Indigenous knowledge while attempting to maintain cultural significance, context, ownership, and control of the resources" (McCann et al., 2016, p. 126; see also Pulsifer et al., 2012).

6.5 Conclusion

Working backwards, the main goal of this chapter is to suggest that digital cultural heritage along with its digital libraries, archives, and museums represent a form of digitalization, which in turn makes possible and, is made possible by, liquid modernity. Furthermore, the context of the Arctic is used to propose the term Liquid Arctic as an extension of the Global Arctic to better understand Arctic change. The chapter does this by arguing that signatures of Liquid Arctic are apparent in (1) the reality of large-scale, pan-Arctic problems, risks, and uncertainties that cannot be addressed unilaterally; (2) the pan-Arctic growth of non-places, aided by migration, urbanization, and consumption in accelerated time; and (3) the ever-expansive, pan-Arctic electronic flows of data, information, and communication in day-to-day life occurring thanks to the transformative process of digitalization. As a relevant example for library and information science, the chapter asserts that Arctic digital cultural heritage is a form of ongoing Arctic digital transformation. Professionals and scholars working in LIS and related sectors already participate in, and are products of, globalization (Witt, 2012), yet the liquid metaphor presented in this chapter that better describes late modernity is not well known in the LIS field. The Liquid Arctic term provides a conceptual vehicle through which those working in LAMs internal to the Arctic, as well as those working in LAMs external to the Arctic with Arctic collections, can understand Arctic change in a new way.

Given what has been said so far about liquid modernity and the Arctic connections this chapter has made, describing the Circumpolar North as a Liquid Arctic—an Arctic beyond simply being Global—is sensible. Nonetheless, the Liquid Arctic term—that is, liquid modernity in the Arctic context—is not without limitations. First, as a grand narrative and metaphor, the 'liquid' aspects of liquid modernity and Liquid Arctic may not apply to all individuals or groups within or related to the Circumpolar North, but the point of the concept is not to do this anyway. That is, Liquid Arctic is not meant to operate at the micro level; it is not applicable in understanding individuality per se but rather aims to provide deeper insight into the Arctic's macro, late modern, and global positioning. After all, the Arctic exists in the world and, therefore, is not immune from the effects of being part of it. Liquid Arctic, much like Global Arctic, is meant to convey a large-scale experience encompassing the Circumpolar North, not one that is attributable to every singular entity within it. However, unlike Global Arctic, the Liquid Arctic concept provides a metaphorical device for visualizing the cascade of Arctic change.

Second, the use of Bauman's liquid modernity may be viewed as problematic because 'modernity' is conceptually and "thoroughly European in its origins and its understanding of current global politics, with a 'civilized centre' and a less than civilized periphery" (Munck, 2016, p. 240), yet the Arctic is not by any measure solely European. Notwithstanding the Eurocentricity of modernity, employing the construct remains a useful technique in conceptualizing major, far-reaching change, the likes of which accurately describes what is occurring across the Circumpolar North and the impacts of that change on the rest of the world. Although the Global Arctic depiction alone falls short of explicating change via the metaphorical lens of liquid modernity, Liquid Arctic is able to introduce the easy-to-understand liquid metaphor toward viewing the kaleidoscopic change of a transforming Arctic. Thus, despite these limitations, describing the Arctic as liquid and enveloped in the tides of liquid modernity remains useful as a theoretical and conceptual framework to depict and understand the late-modern conditions characteristic of today's—and tomorrow's—Circumpolar North.

References

Abildgaard, M. S., Ren, C., Leyva-Mayorga, I., Stefanovic, C., Soret, B., & Popovski, P. (2022). Arctic connectivity: A frugal approach to infrastructural development. *Arctic, 75*(1), 72–85. https://doi.org/k8nt

Acadia, S., & Fjellestad, M. T. (2020). Introduction: Why this book and why the Arctic? In S. Acadia & M. T. Fjellestad (Eds.), *Library and information studies for Arctic social sciences and humanities* (pp. 1–65). Routledge.

Administration, President of Russia/Administratsiya, Prezidenta Rossii. (2017). *Ukaz Prezidenta Rossiyskoy Federatsii ot 09.05.2017 g. No. 203: «O strategii razvitiya informatsionnogo obshchestva v Rossiyskoy Federatsii na 2017–2030 gody»* [Decree of the President of the Russian Federation dated 05/09/2017, No. 203: The strategy for the development of the information society in the Russian Federation for 2017–2030]. https://bit.ly/3uUdNAl. Accessed Dec 21 2023.

Adolf, M., & Stehr, N. (2017). *Knowledge* (2nd ed.). Routledge.

Ahmmed, T., Alidadi, A., Zhang, Z., Chaudhry, A. U., & Yanikomeroglu, H. (2022, June). The digital divide in Canada and the role of LEO satellites in bridging the gap. *IEEE Communications, 60*(6), 24–30. https://doi.org/k8nv

Åland Regional Government/Ålands landskapsregering. (2012). *Digital agenda för landskapet Åland* [Digital agenda for the Åland region]. https://bit.ly/3NqtwNS. Accessed Dec 21 2023.

Alaska Broadband Office (ABO). (2023). *Internet for all Alaska: State of Alaska five-year action plan*. https://bit.ly/3TmKIaO. Accessed Dec 21 2023.

Alberque, W., & Schreer, B. (2022, June/July). Finland, Sweden, and NATO membership. *Survival, 64*(3), 67–72. https://doi.org/k8nw

Aldao, C. & Mihalic, T. A. (2020). New frontiers in travel motivation and social media: The case of Longyearbyen, the High Arctic. *Sustainability, 12*(15), Article 5905, 1–19. https://doi.org/k8nx

Amery, R. (2023, 3 July). Frustrated Orkney council to debate defecting to Norway. *The Scotsman*. https://bit.ly/3Nqvr59. Accessed Dec 21 2023.

Anderson, S., Strawhacker, C., Presnall, A., Butler, V., Etnier, M., Petrov, A., Rasmus, S., Smith, K., & Yamin-Pasternak, S. (2018). *Arctic horizons: Final report*. Jefferson Institute. https://bit.ly/3uYsvGw. Accessed Dec 21 2023.

Andresen, H., Huvila, I., & Stokstad, S. (2020). Perceptions and implications of user participation and engagement in libraries, archives, and museums. In R. Audunson, H. Andresen, C. Fagerlid, E. Henningsen, H.-C. Hobohm, H. Jochumsen, H. Larsen, & T. Vold. (Eds.), *Libraries, archives, and museums as democratic spaces in a digital age* (pp. 185–206). de Gruyter. https://doi.org/gjfphx

Appadurai, A. (1996). *Modernity at large: Cultural dimensions of globalization.* University of Minnesota Press.

Arbo, P., Iversen, A., Knol, M., Ringholm, T., & Sander, G. (2013). Arctic futures: Conceptualizations and images of a changing Arctic. *Polar Geography, 36*(3), 163–182. https://doi.org/gprm26

Arctic Council. (2023). *The Russian Federation.* https://bit.ly/3RIEMrH. Accessed Dec 21 2023.

Arctic Monitoring and Assessment Programme (AMAP). (2021). *AMAP Arctic climate change update 2021: Key trends and impacts.* https://bit.ly/3RH7qJJ. Accessed Dec 21 2023.

Arctic Russia: Tourism. (n.d.-a). *The easternmost, the northernmost, the longest: Anadyr set to construct a cableway like no other in the world.* https://bit.ly/3TrSu3h. Accessed Dec 21 2023.

Arctic Russia: Tourism. (n.d.-b). *The most beautiful village in Russia.* https://bit.ly/3RFRUxr. Accessed Dec 21 2023.

Arctic Russia: Tourism. (n.d.-c). *Russian Arctic National Park.* https://bit.ly/48hxUqm. Accessed Dec 21 2023.

ArcticNet. (2021). *Data management policy.* https://bit.ly/3NqAUJo. Accessed Dec 21 2023.

Atkinson, W. (2007). Beck, individualization, and the death of class: A critique. *British Journal of Sociology, 58*(3), 349–366. https://doi.org/db6n4z

Audunson, R., Aabø, S., Blomgren, R., Hobohm, H.-C., Jochumsen, H., Khosrowjerdi, M., Mumenthaler, R., Schuldt, K., Rasmussen, C. H., Rydbeck, K., Tóth, M., & Vårheim, A. (2019). Public libraries as public institutions: A comparative study of perceptions of the public library's role in six European countries. *Journal of Documentation, 75*(6), 1396–1415. https://doi.org/gf6kbs

Augé, M. (2008). *Non-places: An introduction to supermodernity* (2nd ed.). Verso.

Avango, D., Nilsson, A. E., & Roberts, P. (2013). Assessing Arctic futures: Voices, resources, and governance. *Polar Journal, 3*(2), 431–446. https://doi.org/f24j6c

Baldacchino, G. (Ed.). (2006). *Extreme tourism: Lessons from the world's cold water islands.* Routledge.

Bannykh G., & Kostina, S. (2022). The state's activity on the development of digital capitalism: Evidence from Russia. *Post-Communist Economies, 34*(1), 99–121. https://doi.org/k8nz

Barbour, T. (2020, January). The future of 5G for Alaska: The Last Frontier at the forefront of technology. *Alaska Business.* https://bit.ly/41lreoZ. Accessed Dec 21 2023.

Barbour, T. (2022, December). Leveraging 5G: Faster, more stable, and more secure wireless connectivity. *Alaska Business.* https://bit.ly/3GEZORw. Accessed Dec 21 2023.

Barnes Reports. (2023). *U.S. Industry and Market Report, NAICS 722513: Fast Food Restaurants Industry.*

Basaraba, N., Conlan, O., Edmond, J., & Arnds, P. (2019). Digital narrative conventions in heritage trail mobile apps. *New Review of Hypermedia and Multimedia, 25*(1/2), 1–30. https://doi.org/gn9psw

Bauman, Z. (1997). *Postmodernity and its discontents* (2005 reprint ed.). Polity.

Bauman, Z. (1998). *Globalization: The human consequences.* Columbia University Press.

Bauman, Z. (2000/2012). *Liquid modernity* (2018 reprint ed.). Polity.

Bauman, Z. (2006). *Liquid fear.* Polity.

Bauman, Z. (2007a). *Consuming life* (2013 reprint ed.). Polity.

Bauman, Z. (2007b). *Liquid times: Living in an age of uncertainty* (2017 reprint ed.). Polity.

Bauman, Z. (2011). *Culture in a liquid modern world* (2016 reprint ed.). Polity.

Beck, U. (1992). *Risk society: Towards a new modernity* (1996 reprint ed.). Sage.

Beck, U. (1999). *World risk society* (2008 reprint ed.). Polity.

Beck, U. (2009). *World at risk* (2015 reprint ed.). Polity.

Beck, U., & Willms, J. (2004). *Conversations with Ulrich Beck. Polity.*

Blackshaw, T. (2005). *Zygmunt Bauman.* Routledge.

Borja, J., Castells, M., Belil, M., & Benner, C. (1997). *Local and global: Management of cities in the information age.* Earthscan.

Born, C., Henkel, M., & Mainka, A. (2018). How public libraries are keeping pace with the times: Core services of libraries in informational world cities. *Libri, 68*(3), 181–203. https://doi.org/gd9xhd

Bousquette, I. (2023, 10 March). What will it take to connect the Arctic? $1.2 billion, 10,000 miles of fiber-optic cable, and patience. *Wall Street Journal*. https://bit.ly/3TmpZUA. Accessed Dec 21 2023.

Brigham, L. W. (2007, September/October). Thinking about the Arctic's future: Scenarios for 2040. *Futurist, 41*(5), 27–29, 31–34.

Bryant, A. (2007). Liquid modernity, complexity, and turbulence. *Theory, Culture, and Society, 24*(1), 127–135. https://doi.org/crbf2c

Büscher, M., Sheller, M., & Tyfield, D. (2016). Mobility intersections: Social research, social futures. *Mobility, 11*(4), 485–497. https://doi.org/gf27t7

Bystrowska, M., & Dawson, J. (2017). Making places: The role of Arctic cruise operators in 'creating' tourism destinations. *Polar Geography, 40*(3), 208–226. https://doi.org/k8n2

Cameron, F. (2015). The liquid museum: New institutional ontologies for a complex, uncertain world. In A. Witcomb & K. Message (Eds.), *International handbook of museum studies: Museum theory* (pp. 345–361). Wiley. https://doi.org/gqx7kh

Cameron, F. R. (2021). *The future of digital data, heritage, and curation in a more-than-human world*. Routledge.

Campbell, T. (2013). The temporal horizon of 'the choice': Anxieties and banalities in 'time,' modern and liquid modern. *Thesis Eleven, 118*(1), 19–32. https://doi.org/k8n3

Canadian Cryospheric Information Network (CCIN). (2023). *The Polar Data Catalogue*. https://bit.ly/3RkhhUd. Accessed Dec 21 2023.

Carlson, A., & Isaacs, A. M. (2018). Technological capital: An alternative to the digital divide. *Journal of Applied Communication Research, 46*(2), 243–265. https://doi.org/gf6k9s

Castells, M. (2000). Materials for an exploratory theory of the network society. *British Journal of Sociology, 51*(1), 5–24. https://doi.org/b9csf8

Castells, M. (2010). *The rise of the network society* (2nd ed.). Wiley.

Čeginskas, V. L. A., Kaasik-Krogerus, S., Lähdesmäki, T., & Mäkinen, K. (2021). Constructing social Europe through European cultural heritage. *European Societies, 23*(4), 487–512. https://doi.org/k8n4

CGI. (2021, May 26). *GCI reveals landmark commitment to bring 10 gig internet speeds to Alaska, will deliver 2 gig in 2022* [Blog]. https://bit.ly/3NpfVqd. Accessed Dec 21 2023.

Christensen, J. D., Therkelsen, J., Georgiev, I., & Sand, H. (2018). *Data centre opportunities in the Nordics: An analysis of the competitive advantages*. Nordic Council of Ministers. https://doi.org/k8n5

Church, D. L., Friddell, J. E., & LeDrew, E. F. (2016). The Polar Data Catalogue: A vehicle for collaboration, northern community partnerships, and policy making. In L. Brigham, H. Exner-Pirot, L. Heininen, & J. Pouffe (Eds.), *Arctic yearbook 2016* (pp. 193–207). Geopolitics and Security Thematic Network, University of the Arctic. https://bit.ly/3NqweTF. Accessed Dec 21 2023.

Collins, S. (2017). *Red-hot growth in an ice-cold land: An overview of Iceland's hotel market*. HVS. https://bit.ly/3RkhUx3. Accessed Dec 21 2023.

Companies are getting out of Russia, sometimes at a cost. (2022, October 14). *New York Times*. https://bit.ly/46Zt7Jp. Accessed Dec 21 2023.

Connectivity Working Group (CWG), Arctic Economic Council (AEC). (2021). *Connectivity infrastructure in the Arctic*. https://bit.ly/48jh6j5. Accessed Dec 21 2023.

Conzett, P. (2019). *Disciplinary case study: The Tromsø Repository of Language and Linguistics (TROLLing)*. https://doi.org/k8n7

Cooper, E. A. (2020). Cultural centres: A future for cultural Arctic tourism? *Journal of Tourism Futures, 6*(1), 57–69. https://doi.org/gkx62n

Creswell, J. (2022, March 9). Russia loses fast foods, long symbols of the West. *New York Times*. https://bit.ly/41kpv3s. Accessed Dec 21 2023.

Danish Agency for Digital Government/Digitaliseringsstyrelsen. (2021). *Visions and recommendations for Denmark as a digital pioneer*. https://bit.ly/41sSySw. Accessed Dec 21 2023.

Danish Agency for Digitalisation/Digitaliseringsstyrelsen & Government of Greenland/Naalakkersuisut. (2018). *Det digitale samfund: National digitaliseringsstrategi 2018–2021*

[The digital society: National digitalisation strategy 2018–2021]. https://bit.ly/3v0hdSg. Accessed Dec 21 2023.

Davis, M. (2013). Hurried lives: Dialectics of time and technology in liquid modernity. *Thesis Eleven, 118*(1), 7–18. https://doi.org/k8n8

Davis, M. (2016). Liquid sociology—What for? In M. Davis (Ed.), *Liquid sociology: Metaphor in Zygmunt Bauman's analysis of modernity* (pp. 1–12). Routledge.

Delaunay, M., & Landriault, M. (2020). Connectivity and infrastructure: The Arctic digital divide. In J. Weber (Ed.), *Handbook on geopolitics and security in the Arctic: The High North between cooperation and confrontation* (pp. 231–248). Springer. https://doi.org/k8n9

DeMarban, A. (2022, December 5). Amazon plans to build a sorting facility at former Sears warehouse in Anchorage. *Anchorage Daily News*. https://bit.ly/3GHlmNp. Accessed Dec 21 2023.

DeMarban, A. (2023a, May 8). Alaska state agency gives preliminary approval to Valdez ski resort. *Anchorage Daily News*. https://bit.ly/3tdyrel. Accessed Dec 21 2023.

DeMarban, A. (2023b, May 30). Developers plan 150-room lodge in Girdwood. *Anchorage Daily News*. https://bit.ly/3tm9CwE. Accessed Dec 21 2023.

Demiroglu, O. C., Lundmark, L., Saarinen, J., & Müller, D. K. (2020). The last resort? Ski tourism and climate change in Arctic Sweden. *Journal of Tourism Futures, 6*(1), 91–101. https://doi.org/gjd57b

Department of Tourism and Culture, Government of Yukon/Ministère du Tourisme et de la Culture, Gouvernement du Yukon. (n.d.-a). *What's your next activity? Category: Shopping*. https://bit.ly/46ZjTwP. Accessed Dec 21 2023.

Department of Tourism and Culture, Government of Yukon/Ministère du Tourisme et de la Culture, Gouvernement du Yukon. (n.d.-b). *Klondike treasures*. https://bit.ly/3tfF67I. Accessed Dec 21 2023.

Dodds, K. (2018). Global Arctic. *Journal of Borderlands Studies, 33*(2), 191–194. https://doi.org/k8pb

Dodds, K., & Nuttall, M. (2019). *The Arctic: What everyone needs to know*. Oxford University Press.

Dodds, K., & Woodward, J. (2021). *The Arctic: A very short introduction*. Oxford University Press.

Donner, J. (2015). *After access: Inclusion, development, and a more mobile internet*. MIT Press.

Dufva, T., & Dufva, M. (2019). Grasping the future of the digital society. *Futures, 107*, 17–28. https://doi.org/gfv22k

Edelheim, J., & Lee, Y.-S. (2017). Tourists and narration in the Arctic: The changing experience of museums. In Y.-S. Lee, D. B. Weaver, & N. K. Prebensen (Eds.), *Arctic tourism experiences: Production, consumption, and sustainability* (pp. 37–47). CABI.

Edquist, S., Audunson, R., & Huvila, I. (2023). Do collections still constitute libraries, archives, and museums? In C. H. Rasmussen, K. Rydbeck, & H. Larsen (Eds.), *Libraries, archives, and museums in transition: Changes, challenges, and convergence in a Scandinavian perspective* (pp. 73–86). Routledge. https://bit.ly/3GHjvbr. Accessed Dec 21 2023.

Edvardsen, A. (2022, September 22). Taking network coverage in the Arctic to new heights. *High North News*. https://bit.ly/3NsDuhU. Accessed Dec 21 2023.

Elliott, A., & Urry, J. (2010). *Mobile lives*. Routledge.

Emelyanova, E. E. (2019). Evaluating the performance of the policy and potential investment development of Northern and Arctic municipalities. *Problems of Economic Transition, 61*(7/9), 737–748. https://doi.org/k8pc

Ericsson. (2022, September 30). *Tusass and Ericsson connect Greenland with 5G*. https://bit.ly/470v3kN. Accessed Dec 21 2023.

Ericsson. (2023, March 28). *Faroese Telecom and Ericsson set European 5G mmWave downlink speed record*. https://bit.ly/3NlZdYz. Accessed Dec 21 2023.

Ermolovskaya, O. Y., Sedash, T. N., Cheglov, V. P., Timofeeva, L. L., & Feigin, G. F. (2020). Priority areas of digitalization in Russia. *EurAsian Journal of BioSciences, 14*(2), 3551–3556.

EU-PolarNet. (2017). *Connecting science with society: Deliverable 3.5: Data management recommendations for polar research data systems and infrastructures in Europe*. https://bit.ly/46XPOgM. Accessed Dec 21 2023.

6 The Liquid Arctic and Digitalization

EU-PolarNet. (2023). *History of EU-PolarNet 1*. https://bit.ly/47dnesh. Accessed Dec 21 2023.

European Commission. (2020). *Shaping Europe's digital future*. https://bit.ly/3Rp9moQ. Accessed Dec 21 2023.

European Commission. (2021a). *A stronger EU engagement for a peaceful, sustainable, and prosperous Arctic*. https://bit.ly/48ek0Fv. Accessed Dec 21 2023.

European Commission. (2021b). *2030 digital compass: The European way for the digital decade*. https://bit.ly/3GF1w5o. Accessed Dec 21 2023.

European Commission. (2022a). *Digital Economy and Society Index (DESI) 2022: Denmark*. https://bit.ly/3Rmmjj5. Accessed Dec 21 2023.

European Commission. (2022b). *Digital Economy and Society Index (DESI) 2022: Finland*. https://bit.ly/3GIQc8q. Accessed Dec 21 2023.

European Commission. (2022c). *Digital Economy and Society Index (DESI) 2022: Norway*. https://bit.ly/48h5i0I. Accessed Dec 21 2023.

European Commission. (2022d). *Digital Economy and Society Index (DESI) 2022: Sweden*. https://bit.ly/41javCX. Accessed Dec 21 2023.

European Commission. (2023a). *Digital Decade Country Report 2023: Denmark*. https://bit.ly/3timGDj. Accessed Dec 21 2023.

European Commission. (2023b). *Digital Decade Country Report 2023: Finland*. https://bit.ly/41nBpt9. Accessed Dec 21 2023.

European Commission. (2023c). *Digital Decade Country Report 2023: Sweden*. https://bit.ly/41i883j. Accessed Dec 21 2023.

Eutelsat OneWeb. (2021, June 4). *Pacific Dataport Inc. signs strategic distribution partnership with OneWeb*. https://bit.ly/3RpEKDF. Accessed Dec 21 2023.

Eutelsat OneWeb. (2023a, May 23). *Arctic Space Technologies to support OneWeb's constellation with construction of hyperscale satellite ground station installation*. https://bit.ly/41i8bfv. Accessed Dec 21 2023.

Eutelsat OneWeb. (2023b, May 24). *Space-based internet programme puts Iceland on front foot for 'High North' satcomms connectivity*. https://bit.ly/48b1NIU. Accessed Dec 21 2023.

Evengård, B., Larsen, J. N., & Paasche, Ø. (Eds.). (2015). *The new Arctic*. Springer.

Falk, M. T., & Hagsten, E. (2022). Digital indicators of interest in natural world heritage sites. *Journal of Environmental Management, 324*(15), Article 116250, 1–11. https://doi.org/k8pd

Fay, G., & Karlsdóttir, A. (2011). Social indicators for Arctic tourism: Observing trends and assessing data. *Polar Geography, 34*(1/2), 63–86. https://doi.org/dq9gn7

Federal State Statistics Service/Federal'naya sluzhba gosudarstvennoi statistiki. (2023). *Chislennost' naseleniya Rossiyskoy Federatsii po munitsipal'nym obrazovaniyam na 1 yanvarya 2023 goda* [Population of the Russian Federation by municipalities as of January 1, 2023]. https://bit.ly/3RG53qk. Accessed Dec 21 2023.

Fedorinova, Y. (2021, December 17). The $31 billion plan to make you book your vacation in Siberia. *Bloomberg*. https://bit.ly/4akIe2P. Accessed Dec 21 2023.

Finger, M., & Heininen, L. (Eds.). (2019). *The GlobalArctic handbook*. Springer.

Finger, M., & Rekvig, G. (Eds.). (2022a). *Global Arctic: An introduction to the multifaceted dynamics of the Arctic*. Springer.

Finger, M., & Rekvig, G. (2022b). Introduction. In M. Finger & G. Rekvig (Eds.), *Global Arctic: An introduction to the multifaceted dynamics of the Arctic* (pp. 1–17). Springer. https://doi.org/k8pf

Finnish Government/Valtioneuvosto. (2021). *Finland's strategy for Arctic policy*. https://bit.ly/3NrDrTg. Accessed Dec 21 2023.

Finnish Government/Valtioneuvosto. (2022). *Finland's digital compass*. https://bit.ly/3Nm06jR. Accessed Dec 21 2023.

Finnish Social Science Data Archive/Tietoarkisto. (2014). *Annual report 2014*. https://bit.ly/3NqDqzk. Accessed Dec 21 2023.

Fitch Solutions Group. (2022a). *Canada tourism report, Q2 2022*.

Fitch Solutions Group. (2022b). *Russia tourism report, Q3 2022*.

Fitch Solutions Group. (2022c). *Sweden tourism report, Q2 2022.*

Floridi, L. (2010). *Information: A very short introduction.* Oxford University Press.

Floridi, L. (2014). *The 4th revolution: How the infosphere is reshaping human reality.* Oxford University Press.

Foundation for Strategic Environmental Research/Stiftelsen för Miljöstrategisk forskning. (2012). *Mistra Arctic futures in a global context.* https://bit.ly/481O1sM. Accessed Dec 21 2023.

Franklin, A. (2003). The tourist syndrome: An interview with Zygmunt Bauman. *Tourist Studies, 3*(2), 205–217. https://doi.org/dchtjp

Fredman, P., & Margaryan, L. (2020). 20 years of Nordic nature-based tourism research: A review and future research agenda. *Scandinavian Journal of Hospitality and Tourism, 21*(1), 14–25. https://doi.org/gjcdq7

Gane, N. (2001). Zygmunt Bauman: Liquid modernity and beyond. *Acta Sociologica, 44,* 267–275. https://bit.ly/3TvqwUa. Accessed Dec 21 2023.

Gassen, N. S., & Heleniak, T. (2019). *The Nordic population in 2040: Analysis of past and future demographic trends.* Nordregio. https://doi.org/k8pg. Accessed Dec 21 2023.

Gershkovich, E. (2022, August 19). Starbucks replacement opens in Russia with similar look; coffee chain now owned by a Russian restaurateur and popular rapper, but has a familiar look and feel. *Wall Street Journal.* https://bit.ly/3v1ZKJe. Accessed Dec 21 2023.

Gladkova, A., Vartanova, E., & Ragnedda, M. (2020). Digital divide and digital capital in multiethnic Russian society. *Journal of Multicultural Discourses, 15*(2), 126–147. https://doi.org/gk2tck

Government of Canada/Gouvernement du Canada. (2019). *Canada's Arctic and Northern policy framework.* https://bit.ly/46XR8QM. Accessed Dec 21 2023.

Government of Iceland/Stjórnarráð Íslands. (2021). *Digital Iceland's digital policy.* https://bit.ly/47VKJH8. Accessed Dec 21 2023.

Government of Ireland/Rialtas na hÉireann. (2020). *Ireland's application for Arctic Council observer status.* https://bit.ly/48jjAhp. Accessed Dec 21 2023.

Government Offices of Sweden/Regeringskansliet. (2020). *Sweden's strategy for the Arctic region.* https://bit.ly/47dok7n. Accessed Dec 21 2023.

Grydehøj, A., Grydehøj, A., & Ackrén, M. (2012). The globalization of the Arctic: Negotiating sovereignty and building communities in Svalbard, Norway. *Island Studies Journal, 7*(1), 99–118. https://doi.org/k8ph

Gunkel, D. J. (2003). Second thoughts: Toward a critique of the digital divide. *New Media and Society, 5*(4), 499–522. https://doi.org/cv4tn9

Halegoua, G. R. (2019). *The digital city: Media and the social production of place.* New York University Press.

Hall, C. M., & Saarinen, J. (2010a). Last chance to see? Future issues for polar tourism and change. In C. M. Hall & J. Saarinen (Eds.), *Tourism and change in polar regions: Climate, environments, and experiences* (pp. 301–310). Routledge.

Hall, C. M., & Saarinen, J. (2010b). Polar tourism: Definitions and dimensions. *Scandinavian Journal of Hospitality and Tourism, 10*(4), 448–467. https://doi.org/fv7vrq

Hall, C. M., & Saarinen, J. (2010c). Tourism and change in polar regions: Introduction—definitions, locations, places, and dimensions. In C. M. Hall & J. Saarinen (Eds.), *Tourism and change in polar regions: Climate, environments, and experiences* (pp. 1–41). Routledge.

Hancock, A. (2022, March 9). Accor drops Russia expansion plans. *Financial Times.* https://bit.ly/3Toy5w1. Accessed Dec 21 2023.

Hansen, K. G., Rasmussen, R. O., Olsen, L. S., Roto, J., & Fredricsson, C. (2012). *Megatrends in the Arctic: New inspiration into current policy strategies.* Nordregio. https://bit.ly/3GDfeG5. Accessed Dec 21 2023.

Hantrais, L., & Lenihan, A. T. (2021). Social dimensions of evidence-based policy in a digital society. *Contemporary Social Science, 16*(2), 141–155. https://doi.org/gs7vm7

Harrington, S. (2016, March 2). The new Arctic Oilfield Hotel. *Alaska Business.* https://bit.ly/3NpZQR0. Accessed Dec 21 2023.

6 The Liquid Arctic and Digitalization

Heininen, L. (2019). Special features of Arctic geopolitics: A potential asset for world politics. In M. Finger & L. Heininen (Eds.), *The GlobalArctic handbook* (pp. 215–234). Springer. https://doi.org/k8pj

Heininen, L., & Southcott, C. (2010). Globalization and the Circumpolar North: An introduction. In L. Heininen & C. Southcott (Eds.), *Globalization and the Circumpolar North* (pp. 1–21). University of Alaska Press.

Heleniak, T. (2020). *Polar peoples in the future: Projections of the Arctic populations.* Nordregio. https://doi.org/k8pk

Heleniak, T. (2021). The future of the Arctic populations. *Polar Geography, 44*(2), 136–152. https://doi.org/gjvdwq

Heleniak, T., & Jokinen, J. C. (2020). Migration and mobility: More diverse, more urban. In J. Grunfelder, G. Norlén, L. Randall, & N. S. Gassen (Eds.), *State of the Nordic region 2020* (pp. 40–50). Nordic Council of Ministers. https://bit.ly/3TGgkZt. Accessed Dec 21 2023.

Heleniak, T., & Jokinen, J. C. (2022). Migration. In G. Norlén, L. Randall, N. S. Gassen, & C. Tapia (Eds.), *State of the Nordic region 2022* (pp. 42–58). Nordregio. https://doi.org/k8pm

Herman, R. D. K. (2018). Introduction: Why 'giving back?'. In R. D. K. Herman (Ed.), *Giving back: Research and reciprocity in Indigenous settings* (pp. 1–10). Oregon State University Press.

Herreman, Y. (1998). Museums and tourism: Culture and consumption. *Museum International, L(3)*, 4–12. https://bit.ly/48iNt11. Accessed Dec 21 2023.

Herva, V.-P., Varnajot, A., & Pashkevich, A. (2020). Bad Santa: Cultural heritage, mystification of the Arctic, and tourism as an extractive industry. *Polar Journal, 10*(2), 375–396. https://doi.org/gh8b35

Hoffman, N. (2020). Controlled vocabulary and Indigenous terminology in Canadian Arctic legal research. In S. Acadia & M. T. Fjellestad (Eds.), *Library and information studies for Arctic social sciences and humanities* (pp. 110–132). Routledge.

Hovelsrud, G. K., & Krupnik, I. (2006). IPY 2007–08 and social/human sciences: An update. *Arctic, 59*(3), 341–348. https://doi.org/k8pn

Hovelsrud, G. K., Poppel, B., van Oort, B., & Reist, J. D. (2011). Arctic societies, cultures, and peoples in a changing cryosphere. *Ambio, 40*(Suppl 1), 100–110. https://doi.org/fxtvg7

Hovelsrud, G. K., Kaltenborn, B. P., & Olsen, J. (2020). Svalbard in transition: Adaptation to cross-scale changes in Longyearbyen. *Polar Journal, 10*(2), 420–442. https://doi.org/gn86rx

Huijbens, E. H. (2022). The Arctic as the last frontier: Tourism. In M. Finger & G. Rekvig (Eds.), *Global Arctic: An introduction to the multifaceted dynamics of the Arctic* (pp. 129–146). Springer. https://doi.org/k8pq

Huskey, L., & Southcott, C. (Eds.). (2010). *Migration in the Circumpolar North: Issues and Contexts.* CCI.

Huvila, I., Johnston, J., & Roued-Cunliffe, H. (2023). LAMs and the participatory turn. In C. H. Rasmussen, K. Rydbeck, & H. Larsen (Eds.), *Libraries, archives, and museums in transition: Changes, challenges, and convergence in a Scandinavian perspective* (pp. 158–172). Routledge. https://bit.ly/47MAtB7. Accessed Dec 21 2023.

Hylland, O. M. (2022). Digital cultural policy: The story of a slow and reluctant revolution. *International Journal of Cultural Policy, 28*(7), 813–828. https://doi.org/grgp3r

Ianioglo, A., & Rissanen, M. (2020). Global trends and tourism development in peripheral areas. *Scandinavian Journal of Hospitality and Tourism, 20*(5), 520–539. https://doi.org/ghrz55

IBISWorld. (2022). *U.S. Industry State Report AK72221A: Fast Food Restaurants in Alaska.*

Innovation, Science, and Economic Development Canada/Innovation, Sciences et Développement économique Canada. (2019). *Canada's digital charter in action: A plan by Canadians, for Canadians.* https://bit.ly/3RG3BV1. Accessed Dec 21 2023.

Innovation, Science, and Economic Development Canada/Innovation, Sciences et Développement économique Canada. (2022a). *Governments of Canada and Newfoundland and Labrador invest over $230,000 to bring high-speed internet to more than 650 households in Wabush and Labrador City.* https://bit.ly/4aixTV0. Accessed Dec 21 2023.

Innovation, Science, and Economic Development Canada/Innovation, Sciences et Développement économique Canada. (2022b). *Governments of Canada and Quebec have invested more than*

$1.1 million to bring high-speed internet services to 1171 rural Quebec households. https://bit.ly/3v6kK19. Accessed Dec 21 2023.

Interagency Arctic Research Policy Committee, US National Science and Technology Council. (2021). *Arctic research plan 2022–2026.* https://bit.ly/46WVWGc. Accessed Dec 21 2023.

International Arctic Science Committee (IASC). (2013). *Statement of principles and practices for Arctic data management.* https://bit.ly/3v7CkBS. Accessed Dec 21 2023.

International Arctic Science Committee (IASC). (2021). *2021 state of the Arctic science report.* https://bit.ly/3v4BqWO. Accessed Dec 21 2023.

International Arctic Science Committee (IASC). (2022). *2022 state of the Arctic science report.* https://bit.ly/47Seqcr. Accessed Dec 21 2023.

International Arctic Science Committee (IASC). (2023). *2023 state of the Arctic science report.* https://bit.ly/41nJxdt. Accessed Dec 21 2023.

International Council of Shopping Centers (ICSC). (n.d.). *European shopping-centre classification and typical characteristics.* https://bit.ly/41pEDg2. Accessed Dec 21 2023.

International Polar Year (IPY). (2006). *2007–2008 data policy.* https://bit.ly/41jF0so. Accessed Dec 21 2023.

International Telecommunication Union (ITU). (2021). *Measuring digital development: Facts and Figs. 2021.* https://bit.ly/3Nq0BJQ. Accessed Dec 21 2023.

International Telecommunication Union (ITU). (2022). *Measuring digital development: Facts and Figs. 2022.* https://bit.ly/48etRvg. Accessed Dec 21 2023.

Inuit Circumpolar Council/Inuit Ukiuqtaqtumiuqatigiit Katimajingit. (2010). *Inuit Arctic policy.* https://bit.ly/48b34Qc. Accessed Dec 21 2023.

Iranowska, J. (2020). One mobile app, seven art museums: A case study of Kunstporten. *Nordic Museology, 29*(2), 67–81. https://doi.org/k8ps. Accessed Dec 21 2023.

Jackson, S. (2022, June 13). Former McDonald's stores in Russia just welcomed their first visitors after a rebrand. See inside the grand opening at the restaurants. *Business Insider.* https://bit.ly/3uZ18wd. Accessed Dec 21 2023.

Johnsen, I. H. G., Grunfelder, J., Møller, M. F., & Rinne, T. (2018). Digitalisation for a more inclusive Nordic region. In J. Grunfelder, L. Rispling, & G. Norlén (Eds.), *State of the Nordic Region 2018* (pp. 160–169). Nordic Council of Ministers. https://doi.org/k8pt

Johnston, M., Viken, A., & Dawson, J. (2011). Firsts and lasts in Arctic tourism: Last chance tourism and the dialectic of change. In H. Lemelin, J. Dawson, & E. J. Stewart (Eds.), *Last chance tourism: Adapting tourism opportunities in a changing world* (pp. 10–24). Routledge.

Joy, F. (2019). Sámi cultural heritage and tourism in Finland. In M. Tennberg, H. Lempinen, & S. Pirnes (Eds.), *Resources, social, and cultural sustainabilities in the Arctic* (pp. 144–162). Routledge.

Jungsberg, L., Turunen, E., Heleniak, T., Wang, S., Ramage, J., & Roto, J. (2019). *Atlas of population, society, and economy in the Arctic.* Nordregio. https://doi.org/ghx5b6

Käpylä, J., & Mikkola, H. (2019). Contemporary Arctic meets world politics: Rethinking Arctic exceptionalism in the age of uncertainty. In M. Finger & L. Heininen (Eds.), *The GlobalArctic handbook* (pp. 153–169). Springer. https://doi.org/k8pv

Kasten, E. (2020). Fieldwork on Kamchatka Peninsula and the creation of the Foundation for Siberian Culture: Towards an open-access database of Indigenous languages and knowledge from the Russian Far East. In S. Acadia & M. T. Fjellestad (Eds.), *Library and information studies for Arctic social sciences and humanities* (pp. 329–352). Routledge.

Kekkonen, A., Shabaeva, S., & Gurtov, V. (2017). Human capital development in the Russian Arctic. In K. Latola & H. Savela (Eds.), *The interconnected Arctic: UArctic Congress 2016* (pp. 167–173). Springer. https://doi.org/k8px

Kenter, P. (2019). Hotel Cari-BOO? Renovation of Yukon landmark with supernatural sightings. *Daily Commercial News, 92*(210), 1–2. https://bit.ly/3TjYNGb. Accessed Dec 21 2023.

Keskitalo, E. C. H. (2008). *Climate change and globalization in the Arctic: An integrated approach to vulnerability assessment.* Routledge.

6 The Liquid Arctic and Digitalization

Keskitalo, E. C. H., & Southcott, C. (2014). Globalization. In J. N. Larsen & G. Fondahl (Eds.), *Arctic human development report: Regional processes and global linkages* (pp. 401–425). Nordic Council of Ministers. https://doi.org/k8pw

Kim, H., & Maltceva, N. (2022). Digitization of libraries, archives, and museums in Russia. *Information Technology and Libraries, 41*(4), 1–17. https://doi.org/k8pz

Kirshenblatt-Gimblett, B. (1998). *Destination culture: Tourism, museums, and heritage*. University of California Press.

Kiruna C. (2022, 25 August). *Joo, nu blir det invigning!* [Yeah, now it's opening!]. https://bit.ly/48e2wJB. Accessed Dec 21 2023.

Koivurova, T. (2016). Analysis: The Arctic conflict—truth, fantasy, or a little bit of both? *High North News*. https://bit.ly/4amL3Ao. Accessed Dec 21 2023.

Krueger, A. (2019, August 10). Where libraries are the tourist attractions. *New York Times*. https://bit.ly/3Nvr6O3. Accessed Dec 21 2023.

Krupnik, I., & Crowell, A. L. (Eds.). (2020). *Arctic crashes: People and animals in the changing north*. Smithsonian.

Krupnik, I., & Jolly, D. (2002). *The Earth is faster now: Indigenous observations of Arctic environmental change*. ARCUS. https://bit.ly/47MB3ih. Accessed Dec 21 2023.

Krupnik, I., Bravo, M., Csonka, Y., Hovelsrud-Broda, G., Müller-Wille, L., Poppel, B., Schweitzer, P., & Sörlin, S. (2005). Social sciences and humanities in the International Polar Year, 2007–2008: An integrating mission. *Arctic, 58*(1), 91–101. https://doi.org/k8p2

Kubny, H. (2021, June 8). Russia's Arctic is to become a tourist paradise. *Polar Journal*. https://bit.ly/3tlWTdt. Accessed Dec 21 2023.

Kuchumov, A., Karpova, G., Pecheritsa, E., & Voloshinova, M. (2023). Development of tourism in the Arctic regions of the Russian Federation: The environmental aspect [Conference paper]. In A. Makhovikov & E. Samylovskaya (Eds.), *E3S Web of Conferences*, 378, Article 06020, 1–5. https://doi.org/k8p3

Kuersten, A. (2018). The Arctic digital divide. In B. O'Donnell, M. Gruenig, & A. Riedel (Eds.), *Arctic summer college yearbook: An interdisciplinary look into Arctic sustainable development* (pp. 93–105). Springer. https://doi.org/k8p4

Kugiejko, M. (2021). Increase of tourist traffic on Spitsbergen: An environmental challenge or chance for progress in the region? *Polish Polar Research, 42*(2), 139–159. https://doi.org/k8p5

Kyzer, L. (2022, June 5). New designer shopping and dining centre Hafnartorg Gallery to open downtown. *Iceland Review*. https://bit.ly/3RFxJQf. Accessed Dec 21 2023.

Lancaster, H. (2022). *Iceland: Telecoms, mobile, and broadband – Statistics and analysis*. Paul Budde Communications.

Larsen, H. (2018). Archives, libraries, and museums in the Nordic model of the public sphere. *Journal of Documentation, 74*(1), 187–194. https://doi.org/gcs99v

Larsen, J. K., & Hemmersam, P. (Eds.). (2018). *Future North: The changing Arctic landscapes*. Routledge.

Larsen, J. N., & Huskey, L. (2015). The Arctic economy in a global context. In B. Evengård, J. N. Larsen, & Ø. Paasche (Eds.), *The new Arctic* (pp. 159–174). Springer. https://doi.org/k8p6

Last, J. (2019). The rise and fall of a small-town mall. *CBCNews*. https://bit.ly/46Z4eNY. Accessed Dec 21 2023.

Latola, K., & Savela, H. (Eds.). (2017). *The interconnected Arctic: UArctic Congress 2016*. Springer.

Lavengood, Z. (2021). The evolving Arctic in the world-system. *Journal of World-Systems Research, 27*(2), 468–493. https://doi.org/k8p7

Lee, R. L. M. (2006). Reinventing modernity: Reflexive modernization vs. liquid modernity vs. multiple modernities. *European. Journal of Social Theory, 9*(3), 355–368. https://doi.org/c39ww2

Lee, R. L. M. (2021). Time, space, and power in digital modernity: From liquid to solid control. *Time and Society, 31*(1), 69–87. https://doi.org/k8p8

Lemelin, R. H., & Baikie, G. (2011). Bringing the gaze to the masses, taking the gaze to the people: The sociocultural dimensions of last chance tourism. In H. Lemelin, J. Dawson, &

E. J. Stewart (Eds.), *Last chance tourism: Adapting tourism opportunities in a changing world* (pp. 168–181). Routledge.

Lemelin, R. H., Thompson-Carr, A., Johnston, M., Stewart, E., & Dawson, J. (2013). Indigenous people: Discussing the forgotten dimension of dark tourism and battlefield tourism. In D. K. Müller, L. Lundmark, & R. H. Lemelin (Eds.), *New issues in polar tourism: Communities, environments, politics* (pp. 205–215). Springer. https://doi.org/k8p9

Levin, I., & Mamlok, D. (2021). Culture and society in the digital age. *Information, 12*(2), Article 68, 1–13. https://doi.org/k8qb

Lipscombe, P. (2022, November 17). OneWeb signs connectivity deal with Greelandic telco Tusass. *Data Center Dynamics*. https://bit.ly/4av9DiO. Accessed Dec 21 2023.

Löfving, L., Kamuf, V., Heleniak, T., Weck, T., & Norlén, G. (2022). Can digitalization be a tool to overcome spatial injustice in sparsely populated regions? The cases of Digital Västerbotten (Sweden) and Smart Country Side (Germany). *European Planning Studies, 30*(5), 917–934. https://doi.org/gj4m59

Maher, P. T. (2017). Tourism futures in the Arctic. In K. Latola & H. Savela (Eds.), *The interconnected Arctic: UArctic Congress 2016* (pp. 213–220). Springer. https://doi.org/k8qc

Maher, P. T., Jóhannesson, G. T., Kvidal-Rovik, T., Müller, D. K., & Rantala, O. (2021). Touring the Arctic: Shades of gray toward a sustainable future. In D. C. Natcher & T. Koivurova (Eds.), *Renewable economies in the Arctic* (pp. 81–98). Routledge.

Mainka, A., Hartmann, S., Orszullok, L., Peters, I., Stallmann, A., & Stock, W. G. (2013). Public libraries in the knowledge society: Core services of libraries in informational world cities. *Libri, 63*(4), 295–319. https://doi.org/gpsjgf

MarketLine. (2023a). *Industry profile: Hotels and motels in Canada*.

MarketLine. (2023b). *Industry profile: Hotels and motels in Finland*.

MarketLine. (2023c). *Industry profile: Hotels and motels in Norway*.

MarketLine. (2023d). *Industry profile: Hotels and motels in Sweden*.

Mason, R., Robinson, A., & Coffield, E. (2018). *Museum and gallery studies: The basics*. Routledge.

Massi, M., Vecco, M., & Lin, Y. (Eds.). (2021). *Digital transformation in the cultural and creative industries: Production, consumption, and entrepreneurship in the digital and sharing economies*. Routledge.

Maxi Development Company/Kompaniya «Maksi Development». (2023). *Torgovo-razvlekatel'nyy tsentr «Maksi» v Arkhangel'ske* [Shopping and entertainment center "Maxi" in Arkhangelsk]. https://bit.ly/48i7h4G. Accessed Dec 21 2023.

McBride, K. (2019). Sailing toward digitalization when it doesn't make cents? Analysing the Faroe Islands' new digital governance trajectory. *Island Studies Journal, 14*(2), 193–214. https://doi.org/grs23z

McCann, H. S., Pulsifer, P. L., & Behe, C. (2016). Sharing and preserving Indigenous knowledge of the Arctic using information and communications technology. In C. Callison, L. Roy, & G. A. LeCheminant (Eds.), *Indigenous notions of ownership and libraries, archives, and museums* (pp. 126–144). de Gruyter. https://doi.org/k8qd

Medby, I. A. (2023). Arctic conflict and co-operation. *Geography, 108*(1), 38–43. https://doi.org/k8qf

Middleton, A. (2023). Norwegian and Russian settlements on Svalbard: An analysis of demographic and socioeconomic trends. *Polar Record, 59*, Article e14, 1–13. https://doi.org/k8qg

Ministry for the Development of the Russian Far East and Arctic/Ministerstvo Rossiyskoy Federatsii po razvitiyu Dal'nego Vostoka i Arktiki. (n.d.). *About the Arctic*. Arctic Russia: Investment Portal of the Arctic Zone of the Russian Federation/Investitsionnyy portal Arkticheskoy zony Rossii. https://bit.ly/481QraQ. Accessed Dec 21 2023.

Ministry of Digital Development, Communications, and Mass Communications of the Russian Federation/Ministerstvo tsifrovogo razvitiya, svyazi i massovykh kommunikatsiy Rossiyskoy Federatsii. (2019). *Prikaz No. 22 ot 30.01.2019: «Ob utverzhdenii plana deyatel'nosti rasshireniy razvitiya, svyazi i massovykh kommunikatsiy Rossiyskoy Federatsii na period 2019–2024 godov»* [Order No. 22 of January 30, 2019: On approval of the activity plan for expansion of

6 The Liquid Arctic and Digitalization 145

development, communications, and mass communications of the Russian Federation for the period 2019–2024]. https://bit.ly/4agOQiP. Accessed Dec 21 2023.

Ministry of Finance, Finnish Government/Valtiovarainministeriön, Valtioneuvosto. (2021). *Suomen teknologiapolitiikka 2020-luvulla: Teknologialla ja tiedolla maailman kärkeen* [Finland's technology policy in the 2020s: Leading the world with technology and knowledge]. https://bit.ly/4anb1UD. Accessed Dec 21 2023.

Ministry of Finance, Government of Denmark/Finansministeriet, Regeringen. (2022). *National strategy for digitalisation: Together in the digital development.* https://bit.ly/3Nsic3M. Accessed Dec 21 2023.

Ministry of Finance, Government of Sweden/Finansdepartementet, Regering. (2017). *För ett hållbart digitaliserat Sverige – en digitaliseringsstrategi* [For a sustainable digitized Sweden – A digitization strategy]. https://bit.ly/3Ru7wmK. Accessed Dec 21 2023.

Ministry of Finance, Government of Sweden/Finansdepartementet, Regering. (2021). *Data – en underutnyttjad resurs för Sverige: En strategi för ökad tillgång av data* [Data – An underutilized resource for Sweden: A strategy for increased access to data]. https://bit.ly/3tgrWaB. Accessed Dec 21 2023.

Ministry of Foreign Affairs & Ministry of Finance, Government of the Faroe Islands/Uttanríkis- og vinnumálaráðið & Fíggjarmálaráðið, Føroya landsstýri. (2015). *National digitalisation programme of the Faroe Islands.* https://bit.ly/46WLVsG. Accessed Dec 21 2023.

Ministry of Foreign Affairs, Government of Iceland/Utanríkisráðuneytið, Stjórnarráð Íslands. (2021). *Iceland's policy on matters concerning the Arctic region.* https://bit.ly/3RHIkKP. Accessed Dec 21 2023.

Ministry of Foreign Affairs, Government of Norway/Utenriksministeren, Regjeringen. (2014). *Norway's Arctic policy.* https://bit.ly/3RHI7Y3. Accessed Dec 21 2023.

Ministry of Foreign Affairs, Government of Norway/Utenriksministeren, Regjeringen. (2017). *International cyber strategy for Norway.* https://bit.ly/46S6Z3D. Accessed Dec 21 2023.

Ministry of Foreign Affairs, Government of the Faroe Islands/Uttanríkis- og vinnumálaráðið, Føroya landsstýri. (2022). *The Faroe Islands in the Arctic.* https://bit.ly/3t66ipC. Accessed Dec 21 2023.

Ministry of Foreign Affairs, Kingdom of Denmark/Udenrigsministeriet, Kongeriget Danmark; Department of Foreign Affairs, Government of Greenland/Departement for Udenrigsanliggender, Naalakkersuisut; & Ministry of Foreign Affairs, Government of the Faroe Islands/Uttanríkis- og vinnumálaráðið, Føroya landsstýri. (2011). *Kingdom of Denmark: Strategy for the Arctic, 2011–2020.* https://bit.ly/3GHpqgD. Accessed Dec 21 2023.

Ministry of Infrastructure, Government of Iceland/Innviðaráðuneytið, Stjórnarráð Íslands. (n.d.). *Iceland's Rural Fibre Project.* https://bit.ly/46XyxEz. Accessed Dec 21 2023.

Ministry of Local Government and Modernisation, Government of Norway/Kommunal- og moderniseringsdepartementet, Regjeringen. (2016). *Digital agenda for Norway in brief: ICT for a simpler everyday life and increased productivity.* https://bit.ly/3ToHy6t. Accessed Dec 21 2023.

Ministry of Local Government and Modernisation, Government of Norway/Kommunal- og moderniseringsdepartementet, Regjeringen. (2019). *One digital public sector: Digital strategy for the public sector 2019–2015.* https://bit.ly/3TGhRib. Accessed Dec 21 2023.

Ministry of Local Government and Modernisation, Government of Norway/Kommunal- og moderniseringsdepartementet, Regjeringen. (2021). *Our new digital world: Digitalisation in Norway during the coronavirus pandemic.* https://bit.ly/3TmPIw6. Accessed Dec 21 2023.

Ministry of Transport and Communications, Finnish Government/Liikenne- ja viestintäministeriö, Valtioneuvosto. (2019). *Turning Finland into the world leader in communications networks: Digital infrastructure strategy 2025.* https://bit.ly/48aNKnr. Accessed Dec 21 2023.

Müller, D. K. (2015). Issues in Arctic tourism. In B. Evengård, J. N. Larsen, & Ø. Paasche (Eds.), *The new Arctic* (pp. 147–158). Springer. https://doi.org/f3nc5m

Müller, D. K., Carson, D. A., de la Barre, S., Granås, B., Jóhannesson, G. T., Øyen, G., Rantala, O., Saarinen, J., Salmela, T., Tervo-Kankare, K., & Welling, J. (2020). *Arctic tourism in times of change: Dimensions of urban tourism.* Nordic Council of Ministers. https://doi.org/gjd7jn

Munck, R. (2016). Global sociology: Towards an alternative southern paradigm. *International Journal of Politics, Culture, and Society, 29,* 233–249. https://doi.org/k8qh

Mythen, G., & Walkate, S. (2016). Risk, *nichtwissen,* and fear: Searching for solidity in liquid times? In M. Davis (Ed.), *Liquid sociology: Metaphor in Zygmunt Bauman's analysis of modernity* (pp. 139–156). Routledge.

Newman, A. (2022). Bathed in luxury: The Nordic spa at Alyeska Resort. *Alaska Business.* https://bit.ly/41nE1Ht. Accessed Dec 21 2023.

Nguyen, B. (2022, June 3). Marriott is suspending all hotel operations in Russia, citing sanctions that make it 'impossible' to continue doing business. *Business Insider.* https://bit.ly/3TlR4r2. Accessed Dec 21 2023.

Nikoliers. (2023). *Murmansk Moll Krupneyshiy TRK Zapolyar'ya* [Murmansk Mall: The largest shopping and entertainment complex in the Arctic]. https://bit.ly/48hpwre. Accessed Dec 21 2023.

Nokia. (2023, October 16). *Nokia and Mila bring 10G broadband to Iceland with fiber network upgrade.* https://bit.ly/3tq7bct. Accessed Dec 21 2023.

Nordic Council of Ministers. (2020a). *Ministerial declaration: Digital North 2.0.* https://bit.ly/3GE28s6. Accessed Dec 21 2023.

Nordic Council of Ministers. (2020b). *The Nordic region – Towards being the most sustainable and integrated region in the world: Action plan for 2021 to 2024.* https://doi.org/k8qj

Nordic Council of Ministers. (2022). *Monitoring digital inclusion in the Nordic-Baltic region.* https://doi.org/k8qm

Nordic e-Infrastructure Collaboration (NeIC). (2018). *Annual report 2018.* NordForsk. https://bit.ly/3GHq91l. Accessed Dec 21 2023.

North American Treaty Organization (NATO). (2022, May 18). *Finland and Sweden submit applications to join NATO.* https://bit.ly/3GDh7m9. Accessed Dec 21 2023.

Nyhlén, S., & Gidlund, K. L. (2019). 'Everything' disappears: Reflexive design and norm-critical intervention in the digitalization of cultural heritage. *Information, Communication, and Society, 22*(10), 1361–1375. https://doi.org/gc2c3h

Nyseth, T. (2017). Arctic urbanization: Modernity without cities. In L.-A. Körber, S. MacKenzie, & A. W. Stenport (Eds.), *Arctic environmental modernities: From the age of polar exploration to the era of the Anthropocene* (pp. 59–70). Springer. https://doi.org/k8qn

Office of the President of the Russian Federation/Kantselyariya Prezidenta Rossiyskoy Federatsii. (2020). *Foundations of the Russian Federation state policy in the Arctic for the period up to 2035* (A. Davis, & R. Vest, Trans.). Russia Maritime Studies Institute. https://bit.ly/48fJuT7. Accessed Dec 21 2023.

Organisation for Economic Co-operation and Development (OECD). (2017). *OECD digital government studies: Digital government review of Norway.* https://doi.org/k8qp

Organisation for Economic Co-operation and Development (OECD). (2018). *OECD reviews of digital transformation: Going digital in Sweden.* https://doi.org/k8qq

Organisation for Economic Co-operation and Development (OECD). (2019a). *Going digital: Shaping policies, improving lives.* https://bit.ly/3Tof0tJ. Accessed Dec 21 2023.

Organisation for Economic Co-operation and Development (OECD). (2019b). *OECD digital government studies: Digital government review of Sweden.* https://doi.org/k8qr

Orr, V. (2019). Luxury—Alaska style: Redefining extravagance off-the-grid. *Alaska Business.* https://bit.ly/48cW9pS. Accessed Dec 21 2023.

Orr, V. (2022). Room for more rooms: New hotels welcome resurgent visitors despite supply-chain challenges. *Alaska Business.* https://bit.ly/46WRKGz. Accessed Dec 21 2023.

Orttung, R. W., Anisimov, O., Badina, S., Burns, C., Cho, L., DiNapoli, B., Jull, M., Shaiman, M., Shapovalova, K., Silinsky, L., Zhang, E., & Zhiltcova, Y. (2021). Measuring the sustainability of Russia's Arctic cities. *Ambio, 50,* 2090–2103. https://doi.org/k8qv

Orzkhanova, M., Hubolov, S., & Polyakova, E. (2021). Digitalization of the Russian Federation's economy in the context of global transformation: Problems and development prospects. *SHS Web of Conferences,* 106, Article 01013, 1–7. https://doi.org/k8qw

OurAirports. (n.d.). *OurAirports help*. https://bit.ly/3TqppW8. Accessed Dec 21 2023.

Palsdottir, A. (2021). Data literacy and management of research data: A prerequisite for the sharing of research data. *Aslib Journal of Information Management, 73*(2), 322–341. https://doi.org/gkgkvn

Parks Canada/Parcs Canada. (2023). *How to get here: Quttinirpaaq National Park*. https://bit.ly/3Tpbqjc. Accessed Dec 21 2023.

Pasch, T. J., & Kuhlke, O. (2022). Arctic broadband connectivity and the creative economy: Access, challenges, and opportunities in Nunavut and Alaska. In D. C. Natcher & T. Koivurova (Eds.), *Renewable economies in the Arctic* (pp. 9–45). Routledge.

Pedersen, T. (2021). The politics of research presence in Svalbard. *Polar Journal, 11*(2), 413–426. https://doi.org/k8qx

Pettersson, R., & Müller, D. K. (2023). Museums portraying Indigenous heritage: The case of Sámi museums in Sweden. *Journal of Heritage Tourism, 18*(2), 184–201. https://doi.org/grnm98

Pulsifer, P., Gearhard, S., Huntington, H. P., Parsons, M. A., McNeave, C., & McCann, H. S. (2012). The role of data management in engaging communities in Arctic research: Overview of the Exchange for Local Observations and Knowledge of the Arctic (ELOKA). *Polar Geography, 35*(3/4), 271–290. https://doi.org/gmfqpt

Randall, L., & Berlina, A. (2019). *Governing the digital transition in Nordic regions: The human element*. Nordregio. https://doi.org/k8qz

Randall, L. & Sigurjónsdóttir, H. R. (2019). Reykjavík. In L. Randall & A. Berlina, *Governing the digital transition in Nordic regions: The human element* (pp. 46–50). Nordregio. https://doi.org/k8qz

Randall, L., Vestergård, L. O., & Meijer, M. W. (2020). *Rural perspectives on digital innovation: Experiences from small enterprises in the Nordic countries and Latvia*. Nordregio.

Rasmussen, R. O. (Ed.). (2011). *Megatrends*. Nordic Council of Ministers. https://doi.org/k8q3

Redshaw, T. (2020). What is digital society? Reflections on the aims and purpose of digital sociology. *Sociology, 54*(2), 425–431. https://doi.org/ggcdm8

Ren, C., Jóhannesson, G. T., Kramvig, B., Pashkevich, A., & Höckert, E. (2021). 20 years of research on Arctic and Indigenous cultures in Nordic tourism: A review and future research agenda. *Scandinavian Journal of Hospitality and Tourism, 21*(1), 111–121. https://doi.org/gh8b7x

Rigby, C. (2020). ᓄᓇᕗᒻᒥ ᐅᖃᓕᒫᒐᖃᕐᕕᒻᒥᑦ ᑎᑭᓵᒃᓴᐃᑦ = Nunavummi Uqalimaagaqarvimmit Tikisaaksait = Nunavut's library catalogues and the preservation and promotion of Inuit language materials. In S. Acadia & M. T. Fjellestad (Eds.), *Library and information studies for Arctic social sciences and humanities* (pp. 389–407). Routledge.

Roberts, P., & Paglia, E. (2016). Science as national belonging: The construction of Svalbard as a Norwegian space. *Social Studies of Science, 46*(6), 894–911. https://doi.org/f3rn94

Rosa, H. (2013). *Social acceleration A new theory of modernity* (J. Trejo-Mathys, Trans.; 2015 ed.). Columbia University Press. (Original work published 2005).

Roued-Cunliffe, H., Valtysson, B., & Colbjørnsen, T. (2023). Digital communication in LAMs. In C. H. Rasmussen, K. Rydbeck, & H. Larsen (Eds.), *Libraries, archives, and museums in transition: Changes, challenges, and convergence in a Scandinavian perspective* (pp. 130–143). Routledge. https://bit.ly/47VtdmA. Accessed Dec 21 2023.

Roura, R. (2009). Polar cultural heritage as a tourism attraction: A case study of the airship mooring mast at Ny-Ålesund, Svalbard. *Téoros, 28*(1), 29–38. https://doi.org/k8q4

Royal Ministry of Justice, Government of Norway/Det kongelige justis- og politidepartement, Regjeringen. (1988). *Treaty of 9 February 1920 relating to Spitsbergen (Svalbard), Act of 17 July 1925 relating to Svalbard, The mining code for Spitsbergen (Svalbard)*. https://bit.ly/3Ts1hCj. Accessed Dec 21 2023.

Rydbeck, K., Larsen, H., & Rasmussen, C. H. (2023). Differences and similarities between LAMs and their pursuit of common challenges. In C. H. Rasmussen, K. Rydbeck, & H. Larsen (Eds.), *Libraries, archives, and museums in transition: Changes, challenges, and convergence in a*

Scandinavian perspective (pp. 231–241). Routledge. https://bit.ly/48gnVBL. Accessed Dec 21 2023.

Saarinen, J., & Varnajot, A. (2019). The Arctic in tourism: Complementing and contesting perspectives on tourism in the Arctic. *Polar Geography, 42*(2), 109–124. https://doi.org/k8q5

Sanderson, D. (2023, July 2). Orkney considering becoming part of Norway. *The Telegraph.* https://bit.ly/473oEoN. Accessed Dec 21 2023.

Saunavaara, J., Kylli, R., & Salminen, M. (2021). Telecommunication line infrastructure and the Arctic environment: Past, present, and future. *Polar Record, 57*(e8), 1–12. https://doi.org/k8q6

Saville, S. (2022). Valuing time: Tourism transitions in Svalbard. *Polar Record, 58*(e11), 1–13. https://doi.org/k8q7

Scottish Government/Riaghaltas na h-Alba. (2019). *Arctic connections: Scotland's Arctic policy framework.* https://bit.ly/3GIUvAu. Accessed Dec 21 2023.

Selwyn, N. (2019). *What is digital sociology?* Polity.

Shadian, J. (2018). Finding the Global Arctic. *Journal of Borderlands Studies, 33*(2), 195–198. https://doi.org/k8q8

Sheller, M. (2014). The new mobilities paradigm for a live sociology. *Current Sociology Review, 62*(2), 789–811. https://doi.org/ggw59k

Shiri, A., Howard, D., & Farnel, S. (2022). Indigenous digital storytelling: Digital interfaces supporting cultural heritage preservation and access. *International Information and Library Review, 54*(2), 93–114. https://doi.org/gnqr25

Simon Media Properties. (2023). *About Anchorage 5th Avenue Mall.* https://bit.ly/3ThEbhM. Accessed Dec 21 2023.

Skare, R. (2020). Like, share, and comment! The use of Facebook by public libraries and museums: A case study from Tromsø. In R. Audunson, H. Andresen, C. Fagerlid, E. Henningsen, H.-C. Hobohm, H. Jochumsen, H. Larsen, & T. Vold (Eds.), *Libraries, archives, and museums as democratic spaces in a digital age* (pp. 207–224). de Gruyter. https://doi.org/k8rb

Smith, D. (1999). *Zygmunt Bauman: Prophet of postmodernity* (2004 reprint ed.). Polity.

Sørensen, M. P., & Christiansen, A. (2014). *Ulrich Beck: An introduction to the theory of second modernity and the risk society.* Routledge.

Stalder, F. (2006). *Manuel Castells: The theory of the network society.* Polity.

Statista. (2020a). *Hotels in Norway.*

Statista. (2020b). *Hotels in Sweden.*

Statista. (2022). *Internet usage in the United States.*

Statista. (2023a). *Internet usage in Canada.*

Statista. (2023b). *Internet usage in the Nordics.*

Statista. (2023c). *Internet usage in Russia.*

Statista. (2023d). *Number of hotels in Moscow operated by international hotel brands that suspended operations in Russia due to the war in Ukraine as of June 2022.*

Statista. (2023e). *Quick Service Restaurants in the U.S.*

Statista. (2023f). *Which fast food (quick service) restaurants do you go to, if any? (Finland).*

Statista. (2023g). *Which fast food (quick service) restaurants do you go to, if any? (Norway).*

Statista. (2023h). *Which fast food (quick service) restaurants do you go to, if any? (Sweden).*

Statistics Canada/Statistique Canada. (2023). *Census profile, 2021 Census of Population.* https://bit.ly/48fMC19. Accessed Dec 21 2023.

Statistics Faroe Islands/Hagstova Føroya. (n.d.). *Population.* https://bit.ly/3tguV2N. Accessed Dec 21 2023.

Statistics Finland/Tilastokeskus. (n.d.). *Key figures on population by region, 1990–2022.* https://bit.ly/3NqDiQb. Accessed Dec 21 2023.

Statistics Greenland/Kalaallit Nunaanni Naatsorsueqqissaartarfik. (2023). *Kalaallit Nunaanni Kisitsisit* [Greenland in figures]. https://bit.ly/4dar21x

Statistics Iceland/Hagstofa Íslands. (n.d.-a). *Passengers through Keflavik airport.* https://bit.ly/4aihvE8. Accessed Dec 21 2023.

Statistics Iceland/Hagstofa Íslands. (n.d.-b). *Population by urban nuclei, sex, and age 2001–2023.* https://bit.ly/41lylxH. Accessed Dec 21 2023.

Statistics Norway/Statistisk sentralbyrå. (2022). *Population and land area in urban settlements.* https://bit.ly/3Tk3Ar9. Accessed Dec 21 2023.

6 The Liquid Arctic and Digitalization

Statistics Norway/Statistisk sentralbyrå. (n.d.). *Air transport.* https://bit.ly/47Vu6vq. Accessed Dec 21 2023.

Statistics Sweden/Statistiska centralbyrån. (n.d.). *Population in the country, counties, and municipalities on 31 December 2022 and population change in 2022.* https://bit.ly/4adGXe5. Accessed Dec 21 2023.

Stehr, N. (2001a). *The fragility of modern societies: Knowledge and risk in the information age.* Sage.

Stehr, N. (2001b). Modern societies as knowledge societies. In G. Ritzer & B. Smart (Eds.), *Handbook of social theory* (2009 reprint ed., pp. 494–508). Sage.

Stewart, E. J., Liggett, D., & Dawson, J. (2017). The evolution of polar tourism scholarship: Research themes, networks, and agendas. *Polar Geography, 40*(1), 59–84. https://doi.org/k8rc

Strouk, M. (2021). Opening-up the Arctic through international science: The case of Svalbard, Norway. In L. Heininen, J. Barnes, & H. Exner-Pirot (Eds.), *Arctic yearbook 2021: Defining and mapping the Arctic: Sovereignties, policies, and perceptions* (pp. 632–639). Geopolitics and Security Thematic Network, University of the Arctic. https://bit.ly/47U0Xk1. Accessed Dec 21 2023.

Swann, K. (2015, June). Business-class hotels in Alaska: Comfort, convenience, and unbeatable views. *Alaska Business Monthly,* 112–115. https://bit.ly/48dzSbs. Accessed Dec 21 2023.

Tabet, S. (2017). Interview with Zygmunt Bauman: From the modern project to the liquid world. *Theory, Culture, and Society, 34*(7/8), 131–146. https://doi.org/gshn7d

Task Force on Improved Connectivity in the Arctic (TFICA), Arctic Council. (2019). *Improving connectivity in the Arctic.* https://bit.ly/4avdNHs. Accessed Dec 21 2023.

Taylor, P. (2023). *Number of mobile (cellular) subscriptions worldwide from 1993 to 2022 (in millions).* Statista.

The White House, US Federal Government. (2018). *National cyber strategy of the United States of America.* https://bit.ly/3GGGjIh. Accessed Dec 21 2023.

The White House, US Federal Government. (2022). *National strategy for the Arctic region.* https://bit.ly/3ToMYhL. Accessed Dec 21 2023.

Treasury Board of Canada Secretariat, Government of Canada/Secrétariat du Conseil du Trésor du Canada, Gouvernement du Canada. (2021). *Canada's digital government strategy.* https://bit.ly/48e7wOn. Accessed Dec 21 2023.

Treasury Board of Canada Secretariat, Government of Canada/Secrétariat du Conseil du Trésor du Canada, Gouvernement du Canada. (2022). *Canada's digital ambition 2022.* https://bit.ly/4agcewJ. Accessed Dec 21 2023.

Treasury Board of Canada Secretariat, Government of Canada/Secrétariat du Conseil du Trésor du Canada, Gouvernement du Canada. (2023). *The Government of Canada's digital ambition.* https://bit.ly/48kJwJz. Accessed Dec 21 2023.

Tsatsou, P. (2011). Digital divides revisited: What is new about divides and their research? *Media, Culture, and Society, 33*(2), 317–331. https://doi.org/bv6r29

Tunsjø, Ø. (2020, October–November). The great hype: False visions of conflict and opportunity in the Arctic. *Survival, 62*(5), 139–156. https://doi.org/gmc599

Turunen, E. (2019). *Airports in the Arctic 2019.* Nordregio. https://bit.ly/41t0Gm0. Accessed Dec 21 2023.

United Nations. (2019). *World population prospects 2019: Highlights.* https://bit.ly/3RGZhEY. Accessed Dec 21 2023.

Urry, J. (2000a). Mobile sociology. *British Journal of Sociology, 51*(1), 185–203. https://doi.org/cfth3b

Urry, J. (2000b). *Sociology beyond societies: Mobilities for the twenty-first century.* Routledge.

Urry, J. (2007). *Mobilities.* Polity.

US 115th Congress. (2018). *21st Century Integrated Digital Experience Act* (H.R. 5759). https://bit.ly/3RkZbSe. Accessed Dec 21 2023.

US Agency for International Development (USAID). (2020). *Digital strategy 2020–2024.* https://bit.ly/3RI3c4C. Accessed Dec 21 2023.

US Bureau of Transportation Statistics. (n.d.-a). *Adak Island, AK: Adak (ADK).* https://bit.ly/3RQHVpv. Accessed Dec 21 2023.

US Bureau of Transportation Statistics. (n.d.-b). *Anchorage, AK: Ted Stevens Anchorage International (ANC)*. https://bit.ly/3NqDzCA. Accessed Dec 21 2023.

US Bureau of Transportation Statistics. (n.d.-c). *Fairbanks, AK: Fairbanks International (FAI)*. https://bit.ly/47duLax. Accessed Dec 21 2023.

US Census. (2020). *2020 Census demographic profile: Alaska*. https://bit.ly/4ajw2PS. Accessed Dec 21 2023.

Valtysson, B. (2017). From policy to platform: The digitization of Danish cultural heritage. *International Journal of Cultural Policy, 23*(5), 545–561. https://doi.org/grknq9

Valtysson, B., Kjellman, U., & Audunson, R. (2023). The impacts of digitalization on LAMs. In C. H. Rasmussen, K. Rydbeck, & H. Larsen (Eds.), *Libraries, archives, and museums in transition: Changes, challenges, and convergence in a Scandinavian perspective* (pp. 117–129). Routledge. https://bit.ly/41kbbYu. Accessed Dec 21 2023.

van Kempen, S., van den Dool, A., Lindberg, P., & Parviainen, L. (2021). Trends in the Dutch and Finnish library landscape. *Library Management, 42*(3), 167–183. https://doi.org/gkmz6x

Vannini, P., Baldacchino, G., Guay, L., Royle, S. A., & Steinberg, P. E. (2009). Recontinentalizing Canada: Arctic ice's liquid modernity and the imagining of a Canadian archipelago. *Island Studies Journal, 4*(2), 121–138. https://doi.org/k8rd

Vårheim, A., Jochumsen, H., Rasmussen, C. H., & Rydbeck, K. (2020). The use of LAM institutions in the digital age. In R. Audunson, H. Andresen, C. Fagerlid, E. Henningsen, H.-C. Hobohm, H. Jochumsen, H. Larsen, & T. Vold (Eds.), *Libraries, archives, and museums as democratic spaces in a digital age* (pp. 247–269). de Gruyter. https://doi.org/k8rf

Varnajot, A. (2020). Digital Rovaniemi: Contemporary and future Arctic tourist experiences. *Journal of Tourism Futures, 6*(1), 6–23. https://doi.org/gp6bzn

Veijola, S., & Strauss-Mazzullo, H. (2019). Tourism at the crossroads of contesting paradigms of Arctic development. In M. Finger & L. Heininen (Eds.), *The GlobalArctic handbook* (pp. 63–81). Springer. https://doi.org/k8rg

Visit Faroe Islands. (n.d.). *Shopping in the Faroe Islands*. https://bit.ly/48fHNVF. Accessed Dec 21 2023.

Visit South Iceland. (2022, January 26). *New town center in Selfoss!* https://bit.ly/47Y38Dm. Accessed Dec 21 2023.

Weber, R., Rasmussen, R. O., Zalkind, L., Karlsdottir, A., Johansen, S. T. F., Terräs, J., & Nilsson, K. (2017). Urbanisation and land use management in the Arctic: An investigative overview. In G. Fondahl & G. N. Wilson (Eds.), *Northern sustainabilities: Understanding and addressing change in the circumpolar world* (pp. 269–284). Springer. https://doi.org/k8rh

Webster, F. (2014). *Theories of the information society* (4th ed.). Routledge.

Williams, O. (2023). Yellowknife's lower Centre Square Mall placed up for sale. *Cabin Radio*. https://bit.ly/41oL6b6. Accessed Dec 21 2023.

Willox, A. C., Harper, S. L., Edge, V. L., My Word Storytelling and Digital Media Lab, & Rigolet Inuit Community Government. (2012). Storytelling in a digital age: Storytelling as an emerging narrative method for preserving and promoting Indigenous oral wisdom. *Qualitative Research, 13*(2), 127–147. https://doi.org/ghqfq5

Witt, S. (2012, August 11–17). *Agents of change: International librarianship, development, and globalization theory* [Conference paper]. 78th IFLA General Conference and Assembly, Helsinki, Finland.

Wøien, M., & Randall, L. (2019). Finnmark/Vardø. In L. Randall & A. Berlina, *Governing the digital transition in Nordic regions: The human element* (pp. 51–55). Nordregio. https://doi.org/k8qz

Woodall, S. (n.d.). A traveler's guide to great souvenir shopping in Greenland. *Visit Greenland*. https://bit.ly/46SgkIE. Accessed Dec 21 2023.

World Bank. (2023). *Digital development overview*. https://bit.ly/46ZrzPF. Accessed Dec 21 2023.

Wråkberg, U., & Granqvist, K. (2014). Decolonizing technoscience in northern Scandinavia: The role of scholarship in Sámi emancipation and the indigenization of Western science. *Journal of Historical Geography, 44*, 81–92. https://doi.org/k8rj

Yeasmin, N., Uusiautti, S., & Heleniak, T. (Eds.). (2022). *The future of the Arctic population: Migration in the North*. Routledge.

Chapter 7
The Limits of Everyday Digitalization in the Arctic: A Digital Security Perspective

Mirva Salminen and Laurence Morris ⓘ

Abstract The digitalization of the Arctic is now an everyday phenomenon, but discussion of vulnerabilities embedded within this sociotechnical transformation remains limited and with little historic attention paid to local contexts. Since the early 2000s, the Arctic Council and the Arctic Economic Council have worked to address this situation, producing area-specific information alongside pan-Arctic perspectives on digital development. However, the security questions highlighted in this chapter have only been partially included in such discourse. Consequently, this chapter is an introduction to digital security as an everyday issue in the context of the Arctic based upon regional and national data from the five Arctic states of Finland, Sweden, Norway, Canada, and the United States. The chapter argues that digitalization generates uncertainty for individuals and communities and, therefore, requires greater attention. First, the chapter outlines the opportunities of digitalization for Arctic communities and offers a conceptual discussion of the relationships between information security, cybersecurity, and digital security. Secondly, the chapter examines Arctic digital security questions such as digital connectivity, accessibility of information and digital services, digital literacies and rights, and forms of digital abuse, while considering the role of libraries in particular detail.

Keywords Arctic connectivity · Digital governance · Digital literacies · Digital security · Digital rights · Digital skills · Digitalization · Information access

---

M. Salminen (✉)
UiT – The Arctic University of Norway, Tromsø, Norway
e-mail: mirva.salminen@uit.no

L. Morris
Leeds Beckett University, Leeds, UK

© The Author(s), under exclusive license to Springer Nature
Switzerland AG 2024
S. Acadia (ed.), *Library and Information Sciences in Arctic and Northern Studies*, Springer Polar Sciences, https://doi.org/10.1007/978-3-031-54715-7_7

151

7.1 Introduction

> From a technological perspective, the future of connectivity in the Arctic is—and will continue to be—nonhomogeneous. (Arctic Economic Council, 2021, p. 14)

While this Arctic Economic Council's (AEC) Arctic Connectivity Working Group's (ACWG) observation is valid, the same conclusion could be made, for example, from cultural or socioeconomic perspectives. Such perspectives touch upon the different layers of digital governance—the infrastructure layer, the logical layer, and the economic and societal layer (Internet Corporation for Assigned Names and Numbers, 2015)—and reveal an important insight: Digitalization is not a neutral developmental trajectory which follows its own laws; does not automatically improve the state of affairs; and does not treat every region, social group, community, and individual similarly. Instead, digitalization is a profoundly social and economic trajectory that is influenced by and transforms local contexts. Although digitalization is now an everyday phenomenon in the Arctic, discussion of the vulnerabilities embedded within the sociotechnical transformation remains limited. For example, the Arctic Council (https://www.arctic-council.org/) and the AEC (https://arcticeconomiccouncil.com/) have worked to address connectivity since the early 2000s, developing a pan-Arctic perspective on digital development and producing location-specific information. Nonetheless, while the opportunities of digitalization generate much discussion, the limitations and constraints of the process and their relationship with local contexts is only partially included in pan-Arctic discourse. This relative lacuna in the conversation has significant implications for effective policymaking, with restraining factors a key aspect of the lived experience of digitalization for Arctic communities.

As a minor contribution to a broader literature of Arctic digitalization, this chapter provides an interdisciplinary introduction to the limits of everyday digitalization in the Arctic, using data and examples from the five Arctic societies of Finland, Norway, Sweden, Canada, and the United States, and with a particular focus on digital security. First, the chapter discusses sociotechnical change and outlines ongoing digital developments and opportunities in the Arctic. Second, the chapter covers relevant conceptual discussion of the relationship between information security, cybersecurity, and digital security. Third, after focusing on digital security, the chapter examines related questions such as digital connectivity, access to digital services, digital literacies, digital rights, and forms of digital abuse. Finally, considering solutions to challenges, the role of libraries in everyday digitalization is examined in closer detail, an example chosen due to the digital literacy and service roles envisioned for libraries by various national and regional strategies in Arctic states.

Caution regarding pan-Arctic generalization (O'Donnell et al., 2016) is valid, with information infrastructure varying significantly between Europe and more isolated parts of Alaska, for example. Notwithstanding, some commonalities are evident regarding digitalization. In particular, a common factor is the prevalent influence of local contexts, whether geographical, economic, cultural, or otherwise. This chapter argues that both wider limitations and local challenges must be more rigorously considered alongside potential opportunities in Arctic digitalization and digital security policymaking. Such an approach is necessary due to the ongoing impact of digitalization on everyday life in the Arctic, and in the pragmatic acknowledgement of the historic connectivity gap and its potential long-term consequences while, at the same time, harnessing local knowledge and lived experiences to inform an improved global understanding of the impact of wider historical change—from climate change to geopolitics—on the transformation of Arctic societies.

7.2 Ongoing Digital Development and Opportunities

7.2.1 Digitalization as Sociotechnical Change

The starting point of this chapter is that neither digital technologies nor societies unequivocally determine the outlook of digitalization in the Arctic. Instead, both technology and society become socially constructed in their constantly evolving mutual relations imbued by contextualized knowledge (see Carr, 2012, 2016; Pinch & Bijker, 2012). Thus, digital technologies and Arctic societies vary in different parts of the Circumpolar North and within different knowledge cultures, leading to approximations in broader discussion on digital development in the Arctic. While acknowledging this deficiency, the present chapter nonetheless provides a general idea of the limits of everyday digitalization in the Arctic.

Sociotechnical change refers to a gradual transformation of technologies and societies over the course of time. This change is a holistic process that does not involve only one technology or society but networked relations of multiple technologies and societies, nor does it progress in a linear manner but instead vacillates with varying momentum in different places and times and with different technologies, unequally, sometimes reversely and at other times by leaps, bifurcation, and convergence. Importantly, when this change occurs, there is an observable shift in technologies and knowledges, their uses, and societal practices and structures (Avgerou & McGrath, 2007; Bijker, 1997). Such change leads to discrepancies between expectations and realities which, as pertaining to societal digitalization, are expressed in concepts such as 'digital divide' and 'digital literacy.' In this chapter, sociotechnical change is addressed primarily from the perspective of opportunities (i.e., positive security) and limitations (i.e., negative security) of digitalization in a manner that ties them together despite the main Arctic governance bodies that tend to focus only on opportunities under labels such as 'connectivity' and 'development,' highlighting their emphasis on technical and economic aspects of digitalization.

7.2.2 Infrastructural Development

Recent years have seen reduction of the constraints placed upon digitalization of the Arctic by limited connectivity via technological rollout that extends the range of opportunities open to individuals and communities. The Arctic Council's Task Force on Improved Connectivity in the Arctic (2019) highlights a range of technologies such as low-Earth orbit, medium-Earth orbit, and highly elliptical orbit satellites, narrow-band options, terrestrial and undersea fibre cables, high frequency communication for marine areas, and mobile wireless, alongside improved battery backup, as means of improving digital connectivity and network robustness in different Arctic contexts. These options are acknowledged by the ACWG (2021, p. 4), noting international consensus on the need to improve Arctic connectivity but also the local context of such work as well as the unprecedented extent of broader contemporary changes to climate and regional economies. Specifically, the ACWG report lists unique characteristics of the Arctic as an operational environment: landscape, weather, generally low population densities, cultural diversity, lack of or gaps in infrastructure, differing regulatory structures, and a need for public investment. Recognizing the impact of these factors, ACWG (2021, p. 9) concludes that "Arctic projects [have] to be evaluated on a different set of criteria" to the wider world as performance and cost modelling analyses used for most projects are unsuitable to the Arctic. Such criteria might, for instance, include supporting an Arctic community's longer-term development that requires unconventional cost-benefit analyses and unusual on-the-ground solutions. The highlighting of Arctic contexts and their growing implicit acceptance by national governments is as much a key development as emerging technologies and climate change.

One way in which government acknowledgement of the unique Arctic context can manifest itself is via specific infrastructure projects and their underlying funding arrangements. In Canada, the *Mackenzie Valley Fiber Link* project (https://www.mvfl.ca/) was initiated by the Government of the Northwest Territories to install high-speed fibre optic telecommunication along a corridor of approximately 1270 km (790 mi) initially from McGill Lake to Inuvik, and then on Tuktoyaktuk, connecting local communities to the country's wider fibre optic network. In neighbouring Alaska, a comparable fibre optic line was planned along the Dempster Highway to Inuvik (https://yukon.ca/dempsterfibreproject), improving connection speeds while also increasing wider network robustness. Across the Atlantic, the Svalbard Undersea Cable System connects Svalbard to the wider Norwegian broadband network (Space Norway, 2022), while in Finland the 5G network in rural regions is being rolled out through the Suomen Yhteisverkko [Finnish Shared Network] (https://yhteisverkko.fi/), a company in part owned by the Swedish and Norwegian governments. In European regions, public funding schemes are not necessarily aimed at the Arctic, but Arctic populations still benefit from interventions to address specific issues or rurality, and from obligations to provide universal service to national populations.

7 The Limits of Everyday Digitalization in the Arctic: A Digital Security Perspective 155

While notable as significant information infrastructure developments supported by diverse technological solutions, these projects also demonstrate the extensive use of hybrid public-private funding models to extend Arctic digitalization. In 2021, the Arctic Connectivity Sustainability Matrix recorded the following hybrid models in operation: design-build grants, publicly supported loans and bonds, tax incentives, operation subsidies, design-build-operate support, public-private partnership funding, centralized purchasing, aid-to-construction, long-term purchasing agreement, and one-time funding (ACWG, 2021). The diversity of funding models in use further demonstrates the importance of local contexts to digitalization. However, while specific arrangements depend on local operational and regulatory environments, funding when available is generally in recognition of the specific characteristics of the Arctic operating environment. Such funding supports development which would otherwise be unlikely with exclusively private, state, or community resources due to the high costs of Arctic infrastructure projects, both during construction and longer-term operation (see Hudson, 2015; Salminen & Hossain, 2018).

As well as the range of technological and funding models in use, the extent of state and private sector resources being deployed is striking. For example, the *Connecting Canadians* program aims to extend high speed broadband access with $50 million of the $290 million initially allocated in the 2014 budget earmarked for 12,000 households in Nunavut and Nunavik (Government of Canada, 2020, 2021). The subsequent *Connect to Innovate* project saw funding extended to $585 million, to improve connectivity in "over 975 rural and remote communities, including 190 Indigenous communities, by 2023" (Government of Canada, 2021, para. 2). A significant proportion of the funding was again targeted towards Arctic communities, with, for example, $49.9 million of funding for a project to improve connectivity in Nunavut to be further supplemented by $73 million from Norwestel, a regional telecommunications company (Government of Canada, 2017). Other available resourcing options include the Universal Broadband Fund, Canadian Radio-Television and Telecommunications Commission Broadband Fund, Canada Infrastructure Bank, subsidized access to low-Earth orbit satellite internet, First Nation Infrastructure Fund, and rural and northern communities' stream of the *Investing in Canada Program* (Government of Canada, 2022).

However, even when reviewing technological and financial development, it remains challenging to assess actual on-the-ground process of digitalization at a local level in Arctic communities. Turning to the European Arctic, in the European Commission's (2022) Digital Economy and Society Index for 2021, Finland placed second overall and lead the European Union in human capital and digital public services but with a significant urban-rural division observed, placing 13th for digital connectivity. In practice, 75% of households in the Finnish Arctic municipalities of Enontekiö and Muonio still had broadband of less than 30Mbps in 2021 (Nordregio, 2021). In the nearby Norwegian municipalities of Kautokeino and Karasjok, the same figure was 25–50%, but only 5% in Sweden's neighbouring Kiruna municipality (Nordregio, 2021). Such statistical discrepancies reflect population patterns as much as infrastructure and investment, illustrating the complexity of assessing pan-Arctic digitalization, with pleas for additional data a continuing presence in the literature of Arctic development.

7.2.3 Opportunities

> Internet access is now an essential part of everyday life... We can no longer consider high-speed internet a luxury. (Government of Canada, 2017, para. 7)

As noted in the above quote by Navdeep Bains, Minister of Innovation, Science, and Economic Development, the internet is now used for standard, everyday access to education, health services, entertainment, shopping, training, well-paying jobs, and the global marketplace. Nowadays, everyday life in the contemporary Arctic depends on functioning information and electricity infrastructures and information and communication technologies (ICT) and solutions (see also Salminen, 2021). Similarly, in a series of five resolutions passed between 2012 and 2021, the United Nations Human Rights Council (2021, p. 2) recognized "the importance of access to information and communications technology for the full enjoyment of human rights," including civic engagement and "means of participation in civil, political, economic, social, and cultural life." Although there were four abstentions—from Cameroon, China, Eritrea, and Venezuela—on the most recent resolution, there is still a broad international consensus on internet access as necessary for full participation in twenty-first century societies.

Most opportunities of Arctic digitalization are associated with economic development in some way. The ACWG (2021, p. 4) notes that "sustainable economic development and the resilience of local Arctic communities are two sides of the same coin," and the first principle of the Arctic Investment Protocol is to "build resilient societies through economic development" (AEC, 2021, p. 1). What is noteworthy here is the emphasis on resilience, not on everyday security. In other words, Arctic societies are to be supported mostly to help themselves when it comes to digital security threats. Development of more traditional economic activities in the Arctic (e.g., reindeer herding and extractive industry) is also supported by digitalization, while north-specific technological innovation may help embed economic development locally alongside other activities such as tourism (Larsen & Petrov, 2020). The extent to which poorer and vulnerable communities can access associated new jobs may be constrained (Wilson, 2019), but the tools to support requisite upskilling, as well as access to global markets and employment opportunities, have been extended. As the same could be said for other global communities that are already more digitalized than the Arctic, the AEC has included "closing the digital divide" as one of its core principles for sustainable Arctic connectivity projects (ACWG, 2021, p. 13). However, tangible details on what this might mean in practice, and whether social-economic and cultural development might be practically addressed alongside connection speeds, remain scarce. Nonetheless, parallel to

7 The Limits of Everyday Digitalization in the Arctic: A Digital Security Perspective 157

economic development, digitalization can at least assist with social challenges where access to state and other services is historically a constraining factor. From education, health, and social services to support with domestic violence and substance abuse, digital engagement of communities can significantly extend the reach of relevant programs and services. This support is increasingly reflected in governmental planning, with, for example, a report published by the Nordic Council of Ministers (Lundgren et al., 2020), noting that "digitalisation and smart digital solutions in health care and social care are expected to contribute to raising health and health care performance in the Nordic region" (p. 10). However, as with connection speeds, the same report also notes a strong urban-rural discrepancy in engagement, and an age divide with take-up of online medical services surprisingly low until recent changes were necessitated by the outbreak of the COVID-19 pandemic.

Opportunities also exist for enhanced support of Indigenous languages alongside concern at their potential online amalgamation into and appropriation by relatively homogenized online national and global cultures. Digitalization allows wider access to language revitalization initiatives, additional connections between Indigenous language speakers, and greater capacity to showcase related cultures. *Ságastallamin* (https://site.uit.no/sagastallamin/) was initially a travelling exhibition on Indigenous languages produced by UiT—Norges arktiske universitetsbiblioteket [UiT—The Arctic University of Norway Library] (https://uit.no/ub) and the Arctic Council Indigenous Peoples' Secretariat (https://www.arcticpeoples.com/), but later became an online educational resource aiming to complete a peer-reviewed GIS map of Arctic Indigenous languages to support further research in the field. The President of the Sámi Parliament of Norway noted such opportunities at an Arctic Leaders' Summit in Rovaniemi in 2019: "I think of digitalization and the internet as the western world's big gift to Indigenous peoples because it has opened so many possibilities" (Arctic Council, 2022, para. 13). However, Darling Anderson, an Aleut youth representative at the AEC's Arctic Frontiers panel also notes that further investment was required to support Indigenous languages' "use and relevance in today's society" (Arctic Council, 2022, para. 16). This argument can be extended to other minority languages of the Arctic whose relative digital non-existence is noted in existing research (Dymet, 2019).

Improved connectivity that extends opportunities for support applies broadly to all Arctic communities and is perhaps of practical relevance to historically disadvantaged social groups (e.g., the LGBTQ+ community or people with disabilities). Increased connectivity provides opportunities for greater engagement with the global communities of which they are also a part, allowing them to disseminate their experiences and access additional support from peers and services online via forums, online groups, and one-to-one interaction a potential lifeline for the physically or socially isolated (Olsén-Ljetoff & Hokkanen, 2020.) Nonetheless, constraints and vulnerabilities remain (e.g., Is exclusion of Arctic citizens from participating in video forms of voice over internet protocol (VoIP) communication due to intermittent connectivity from mere lack of infrastructure or more so lack of support for and attention to historically disadvantaged groups to organize online?).

Improved household connectivity also increases potential capacity to address gaps in the availability of relevant, contextualized information and disinformation on key developments in Arctic communities. The former requires, for example, resources to provide such information and willingness to make it publicly available, while the latter can be carried out, for instance, by extending access to programs such as the *EUvsDiSiNFO* project (https://euvsdisinfo.eu/) and its work to highlight vaccine safety and effectiveness alongside addressing geopolitical controversies (EUvsDiSiNFO, 2021). Digitalization is not a panacea for disinformation, particularly given the acerbation of its spread by digital networks. As Berman (2020) notes, anti-vaxx actors and others often disrupt information environments by providing contradictory information but doing so does not mean they suffer from an information deficit. However, as with state services, an extended digital sphere at least provides additional capacity for addressing these challenges.

While concern of local gaps and pace of development relative to the wider world remains valid, recent digitalization in the Arctic has extended the range of opportunities open to most of its communities. Information infrastructure development often has specific Arctic characteristics, manifesting in a range of associated hybrid funding, technological, and organizational structures, and in the diverse potential impacts on Indigenous and other Arctic communities. Equally, though, physical geography remains a constraining factor on digitalization, while public-private partnerships used as resourcing solutions have their own issues of long-term robustness. In a comparable way to which improved digital connectivity can both accelerate and address the spread of online (dis)information, vulnerabilities, and limitations are embedded along with the opportunities of Arctic digitalization.

7.3   Digital, Cyber, and Information Security

The realization of opportunities that digitalization provides to individuals, organizations, communities, and societies is protected through various security frameworks, including information security, cyber security, and digital security. These frameworks coexist, overlap, and enmesh, often supporting one another, but the choice between which specific one to be applied or emphasized is a political act which influences the construction of both technology and society as well as the direction of sociotechnical change. Whereas information security and cybersecurity are becoming more established frameworks, digital security or human-centric cybersecurity is only emerging. Differences in these frameworks build upon their varying referent objects, that is, what is being protected. In information security, the referent object is either moving or stationary information both offline and online. The main aim is to ensure the confidentiality, integrity, and availability of information in all circumstances—under stress and in normal conditions. Thus, information security also incorporates issues of data protection and privacy. The definition of the referent object impacts how threats to it become constructed and the alternative security measures available. Threats in information security are most constructed in

7 The Limits of Everyday Digitalization in the Arctic: A Digital Security Perspective

technical terms (e.g., malware, information breaches, and denial of service attacks). However, the possibilities of human mistakes and insider malevolence are also included. Security measures then entail inter alia technical, organizational, and educational arrangements, and interventions to prepare for, prevent, or counter these threats, and to recover from their realization.

Whereas information security generally operates at the level of organizations, and is integrated in ICT architecture and operations, cybersecurity lifts this challenge to the level of society and the state, hence multiplying its complexity. While integrating information security, cybersecurity focuses on the protection of digitalized infrastructure deemed critical for the functioning of society, vital societal functions and flows, and, increasingly, the fundamental values of a society (e.g., democracy and the protection of human rights). The respective threat imagery centres upon strategic conceptualizations such as hostile operations in the cyber domain, digital espionage, and cybercrime. Most states emphasize a 'whole-of-society' or comprehensive security approach to prepare for, pre-empt or prevent, counter, and mitigate the effects of such threats, as well as to recover from them. In such approaches, the responsibility for security production is allocated to all societal actors ranging from individuals to the state and inter–/supra–/trans-national organizations in their respective roles. Security measures expected from and resorted to by the societal actors vary, but generally also revolve around technology and organizational arrangements, as well as awareness and skills.

Another security approach, and one pivotal for this chapter, goes by many names and fluctuating conceptualizations, but its main characteristic is to emphasize the security of individuals amidst their digitalizing everyday life. What is being protected in this framework, named as digital security in this chapter (Salminen, 2019, 2022; Zojer, 2019), is the well-being of individuals and communities in the Arctic when an increasing share of their lived experience somehow integrates digitality. Digital security incorporates digital rights and the realization of human rights, which increasingly depend upon functioning infrastructures, and emphasizes data protection and privacy because of the consequences that data breaches and involuntary exposure can generate in everyday life.

Threat depictions in digital security are more concrete than in information security and cybersecurity and highlight the interplay of digital and physical spheres such as the everyday difficulties caused by incapability or unwillingness to use digital products and services or their non-functionality, cybercrime and digital abuse, and the implications of digital connectivity for emotional well-being and belongingness. Security measures then entail (non-) actions in all societal spheres that support human well-being. Often such issues are discussed as part of cyber resilience (i.e., from the top down), but for this chapter more important are everyday security perspectives (i.e., from the bottom up). The pool of actors participating in the definition of what security is and how it is to be produced is thus extended from security specialists and societal and economic decision makers to every participant in a space. Furthermore, alongside negative security (i.e., freedom from some threats) the aspects of positive security (i.e., freedom to something) are integrated in the framework (Hoogensen Gjørv, 2012). Dunn Cavelty (2014) and

Salminen et al. (2020) provide similar elaborations on cybersecurity discourses and practices.

All security frameworks just discussed perceive security as both an objective situation, or a collective evaluation of the situation, and a subjective emotion, or a subjective evaluation of the situation (see Wolfers, 1952). In addition, (in)security has both structural and agential aspects (see Galtung, 1969), which are emphasized varyingly in the security frameworks. Whereas information security and cybersecurity are referred to relatively little by the main Arctic governance bodies in their discussion of digitalization, such discourse does touch upon digital security, usually under the label of 'Arctic resilience' and without discussing it much further (Salminen, 2022). Digital security is closely related to people's everyday experience when using ICT and digital services. For example, in the Arctic, poor service design quickly turns into a safety issue, and digitalization of cars and snow mobiles into a question of economic security and even survival. Also, a mobile phone and functioning mobile networks may save lives, whereas hostile or derogatory behaviour in social media may endanger social integrity (see Salminen, 2021).

7.4 Digital Security Issues

7.4.1 *Applying Connectivity*

Digital connectivity is a priority of the AEC with potential benefits acknowledged by national and regional authorities in the Arctic region (Telecommunications Infrastructure Working Group, 2016). However, the extent to which improved connectivity impacts Arctic societies differs from the more utopian aspirations and pessimistic assumptions. The image of an isolated North is an enduring cultural trope, but while Arctic regions may lag in infrastructure, their communities also have extensive collective experience applying new technological options in their geographical contexts (Hudson, 2015; O'Donnell et al., 2016). From a digital security point of view, connectivity is not only a question of network coverage but also of its redundancy and fault tolerance. Whereas information infrastructure remains thinly spread and its functionality dependent on single points of failure, or the weather, people remain untrusting of the infrastructure even while acknowledging improvement in its reliability in recent years (Salminen, 2021).

Digitalization brings fresh opportunities and challenges, but the community-level skill set and resources necessary for engaging with them is comparable to that required to access, evaluate, and apply previous technologies. Nonetheless, individual capacity remains a constraint on everyday digitalization. In low-income households, for instance, individuals might lack access to the devices and bank accounts necessary for many forms of online participation, while improved educational, healthcare, and community resilience opportunities require individuals to engage with them. Part of this skillset can be acquired by outsourcing the running of digital errands to relatives and friends and through the guidance and support provided by public, private, and third and voluntary sectors. However, what is more difficult to influence is people's attitudes and worldviews, and it also should be asked to what extent this even ought to occur. Even if digitalization eases everyday life, it may still primarily advance the interests of ICT companies, service providers, and Arctic states, not individuals and communities (Kairala, 2014, p. 64).

The COVID-19 pandemic provides a practical example of the potential impact of connectivity on everyday service access. In most Nordic communities, basic healthcare services moved away from face-to-face provision where feasible, although specialist healthcare was still provided in person, albeit subject to a delay. Access to online health support and social security services was inevitably dependent on connectivity (e.g., if individuals could access video VoIP services). In 2020, the number of visitors from Finnish Lapland to a national virtual health and social security centre was 524,600, a 13% increase, while use of municipalities' online health and social security service channels rose by 12% to 12,467, with more than 900 distance health appointments and social security services visits provided (Yliräisänen-Seppänen, 2020). For all that attitudes to online engagement evidently changed in the exceptional pandemic circumstances, it also exacerbated the pre-pandemic situation of a broad social and technological trajectory with limited alternatives, posing new challenges to professionals in healthcare and social work (Kilpeläinen, 2016; Kilpeläinen & Päykkönen, 2014; Poikela & Turpeenniemi, 2015). Online engagement, in turn, shows the capacity to reinforce existing social and health inequalities (Heponiemi et al., 2020), excluding those with less capacity to access and apply online services, an area in which Arctic communities often start from a position of relative historic deficit.

In Finnish Lapland, welfare technology has developed since the 1990s and is perceived as particularly important for remote areas because of its capacity to erode distances in service provision (Poikela & Turpeenniemi, 2015). Cooperation with customers in service development is a key to success in service adoption and satisfaction. However, these remote areas still lag in connectivity and people in these areas must pay for the equipment and acquire necessary skills to use it. Digitalization of health and welfare services also pushes more responsibility onto the shoulders of customers (e.g., in citizen self-care processes) (Poikela & Turpeenniemi, 2015; Salminen, 2022).

7.4.2 Digital Literacies

The range of skills required to effectively transcend the challenges of digitalization is another limit on everyday opportunity. In Arctic scenarios, as elsewhere, such skills and competencies could take the form of working knowledge of the use of ICT and digital services, disinformation, cybercrime, online abuse, and online economies and cultures, as well as the underlying power structures of the digital sphere. More broadly, digital rights, digital literacy, digital communication, digital emotional intelligence, digital security and safety, digital use, and digital identity are identified as key areas of digital life (DQ Institute, 2019). The same framework also notes differing levels of digital maturity, ranging from digital citizenship to digital competitiveness (DQ Institute, 2019). Given such a diverse range of knowledge areas and competencies, there is clear potential to increase the vulnerability of individuals, as well as their opportunities, by extending connectivity and inclusion in broader networks of human and machine interaction. The point is particularly salient in the Arctic where the rapid pace of change noted by the Arctic Council (2022) could result in individuals with more limited skills being exposed to, for example, social engineering or forms of digital abuse as they engage with more digitally experienced elements of wider online society.

Arctic digital literacies and practices are consequently vulnerable if they do not incorporate wider awareness of the underlying societal and technological power structures of digitalization such that individuals are aware of the influences acting upon them. While digitalization may support positive outcomes such as enabling Arctic communities to disseminate their local perspectives upon climate change (Young, 2021), they also make communications through a technological, regulatory, and social framework mediated by non-Arctic national and international corporate, social, and economic structures and power dynamics (Yunes, 2016). In that sense, digitalization serves to extend control of existing spheres of influence into new territories in a form of twenty-first century online colonialism, further propagating state, race, gender, financial, and other forms of societal power imbalance. To take a practical example, information available to Arctic communities through digitalization and other processes is likely to be mainstream, not necessarily meeting the needs of a particular community or even available in that community's languages, although work continues to address this challenge. Equally, not all welcome the digitizing and dissemination of the traditional knowledge and cultures of Indigenous communities, such activity raising its accessibility but also its susceptibility to cultural appropriation. In a similar manner, some minorities may not wish their health data to be collated due to the capacity for that information to be used to reinforce stereotypes and social segregation. To take another example, reindeer herders in the European Arctic may not wish to share data on the movement of their herds in case it be used to direct their activities. The issue here is that data collection is contested depending on local and individual priorities within Arctic communities as in the wider world.

At an individual level, there is also potential for digitalization to exacerbate capacity for abuse in isolated communities, for example, if one party in a relationship is dependent upon another's greater access or digital literacy, even if just for running errands. Also, worth noting is that the representative definition of digital literacy used by the American Library Association (ALA) (2022a) includes the ability to evaluate information, noting the requirement for both technical and cognitive skills. Given prevalent concerns about online misinformation, and disinformation campaigns from state and other actors, ability to critically evaluate and apply information is a significant factor in the impact of digitalization on individual life. To limit individual vulnerability, such literacies should involve awareness of how forms of online communication influence individual experience of wider power structures, whether through spelling and grammar or activity in more image-based environments such as Instagram.

From a broader perspective, individual awareness could also usefully incorporate awareness of the extent to which personal well-being, safety, and digital literacies are often comparatively minor factors in digitalization planning compared to other factors such as economic development. Such prioritization, while understandable, leaves capacity for knowledge gaps in available information and wider literacies. To take a practical example, while general statistical information on the Arctic is limited, gender and intersectional information is more limited (Hoogensen Gjørv, 2017), with gaps particularly prevalent regarding Indigenous communities. For instance, only in 2020 did Nunavut authorities begin recording when a social services call was made related to child abuse (Brown, 2020). This lack of information has practical significance for the planning of services accessed by individuals and such issues will not necessarily be addressed by economically orientated digitalization, even when considering deliberate acts of abuse.

7.4.3 Digital Abuse

Digitalization is used in various forms of domestic abuse and coercive control, including but not limited to control of passwords and contacts, harassment, hate speech, use of tracking technologies, demands for swift responses, and non-consensual obtaining and sharing of intimate images. Such issues are aside of the potential exploitation of differing levels of digital literacies, and the potential for abuse of technologies such as the Internet of Things for coercive control of household tools like locks and temperature controls, stalking, and other forms of abuse such as gaslighting (Lopez-Neira et al., 2019). In Arctic scenarios, the relative social isolation of more remote communities and households has capacity to exacerbate the impact and (in)visibility of such abuse.

If intersectional information on the Arctic is limited (Hoogensen Gjørv, 2017), the exacerbation of issues such as sex trafficking in North American regions by digitally adjacent contemporary Arctic developments (e.g., natural resource exploitation and population movement) are noted (Sweet, 2014), as well as the general use of digital technologies in trafficking (Sethi, 2007). Bailey and Shayan (2021) also highlight how technology facilitates multiple forms of violence against women in the Arctic, as well as the vulnerability of Indigenous women and girls due to interlocking forms of systematic oppression. The internet can be used both to lure individuals away from home with the imagery of 'better lives' while advertising them to criminal clientele and in online pornography of varying levels of legality and consent (Bailey & Shayan, 2021). In addition, there are issues of system design, for example, revealing the location of an individual through their use of online platforms and apps, increasing the vulnerability of individuals in general and, in particular, female participants within the digital sphere.

Regarding other forms of abuse, it should also be noted that Nordic regions have previously been identified as attractive potential targets for cybercrime (FireEye, 2015), that significant numbers of such crimes are undetected or unreported (Leppänen et al., 2016), and that malware and online fraud have potential to significantly disrupt individual lives. Similarly, greater online activity equates to greater capacity for individuals to participate in and be exposed to forms of online hate speech with potential for the greater marginalization of minority communities within Arctic populations. Data on this topic is limited not least due to the subjective challenges of defining hate speech and abuse, distinguishing between permissible freedom of expression and what requires negotiation through legislation, court cases, and independent review. However, in the youth sphere, a large-scale study of five schools in Tromsø found that while cyberbullying is less common than traditional bullying, it has a statistically significant impact on students' self-reported quality of life and academic achievement (Rønning et al., 2017). Similarly, a later study of over 2000 adolescents in the three northernmost Norwegian counties found that nearly 10% report experiencing cyberbullying as a victim with a negative impact on mental health, particularly for female participants (Kaiser et al., 2020).

Negative impacts can also take the form of self-harm. For every worthy success story, such as finding that Alaska Native young people generally represent positive self-images in digital stories (Wexler et al., 2014), there is capacity for negative impact, such as the exacerbation of eating disorders and mental health issues through use of platforms such as Instagram and TikTok to reinforce negative self-image. Even a favourable study such as Wexler et al.'s (2014) found lack of male young adult role models reflected in young people's online environment. To be sure, the internet extends into the realms of human activity for better and worse, and this point stands in the Arctic as elsewhere.

7.5 The Role of Libraries

7.5.1 Governmental Frameworks

> The library should be the most natural place to turn to for those who wish to distinguish between real and fake news, and between good and bad sources of knowledge. It is crucial that staff have broad, updated skills in order to ensure that libraries can fulfil their social tasks and deliver a good range of library services. (Royal Norwegian Ministry of Culture and Equality, 2019, p. 34)

Turning to potential solutions and their limitations, it is apparent from legislative and other government literature that public libraries are expected to be active in addressing the challenges and opportunities of digitalization alongside their other roles. Libraries are, therefore, a useful example in considering further capacity to influence the everyday impact of digitalization on individuals. In official literature, particular attention is paid to information, facility access, and user education regarding digital skills and literacies, with some discussion of the impact of such services on wider society. This common governmental expectation is an evolution of the perceived and actual long-term role of libraries in enabling information access, evaluation, and application. This expectation manifests in varying forms throughout the Arctic and its corresponding states, but its broad existence is demonstrable.

For example, in Finland's *Laki yleisistä kirjastoista* [Public Libraries Act] (2016, section 6), together with traditional tasks like collection development and promotion of reading, public libraries are directed to provide information services, such as "guidance and support in information acquisition and application, as well as in versatile literacy." Similarly, the Swedish *Bibliotekslag* [Library Act] (2013, section 2, 7) directs public libraries to contribute to "free opinion formation" and "work to increase knowledge about how information technology can be used for knowledge acquisition, learning and participation in cultural life." In North America, the *2018–2022 Alaska State Plan* for libraries includes in its first goal supporting individuals' needs for "digital literacy skills," "improving the quality of and access to library and information services," and targeting individuals with limited functional literacy or information skills (Alaska State Library and the Governor's Advisory Council on Libraries, n.d., pp. 1, 3). Norwegian legislation is less specific: The 2013 amendment to the 1985 *Lov om folkebibliotek [Public Library Act]* (section 1) simply retains a broad clause about the role of public libraries promoting "information, education, and other cultural activities." However, the National Libraries Strategy excerpted above in collaboration with public and school libraries, and with the Faktisk fact-checking cooperative project (https://www.faktisk.no/), demonstrate the practical manifestation of their expectations with regard to digitalization. Similarly, while the Canadian Northwest Territories' *Public Library Act* (2009) is primarily concerned with library organization, the Government of Northwest Territories (n.d., para. 1) defines their public libraries' role as meeting residents' "educational, cultural, informational and recreational needs." In neighbouring Nunavut, the Public Library Service (NPLS) (2019) goes further, stating their support of social wellbeing, debate, discussion, and lifelong literacy. Such work necessarily involves engagement with the digitalized information landscape and its participants. Other broad similarities relating to digitalization are apparent elsewhere in government library literature. While the Alaskan state plan sets goals of improving support for underserved and rural communities, the NPLS provides special events to promote Nunavut's culture and literacy. Both Finnish and Swedish library legislation directs resource allocation to support national minority languages and bilingual communities. In the case of Finland, libraries are explicitly directed to consider the needs of Finnish, Swedish, and Sámi speakers 'on equal grounds.' Even a partially digitalized information landscape provides new opportunities for libraries to provide such services even with its accompanying challenges.

Obvious limitations to such comparisons exist (e.g., the communalities regarding library engagement with digitalization in their governmental literature are broad and the practicalities of that engagement will be determined by local contexts). Nonetheless, broad similarities do exist, demonstrating an international acknowledgement by Arctic governments of the potential role of libraries in addressing the opportunities and challenges of digitalization along with their more traditional activities. How significant that role is relative to other participants in the twenty-first century information landscape, and the extent to which Arctic public libraries have the capacity to fulfil it, is more questionable.

7.5.2   Operational Contexts

Several Arctic libraries work towards their assigned roles in addressing the opportunities and challenges of digitalization in distinct ways. If users can access suitably resourced physical libraries, they should be able to access computers and onsite space for a range of civic, educational, leisure, and work activities. Equally, through their online resources, Arctic libraries extend public access to information. Local collections such as the Rovaniemi City Library's extensive Sámi materials support specific communities, while initiatives like the Open Polar research data and publications portal (https://site.uit.no/open-polar/) support the wider dissemination of pertinent information and the Polar Libraries Colloquy (https://polarlibraries.org/) helps Arctic libraries to pool best practice.

However, even for those able to access library collections online, information access remains an issue, particularly given the COVID-19 pandemic's understandable acerbation of existing tendencies to prioritize other areas of public spending. While Finland's public libraries are regarded as among the best supported in the world, and library spending in Arctic municipalities grew by 8.3% between 2010 and 2019, this increase was outstripped by rises in digital operating costs, dropping to 1.63% in 2020 (Kirjastot.fi, 2021). Even when libraries are adequately funded for resource acquisition in the digital age, e-books, e-audiobooks, and online databases are often not offered by publishers to libraries on sustainable pricing models, at least relative to print, and some key texts are unavailable to libraries in a usable online format. A recent ALA campaign, with the comparable #eContentforLibraries campaign in Canada, emphasized that major bestsellers are sometimes unavailable through libraries: "Limiting access to eBooks for libraries means limiting access for readers like you" (ALA, 2019, para. 1; Canadian Urban Libraries Council, n.d.).

Libraries directing some of their user communications to explain gaps in their collection and harness users as advocates highlights the complexities of the digital information landscape to patrons and demonstrates some of the practical and ethical challenges facing librarians as instructors in a digital environment in which they are active participants. Additionally, while librarians have long-term expertise in information access and resource evaluation, they are not necessarily trained instructors nor familiar with highly specific digital developments in a fast-changing landscape. The need for staff training is covered by the Alaska State Plan, while the *Norwegian National Strategy for Libraries* describes staff having "updated skills" as "crucial" to libraries fulfilling their "societal tasks" (Alaska State Library and Governor's Advisory Council on Libraries, n.d.; Royal Norwegian Ministry of Culture and Equality, 2019, p. 33). Digital education content is also a challenge, particularly given the emphasis placed by news media, politicians, and librarians themselves on disinformation and contested facts rather than, for example, the impact of advertising algorithms on consumer behaviour. Even regarding contested facts, as Wilkinson (2016) observes, the tendency of librarians to stress how they can assist reflects contemporary concerns as much as long-term professional discourse, and it would perhaps be more effective to see librarians as supporting the negotiation of meaning.

User engagement is also required for library-based digital literacy instruction to be effective. In this context, it is worth revisiting the position of libraries in the wider information landscape. In a respected study of the World's Most Literate Nations, Finland placed first overall, and in the top ten for libraries (Miller & McKenna, 2016); its Arctic region public libraries were visited 8.56 times per inhabitant in 2019, with 21.62 loans per inhabitant (Kirjastot.fi, 2021). However, internet penetration in Finland is 95% of the population and there are 4.46 million Finnish social media users (Kemp, 2021). A survey of Finns aged 16–74 found that 84% uses WhatsApp at least weekly, YouTube 77%, Facebook 74%, Instagram 54%, and Twitter 26% (Nepa, 2021). Even accepting that some may use public libraries to access such platforms, particularly in underprivileged communities, the relatively insignificant position of libraries as a single actor in a complex digital information environment is apparent.

Unsurprisingly, individuals may seek to develop their information and digital literacies in spaces in which they are more regularly active than libraries. However, engagement with digital skills development at all is a broader issue. Remaining with the example of Finland, a recent Eurobarometer survey found that 90% of those surveyed think they have the digital technologies skills necessary for their jobs and 76% their daily lives, with a striking 25% stating that they do not need to improve their skills when asked about barriers to extending them. In Sweden, the comparable figures were 96%, 87%, and 20%. (European Commission, 2020). Elsewhere, a study of nearly 500 Swedish teenagers found many unable to determine the credibility of different news sources with those who self-reported as being good at finding information online generally less effective at civic reasoning (Nygren & Guath, 2019).

Security and wider societal implications arise from disinterest in extending digital skills and literacy, even apart from the capacity of libraries to support such work. Nonetheless, the reach of library training in multiple forms of literacy, from digital skills to critical thinking, can be extended when interlinked with wider society. The Faktisk collaboration is a useful example here with discussion of fact-checking that incorporates media, schools, and libraries, and presents media literacy as part of the wider public sphere (Magazines Canada, 2020). COVID-19 provides another example with online misinformation linked to vaccine hesitancy (see Loomba et al., 2021; Pierri et al., 2022), and the ALA (2022b) explicitly links their work to pandemic response. Even as addressing COVID-19 with facts via outreach, as a memorable *American Libraries* headline proclaimed (Ewen, 2020), Berman's (2020) caution on how to engage with anti-vaxx communities and vaccine hesitancy remains valid. Looking beyond user guidance, it is welcome that libraries are categorized with other public sector organizations by both the AEC

(2021) and the US *Infrastructure Investment and Jobs Act* (2021) when it comes to extending broadband provision.

The effectiveness of public libraries at specific tasks relates to the priorities of the societies of which they are a part and the extent to which libraries connect with those priorities, technologies, and societies. Arctic governments acknowledge that librarians and public libraries have expertise and resources applicable to the opportunities and challenges of digitalization. However, the effectiveness of such work is dependent upon resourcing, skills, engagement, and the impact of other actors in the information sphere, as well as broader and localized societal developments. For all the distinctiveness of the Arctic and digital contexts, these challenges are not new for libraries.

7.6 Conclusion

For all the caveats expressed in this chapter, recent years have seen a significant reduction in the constraints placed upon the everyday digitalization of the Arctic by limited digital connectivity. As the Arctic Council and AEC note, traditional challenges of the Arctic as a digital environment are addressed through the rollout of technologies such as fibre cabling and low-Earth orbit satellites, often supported by innovative hybrid funding models. Such activity acknowledges the Arctic as a unique operational context, but pan-Arctic discussion of the vulnerabilities embedded in Arctic digitalization remains limited, particularly regarding digital security. Significant local exceptions to the communalities explored in this chapter also remain, with data still limited on the local progress of digitalization in specific Arctic communities and for specific sub-sections of those communities.

Such gaps in the data and discourse have potential to impact the everyday lives of individuals, given the extent to which digitality is increasingly fundamental to 'conventional' twenty-first century life. Digitalization assists with many challenges facing Arctic communities, particularly those where physical access to state and other services is a constraining factor. Digitalization also provides enhanced economic and cultural opportunities, contributing to community resilience (e.g., supporting Indigenous languages through activities such as the *Ságastallamin* project, and amplifying Arctic voices on key issues such as climate change). However, urban-rural, cultural, and age-based divides are noted in the uptake of such services and, as a legacy of past connectivity issues, some Arctic citizens start with a digital skills gap, even with all their enduring collective experience of adapting and applying new technologies to local scenarios.

Further challenges also exist. Particularly in less well-off communities, those who wish to engage with digital services and opportunities may lack the technological, financial, and social means to do so. Those who do connect may still lose out in digital competitiveness to more digitally mature societies, or see their local cultures further eroded or appropriated through greater exposure to homogenized online national and global cultures. Individuals are also potentially more vulnerable to

7 The Limits of Everyday Digitalization in the Arctic: A Digital Security Perspective

extended, and new, online forms of abuse and coercive control (e.g., hate speech, stalking, and sex trafficking). Other vulnerabilities include cybercrime, youth bullying, and capacity for mental health issues to be exacerbated by online interaction. Then, at a broader societal level, while digitalization provides opportunities for historically oppressed subgroups and individuals to network and organize, it also reflects and reconstructs existing societal power structures.

The extent to which individual actors such as libraries can presently assist with such challenges is limited. For all the enduring resonance of their historic roles in some state plans, libraries are relatively minor players in the digital sphere, constrained by funding, engagement, and the relative power of publishers and social media platforms, among others. These challenges are universal rather than Arctic-specific, but the Arctic has unique potential to address them, for example, through the additional forms of state leverage over the private sector offered by hybrid funding, should the broadened view of digitalization as incorporating sociotechnical change and digital security represented by this chapter be adopted in policymaking. However, unique funding models also bring unique vulnerabilities, themselves meriting further research (e.g., in the short-term, it remains the case that the broader limits of Arctic digitalization can disproportionately influence specific communities due to their local historical contexts).

Digitalization as sociotechnical change is mutually constructed in relations between society and technology. The current chapter depicts this transformation in the Arctic from the perspective of digital security in individuals' and communities' everyday lives. Digitalization remains flawed as its limitations are embedded alongside its opportunities in local contexts and, in this sense at least, the Arctic experience may be universal.

References

Alaska State Library and the Governor's Advisory Council on Libraries. (n.d.). *Library Services and Technology Act: Alaska State Plan 2018–2022.* https://bit.ly/3Ur7FXq. Accessed 9 Dec 2023.

American Library Association (ALA). (2019). *#eBooksForAll.* https://bit.ly/3Ur810c. Accessed 9 Dec 2023.

American Library Association (ALA). (2022a). *Digital literacy.* https://bit.ly/3h20jMo. Accessed 9 Dec 2023.

American Library Association (ALA). (2022b). *Libraries respond: Combating xenophobia and fake news in light of COVID-19.* https://bit.ly/3UzELEm. Accessed 9 Dec 2023.

Arctic Connectivity Working Group (ACWG). (2021). *The Arctic connectivity sustainability matrix.* AEC. https://bit.ly/3VF2gxu. Accessed 9 Dec 2023.

Arctic Council. (2022). *How Arctic Indigenous peoples are revitalizing their languages.* https://bit.ly/3Y0HNVp. Accessed 9 Dec 2023.

Arctic Economic Council (AEC). (2021). *Arctic investment protocol: Guidelines for responsible investment in the Arctic.* https://bit.ly/3P8PMvy. Accessed 9 Dec 2023.

Avgerou, C., & McGrath, K. (2007). Power, rationality, and the art of living through sociotechnical change. *MIS Quarterly, 31*(2), 295–315.

Bailey, J., & Shayan, S. (2021). The missing and murdered indigenous women crisis: Technological dimensions. In J. Bailey, A. Flynn, & N. Henry (Eds.), *Emerald international handbook of technology facilitated violence and abuse* (pp. 125–1440). Emerald.

Berman , J. M. (2020). *Anti-vaxxers: How to challenge a misinformed movement*. MIT Press.

Bibliotekslag [Library Act]. (2013). Sveriges Riksdag/Parliament of Sweden. https://bit.ly/3XZ46uj. Accessed 9 Dec 2023.

Bijker, W. E. (1997). *Of bicycles, bakelites, and bulbs: Toward a theory of sociotechnical change*. MIT Press.

Brown, B. (2020). Long-time Inuk social worker says abuse is normalized in Nunavut households. *CBC News*. https://bit.ly/3XW4Wbo. Accessed 9 Dec 2023.

Canadian Urban Libraries Council/Conseil des Bibliothèques Urbaines du Canada. (n.d.). *#eContentforlibraries*. https://bit.ly/3uJclO5. Accessed 9 Dec 2023.

Carr, M. (2012). The political history of the internet: A theoretical approach to the implications for U.S. power. In S. S. Costigan & J. Perry (Eds.), *Cyberspaces and global affairs* (pp. 173–188). Ashgate.

Carr, M. (2016). *US power and the internet in international relations: The irony of the information age*. Palgrave Macmillan.

DQ Institute. (2019). *DQ global standards report 2019: Common framework for digital literacy, skills, and readiness*. https://bit.ly/3P0YJ9U. Accessed 9 Dec 2023.

Dunn Cavelty, M. (2014). Breaking the cyber-security dilemma: Aligning security needs and removing vulnerabilities. *Science and Engineering Ethics, 20*(3), 701–715.

Dymet, M. (2019). Digital language divide in the European High North: The level of online presence of minority languages from northern Finland, Norway, and Sweden. *Yearbook of Polar Law Online, 10*(1), 245–274.

European Commission. (2020). *Attitudes towards the impact of digitalisation on everyday lives*. https://bit.ly/3VVcgSC. Accessed 9 Dec 2023.

European Commission. (2021). *Digital Economy and Society Index (DESI) 2021: Finland*. https://bit.ly/3VVcTvs. Accessed 9 Dec 2023.

European Commission. (2022). *Digital Economy and Society Index: Countries' performance in digitisation*. https://bit.ly/3BaaDZC. Accessed 9 Dec 2023.

EUvsDiSiNFO. (2021). *Coronavirus*. https://bit.ly/3UyUHqL. Accessed 9 Dec 2023.

Ewen, L. (2020, March 5). Libraries and pandemic preparedness: Addressing COVID-19 with facts and outreach. *American Libraries*. https://bit.ly/3iHPIq8. Accessed 9 Dec 2023.

FireEye. (2015). *Cyber threats to the Nordic region*. https://bit.ly/488c7RX. Accessed 9 Dec 2023.

Galtung, J. (1969). Violence, peace, and peace research. *Journal of Peace Research, 6*(3), 167–191.

Government of Canada/Gouvernement du Canada. (2017). *Communities across Nunavut will benefit from faster internet*. https://bit.ly/3gZ73dQ. Accessed 9 Dec 2023.

Government of Canada/Gouvernement du Canada. (2020). *Connecting Canadians: Digital Canada 150*. https://bit.ly/3ivL2DN. Accessed 9 Dec 2023.

Government of Canada/Gouvernement du Canada. (2021). *Connect to innovate*. https://bit.ly/3iDhIeO. Accessed 9 Dec 2023.

Government of Canada/Gouvernement du Canada. (2022). *Investing in Canada plan: Building a better Canada*. https://bit.ly/3ustuuX. Accessed 9 Dec 2023.

Government of Northwest Territories. (n.d.). *NWT public libraries*. https://bit.ly/3iGuFVe. Accessed 9 Dec 2023.

Heponiemi, T., Jormanainen, V., Leemann, L., Manderbacka, K., Aalto, A.-M., & Hyppönen, H. (2020). Digital divide in perceived benefits of online health care and social welfare services: National cross-sectional survey study. *Journal of Medical Internet Research, 22*(7), e17616.

Hoogensen Gjørv, G. (2012). Security by any other name: Negative security, positive security, and a multi-actor security approach. *Review of International Studies, 38*(4), 835–859.

Hoogensen Gjørv, G. (2017). Finding gender in the Arctic: A call to intersectionality and diverse methods. In K. Latola & H. Savela (Eds.), *The inter-connected Arctic: UArctic congress 2016* (pp. 293–303). Springer.

Hudson, H. E. (2015). *Connecting Alaskans. Telecommunications in Alaska from telegraph to broadband*. University of Alaska Press.

Infrastructure Investment and Jobs Act, Pub. L. No. 117-58, 135 Stat. 429. (2021). US Government Publication Office. https://bit.ly/3UzhiDw. Accessed 9 Dec 2023.

Internet Corporation for Assigned Names and Numbers (ICANN). (2015). *Three layers of digital governance infographic*. https://bit.ly/3h1LMAg. Accessed 9 Dec 2023.

Kairala, M. (2014). Social work and technological challenges. In A. Kilpeläinen & K. Päykkönen (Eds.), *eCompetence for social work* (pp. 63–72). University of Lapland.

Kaiser, S., Kyrrestad, H., & Fossum, S. (2020). Cyberbullying status and mental health in Norwegian adolescents. *Scandinavian Journal of Psychology, 61*(5), 707–713.

Kemp, S. (2021, February 11). *Digital 2021: Finland*. DataReportal. https://bit.ly/3UrG4W0. Accessed 9 Dec 2023.

Kilpeläinen, A. (2016). *Teknologiavälitteisyys kyläläisten arjessa. Tutkimus ikääntyvien sivukylien teknologiavälitteisyydestä ja sen rajapinnoista maaseutusosiaalityöhön* [Technology mediation in the everyday life of villagers: A study of the technology mediation of aging side villages and its interfaces with rural social work] [Doctoral dissertation, University of Lapland]. https://bit.ly/3ByIWdh. Accessed 9 Dec 2023.

Kilpeläinen, A., & Päykkönen, K. (Eds.). (2014). *eCompetence for social work*. University of Lapland. https://bit.ly/3Baqibp. Accessed 9 Dec 2023.

Kirjastot.fi. (2021). *Suomen yleisten kirjastojen tilastot* [Finnish Public Library Statistics]. https://bit.ly/3HagMss. Accessed 9 Dec 2023.

Laki yleisistä kirjastoista [Public Libraries Act]. (2016). Opetus- ja kulttuuriministeriö/Ministry of Education and Culture. https://bit.ly/3gYW3gK. Accessed 9 Dec 2023.

Larsen, J. N., & Petrov, A. N. (2020). The economy of the Arctic. In K. Coates & C. Holroyd (Eds.), *Palgrave handbook of Arctic policy and politics* (pp. 79–95). Palgrave Macmillan.

Leppänen, A., Linderborg, K., & Saarimäki, J. (2016). *Tietoverkkorikollisuuden tilannekuva* [Cybercrime snapshot]. https://bit.ly/3P3AYht. Accessed 9 Dec 2023.

Loomba, S., de Figueiredo, A., Piatek, S. J., de Graaf, K., & Larson, H. J. (2021). Measuring the impact of COVID-19 vaccine misinformation on vaccination intent in the UK and USA. *Nature Human Behaviour, 5*(3), 337–348.

Lopez-Neira, I., Patel, T., Parkin, S., Danezis, G., & Tanczer, L. (2019). 'Internet of things': How abuse is getting smarter. *Safe: The Domestic Abuse Quarterly, 63*, 22–26.

Lov om folkebibliotek [Public Library Act]. (1985/2013). Det kongelige kultur- og likestillingsdepartement/Royal Norwegian Ministry of Culture and Equality. https://bit.ly/3upGgKP. Accessed 9 Dec 2023.

Lundgren, A., Randall, L., & Norlén, G. (Eds.). (2020). *State of the Nordic region 2020: Wellbeing, health, and digitalisation edition*. Nordic Council of Ministers. https://doi.org/jppf

Magazines Canada. (2020). *Faktisk: Norway's fact-checking cooperative*. https://bit.ly/487AP52. Accessed 9 Dec 2023.

Miller, J. W., & McKenna, M. C. (2016). *World literacy: How countries rank and why it matters*. Routledge.

Nepa. (2021). *DNA: Digitaaliset elämäntavat -tutkimus* [Digital lifestyle research]. https://bit.ly/3Fua9Aa. Accessed 9 Dec 2023.

Nordregio. (2021). *Households without access to fixed broadband at downloads speed 30 Mbps, 2018* [Map]. https://bit.ly/3BaSqei. Accessed 9 Dec 2023.

Nunavut Public Library Service (NPLS). (2019). *About Nunavut public libraries*. https://bit.ly/3uKeOYB. Accessed 9 Dec 2023.

Nygren, T., & Guath, M. (2019). Swedish teenagers' difficulties and abilities to determine digital news credibility. *Nordicom Review, 40*(1), 23–42.

O'Donnell, S., Beaton, B., McMahon, R., Hudson, H. E., Williams, D., & Whiteduck, T. (2016, May 30–June 3). *Digital technology adoption in remote and northern Indigenous communities in Canada* [Conference paper]. Canadian Sociological Association Annual Conference, Calgary, Alberta, Canada. https://bit.ly/3Rjc1jX. Accessed 9 Dec 2023.

Olsén-Ljetoff, L., & Hokkanen, L. (2020). The interconnection between digitalisation and human security in the lives of Sámi with disabilities. In M. Salminen, G. Zojer, & K. Hossain (Eds.), *Digitalisation and human security. A multi-disciplinary approach to cybersecurity in the European high north* (pp. 295–322). Palgrave Macmillan.

Pierri, F., Perry, B., DeVerna, M. R., Yang, K.-C., Flammini, A., Menczer, F., & Bryden, J. (2022). *Online misinformation is linked to early COVID-19 vaccination hesitancy and refusal*. https://doi.org/jpph

Pinch, T. J., & Bijker, W. E. (2012). Social construction of facts and artifacts: Or how the sociology of science and the sociology of technology might benefit each other. In W. E. Bijker, T. P. Hughes, & T. Pinch (Eds.), *Social construction of technological systems: New directions in the sociology and history of technology* (Anniversary ed., pp. 11–44). MIT Press.

Poikela, P., & Turpeenniemi, S. (Eds.). (2015). *Distance is not a barrier to health: Welfare technology makes life easier*. Lapland University of Applied Sciences. https://bit.ly/3UA6GnU. Accessed 9 Dec 2023.

Rønning, J. A., Thorvaldsen, S., & Egeberg, G. (2017). Well-being in an Arctic city: Designing a longitudinal study on student relationships and perceived quality of life. In K. Latola & H. Savela (Eds.), *The inter-connected Arctic: UArctic Congress 2016* (pp. 185–194). Springer. https://doi.org/jppk

Royal Norwegian Ministry of Culture and Equality/Det kongelige kultur- og likestillingsdepartement. (2019). *Nasjonal bibliotekstrategi 2020–2023—Rom for demokrati og dannelse* [A space for democracy and self-cultivation: National strategy for libraries 2020–2023]. https://bit.ly/3UxReJ0. Accessed 9 Dec 2023.

Salminen, M. (2019). Refocusing and redefining cybersecurity: Individual security in the digitalising European high north. *Yearbook of Polar Law Online, 10*(1), 321–356.

Salminen, M. (2021). Arkipäivän digitaalinen turvallisuus Euroopan pohjoisilla alueilla: Tapaustutkimus Tunturi-Lapista [Everyday digital security in the European High North: A case study from Fjeld Lapland]. *Media ja viestintä* [Media and Communication], *44*(1), 158–180.

Salminen, M. (2022). *"Et nää on näitä meiän kyberhyökkäyksiä nämä"* ["These are these our cyberattacks"]: The government of one and all in everyday digital security in Finnish Lapland. [Doctoral dissertation, University of Lapland]. https://bit.ly/3Y1VuU3. Accessed 9 Dec 2023.

Salminen, M., & Hossain, K. (2018). Digitalisation and human security dimensions in cybersecurity: An appraisal for the European high north. *Polar Record, 54*(2), 108–118.

Salminen, M., Zojer, G., & Hossain, K. (2020). Comprehensive cybersecurity and human rights in the digitalising European high north. In M. Salminen, G. Zojer, & K. Hossain (Eds.), *Digitalisation and human security. A multi-disciplinary approach to cybersecurity in the European high north* (pp. 21–55). Palgrave Macmillan.

Sethi, A. (2007). Domestic sex trafficking of aboriginal girls in Canada: Issues and implications. *First Peoples Child and Family Review, 3*(3), 57–71.

Space Norway. (2022). *The Svalbard fibre optic cable connection*. https://bit.ly/3BeGdVQ. Accessed 9 Dec 2023.

Sweet, V. (2014). Rising waters, rising threats: The human trafficking of indigenous women in the circumpolar region of the United States and Canada. *Yearbook of Polar Law Online, 6*(1), 162–188.

Task Force on Improved Connectivity in the Arctic (TFICA). (2019). *Report: Improving connectivity in the Arctic*. Arctic Council. https://bit.ly/3BaWBad. Accessed 9 Dec 2023.

Telecommunications Infrastructure Working Group (TIWG). (2016). *Arctic broadband: Recommendations for an interconnected Arctic*. AEC. https://bit.ly/3iFoUqQ. Accessed 9 Dec 2023.

United Nations Human Rights Council (UNHRC). (2021). *The promotion, protection and enjoyment of human rights on the internet*. https://bit.ly/3UwVWXb. Accessed 9 Dec 2023.

Wexler, L., Eglinton, K., & Gubrium, A. (2014). Using digital stories to understand the lives of Alaska Native young people. *Youth and Society, 46*(4), 478–504.

Wilkinson, L. (2016, December 1). Post-truth and information literacy [Blog post]. *Sense and reference: A philosophical library blog*. https://bit.ly/3h1NrpE. Accessed 9 Dec 2023.

Wilson, E. (2019). What is benefit sharing? Respecting Indigenous rights and addressing inequities in Arctic resource projects. *Resources, 8*(2), 1–23.

Wolfers, A. (1952). "National security" as an ambiguous symbol. *Political Science Quarterly, 67*(4), 481–502.

Yliräisänen-Seppänen, P. (2020). *Vuoden 2020 sähköisten palveluiden tilastot* [Statistics of electronic services in 2020]. Pohjois-Suomen sosiaalialan osaamiskeskus/Northern Finland Center for Social Affairs. https://bit.ly/3iFgdg3. Accessed 9 Dec 2023.

Young, J. C. (2021). Environmental colonialism, digital indigeneity, and the politicization of resilience. *Environment and Planning E: Nature and Space, 4*(2), 230–251.

Yunes, E. (2016). Arctic cultural (mis)representation: Advocacy, activism, and artistic expression on social media. *Public, 27*(54), 98–103.

Zojer, G. (2019). Free and open-source software as a contribution to digital security in the Arctic. In L. Heininen, H. Exner-Pirot, & J. Barnes (Eds.), *Arctic Yearbook 2019* (pp. 1–16). Geopolitics and Security Thematic Network, University of the Arctic. https://bit.ly/3HjSOem. Accessed 9 Dec 2023.

Chapter 8
Polar Research Data Management: Understanding Technical Implementation and Policy Decisions in the Era of FAIR Data

Gregory Vey (ID), **Wesley Van Wychen** (ID), **Chantelle Verhey** (ID), **Peter Pulsifer** (ID), **and Ellsworth LeDrew** (ID)

Abstract This chapter examines current and emerging trends, practices, and technological methods relating to polar research data management. The authors discuss metadata standards, data architecture, semantics, interoperability, dissemination, knowledge mobilization, and organizational policy with respect to how they apply in the context of contemporary issues such as FAIR data principles (i.e., findability, accessibility, interoperability, and reusability), automated metadata harvesting, and data science interests such as data visualization. The chapter begins with a brief history of the beginnings of polar research data management as motivated primarily by domain specific informational needs, followed by description of the progressive changes and emerging criteria that have iteratively shaped disparate ad hoc repositories, propelling them toward the current state of data management that challenges many legacy systems. The Polar Data Catalogue is used as a working example throughout this chapter to illustrate the needs, impacts, challenges, and solutions relating to modern polar research data management. Five specific technical topics are discussed in this chapter. First, metadata standards: The ISO 19115 schema is examined, including its congruence to emerging trends like the schema.org vocabulary, as well as its limitations and future challenges. Second, data architecture: The modelling, representation, and storage of metadata and data are considered with

G. Vey (✉)
Waterloo Climate Institute, University of Waterloo, Waterloo, ON, Canada
e-mail: gvey@uwaterloo.ca

W. Van Wychen · E. LeDrew
Department of Geography and Environmental Management, University of Waterloo, Waterloo, ON, Canada

C. Verhey
Polar Data Catalogue, University of Waterloo, Waterloo, ON, Canada

P. Pulsifer
Geomatics and Cartographic Research Centre, Carleton University, Ottawa, ON, Canada

© The Author(s), under exclusive license to Springer Nature Switzerland AG 2024
S. Acadia (ed.), *Library and Information Sciences in Arctic and Northern Studies*, Springer Polar Sciences, https://doi.org/10.1007/978-3-031-54715-7_8

respect to the traditional relational model versus recent NoSQL technologies, particularly from the perspective of their suitability for supporting the requirements discussed in the other sections. Third, semantics and interoperability: The FAIR data principles are discussed with a particular focus on semantics and interoperability, including challenges in implementing schema.org capabilities, search engine optimization, and participation in federated search initiatives with other organizations and partners. Fourth, dissemination and knowledge mobilization: The modernization of data availability and means of data acquisition are explored, with consideration for the growing interest and impact of data science. The emergence of REST APIs and their consumption to support automated harvest for activities such as real-time data visualization are examined as working examples. Fifth, organizational policy: The interplay between organizational policies and technical implementations is examined from the perspective of reciprocal impacts. The chapter concludes with our impressions of what challenges remain to be addressed and what others might arise in the future for polar research data management.

Keywords Data architecture · Interoperability · Knowledge mobilization · Metadata standards · Organizational policy · Polar data · Research data management

8.1 Introduction

Given the harsh environmental conditions and significant logistical costs, collecting quality data in polar regions poses a considerable challenge and efforts to ensure the longevity and re-use of any data collected in these environments is crucial. In response to this need, various data repositories have been developed to ensure that datasets collected in polar environments are securely saved and made broadly available to the wider community, including researchers, policy makers, local northern communities, and the public.

Within Canada, tangible efforts to tackle the challenge of national polar data management and contribution to the global needs for monitoring the cryosphere was recognized in the 1990s (Barry, 1995), leading to the formation of the Cryosphere System (CRYSYS) project. CRYSYS was a network of scientists from government, universities, and the private sector who were working to develop capabilities to monitor and better understand variations in major components of the cryosphere (Goodison et al., 1999). Within the CRYSYS framework, a series of consultations were held with an interested cross-section of Canadians from education, research, government, and industry. Based on these consultations, it was determined that the best mechanism to achieve both access to data and improved information flow to the public and decision makers was to establish a non-government information node.

8 Polar Research Data Management: Understanding Technical Implementation...

As a result, the Canadian Cryospheric Information Network (CCIN) (https://ccin.ca/) was born in 2001. Based at the University of Waterloo in Ontario and founded in partnership with support from federal agencies and the private sector, the CCIN archives and publicly distributes metadata and datasets contributed by scientist working in polar regions.

The early 2000s was a transformative time for Arctic research within Canada. New research programs, such as the ArcticNet Network Centre of Excellence of Canada (2022) that was established in 2004 and the International Polar Year 2007–2008 (Krupnik et al., 2011) meant that there was a greater need for a formal online data management system for scientists to archive information about their datasets and give the public a means to access them, especially for local northern residents where the research was occurring. Although the CCIN was recognized as a data repository for its multitude of research projects, significant upgrades to its data management capabilities and infrastructure were needed to make it a modern and robust data repository. The result was the creation of the Polar Data Catalogue (PDC) (https://www.polardata.ca/). Launched in 2007, the PDC was initially developed as a metadata-only discovery portal to allow for the exchange of information about datasets between researchers, northern communities, international programs, decision makers, and the interested public. By 2011, functionality was added to archive and share data files to accompany the rapidly growing metadata collection. As of 1 July 2022, the number of publicly available metadata records in the PDC reached nearly 3000. Today, the PDC is one of the premier data repositories within Canada and is certified by the World Data System (https://worlddatasystem.org/) of the International Science Council as a CoreTrustSeal repository (https://www.coretrustseal.org/), meaning that the PDC is internationally certified as a sustainable and trustworthy data repository.

In recent years, PDC efforts have focused on the interoperability and discoverability of datasets between various data repositories and implementing modern standards for data management. These efforts help ensure that the metadata and datasets stored within the PDC are available to the broadest audience possible in easy-to-use formats; in the world of 'big data,' this helps ensure maximum use and utility of PDC holdings. For complex environmental problems in particular, these efforts are of paramount importance because they provide opportunities to make new predictions, discoveries, and solutions to human-induced change and other challenges facing the polar regions. In this chapter, we examine emerging trends, practices, and technological methods relating to polar data management with particular attention to metadata standards, data architecture, data interoperability, data dissemination, and how these apply to Canada's Polar Data Catalogue to ensure it maintains its status as a key resource for serving polar metadata and datasets. Furthermore, this chapter is meant to provide a template and resource for other data repositories that aim to build similar research data management (RDM) infrastructure.

8.2 Metadata Standards

The polar RDM community operates in a multidisciplinary space. Options for standards are numerous, detailed, and cover information about the data itself; the machines and instruments used to collect the data (e.g., make, model, and manufacturer); and any steps or scripts used to clean, analyse, process, or create data and data products. Along with metadata standards, controlled vocabularies supply standardized sets of property values such that common metadata elements (i.e., fields) and their respective values (i.e., contents) uniformly describe features using the same terms. Combining both strategies improves the ability of an individual or machine to find data for which they are searching while also providing the opportunity for communities of practice to actively share data. All these factors are pertinent to curating robust metadata. Due to the complexity and cross-domain nature of the data, a single metadata standard has yet to emerge for the polar RDM community. Although there have been initiatives to create a universal metadata standard in the past, pursuing a one-size-fits-all solution has proven unrealistic as adoption requires broad consensus among heterogeneous stakeholder groups. Instead, and so far, this situation has resulted in a more collaborative approach of establishing crosswalks between standards. Repositories currently have no obligation to choose a standard or schema from existing inventory, and some organizations and repositories elect to create their own formats, such as the Socioeconomic Data and Applications Center's (2022) CEISIN standard. From the vast number of standards that have emerged, there are several that are common throughout the polar RDM community, including the International Organization for Standardization (ISO) 19115 in XML, Federal Geospatial Data Committee (FGDC) in XML, GCMD Directory Interchange Format (DIF) in XML, DataCite Schema in XML, Dublin Core in XML, and Data Catalog Vocabulary in JSON (Jones et al., 2014). Important to note is that format (e.g., XML, JSON, etc.) is irrespective of standard.

In the case of the PDC, the ISO 19115 standard (https://www.iso.org/standard/53798.html) is the core standard used to implement metadata, along with translations to other formats such as FGDC. The PDC uses a standardized ISO 19115 web schema for its users to fill out alongside their datasets. Once submitted, a dedicated data manager reviews the records for consistency and robustness. While this process can vary across repositories, the ISO 19115 standard is compatible with the FGDC and DIF standards to abide by the Antarctic Treaty (Secretariat of the Antarctic Treaty, n.d.). ISO 19115 was established by the International Standards Organization (https://www.iso.org/) in 2003 and is predominately used with geospatial data within the earth sciences. The standard allows for tailored metadata records. For example, ISO 19115 provides information about the description, extent, quality, spatial and temporal schema, spatial reference, keywords, and distribution of digital geographic data (i.e., source). However, while the standard is well known and documented, it is a proprietary standard, and potential implications of this facet should be well understood by adopting repositories.

As standards continue to evolve, the PDC remains engaged with the current community trends and requirements to ensure its metadata and data holdings meet these needs. A current example is the adoption of the findability, accessibility, interoperability, and reusability data principles known as FAIR (GoFAIR, n.d.; Wilkinson et al., 2016). Currently, the PDC is challenged by how to reconcile legacy infrastructure design decisions to best implement this important policy shift as it continues to emerge for the betterment of the data management landscape. The sections that follow elucidate various factors and considerations raised by implementing FAIR data from a variety of relevant perspectives.

8.3 Data Architecture

Data architecture represents a core consideration for any organization. Decisions with respect to policy and technical implementation have a tremendous cascading impact on how organizational activities are executed and shape how organizations interact with their intended usage domain and target users. Furthermore, decisions on data architecture are difficult to retract or modify both in terms of policy and technical implementation; therefore, this is typically something that must be well planned in the formative stages of the organization. In the case of the PDC, implementation of geographic metadata standards, heterogeneity of the contributed data, and repository futureproofing all exert an effect on data modelling and data architecture perspectives, policies, and implementation.

Influenced by the factors listed above, the PDC implements metadata architecture using a normalized relational model, a data management paradigm that uses structure and language consistent with first-order predicate logic. This model is used for PDC data and other assets such as the Canadian Space Agency's RADARSAT collections. The relational model (RM) (Codd, 1970) offers benefits such as low data redundancy, data consistency, and physical data independence (Ward & Dafoulas, 2006). In terms of implementation, the RM rests on the formal mathematical basis of tuple relational calculus, a declarative language that provides formal description of a domain or data model, and relational database (RDB) design is accomplished through a formal normalization process (Ward & Dafoulas, 2006). However, there are multiple aspects of data representation and entity-relationship (ER) modelling that are not effectively captured by the RM. ER modelling characterizes a specific domain of knowledge using entity types that describe objects or things, while specifying the relationships that can exist between the various entity types.

RDBs are unable to directly represent many real-world objects, especially those that are complex and composed of other objects, a result of the inability of the RM to distinguish between entities versus relationships. This outcome occurs because relationships identified during ER modelling are not directly represented within the RM and therefore do not persist in an explicit fashion, preventing the RM from offering a means to directly recover the relationships between entities (e.g., the *Works In* relationship between *Employee* and *Department* entities). Consequently, users must possess prior knowledge about such relationships to compensate for the semantic overloading that occurs because relations from the RM are used to represent both the entities and relationships from the corresponding ER model (Ward & Dafoulas, 2006).

Other challenges for the RM include excessive fragmentation that can require numerous joins to meet queries, inability to directly capture lists or sets, and inability to directly include a composite attribute (Ward & Dafoulas, 2006) (e.g., *Name*, which might contain member attributes like *First Name* and *Last Name*). Related to this latter challenge, the range of available datatypes is limited, and no way exists to create user-defined types required for specific application domains (Ward & Dafoulas, 2006). Similarly, the RM cannot depict hierarchical or inheritance associations (Ward & Dafoulas, 2006), such as inferring that entities like *Employee* and *Student* both inherit the attributes of a mutual parent entity like *Person*, or that the set of all *Employees* is a subset of all *Persons*.

To better appreciate the technical formalities discussed so far, we can consider a usage scenario taken from the polar RDM domain. Figure 8.1 shows an example of an ER diagram modelling a polar metadata record based on the actual RM implementation used at the PDC. The sample diagram shows the fields (i.e., columns) contained in the primary Metadata table in the centre as well as three other associated tables, each with their own respective fields. In particular, the first field (i.e., the primary key) in the Metadata table, *metadata_id*, also occurs as a field in each of the three associated tables. This design provides a retrieval process where the *metadata_id* associated with any metadata record can be used to lookup additional information, such as the Research Program associated with that instance of metadata. Decoupling the data across associated tables is the result of the previously mentioned process of normalization, providing benefits such as low data redundancy while enforcing strong data integrity. However, a report generated on the contents of current metadata would necessitate fetching back information from the associated tables through numerous *Join* operations. For example, if the report requires the name of Research Program or the name of Responsible Party for each record, these are not directly contained within the primary Metadata table, therefore increasing the overall retrieval cost to obtain this more comprehensive information.

Despite its limitations, the RM and RDBs offer a gold standard of reliability, serving as the core data persistence and data management components of a vast number of commercial, financial, and academic organizations. Nevertheless, the growing adoption of non-relational database implementation, or Not Only SQL (NoSQL), lends motivation to consider possible advantages, particularly with respect to trends such as 'big data.' Some key advantages of NoSQL databases include distributed database capability, horizontal scalability, and schema-free insertion of data (Chen & Lee, 2018). Schema-free representation of data is an important capability for many application domains and is of high interest to PDC data architecture considerations.

One example of an issue that has prompted reconsideration of PDC metadata architecture is the assignment of Digital Object Identifiers (DOIs) (ISO, 2012). A DOI is an ISO-standardized persistent identifier that is used to uniquely identify various objects, including published datasets. In the case of the PDC, DOI

8 Polar Research Data Management: Understanding Technical Implementation... 181

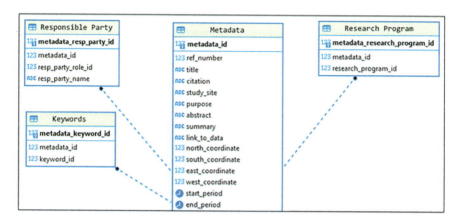

Fig. 8.1 Example of an entity-relationship (ER) diagram modelled from metadata tables at the Polar Data Catalogue. (Screenshot credit: G. Vey)

assignment is an organizational practice that began after the design and implementation of the metadata tables that comprise the internal representation and storage of PDC metadata, resulting in an alteration to the specification of internal metadata. In terms of implementing this change, one solution is to alter the core metadata table by adding a column to store DOI values; however, doing so would introduce notable risk for a live production system even after thorough testing in an offline version. In addition, an issue of sparsity is present as many previous records might not have values for this column. An alternative to altering the core metadata table is to create a separate table with only the two columns of the unique metadata record identifier from the core table and the DOI associated with it. This approach both reduces risk and resolves sparsity but violates the concept of normality that is central to using an RDB because the unique metadata record identifier is used as the primary key in both cases. Therefore, according to ER modelling, the DOI value should be a field (i.e., column) within the core Metadata table rather than a field in an ancillary table. In contrast, using a schema-free NoSQL allows for the direct inclusion of DOI values within impacted metadata records, beginning when this organizational decision is adopted.

The previous example shows how NoSQL implementation offers crucial flexibility in the event of a changing data model; however, there are costs and benefits associated with using NoSQL implementation versus an RDB. RDBs are well suited for usage domains where the data are structured, and low data redundancy is important. Furthermore, RDBs are implemented to support broad range queries with good performance, although excessive joins can impact performance. Moreover, this feature can be useful if new queries are likely to be required with emerging organizational needs. In contrast, NoSQL is not bound by a fixed schema and is therefore well suited for semi-structured or irregular data. However, this flexibility can result in redundancy and does not necessarily support general purpose querying. This makes a NoSQL implementation, such as a MongoDB document-oriented database (https://www.mongodb.com), a good fit when a recurrent usage domain is well understood (e.g., a web-based application that fetches and updates user profiles and the artefacts associated with a user account). This last perspective aligns well with the concept of maintaining PDC user profiles and their associated metadata and data contributions.

Another area of interest for the PDC with respect to MongoDB relates to the JSON-like structure of the stored documents. JavaScript Object Notation (JSON) is a self-describing, lightweight format for storing and transporting data; it is commonly used in web and client-server application development. In particular, the ease of conversion between JSON used for APIs and data driven web apps versus the internal binary JSON representation—known as BSON—within MongoDB is also a noteworthy feature when considering data architecture. So far, the present discussion of data architecture and technological implementations has been driven by conventional organizational pursuits. As a final thought on data architecture, we would like to draw attention to potential limitations and challenges faced when a central goal is the inclusion and representation of Indigenous knowledge, especially within the context of Indigenous knowledge paradigms themselves. Based on the discussion above, it seems that a schema-free design might be more successful than a structured table approach, and such designs have been previously implemented (e.g., Hayes et al., 2014; Vey & Charles, 2014) as solutions in this domain. However, design and implementation ultimately depend on the perspective of how content should be best decomposed, if at all, and represented for internal storage and subsequent reconstruction. No immediate recommendation is offered here, but we do believe that this topic embodies a crucial issue that should be central to future data architectures.

8.4 Semantics and Interoperability

Recent years have seen a strong interest in FAIR data (Wilkinson et al., 2016) as a premise, while also noting the disparity between advocating for policy versus actual technical implementations (Deniz Beyan et al., 2020; Sinaci et al., 2020). This sentiment was reiterated by the European Commission Expert Group on FAIR Data in the 2018 report *Turning FAIR Into Reality* that addresses the well-established concept of a technical ecosystem (Parsons et al., 2011; Pulsifer et al., 2020). However, while recognizing that FAIR data implementations involve technical facets, these works are not aimed at providing stepwise guidance for software development required to FAIR data compliance. Large RDM systems and metadata platforms do exist that explicitly address FAIR data management considerations, including the German Network for Bioinformatics Infrastructure (Mayer et al., 2021), National Science Foundation Arctic Data Center (Schildhauer et al., 2019), Ocean FAIR Data Services (Tanhua et al., 2019), and several others in areas such as the earth and life sciences. However, again, the focus of these ventures relates to the provision of

FAIR capabilities rather than an exhaustive presentation of how to carry out technical implementations and/or refactoring of existing RDM systems.

Interoperability is a key component of the FAIR data principles (Wilkinson et al., 2016). Interoperability in RDM entails systems exchanging services and data with one another (Heiler, 1995). This component of FAIR is essential for large scale user consumption and information exchange between repositories. Linked open data (LoD) follows a set of design principles for sharing machine-readable interlinked data on the web and can be freely used and distributed (Berners-Lee et al., 2001; Holdborn, 2014). Challenges that arise from these information exchanges include systems having to agree upon common standards, algorithms, and semantics in general. The advantage of using LoD is that the Resource Description Framework (RDF) and associated formats (e.g., JSON-LD) can be used to represent metadata and data, as well as explicitly define the semantics (e.g., labels, definitions, hierarchical and logical relationships, etc.) of the metadata and data represented.

One solution that the World Wide Web Consortium (W3C) (https://www.w3.org/) community uses to establish a common lightweight metadata standard that can be implemented on a large-scale basis is schema.org's service data object (SDO) markup. Schema.org was created in 2011 by major search engine organizations, including Google, Yahoo, Bing, and Yandex. Typically, SDO is utilized for marking-up webpages to enhance their discoverability by search engines. With this concept of LoD, published datasets described by schema.org can be linked to other datasets and resources. Google has also established a Google Dataset Search that aims to do what Google Scholar has done for published articles but for dataset discoverability. The W3C provides guidance on how repositories can mark-up their existing metadata schemas to be included in their search interfaces (Holdborn, 2014).

The RDM community has since identified semantic mark-up as the most viable way to enhance interoperability between and among data repositories. Specific to the polar community, Polar Data Discovery Enhancement Research (POLDER) (https://polder.info/) is working to find the best path forward for polar data discovery. The international working group has collaborated since 2017 to establish a federated search tool. POLDER is a collaboration between the Southern Ocean Observing System, Arctic Data Committee, and Standing Committee on Antarctic Data Management. Federated metadata search for the polar regions will dramatically simplify data discovery for polar scientists. Instead of searching dozens of metadata catalogues separately, a single search page can be used. Other domains have already completed similar projects, although challenges unique to the polar community has delayed the full adoption development. Firstly, the polar community is a diverse and dynamic community producing multidisciplinary datasets and data from local communities across the Arctic, including Indigenous data and information. During the International Polar Year 2007–2008, a common metadata profile was developed and implemented by several data centres (Parsons et al., 2011), including the PDC. Similarly, the Arctic Data Explorer was launched in 2013 and operated until 2019 (Liu et al., 2013). These tools, while useful, were driven by specific data centres and funding rather than community-driven initiatives; thus, broad adoption went unrealized. The POLDER effort builds on community-wide collaboration from the outset and builds on SDO, a model that is increasingly used across many communities of practice. For example, since the release of basic SDO vocabulary, the environmental science domain has created a 'science-on-schema. org' set of guidelines and recommendations that is utilized to guide polar repositories for inclusion in the POLDER's federated search tool. The guidelines provide direction for members of that domain to complete mark-up with only the relevant terms that are applicable to their schemas, no matter which one the repository uses. Secondly, POLDER's federated search tool has developed slowly due to lack of capacity and funding within the community, specifically funding for repositories to dedicate development resources on their own infrastructure needs to include semantic mark-up within their existing landing pages, or for the creation of one if needed. For example, funding for Antarctic initiatives and repository management is scarce, further exacerbating the problem that is already so prevalent. Toward alleviation of some of these issues, the POLDER group works together for fundraising and providing web developmental resources on a *pro bono* basis so that underfunded repositories with valuable polar data can be included in the federated search tool.

8.5   Dissemination and Knowledge Mobilization

Over the past few years, the single most requested new feature from PDC users is the development of a server-side web application programming interface (API) to expose PDC metadata through a collection of endpoints. Representational state transfer (REST) defines an architectural paradigm intended to facilitate web-based communication in the form of client and server requests and responses under the constraint of statelessness. RESTful web APIs offer a means to handle stateless requests made to an endpoint through a response payload that supports a specific format, including human-readable and machine-readable text (e.g., JSON and XML). Therefore, the development of a RESTful web API for PDC metadata is a major opportunity to meet user needs while implementing some of the previously discussed issues relating to interoperability. Specifically, the implementation of JSON-LD endpoints provides a mechanism to expose metadata while supporting schema.org capability and facilitating findability through search engine optimization (SEO). Implementing equivalent XML responses and endpoints is also an essential consideration for the PDC to support legacy formats, specifically the common ISO 19115 XML standard.

Internet search engines are a common tool in the discovery and acquisition of research datasets. As a result, SEO is an increasingly relevant pursuit for data repositories. SEO involves optimizing webpages such that the algorithmic search results of relevant keywords will increase the rank of the given webpages (Li et al., 2014). In turn, this improved ranking leads to improved discoverability of assets and, in the case of data repositories and FAIR principles, the improved findability of data. These considerations of SEO impact PDC metadata API implementation such that the JSON-LD endpoints provide schema.org compliant responses because of intentional congruence between the JSON representation that is designed for embedding into a webpage corresponding to a PDC metadata record and the JSON representation of the same record provided as an API response.

For the JSON-LD endpoints, any given API response is composed of JSON elements corresponding to schema.org types and properties. Each individual metadata record is structured and nested to represent a *Dataset* instance. Furthermore, if a response contains one or more metadata records, each individual *Dataset* element is contained within a wrapping *itemListElement*, where the set of *itemListElements* are contained within an *itemList* (i.e., an array of *itemListElements*). Understanding the structure of metadata within the API response is necessary to effectively extract content of interest. Figure 8.2 illustrates the nested topology of PDC JSON-LD metadata with validated content shown on the left and raw JSON code shown on the right.

One of the core motivations for providing these APIs relates to supporting knowledge mobilization objectives. In general, APIs necessarily meet the goal of broad data dissemination and thus are central to knowledge mobilization. The specific APIs discussed here also serve to push appropriate data into the public domain, another important facet of knowledge mobilization. Beyond these features, we expect that these APIs will drive knowledge synthesis, reinterpretation, and subsequent redistribution, thereby extending the scope of dissemination. We expect that the API endpoints will be harvested and consumed by automated processes and scheduled tasks, will become data sources for real-time data visualizations and

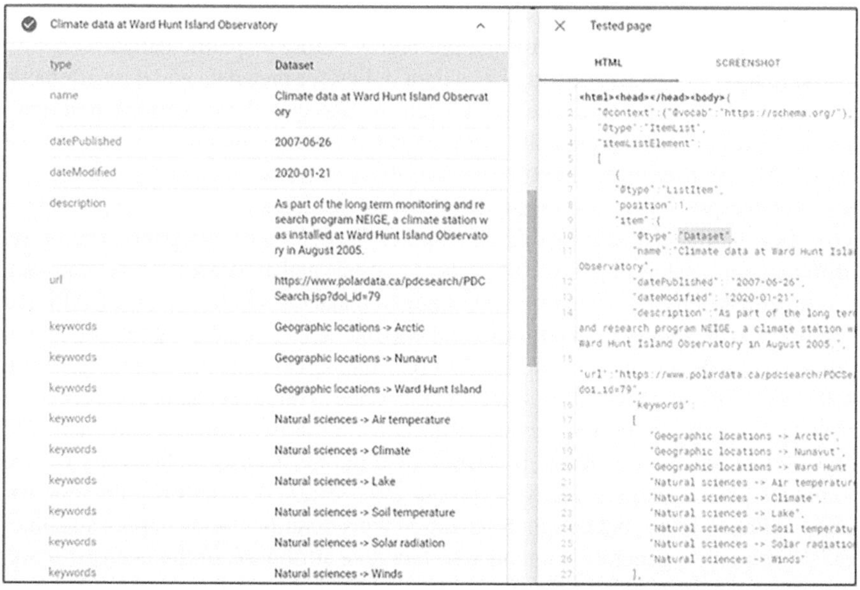

Fig. 8.2 Example of JSON-LD metadata topology using a metadata record at the Polar Data Catalogue. (Screenshot credit: G. Vey)

machine learning applications, and their contents will be used to populate other repositories and catalogues.

Overall, the metadata APIs described here are of benefit to government and university researchers and scientists, as well as graduate and undergraduate students, who are involved in polar research. However, in addition to polar and geographic domains, we believe that these resources also of interest to, and facilitate access for a wider domain of, data scientists, modelers, and the public. Indeed, one of the main goals of these ventures is to achieve knowledge mobilization by linking currently available polar research to broader arenas where it can contribute to pressing large-scale issues and help inform policy and action.

8.6 Organizational Policy

Much of the previous discussion focuses on standards, architecture, and technical implementation. While the topic of policy, whether from an external user policy perspective or from an internal organizational perspective, might seem unrelated, there is considerable interplay among these facets because policy choices inform downstream decisions on standards, architecture, and technical implementations, while policy implementations are necessarily bound by the standards, architecture, and technical capabilities of the repository. That is, a repository cannot simply elect to support FAIR data principles if its current implementation lacks the capability to provide the corresponding functionality. Thus, understanding the resonance between these two key drivers of RDM is crucial and should be undertaken as early as possible in the lifecycle of any repository, preferably before its public launch.

The PDC (2011, 2021) already has a data policy for metadata and data artefacts, as well as a general terms of use for its website, associated applications, and databases. However, these constraints are predicated on a paradigm of manual usage where a human user must click to assent to these usage agreements to use the service. For the previously discussed APIs, the usage domain needs to support scenarios beyond manual activity (e.g., automated harvesting of metadata). Therefore, a different approach is required with respect to usage and agreements. One approach is to require API users to acquire an API key to make calls to the metadata API. An API key acts as a unique identifier to authenticate a user and ensure that the client acquiesces to all applicable policies, licenses, and agreements prior to the granting of the key. This practice allows automated usage without manual acceptance of terms because the client has previously accepted all terms. Another approach is to forgo repository-specific terms in favour of a public license, such as a Creative Commons license (https://creativecommons.org/). These licenses offer flexible features, including reuse and commercialization considerations, and support machine-readable metadata generation intended to facilitate attribution of the licensed work. The Apache license version 2.0 from the Apache Software Foundation (2004) is another popular public license but its usage is primarily intended for software licensing, while the Creative Commons licenses are more broadly applicable to creative works in general.

Understanding and determining the best suited policies and applicable licenses is mission critical for any data repository. These decisions are even more imperative when a repository requires user registration because changing, updating, or revoking existing agreements and licenses is a nearly insurmountable issue. These issues are exacerbated by the definition of ownership: While data submitters often maintain ownership of their data assets, they typically have no dominion over the corresponding metadata that describes these artefacts. Thus, careful planning must be built into repository policy design and the selection of corresponding licensing and agreements.

Modern trends in cloud infrastructure have given rise to another major policy choice for data repositories; specifically, there now exists the opportunity to implement serverless architectures for selected services or the entire repository. The concept of a serverless architecture involves removing the concern of server management at the repository level and delegating this to a cloud services provider such as Amazon Web Services or Google Compute Engine. The motivation for this approach is that data repositories are able to focus their technical efforts on domain-specific application and database development without the considerable burden of maintaining physical infrastructure. However, this premise, while appearing to be purely of a technical nature, carries significant policy ramifications. One of the primary concerns relates to the geographic location of stored data as there can be caveats stemming from the transitive imposition of laws and regulations that are inherent to a given country, state, or other entity; this is often major concern for submitters of data, and with good reason. Therefore, substantial diligence is required before adopting this type of design to manage and mitigate organizational risk, as well as to understand potential changes in user patterns and demand. Thus, the decision to use a serverless architecture provides a compelling example of the powerful coupling between technical and policy perspectives.

8.7 Conclusion

Data repositories, such as the Polar Data Catalogue, face a myriad of complexities and challenges from both technical and policy perspectives. In addition to the ongoing evolution of new technologies and progressive changes in policy and goals, there is the complication of reconciling the dependencies that arise from the interplay between all these factors. That is, the decision to implement FAIR data principles cannot be done in the absence of supporting technical infrastructure. Similarly, electing to implement a metadata API while deprecated another older metadata harvesting service, such as an Open Archives Initiative Protocol for Metadata Harvesting (OAI-PMH) (https://www.openarchives.org/pmh/) endpoint, cannot be done without assessing and understanding policy issues relating to potential impacts to users of the deprecated service.

Future planning for the PDC includes a full public release of its metadata API with support for legacy ISO 19115 XML, as well as schema.org compliant JSON-LD. In conjunction with the API release, the PDC will also integrate its metadata to become available through the CCADI metadata API and will update, strengthen, and clarify the content and language that comprise its data policy and terms of use. Specifically, the PDC's goal is to modernize the context for these documents so that they better reflect and support the interests and activities of the polar RDM community as well as the broader data management community at large. The PDC will also broaden its dissemination efforts beyond metadata to include data by developing infrastructure to expose selected datasets through OPeNDAP services (https://www.opendap.org/).

A key challenge for many data repositories, including the PDC, is to begin planning for the integration and adoption of Indigenous knowledge, and more generally any cross-cultural knowledge, which is not yet directly supported from a technical perspective. This undertaking serves as another paramount example of the reciprocal nature of organizational policy and technical implementation with respect to their impacts upon one another. Methodical planning is essential to effectively implement a design that is both powerful and sufficiently malleable for current needs while offering capabilities to meet future contingencies.

Overall, the convergence of many exciting technological trends and progressive policy trajectories combine to offer tremendous opportunities for both existing and emerging data repositories. Nevertheless, careful planning is required to ensure maximum compatibility with domain specific needs and standards while meeting an appropriate policy position. In addition, wherever possible, maintaining organizational flexibility and manoeuvrability is a central goal, both in terms of technical evolution and changing trajectory for goals and policies.

Acknowledgements The authors acknowledge financial support from the following organizations and programs: Amundsen Science, Université Laval; CFI-Cyberinfrastructure (Canadian Consortium for Arctic Data Interoperability), University of Calgary; Institutional Support (Canadian Consortium for Arctic Data Interoperability), University of Waterloo; Northern Contaminants Program/Crown-Indigenous Relations and Northern Affairs Canada; Nunavut General Monitoring Plan/Crown-Indigenous Relations and Northern Affairs Canada; and Polar Knowledge Canada/Canadian High Arctic Research Station.

References

Apache Software Foundation. (2004). *Apache license, version 2.0.* https://bit.ly/3ug5hrY. Accessed 9 Dec 2023.

ArcticNet Network Centre of Excellence of Canada. (2022). *ArcticNet: Working towards a sustainable and prosperous North.* https://bit.ly/3AV9vsM. Accessed 9 Dec 2023.

Barry, R. G. (1995). Observing systems and data sets related to the cryosphere in Canada. A contribution to planning for the global climate observing system. *Atmosphere-Ocean, 33*(4), 771–807.

Berners-Lee, T., Hendler, J., & Lassila, O. (2001, May). The semantic web: A new form of web content that is meaningful to computers will unleash a revolution of new possibilities. *Scientific American, 284*(5), 34–43.

Chen, J.-K., & Lee, W.-Z. (2018). An introduction of NoSQL databases based on their categories and application industries. *Algorithms, 12*(5), 1–17.

Codd, E. F. (1970). A relational model of data for large shared databanks. *Communications of the ACM, 13*(6), 377–387.

Deniz Beyan, O., Chue Hong, N., Cozzini S., Hoffman-Sommer, M., Hooft, R., Lembinen, L., Marttila, J., & Teperek, M. (2020). *Seven recommendations for implementation of FAIR practice.* https://doi.org/jn47

European Commission Expert Group on FAIR Data. (2018). *Final report and action plan: Turning FAIR into reality.* European Union. https://bit.ly/46PzS0k. Accessed 9 Dec 2023.

GoFAIR. (n.d.). *FAIR principles.* https://bit.ly/3AZoH8a. Accessed 9 Dec 2023.

Goodison, B. E., Brown, R. D., Brugman, M. M., Duguay, C. R., Flato, G. M., LeDrew, E. F., & Walker, A. E. (1999). CRYSYS—Use of the cryospheric system to monitor global change in Canada: Overview and progress. *Canadian Journal of Remote Sensing, 25*(1), 3–11.

Hayes, A., Pulsifer, P. L., & Fiset, J. P. (2014). The Nunaliit cybercartographic atlas framework. In D. R. Fraser Taylor (Ed.), *Developments in the theory and practice of cybercartography: Application and Indigenous mapping* (Vol. 5, 2nd ed., pp. 129–140). Elsevier.

Heiler, S. (1995). Semantic interoperability. *ACM Computing Surveys, 27*(2), 271–273.

Holborn, T. (2014, January 17). *What is 5 star linked data?* [Blog post]. https://bit.ly/3FgImmu. Accessed 9 Dec 2023.

International Organization for Standardization (ISO). (2012). *ISO 2634:2012(en) Information and documentation—Digital object identifier system.* https://bit.ly/3GZHhkj. Accessed 9 Dec 2023.

Jones, P. R., Ritchey, N. A., Peng, G., Toner, V. A., & Brown, H., (2014, December 15–19). *ISO, FGDC, DIF, and Dublin Core: Making sense of metadata standards for Earth science data* [Conference paper]. American Geophysical Union, Fall meeting, San Francisco, California, USA.

Krupnik, I., Allison, I., Bell, R., Cutler, P., Hik, D., López-Martínez, J., Rachold, V., Sarukanian, E., & Summerhayes, C. (2011). *Understanding Earth's polar challenges: International Polar Year 2007–2008.* World Meteorological Association and International Council for Science. https://bit.ly/3AZzhfr. Accessed 9 Dec 2023.

Li, K., Lin, M., Lin, Z., & Xing, B. (2014, January 6–9). Running and chasing: The competition between paid search marketing and search engine optimization [Conference paper]. *Proceedings of the 47th Hawaii International Conference on System Science (HICSS)* (pp. 3110–3119), Waikoloa, Hawaii, USA. https://doi.org/jn49

Liu, M., Truslove, I., Yarmey, L., Lopez, L., Reed, S. A., & Brandt, M. (2013, December 9–13). *Arctic data explorer: A Rich Solr powered metadata search portal* [Conference paper]. American Geophysical Union, Fall meeting, San Francisco, California, USA.

Mayer, G., Müller, W., Schork, K., Uszoreit, J., Weidemann, A., Wittig, U., Rey, M., Quast, C., Felden, J., Glöckner, F. O., Lange, M., Arend, D., Beier, S., Junker, A., Scholz, U., Schüler, D., Kestler, H. A., Wibberg, D., Pühler, A., et al. (2021). Implementing FAIR data management within the German network for bioinformatics infrastructure (de.NBI) exemplified by selected use cases. *Briefings in Bioinformatics, 22*(5), 1–14.

Parsons, M. A., Godøy, Ø., LeDrew, E., De Bruin, T. F., Danis, B., Tomlinson, S., & Carlson, D. (2011). A conceptual framework for managing very diverse data for complex, interdisciplinary science. *Journal of Information Science, 37*(6), 555–569.

Polar Data Catalogue (PDC). (2011). *Data policy.* https://bit.ly/3OWQHir. Accessed 9 Dec 2023.

Polar Data Catalogue (PDC). (2021). *Terms of use of the Polar Data Catalogue.* https://bit.ly/3gLSwCj. Accessed 9 Dec 2023.

Pulsifer, P. L., Kontar, Y., Berkman, P. A., & Fraser Taylor, D. R. (2020). Information ecology to map the Arctic information ecosystem. In O. R. Young, P. A. Berkman, & A. N. Vylegzhanin (Eds.), *Governing Arctic seas: Regional lessons from the Bering Strait and Barents Sea* (Vol. 1, pp. 269–291). Springer.

Schildhauer, M., Chong, S., O'Brien, M., Mecum, B., & Jones, M. B. (2019, December 9–13). *Semantic approaches to enhancing data findability and interoperability in the NSF DataONE and Arctic Data Center Data Repositories* [Conference paper]. American Geophysical Union, Fall meeting, San Francisco, California, USA. https://bit.ly/3XOrpa8. Accessed 9 Dec 2023.

Secretariat of the Antarctic Treaty. (n.d.). *Antarctic Treaty.* https://bit.ly/3ONnG8O. Accessed 9 Dec 2023.

Sinaci, A. A., Núñez-Benjumea, F. J., Gencturk, M., Jauer, M.-L., Deserno, T., Chronaki, C., Cangioli, G., Cavero-Barca, C., Rodríguez-Pérez, J. M., Pérez-Pérez, M. M., Laleci Erturkmen, G. B., Hernández-Pérez, T., Méndez-Rodríguez, E., & Parra-Calderón, C. L. (2020). From raw data to FAIR data: The FAIRification workflow for health research. *Methods of Information in Medicine, 59*(S01), e21–e32.

Socioeconomic Data and Applications Center (SEDAC). (2022). *Metadata.* https://bit.ly/3FhSueV. Accessed 9 Dec 2023.

Tanhua, T., Pouliquen, S., Hausman, J., O'Brien, K., Bricher, P., de Bruin, T., Buck, J. J. H., Burger, E. F., Carval, T., Casey, K. S., Diggs, S., Giorgetti, A., Glaves, H., Harscoat, V., Kinkade, D., Muelbert, J. H., Novellino, A., Pfeil, B., Pulsifer, P. L., et al. (2019). Ocean FAIR data services. *Frontiers in Marine Science, 6,* 1–17.

Vey, G., & Charles, T. C. (2014). MetaProx: The database of metagenomic proximons. *Database: The Journal of Biological Databases and Curation, 2014,* 1–8.

Ward, P., & Dafoulas, G. (2006). *Database management systems.* Thompson.

Wilkinson, M. D., Dumontier, M., Aalbersberg, I. J., Appleton, G., Axton, M., Baak, A., Blomberg, N., Boiten, J.-W., da Silva, B., Santos, L., Bourne, P. E., Bouwman, J., Brookes, A. J., Clark, T., Crosas, M., Dillo, I., Dumon, O., Edmunds, S., Evelo, C. T., Finkers, R., et al. (2016). The FAIR guiding principles for scientific data management and stewardship. *Scientific Data, 3,* 160018.

Chapter 9
Tracking and Unlocking the Past: Documentation of Arctic Indigenous Languages

Lenore A. Grenoble ⓘ **and Vanda B. Ignatieva** ⓘ

Abstract This chapter considers the types of materials available in libraries, archives, special collections, and shoeboxes for studying and understanding Arctic Indigenous languages. Indigenous peoples account for approximately 12.5% of the overall Arctic population and, for centuries, have been in contact with non-Indigenous peoples (e.g., explorers, colonists, traders, and other visitors). Until recently, these 'outsiders' were the ones who created most of the records about Arctic languages, documenting language forms and linguistic practices from their own distanced perspectives. There is no single archive or repository for Arctic Indigenous languages, nor is there a centralized catalogue which lists what resources exist and where they are located. The resources are scattered, not only across the Arctic but also many important recordings are in the archives or personal holdings of the people who made them. We map out existing records and provide information about how to work with them, and then provide a close analysis of the holdings in one archive located in Yakutsk, Russia to exemplify the possibilities of finding language materials in regular archives.

Keywords Arctic Indigenous history · Arctic Indigenous languages · Linguistic practices · Language archives · Language repositories · Republic of Sakha (Yakutia)

L. A. Grenoble (✉)
University of Chicago, Chicago, IL, USA
e-mail: grenoble@uchicago.edu

V. B. Ignatieva
Institute for Humanitarian Research and the Problems of Indigenous Minorities of the North, Siberian Branch of the Russian Academy of Sciences, Yakutsk, Russia

© The Author(s), under exclusive license to Springer Nature
Switzerland AG 2024
S. Acadia (ed.), *Library and Information Sciences in Arctic and Northern Studies*, Springer Polar Sciences, https://doi.org/10.1007/978-3-031-54715-7_9

191

9.1 Introduction

Among the many threats facing Indigenous peoples in the Arctic, language and concurrent cultural shift is one that speaks to the heart of identity and self-worth. One response from Indigenous communities is to actively increase the vitality of their languages and instate measures to ensure long-term sustainability of those languages. For many revitalization programs, this response involves not only actively speaking and teaching the languages, but also looking to records of the past to resurrect language and culture as a way of building new Indigenous futures. These initiatives involve cultural reclamation and both a present and future assertion of self-control. Increasingly, academic scholars and Indigenous community members alike are interested in locating materials about Indigenous languages.

This chapter considers the kinds of materials available in libraries, archives, special collections, and shoeboxes for studying and understanding Arctic Indigenous languages. Indigenous peoples account for approximately 12.5% of the overall Arctic population and, for centuries, have been in contact with non-Indigenous peoples (e.g., explorers, colonists, traders, and other visitors). Until recently, these 'outsiders' were the ones who created most of the records about Arctic languages, documenting language forms and linguistic practices from their own distanced perspective. Alongside Indigenous languages of the Arctic are the majority languages of Arctic colonizers and national governments of which the Arctic is a part, namely Danish, English, Finnish, Norwegian, Russian, and Swedish. Other common languages are French, German, Icelandic, and Japanese. Because many outside explorers of the past collected word lists and made observations about language practices, early records are written in these majority, common, non-Indigenous languages.

There exists no single archive or repository for Arctic Indigenous languages (henceforth Arctic languages), nor is there a centralized catalogue of what resources exist and where they are located. Instead, the resources are scattered across the Arctic and non-Arctic, and many important records are held in the archives and personal collections of those who created them. Adding further complication is that, for many Arctic communities, the multiple outsiders who produced early and more recent records reside in different geographies, speak and created records in different languages, and possessed differing interest and expertise. All these factors influence the nature of the documentary records and where they are housed. Thus, finding and interpreting these records requires focused and dedicated detective work.

To illustrate these claims, this chapter maps out a general overview of the current situation regarding Arctic languages materials. The chapter then illustrates the rich existing documentation, along with the difficulties accessing it, via discussions of, first, Kalaallisut [Greenlandic] (ISO 639-3 kal), the Inuit language spoken in Greenland, and, second, the archives of the Manuscript Department of the Institute for Humanitarian Research and the Problems of Indigenous Minorities of the North, Siberian Branch of the Russian Academy of Sciences, Manuscript Division [Institut gumanitarnyx issledovanij i problem malochislennyx narodov Severa SO RAN—obosoblennoe podrazdelenie] (https://www.sbras.ru/ru/organization/2314).

9.2 Finding Language Materials

No designated, single archive exists for all Arctic languages, although there are some regional ones such as the Alaska Native Languages Archives (ANLA) (https://www.uaf.edu/anla/). Typically, Arctic language materials are consolidated with other, larger language archives; grouped in more general, non-language archives; or not archived at all. Thus, locating these materials is challenging. A first step in locating materials is to consult known language archives; identify and recruit the assistance of linguists who have worked on the language(s) of interest; and track down various related sources provided by linguists, historians, anthropologists, archivists, and others that are often housed on university campuses. Community archives may reside in some local area libraries and museums.

Second, consideration of early explorers to Arctic and Northern regions must be made as some kept records of languages they encountered while on expedition. For example, the Vega Expedition (1878–1880), named after the ship the *SS Vega* and under the direction of the of Swedish-Finnish explorer Adolf Erik Nordenskiöld (1832–1901), navigated through the Northeast Passage and around Eurasia. The ship was icebound not far from the Chukotka Peninsula for a long winter, from late September 1878 until August of the following year. During this time, the travellers on board frequently encountered the local Chukchi peoples. Records from this expedition provide valuable information about a simplified Chukchi variety of language that was used with outsiders (de Reuse, 1996; Nordenskiöld, 2012). Another example is the Jesup North Pacific Expedition (1897–1902) led by anthropologist Franz Boas (1858–1942). The purpose of this expedition was to study the peoples and cultures of North America's Pacific Northwest coast and the eastern coast of Siberia, during which extensive recordings and notes were created about languages and cultural practices. While many of these materials have since been published, valuable and unpublished archives from the expedition remain. The expedition was funded by the American Museum of Natural History in New York and many papers of Waldemar Bogoras (1865–1936) and Waldemar Jochelson (1855–1937) are now located in the New York Public Library (NYPL), a great example of a core Arctic collection that is housed in an unexpected repository. Other key explorers include Knud Rasmussen (1879–1933), a Greenlandic-Danish anthropologist born in Greenland, who spent many years collecting folklore from local Inuit throughout Greenland and Canada, as well as Vilhjalmur Stefansson (1879–1962), a Canadian of Icelandic descent, who surveyed the central Arctic regions of North America with the support of the American Museum of Natural History. Although neither explorer was a linguist, both made important contributions to early documentation of Arctic languages.

Of all Arctic languages, considerably more written and oral recordings of Kalaallisut exist than any others, albeit their locations are widely dispersed. Greenland was colonized without massive settlement, and written Kalaallisut was developed in the early 1700s for local religious and administrative purposes; spoken Kalaallisut existed in Greenland much earlier. Publication of the first Inuit newspaper, *Atuagagdliutit*, dates to 1861 (Hoh, 2016) and the first issues from 1861 to 1864 are located at the United States Library of Congress. Bible translations into Kalaallisut are even older, as Poul Egede's (1708–1789) Kalaallisut version of the Gospels was published in part in Copenhagen in 1744 (published fully as Egede 1766). The Oqaasileriffik [Greenland Language Secretariat] (https://oqaasileriffik. gl/) has many digital resources, including recently created materials and digital versions of earlier print materials such as the dictionaries of Kleinschmidt (1871), Rasmussen (1873), and Schultz-Lorentzen (1926, 1927).

The Nunatta Katersugaasivia Allagaateqarfialu [Greenland National Archives] (https://nka.gl/) contains a trove of both public documents and private, personal materials. Many of these materials are in Kalaallisut, although plenty are also in Danish. Few materials are available online, although various church records and the guest book from the ship *Umanak* from 1949–1952 are digitally available. In addition, the Kalaallit Nunaata Radio [Greenland Radio Station], or KNR, was founded in 1958 and maintains a collection of its radio broadcasts, serving as important documentation of spoken Kalaallisut, although many of the older broadcasts have not yet been digitized. Finally, Knut Bergslund's (1914–1998) materials on Kalaallisut are in the ANLA.

In the case of Greenland, resources are abundant because the language is robustly used. The challenge, however, is accessing and understanding the resources as they are often monolingual in Kalaallisut, a language which is extraordinarily difficult to learn as an adult. In contrast, although Imperial Russian expansion had reached the far eastern Pacific coast by 1639, albeit in small numbers as explorers and trappers, there is no current evidence that they made any attempts to learn or record the languages they encountered. Rather, the earliest recordings of the languages of Siberia and the Russian Far North were made only in the late nineteenth century by explorers and political exiles.

Tracking down resources on the languages of the Russian Arctic is even more challenging as they appear in unlikely places often not readily discoverable due to insufficient cataloguing and lack of digitization. Early phonogram recordings are housed in the Pushkinski dom [Pushkin House] (http://ro.pushkinskijdom.ru/) in St. Petersburg, Russia and a large project led by Tjeerd de Graaf (2009) digitized some of these to improve accessibility. Archives from early Russian explorers are also found in the Kunstkamera (https://www.kunstkamera.ru/), as well as the NYPL and ANLA. More recent linguistic documentation is available in other recognizable language archives and websites, including the Endangered Language Archive (ELAR) (https://www.elararchive.org/) and Kulturstiftung Sibirien [Foundation for Siberian Cultures] (https://dh-north.org/). Plus, just about anything published about Evenki people can be found online at *Evenkiteka* (www.evenkiteka.ru), although that site is limited to published materials.

Despite the great value and utility of these mentioned resources, other challenges remain, including having working knowledge of the requisite contact language(s) because many materials contain descriptions and other essential information, and are catalogued, in at least one colonizing language that may not be English. Moreover, even though English is an Arctic nation-state language due to the United

9 Tracking and Unlocking the Past: Documentation of Arctic Indigenous Languages   195

States' state of Alaska, much scholarly research about the Arctic generally, including about Arctic languages specifically, is not published in English. In fact, sizeable and impressive Arctic collections worldwide are in Danish, Finnish, Japanese, Norwegian, Russian, and Swedish.

9.3 Archives and Repositories

The following is a non-exhaustive list of existing repositories and archives holding Arctic materials. Inclusion of this list in the present chapter is an attempt at beginning an inventory of archives that are paramount for Arctic studies generally and Arctic languages specifically. In addition to physical and digital Arctic archives, there exist many companion and supplementary websites also containing digital files of Arctic relevance. These sites are not included here, however, because they are not archives in the technical sense and can be quite short-lived; that is, there is no guarantee of their long-term viability.

9.3.1 Archives and Repositories Dedicated to Arctic Materials

9.3.1.1 Alaska Native Language Archive (ANLA) (https://www.uaf. edu/anla/)

The ANLA is part of the University of Alaska Fairbanks. The archive houses materials on over 20 Indigenous languages spoken in Alaska, including those not considered to be 'Arctic,' as well as materials on neighbouring languages, both Arctic and non-Arctic. Materials in the archive encompass published and unpublished materials in print, audio, and video formats; linguistic fieldnotes of Alaskan Native languages; wordlists collected by early Arctic explorers; dictionaries; pedagogical items; copies of primary materials. and grey literature of locally- and self-published materials. The Knut Bergslund Special Collection and Bergslund's materials relating to the Kalaallisut (Greenlandic) and Unangan (Aleut) languages are notable features of the archive, as are some original manuscripts from the Russian-American period of the early 1700s to mid-1800s. Much of the ANLA's collection is digitally available and accessible online.

9.3.1.2 Nunatta Katersugaasivia Allagaateqarfialu [Greenland National Archives] (NKA) (https://nka.gl/)

The NKA in Nuuk, Greenland contains language and other materials related to Greenland. Materials are mostly in Kalaallisut or Danish. As mentioned earlier, historical church ledgers are available online, as is the *Umanak* ship guest book, covering the time period from 1949 to 1958, with cargo and guestlists. The NKA also contains governmental records from colonial times and more modern records from Greenland Home Rule instituted in 1979. The holdings include records from trade managers, and private archival records. Most of the collections are accessible after 25 years, although some are held for 80 years until publicly accessible.

9.3.1.3 Kulturstiftung Sibirien [Foundation for Siberian Cultures] (https://dh-north.org/)

Kulturstiftung Sibirien operates *Digital Humanities of the North*, a digital repository of wide-ranging materials on Siberian languages and peoples, including Sámi in Scandinavia, with ethnographies, photographs, and videos. Kulturstiftung Sibirien has its own publishing house, and regularly publishes new material in French, German, Japanese, Russian, and English. The organization's output features a strong focus on the languages of the Russian Far East and, as such, many materials are in Russian and target languages. Kulturstiftung Sibirien's collections are mostly secondary materials, including research and pedagogical products.

9.3.1.4 Kunstkamera (https://www.kunstkamera.ru/)

Located in St. Petersburg, Russia, the Kunstkamera maintains a vast and varied collection of materials that primarily come from scholars, collectors, and other St. Petersburg institutions. The Kunstkamera is also known as the Muzej antropologii i etnografii imeni Petra Velikogo Rossijskoj akademii nauk [Russian Academy of Science's Peter the Great Museum of Anthropology and Ethnography] and is most widely known for keeping Tsar Peter I's (1672–1725) collection of oddities. In addition, the museum contains the archives, field notes, and other materials of various Arctic and Northern ethnographers, as well as those of scholars from the Institute of the Peoples of the North in Leningrad during 1929–1941. Most of the Kunstkamera's collection is digitally unavailable, though there is an online catalogue of archived language-related materials (https://www.kunstkamera.ru/museums_structure/nauchnyj_arhiv_mae).

9.3.1.5 New York Public Library, Archives, and Manuscripts (http://archives.nypl.org/)

The NYPL keeps many materials of the New York Historical Society, including those of Waldemar Bogoras and Waldemar Jochelson, both mentioned earlier. In fact, part of the collection are Jochelson's extensive notes and card files on the Itelmen language of the Kamchatka Peninsula in the Russian Far East. The collection contains five linear feet of Jochelson's papers, including his work on Aleut (i.e., folktales, Aleut-Russian dictionary, and an Aleut grammar) and his extensive

9 Tracking and Unlocking the Past: Documentation of Arctic Indigenous Languages

holdings of Itelmen (Kamchadal) with folktales and dictionary materials. The Bogoras archive is much smaller and focuses on the Aiwan Yupik dialects, annotated by Roman Jakobson. There are with also some folktales in Fox Island Aleut with an interlinear translation by Jay Ransom.

9.3.1.6 Rauner Special Collections (RSC), Vilhjalmur Stefansson Papers (https://archives-manuscripts.dartmouth.edu/repositories/2/resources/1204)

The Rauner Special Collections (RSC) are part of the library system of Dartmouth College in Hanover, New Hampshire. Notably, the RSC contains most of the explorer Vilhjalmur Stefansson's (1879–1962) materials, including his wordlists and language notes. Stefansson's collections of materials also include photographs, reports, and personal correspondence. Among the materials are also works by other researchers on the Arctic peoples whom Stefansson encountered in his explorations. Another part of the collection is the unpublished, 15-volume reference work, the *Encylopedia Arctica* (https://collections.dartmouth.edu/arctica-beta/index.html). Volume 8 is dedicated to the anthropology and archaeology of the Arctic and Volume 10 to the Soviet North. There is scattered information about languages and peoples in both volumes. A brief overview of the project is published in Stefansson (1948), providing a remarkable snapshot view of thinking about the Arctic at the time.

9.3.2 Archives and Repositories Devoted to Individual Languages or Language Families

9.3.2.1 Evenkiteka (https://www.evenkiteka.ru/)

Evenkiteka is a vast repository of digital copies of publications about Evenki people and culture. With an emphasis on the Evenki language, a Tungusic language found over a large area of Siberia, the site contains digitized materials of and on ethnography, folklore, poetry, and much more. The site opened in 2011 and now contains over 300 books and other works in Evenki and other languages (*Evenkiteka*, n.d.).

9.3.2.2 Sámi Archives

The Sámi people are from, and live in, northern Finland, Norway, Russia, and Sweden and Sámi archives are in various places across these countries. The national archivists of Finland, Norway, and Sweden collaborate to make Sámi archives digitally accessible to the disparate Sámi communities across the European and Russian North. Mentioned here are some of the major existing Sámi archives.

First is the Arctic Indigenous Design Archives (AIDA) (https://kansal-lisarkisto.fi/aida/), a tripartite enterprise between the Sámi Arkiiva [Sámi Archives] of the Kansallisarkisto [National Archives of Finland] (https://kansal-lisarkisto.fi/); the Ájtte, Svenskt fjäll- och samemuseum [Swedish Mountain and Sámi Museum] (https://www.ajtte.com/) in northern Sweden; and the Sámi allaskuvla [Sámi University of Applied Sciences] (https://samas.no/nb) in northern Norway. Many of the holdings contain material culture, as well as language-related materials.

Maintained by the Kansalliskirjasto [National Library of Finland] (https://www.kansalliskirjasto.fi/), Finna.fi (n.d.) (https://www.finna.fi/) provides access to an extensive network of the country's libraries, archives, and museums, including immense records of scientific and cultural materials relevant throughout Finland. More specifically, physical archives for Sámi in Finland are found in Inari (https://arkisto.fi/samiarchives) in the far north of the country. The Arkivverket [National Archives of Norway] (https://www.arkivverket.no/) maintains the Samisk arkiv [Sámi Archives] in Norway (https://www.arkivverket.no/om-oss/samisk-arkiv) in Kautekeino. In Sweden, and in addition to the Ájtte museum mentioned previously, the Riksarkivet [National Archives of Sweden] (https://riksarkivet.se/) offers plenty of digitized Sámi content.

9.3.3 General Language Archives

9.3.3.1 Endangered Languages Archive (ELAR) (https://www. elararchive.org/)

The Endangered Languages Archive (ELAR) was created in 2002 in conjunction with the Endangered Languages Documentation Programme (ELDP) (https://www.eldp.net/) and contains content and links to an abundance of language mate-rials (e.g., audio, video, transcriptions, translations, dictionaries, and primers). The scope of ELAR extends to languages spoken all over the world, including Arctic languages.

9.3.3.2 Documentation of Endangered Languages (DoBeS) (https://dobes. mpi.nl/)

The DoBeS Archive takes its name from the original German name of the project, Dokumentation Bedrohte Sprachen, and is funded by Volkswagung Stiftung. The archive contains materials collected by researchers, some receiving DoBeS funding, and accepts new deposits. Arctic languages covered in the DoBeS Archive include Délı̨nę in northern Canada and Kola Sámi, Enets, Forest Nenets, and Even in north-ern Russia.

9 Tracking and Unlocking the Past: Documentation of Arctic Indigenous Languages

9.3.3.3 California Language Archive (CLA) (https://cla.berkeley.edu/)

The California Language Archive (CLA) at the University of California Berkeley is both a physical and digital archive dedicated to the Indigenous languages of the Americas. The CLA (n.d.) was formally established in the early 1950s as the Survey of California Indian Languages. Regarding Arctic languages, the archive contains images and recordings pertaining to Alaska and northern Canada.

9.4 Documentation in Northeast Asia: Archives in Yakutsk, Russia

As an illustrative example and descriptive case study of Arctic records, the chapter now turns to the archives in Yakutsk in the Republic of Sakha (Yakutia). During the Soviet period, this region was officially known as the Yakut Autonomous Soviet Socialist Republic, or Yakut ASSR, founded on 27 April 1922 until 1991 when it was transformed into the modern Republic of Sakha (Yakutia). As the name suggests, there are two ethnonyms at play for referring to the majority population and language of the region: the Sakha people and language, and the Yakut people and language. *Sakha* is a Turkic language (ISO 639-3 sah), named from the English version of the word *saxa* from the proto-Turkic word **jaka,* meaning edge or collar. The alternate name, *Yakut,* or *jakut,* is a translation from Russian adjective *jakutskij,* or the noun *jakut,* which is itself derived from the Tungusic name for the people *yeket* (Forsyth, 1992, p. 52). For present purposes, the name as it occurs in the Sakha language is used, however, Russian-language sources instead mostly use the word Yakut to this day.

Although many resources are housed locally, documentation of the languages of the Sakha Republic are also found in international archives because much research has been conducted by foreign specialists or funded by external granting agencies. The Manuscript Department of the Institute of Humanitarian Research and the Problems of Indigenous Minorities of the North, formally known as the Manuscript Fond of the Archives of the Yakut Scientific Centre, contains valuable original sources on the languages and cultures of ethnic communities of North Asia, including the Yakuts (Sakha), Evenki (or Tungus), Even (or Lamuts), Dolgans, Yukaghirs, and the Old Believer Russian population. Because the names of these groups have varied over time, all possible names must be known to locate materials related to them. Moreover, linguistic classification has changed throughout history; for example, Dolgan historically is treated as a dialect of Sakha and the two distinct Yukaghir languages (i.e., Forest and Tundra) are considered a single language in official Russian documents and, thus, are treated collectively in the Russian archives.

At present, the archive collection of the Manuscript Department consists of about 6895 items in two fonds: (1) Fonds No. 4: Dejateli nauki, literatury i istorii [Workers of science, literature, and history], and (2) Fonds No. 5: Institut jazyka, literatury i istorii Sibirskogo otdelenija Akademii nauk SSR [Institute of Language, Literature, and History of the Siberian Branch of the Academy of Sciences of the USSR]. Fonds No. 4 contains materials from 1730 to 2006 and includes a large corpus of the written heritage of the first Sakha writers Alexei Eliseevich Kulakovsky (1877–1926), Anempodist Ivanovich Sofronov (1886–1935), Nikolai Denisovich Neustroev (1895–1929), as well as materials of the first scientists to study North-East Asia: Semen Andreyevich Novgorodov (1892–1924), Petr Vonifat'evich Sleptsov (1880–1932), and Gavril Vasilyevich Ksenofontov (1889–1938). In addition, Fonds No. 4 contains materials of the research society Sakha keskile [The Future of the Sakha], which operated during 1925–1929, as well as documents of the Sakha Committee for Written Language at the Sakha Central Executive Committee during 1928–1930. Fonds No. 5 consists of materials from 1905 to 2011, including an array of scientific documentation of the Institute of Humanitarian Research and the Problems of Indigenous Minorities of the North since its foundation in 1935. The materials in Fonds 5 comprise field expeditions, scientific reports, excerpts from archival documents, and handwritten records of oral intangible heritage of the peoples of the Republic of Sakha (Yakutia) with local peculiarities.

Within Fonds No. 4 is Ksenofontov's personal collection, comprising 18 recordings, albeit incomplete, of the Sakha epic *Olonkho* with 50 tales, over 200 legends, and more than 100 texts on shamanism; these were recorded by Ksenofontov in 1925–1926. Ksenofontov's expedition covered a route from the Republic of Sakha (Yakutia) all the way west to Western Buryatia, beginning in Yakutsk and following the route: Toyon Ary Island, Western Kangalass District, Srednevilyuysk District, Vilyuysk, Verkhnevilyuysk, Markha, Nyurba, Sheya, Suntar, Khochin District, Brangatskij village, Chona River, Erbogachen, Nizhnyaya Tunguska River, Krasnoyarsk, and Khakassia, ending in Western Buryatia.

Fonds No. 4 also contains Sleptsov's personal collection of early manuscripts and materials from expeditions to the Bulun District in 1924 and Khatango-Anabar District from 1928 to 1929, both part of the Yakut ASSR. The philological portion of the collection contains *Russko-jakutsko-tungusskij slovar'* [The Russian-Sakha-Tungus (Evenki) Dictionary] (material 298, sheet 38); *Nazvanija predmetov domashnego obixoda* [The Names of Household Items] in the Dolgan language (material 287, sheet 36); and *Etnograficheskie zametki iz zhizni Bulunskogo uezda* [Ethnographic Notes from the Life of Bulun District] (material 292, sheet 78). Figure 9.1 is taken from Sleptsov's materials; it is a representative page from the handwritten manuscript of his trilingual dictionary from 1908.

A significant place in the Fonds No. 4 collection belongs to the materials of the folklore and dialectological expeditions of the researchers Sesen Bolo Dyachkovsky Dmitry Ivanovich (1905–1948) and Andrej Andreevich Savvin (1896–1951) of the Institute of Language and Culture of the Yakut ASSR during 1938–1939 in Vilyui District and 1939–1941 in the northern districts of Abyisk, Allaihisky, and Bulunsk. Figure 9.2 provides a fragment from Savvin's records of the Sakha text *Aiyyhyt algyha* [The Good Wishes of Aiyyhyt]. In Sakha mythology, Aiyyhyt is the patron goddess of fertility who brings children to people and gives offspring to domestic animals.

9 Tracking and Unlocking the Past: Documentation of Arctic Indigenous Languages 201

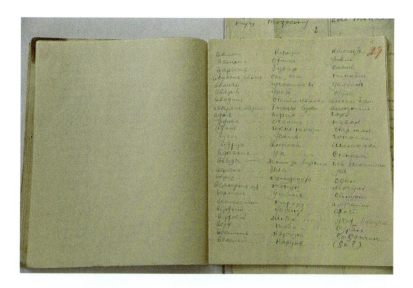

Fig. 9.1 *Russko-jakutsko-tungusskij slovar'* [The Russian-Sakha-Tungus Dictionary] written by P. V. Sleptsov in 1908. Figure credit: Manuscript Department of the Institute for Humanities Research and Indigenous Studies of the North, Siberian Branch of Russian Academy of Sciences. Funds No. 5, inventory 3, matter 298, sheet 29

Among Bolo's and Savvin's expedition materials are texts of the *Olonkho*, the Sakha national epic, a series of poetic tales ranging in length from 10 to 10,000 verses. Many of the texts are believed to predate the migration of the Sakha to northeast Russia in the fourteenth century, making them among the oldest known Turkic epics. In 2008, the *Olonkho* was inscribed in UNESCO's (2022) Intangible Cultural Heritage list. The Manuscript Division has written records of legendary *Olonkho* narrators such as Semen Nikolaevich Karataev's *Tong Saar-buhatyir* [Impressive Cold Hero], Semen Semenovich Afanasiev's *Odun Churaa* [Upper Chura], and Mitrofan Zaxarovich Martynov's *Oğo Duolan* [Huge Child]. The archives also contain audio recordings but access to them is closed. The collection also includes Bolo's recordings of shamanic incantations and incantations into the upper and lower worlds as chanted by the 84-year-old shaman Spiridon Gerasimovich Ignatyev, as well as Savvin's recordings of the incantations *Kut araaryyta* [Division of the Soul] and *Doidu ichchitiger kiyiriya* [An Appeal to the Earth Spirit] from shaman Vasilij Nikolaevich Dmitriev. Both Bolo and Savvin created a rich collection of different genres of oral literature, including *byrgy sehenen* [legends], *ostuoruya* [fairy tales], *ühuyayen* [myths], and *nomokh* [legends]; shorter text types such as *taabyryn* [riddles], *chabyrğakh* [sayings], *ös hohono* [proverbs], *tyl nomoğo* [proverbs], variations of *yrya* [songs] about the universe, seasons, natural phenomena, birds, and animals.

Several resources focused on the languages of the Sakha region are contained within Fonds No. 4. These resources pertain to descriptions of Dolgan, a Turkic variety that is closely related to Sakha and historically classified as a dialect of

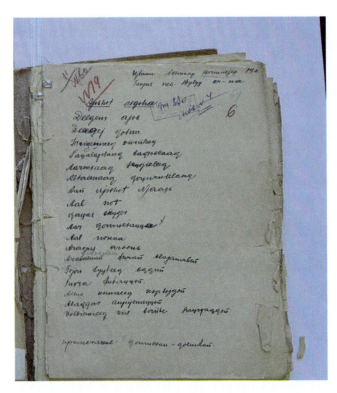

Fig. 9.2 *Aiyyhyt algyha* [Good Wishes of Aiyyhyt] recorded by A. A. Savvin in 1938. Figure credit: Manuscript Department of the Institute for Humanities Research and Indigenous Studies of the North, Siberian Branch of Russian Academy of Sciences. Funds No. 5, inventory 3, matter 101, sheet 6

Sakha, not a distinct language. Much study of Dolgan has been focused in the Taimyr Region to the east of the Sakha Republic and these resources include: *Jazyk dolgan Turuxanskogo kraja* [The Dolgan Language of the Turukhan Territory], *Materialy po govoram (terminy) dulgano-jakutov Turuxanskogo kraja na slovax kuljatskix jakutov* [Materials on the Dolgan-Yakut Dialects (Terminology) of the Turukhan Territory in the Words of the Kulat Yakuts], and *Dulgan-saxalaryy tyyllara* [Dolgan-Sakha Language]. Additional resources relate to Chukchi, including *Imennye zvanija luoreovetlanov Nižnekolymskogo rajona Jakutskoj SSR* [Names of Luorovetlans (Chukchi) in the Nizhnekolymsk District of the Yakut ASSR], a record of 57 personal names of the Chukchi living in the Khalarchin Tundra translated into Sakha with comments by Bolo (file 449, sheet 14). The collection further includes *Materialy po govoram evenkov/evenov Nižnekolymskogo rajona* [Materials on the Evenki/Even Dialects of the Nizhnekolymsk District] with interesting records of the *xangaayy* [dancing shouts] (13 words in total), seen in Fig. 9.3.

Finally, Fonds No. 4 contains a word list from Kolmya Evenki dialects (124 words) and Indigenous names of natives (i.e., the Evenki of the Far East, coastal

9 Tracking and Unlocking the Past: Documentation of Arctic Indigenous Languages

Fig. 9.3 *Tanceval'nye vozglasy kolymskix evenov* [Dancing Shouts of the Kolyma Even] recorded by G. N. Tretyakov in 1940. Figure credit: Manuscript Department of the Institute for Humanities Research and Indigenous Studies of the North, Siberian Branch of Russian Academy of Sciences. Funds No. 5, inventory 3, matter 442, sheet 4

Chukchi, Koryaks, Yukaghirs, Chuvans, Sakha, and Russians) recorded in Even and translated into Sakha, with some parts in Russian. Archival data indicate that despite the construction of the 'ethnic' identity of the peoples of the North during both the Imperial and Soviet periods, such identifiers as Tungus, Lamuts, Chukchi and Yukaghirs existed rather formally until the 1970s. In everyday life, they continued to use 'old' identities—both their own and those of neighbouring peoples—to navigate in social space. In particular, according to the materials of the scientific expedition of Bolo, the Lower Kolyma Evens called themselves *yvyn*, while the Chukchi identified them as *xórom-tele*; the Chukchi, they called *luoravetlanami* or *chauchu*; the reindeer group were called *heej-ex*; those who roamed the Dezhnev Cape on dogs were called *kauralit*; Koryaks were *chauchi-ba* or *lich'e-tanin*; Chuvans were called *buyat'i* [reindeer]; Yukaghirs, *alad'i* or *hul-hacha*; Sakha people were called *n'oxo*; and Russians, *n'uch*.

For many representatives of northern communities seeking a foothold for their identity, language, and culture in the modern world, archival sources can help to at least partially fill in some of the lost cultural memory and social experience accumulated throughout their pre-Russian history, applying not only to ethnonyms but also to personal so-called pagan names and cultural practices that were lost during the Christianization of the Republic of Sakha (Yakutia) and conversion to the Russian anthroponymic system, as well as during Sovietization.

Fonds No. 5 is of particular interest for researchers of Turkic oral epic traditions and the Sakha *Olonkho*. The archives hold more than 600 items about the heritage of the peoples of Yakutia. These materials, recorded during 1940–1946 as part of a Soviet project collecting the best ethnic traditions of the peoples of the region, include records of 150 full texts of the *Olonkho* and 80 shorter versions performed by 83 different *Olonkho* performers from 13 regions of the Republic of Sakha (Yakutia). The goal of the Soviet project was to compile a single authoritative version of the *Olonkho* together with records of rare details of verbal culture. When completed, the project had more than 160 full versions, excerpts, and short summaries of the *Olonkho*.

In addition to records of early forms of the *Olonkho*, Fonds No. 5 also contains *kyryry* [shamanic incantations], *algys* [good wishes], *kyryys* [curses], and occasional rites, all recorded in their living, natural forms. These performances most likely will not be repeated again in human history. Noteworthy is that this oral tradition preserved *Olonkho* epics by famous performers of the seventeenth century such as Yrya Chongkunaan [Singer with a Piercing Voice], Yrya Chekat Tur [The Singer Chekat Tur], Sehenneh Selykidien [The Good Storyteller Selykidien], and Oloodo (personal name)—that have been maintained in today's living folklore. Within the *chabyrğakh* [tongue twisters] genre, the text *Bilbit-korbut* (*Knew-saw*, about a knowledgeable man who is always astute and alert) preserves layers from the legendary singers of these tongue twisters, or *chabyrgasyt*, who lived in the second half of the nineteenth and early twentieth centuries in the Meghina District of Dyulay-Boken.

Fonds No. 5's assortment of spiritual folklore, with approximately 500 samples of mainly shamanic texts, is recorded from the mouths of the bearers of shamanic tradition themselves, presenting thorough accounts of shaman birth and initiation, ritual activities, and healing practices. The collection includes records of rare shamanic incantations to deities and spirits of Earth, water, and fire as descriptions of live ceremonies in real time aimed at the maintenance of harmonic interactions between nature and humankind. In 1944, the journalist Petr Terent'evich Stepanov from the Megino-Kangalassk District managed to record six live shamanic ceremonies performed in archaic shamanic language as recited by the Nakhar shaman Petr Alekseevich Abramov-Alaadya. Samples of archaic *Olonkho* texts were also recorded from the Sakha shamans Nikita Petrovich Yakovlev-Kuruppa and Ivan Andreevich Suzdalov-Sappalai.

9.4.1 Palaeographic Features of Manuscripts from the 1908–1940s

All entries in the Yakutsk archives relating to the period 1908–1940s are made in student or ordinary notebooks, with normal standard writing paper (A4) or nonstandard (15 × 11 cm) paper, written either in pencil or black or blue ink. Text is written in Romanized Sakha language and mostly double-sided throughout the notebooks. Most of the records are in satisfactory condition, but some are at risk of disappearing through erasure and wear-and-tear rubbing, folding, and tearing of the paper.

9 Tracking and Unlocking the Past: Documentation of Arctic Indigenous Languages   205

Among the philological sources are materials of the Indigir ethnographic-linguistic expedition of Teodor Abramovich Shub, Nikolaj Alekseevich Gabyshev, and others. These materials include the *Zapisi po folkloru Russkogo Ust'ja* [Folklore records of the Russian Ust'], various songs, *bylinas* [oral epics], and tales of Russian Old Believers from the village of Polar in the Allaihov District (matter 769, sheet 49) and Kosuhino village (inventory 3, matter 769, sheet 203), as well as records of word formation and suffixes, descriptive phrases, words denoting nature and natural phenomena, dictionaries with lexical meanings, and dialect dictionaries made in the village of Russkoye Ustye (inventory 3, matter 768b, sheet 775). Figure 9.4a, b show excerpts from a word list of the Old Believers' Russian dialect in the Russko-Ustinsky region where Russkoe Ustye is located in the far northern part of the Sakha Republic.

9.4.2 Palaeographic Features of Manuscripts from the 1950s and 1970s

Records from the 1950s and 1970s were written in an ordinary A4-sized standard inventory notebook of yellow writing paper and on non-standard cards and sheets of paper in plain pencil, ink, and ballpoint pen; later records were composed using a

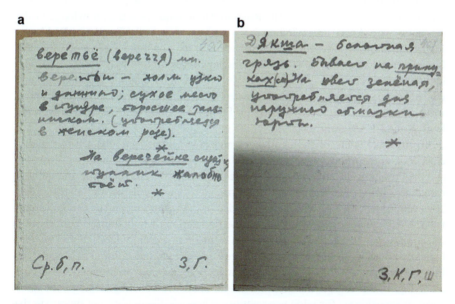

Fig. 9.4 (a) Word sample in Russian from the Russko-Ustinsky region. The word *veret'e* was recorded by G. A. Shub, N. A. Gabyshev, et al. in 1946. Figure credit: Manuscript Department of the Institute for Humanities Research and Indigenous Studies of the North, Siberian Branch of Russian Academy of Sciences. Fund No. 5, inventory 3, matter 7668, sheet 400. (b) Word sample in Russian from the Russko-Ustinsky region. The word *jakša* was recorded by G. A. Shub, N. A. Gabyshev, et al. in 1946. Figure credit: Manuscript Department of the Institute for Humanities Research and Indigenous Studies of the North, Siberian Branch of Russian Academy of Sciences. Fund No. 5, inventory 3, matter 7668, sheet 407

typewriter. Text is written using the Cyrillic alphabet in Sakha, Russian, Evenki, Even, and Chukchi, and entries are made on either one side or both sides of the paper. Most of the records are in satisfactory physical condition, but some are yellowed and worn, and some of the erasable records have been erased. Folding and tearing is evident in some of the paper, and some pages are missing entirely.

9.5 Conclusion

One of the biggest challenges in working with archival materials of Arctic languages is locating them. There are limited dedicated language archives for Arctic materials, with the Alaska Native Language Archive an exception. Recent recordings of language materials can be found in general language archives. Due to the current standards for language documentation, such recordings are often readily usable for researchers as many have audio and video and are transcribed and glossed. But these conditions refer primarily to recordings made in the last few decades. For earlier records, a trove of materials can be found in other archives, and in particular archives of Arctic explorers and ethnographers. Finding such materials requires some detective work, as it may be necessary to first identify an explorer or expedition that made contact with Arctic speakers. Thus, for example, a search of early records of languages spoken in the Russian Arctic requires some knowledge of the Russians who knew these languages, such as Vladimir Bogoraz, Waldemar Jochelson, and Lev Shternberg. In other areas, it may be more a question of identifying linguists who worked with a specific language and finding where they deposited their materials. Thus, the archive of the Norwegian linguist Knud Bergsland, who did extensive work on Aleut, is located in the Alaska Native Language Archive, while more recent linguists working on Even have archived their materials in the DoBeS and ELAR archives.

To illustrate some of the challenges and possibilities, this chapter provided a close look at the Manuscript Department of the Institute of Humanitarian Research and the Problems of Indigenous Minorities of the North. The linguistic and cultural resources as described here do not comprise an exhaustive listing of their holdings, however. Rather, they provide a general idea of the various resources and key archival Yakutsk collections that constitute the foundation of the cultural memory of a selection of peoples across North Asia. The methodologically modern and technologically advanced documentation of linguistic diversity and cultural heritage at the Institute currently is hampered by the lack of appropriate equipment and digital archiving. In this regard, the Institute cannot make available digital linguistic databases or repositories for wide accessibility. These challenges are not unique to the Institute, however, as Arctic language archives and resources generally are difficult to access.

9 Tracking and Unlocking the Past: Documentation of Arctic Indigenous Languages

Acknowledgments This chapter was written within the framework of the project "Preservation of Linguistic and Cultural Diversity and Sustainable Development of the Arctic and Subarctic of the Russian Federation" via a mega-grant from the Government of the Russian Federation (No. 075-15-2021-616). Author Vanda Ignatieva expresses gratitude to the Centre for Collective Research at the Institute of Humanitarian Research and the Problems of Indigenous Minorities of the North, Siberian Branch of the Russian Academy of Sciences for the opportunity to conduct research on the scientific equipment purchased with the help of grant No. 13.CKK.21.0016.

References

California Language Archive (CLA). (n.d.). *History*. https://bit.ly/47Q6Gri. Accessed 10 Dec 2023.
de Graaf, T. (2009). Das phonogrammarchiv am Institut für Russische Literatur (Pushkinski Dom) der Russischen Akademie der Wissenschaften in St. Petersburg [The phonogram archive at the Institute of Russian Literature (Pushkin House) of the Russian Academy of Sciences in St. Petersburg]. In E. Kasten (Ed.), *Schamanen Sibiriens, Magier-mittler-heiler* [Shamans of Siberia: Magicians, mediators, healers] (p. 227). Reimer Verlag.
de Reuse, W. J. (1996). Chukchi, English, and Eskimo: A survey of jargons in the Chukotka peninsula area. In E. Håkon Jahr & I. Broch (Eds.), *Language contact in the Arctic: Northern pidgins and contact languages* (pp. 47–62). de Gruyter.
Egede, P. H. (1766). *Testamente Nutak, eller, det Nye Testament: oversat i det Grönlandske Sprog, med Forklaringer, Paralleler og udförlige Summarier* [The New Testament, or the New Testament: Translated into the Greenlandic language, with explanations, parallels texts, and detailed summaries]. Gerhard Giese Salikath.
Evenkiteka. (n.d.). *O biblioteke* [About the library]. https://bit.ly/47WwB0E. Accessed 10 Dec 2023.
Finna.fi. (n.d.). *Finna—hakupalvelujen kokonaisuus* [Finna—Search services as a whole]. https://bit.ly/46U8CxJ. Accessed 10 Dec 2023.
Forsyth, J. (1992). *A history of the peoples of Siberia: Russia's north Asian colony 1581–1990.* Cambridge University Press.
Hoh, A. (2016, November 7). *Atuagagdliutit*: The first Inuit newspaper published in Greenland (*Kalâtdlit-Nunât*). http://bit.ly/3WNMxf7. Accessed 10 Dec 2023.
Kleinschmidt, S. (1871). *Den Grønlandske ordbog* [The Greenlandic dictionary]. L. Kleins bogtrykkeri. https://bit.ly/3RfGH5A. Accessed 10 Dec 2023.
Nordenskiöld, A. E. (2012). *The voyage of the Vega around Asia and Europe, with a historical review of previous journeys along the north coast of the Old World* (A. Leslie, Trans.). Cambridge University Press. (Original work published 1882).
Rasmussen, C. (1873). *Supplement til Den Grønlandske ordbog* [Supplement to the Greenlandic dictionary]. https://bit.ly/47QTq5B. Accessed 10 Dec 2023.
Schultz-Lorentzen, C. W. (1926). *Den Grønlandske ordbog* [The Greenlandic dictionary]. https://bit.ly/3v0VIR1. Accessed 10 Dec 2023.
Schultz-Lorentzen, C. W. (1927). *Dictionary of the West Greenland Eskimo language*. https://bit.ly/47SFKXS. Accessed 10 Dec 2023.
Stefansson, V. (1948). Encyclopedia Arctica. *Arctic, 1*(1), 44–46.
UNESCO. (2022). *Olonkho, Yakut heroic epics*. http://bit.ly/3HjppPO. Accessed 10 Dec 2023.

Chapter 10
Enhancing Digital Libraries through Digital Storytelling: The Case of the Inuvialuit Digital Library

Sharon Farnel ⓘ**, Ali Shiri, Ethel-Jean Gruben, Beverly Siliuyaq Amos, and Lena Kotokak**

Abstract Indigenous communities around the world have been turning to digital media and platforms to preserve and revitalize their culture, language, and ways of life as part of their broader struggle for self-determination and self-representation. This chapter provides an overview of digital storytelling as a methodology and provides examples of its use in systems and approaches for working with Indigenous communities. The chapter introduces the *Inuvialuit Voices* project, a federally funded collaborative project underway in Canada to explore the use of digital storytelling technologies to enhance digital libraries and provide a seamless platform for cultural heritage preservation and access in Indigenous communities. In addition, the chapter outlines the benefits of a real-time, seamless digital storytelling system, presents a community-focused participatory design methodology as a basis for working with Indigenous communities, and addresses the contribution of information practitioners to the project.

Keywords Arctic cultural heritage · Digital archives · Digital libraries · Digital storytelling · Indigenous storytelling · Indigenous knowledge · Inuvialuit Settlement Region

---

S. Farnel (✉) · A. Shiri
University of Alberta, Edmonton, AB, Canada
e-mail: sharon.farnel@ualberta.ca

E.-J. Gruben · B. S. Amos · L. Kotokak
Inuvialuit Cultural Centre, Inuvialuit Regional Corporation, Inuvik, NT, Canada

© The Author(s), under exclusive license to Springer Nature
Switzerland AG 2024
S. Acadia (ed.), *Library and Information Sciences in Arctic and Northern Studies*, Springer Polar Sciences, https://doi.org/10.1007/978-3-031-54715-7_10

10.1 Introduction

Article 13 of the United Nations' (2007, pp. 12–13) *Declaration on the Rights of Indigenous Peoples* states that "Indigenous Peoples have the right to revitalize, use, develop and transmit to future generations their histories, languages, oral traditions, philosophies, writing systems" and literatures. The Truth and Reconciliation Commission of Canada's (2015, p. 2) *Calls to Action* reiterate and clarify the rights of Indigenous Peoples by stating that "the preservation, revitalization, and strengthening of Aboriginal languages and cultures are best managed by Aboriginal people and communities." These inalienable rights are evidenced by the fact that Indigenous communities around the world turn to digital media and platforms to preserve and revitalize their culture, language, and ways of life as part of their broader struggle for self-determination and self-representation (Ginsburg, 2016; O'Sullivan, 2013). These initiatives, though leveraging contemporary technology, continue to be deeply rooted in Indigenous traditions such as storytelling. The result is a trend toward integrating storytelling practices into digital platforms to allow for a more dynamic, holistic approach to memory making. According to the Canadian Federation of Library Associations Truth and Reconciliation Committee Report (2017), the role of librarians and information professionals is to work collaboratively in the spirit of reconciliation with Indigenous Peoples to "support and promote Indigenous Libraries, Archives and Cultural Memory Institutions and library, archives and cultural memory organizations serving Indigenous People" (p. 17).

This chapter introduces a federally funded collaborative project underway in Canada that explores the use of digital storytelling technologies in enhancing digital libraries and providing a seamless platform for Indigenous community cultural heritage preservation and access. The project, *Inuvialuit Voices* (n.d.), is currently researching and developing an interactive, real-time digital storytelling system for the Inuvialuit Digital Library (https://inuvialuitdigitallibrary.ca/), which provides access to cultural and language resources by and for the Inuvialuit communities in the Northwest Territories. Using the project as a case study, the role of digital technologies in preserving diverse First Nations, Métis, and Inuit heritage, memory, and identity is examined; the benefits of a real-time, seamless digital storytelling system is outlined; and the community-focused participatory design methodology as an example of how library and information science (LIS) practitioners and researchers can work with Indigenous communities to develop such systems is presented.

10.2 The Inuvialuit and the Inuvialuit Settlement Region

The Inuvialuit, meaning 'real people' in Inuvialuktun, are the Inuit of the western Arctic region of what is now Canada and are likely the descendants of the Thule people who inhabited the Bering Sea region, eventually migrating to the areas around the mouth of the Mackenzie River. Even though the Inuvialuit actively participate in modern society and generally welcome the modern conveniences of life, they retain strong, traditional ties to the Western Arctic lands (Arnold et al., 2011; *Inuvialuit Living History Project*, n.d.; Inuvialuit Regional Corporation, n.d.). In 1984, the Inuvialuit represented by the Committee for Original Peoples' Entitlement, and the Government of Canada represented by the Minister of the then-called Department of Indian Affairs and Northern Development, signed the *Inuvialuit Final Agreement* (Indian and Northern Affairs Canada, 1984). This comprehensive land claim agreement acknowledged Inuvialuit ownership of lands within their traditional homeland, now known as the Inuvialuit Settlement Region (ISR) (Fig. 10.1) and was designed to preserve and promote Inuvialuit culture and values, ensuring that the Inuvialuit were equal participants in northern social,

Fig. 10.1 Map of the Inuvialuit Settlement Region (ISR), Canada. (Map credit: Joint Secretariat)

economic, and environmental activities and initiatives (Inuvialuit Regional Corporation, 2018).

The ISR covers approximately 90,000 km^2 (34,750 mi^2) in the northern Northwest Territories of Canada and includes both Inuvialuit private and territorial lands. The population of the region is roughly 6500 persons, the majority of whom reside in the region's capital of Inuvik. The other five communities within the region are Aklavik, Paulatuk, Sachs Harbour, Tuktoyaktuk, and Ulukhaktok (Inuvialuit Regional Corporation, n.d.). Many Inuvialuit also make their homes in southern Canada and elsewhere (Smith, 2018).

The language of the Inuvialuit is collectively known as Inuvialuktun and consists of three dialects or languages: Uummarmiutun, meaning 'people of the evergreens,' spoken in Aklavik and Inuvik; Sallirmiutun, meaning 'people closest to the shore,' spoken in Paulatuk, Sachs Harbour, and Tuktoyaktuk; and Kangiryuarmiutun, meaning 'people of the large bay,' spoken in Ulukhaktok. Inuvialuktun is an endangered language, but many community initiatives and efforts are underway to ensure continued use and preservation (Inuvialuit Cultural Centre, n.d.; Inuvialuit Regional Corporation, n.d.).

10.3   The Inuvialuit Cultural Centre and the Inuvialuit Digital Library

The Inuvialuit Cultural Centre Pitquhiit-Pitqusiit (ICRC) (Fig. 10.2) was established in 1998 in Tuktoyaktuk with a mandate to preserve and revitalize Inuvialuit language and culture, as well as create resources for teaching in the ISR. In 2000, the ICRC relocated to Inuvik to better serve all communities within the region through the development of teaching and learning resources, organization and hosting of culture and language workshops and projects, and provision of support to individuals and groups for developing and carrying out their own culture and language activities (Inuvialuit Cultural Centre, n.d.; Inuvialuit Cultural Centre, University of Alberta, 2014).

The ICRC staff are community members and cultural heritage practitioners, entrusted by the Inuvialuit with stewarding their culture and language resources, as well as engaging the entire community in the sharing and creation of knowledge. However, the ICRC faced challenges in making its growing number of digital resources—both born digital and digitized—available to community members not located in Inuvik. In 2013, the manager of the ICRC at the time, who also held a master's in library science degree from the University of Alberta, reached out to librarians and LIS researchers at the university to discuss possible approaches to addressing the challenge of access. Through collaborative discussion and exploration, the idea for a digital library was formed and the *Digital Library North* project was born (Shiri et al., 2013).

The *Digital Library North* (DLN) (https://sites.google.com/ualberta.ca/dln/home) project was a four-year collaboration, from 2014–2018, between LIS

Fig. 10.2 Photograph of the Inuvialuit Cultural Centre Pitquhiit-Pitqusiit (ICRC) in Inuvik. (Photo credit: A. Shiri)

researchers and librarians at the University of Alberta, staff at the ICRC in Inuvik, and communities within the ISR to develop a digital library infrastructure to support access to cultural resources. Project research and development were carried out along several themes: digital libraries, culturally responsive metadata, information needs and behaviours, stewardship of cultural heritage, multilingual user interfaces, user evaluation, theories and methods of community driven research, and appropriate partnerships and relationship building. The goals of the project were to investigate and identify the information needs and seeking behaviours of community members within the ISR, develop a digital library of cultural heritage resources, explore appropriate methodologies for treatment of Indigenous cultural heritage information, create a culturally appropriate metadata framework as a basis for resource description, develop requirements for a multilingual user interface for the digital library, conduct a user-centred evaluation of the digital library, develop a sustainability strategy for the digital library to ensure long-term access to digital resources, and provide training in information management to local project collaborators and participants (*Digital Library North*, n.d.).

The digital library that grew out of the DLN project is the Inuvialuit Digital Library (IDL), which soft-launched in late 2017 and had a more formal launch on 5 June 2019 to coincide with Inuvialuit Day. A screenshot of the IDL homepage taken in 2021 is provided as Fig. 10.3. As of July 2021, the IDL includes just under 5700 digital resources of four different types (i.e., audio, video, text, and image) organized into 53 collections. The resources are organized and described according to a dynamic community-driven metadata framework, surfaced through collaboration and iterative development, both of which are ongoing. The IDL offers multiple pathways into its collections (e.g., by resource type, place, curated exhibit, or theme). Basic and advanced search allows targeted access to collections, and rich metadata with linking fields enable navigation through resources that share one or more properties such as subject, language, people, or place. Although detailed statistics on IDL usage are not yet available, conversations with ICRC and IRC staff, as well as the regular flow of comments and queries about the site that come into the IDL email, indicate strong awareness and use of the IDL.

The platform chosen for the IDL was Omeka (https://omeka.org/classic/). Community collaborators indicated that the platform used must be cost-effective, ideally free and open-source; flexible in terms of customization and adding additional functionality; easy to install, configure, and upgrade; capable of handling multiple layers of access permissions; and able to handle multilingual content and interfaces. The other platforms of Fedora, Mukurtu, DSpace, and Drupal were also examined, but Omeka was the best choice based on broad community uptake, project team expertise and experience, and long-term sustainability. Although there may already be existing commercial platforms (e.g., social media) that serve these needs, issues of ownership, intellectual property, privacy, and lack of control were of critical importance. Therefore, adoption of a user-friendly, culturally sensitive, non-commercial digital platform was the path chosen.

A project of this size is complex, multifaceted, and not without challenges. Creation and development of the IDL was completed by a project team in Edmonton along with the Arts Resource Centre at the University of Alberta. Eventually, the IDL infrastructure will be maintained and hosted by the Inuvialuit community, and

Fig. 10.3 Screenshot of the Inuvialuit Digital Library (IDL) homepage, 2021. (Screenshot credit: A. Shiri)

steps have been taken to make that transfer when the time is right for the community. The IRC technical lead and team have been involved with the project from the start and have full access to the IDL infrastructure so that they can familiarize themselves with the platform. The final transfer of hosting and maintenance of the IDL will occur when the IRC technical staff indicate that they are ready to take on that responsibility. Much time was spent by the project team gathering input into IDL's design and functionality via interviews and informal conversations, displays and demonstrations at the ICRC as well as locations and events around Inuvik, open houses and user testing sessions with ISR communities, and discussions and information sessions with ICRC staff. All feedback was incorporated into the IDL in an iterative fashion and new information continues to feed into its ongoing development. The ICRC staff continue to add to and enhance the content and descriptions of resources in the IDL based on priorities from users. Understanding and documenting an appropriate structure for knowledge organization and resource description for the IDL is a focus of the collaborative work as evidenced in the way in which IDL is organized and functions. Certain areas of the framework (e.g., definition of more nuanced rights scenarios and expressions for the content, as well as additional organizational paths focused on people, themes, and seasons) are still in need of development.

Although the composition of community and university members involved in the project has changed over the years, commitment to the IDL has not wavered. Positive relationships between university and community members have led to continued efforts to enhance the IDL, and one such effort grew into a new, related project called *Inuvialuit Voices* that focuses on adding real-time digital storytelling functionality to the IDL.

10.4 Digital Storytelling and the Inuvialuit Digital Library: The *Inuvialuit Voices* Project

Inuvialuit Voices, which began in 2019, builds on previous work conducted in the ISR, including development of the IDL, and involves a team of community collaborators from the ICRC, Inuvialuit Regional Corporation (IRC), and University of Alberta. Figure 10.4 shows team members of the *Inuvialuit Voices* project while in Edmonton. The overarching objective of this project is to investigate, develop, and evaluate a real-time user interface that allows for the audio-recording of digital storytelling and implementation of direct commenting into the IDL to facilitate live capturing of Inuit community input, including stories, while interacting with, or for deposit into, the IDL. More specifically, the project aims to establish a novel community-driven participatory design methodology for developing an audio-recording digital storytelling user interface; designing, prototyping, and developing the interface with Inuvialuktun features such as storytelling and commenting functionalities that can be captured in real time; exploring the enhancement of the

Fig. 10.4 The *Inuvialuit Voices* team at lunch in Edmonton, Alberta, Canada. (Photo credit: A. Shiri)

currently available digital materials of cultural heritage within the IDL through real-time stories and comments by Inuvialuit community members; and conducting a community-driven usability evaluation of the real-time digital storytelling and audio-recording interface.

Erstad and Wertsch (2008) argue that narratives are cultural tools that all people relate to and use in activities to make meaning. According to Couros et al. (2013, p. 550), "story or narrative imagining is our primary mode of making meaning and understanding lived experience, both our own and others." For Indigenous Peoples in particular, story is a critical method of sharing and preserving knowledge, culture, and history. Unfortunately, the histories of Indigenous communities have long been excluded or misconstrued in institutionalized settings and have thus been taken up at the grassroots, community level for autonomous documentation (Flinn et al., 2009). Holland and Smith (2000) observe that as Indigenous communities endeavour to maintain their traditional ways of knowing, many are turning to information and communications technologies to sustain and stimulate their Indigenous knowledge traditions. Technology provides opportunities for communities to preserve and pass on their traditional knowledge and stories in their own way and according to their own protocols (Christie, 2005; Eagles et al., 2005; Nakata, 2007). Thus, through digital media projects, Indigenous Peoples foster a sense of community resistance to and power against dominant colonial narratives, exerting control over their collective memory (Flinn et al., 2009, p. 82).

The importance of community networking and community building in the development of digital libraries and archives is widely emphasized in existing literature

(Aparac-Jelušić, 2017; Caidi & Clement, 2004; Williams, 2015). Lynch (2002) notes that digital libraries are not only collections of content and tools that build communities, but also allow members of communities to communicate with each other. Digital storytelling as a powerful technique has tremendous potential for Indigenous communities who are increasingly leveraging technology to bequeath and generate knowledge on their own terms (Christen, 2015; Christie, 2004; Stevens, 2008). As the IDL was developed, valuable feedback was received from community Elders, and members of the community emphasized the need for developing new user interfaces that would allow Elders and members to document stories in Inuvialuktun as well as make comments and corrections in that language directly within the IDL interactively and in real time.

10.5 Digital Storytelling

Digital storytelling is a technique or method that draws on narrative theory which argues that story is a tool for empowerment by allowing individuals and communities to (re)construct and share stories based on their own worldviews (Perone, 2014, p. 114). McWilliam (2008) provides a useful distinction between two types of digital storytelling: specific and generic. Specific digital storytelling refers to the "co-creative filmmaking practice developed by Dana Atchley, Joe Lambert, and Nina Mullen in California in the early 1990s" (p. 146); it follows a standard format and process and has been reproduced in many iterations around the world since its inception. Generic digital storytelling, on the other hand, reflects the myriad ways in which our understanding of what digital storytelling is has evolved, including how it is done, what it is for, and where it is located. This version of digital storytelling is understood broadly as "any media form that digitally facilitates interactive storytelling" (p. 145), or "the whole range of personal stories now being told in potentially public form using digital media resources" (Couldry, 2008, p. 42). Thus, digital storytelling is part of a broader shift away from one-way, top-down models of communication toward two-way, bottom-up models, like those in community and participatory media (McWilliam, 2008, pp. 145–147) and is a "method for local action as well as a means for preservation of local culture" (Bratteteig, 2008, p. 279). Digital storytelling gives voice and agency back to communities and provides the potential for community members to challenge established institutions which, for too long, have held the power to represent Indigenous communities without their input.

Digital storytelling as a bottom-up, user-driven means of applying technology to transform the act of storytelling enables people to connect with objects, places, events, and other people (Detlor et al., 2017; Lambert, 2006; Lundby, 2008). Enhancing the IDL with a mechanism for digital storytelling is both reflective of the living character of the cultural resources it holds and respectful of oral tradition, allowing the resources to come alive through story (Burgess, 2006; Powell, 2007) and generating new resources that aid in knowledge transfer and preservation as well as language revitalization (Christal et al., 2005; Hunter et al., 2003). As noted by Detlor et al. (2017), "digital storytelling can play an important role in strengthening the connection between people and their communities by providing relevant, timely and location-based information" (p. 651).

Digital storytelling methods and platforms are diverse with some delivered in-person while others are online. Several ongoing projects are in the process of integrating, or have already integrated, digital storytelling features via audio features within digital libraries and archives. For example, *Yamoria: The One Who Travels* (https://www.nwtexhibits.ca/yamoria/) is a companion website to a physical exhibit featuring stories of Yamoria, the legendary Dene traveller and lawmaker, as told by Dene Elders. *Tuhaalruuqtut, Ancestral Sounds* (https://www.communitystories.ca/v1/pm_v2.php?lg=English&ex=00000370), part of the Virtual Museum of Canada, gathers stories in English and Inuktitut from Elders of Baker Lake, Nunavut, highlighting the rich traditions and exploits of the Inuit of the eastern Arctic. The *Arviat Iglu* website (https://epe.lac-bac.gc.ca/100/205/301/ic/cdc/arviat/enghome.html) is one of several efforts to support both language learning and the development of traditional skills through the capturing of stories from Elders related to aspects of traditional shelters including the igloo. As part of a larger project to document the impacts of climate change, the Rigolet Inuit Community Government (2017) in Nunatsiavut leveraged digital technology to capture personal narratives from Elders and community members from 2009–2010. Moreover, the *My Word Storytelling and Digital Media Lab* that was a part of the project continues to operate, capturing community stories on a wide range of topics. Finally, Nordin (2020) and Moradi et al. (2020) discuss a project to prototype a potential digital archive and storytelling platform for the Sámi people of Scandinavia.

Mukurtu, Omeka, and Ara Irititja, three digital content management systems used for creating digital libraries and archives, provide functionalities for audio-commenting and recording (Christen, 2008; Omeka Audio-Recorder, 2021; Oppenneer, 2008). The mobile version of Mukurtu allows users to upload media content on-the-go and in real-time (Mukurtu CMS, 2015). Ara Irititja is a platform that is used by *Storylines*, a digital repatriation project for Indigenous Peoples of Australia, and allows text and video annotations (Webb, 2015). In addition, examples of digital technology use for Indigenous language revitalization exist, including learning of the Inuttitut language in Labrador (Dicker et al., 2009), *Blackfoot Lullaby* documentation project (Miyashita & Crow Shoe, 2009), Darug language of the Darug people of Sydney (Kutay, 2013; Kutay & Green, 2013), and use of YouTube as a digital storytelling platform by Inuit youth (Wachowich & Scobie, 2010). The *Inuit Qaujimajatuqangit Adventure* website (http://www.inuitq.ca/), which is bilingual in Inuktitut and English, allows Inuit youth to experience a virtual journey from Nunavut to Cape Dorset with Inuit Elders by participating in an interactive film about the Inuktitut language and the Inuit hero Kiviuq and navigating contemporary challenges (Alexander et al., 2009, p. 232).

While a few of the above projects allow audio commenting, most of them require offline recording and file upload onto a digital library or archive. Therefore, developing seamless, user-friendly, interactive, and real time digital storytelling user interfaces, such as that used in *Inuvialuit Voices*, for digital libraries and archives is of importance because they allow users to interact with digital library content to record their comments and stories to the collection in real time rather than capturing and recording offline for later upload.

10.6 Theoretical and Methodological Considerations

In the *Inuvialuit Voices* project, the digital storytelling interface is still being created through a process of community-based co-design, influenced by Indigenous methodologies. Participatory research focuses on understanding community needs and engaging community members in all research activities (Park, 1993, 1999). As a methodology, participatory design provides a suitable framework for developing systems and technologies in an inclusive and engaging manner. Spinuzzi (2005) argues that participatory design cuts through the entire research project and the goal is not just to empirically understand the activity, but to account for participants' co-interpretation of research, including its development, execution, and evaluation. Bishop et al. (2000, 2003) argues that design and evaluation of community-focused digital library interfaces should include close attention to traditionally marginalized groups in all stages of the system's lifecycle, from design and testing through implementation and evaluation. Oppenneer (2008) argues for design that respects how various Indigenous communities interact with their cultural heritage, as well as technological solutions that adhere to the cultural practices and ways of knowing of those communities. Ethnography has also been used to engage community leaders in the design of community-based information systems (Srinivasan, 2007, p. 723; Srinivasan & Huang, 2005). Crabtree et al. (2000, p. 667) notes that ethnography, with its emphasis on the situational observation of interactions within natural settings, is suitable for gaining a social perspective on how to design systems. In *Inuvialuit Voices*, the idea of digital storytelling based on a community-created digital library originates from the Inuvialuit community and their needs. These methodologies were used extensively in the development and evaluation of the IDL (Rathi et al., 2017; Shiri, 2018; Shiri & Stobbs, 2018).

Developing digital storytelling technologies for Indigenous communities requires community-based and culturally aware methodological frameworks. Lee (2011) and Denzin et al. (2008) report that obtaining Indigenous research participants and involving them in research is challenging due to a long history in which Indigenous communities have not benefited from research results. Balanoff et al. (2006) stresses the need to decolonize methodologies by collaborating with community members at every stage of a research project (Bushnell, 2009; Hollowell & Nicholas, 2009). Elders and community participants must understand the purpose and application of the research, as well as be remunerated for their contributions, given credit for their input, and given the opportunity to review and approve work before it is disseminated (Hollowell & Nicholas, 2009; Tyson, 1999). The First Nations Information Governance Centre (FNIGC) (2014) outlines principles related to data ownership, control, access, and possession—known as OCAP—and recommends that community-based and participatory approaches be the predominant ones within Indigenous research. Through collaboration on the IDL, extensive partnerships were developed with community Elders, leaders, and members in the ISR region, including the IRC, ICRC, Aurora Research Institute, Aurora College, Centennial Public Library, and several community corporations in which digital library workshops were held. These experiences and relationships continue to inform work on the development of the digital storytelling interface and ensure work is community driven.

10.7 Inuvialuit Elders' Storytelling Event

A critical step in developing the digital storytelling interface is gaining a better understanding of in-context storytelling. Towards that goal, the research team organized a four-day storytelling event in November 2019 in Inuvik. The organization of the gathering was driven by our expert community collaborators at the ICRC. Their knowledge and community connections ensured that the local context was considered and accommodated, including the dates of the gathering; who might attend; location; how the days should be scheduled; and what was appropriate in terms of food and beverages, honoraria, and travel and accommodations. Working closely with the local community corporations, the ICRC invited two or three Elders from each of the six ISR communities to attend and share their stories. Representation from each community was important, not only to ensure inclusion of voices from the entire region, but also so speakers from each of the three regional dialects would be in attendance. Also, a deliberate attempt was made to have both Indigenous men's and women's experiences and stories represented. A total of 12 Elders and community members were able to attend.

All 4 days of the event were moderated by the regional language consultant for the ICRC, and most of the stories were told in Inuvialuktun. The consultant invited everyone to introduce themselves and share stories of their own choosing, and presented topics of interest for discussion (e.g., genealogy and the pronunciation of names, preservation of language, etc.). The second day included time spent with the IDL displayed on a smart board so that attendees could explore photo collections as a group and share their recollections about different people and families they saw. This activity was a great way to explore how technology might be incorporated into the storytelling context as well as for listening to the stories people want to share about existing items in the ICRC collections. For this gathering, the goal was to explore storytelling practices and traditions to see how they might be reflected in the online interface while also having the opportunity to listen to and record stories that will be preserved and made available for the community in the future. On the final day, one participant brought some hymnals that included Inuvialuktun translations, and the attendees enjoyed a sing-along. In addition, much discussion took place about drum dancing and Inuvialuktun language learning. Overall, the event was successful and rewarding for all involved; it resulted in many stories being told and recorded and provided insight into how to best move forward with the *Inuvialuit Voices* project. The entirety of the gathering was photographed and recorded so that the stories told could be preserved and added to the IDL. After the four-day event concluded, the video was edited into smaller segments to facilitate easy online viewing and digital copies on a flash drive were shared with event participants.

10.8   Working with Librarians and Information Professionals

LIS practitioners and researchers are critical participants in the work of the digital storytelling interface described in this chapter. Both the DLN and the *Inuvialuit Voices* research projects were, and are, led by researchers in LIS from the University of Alberta. To this work they bring a deep understanding of digital library technologies, information behaviour, and community driven collaborative research. Through these projects, numerous masters and doctoral students in the information sciences have contributed to and learned to work with Indigenous communities in development of digital library functionality and worked on all project aspects from developing and conducting interviews and usability sessions to working with community members on resource description and investigating technical aspects of the proposed platform. Project collaborators from the University of Alberta have included academic librarians with experience and expertise in aspects of the research such as metadata, Northern research and information practices, research data management, and web design and coding for usability.

The roles played by information practitioners from within the Inuvialuit community itself have been particularly important and instrumental. Mentioned earlier, a key instigator of the DLN project was the former manager of the ICRC, a community Elder who also holds an MLIS degree. The records manager for the IRC has been a core collaborator throughout both the DLN and IDL projects, advising on various components of them and providing consultation on how to work with local Indigenous communities appropriately and effectively. A contract Inuvialuktun language specialist from the Inuvialuit community with expertise in the description of oral recordings contributed by way of describing resources and developing localized- and community-relevant topic, place name, and person name lists. The staff of the ICRC, who are stewards of the community's cultural and linguistic record and serve the community through the collection, organization, and description of resources and the provision of associated services, drive the IDL digital storytelling initiative forward and guide its direction to ensure it is of greatest benefit to the community.

The work to develop and grow the IDL has brought together community collaborators, researchers, and LIS practitioners who each bring their own specific understanding of, and interest in, what information means in their specific context. Together, these varied worldviews, skills, and knowledge(s) come together in service of the Inuvialuit community of today and tomorrow.

10.9 Conclusion

The *Inuvialuit Voices* project builds on successful collaborations and community relationships to enhance the Inuvialuit Digital Library (IDL) with a digital storytelling platform in support of language and culture sharing and revitalization. The IDL demonstrates the potential power of projects that combine the knowledge and expertise of community members and information science practitioners and researchers to co-develop knowledge creation and sharing tools that are responsive to the needs and interests of Indigenous communities. Throughout the *Digital Library North* and *Inuvialuit Voices* projects, many lessons were learned. The diversity of theoretical basis and the methodological techniques used for gathering, analysing, and sharing data on these two projects is noteworthy. These projects also provide deeper insight into the importance of community engagement as the foundation of research and development work with Indigenous communities. Furthermore, involving graduate students from LIS education programs proved to be an influential step in promoting social responsibility in LIS educational practices.

The IDL is a living entity and continues to grow and develop. As part of the *Inuvialuit Voices* project, development of the real-time digital storytelling interface and functionality is ongoing. In addition, work continues with the technical team at the Inuvialuit Regional Corporation to plan for the sustainable transfer of the platform to be hosted and maintained by the community. Staff at the Inuvialuit Cultural Centre Pitquhiit-Pitqsiit are currently scanning, uploading, and describing images of community events, people, and places that are held in their vast collection.

References

Alexander, C. J., Adamson, A., Daborn, G., Houston, J., & Tootoo, V. (2009). Inuit cyberspace: The struggle for access for Inuit Qaujimajatuqangit. *Journal of Canadian Studies, 43*(2), 220–249. https://doi.org/g8fh

Aparac-Jelušić, T. (2017). Digital libraries for cultural heritage: Development, outcomes, and challenges from European perspectives. *Synthesis Lectures on Information Concepts, Retrieval, and Services, 9*(4) https://doi.org/gksmxr

Arnold, C., Stephenson, W., Simpson, B., & Ho, Z. (Eds.). (2011). *Taimani – At that time: Inuvialuit timeline visual guide*. Inuvialuit Regional Corporation. https://bit.ly/3TeY0X1. Accessed 10 Dec 2023.

Balanoff, H., Chambers, C., Kaodloak, A., & Kudlak, E. (2006, October 26–28). "This is the way we were told...": Multiple literacies in Ulukhaktok, Northwest Territories. In B. Collignon & M. Therrien (Eds.), *Orality in the 21st century: Inuit discourse and practices. Proceedings of the 15th Inuit studies conference*, Paris, France. Institut national des langues et civilisations orientales. https://bit.ly/3t15e6o. Accessed 10 Dec 2023.

Bishop, A. P., Mehra, B., Bazzell, I., & Smith, C. (2000). Socially grounded user studies in digital library development. *First Monday, 5*(6) https://doi.org/g8fj

Bishop, A. P., Van House, N. A., & Buttenfield, B. (2003). *Digital library use: Social practice in design and evaluation*. MIT Press.

Bratteteig, T. (2008). Does it matter that it's digital? In K. Lundby (Ed.), *Digital storytelling, mediatized stories: Self-representations in new media* (pp. 271–284). Peter Lang.

Burgess, J. (2006). Hearing ordinary voices: Cultural studies, vernacular creativity, and digital storytelling. *Continuum: Journal of Media and Cultural Studies, 20*(2), 201–214. https://doi.org/cmjnf4

Bushnell, J. (2009). *"I can think of a lot of stories.": Shared knowledges, Indigenous methodology and purposeful conversations with sixteen native women in Seattle* [Doctoral dissertation, University of Washington]. ProQuest Dissertations and Theses Global.

Caidi, N., & Clement, A. (2004, June 7–11). Digital libraries and community networking: The Canadian experience. In *Proceedings of the 4th ACM/IEEE-CS joint conference on digital libraries* (p. 386), Tucson, Arizona, USA. Association for Computing Machinery. https://doi.org/bkbczk

Canadian Federation of Library Associations Truth & Reconciliation Committee / Fédération canadienne des associations de bibliothèques comité vérité et réconciliation. (2017). *Truth and Reconciliation Report and Recommendations.* https://bit.ly/3GDLIQi. Accessed 10 Dec 2023.

Christal, M., Roy, L., & Cherian, A. (2005). Stories told: Tribal communities and the development of virtual museums. *Journal of Internet Cataloging, 7*(1), 65–88. https://doi.org/fs7jc4

Christen, K. (2008). Archival challenges and digital solutions in Aboriginal Australia. *SAA Archaeological Record, 8*(2), 21–24.

Christen, K. (2015). A safe keeping place: Mukurtu CMS innovating museum collaborations. In J. Decker (Ed.), *Technology and digital initiatives: Innovative approaches for museums* (pp. 61–68). Rowman & Littlefield.

Christie, M. (2004). Computer databases and Aboriginal knowledge. *Learning Communities: International Journal of Learning in Social Contexts, 1*, 4–12. https://bit.ly/3NlttTu. Accessed 10 Dec 2023.

Christie, M. (2005). Words, ontologies, and Aboriginal databases. *Media International Australia, 116*(1), 52–63. https://doi.org/gfj877

Couldry, N. (2008). Digital storytelling, media research, and democracy: Conceptual choices and alternative futures. In K. Lundby (Ed.), *Digital storytelling, mediatized stories: Self-representations in new media* (pp. 41–60). Peter Lang.

Couros, A., Montgomery, K., Tupper, J., Hildebrandt, K., Naytowhow, J., & Lewis, P. (2013). Storytelling treaties and the treaty relationship: Enhancing treaty education through digital storytelling. *International Review of Qualitative Research, 6*(4), 544–558. https://doi.org/gmpr8n

Crabtree, A., Nichols, D. M., O'Brien, J., Rouncefield, M., & Twidale, M. B. (2000). Ethnomethodologically informed ethnography and information system design. *Journal of the American Society for Information Science, 51*(7), 666–682. https://doi.org/c7mzxx

Denzin, N. K., Lincoln, Y. S., & Smith, L. T. (2008). Introduction: Critical methodologies and Indigenous inquiry. In N. K. Denzin, Y. S. Lincoln, & L. T. Smith (Eds.), *Handbook of critical and Indigenous inquiry* (pp. 1–20). SAGE.

Detlor, B., Nosrati, F., & Crippa, C. (2017). Connecting people with their communities through proximity-based digital storytelling. *Proceedings of the Association for Information Science and Technology, 54*(1), 650–651. https://doi.org/g8fk

Dicker, J., Dunbar, E., & Johns, A. (2009). Developing intermediate language learning materials: A Labrador Inuttitut story database. In J. Reyhne & L. Lockard (Eds.), *Indigenous language revitalization: Encouragement, guidance, and lessons learned* (pp. 155–166). Northern Arizona University. https://bit.ly/46UW6Oe. Accessed 10 Dec 2023.

Digital Library North (n.d.). Retrieved from https://sites.google.com/ualberta.ca/dln/home

Eagles, D., Woodward, P., & Pope, M. (2005, April 13–15). *Indigenous learners in the digital age: Recognising skills and knowledge* (Paper 045). AVETRA 8th Annual Conference, Emerging Futures: Recent, Responsive, and Relevant Research, Brisbane, Queensland, Australia. Australian Vocational Education and Training Research Association. https://bit.ly/482NeaE. Accessed 10 Dec 2023.

Erstad, O., & Wertsch, J. V. (2008). Tales of mediation: Narrative and digital media as cultural tools. In K. Lundby (Ed.), *Digital storytelling, mediatized stories: Self-representations in new media* (pp. 21–40). Peter Lang.

First Nations Information Governance Centre (FNIGC). (2014). *Ownership, control, access, and possession (OCAPTM): The path to First Nations information governance*. https://bit.ly/3NlzNuj. Accessed 10 Dec 2023.

Flinn, A., Stevens, M., & Shepherd, E. (2009). Whose memories, whose archives? Independent community archives, autonomy, and the mainstream. *Archival Science, 9*(1–2), 71–86. https://doi.org/fwpd56

Ginsburg, F. (2016). Indigenous media from U-Matic to YouTube: Media sovereignty in the digital age. *Sociologia and Antropologia, 6*(3), 581–599. https://doi.org/gjqr5p

Holland, M., & Smith, K. (2000). Using information technology to preserve and sustain cultural heritage: The digital collective. In *UNESCO World Culture Report 2000: Cultural diversity, conflict, and pluralism* (pp. 186–196). https://bit.ly/47N3NaP. Accessed 10 Dec 2023.

Hollowell, J., & Nicholas, G. (2009). Using ethnographic methods to articulate community-based conceptions of cultural heritage management. *Public Archaeology, 8*(2/3), 141–160. https://doi.org/cqtt3z

Hunter, J., Koopman, B., & Sledge, J. (2003). Software tools for Indigenous knowledge management. *Museums and the Web 2003*. https://bit.ly/3RBEO4q. Accessed 10 Dec 2023.

Indian and Northern Affairs Canada/Affaires autochtones et du Nord Canada. (1984). *The Western Arctic Claim: The Inuvialuit Final Agreement* (Bill C-49). https://bit.ly/4ag4niU. Accessed 10 Dec 2023.

Inuvialuit Cultural Centre (ICRC). (n.d.). *Inuvialuit Cultural Centre Pitquhiit-Pitqusiit*. https://bit.ly/3Rp4aRY. Accessed 10 Dec 2023.

Inuvialuit Cultural Centre (ICRC), University of Alberta. (2014). *Inuvialuit Digital Library*. https://inuvialuitdigitallibrary.ca/. Accessed 10 Dec 2023.

Inuvialuit Living History Project. (n.d.). *The Inuvialuit*. https://bit.ly/3GFkzN3. Accessed 10 Dec 2023.

Inuvialuit Regional Corporation (IRC). (2018). *Inuvialuit Final Agreement 101*. http://ifa101.com/. Accessed 10 Dec 2023.

Inuvialuit Regional Corporation (IRC). (n.d.). http://www.irc.inuvialuit.com/. Accessed 10 Dec 2023.

Inuvialuit Voices. (n.d.). *About*. https://bit.ly/3TlHsfU. Accessed 10 Dec 2023.

Kutay, C. (2013). Collecting Aboriginal stories for education through immersion. In Z. Pan, A. D. Cheok, W. Mueller, I. Iurgel, P. Petta, & B. Urban (Eds.), *Transactions on edutainment X* (pp. 102–121). Springer. https://doi.org/gr35cn

Kutay, C., & Green, R. (2013). Culture online. In L. Ormond-Parker, A. Corn, C. Fforde, K. Obata, & S. O'Sullivan (Eds.), *Information technology and Indigenous communities* (pp. 89–104). Australian Institute of Aboriginal and Torres Strait Islander Studies. https://bit.ly/3GAn570. Accessed 10 Dec 2023.

Lambert, J. (2006). *Digital storytelling: Capturing lives, creating community*. Digital Diner.

Lee, D. (2011). Indigenous knowledge organization: A study of concepts, terminology, structure, and (mostly) Indigenous voices. *Partnership: The Canadian Journal of Library Information Practice and Research, 6*(1), 1–33. https://doi.org/g8fm

Lundby, K. (2008). Introduction: Digital storytelling, mediatized stories. In K. Lundby (Ed.), *Digital storytelling, mediatized stories: Self-representations in new media* (pp. 1–20). Peter Lang.

Lynch, C. (2002). Digital collections, digital libraries, and the digitization of cultural heritage information. *Microform and Imaging Review, 31*(4), 131–145.

McWilliam, K. (2008). Digital storytelling as a 'discursively ordered domain'. In K. Lundby (Ed.), *Digital storytelling, mediatized stories: Self-representations in new media* (pp. 145–160). Peter Lang.

Miyashita, M., & Crow Shoe, S. (2009). Blackfoot lullabies and language revitalization. In J. Reyhner & L. Lockard (Eds.), *Indigenous language revitalization: Encouragement, guidance, and lessons learned* (pp. 155–166). Northern Arizona University. https://bit.ly/482NC96. Accessed 10 Dec 2023.

Moradi, F., Öhlund, L., Nordin, H., & Wiberg, M. (2020, October 25–29). Designing a digital archive for Indigenous people: Understanding the double sensitivity of design (Article 26). *NordiCHI '20: Proceedings of the 11th Nordic conference on human-computer interaction: Shaping experiences, shaping society*, Tallinn, Estonia. Association for Computing Machinery. https://doi.org/gjd6zm

Mukurtu CMS. (2015). *Mukurtu mobile*. https://bit.ly/46Y4sEN. Accessed 10 Dec 2023.

Nakata, M. (2007). Indigenous digital collections. *Australian Academic and Research Libraries, 38*(2), 99–110. https://doi.org/g8fn

Nordin, H. (2020). Storing stories: Digital render of momentous living archives [Master thesis, Umeå University]. https://bit.ly/4aghCQI. Accessed 10 Dec 2023.

O'Sullivan, S. (2013). Reversing the gaze: Considering Indigenous perspectives on museums, cultural representation, and the equivocal digital remnant. In L. Ormond-Parker, A. Corn, C. Fforde, K. Obata, & S. O'Sullivan (Eds.), *Information technology and Indigenous communities* (pp. 139–149). Australian Institute of Aboriginal and Torres Strait Islander Studies. https://bit.ly/3GAn570. Accessed 10 Dec 2023.

Omeka Audio-Recorder [Computer software component]. (2021). https://bit.ly/47Hv7Hj. Accessed 10 Dec 2023.

Oppenneer, M. (2008). *A value sensitive design approach to Indigenous knowledge management systems*. https://bit.ly/4adqFSa. Accessed 10 Dec 2023.

Park, P. (1993). What is participatory research? A theoretical and methodological perspective. In P. Park, M. Brydon-Miller, B. Hall, & T. Jackson (Eds.), *Voices of change: Participatory research in the United States and Canada* (pp. 1–19). Praeger.

Park, P. (1999). People, knowledge, and change in participatory research. *Management Learning, 30*(2), 141–157. https://doi.org/b5pvjh

Perone, K. E. (2014). Digital storytelling: A technological approach [Review of the book *Digital storytelling: Capturing lives, creating community*, by J. Lambert]. *Journal of Community Engagement and Scholarship, 7*(2), 113–114. https://doi.org/k79x

Powell, T. B. (2007). A drum speaks: A partnership to create a digital archive based on traditional Ojibwe systems of knowledge. *RBM: A Journal of Rare Books, Manuscripts, and Cultural Heritage, 8*(2), 167–180. https://doi.org/g8fp

Rathi, D., Shiri, A., & Cockney, C. (2017). Environmental scan: A methodological framework to initiate digital library development for communities in Canada's North. *Aslib Journal of Information Management, 69*(1), 76–94. https://doi.org/f9sj8x

Rigolet Inuit Community Government. (2017). *The stories*. https://bit.ly/3tdsrlH. Accessed 10 Dec 2023.

Shiri, A. (2018, June 3–6). Methodological considerations in developing cultural heritage digital libraries: A community-driven framework [Conference poster]. *JCDL '18 Proceedings of the 18th ACM/IEEE Joint Conference on Digital Libraries: From data to wisdom: Resilient integration across societies, disciplines, and systems*, Fort Worth, Texas, USA. Association for Computing Machinery.

Shiri, A., & Stobbs, R. (2018, November 10–14). Community-driven user evaluation of the Inuvialuit cultural heritage digital library. *Proceedings of the Association for Information Science and Technology annual conference, 55*(1), 440–449, Vancouver, British Columbia, Canada. https://doi.org/g8fq

Shiri, A., Cockney, C., Campbell, S., Day Nuttall, A., & Rathi, D. (2013). *Digital Library North: Creating a path for information access in Canada's north* [Unpublished grant application]. Social Sciences and Humanities Research Council of Canada/Conseil de recherches en sciences humaines.

Smith, D. N. (2018). *Letter to Inuvialuit*. https://bit.ly/3NkWW03. Accessed 10 Dec 2023.

Spinuzzi, C. (2005). The methodology of participatory design. *Technical Communication, 52*(2), 163–174.

Srinivasan, R. (2007). Ethnomethodological architectures: Information systems driven by cultural and community visions. *Journal of the American Society for Information Science and Technology, 58*(5), 723–733. https://doi.org/b899hp

Srinivasan, R., & Huang, J. (2005). Fluid ontologies for digital museums. *International Journal on Digital Libraries, 5*(3), 193–204. https://doi.org/bmf63p

Stevens, A. (2008). A different way of knowing: Tools and strategies for managing Indigenous knowledge. *Libri, 58*(1), 25–33. https://doi.org/c8qwbz

Truth and Reconciliation Commission of Canada/Commission de vérité et réconciliation du Canada. (2015). *Calls to action.* https://bit.ly/46SG9Ik. Accessed 10 Dec 2023.

Tyson, M. (1999). *TK for dummies: The Dene Nation guide to traditional knowledge.* Dene Nation.

United Nations (UN). (2007). *Declaration on the rights of Indigenous peoples.* https://bit.ly/3Rzq7iq. Accessed 10 Dec 2023.

Wachowich, N., & Scobie, W. (2010). Uploading selves: Inuit digital storytelling on YouTube. *Études/Inuit/Studies, 34*(2), 81–105. https://doi.org/g8fr

Webb, D. (2015, August 15–21). *Curating with community.* [Conference paper]. IFLA World Library and Information Congress: 81st IFLA General Conference and Assembly, Cape Town, South Africa. https://bit.ly/3RB1At6. Accessed 10 Dec 2023.

Williams, A. (2015). Participation, collaboration, and community building in digital repositories. *Canadian Journal of Information and Library Science, 39*(3/4), 368–376. https://bit.ly/3TeZAYX. Accessed 10 Dec 2023.

Chapter 11
Digital Humanities of the North: Open Access to Research Data for Multiple User Groups

Erich Kasten

Abstract By means of the *Digital Humanities of the North* (DHN) website, this chapter shows how free access to social and cultural anthropology research is provided not only to scientific communities, but also to interested public and Indigenous communities of Siberia and other parts of the Circumpolar North. The DHN site is primarily targeted at local community use as endangered Indigenous knowledge and languages are best preserved and sustained if their everyday use is encouraged. At the same time, DHN also contributes to the overall preservation of cultural diversity in global perspective. The increasingly important role that use of new technology and social media plays now, and will play in the future, to involve the Indigenous youth is explored as they make use of documented but at-risk Indigenous knowledge of experienced elder community members. A particular focus of this chapter is on the new Environmental Knowledge of the North website, with the aim to bring together both Indigenous knowledge and Indigenous science with mainstream disciplinary social and cultural research combined with methods and data of the natural sciences. Another goal of the chapter is to connect museum collections virtually with fieldwork documentaries of corresponding knowledge and techniques of craftsmen, craftswomen, and artists from Indigenous communities.

Keywords Co-production of knowledge · Digital Humanities · Environmental knowledge · Knowledge repatriation · Knowledge equity · Museum research · Open access · Open science

---

E. Kasten (✉)
Kulturstiftung Sibirien, Fürstenberg/Havel, Germany
e-mail: kasten@kulturstiftung-sibirien.de

© The Author(s), under exclusive license to Springer Nature
Switzerland AG 2024
S. Acadia (ed.), *Library and Information Sciences in Arctic and Northern Studies*, Springer Polar Sciences, https://doi.org/10.1007/978-3-031-54715-7_11

227

11.1 Introduction

One of the objectives and tasks of the Foundation for Siberian Cultures (FSC) [Kulturstiftung Sibirien] (https://dh-north.org/themen/kulturstiftung-sibirien/) and its affiliated publishing house (https://dh-north.org/verlag/) is to provide free access to social and cultural anthropology research. This service is provided via the *Digital Humanities of the North* (DHN) website (https://dh-north.org/). DHN is aimed not only at scientific communities, but also interested public and Indigenous communities of Siberia and of other parts of the Circumpolar North.

In addition to published research, DHN provides access to primary research data on which published findings are based, notably video and audio recordings of activities and interviews, along with corresponding transcriptions and translations, that document Indigenous knowledge and practices. Often, it is more comfortable for researchers to keep their own primary research data in their own private archive. However, this practice is not ideal because conclusions, interpretations, and theory-building cannot easily be double-checked, replicated, or questioned by others. Linking primary research data with resulting digital publications and presenting them in combination via the internet appeals also to interested user groups beyond the scientific community. For example, availability of research data allows it to be reused by others or returned to their communities of origin where the data may play an important role in sustaining local cultural heritage, especially for Indigenous communities.

On the DHN site, provision of recorded and free, easily accessible Indigenous data that are used and published in studies is targeted in particular for Indigenous communities' use. There, these materials find wide resonance as local learning tools (Fig. 11.1). By planning and pairing these data and publications together, long-lasting research collaborations with Indigenous communities have developed over the years. These relations are based more on mutual trust and less on short-term formal or business-like agreements (see Allemann & Dudeck, 2019). This methodological approach is in line and further promotes up-to-date concepts of co-production between 'outside' researchers and Indigenous communities (Kasten, 2021a; Krupnik, 2021; Krupnik & Bogoslovskaja, 2021), which has become the foundation for most social and cultural anthropology research in the North for the last two decades.

11.2 History and Contents of Digital Humanities of the North (DHN)

Content on the DHN site is open access and always has been even with the FSC's previous web domains (http://www.siberian-studies.org/ and http://www.kulturstiftung-sibirien.de) that were set up in 2004 and 2010, respectively. With the establishment of the FSC in 2010, content on the site was expanded to include

Fig. 11.1 Use of the FSC's digital learning tools during a school class in Lesnaya, Kamchatka, Russia in 2012. (Photo credit: E. Kasten)

audiovisual media. The problem soon arose of how to best organize and present the rapidly growing digital collections in a user-friendly way that could be shared easily with others to facilitate productive scientific exchanges, as well as return collected data to the communities of their origin. Early on, the 2010 site well-served the FSC's needs until technical limitations became increasingly apparent regarding attractive layout and when rapidly growing smartphone use, especially in Indigenous communities, set restrictions for its intended application because of its outdated HTML structure. Therefore, a workshop was held in 2018 at the FSC in Fürstenberg/Havel, Germany that brought together social and cultural anthropologists with strong interest and experience in data management to discuss and outline adequate responses and future strategies (Kasten, 2021b).

Consequently, the new DHN site was created and went live in 2019. The site offers sought-after new opportunities to make rich digital collections available to multiple user groups in a well-integrated and attractive way. Like its forerunner, the kulturstiftung-sibirien site, DHN is multilingual in German, English, and Russian, whereas most other databases and web portals are in English or, at best, bilingual in German and English only, excluding their use by Indigenous communities of other-language-speaking countries. Plans are underway to add French to the DHN's multilingual site and coverage of Canadian Arctic content will soon more prominently materialize. French is an official language of Canada and some Indigenous members in Canada speak various types of French. Thus, adding this language to the DHN site complies with the FSC's principal objective of targeting Indigenous groups as current and future users of the site.

The digital collections of the FSC are manifold, belonging to diverse formats such as photo, video, audio, and text collections. Among the latter are digital editions from the FSC's publishing house; other books, journal articles, and book chapters; and scanned rare books from the FSC's physical library. To meet the challenge of bringing together information from different formats in a well-integrated way, dossiers are created on certain themes. In addition, pathways are created to improve discoverability of content surrounding regional or thematic interests of various user groups, such as Indigenous community members, scientists, and the wider public. One possible access route, for instance, is by way of ethnographies if site users are interested to learn more about a certain ethnic group. On the main page for a selected ethnic group, general and illustrated information is provided, while more specific themes are addressed in the subsequent text. Text highlights are then linked to subpages, most often dossiers, where diverse materials on certain themes are compiled in a well-structured way, allowing and encouraging users to navigate freely across themes in their own explorative and creative ways. Indeed, another access mode is by way of themes. Here, a selected theme is first generally outlined with links embedded in the text to subthemes that are then more comprehensively and thoroughly presented in the form of dossiers. In addition, the DHN site provides from its main menu information on the FSC and its recent activities, including direct access for download of digital editions from the FSC's publishing house. However, as the new DHN site was created only a few years ago in 2019, not all categories are fully complete yet and still under in-progress status.

11.3 Linking Digital Collections of the FSC for Multiple and Notably Indigenous Community Uses

The FSC's published research (i.e., monographs, collective volumes, and essays; research data of more than 200 hours of audio-visual documentation of Indigenous knowledge; and new editions of historical ethnographic sources such as travelogues and early ethnographies in the public domain) is easily linked to each other in electronic form on the DHN site. Combinations of selected modules from the aforementioned varied formats can be arranged by users themselves about interests and research questions.

For the digital collections of the FSC, much audio and video data are from my own fieldwork recordings with the Itelmen, Even, and Koryak peoples on the Kamchatka Peninsula from the 1990s through the mid-2010s (Kasten, 2021b). At that time, true co-production of knowledge evolved and could flourish with Indigenous communities, whereas in recent years the impacts of political Russian propaganda towards the West and impediments for non-Russian researchers are increasingly felt, along with already earlier trends of Indigenous and local culture commodification (Kasten, 2004). Together, these phenomena gradually impaired the basis for open discourses on Indigenous knowledge and dissemination of printed learning tools from my original recordings. After being urged by local communities, the Koryak co-editor of some textbooks published by the FSC, Galina Khariutkina, forwarded in 2016 a request by the FSC to the Kamchatka Ministry of Education championing for wider use of these learning tools in the regular local school curricula. Unfortunately, no response was received. Since then, the FSC's focus is on processing the collections of recorded existing materials in electronic form with the principle aim of making them available for community use to sustain endangered Indigenous languages and knowledge and, in this way, contribute to the preservation of cultural diversity in global perspective.

In addition, more collections have been and will be solicited by other colleagues for digital publication and presentation via DHN, including the edited volumes by Raisa Bel'dy et al. (2012) and Tat'iana Bulgakova (2016) on the Nanai people, Brigitte Pakendorf and Nataliia Aralova (2019) on the Negidal people, Alexandra Lavrillier and Dejan Matic (2013) on the Even people, Cecilia Odé (2016a, b) on the Yukaghir people, and, currently in preparation, Zsófia Schön and Stephan Dudeck on the Khanty people, Roza Laptander on the Nenets people, and Michael Riessler on both the Komi and Sámi peoples. Most recently in 2021 and on behalf of the FSC, Viacheslav Shadrin recorded Indigenous knowledge on sustainable relations with nature in times of climate change among the Chukchi, Yukaghir, and Even peoples living in Sakha (Yakutia) in their respective Indigenous languages (Fig. 11.2).

Most of my own annotated recordings on Itelmen, Even, and Koryak language and culture are hosted at the Endangered Languages Archive (ELAR) (https://www.elararchive.org) at the Berlin-Brandenburgische Akademie der Wissenschaften [Berlin-Brandenburg Academy of Sciences] for long-term storage. All the full-resolution video recordings will also be stored at the Ethnological Museum [Ethnologisches Museum] (https://www.smb.museum/museen-einrichtungen/ethnologisches-museum/home/) in Berlin, together with my already deposited video recordings from the 1980s made with the First Nations of the Canadian Pacific Northwest. For ELAR and DHN, the film quality is compressed for faster download. While ELAR is addressed more to the scientific community and scholars of

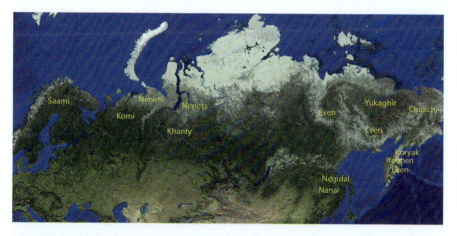

Fig. 11.2 Map with documented languages presented on or in preparation for the Digital Humanities of the North website. (Map credit: Kulturstiftung Sibirien)

Fig. 11.3 Video seminar in Kazym, Western Siberia with, from left to right, Stephan Dudeck, Tat'iana Liubavina, and Anastasiia Brusnitsina, 2021. (Photo credit: E. Fedotova and S. Dudeck)

linguistic studies, DHN is targeted at local community use. Endangered Indigenous knowledge and languages is best preserved and sustained if their everyday use is encouraged by faster and easier access to content which is what DHN is designed to do.

Detailed surveys have been carried out to determine how additional attention can be drawn to use of open access resources provided by the FSC for its primary target groups. Among these surveys is one carried out by Stephan Dudeck (2021) for the FSC as part of its recent project on sustainable relations with nature (Fig. 11.3). Dudeck explores the increasingly important role that the use of new technology and social media plays now, and will play in the future, to involve the Indigenous youth in sustaining the Indigenous knowledge of experienced community members—most often elders—that is at risk of fading into oblivion. By motivating the younger generation this knowledge can be preserved.

11.4 Environmental Knowledge of the North (EKN)

In 2021, the FSC launched an additional website: *Environmental Knowledge of the North* (EKN) (https://ek-north.org/en). This site integrates social media algorithms to encourage interactive discourses with and among Indigenous users in the North, providing additional pathways to the common pool of online publications and research data similarly as the DHN site. The structure of EKN is slightly different from DHN and more closely tuned to participatory Indigenous community users. The main access structure to seek information (e.g., themes, regions, peoples, dossiers, etc.) remains the same. However, to stimulate vivid interactive exchanges, an alternating new 'video of the week' on a certain theme is posted on the first page. Community members can respond with their own video posts, often spontaneously taken with their smartphones, which appears under videoblogs. By providing their own content, users become co-producers of the EKN site. For Indigenous community users and foreign researchers, this user-added content provides informative data for further comparatives analyses.

Under themes, another issue is more strongly emphasized on EKN: natural science research. This category brings together Indigenous knowledge and Indigenous science (see Lavrillier & Gabyshev, 2017) with social and cultural research and the natural sciences. For both Indigenous partners and natural scientists, it is useful to learn about their different methodological approaches and each other's complementing observations and results. This focus contributes to bridging gaps between differing methods and outcomes, often recognized in the past but about which both sides now have become increasingly interested in learning. Thus, short films are posted made by natural scientists of the Alfred-Wegener-Institut, Helmholtz-Zentrum für Polar- und Meeresforschung [Alfred Wegener Institute for Polar and Marine Research] (AWI) (https://www.awi.de/) in Bremerhaven, in collaboration with film universities in Berlin and Potsdam, that show the output of their teams working in the Arctic. The videos inform in an understandable and visually appealing way complex content in the natural sciences, in this case regarding climate change, that dramatically effects and is of great interest for Indigenous peoples in their corresponding regions.

At the FSC, it is important that all video posts contain both Russian and English subtitles for the promotion of dialogue between and among Indigenous communities in Russia and the entire North on important themes and concerns that most of them have in common. Unfortunately, the phase when these new social media tools were about to be tested and fully implemented for users in Siberia coincided with the escalation of the Russian invasion of Ukraine in early 2022 and subsequent restrictions and shutdowns of some social media platforms in Russia that the FSC intended to use. However, these initiatives will be taken up again as soon as possible. Then, the FSC plans to establish a network of local administrators to enact and oversee additional participatory community-based, self-determined social media activity.

11.5 Prospects to Further Expanding Digital Humanities of the North (DHN)

DHN has rapidly developed since its implementation in 2019 in ways that were not anticipated at the beginning. Therefore, increasing complexity urged the FSC to split the site step-by-step into more specific sub-websites that remain linked to each other for cohesiveness.

The initial focus on the documentation of Indigenous languages under the program *Languages and Cultures of the Russian Far East* has recently been, and will continue to be, expanded to become *Languages of the North*; it will be presented and accessed through a separate forthcoming website. As before, this website will provide even more comprehensive information for linguistic research, allowing a more wide-ranging exchange of relevant cultural and language issues among Indigenous communities of the North.

In the future, other themes will be emphasized. One of these themes was already initiated in 2021 with the project *Indigenous Environmental Knowledge and Sustainable Relations with Nature in Times of Climate Change* funded by the Eastern Partnership and Russia program of the Auswärtiges Amt der Bundesrepublik Deutschland [Federal Foreign Office of the Federal Republic of Germany] (2022). For that project, environmental knowledge was recorded in co-production with local partners in Western Siberia, Sakha (Yakutia), and Kamchatka. The short films are shown with Russian and English subtitles on the EKN website. In the future, the information on Indigenous environmental knowledge and corresponding practices will be further enhanced through interactive tools (e.g., with posts by users from local communities).

Another important goal of the project is to stimulate exchanges between the humanities and natural sciences dealing with pressing issues in the North (e.g., the effects of climate change) whose consequences are already experienced dramatically in northern Siberia. Therefore, beyond findings of social sciences research, an environmental assessment was undertaken by ethnobotanists and climatologists (Černjagina & Kiričenko, 2021) of the Tikhookeanskiy institut geografii Dal'nevostochnogo otdeleniya Rossiyskoy akademii nauk [Kamchatka Branch of the Pacific Institute of Geography of the Far Eastern Branch of the Russian Academy of Sciences] with whom the FSC maintains long-lasting partnerships ever since the first joint resource assessment project in 1995 that was funded by the European Union's International Association for the Promotion of Cooperation with Scientists from the Independent States of the Former Soviet Union (Kasten & Dul'chenko, 1996). Bringing together social and natural sciences on relevant issues in the North has been a continuing concern for the FSC as myself and other FSC associates participate each year since 2015 in the Franco-German workshop series *Gateway to the Arctic* put on by the AWI in Germany and, in France, the Cultures, Environnements, Arctique, Répresentations, Climat Cultures [Environments, Arctic, Representations, Climate] research centre (https://www.cearc.fr/) at the University of Versailles Saint-Quentin-en-Yvelines. Consequently, colleagues from the AWI contributed a chapter to the project proceedings (Treffeisen & Grosfeld, 2021). More authors brought the environmental challenges also into its broader perspective about Russian state environmental politics (Tynkkynen, 2021), and Russian editions of the volume were published and made freely available online. Thus, on the EKN website, social and natural science research results can be linked to the recorded environmental knowledge by Indigenous community members where it can be openly accessed.

Currently, this methodological approach is further expanded to the Western Arctic as well, partly motivated by the fact that former co-productions with our

11 Digital Humanities of the North: Open Access to Research Data for Multiple User...

Russian partners have been halted for political reasons, hopefully only temporary. Therefore, within Germany, the FSC is partner in the recent new Circumpolar Research Co-Creation initiative at the Helmholtz-Zentrum für Umweltforschung [Helmholtz Centre for Environmental Research] in Leipzig and the Institut für fortgeschrittene Nachhaltigkeitsstudien [Institute for Advanced Sustainability Studies] in Potsdam. Currently, the forthcoming project is in its initial phase and has been further elaborated during a workshop in July 2022 at the FSC, incorporating Indigenous knowledge from Indigenous communities living across the Circumpolar North.

A primary issue to be elaborated with partners from Indigenous communities is future forms of co-production, in particular about Free Prior Informed Consent (FPIC) (Food and Agriculture Organization of the United Nations, 2016) and being alert about data privacy laws in Russia that can declare any publication of recorded personal data without FPIC as illegal and an administrative offence (*O personal'nykh dannykh*, 2006). Especially regulated are personal data (i.e., any data that allow the identification of an individual, including information on ethnicity, religion, or worldview). Data such as this must be anonymized—impossible for photo and video data. Common practice by Russian state authorities is to arbitrarily apply a certain law or not,[1] opening the door to put pressure on or block any (foreign) journalists or ethnographers, while at the same time allowing state-controlled institutions to proceed with their work if those researchers follow Russian political guidelines. Therefore, formalized regulations must be viewed with caution as they can be (ab)used by political stakeholders over the vested interests of those affected.

Regarding future thematic contents, a particular emphasis will be on material culture such as handicrafts and tools. This emphasis connects to another program and earlier research focus with which the FSC has already engaged in the past: to connect museum collections virtually with fieldwork documentaries of corresponding knowledge and techniques of craftsmen, craftswomen, and artists from Indigenous communities. In 2000, I commissioned a full set of an Even festive garment made by Maja Lomovtseva in Esso, Kamchatka for the Ethnological Museum in Berlin (museum identity numbers: I A 5634 a–b and I A 5635 a–f). During this time, I was invited by Even craftswomen to document their work by video recording so that their knowledge and expertise could be preserved and used later by following generations as these women felt that earlier ways of how this knowledge was passed down to children and grandchildren within the communities was no longer fully effective. In the meantime, these informative recordings of the craftswomen's work were transcribed and translated from the Even language. Eventually, these films were made available with optional Russian and English subtitles on the DHN site. For the local community, the videos serve as useful learning tools because detailed information is conveyed as well in spoken Even language that can be studied also in a corresponding textbook (Kasten & Avak, 2018).

---

[1] A Russian saying goes: "The strictness of our laws is relieved by their not unconditional observability" (Mikhail Efgrafovich Saltykov Shchedrin), Stephan Dudeck, personal communication.

Virtual presentation offers wide-ranging comparative possibilities. For example, while looking for incised drawings in walrus tusk in the collections of the Ethnological Museum in Berlin, I came across an older but similar Even garment from 1887 (museum identity number: I A 2247). The scant documentation that was common at the time stated only that it was acquired somewhere in Siberia northwest of Kamchatka, presumably in Sakha (Yakutia). During my next visit to Yakutsk, I organized a seminar at the Institute for Humanities Research and Indigenous Studies of the North (http://igi.ysn.ru/) where an Even craftswoman, Alyona Nikolaevna Khabarovskaia (2019), commented on the garment in detail with help of its image from the museum object projected on a full screen (Fig. 11.4). As soon as this annotated film was put online, Maia Lomovtseva from Kamchatka sent a series of Whatsapp messages to me further discussing this image, tracing similarities of her own work to her ancestry. Discourses such as these are exciting and of great value for local craftswomen and artists, the same as they enhance the documentation of a given object for the museum and its visitors considerably.

The same approach was applied again with regard to two other objects in the collections of the Ethnological Museum in Berlin that I noticed during the same investigation, specifically two Koryak festive garments—*Kukhliankas*—from 1900 (museum identity numbers: I A 2911 and 2913). During a workshop under the Endangered Languages Documentation Programme (https://www.eldp.net/) on transcribing Koryak texts for ELAR, a Koryak craftswoman from Kamchatka, Lydiia Chechulina, stayed for a week at the FSC to comment extensively on these two objects with the help of a photo (Fig. 11.5). During this investigation, she became increasingly excited to see for the first time such an old item that supposedly originated from her home village. Additionally, she later discovered previously unknown materials and ornaments that made study of them not only informative for her but also cultural and social anthropological and museum research in the

Fig. 11.4 Alyona Khabarovskaia comments on an Even old garment during a seminar in Yakutsk, Russia in 2019. (Video still credit: E. Kasten)

11 Digital Humanities of the North: Open Access to Research Data for Multiple User… 237

Fig. 11.5 Lydiia Chechulina comments on a Koryak festive garment from 1900 during a workshop at the FSC, 2020. (Video still credit: E. Kasten)

Fig. 11.6 Koryak fur coat made and worn by Tamara Khupkhi in Tilichiki, Kamchatka, Russia in 2002. (Photo credit: E. Kasten)

exploration of cultural dynamics at different times (Kasten, 2021c). Another similar object that I commissioned for an exhibition from a Koryak craftswoman, Tamara Khupkhi, from Tilichiki in 2002 and now in the collections of the FSC (Fig. 11.6), was paired with fully annotated video commentary. Such full comparative documentation is of mutual benefit and inspiration for Indigenous craftswomen, the Ethnological Museum, social and cultural anthropologists, and the wider public.

Because of these promising first results, the Ethnological Museum in collaboration with the FSC prepared a research project on the museum's collection from the Nanai people in the Russian Far East. In 2021, the custodian of the depository Claudius Kamps and I began photographing the objects that would then be discussed in a field project in 2022 with craftsmen and craftswomen in the Amur Region. The project was frozen—the only one to be so—in April 2022 due to sanctions resulting from Russia's war in Ukraine. Part of the project is to create another FSC website, *Museums of the North*, where images of German museum collections are shown together with annotated video documentaries on the knowledge and techniques of present-day craftswomen, artists, and craftsmen from the corresponding Indigenous communities. Beyond the benefit of such useful contextual information and vivid presentation for museum visitors and scientists, these virtual exhibitions have great impact on the Indigenous communities from where these objects originate, especially by stimulating other creative artwork. Plus, online accessibility gives those local community members who do not have the chance to travel abroad to visit distant museums a chance to view and learn about the collections.

Together with the FSC's partner institution, the Hokkaidō-ritsu Hoppō Minzoku Hakubutsukan [Hokkaido Museum of Northern Peoples] (https://hoppohm.org/) in Abashiri, Japan, plans are in place to translate the FSC's websites into Japanese to reach additional audiences and integrate complementing collections and digital presentations from and about Japan. Another extension of DHN is a planned subwebsite on life histories where videos held by the FSC can be linked and shown together with academic works by historians on issues or events. For example, if a person wants to learn more about the socioeconomic transitions in Siberia during *kolkhoz, sovkhoz,* or *perestroika* times, analyses and assessments by historians and other scholars—which may be biased through their given academic or political zeitgeist—can be contrasted here with original statements of Indigenous peoples in their recorded life histories, providing broader and more balanced perspectives showing how local peoples were directly affected by these changes as well as how differently changes were perceived.

11.6 Conclusion: Future Perspectives in Politically Uncertain Times

In April 2022, with the war in Ukraine in mind, the FSC launched its new program *Escape and Displacement in Eastern Europe due to the War in Ukraine*. As former connections with state-controlled institutions in Russia cannot be maintained for the time being, it is all the more important for the FSC to keep the ties with individual partners in Siberia. The FSC, in collaboration with its partners in Canada, the United States, and Europe, is considering the launch of an open publication platform for scholars working on Siberian topics in the social sciences, humanities, and natural sciences, featuring contributions by authors separated by boundaries and newly

11 Digital Humanities of the North: Open Access to Research Data for Multiple User... 239

erected barriers in international collaboration (Kasten et al., 2024). By maintaining these and other connections as much as possible, the FSC and Indigenous communities can be better prepared for the future when fruitful collaborations and partnerships with Russia may be resumed for mutual benefit as it was prior to 2022.

References

Allemann, L., & Dudeck, S. (2019). Sharing oral history with Arctic Indigenous communities: Ethical implications of bringing back research results. *Qualitative Inquiry, 25*(9/10), 890–906. https://doi.org/gmw5d8

Bel'dy, R., Bulgakova, T., & Kasten, E. (Eds.). (2012). *Nanaiskie skazki* [Nanai tales]. Kulturstiftung Sibirien. https://bit.ly/3aUzDKj. Accessed 10 Dec 2023.

Bulgakova, T. (2016). *Kamlaniia nanaiskikh shamanov* [Rites of Nanai shamans]. Kulturstiftung Sibirien. https://bit.ly/3ROEL3k. Accessed 10 Dec 2023.

Černjagina, O., & Kiričenko, V. (2021). Kamtschatka: Klimatrends, öffentliche Wahrnehmung des Wandels und Reaktion der Ökosysteme [Kamchatka: Climate trends, public perceptions of change, and ecosystem response]. In E. Kasten (Ed.), *Mensch und Natur in Sibirien: Umweltwissen und nachhaltige Naturbeziehungen in Zeiten des Klimawandels* [Man and nature in Siberia: Environmental knowledge and sustainable relationships with nature in times of climate change] (pp. 199–235). Kulturstiftung Sibirien. https://bit.ly/3RW58Er. Accessed 10 Dec 2023.

Dudeck, S. (2021). Ethnoblogging – Synergien und Herausforderungen für indigenes umweltwissen auf Social-Media-Plattformen [Ethnoblogging: Synergies and challenges for Indigenous environmental knowledge on social media platforms]. In E. Kasten (Ed.), *Mensch und Natur in Sibirien: Umweltwissen und nachhaltige Naturbeziehungen in Zeiten des Klimawandels* [Man and nature in Siberia: Environmental knowledge and sustainable relationships with nature in times of climate change] (pp. 279–302). Kulturstiftung Sibirien. https://bit.ly/3olaeN3. Accessed 10 Dec 2023.

Federal Foreign Office of the Federal Republic of Germany/Auswärtiges Amt der Bundesrepublik Deutschland. (2022). *Russian Federation.* https://bit.ly/3B8Y0Po. Accessed 10 Dec 2023.

Food and Agriculture Organization of the United Nations. (2016). *Free prior and informed consent: An Indigenous peoples' right and a good practice for local communities.* United Nations. https://bit.ly/3RfmU6k. Accessed 10 Dec 2023.

Kasten, E. (Ed.). (2004). *Properties of culture – Culture as property: Pathways to reform in post-Soviet Siberia.* Dietrich Reimer Verlag.

Kasten, E. (2021a). Einführung [Introduction]. In E. Kasten (Ed.), *Mensch und Natur in Sibirien: Umweltwissen und nachhaltige Naturbeziehungen in Zeiten des Klimawandels* [Man and nature in Siberia: Environmental knowledge and sustainable relationships with nature in times of climate change] (pp. 9–15). Kulturstiftung Sibirien. https://bit.ly/3yYUcNN. Accessed 10 Dec 2023.

Kasten, E. (2021b). Fieldwork on Kamchatka peninsula and the creation of the Foundation for Siberian Cultures: Towards an open-access database of Indigenous languages and knowledge from the Russian Far East. In S. Acadia & M. T. Fjellestad (Eds.), *Library and information studies for Arctic social sciences and humanities* (pp. 329–352). Routledge.

Kasten, E. (2021c). Erschließen von Museumsbeständen in Koproduktion mit indigenen Gemeinschaften, mit einer Einführung von Henriette Lavaulx-Vrecourt [Cataloguing museum collections in co-production with Indigenous communities, with an introduction by Henriette Lavaulx-Vrecourt]. *Baessler Archiv* [Baessler Archive], *67*, 141–157.

Kasten, E., & Avak, R. (Eds.). (2018). *Clothing and decorative arts: Evens, Kamchatka, Bystrinski district.* Kulturstiftung Sibirien. https://bit.ly/3aVjc0v. Accessed 10 Dec 2023.

Kasten, E., & Dul'chenko, E. V. (Eds.). (1996). *Resursy tradicionnogo prirodopol'zovaniia narodov Severa i dal'nego vostoka Rossii* [Resources of traditional nature management of the peoples of the North and the Far East of Russia]. Kamšat. https://bit.ly/3bBKF7J. Accessed 10 Dec 2023.

Kasten, E., Krupnik. I., & Fondahl. G. (Eds.). (2024). A fractured North: Facing dilemmas. Kulturstiftung Sibirien (in print). https://bit.ly/4aj6vWO. Accessed 10 Dec 2023.

Khabarovskaia, A. N. (2019). *Commentary on festive clothing of the Evans* [Video]. https://bit.ly/3Ptfnym. Accessed 10 Dec 2023.

Krupnik, I. (2021). Foreword: Running up the Arctic information highway. In S. Acadia & M. T. Fjellestad (Eds.), *Library and information studies for Arctic social sciences and humanities* (pp. xxxiv–xxxix). Routledge.

Krupnik, I., & Bogoslovskaja, L. (2021). Unser Eis, unser Schnee und unsere Winde: Von Wissens-"Integration" zur Wissens-"Koproduktion" im russischen SIKU-Projekt, 2007–2013 [Our ice, our snow, and our winds: From knowledge "Integration" to knowledge "co-production" in the Russian SIKU project, 2007–2013]. In E. Kasten (Ed.), *Mensch und Natur in Sibirien: Umweltwissen und nachhaltige Naturbeziehungen in Zeiten des Klimawandels* [Man and nature in Siberia: Environmental knowledge and sustainable relationships with nature in times of climate change] (pp. 175–197). Kulturstiftung Sibirien. https://bit.ly/3yVYu8M. Accessed 10 Dec 2023.

Lavrillier, A., & Gabyshev, S. (2017). *An Arctic Indigenous knowledge system of landscape, climate, and human interactions: Evenki reindeer herders and hunters*. Kulturstiftung Sibirien. https://bit.ly/3z0ItOB. Accessed 10 Dec 2023.

Lavrillier, A., & Matic, D. (Eds.). (2013). *Evenskie nimkany Dar'i Mikhailovny Oseninoi* [Even folk tales of Daria Mikhailovna Osenina]. Kulturstiftung Sibirien. https://bit.ly/3PLmXUZ. Accessed 10 Dec 2023.

O personal'nykh dannykh [On Personal Data]. (2006). Federal law No. 152-FZ.

Odé, C. (Ed.). (2016a). *Akulina Innokent'evna Struchkova: Various tales, for the Yukaghir children*. Kulturstiftung Sibirien. https://bit.ly/3PHBNwh. Accessed 10 Dec 2023.

Odé, C. (Ed.). (2016b). *Il'ia Kurilov: My life, songs*. Kulturstiftung Sibirien. https://bit.ly/3Opc9uz. Accessed 10 Dec 2023.

Pakendorf, B., & Aralova, N. (Eds.). (2019). *Negidal'skie skazki, rasskazy i obychai* [Negidal's tales, stories, and customs]. Kulturstiftung Sibirien. https://bit.ly/3op0RMp. Accessed 10 Dec 2023.

Treffeisen, R., & Grosfeld, K. (2021). Klimawandel in Sibirien – eine Region im Umbruch [Climate change in Siberia: A region in transition]. In E. Kasten (Ed.), *Mensch und Natur in Sibirien: Umweltwissen und nachhaltige Naturbeziehungen in Zeiten des Klimawandels* [Man and nature in Siberia: Environmental knowledge and sustainable relationships with nature in times of climate change] (pp. 17–37). Kulturstiftung Sibirien. https://bit.ly/3BJWkMd. Accessed 10 Dec 2023.

Tynkkynen, P. (2021). Russland und die arktische Umwelt: Ströme von Kohlenwasserstoffkulturen [Russia and the Arctic environment: Flows of hydrocarbon cultures]. In E. Kasten (Ed.), *Mensch und Natur in Sibirien: Umweltwissen und nachhaltige Naturbeziehungen in Zeiten des Klimawandels* [Man and nature in Siberia: Environmental knowledge and sustainable relationships with nature in times of climate change] (pp. 306–322). Kulturstiftung Sibirien. https://bit.ly/3A0zL4T. Accessed 10 Dec 2023.

Chapter 12
Selected Sources of Information about the History of Exploration of the Arctic Region from the Collection of the Siberian Federal University Scientific Library

Elena N. Kasyanchuk ⓘ, **Valentina A. Koreshkova, Olga I. Babina** ⓘ, **Irina A. Tsvetichkina** ⓘ, **and Ruslan A. Baryshev** ⓘ

Abstract This chapter describes activities of the Scientific Library of the Siberian Federal University (SibFU) on the development and implementation of the project *Creation of a Scientific and Educational Geographical Library in SibFU*. This project, launched jointly with the Russian Geographical Society, aims to provide users with high-quality informational and educational resources on the profile and topics of the main directions of development of geographical sciences and popularization of geographical knowledge among the population of the cities and region of Yenisei Siberia. Study of the Arctic is a priority task of the SibFU, and the activity of the SibFU library reflecting this priority is analysed in this chapter. The Arctic plays an important role in creating a new library model within the context of the formation of information resources via the works of SibFU scientists related to the study of Siberia and the Arctic by providing public access to their accumulated knowledge. The basis of this project's collection is the unique documents of S. B. Slevich of the Russian Ecological Academy wherein topics include Arctic Indigenous peoples, ecology of the Far North, industrial development of northern territories, and construction on permafrost. In addition, this chapter identifies ways to further promote the project. For example, a plan of collaboration with the Institute of the North and the Arctic at SibFU is under development to train Indigenous peoples of the Russian Arctic on research activities, as well as publish a digest of scientific information on Arctic research carried out by universities throughout Yenisei Siberia.

Keywords Arctic archives · Arctic expeditions · Arctic libraries · Russian Geographical Society · Siberian Federal University Scientific Library · Solomon Borisovich Slevich · Yenisei Siberia

---

E. N. Kasyanchuk (✉) · V. A. Koreshkova · O. I. Babina · I. A. Tsvetichkina · R. A. Baryshev
Siberian Federal University, Krasnoyarsk, Siberia, Russia
e-mail: ekasyanchuk@sfu-kras.ru

© The Author(s), under exclusive license to Springer Nature Switzerland AG 2024
S. Acadia (ed.), *Library and Information Sciences in Arctic and Northern Studies*, Springer Polar Sciences, https://doi.org/10.1007/978-3-031-54715-7_12

241

12.1 Introduction

The Arctic Zone is one of the most undeveloped territories on Earth due to its extreme natural and climatic conditions, low population density, and relative spatial distance. At the same time, a large amount of minerals and biological resources are present in the Far North and Arctic, making the zone a promising area for development, especially of the Northern Sea Route. To accomplish this task, comprehensive scientific research must be carried out to develop new technologies and materials that ensure successful production activities, create conditions for comfortable living, fulfil environmental requirements, and ensure the rights and preservation of the activities and possibilities of living for the Indigenous peoples of the Russian North.

For the Krasnoyarsk Territory, the issue of the study and development of the Arctic is priority as a significant portion of the territory (40%) lies within the Arctic Zone. In fact, the northernmost continental point of Russia is within the Krasnoyarsk Territory, and polar aviation by Russia and the world began from that location. In 2014, the agreement *O sukhoputnykh territoriyakh Arkticheskoy zony Rossiyskoy Federatsii* [On the land territories of the Arctic Zone of the Russian Federation] (Decree No. 296 (2014)) was signed on the formation of the Arctic Union of Russian Regions which included the eight Arctic constituent entities of the Russian Federation: Krasnoyarsk Territory along with the territories of Murmansk, Nenets, Yamalo-Nenets, Chukotka, Komi, Arkhangelsk, and Sakha (Yakutia). The Krasnoyarsk Territory contains the largest deposits of oil and gas, copper, gold, nickel, platinum, and other minerals in all of Russia. The city of Norilsk in Krasnoyarsk is located beyond the Arctic Circle and the largest Russian companies operate there and throughout the northern and Arctic territories. For instance, the public joint-stock companies Noril'skij nikel' [Norilsk Nickel], a mining and metallurgical company that is the world's largest producer of copper, nickel, and platinum, and Rosnéft' [NK Rosneft], the world's largest oil production and refining company, both operate in Norilsk. The area comprising Krasnoyarsk Territory is shown in Fig. 12.1.

At the same time, several problems are currently inherent in the northern and Arctic areas of the Krasnoyarsk Territory (e.g., damage to permafrost due to the creation of infrastructure, construction, and operation of buildings; poor development of transport infrastructure; and the low resistance of ecological systems to anthropogenic impact). Moreover, these problems are enhanced by harsh climatic conditions, remoteness, and low quality of life found in the North and Arctic. Overcoming these problems is possible only with the involvement of innovative scientific solutions that create conditions for advanced development of the northern and Arctic areas of the Krasnoyarsk Territory. To implement these tasks, the *Strategija social'no-ekonomicheskogo razvitija Krasnojarskogo kraja do 2030 goda* [Strategy for the Social and Economical Development of the Krasnoyarsk Territory until 2030] was approved in 2018 by the Krasnoyarsk Territory Government that defines the goals and objectives of ensuring northern and Arctic development of Krasnoyarsk. One goal of the Strategy is the creation of the Institute of the North and the Arctic at SibFU (2020).

Fig. 12.1 Map of Russia showing Krasnoyarsk Territory and the cities of Krasnoyarsk and Norlisk in Russia. (Map credit: Yu. Afanas'eva and SibFU Scientific Library)

12.2 Institute of the North and the Arctic at SibFU

The purpose of the creation of the Institute of the North and the Arctic at SibFU is to solve the strategic tasks of the Russian Federation for the effective development of the Russian Arctic and North, including development of the scientific and creative potential of people living in the Russian Arctic for the interests of society and state based on innovative advanced training and education technologies. Achieving this goal is possible via a broad range of activities: the creation of modern scientific, laboratory, and educational infrastructure for fundamental and applied research and production technologies; provision of advanced (re)training of personnel for the implementation of both federal and foreign northern and Arctic investment projects; monitoring of social and anthropological research in the North and Arctic; development and support of innovations for northern communities and settlements, including places of compact residences of the Indigenous peoples across Siberia and the Far East; development and management of methods and tools for biodiversity conservation management and use of biological resources as an object of economic activity; and, finally, development of indicators for integrated environmental monitoring and assurance of environmental safety. The Institute is expected to become the leading intellectual centre in Siberia on the field of research, innovative technological developments, and personnel training for the development of the Arctic and northern territories in Russia.

The implementation of the educational tasks of the Institute is achieved through modern educational programs for master's degrees and additional professional education, including the advanced training of specialists to work in northern areas and the Arctic Zone. The Institute concentrates on conducting fundamental and applied multidisciplinary research in and development of the Krasnoyarsk North; monitoring of natural, climatic, and ecological processes; analysis of the specifics of human life and activities, including the preservation of cultures and languages of the Indigenous peoples of northern and Arctic Russian territories; and organizing and conducting scientific expeditions in northern Krasnoyarsk.

Since 2014, the SibFU has been a member of the University of the Arctic (UArctic) (https://www.uarctic.org/). UArctic members are more than 170 universities and scientific organizations in Russia, as well as Canada, Denmark, Finland, Greenland, Iceland, Norway, Sweden, the United States, and other countries, making it possible for students to take part in research on the problems of the Arctic together with the universities of the countries of northern Europe and North America. The SibFU organized more than a dozen expeditions to the Siberian Arctic, including some villages of Indigenous peoples of the North located in Taimyr, Evenkia, Turukhansk regions, Republic of Sakha (Yakutia), and Republic of Tuva. Field studies were carried out where ethnographic and ethnological scientific material was collected, technical assessment of the northern villages conducted, and quality of medical services assessed along with the current state of traditional crafts and domestic reindeer husbandry. On 5 May 2015, 36 students and staff of the SibFU, following in the custom of Russian victory day parades, organized in the village of Dikson, an urban settlement in the Taymyrsky Dolgano-Nenetsy District of Krasnoyarsk, for a solemn procession dedicated to victory in the Great Patriotic War (1941–1945). In addition to the procession, SibFU students and cadets cleaned a monument to the sailors of the warship *Semyon Dezhnev* and performed a concert for residents of the village. In addition, SibFU scientists (e.g., Abovskiy, 2007; Koptseva, 2020; Makarov & Batashev, 2007; Shelopaev et al., 2006) have prepared more than 40 monographs on the operation of highways in Siberia and the North, environmental problems of the Arctic region, history and culture of the peoples of Yenisei Siberia, and development of strategic approaches to Arctic development. These monographs are held at the SibFU's Scientific Library.

12.3   Library Research Work

The Scientific Library of the SibFU library and Publishing Complex (https://www. sfu-kras.ru/en/research/library) was created by combining five scientific libraries of Krasnoyarsk universities that were part of the SibFU: (1) the Scientific Library of the Krasnoyarsk State University, (2) Scientific and Technical Library of the Krasnoyarsk State Technical University, (3) Library of the State University of Nonferrous Metals and Gold, (4) Library of the Krasnoyarsk State Architectural and Construction Academy, and (5) Library of the Krasnoyarsk State Trade and Economic Institute. As discussed by Kasyanchuk et al. (2018), the innovative educational project developed by the SibFU Scientific Library called *Sozdanie i razvitie bibliotechno-informacionnogo kompleksa Sibirskogo federal'nogo universiteta*

12 Selected Sources of Information about the History of Exploration of the Arctic... 245

[Creation and Development of the Library and Information Complex of the Siberian Federal University] defined the development vectors of the newly created library as the main part of the unified information environment of the university, including its resources, communications, and status as a social and cultural centre. The SibFU Scientific Library was created as an open electronic library for university users and residents of the region. In servicing readers, the library uses document collections along with traditional and modern information technologies to provide access to global information. The network of multifunctional reading rooms serves as a computer hardware and software hub for regulated access to educational and scientific content using modern interactive technologies.

The fund, or total collection, of the SibFU's Scientific Library contains over 1.8 million printed documents of various types of scientific and educational literature, dissertations, periodicals, and foreign editions in 41 world languages. Additionally, the library provides access to licensed Russian and world scientific abstract and full-text databases. Guided by the strategic goals of information support of innovative, scientific, and educational activities of the SibFU, the Boris N. Yeltsin Presidential Library electronic reading room provides access to unique materials for Arctic study such as, for example, the *Sovetskaja Arktika: Ezhemesjachnyj politiko-jekonomicheskij zhurnal* [Soviet Arctic: Monthly Political and Economic Journal] (https://www.prlib.ru/item/1152643) published from 1935–1941 and the *Enisejskaja gubernija. Karta Tobol'skogo namestnichestva...* [Yenisei Province: Map of the Tobolsk Governorship...] (https://www.prlib.ru/en/node/680484) from the nineteenth century. To attract attention of the world community to environmental and geopolitical issues, as well as the popularization of Russian science, culture, and education, the library participates in the annual conference-webinar *Days of the Arctic in the Presidential Library* where representatives of leading Russian universities take part in discussions of the issues of modern Arctic development, including its ecological and political situations. In addition, the now-traditional video lecture hall named 'Arctic and North' is used for showing documentaries about northern development.

In 2013, the Department of Geography opened at the SibFU with the support of the Russian Geographical Society (RGO). The SibFU and RGO conduct joint expeditions, including to the regions of the Far North, and engage in projects such as the *Sozdanie nauchno-obrazovatel'noj geograficheskoj biblioteki v SFU* [Creation of a Scientific and Educational Geographic Library in the Siberian Federal University]. This geographical library is an information centre for science and education in the Yenisei Siberia region. At this library, a collection of documents was assembled on the following topics: northern Indigenous peoples, ecology of the Far North, industrial development of northern territories, and construction on permafrost soils. The library fund includes more than 2000 titles of educational and scientific literature and geographical maps, including unique documents from the collection of Solomon Borisovich Slevich (1919–2006), formerly of the Russian Ecological Academy. Slevich described in detail the features of polar stations, logistic support missions, protection of the environment, and human health. Slevich's scientific interests are reflected in the collection of books donated to the SibFU by Slevich's widow in

2014, consisting of 363 titles of publications during 1941–2005 on geography, biology, water transport, and regional studies. The collection includes four monographs written by Slevich (1968, 1977, 1988, 1995 with Korotkevich). The collection further contains materials (e.g., Belov, 1956; Treshnikov, 1956; Treshnikov & Tolstikov, 1956) about scientific drifting stations in the central Arctic, including scientific collections and textbooks; popular science literature on the history of the discovery and development of the Northern Sea Route; details about Russian Arctic expeditions of the seventeenth to twentieth centuries; geographical research of the *Dekabristy* [Decembrists], an anti-government liberalist group active from 1821–1826; and works by Umberto Nobile (1885–1978), the famous Italian airship designer and participant and leader of various Arctic expeditions.

In the past few years, there has been an increase in the interest in Arctic research, and the need for reliable sources of information is growing. To provide information in support of Arctic scientific research, the SibFU Scientific Library is preparing to launch the publication *Information and Analytical Digest* of Arctic topics; it will be compiled and published quarterly by monitoring electronic and printed research resources.

12.4   Rare Editions

Promotion of the educational and research endeavours of universities is the main task of university libraries in Russia; therefore, it is necessary to ensure both the safety and accessibility of the unique fund of rare books in university library collections. The rare fund of the SibFU Scientific Library has been curated since 2012. Currently, the fund contains more than 2000 storage units of rare books and periodicals of the eighteenth to nineteenth centuries. Rare modern editions in the fund include miniature editions, autographed books, publications on the history of the university, works by SibFU scientists, and important and valuable private book collections. Based on the results of a study of the collection of pre-revolutionary publications held by the library, a bibliographic index titled *Knigi XIX – nachala XX vekov chast' 1* [Books Published in the 19th and Early 20th Centuries, Part 1] was created and is available via the SibFU Library. The first part of the index includes a complete scientific description of pre-revolutionary editions of more than 350 volumes of 142 unique titles stored in the library. The publications in the index are arranged by branch of knowledge and, within those sections, in alphabetical order of authors and titles.

One of the main directions of work with the rare fund is the introduction of book monuments into scientific, cultural, and educational circulation. Within the framework of this direction, tasks are solved in two ways: first, providing access for researchers and students to study book monuments, including consulting and selection of literature on research topics; and second, completing full scientific descriptions of collections, including in-depth historical study of book monuments.

12 Selected Sources of Information about the History of Exploration of the Arctic...   247

The Scientific Library staff have extensive experience in the scientific description of memorial libraries and collections. Examples include the library of academician N. P. Abovskiy, collection of architect E. M. Panov (https://bik.sfu-kras.ru/elib/libguides/panov), collection of geographer S. B. Slevich, and collection of the Krasnoyarsk House of Architects. On 16 December 2014, the memorial office-library was named after Naum Petrovich Abovskiy (1929–2012), a well-known scientist, academician of the International Academy of Sciences of Higher Education, and professor at the SibFU. Abovskiy was engaged in the study of construction and seismic resistance in the regions of the Far North. The funds of the memorial office-library were formed based on Abovskiy's personal collection of books: over 1500 books and monographs on structural mechanics, the theory of elasticity, mathematics, and physics.

Rare books are used not only by readers from the university, but also by researchers and students from other universities in the city and region. The library has established contacts with the SibFU's Institute of Philology and Language Communication where teachers are given the opportunity to conduct practical classes and seminars, and students can research and write term papers and theses based on rare funds using primary sources. Thus, the rare collections of the SibFU Scientific Library are not only research tools, but also subjects of research themselves by providing material for historical book research, where a book is viewed as both an object of material culture via printing production as well as a reflection of social and cultural interests and the needs of civilization.

In total, the Scientific Library contains 935 books on the topic of Arctic research, but 15 of them are distinguished and part of a rare fund. Some of them are especially noteworthy such as, for example, *Zapiski polyarnika* [Notes of a Polar Explorer] (1936) by Nikolai Vasilyevich Pinegin (1883–1940), a book about Georgy Yakovlevich Sedov (1877–1914). Sedov was a Russian hydrographer, polar explorer, and senior lieutenant in the navy who took part in expeditions to explore Kara Sea and the mouth of Kara River, Vaigach Island, Novaya Zemlya, Caspian Sea, Kolyma Gulf and the mouth of Kolyma River, and Krestovaya Bay. Sedov was the organizer of an ill-fated expedition to the North Pole, travelling 200 kilometres, or about 125 miles, but died before reaching the declared goal. Until Pinegin's book in 1936, no books were written about Sedov, and only in this book—its only edition—was the fateful expedition of Sedov to the North Pole described.

A few years later in 1939, the book *Sedov* by Semyon Grigorievich Nagorny (1905–1992) was published based primarily on archival items held at the Academy of Sciences as well as the personal diary of Sedov. The book is devoted to the expeditions of Sedov, especially the 1912 expedition to the North Pole on the ship *Saint Fok*. Nagorny's study of the materials of the Central State Naval Archive, Archive of the Academy of Sciences, and personal archive of Sedov's widow, Vera Valerianovna Sedova (1876–1962), who preserved Sedov's letters and notebooks during the expedition as well as a copy of Sedov's diary during the final trip to the North Pole, made it possible to supplement and expand what was previously known about Sedov, serving as the basis for new conclusions about the personality of the polar explorer. Additionally, the book resulted in newer interest in and coverage of Sedov's final expedition, the relationship between its participants, and reasons for Sedov's tragic death.

Russian, and especially Soviet, science has accumulated a great deal of material on the ethnography of the peoples of Siberia. Within the vast expanses of Siberian tundra, forests, and steppes that make up half of the territory of the entire Russian Federation live more than 30 different nationalities and ethnographic groups, in addition to Russians. Of all those living across Siberia, Indigenous peoples—including hunters, fishers, and reindeer herders—have been, and are among, the most economically disadvantaged as well as the most socially and culturally isolated in Russia, and the 1956 edition of the book *Narody Sibiri* [*Peoples of* Siberia] edited by Levin and Potapov, is devoted to this topic (Fig. 12.2). The book consists of two sections: "Peoples of the Far North" and "Far East and Peoples of Southern Siberia," each containing essays and images of history, ethnography, economy, culture, and more as seen, for instance, in Fig. 12.3.

Ethnographic essays such as those found in Levin and Potapov's book are the first experience of a generalizing work on the ethnography of the peoples of Siberia. Numerous expeditions to Siberia organized by various scientific institutions in Russia expanded the range of resources about the Indigenous Siberian peoples,

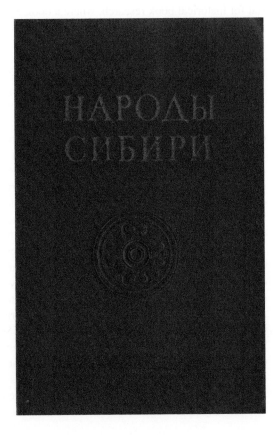

Fig. 12.2 Book cover of *Narody Sibiri* [Peoples of Siberia], 1956 edition, edited by M. G. Levin and L. P. Potapov, published by the Publishing House of the USSR Academy of Sciences. (Image credit: SibFU Scientific Library)

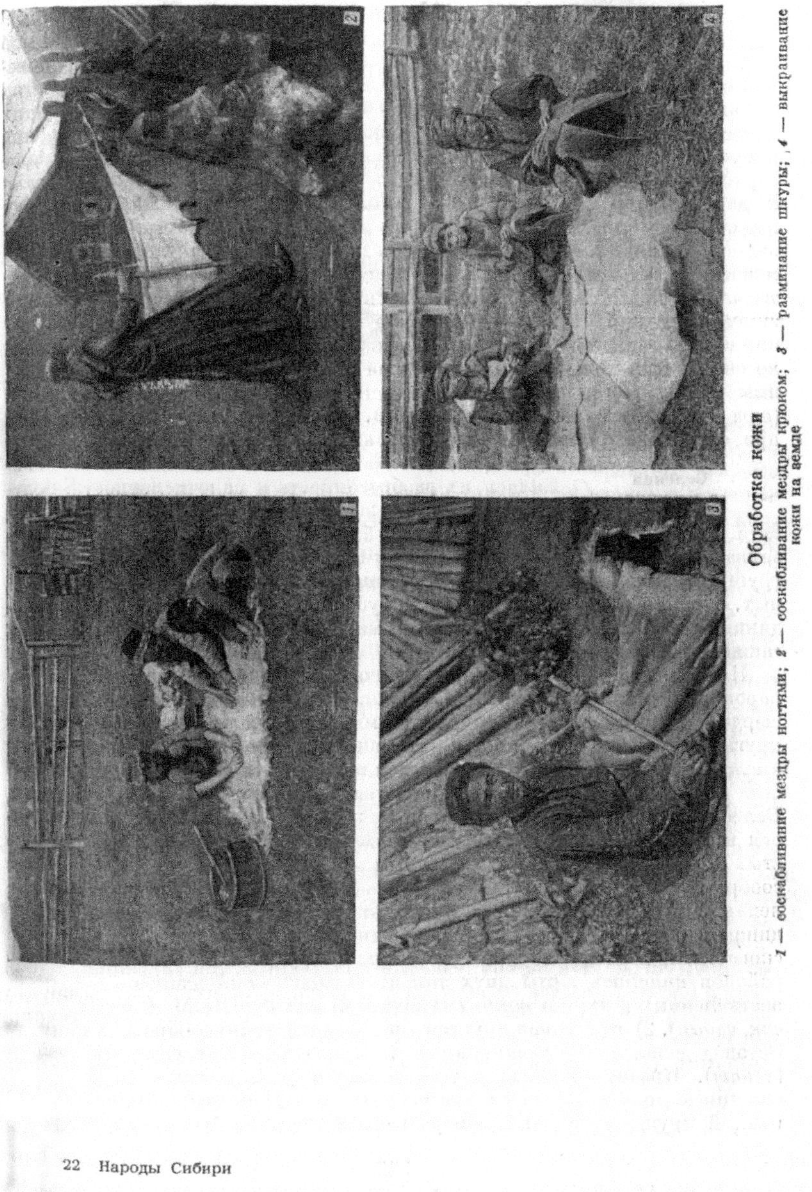

12 Selected Sources of Information about the History of Exploration of the Arctic... 249

Fig. 12.3 Page 22 of *Narody Sibiri* [Peoples of Siberia] (1956). The four images depict leather processing, including scraping the mezdra with nails, scraping the mezdra with a hook, kneading the leather, and cutting out the skin on the ground. Published by the Archive of the Museum of Anthropology and Ethnography of the USSR Academy of Sciences. (Image credit: SibFU Scientific Library)

enriching collections with new and valuable materials. The peoples of Siberia and terms describing them now, and in the past, include Aleuts, Chukchi, Dolgans, Enets, Eskimos, Evenks, Evens, Itelmens, Kets, Khanty and Mansi, Koryaks, Nanais, Negidal, Nenets, Nganasans, Nivkhs, Orochi, Oroks, Selkups, Udege, Ulchi, and Yukagirs. Descriptions about these groups were formed via research in ethnography, archaeology, and anthropology, including study of collections from both the Museum of Anthropology and Ethnography of the Academy of Sciences of the USSR, now known as the Kunstkamera, or Muzey antropologii i etnografii imeni Petra Velikogo Rossiyskoy akademii nauk [Museum of Anthropology and Ethnography named after Peter the Great of the Russian Academy of Sciences] (https://www.kunstkamera.ru/en/) and the Museum of Ethnography of the Peoples of the USSR, now the Rossiyskiy etnograficheskiy muzey [Russian Museum of Ethnography] (https://ethnomuseum.ru/en/), as well as ethnographic literature published both in the pre-Soviet and Soviet periods.

In the rare fund of the SibFU Scientific Library is a book that is the first known generalization on the ethnography of Siberia. That book, as shown in Fig. 12.4, is *Uraangkhai Sakhalar: Ocherki drevnej istorii yakutov* [Uraangkhai – Sakhalar: Essays on the Ancient History of the Yakuts] from 1937 by Gavriil Vasilyevich Ksenofontov (1888–1938). This monograph is a bibliographic rarity; even specialists know little about it. Both the author and the book itself faced a difficult fate. In fact, there was a time when the book could not be quoted. Ksenofontov was born in the Yakutsk region to the family of a wealthy Yakut and graduated from Tomsk University with a law degree. During 1913–1917, Ksenofontov worked as a lawyer in Yakutsk city then began scientific work in 1920, entering Irkutsk University and working as an assistant in the Faculty of Social Sciences under the guidance of Professor Bernard Eduardovich Petri (1884–1937) and began to study the history and ethnography of the peoples of Asia, cooperating with the East Siberian Branch of the RGO. In 1923, Ksenofontov returned to Yakutsk city to engage in thorough collection of ethnographic and folklore materials, and, during 1925–1926, undertook a lengthy trip stopping at the following locations: Toyon Ary Island on the River Lena, the naslegi of West Kangalassky and Srednevilyuisk uluses, and the localities of Vilyuisk, Verkhnevilyuysk, Markha, Nyurba, Sheya, Suntar, Khadan, Sadyn, Chona, Novotukhansk, and Krasnoyarsk. Then, in 1937, Ksenofontov and family relocated to the town of Dimitrov, Moscow region. There, Ksenofontov began preparing for the publication of the first volume of *Uraangkhai Sakhalar*. For this first volume, Ksenofontov did not have time to formulate a complete and comprehensive theory of the origin of the Yakut people; this most important and fundamental part would be presented in the second volume. However, On 22 April 1938, Ksenofontov was arrested on unfounded charges before the second volume could be finished. Then, by verdict of the military collegium of the Supreme Court of the USSR of 28 August of the same year, Ksenofontov was convicted, sentenced to death, and executed all on the same day. The case was revised 19 years later and, in August 1957, Ksenofontov was fully exonerated. Today, Ksenofontov's work plays a major part in modern Yakut studies.

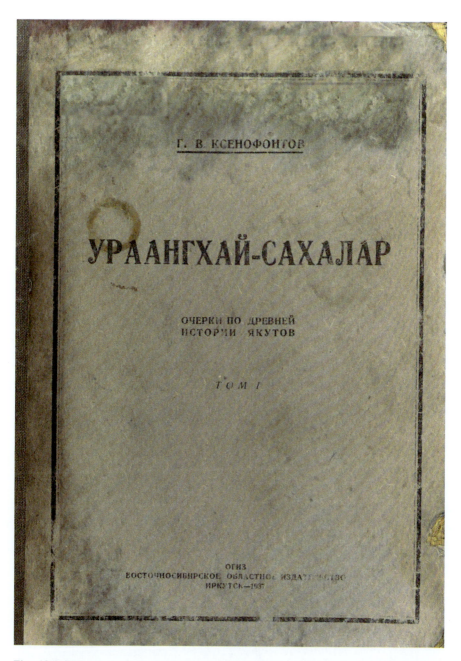

Fig. 12.4 Title page of the book *Uraangkhai Sakhalar: Ocherki drevnej istorii yakutov* [Uraangkhai – Sakhalar: Essays on the Ancient History of the Yakuts] (1937) by G. V. Ksenofontov, published by East Siberian Regional Publishing House. (Image credit: SibFU Scientific Library)

The folklore and ethnographic journal *Sibirskaja Zhivaja Starina* [Siberian Living Starina] of 1929 was created on the initiative of professors Mark Konstantinovich Azadovsky (1888–1954) and Georgii Semenovich Vinogradov (1886–1945) in Irkutsk (Fig. 12.5). This work is notable because it was the first publication of its type in Soviet times. The journal widely published works of folklore recorded during expeditions, including children's fairy tales, songs, counting rhymes, and more, as well as research works of Siberian scientists (Fig. 12.6). The materials and articles of Vinogradov on the pages of the magazine devoted to children's folklore laid the foundation for its systematic study in Russia. The journal

Fig. 12.5 Journal cover of *Sibirskaja Zhivaja Starina* [Siberian Living Starina] (1929), published by the Russian Geographical Society, East Siberian Department. (Image credit: SibFU Scientific Library)

Палеолитическое жилище. Буреть

1 — реконструкция; 2 — общий вид раскопок

изображают обнаженных женщин с одной лишь великолепно убранной пышной шевелюрой на голове. Однако в 1936 г. в Бурети была найдена довольно крупная статуэтка, изображающая женщину в шитой одежде с отчетливо выраженным головным убором в виде капюшона, накинутого на голову. Такие же две статуэтки, только лишь миниатюрные.и оттого более схематично трактованные, оказались в Мальте. Подобно палеоазиатским племенам и эскимосам, древнейшее, верхнепалеолитическое население жило охотой, имело метательные дощечки и так называемые «жезлы начальников», т. е., повидимому, орудия для разминания ремней, выделывало реалистически трактованные изображения животных из кости

25

Fig. 12.6 Page 25 of *Narody Sibiri* [Peoples of Siberia] (1956). The two images depict an illustration of reconstruction of a palaeolithic dwelling Buret' and an archaeological site. Top image by V. Zaporozhskaja. Bottom image by N. Tyumentcev. Published by the Archive of the Museum of Anthropology and Ethnography of the USSR Academy of Sciences. (Image credit: SibFU Scientific Library)

and its founders, especially Azadovsky, discovered eastern Siberia as the land of outstanding masters of the Russian oral and poetic word.

The 1930 publication *Turukhanskij kraj: ekonomicheskoe obozrenie s istoricheskoj spravkoj* [Turukhansk Territory: An Economic Review with a Historical Outline] by George Nikanorovich Tarasenkov is devoted to the nature of the Turukhansk Territory (Fig. 12.7). The publication includes several valuable digital data for 1930 on the physical and geographical conditions of the Turukhansk region (Fig. 12.8). When compiling the review, Tarasenkov used materials of the Central Siberian Geographical Society and Subpolar Census of 1920–1927 along with the works of the Siberian Scientific Fisheries Station, including unpublished departmental reports and primary statistical data. The publication is provided with illustrations in the text, a significant amount of tabular material, and a geographic map.

Based on the Scientific Library's unique book collections, the permanent exposition *History of the Arctic* was designed with a demonstration of both rare and modern editions. The exposition was first put on display at the SibFU's Scientific Library on 8 February 2021, coinciding with the Day of Russian Science.

12.5 Conclusion

University education aimed at training specialists to study and work in the Arctic requires a special approach and focus on practical disciplines. The Institute of the North and the Arctic was created in accordance with the strategic goals of the Russian Federation and the provision of its research activities in the Arctic Zone. The programs of the Institute are provided with information resources of the SibFU Scientific Library to create a scientific and educational geographic library, organize a collection of rare documents, and cooperate with the Boris N. Yeltsin Presidential Library. As an important social and cultural centre, the Scientific Library takes an active part in activities related to the study of the Arctic. Soon, the Scientific Library will create an information and analytical digest to provide up-to-date information about Arctic research and develop the Intellektual'noe nasledie universitetov Enisejskoj Sibiri [Intellectual Heritage of the Universities of Yenisei Siberia] repository to include materials in priority areas of the SibFU's research.

Fig. 12.7 Title page of the book *Turukhanskij kraj: ekonomicheskoe obozrenie s istoricheskoj spravkoj* [Turukhansk Territory: An Economic Review with a Historical Outline] (1930) by G. N. Tarasenkov, published by Turukhansk RIK. (Image credit: SibFU Scientific Library)

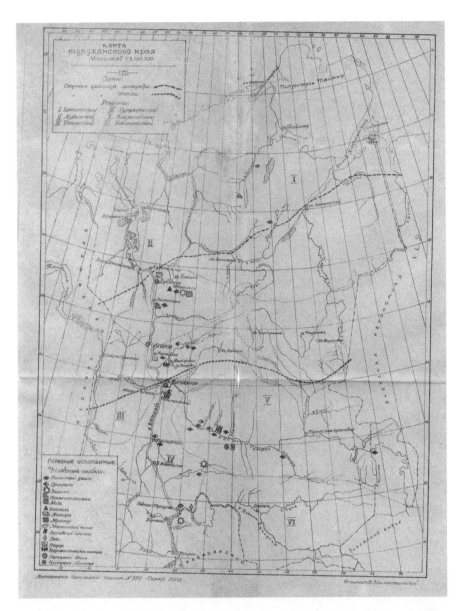

Fig. 12.8 Map of Turukhansk Territory published in the book *Turukhanskij kraj: ekonomicheskoe obozrenie s istoricheskoj spravkoj* [Turukhansk Territory: An Economic Review with a Historical Outline] (1930). (Image credit: V. Konstantinovskij)

12 Selected Sources of Information about the History of Exploration of the Arctic...

References

Abovskiy, N. P. (2007). *Stroitel'nye problemy ekologicheskogo osvoenija severnyh rajonov Krasnoiarskogo kraja* [Construction problems of ecological development of the northern regions of the Krasnoyarsk Territory]. Krasnoyarsk State Academy of Architecture and Construction.

Belov, M. I. (1956). *Istorija otkrytija i osvoenija Severnogo morskogo puti* [History of the discovery and development of the Northern Sea Route] (Vol. 1). Sea Transport.

Kasyanchuk, E. N., Kazantseva, V. P., & Baryshev, R. A. (2018). Nauchnaya biblioteka Sibirskogo federal'nogo universiteta: itogi raboty, zadachi, oriyentiry [Scientific Library of the Siberian Federal University: Results of work, tasks, guidelines]. *Scientific and Technical Libraries, 4*, 23–32. https://doi.org/h6ns

Koptseva, N. P. (Ed.). (2020). *Strategicheskie podhody k razvitiju Arktiki i podderzhke korennyh malochislennyh narodov severa (na materiale Krasnojarskogo kraja)* [Strategic approaches to the development of the Arctic and support of the Indigenous peoples of the North (based on the Krasnoyarsk Territory)]. Siberian Federal University.

Ksenofontov, G. V. (1937). *Uraangkhai – Sakhalar: Ocherki drevnej istorii yakutov* [Uraangkhai – Sakhalar: Essays on the ancient history of the Yakuts]. East Siberian Regional Publishing House.

Levin, M. G., & Potapov, L. P. (Eds.) (1956). *Narody Sibiri* [Peoples of Siberia]. Publishing House of the Academy of Sciences of the USSR.

Makarov, N. P., & Batashev M. S. (2007). *Istorija i kul'tura narodov PriYenisejskogo kraja* [History and culture of the peoples of the Yenisei region]. Siberian Federal University Publishing Complex.

Nagorny, S. G. (1939). *Sedov: Zhizn' zamechatel'nyh ljudej: Serija biografii* [Sedov: The life of remarkable people: Series of biographies], 12(156). Young Guard.

O sukhoputnykh territoriyakh Arkticheskoy zony Rossiyskoy Federatsii [On the land territories of the Arctic Zone of the Russian Federation], Decree No. 296. (2014). https://bit.ly/3Jj7Hgb. Accessed 11 Dec 2023.

Pinegin, N. V. (1936). *Zapiski poljarnika: Vospominanija o pohodah v Arktiku v dorevoljucionnoe i sovetskoe vremja* [Notes of a polar explorer: Memoirs about campaigns in the Arctic in prerevolutionary and Soviet times]. Sevkraigiz.

Sibirskaja Zhivaja Starina: VIII–IX. (1929). [Siberian Living Starina: Years 8–9]. Russkoe Geograficheskoe Obshhestvo [Russian Geographical Society].

Shelopaev, E. I., Zhukov, V. I., & Kapranov, V. V. (2006). *Ekspluatacija avtomobil'nyh dorog v rajiona Sibiri i Severa: avtomobil' nye dorogi i aerodromy* [Operation of highways in the regions of Siberia and the North: Roads and airfields]. Krasnoyarsk State Academy of Architecture and Construction.

SibFU (Siberian Federal University). (2020). *The School of the North and the Arctic launched.* https://bit.ly/3Q9TDb4. Accessed 11 Dec 2023.

Slevich, S. B. (1968). *Ledjanoj materik segodnja i zavtra* [Ice continent today and tomorrow]. Gidrometeoizdat.

Slevich, S. B. (1977). *Shel'f: osvoenie, ispol'zovanie* [Shelf: Development, use]. Gidrometeoizdat.

Slevich, S. B. (1988). *Okean: resursy i hozjajstvo* [Ocean: Resources and economy]. Gidrometeoizdat.

Slevich, S. B., & Korotkevich, E.S. (1995). *Chelovek v Antarktide* [Man in Antarctica]. Gidrometeoizdat.

Strategija social'no-ekonomicheskogo razvitija Krasnojarskogo kraja do 2030 goda [Strategy for the Social and Economical Development of the Krasnoyarsk Territory until 2030], Decree No. 647-P. (2018).

Tarasenkov, G. N. (1930). *Turukhanskiy kray: ekonomicheskoe s istoricheskoj spravkoj* [Turukhansk territory: An economic overview with a historical sketch]. Krasnoyarsk.

Treshnikov, A. F. (1956). Godnal'dine: izdnevnika poljarnika [Year on the ice: From the diary of a polar explorer]. Sea Transport.

Treshnikov, A. F., & Tolstikov, E. I. (1956). *Drejfuyushhie stancii v Central'noj Arktike «Severnyj poljus-3» i «Severnyj poljus-4»* [Drifting stations in the Central Arctic: "North Pole-3" and "North Pole-4"]. Knowledge.

Chapter 13
A Descriptive Review of Research Studies by the Central Libraries of the Far Northern Regions of the Northwestern, Ural, and Siberian Federal Districts and the Far Eastern Federal District During 2017–2020

Alesia G. Kuznetsova 📵

Abstract This chapter is based on data about studies and projects conducted by the regional Central Libraries of Russia collected and published in the report *O nauchnykh issledovaniyakh, provodimykh tsentral'nymi bibliotekami regionov Rossiyskoy Federatsii* [On Scientific Studies Carried out by Central Libraries of Russian Federation Regions] presented at the All-Russian research conference "Traditions and innovations" held 26–27 November 2020. The current chapter's scope is geographically limited to the Russian regions that have land in Far North areas. This chapter updates and extends the author's previous work with some 2020 data not found in the original report.

Keywords Central Libraries of Russia · Library research · Regional Libraries of Russia · Russian Far North

13.1 Scientific Studies by Regional Libraries: Legal Aspects

Methodology and research are mentioned as one of the activities of library institutions in Russia per the federal law *O bibliotechnom dele* [On Library Services] (No. 78–FZ) of 29 December 1994, updated 08 June 2015 (*O bibliotechnom dele*, 1994). As dictated by the law in Article 15, Section 5, the state facilitates, funds, and

---

A. G. Kuznetsova (✉)
National Library of Russia, Saint Petersburg, Russia

© The Author(s), under exclusive license to Springer Nature
Switzerland AG 2024
S. Acadia (ed.), *Library and Information Sciences in Arctic and Northern Studies*, Springer Polar Sciences, https://doi.org/10.1007/978-3-031-54715-7_13

259

promotes the research activities of library institutions. To improve coordination of research projects among Russian libraries, the Russian Library Association (RLA) (2022) established an official section on research (Section 31) in 2002. Since 2011, the Research and Methodological Department of the Russian National Library (RNL) accumulates and monitors statistical and analytical data submitted by the regional Central Libraries of Russia (CLR) in the professional full-text database of the same name: Tsentral'nyye biblioteki sub"yektov Rossiyskoy Federatsii (http://clrf.nlr.ru/). The CLRs annually upload to the database reports about their own activities, as well as those of municipal libraries within their regions, and other important documents, allowing for the monitoring of CLR activity and diagnosing the whole system of Russian public libraries.

In 2015, at the 20th RLA annual conference, the framework policy *O nauchno-metodicheskoy deyatel'nosti tsentral'noy biblioteki regiona Rossiyskoy Federatsii* [On Research and Methodological Activity by a Central Library of a Russian Federation Region] was created and can be adopted by any CLR to form a legal basis of its research work. Additionally, the RNL prepared several versions of the guidelines *O pravovom obosnovanii metodicheskih uslug (rabot) vypolniaemykh tsentral'nymi gosudarstvennymi (munitsipal'nykh) bibliotekami* [On Legal Grounds of Research Services (Works) Provided by Central Public (Municipal) Libraries] with the most recent in 2018 (Taktaikina, 2018). In 2016, the RNL passed in a resolution at the annual meeting of directors of regional and federal libraries the requirement to include applied research studies, consulting services, and publication of books and periodicals in the list of public services provided by CLRs (RLA, 2016). In December of that year, the Russian Ministry of Culture (RMC) included research and methodology in the activity of libraries in the sector-wide list of missions (2016). In 2019, the participants of the 24th RLA annual conference requested that the RMC re-establish the All-Russian contest for best projects in library science, bibliography, and bibliology; previously, it was held annually since 1978 and bi-annually since 1994 for 36 years, 1978–2014. The RMC supported this initiative and became the founder of this contest, co-organized by the RNL and the Russian State Library in Moscow. Other contests include best professional book of the year, library analytics, and innovations in library services.

In 2021, the Russian government accepted the *Strategia razvitia bibliotechnogo dela v Rossijskoj Federatsii do 2030 goda* [Strategy of Development of Library Services in the Russian Federation until 2030] (2021b). In the Strategy's chapter «Razvitie osnovnykh napravlenij bibliotechnogo dela» ["Development of the Main Library Services"], section six «Nauchnoe i metodicheskoe obespechenie dejatelnosti bibliotek» ["Scientific and Methodical Foundations of Library Services"], this government-level document describes in detail that scientific research is a primary library service.

13.2 Specifics of the Russian Far North

In the work *Osvoeniye Severa Sovetskogo Soyuza* [Development of the Soviet North], Slavin (1982) characterizes the Far North region by the following factors: remote geographic location from large urban centres—although some large urban centres such as Murmansk, Yakutsk, and Norilsk are located in Far North areas; severe climatic conditions; low density of population; underdeveloped engineering; and social and transport infrastructure. Tarakanov (2010) states in an article on the evolution of 'Far North' and 'North' concepts that the definition and area of the Far North differs in each case, act of law, and scientific study; that is, there are no universal parameters of what constitutes the Far North for every situation. The Russian Government uses a three-tier hierarchy to scale salaries and benefits of state employees: (1) areas of the Far North, (2) areas equivalent to the Far North, and (3) areas of the North with applicable local coefficients. Moreover, the specific areas within this hierarchy are modified regularly by the government regulations most recently updated in 2021 (2021a) —and the hierarchy may or may not coincide with regional administrative borders. Any given region (e.g., Krasnoyarsk Krai) can include areas with all three statuses. Various institutions (e.g., those creating engineering and architectural standards and regulations) use customized classifications that may be detailed to more or lesser extents than the above hierarchy. The RMC does not have its own regulations on Far North status corresponding to libraries, meaning that libraries have no particular status as institutions, although individually their employees may have a 'Far North dweller' status. Figure 13.1 is a map of the Russian Far North.

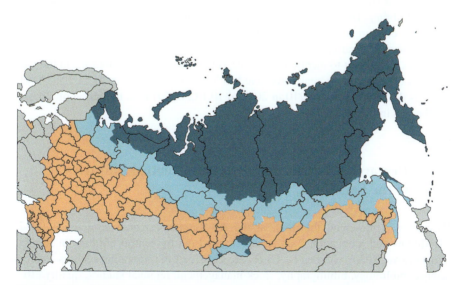

Fig. 13.1 Map of the Russian Extreme North. (Map credit: Hellerick. CC BY-SA 3.0 DEED. https://commons.wikimedia.org/wiki/File:Map_of_the_Russian_Extreme_North.svg)

The main modern demographic trend in the Far North is the extremely high tempo of depopulation caused by migration to other, more southern Russian regions. As indicated by the *Great Russian Encyclopaedia* (2015) during 1991–2012 the population of Chukotka Autonomous Okrug shrunk significantly, the Magadan Oblast population decreased by nearly 60%, and the number of residents in both Kamchatka Krai and Sakhalin was reduced by one-third (Avramova & Basov, 2020). Companies exploiting resources in the Far North prefer using a rotational basis where their mines, oil and gas deposits, and other natural resources are serviced by employees recruited from other regions or countries (i.e., migrant labour), altering the Far North's society and culture. The *Kontseptsiya gosudarstvennoy podderzhki ekonomicheskogo i sotsialnogo razvitiya rayonov severa* [Concept of State Support of Economical and Social Development of Northern Areas] (2000) was adopted by the Russian Government on 17 March 2000 and suggests that reducing the pace of depopulation by such measures as favourable taxation or small business grants is possible, but it does not mention any cultural institutions or projects.

In line with the depopulation, the number of Russian regions in the Far North, and consequently the number of central libraries located there, were reduced after the consolidation of Russian regions in 2005–2008. In 2007, for instance, the Taymyr Dolgano-Nenets and Evenk Autonomous Okrugs became part of Krasnoyarsk Krai. Consequently, Taymyr and Evenk Okrug libraries lost their CLR status and became municipal. In another instance in the same year, Kamchatskaya Oblast and Koryak Autonomous Okrug merged into Kamchatka Krai. Later, in 2013, the Chukotka Autonomous Okrug transferred possession of the Tan-Bogoraz Public Library to the city of Anadyr. The library, thus, became municipal property and lost CLR status. As a result, Chukotka became the only Russian region without a central library. The population of Anadyr is approximately 15,000 people, while the region contains about 50,000 people.

All Russian libraries and archives mentioned in this chapter are listed in the Appendix; important to mention, however, is that the number of libraries in the Far North is on a steady decrease. As noted in Table 13.1, the quantity of Far North libraries decreased from 10,210 in 2017 to 10,132 in 2019—a reduction of almost 80 libraries in a mere two-year timeframe.

13.3 Research Studies and Projects by Central Libraries of the Far North, 2017–2019

Previously, I presented this data at the All-Russian research conference titled "Traditions and innovations" on studies carried out by central libraries in Russia (Kuznetsova, 2020). Studies by CLRs are classified into domains such as library science, bibliology, bibliography, stock management, regional studies, quality/efficiency assessment of library services, and more. In 2017–2019, 18 central libraries

13 A Descriptive Review of Research Studies by the Central Libraries of the Far... 263

Table 13.1 Number of libraries in the Far North, 2017–2019

Districts in the Far North[a] (as of 1 January 2020)	Number of libraries of all departments by year			
	2017	2018	2019	2017–2019 +/−
Altai Republic	157	158	157	No change
Amur Oblast	345	345	345	No change
Arkhangelsk Oblast (including Nenets Autonomous Okrug)	464	463	464	No change
	34	34	34	No change
Buryatia Republic	435	436	436	+1
Chukotka Autonomous Okrug	44	44	44	No change
Irkutsk Oblast	759	754	748	−11
Kamchatka Krai	102	101	101	−1
Karelia Republic	195	196	194	−1
Khabarovsk Krai	309	308	307	−2
Komi Republic	332	325	322	−10
Krasnoyarsk Krai	1153	1147	1146	−7
Magadan Oblast	48	48	48	No change
Murmansk Oblast	146	144	143	−3
Perm Krai	719	712	709	−10
Primorsky Krai	390	387	387	−3
Sakha (Yakutia) Republic	507	504	506	−1
Sakhalin Oblast	163	163	161	−2
Tomsk Oblast	326	326	321	−5
Tuva Republic	173	173	173	No change
Tyumen Oblast (including Yamalo-Nenets Autonomous Okrug and Khanty-Mansi Autonomous Okrug–Yugra)	475	470	469	−6
	84	81	81	−3
	226	224	217	−9
Zabaykalsky Krai	607	602	600	−7
Total =	10,210	10,163	10,132	−78

Table credit: A. G. Kuznetsova using data from the Russian National Library's report *Obshchedostupnyye biblioteki ministerstva kultury Rossiiskoy Federatsii: itogi monitoringa seti – 2020 god* [Public Libraries under the Ministry of Culture of the Russian Federation: Results of Monitoring in 2020] compiled by M. B. Avramova and S. A. Basov
[a]Districts are listed alphabetically

in the Far North submitted to the CLR database 65 annual reports mentioning 84 studies (Table 13.2), including 16 studies on bibliology and book publishing, 17 regional studies, 11 readership surveys, nine stock management studies, seven human resources management studies, five library science studies, and 11 library service quality assessments; however, these research areas often interlace. These reports enumerate studies and projects—but not necessarily publications—conducted by the CLRs and their dependent municipal libraries. Some projects and studies are collaborative, but the extent of each library's participation is not always clear as reports contain only study names. Other information such as, for example, scope and nature of each project is found only in other resources. Figure 13.2 shows percentages by theme of the total output during 2017–2019 by CLRs, indicating that the two most common themes are regional (22%) and bibliological (21%) studies, accounting for over 40%.

13.4 History Studies and Projects

History studies are among the most popular fields of research by the CLRs. These studies are carried out together with local history experts, museums, municipal archives, educational institutions, regional senior councils, and other relevant organizations. As Fig. 13.2 indicates, the 'regional studies' category comprises the highest proportion of CLR studies (22%). These regional studies are, in fact, a type of history study. Other types of history studies and projects are those of library history and bibliology (i.e., book history and culture). These categories—regional history, library history, and bibliology—are discussed in more depth below.

13.4.1 Regional History

In many settlements and areas, libraries are the only or among the few cultural institutions, acting also as exhibition halls, centres for ethnographic and sociological research, and sites for local club meetings. Involvement of local peoples allows them to become active colleagues in historic research projects and sources of local lore in ethnographic studies as well as respondents in community studies rather than passive readers. Local involvement also increases the status of libraries. For example, since 2009, the Yeniseysk City Library, a town within Krasnoyarsk Krai with a population of 17,000 people, reunites the local genealogic club *Rodoslovie*. The club publishes, in collaboration with the Yeniseysk Municipal Archives, the *Yeniseyskiy rodoslov* [Yeniseysk Genealogy] yearbook that has 11 volumes as of this writing. The yearbooks are created in conjunction with local genealogists and contributors from other towns, containing historical documents with facts and evidence about people and events in local history. The entire project was founded and is implemented by enthusiasts—including librarians—without any state or other institutional support (Vlassova et al., 2021).

Far North libraries can also be involved in international projects. For example, in 2019–2021, the Karelia Republic National Library began collaborating with the National Archives of Finland on the project *Finns in Russia 1917–1964* with the

13 A Descriptive Review of Research Studies by the Central Libraries of the Far... 265

Table 13.2 Number of research studies published by central libraries of the Far North, 2017–2020

Districts in the Far North[a] (as of 1 January 2020)	Russian Region Central Library	Year[b]				Total[b] 2017–2020
		2017	2018	2019	2020	
Altai Republic	Altai Republic National Library	–	1	–	1	2
Amur Oblast	Amur Oblast Research Library	–	–	1	–	1
Arkhangelsk Oblast (including Nenets Autonomous Okrug)	Arkhangelsk Oblast Research Library	–	2	1	–	3
	Nenets Central Library	1	–	–	–	1
Buryatia Republic	Buryatia Republic National Library	1	1	1	1	4
Chukotka Autonomous Okrug	N/A	–	–	–	–	–
Irkutsk Oblast	Irkutsk Regional Scientific Library	1	2	–	–	3
Kamchatka Krai	Kamchatka Krai Regional Research Library	–	3	–	1	4
Karelia Republic	Karelia Republic National Library	–	1	1	2	4
Khabarovsk Krai	Far Eastern Public Research Library	2	3	7	5	17
Komi Republic	Komi Republic National Library	–	–	2	1	3
Krasnoyarsk Krai	Krasnoyarsk Krai Scientific Library	–	1	–	1	2
Magadan Oblast	Magadan Oblast Research Library	–	1	–	1	2
Murmansk Oblast	Murmansk Oblast Research Library	–	1	1	4	6
Perm Krai	Perm Krai Universal Library	1	–	1	3	5
Primorsky Krai	Primorsky Krai Public Library	–	2	1	1	4
Sakha (Yakutia) Republic	Sakha Republic (Yakutia) National Library	–	1	4	5	10
Sakhalin Oblast	Sakhalin Oblast Research Library	–	–	1	4	5
Tomsk Oblast	Tomsk Regional Universal Scientific Library	–	–	1	1	2
Tuva Republic	Tuva Republic National Library	–	1	–	1	2

(continued)

Table 13.2 (contined)

Districts in the Far North[a] (as of 1 January 2020)	Russian Region Central Library	Year[b] 2017	2018	2019	2020	Total[b] 2017–2020
Tyumen Oblast (including Yamalo-Nenets Autonomous Okrug and Khanty-Mansi Autonomous Okrug–Yugra)	Tyumen Regional Scientific Library	–	–	–	–	–
	Yamalo-Nenets Autonomous Okrug National Library	–	–	1	–	1
	Ugra State Library	–	–	1	–	1
Zabaykalsky Krai	Zabaykalsky Krai Regional Universal Scientific Library	–	–	–	2	2
Total =		6	20	24	34	84

Table credit: A. G. Kuznetsova using data from the Tsentral'nyye biblioteki sub"yektov Rossiyskoy Federatsii [Central Libraries of Russian Regions] database
[a]Districts are listed alphabetically
[b]A hyphen ("–") in any of these columns indicates zero studies were conducted

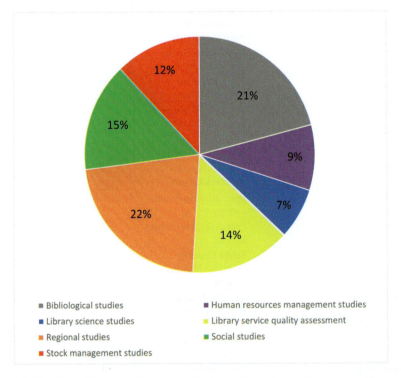

Fig. 13.2 Pie chart of themes and corresponding percentages for studies conducted by central libraries in the Far North of Russia, 2017–2019. (Chart credit: A. G. Kuznetsova using data from the Tsentral'nyye biblioteki sub"yektov Rossiyskoy Federatsii [Central Libraries of Russian Regions] database)

goal to uncover archives about and provide materials pertaining to Finns living in Russia. The ongoing project plans to result in the creation of an interactive database, including photos and documents on all ethnic Finns living in Russian territory during those years.

Libraries also participate in ethnographic projects by publishing materials from their archives. For example, in 2017–2020, the Sakha Republic National Library worked jointly with the Institute for Humanities Research and Indigenous Studies of the North, Siberian Branch of the Russian Academy of Sciences (http://igi.ysn. ru/) to publish Oroch-Russian and Russian-Oroch dictionaries. Oroch was the language of the Oroch people of Siberia; it is now extinct. The dictionaries were prepared in 1912–1913 by anthropologist Sergei Mikhailovich Shirokogorov (1887–1939) (Missonova, 2020; Shirokogorov, 1991). The similar project *Vizual'noye naslediye G. M. Vasilevicha v fonde Natsional'noy biblioteki Respubliki Sakha (Yakutiya)* [Visual Heritage of G. M. Vasilevich in the Fund of the National Library of the Republic of Sakha (Yakutia)] is a publication of photographs documenting various aspects of Evenki life in the middle of the twentieth century taken by ethnographer Glafira Makaryevna Vasilevich (1895–1971) (Zakharova, 2019). The Sakha Republic National Library contributed to another project, *Arkhivnoye naslediye I. S. Gurvicha v fondakh Natsional'noy biblioteki Respubliki Sakha (Yakutiya): rukopisnyye materialy i fotografii po etnografii Yakutii* [Archival Heritage of I. S. Gurvich in the Funds of National Library of the Republic of Sakha (Yakutia): Handwritten Materials and Photographs on the Ethnography of Yakutia], consisting of notes written by ethnographer Ilya Samuilovich Gurvich (1919–1992) during expeditions to the Far North (Neustroeva, 2019).

13.4.2 Library History and Bibliology

The CLRs can conduct projects on their own history such as, for instance, *Istoriya Natsional'noy biblioteki Respubliki Komi v XIX–XX vv.* [History of Komi Republic National Library in the 19th–20th Centuries] during 2019–2020 and *Istoriya Vologodskoy oblastnoy nauchnoy biblioteki v svyazi s istoriyey Vologdy i oblasti* [History of Vologda Oblast Research Library in Connection with the History of Vologda and Region] in 2019. The CLRs conduct bibliological studies of various directions and depth focusing on local history and book culture. For example, during 2017–2018, the Arkhangelsk Oblast Research Library carried out two bibliographic projects: *Rukopisi XV–XVII vekov v arkhive Arkhangel'skoy oblasti* [Manuscripts of the 15th–17th Centuries in the Archives of Arkhangelsk Oblast] and *Knigi na kirillitse XVI–XVII vekov v arkhive Arkhangel'skoy oblasti* [Cyrillic Script Books of the 16th–17th Centuries in the Archives of Arkhangelsk Oblast]. Both projects resulted in the creation of consolidated catalogues accessible via the Arkhangelsk Regional Scientific Library (https://conserv.aonb.ru/raritet/catalog.html).

The Far Eastern State Research Library carries out bibliological studies by way of the project *Redkiye i tsennyye dokumenty v sisteme sokhraneniya istoricheskoy pamyati* [Rare and Valuable Documents in the System of Historical Memory Preservation] (Naumova et al., 2021). In 2019, a study of the regional press resulted in publication of the catalogue by the Library of the Russian Geographical Society (2022) for the *Izvestiya Amurskogo otdeleniya Imperatorskogo Russkogo geograficheskogo obshchestva* [Proceedings of the Amur Chapter of the Imperial Russian Geographical Society], as well as a monograph titled *Zhurnaly Dal'nego Vostoka XIX– nachala XXI vekov: istoriya izdaniya i ispol'zovaniya v Tsentral'noy biblioteke Khabarovskogo kraya* [Magazines at the Far East in the 19th–Beginning of the 21st Centuries: The History of Publication and Usage in the Central Library of Khabarovsk Krai].

Boitunova (2020), a researcher working in the Sakha Republic National Library, published the thesis *Knigorasprostranenie v Yakutii v 1638–1917* [Book circulation in Yakutia in 1638–1917], aiming to reconstruct a general picture and examine the evolution and local specifics of book circulation in a mostly permafrost region with a surface of three million km^2 (1.16 million mi^2) and a population below one million people. The author concludes that climate was the main factor determining book circulation in the region, even more so than other variables such as social, economic and demographic factors. Furthermore, the thesis describes the foundation, functioning, and specifics of libraries and bookshops in the region, as well as development of local book culture.

The Far Eastern State Research Library published the study *Knizhnaya kul'tura korennykh narodov Dal'nego Vostoka* [Book Culture of Indigenous Far Eastern People] (Naumova et al., 2018), resulting in publication of the namesake monograph. The book covers the period before 1945 and positions publishing as an independent cultural phenomenon, focusing on books written in Indigenous languages rather than those by Indigenous authors published in Russian. The study suggests that printed books using Chinese technologies could have existed in the Jurchen Empire in the twelfth to thirteenth centuries, predating printing in Medieval Rus and Europe. Thus, the Far East might be the most ancient centre of printing in Russian territory. Unfortunately, Mongol invasion would have destroyed any solid evidence of this claim. In any case, known printed books are connected to Russian colonization of the Far East through the work of Russian officials, scientists, and missionaries who communicated and proselytized in local languages. Therefore, the earliest books in those languages were dictionaries, manuals, and religious texts written with a Cyrillic or Latin alphabet used by non-native speakers as Far East natives had no written language. These books were published in Moscow, St. Petersburg, and Kazan in the absence of printing facilities in the Far East. Only via scholar education and literacy programs that began in the late 1920s to early 1930s did broad readership in local Far Eastern languages arise, consequently creating the first national writers and poets from those geographic areas.

13.5 Library Science

Another group of studies and projects focuses on assessment of current library services, the tastes and social characteristics of library audiences, problems of book-stock management, and library human resources surveys. As a descriptive example, this section focuses on study of library services provided to Indigenous people of Buryatia.

13.5.1 Library Services to the Indigenous Peoples of the North: A Case Study in Buryatia

During 2018–2019, the Buryatia Republic National Library conducted the survey *Bibliotechnoye obsluzhivaniye korennykh malochislennykh narodov Severa, prozhivayushchikh v Respublike Buryatiya* [Library Services to the Indigenous Peoples of the North Living in Buryatia Republic] (Murzakina, 2019). Conducted in 11 districts within Buryatia, the survey aimed to assess problems of keeping book stock in Indigenous languages and determine best practices of providing library services to nomadic readers (e.g., reindeer herders, hunters, and fishers).

The Bauntovo Inter-Settlement Library is an exemplary case study. This library is a centre for library services to Evenki people in Buryatia. About 3000 Evenks, or roughly 0.3% of the total 2010 population of Buryatia Republic, live nomadically. Within Buryatia there are four boarding schools where Evenki language is taught, several cultural centres, and, since 1991, a university program for Evenki language and literature at Buryatia State University in the city of Ulan-Ude. The Bauntovo library contains a range of publications in Evenki language, including glossaries, collections of tales, learning materials, and school manuals. The library provides services to local nomadic peoples and develops programs to preserve their cultural artefacts and practices. Topics of program include, for instance, the searching of memorial sites, preserving of sacred sites, folklore from taletellers, and photo documentation of the traditional lifestyle of Evenki families in the Bauntovo District. The library communicates with other libraries, publishing houses, and Evenki spiritual leaders, and organizes book exhibitions and public events, such as lessons on Evenki language and discussions of texts, as well as facultative circles on history, folklore, and applied arts. Additionally, the library operates conferences, Olympiads, and local boarding school contests, and provides mobile library service to the nearby Taloi and Karatal reindeer farms.

The replenishment of book stock at the Bauntovo library, however, remains a problem. In the past, the Russian Association of Indigenous Peoples of the North (RAIPON) (https://raipon.info/) distributed literature on northern Indigenous peoples. At that time, libraries sent their requests and received materials by post. Presently, however, many relevant periodicals are either discontinued or require a cost. Publications by the RAIPON (2021), such as the yearbook *Zhivaya Arktika:*

Vselennaya korennykh narodov [Live Arctic: The Universe of Indigenous People] and various learning materials and collections of literary works sent to the «Golos Severa» ["Voice of the North"] contest are distributed for free, but can be obtained only in print—and only in person—at the RAIPON's Moscow office.

The Bauntovo library subscribes to the current periodical *Mir Severa* [Northern World] and the *Zhivaya Arktika* [Live Arctic] yearbook. In addition, the library keeps an archive of discontinued periodicals, such as *Bagul'nik na vetru* [Wild Rosemary in the Wind], *Voprosy Severa* [Northern Studies], *Severnyye prostory* [Northern Expanses], *Zhizn' natsional'nostey* [National Life], *Volika: Lastochka* [Vjolika: Swallow], and *Ulgur*.

13.5.2 Readership Surveys and Projects

Surveys on readership are useful for monitoring the needs and demands of audiences. Since 1995, the RNL (2022) has worked on the research project *Chitatel'skaya auditoriya v rossiyskikh bibliotekakh* [Readership in Russian Libraries]. In 2014, the project resulted in the Chitatel'skaya i bibliotechnaya auditoriya: biblioteka i obshchestvoznaniye [Readership and Library Audience: Library and Social Studies] database, allowing the collection of data on readership and audiences from studies carried out by libraries alone and those collaborating with other institutions.

To see which CLR projects are considered a success is interesting. One successful project during 2017–2020, *Yamal chitayet!* [Yamal Reads!], was conceived by the RMC and coordinated by the Yamalo-Nenets Autonomous Okrug National Library (2021). In the frame of this project, local companies were requested to bring to the library at least 50% of their employees. Visitors listened to a presentation about activities and services provided by the library, were given certificates and stickers, and became registered as subscribers. Additional souvenirs were distributed in a monthly lottery on social platforms among subscribers who read at least one book from the library during each month. Frequent readers and lottery winners were invited to prize-giving ceremonies featuring the mascot Platosha, the reading reindeer. The project aimed to form a steady interest in reading among the population and increase the percentage of subscribed readers in the region.

13.5.3 Book Stock Management

Stock management studies investigate book stock content, usage, and dynamics with the aim to optimize efficiency and increase cohesion with the needs of library audiences. Stock management departments of many libraries, including the Karelia Republic National Library and bookkeeping department of the Primorsky Krai Public Library, participate in the RNL centralized study *Vserossiyskiy monitoring fizicheskogo sostoyaniya bibliotechnykh fondov* [All-Russian Monitoring of *Library*

13   A Descriptive Review of Research Studies by the Central Libraries of the Far...   271

Collections' Physical Condition] (2020) of which «Vserossiyskiy monitoring sokhrannosti knizhnogo fonda» ["All-Russian Monitoring of Book Stock Preservation"] is a part. The study's main purpose is to define the problems of bookkeeping in Russian libraries, assess existing bookkeeping facilities and availability of conservation equipment and skilled personnel, and define necessary conservation and restoration tasks for each book-stock category.

13.5.4   Human Resources (HR) Management

Human resources (HR) management is the subject of several projects and studies based on detailed surveys conducted among librarians to learn how they feel about their work, determine existing problems, and discover suggestions on the improvement of various library workflows. A good example of such survey data is the study *Metodicheskiy otdel: ozhidaniya i real'nost'* [Methodology Department: Expectations and Reality] (Zhalsaraeva, 2017) by the Buryatia Republic National Library. Another good example is Reshetnikova and Neustroeva's (2020) study *Biblioteka glazami bibliotekarey* [Library in the Eyes of Librarians] by the Sakha Republic National Library, showing that only about one-quarter of librarians are satisfied with their working conditions. According to the study, the most common need is specific training as about 80% of employees feel they need more training to operate computers and about 30% feel they would benefit from grant and project writing training. When required to evaluate tasks by attractiveness, employees prefer routine services to writing documents—including research—and public speaking because the former is less stressful. The study *Kadrovyy potentsial bibliotek Krasnoyarskogo kraya: tekushchaya situatsiya i tendentsii* [HR Potential in Krasnoyarsk Krai Libraries: Present Situation and Tendencies] by Popova (2020) reveals demographic considerations: only 13% of employees are less than 30 years old, while 40% are above the age of retirement. In each of these conducted surveys, librarians indicate that they wish to see their libraries become modernized technologically by transforming into information centres or hubs for innovative activities.

13.6   Conclusion

Research activity of the CLRs is manifold and the actualization of their potential is high priority. The main problem with research projects carried out by CLRs is the discrepancy between their potential and the fact that such potential is not used in the context of national cultural policy; no regular demand exists for research work by libraries from the Russian Ministry of Education and Science or the Russian Ministry of Culture. Although these institutions support regular library services, they do not consider libraries as research institutions nor include research activities in their yearly plans. Many research projects are proposed by libraries thanks in large part by individuals' and organizational commitment to research and publication. These projects are not carried out systematically and their results often remain within the undertaking library or, at best, libraries within the same region. In addition, not all projects and studies result in publications, thus making it sometimes difficult to obtain details about and outcomes of them.

In the areas of the Far North, both stationary and mobile library services are a unique cultural institution, possessing boundless potential for improvement. However, the human resources problems and demographic issues that are characteristic in Far North libraries manifest even more acutely than anywhere else in Russia. The most topical studies on these concerns within the Far North take place at leading regional CLRs, such as the Far Eastern Public Research Library and Sakha Republic National Library. Development and support of CLR research activities is an important prerequisite for revealing their potential with the purpose of increasing their role in science, education, culture and quality of life in Russia.

Appendix

Alphabetical list of Russian libraries and archives mentioned in this chapter

Institution name	Location	Website
Arkhangelsk Oblast Research Library	Arkhangelsk, Arkhangelsk Oblast	https://www.aonb.ru/
Bauntovo Inter-Settlement Library	Bauntovo, Bauntovsky District, Buryatia Republic	http://cbsbaunt.ru/
Buryatia Republic National Library	Ulan-Ude, Buryatia Republic	http://nbrb.ru/
Far Eastern State Research Library	Khabarovsk, Khabarovsk Krai	https://fessl.ru/
Karelia Republic National Library	Petrozavodsk, Karelia Republic	http://library.karelia.ru/
Komi Republic National Library	Syktyvkar, Komi Republic	https://www.nbrkomi.ru/
Krasnoyarsk Krai Public Research Library	Krasnoyarsk, Krasnoyarsk Krai	https://www.kraslib.ru/
Primorsky Krai Public Library	Vladivostok, Primorsky Krai	https://pgpb.ru/
Sakha Republic National Library	Yakutsk, Sakha Republic	https://nlrs.ru/
Tan-Bogoraz Public Library	Anadyr City, Chukotka Autonomous Okrug	https://www.library-chukotka.ru/
Vologda Oblast Research Library	Vologda, Vologda Oblast	https://www.booksite.ru/
Yamalo-Nenets Autonomous Okrug National Library	Salekhard, Yamalo-Nenets Autonomous Okrug	https://nb.yanao.ru/

(continued)

Institution name	Location	Website
Yeniseysk City Library	Yeniseysk, Yeniseysk District, Krasnoyarsk Krai	http://biblen.ru/
Yeniseysk Municipal Archives	Yeniseysk, Yeniseysk District, Krasnoyarsk Krai	https://www.eniseysk.com/gorod%20segodnya/Enis_arh/

Table credit: A. G. Kuznetova

References

Avramova, M. B., & Basov, S. A. (2020). *Obshchedostupnyye biblioteki ministerstva kultury Rossiiskoy Federatsii: itogi monitoringa seti – 2020 god* [Public Libraries under the Ministry of Culture of the Russian Federation: Results of monitoring in 2020]. Russian National Library. https://bit.ly/3AAymlH. Accessed 11 Dec 2023.

Boitunova, S. I. (2020) *Knigorasprostranenie v Yakutii v 1638–1917* [Book circulation in Yakutia in 1638–1917] [Thesis, Arctic State Institute of Culture and Arts]. https://bit.ly/3BdM1jp. Accessed 11 Dec 2023.

Kontseptsiya gosudarstvennoy podderzhki ekonomicheskogo i sotsialnogo razvitiya rayonov severa [Concept of state support of economical and social development of northern areas]. Regulation No. 198. (2000). https://bit.ly/3owKHjT. Accessed 11 Dec 2023.

Kuznetsova, A. G. (2020, November 26–27). *O nauchnykh issledovaniyakh, provodimykh tsentral'nymi bibliotekami regionov Rossiyskoy Federatsii* [On scientific studies carried out by central libraries of Russian Federation regions] [Conference paper]. Scientific and Practical Conference of Young Specialists to the 225th Anniversary of the Founding of the Russian National Library: Traditions and Innovations. St. Petersburg, Russia. Russian National Library.

Library of the Russian Geographical Society/Biblioteka Russkogo geograficheskogo obshchestva. (2022). *Izvestiya Amurskogo otdeleniya Imperatorskogo Russkogo geograficheskogo obshchestva* [Proceedings of Amur Chapter of the Imperial Russian Geographical Society]. https://bit.ly/3PEr1qv. Accessed 11 Dec 2023.

Ob utverzhdenii basovogo (otraslevogo) perechnia uslug i rabot v sfere «Kul'tura, kinematografiya, arkhivnoye delo, turizm» [On the basic (sector-wide) list of works and services in the sphere of "culture, cinematography, and tourism"]. Order No. 1197. (2016). https://bit.ly/3b69KaD. Accessed 11 Dec 2023.

Ob utverzhdenii perechnya rajonov Krajnego Severa i mestnostej, priravnennyh k rajonam Krajnego Severa... [On the list of areas of Far North, areas equivalent to Far-North...]. Regulation No. 1946. (2021a). https://bit.ly/3z3nL0P. Accessed 11 Dec 2023.

Strategia razvitia bibliotechnogo dela v Rossijskoj Federatsii do 2030 goda [Strategy of development of library services in the Russian Federation until 2030] Regulation No. 608.(2021b). https://bit.ly/3RTunr4. Accessed 11 Dec 2023.

Missonova, L. (2020). Novyy etap vozvrashcheniya naslediya S. M. Shirokogorova: stranitsy intellektual'noy biografii (1912–1939 gg) [A new stage in the retrieval of the heritage of S. M. Shirokogorov: The pages of his intellectual biography (1912–1939)]. *Etnografia* [Ethnography], 2(8), 184–203. https://doi.org/g7zt

Murzakina, L. V. (2019). *Bibliotechnoye obsluzhivaniye korennykh malochislennykh narodov Severa, prozhivayushchikh v Respublike Buryatiya* [Library services to the Indigenous peoples of the North living in Buryatia Republic]. Buryatia Republic National Library and MBUK «Bauntovskaya TsBS». https://bit.ly/3cwYYdI. Accessed 11 Dec 2023.

Naumova, R. V., Filatkina, I. V., Voropaeva, A. V., Radishauskaite, N. V., & Zagorodnaya, K. A. (2018). *Knizhnaya kul'tura korennykh narodov Dal'nego Vostoka* [Book culture of

Indigenous Far Eastern people]. Khabarovsk Krai Ministry of Culture. https://bit.ly/3RUqF0l. Accessed 11 Dec 2023.

Naumova, R. V., Radishauskaite, N. V., Voropaeva, A. V., Zagorodnaya, K. A., & Filatkina, I. V. (2021). *Redkiye i tsennyye dokumenty v sisteme sokhraneniya istoricheskoy pamyati* [Rare and Valuable Documents in the System of Historical Memory Preservation]. Khabarovsk Krai Ministry of Culture. https://bit.ly/3S73yQu. Accessed 11 Dec 2023.

Neustroeva, V. A. (2019). Arkhivnoye naslediye I. S. Gurvicha v fondakh natsional'noy biblioteki respubliki Sakha (Yakutiya): rukopisnyye materialy i fotografii po etnografii Yakutii [Archival heritage of I. S. Gurvich in the funds of National Library of the Republic of Sakha (Yakutia): Handwritten materials and photographs on the ethnography of Yakutia]. In L. I. Vinokurova, L. S. Zamorschikova, S. V. Maksimova, N. V. Pokatilova, L. B. Stepanova, & E. N. Romanova (Eds.), *Ekho arkticheskoy odissei: sud'by etnicheskikh kul'tur v issledovaniyakh uchenykh-severovedov: Sbornik materialov Vserossiyskoy nauchno-prakticheskoy konferentsii s mezhdunarodnym uchastiyem* [Echo of the Arctic odyssey: The fate of ethnic cultures in the studies of North scientists: Collection of materials of the All-Russian Scientific and Practical Conference with International Participation] (pp. 65–69). Sakha (Yakutia) Republic National Library Publishing House.

O bibliotechnom dele [On Library Services]. Federal law No. 78-FZ. (1994). https://bit.ly/3cGfIiE. Accessed 11 Dec 2023.

Popova, I. N. (2020). *Kadrovyy potentsial bibliotek Krasnoyarskogo kraya: tekushchaya situatsiya i tendentsii* [HR potential in Krasnoyarsk Krai libraries: Present situation and tendencies]. Krasnoyarsk Region State Universal Scientific Library. https://bit.ly/3PPUygx. Accessed 11 Dec 2023.

Reshetnikova, N. P., & Neustroeva, A. B. (2020). *Biblioteka glazami bibliotekarey* [Library through the eyes of librarians]. https://bit.ly/3PRBeiQ. Accessed 11 Dec 2023.

Russian Association of Indigenous Peoples of the North (RAIPON)/Assotsiatsiya korennykh malochislennykh narodov Severa, Sibiri i Dal'nego Vostoka. (2021). *Zhivaya Arktika: Vselennaya korennykh narodov* [Live Arctic: The universe of Indigenous people]. https://bit.ly/3oz5i7w. Accessed 11 Dec 2023.

Russian Library Association (RLA)/Rossiyskaya bibliotechnaya assotsiatsiya. (2015). *O nauchno-metodicheskoy deyatel'nosti tsentral'noy biblioteki regiona Rossiyskoy Federatsii* [On research and methodological activity by a central library of a Russian Federation region]. https://bit.ly/3cDBaou. Accessed 11 Dec 2023.

Russian Library Association (RLA)/Rossiyskaya bibliotechnaya assotsiatsiya. (2016). *Itogovyy dokument Yezhegodnogo soveshchania rukovoditeley federal'nykh i tsentralnykh bibliotek Rossii* [Summary document of the early meeting of directors of federal and central Russian libraries]. https://bit.ly/3vcaXnE. Accessed 11 Dec 2023.

Russian Library Association (RLA)/Rossiyskaya bibliotechnaya assotsiatsiya. (2022). *31. Sektsiya po nauchno-issledovatel'skoy rabote* [31. Research section]. https://bit.ly/3BgNPbl. Accessed 11 Dec 2023.

Russian National Library (RNL)/Rossiyskaya natsional'naya biblioteka. (2022). *Chitatel'skaya auditoriya v rossiyskikh bibliotekakh* [Readership in Russian libraries]. https://bit.ly/3b0yP6G. Accessed 11 Dec 2023.

Severa krajnego rajony i priravnennye k nim mestnosti [Far North and equivalent areas]. (2015). In *Bol'shaya rossijskaya enciklopediya* [Great Russian encyclopaedia] (Vol. 29). Russian Academy of Sciences.

Shirokogorov, S. M. (1991). Tungus literary language. *Asian Folklore Studies, 50*(1), 35–66. https://doi.org/fc4hqf

Slavin, S. V. (1982). *Osvoeniye Severa Sovetskogo Soyuza* [Development of the Soviet North]. Nauka.

Taktaikina, T. I. (2018). *O pravovom obosnovanii metodicheskikh uslug (rabot) vypolniaemykh tsentral'nymi gosudarstvennymi (munitsipal'nykh) bibliotekami.* [On legal grounds of research services provided by central public (municipal) libraries]. https://bit.ly/48cZchL. Accessed 11 Dec 2023.

Tarakanov, M. A. (2010). Evolyutsiya prostranstvennoy lokalizatsii ponyatiy «Krayniy Sever» i «Sever» v Rossii. [Evolution of spatial location of the concepts "Far North" and "North" in Russia]. *Natsional'nyye interesy: prioritety i bezopasnost* [National interests: Priorities and security], 6(26), eLibrary ID 15213325, 32–41.

Vlassova, I. I., Galeeva, F. A., Eremeeva, L. K., Zyryanova, A. L., Maksimova, N. G., Mikhalkova, L. E., Nikitina, O. V., Pirogova, N. V., Ramenskaya, T. M., & Sidorenko, Z. F. (2021). *100 let vmeste s chitatelyami* [100 years with our readers]. Yeniseisk. https://bit.ly/3vaslZI. Accessed 11 Dec 2023.

Vserossiyskiy monitoring sostoyaniya bibliotechnykh fondov [All-Russian monitoring of library collections' physical condition]. (2020). *Bibliotekovedenie* [Russian Journal of Library Science], 69(4), 408. https://bit.ly/3oKKsCh. Accessed 11 Dec 2023.

Yamalo-Nenets Autonomous Okrug National Library (2021). *Yamal chitayet!* [Yamal reads!]. https://bit.ly/4ac8UTj. Accessed 11 Dec 2023.

Zakharova, E. I. (2019). Vizual'noye naslediye G. M. Vasilevich v fonde natsional'noy biblioteki respubliki Sakha (Yakutiya): materialy po shamanizmu Evenkov [Visual heritage of G. M. Vasilevich in the fund of the National Library of the Republic of Sakha (Yakutia): Materials on the shamanism of the Evenks]. In L. I. Vinokurova, L. S. Zamorschikova, S. V. Maksimova, N. V. Pokatilova, L. B. Stepanova, & E. N. Romanova (Eds.), *Ekho arkticheskoy odissei: sud'by etnicheskikh kul'tur v issledovaniyakh uchenykh-severovedov: Sbornik materialov Vserossiyskoy nauchno-prakticheskoy konferentsii s mezhdunarodnym uchastiyem* [Echo of the Arctic odyssey: The fate of ethnic cultures in the studies of North scientists: Collection of materials of the All-Russian Scientific and Practical Conference with International Participation] (pp. 408–413). Sakha (Yakutia) Republic National Library Publishing House.

Zhalsaraeva, N. (2017). *Itogi issledovaniya «Metodicheskaya sluzhba: ozhidaniya i real'nost'»* [Results of the study "Methodological service: Expectations and reality"]. Buryatia Republic National Library. https://bit.ly/3aZ8DJE. Accessed 11 Dec 2023.

Chapter 14
The Irish Impact: Charting a Course for the Development of Historical Arctic and Northern Studies on the Island of Ireland

Sarah Milne and Chelsi Slotten ⓘ

Abstract As an island nation in the North Atlantic, Ireland's relative proximity to the Arctic raises the question of whether Ireland can be categorized as an Arctic-adjacent state. In support of this claim, this chapter argues that Irish links to Arctic and Northern areas are underexplored but go back millennia, defining Ireland's identity in the North and can be utilized towards promoting Ireland's cultural diplomacy activities with Nordic states. Ireland's growing interest in the Arctic region can be witnessed through its application for Arctic Council Observer status in December 2020 and the release of Ireland's Nordic Strategy in June 2021 as part of its Global Ireland foreign policy. This chapter outlines the importance of the creation of the Network of Arctic Researchers Ireland (NARI) in February 2020 as a means for cross-disciplinary Arctic researchers to collaborate and develop new networking opportunities. The authors of this chapter were instrumental in developing the NARI Humanities and Social Science (HSS) Working Group and have organized it into three key research areas, which have a pivotal role in shaping future research outcomes in this multidisciplinary field. The NARI is an important means through which Irish HSS research with Arctic or Northern foci can be highlighted and existing research studies across multiple academic disciplines, including library and information science (LIS), and fields within HSS can be reorganized through the lens of Arctic and Northern studies to produce a more effective way of sharing resources and data while encouraging cross-disciplinary collaboration. This chapter focuses on the development of the *Irish Impact* project as a mapping exercise within the NARI HSS Working Group that seeks to demonstrate Ireland's historical, cultural, social, and political ties to the North Atlantic and Arctic regions. Indeed, the

---

S. Milne (✉)
National Maritime College of Ireland, Munster Technological University Cork, Cork, Ireland
e-mail: sk.milne985@gmail.com

C. Slotten
Sage Publishing, Edinburgh, UK
e-mail: contact@chelsislotten.com

© The Author(s), under exclusive license to Springer Nature
Switzerland AG 2024
S. Acadia (ed.), *Library and Information Sciences in Arctic and Northern Studies*, Springer Polar Sciences, https://doi.org/10.1007/978-3-031-54715-7_14

277

Irish Government has outlined the importance of shared cultural heritage in its Strategy and this chapter discusses Ireland's historical connections to the North and Arctic through two significant eras: (1) the migration of Irish missionaries to Scandinavia in the early Christian era from the fifth through twelfth centuries, with a focus on Norway, the Faroe Islands, and Iceland; and (2) Ireland's strong Viking heritage because of successive waves of Nordic invasions during the Middle Ages. The Irish Government is already using these two historical themes for cultural engagement and to foster greater diplomatic ties with Nordic countries. However, to further the policy objectives of Ireland's Nordic Strategy, LIS systems must be further developed, and new research supports installed. The chapter concludes by outlining the importance of creating digital LIS systems towards the emergence of a visible and robust Irish Arctic and Northern studies university program that could meaningfully contribute to current discourse in the field. To further this objective, two projects are proposed: (1) the creation of an Irish Arctic digital library; and (2) the creation of an Irish university consortium for Arctic and Northern studies in HSS with a supporting university database listing Irish and Nordic partner universities involved in HSS research for Arctic and Northern Studies.

Keywords Arctic Council · Arctic digital library · Cultural diplomacy · Early Christian Ireland · Irish foreign policy · Irish-Nordic studies · Irish Viking studies · Medieval studies · Network of Arctic Researchers Ireland (NARI)

14.1 Introduction: International Relations at Work: Ireland's Application for Arctic Council Observer Status as a Catalyst to Develop Arctic and Northern Studies in Ireland

Ireland was one of three countries that applied in 2020 for Arctic Council (AC) observer status alongside Estonia and the Czech Republic. Even though there was little media or public attention following the Irish Government's announcement on the 1st of December 2020, the decision was seen as a milestone for Arctic researchers in Ireland of all disciplines. The Irish Department of Foreign Affairs' (DFA) (2021a, b) growing interest in the AC signifies that Ireland has become more invested in Arctic and Northern affairs and is finally ready to take its place alongside its other Western European neighbours that have been observers for many years. Unfortunately, lack of consensus at the AC Ministerial meeting in Reykjavík on 20 May 2021 meant that no new observer states were admitted at that time (Quinn, 2021). Despite this setback, the Irish Government is likely to pursue another bid for obtaining AC observer status within the Arctic Council in 2023, when the chair will pass from Russia to Norway.

Meanwhile, it is important to consider what the key motivational factors were for the Irish Government when it chose to apply for AC observer status toward helping to determine Ireland's strategic interests in the Arctic region and thus potentially steering future opportunities for Ireland's Arctic and Northern studies researchers. In December 2020, Ireland's Minister for Foreign Affairs, Simon Covney, declared that AC observer status would enhance Ireland's understanding of climate change in the Arctic and its effects on sea levels, a problem that Minister Covney perceived as being one that will increasingly affect Ireland given its geographic location in the northeast Atlantic. He explained that economic factors were also an important determinant underpinning Ireland's application for AC observer status, in particular fisheries and maritime policy (Cunningham, 2020).

Undoubtedly, Ireland's Arctic interests are multifaceted, however in this chapter we are interested in exploring Ireland's historical ties to the Arctic and Northern regions. The expansion of research in this area could lead to new library and information science (LIS) services being developed to assist academic research and tourism, in addition to political benefits with respect to raising international awareness of Irish historical and cultural events that could strengthen diplomatic connections with Arctic states.

Political scientist Marc Lanteigne, an Arctic expert at the Arctic University of Norway in Tromsø (UiT), conducted research on current and future AC observer states to determine why they seek to engage in Arctic affairs. Lanteigne (2020) created distinct categories for AC observer states based on specific 'Arctic identities' that help to explain the ways in which these non-Arctic states justify their interest in Arctic affairs and the reasons for why they applied for observer status with the AC. The first of Lanteigne's three categories includes those states that have an 'Arctic legacy' and claim to have extensive historical experience in the Arctic that includes explorative and scientific expertise in the region, all of which long predate the creation of the AC. The second category consists of 'all-rounders,' states that focus less on claims of having a historical background, instead stressing the modern economic, environmental, political, and scientific goods they can provide to the AC specifically and Arctic affairs generally. In 2021, Lanteigne created a third category of 'Arctic-adjacent' states that includes those countries that are geographically close to the Arctic region on the assumption that they share various physical, cultural, historical, and economic characteristics with Arctic states. Although it makes sense that Ireland would fall into the Arctic-adjacent category given its geographic location in the North Atlantic and relative proximity to the Arctic North, Ireland may also equally adhere to the all-rounder grouping. In a parliamentary debate held in May 2019, Minister Covney outlined how the AC's work is carried out in several areas such as climate change, biodiversity, and sustainable development that are of importance to Ireland (Houses of the Oireachtas, 2019). Economic interests, however, also served as a key driver for Ireland's AC observer application, particularly fisheries and maritime policy, despite the former policy area not being discussed within AC fora. If Ireland fits the criteria of these two categories, what of the last remaining category of 'Arctic legacy?' Minister Covney answered this quite clearly during his keynote address during an event held by the Institute for International and European Affairs and the Department of Foreign Affairs on 1 March 2021:

> Why is Ireland applying to the Arctic Council is a question I have been asked on a number of occasions in recent months. I believe that the answer is quite simple. Ireland needs to become involved in the work of the Council because we are an island nation at the edge of Europe in the North Atlantic and we have a culture, heritage and identity intrinsically linked to the seas that surround us. We are not in the Arctic, but we can certainly say that we are part of the wider Arctic neighbourhood. (DFA, 2021a, para. 3)

Taking into consideration that Ireland may in fact align with all three of Lanteigne's identity categories, one way to further clarify this possibility is to briefly engage in policy analysis. This method serves as a useful way to evaluate official policy documents in the review of how the Irish Government intend to develop a Northern and Arctic political identity, as well as enable discernment as to what are their priorities. By doing so, this chapter demonstrates that Ireland does indeed engage with all three of Lanteigne's categorizations but emphasizes the importance of the Arctic legacy category with respect to Ireland's Arctic identity.

To date, Ireland does not have a strategy for the entire circumpolar Arctic region, suggesting that the Irish Government's objectives for Arctic engagement are limited to specific subregions of the Arctic, namely the Nordic area. In June 2021, the Government of Ireland published *A Strategy for the Nordic Regions* (hereafter referred to as 'Nordic Strategy'). This document was released as an add-on to the current Irish foreign policy strategy, published by the Government of Ireland in 2018, titled *Global Ireland: Ireland's Global Footprint to 2025*. The Nordic Strategy indicated that the Irish Government aims to strengthen ties with its Nordic neighbours as one of its current priorities. Ireland's 2020 application for observer status in the AC is referred to within the Nordic Strategy as being one way Ireland is seeking to increase its impact in the region. Then, in December 2021, the DFA released a follow-on document, titled *Global Ireland: Ireland's Strategy for the Nordic Region to 2025—Action Plan* (hereafter referred to as 'Action Plan') which set out priorities for the Nordic strategy for the year 2021 and 2022. Described as a living document, the DFA expects that the Action Plan will evolve over time and will likely be updated on a yearly basis. The Action Plan contains 25 action points in total with at least 10 focusing on strengthening scientific research on Arctic and Northern issues either through direct academic linkages with Nordic states, or through the AC if future observer status is achieved, as well as scientific cooperation under the auspices of the European Union (EU). However, the Action Plan discusses action points for just two of the five strategic objectives that are outlined within the Nordic Strategy The five strategic objectives outlined within the Nordic Strategy are below:

I. Ireland will work with Denmark, Finland, Sweden, Iceland, and Norway to advance and safeguard shared interests and values across the world, including in the UN and via European partnerships.
II. Ireland will facilitate deepening trade, tourism, and knowledge exchanges with the Nordic region consistent with our climate action agenda.
III. Ireland will strengthen people-to-people links and links to the Global Irish Community in the Nordic region.

IV. Ireland will grow its reputation across the Nordic countries through enhancing promotion of culture, heritage, and linkages.
V. A strong Government-led Team Ireland will significantly increase its impact to 2025. (Government of Ireland, 2021, p. 5)

Two of these objectives (III and IV) directly correspond to recognizing Irish cultural and historical links with the Nordic region, while objective II relates to developing knowledge exchanges between and academic collaboration with partner universities in Northern and Arctic regions. Additionally, cultural and historical linkages to the North could also be fostered through developing sustainable tourism. These strategic objectives verify that the Irish government intends to pursue historical and cultural diplomacy, hence qualifying Ireland for Lanteigne's Arctic legacies category as one way in which the country can strengthen its connections to the Nordic region. According to Rynijska-Kieldanowcz (n.d., p. 2), the concept of public and cultural diplomacy can be understood "as a form of state 'branding' in a similar manner to the way in which companies endorse brand management and identity building." In addition, because art and culture are at the forefront of many countries' promotional efforts, governments recognize that presenting their cultural heritage to international audiences provides them with an opportunity of not only showing who they are, but also creating a positive image and thus helping to achieve their political aims.

Nonetheless, to create an honest appraisal of Ireland's Northern heritage is to recognize that no country's past is without conflict and struggle. For Ireland, as with many other countries, there is always a balancing act between local and national politics on one hand and international relations on the other. The effects of British colonialism, the historic plantations of Scottish and English settlers, the influence of the Roman Catholic church, and the quest for Irish home rule and independence during the eighteenth, nineteenth, and early twentieth centuries must be acknowledged because all have significantly shaped politics and social identity on the island of Ireland. Following independence from Great Britain in 1922, and the formal creation of the Republic of Ireland in 1949, Ireland worked hard to engage in global affairs, joining the United Nations on the 14 December 1955, on the same day as Finland, and two decades later becoming a member of the European Community, now the EU, in 1973.

Although the island of Ireland may be considered small on a worldly scale covering a total of 84,431 km² (32,599 mi²), there are distinct differences between the north of Ireland, which remains a separate country and part of Great Britain with its own history and heritage, and the Republic of Ireland in the south. However, what both north and south have in common is that they are administratively divided into counties, with six counties in the north of Ireland and 26 in the Republic. County identity is strong on the island of Ireland and local places are always suffixed with their respective county, usually abbreviated as 'Co.,' followed by the county name (e.g., Co. Cork). When a place is mentioned without the Co. suffix, it implies a major town or city within a county of the same name (e.g., Dublin, Cork, Limerick, Galway, etc.). As much as possible, this chapter aims to take an all-island approach to include research contributions from all of Ireland, in addition to discussing cultural events, academic papers, and research projects on Irish-Nordic and Arctic historical linkages.

Going far back in history can help broaden and reassess Irish concepts of 'Northernness' that have arguably become distorted by nationalist politics. Not only could this lead to strengthening Ireland's cultural diplomacy with Arctic nations, but also could assist with reclaiming a more complete understanding of Northernness for Irish identity, one that transcends the partition of Ireland into north and south and their distinct polities. This division harkens back to the separation of the Republic from Great Britain that resulted in a bitter Irish civil war (1922–1923) and long decades of sectarian conflict referred to as 'the Troubles' of the 1970s and 1980s in Northern Ireland.[1] Fortunately, this dark period of Irish history came to an end when the internationally esteemed peace process in Northern Ireland took effect and culminated with the historic signing of the *Comhaontú Aoine an Chéasta* [Good Friday Agreement] in 1998 by the British and Irish governments (DFA, n.d.) and mediated by the Clinton Administration in the United States.

Ongoing north-south relations between the Republic, Northern Ireland, Great Britain, and the EU have intensified both during and in the aftermath of Great Britain officially leaving the EU in January 2020. Commonly referred to as 'Brexit,' this political issue has, and will continue to be, a pivotal focus for the Irish Government as it navigates the uncharted waters of the Northern Ireland protocol. Thus, the aspiration for developing a new Irish understanding of North and Northernness comes at a critical time in the history of Ireland and can be aided by recognizing Ireland's rich Northern and Arctic heritage (Dybris McQuaid et al., 2019, p. 5). The development of Irish Arctic and Northern studies in the humanities and social sciences (HSS) could have many positive benefits for academia on the island of Ireland, with the possible creation of new fields of multidisciplinary studies within HSS, in addition to new university partnerships between north and south, both within Ireland and in cooperation with Arctic countries. As will be explained in this chapter, the development of new library and information science (LIS) services is an essential component in support of Arctic and Northern HSS.

If greater numbers of Irish researchers are to pursue studies involving the Arctic or the North, it is imperative that this new research area is given shape through active engagement by existing Irish Arctic researchers with the sharing of ideas and input from their international colleagues who hail from Arctic states. Therefore, Part I of this chapter discusses the creation of the Network of Arctic Researchers in Ireland (NARI), including how NARI was established, outlining its internal

---

[1] The political division of Ireland came into force on 3 May 1921 under the *Government of Ireland Act* 1920. Located in the northeast of the island, Northern Ireland is divided into six counties: Antrim, Armagh, Down, Fermanagh, Londonderry (Derry), and Tyrone. These six counties were areas that had undergone historical plantation of settlers from England and Scotland. With a predominant Protestant population who proclaimed loyalty to the Union with Great Britain, this led to oppression and violence breaking out between the Protestant majority and the Catholic minority, many of whom were nationalists seeking a reunited Ireland.

structure, and describing how it functions. Next, the specific role that the HSS Working Group has within NARI in promoting Northern and Arctic research is also described.

Part II focuses on two key historical eras through which to view Irish-Northern and Arctic linkages. Ireland's Northern and Arctic heritage is best viewed as one which covers a broad span of history and explored through an interdisciplinary HSS approach, drawing on fields as diverse as political science, environmental history, identity and cultural studies, archaeology, anthropology, and visual ethnography, in addition to Irish and Celtic studies. Such an approach serves as a multidimensional lens through which to view and fully appreciate the rich historical heritage that Ireland shares with the North by framing these activities within time and space. Importantly, recognition of how these Irish-Nordic historical and cultural linkages can serve to strengthen multicultural political agendas through highlighting shared histories and reinforcing political, ethnic, cultural, and religious diversity and tolerance is key. Toward this end, this chapter advocates that Irish academia has a large role to play to ensure that accurate information and research is available to support these endeavours, in addition to Irish scholars and researchers who can contribute their expertise.[2]

Part III seeks to highlight potential projects that serve to further the development of Arctic HSS research in Ireland. Having analysed and examined potential research gaps in Part II through discussion of projects pertaining to the six key historical research areas, the chapter puts forward four specific policy recommendations, including two key projects: (1) the creation of a central online portal of resources for Arctic HSS researchers in Ireland and internationally who are interested in studying Irish-Arctic linkages; and (2) the creation of a university consortium to coordinate and strengthen the availability of relevant academic courses being offered on the island of Ireland as it relates to Arctic and Northern studies in the fields of HSS.

---

[2] The same can also be applied to the other subjects identified by the NARI HSS Working Group. Although in this chapter we focus primarily on those linkages with the Nordic region to coincide with Ireland's Nordic Strategy, we similarly acknowledge that the Irish Canadian and Irish American diaspora to northern regions have produced a rich profusion of historical literature in the social sciences that we hope will be engaged with by others at a later date.

14.2 Part I: The Coordination of Arctic and Northern Studies in HSS Research in Ireland

14.2.1 NARI: Creating a Focus Point for Irish Arctic Research in Support of Ireland's Application for AC Observer Status

NARI was officially launched on 28 February 2020 with an event held at DFA headquarters in Dublin. Several high-ranking government officials were in attendance including the Irish Ambassador to Norway, Keith McBean, and Ciara Delaney, who at the time was director of the EU division at DFA. The inspiration for NARI can be traced back to April 2019 when an Arctic roundtable meeting was organized by the DFA and Marine Institute to identify the scope of Irish Arctic research. The main purpose behind the DFA hosting this meeting was to assess the potential for Ireland to contribute to AC working groups. At the time, Ireland had not yet applied for AC observer status, though it was under consideration. An additional aim of the meeting was to consider the possibility of creating an Irish Arctic network. Consisting of about 20 Irish researchers from natural and social sciences, the proposed network would seek to promote information sharing and collaboration among Irish researchers and have an inclusive approach to membership from all higher educational institutes located across Ireland. Thus, the basis for creating an all-island research network for Arctic studies emerged, and it was agreed during the discussion to create the NARI title of 'Associate Member,' a status granted to Irish professionals working in areas that have linkages to the Arctic as well as international Arctic researchers outside of Ireland. The network would not be dominated by any single academic institution to avoid the emergence of inequalities. Instead, two biannual meetings would be hosted on a rotational basis while an online presence would be maintained through the creation of a website and social media platforms.

NARI decided to design its organizational structure on that of the International Arctic Science Committee (IASC) (https://iasc.info/). Like those of the IASC, the NARI devised three working groups: Marine, Terrestrial; and Humanities and Social Sciences. All three NARI working groups could facilitate the growth of Irish Arctic research and demonstrate that some Irish research projects aligned with the activities of the AC working groups.[3] If Ireland should obtain AC observer status, the Irish Government could utilize NARI expertise to assist with the country's contribution to AC working group activities. Although the NARI's first Annual General Meeting (AGM) was intended to take place in late 2020 at the National University of Ireland Galway, plans were revised due to the COVID-19 pandemic. The AGM was instead held online on 22 October 2020 and a new committee was voted in to govern the

---

[3] Where NARI's HSS Working Group is concerned, contributions and project ideas will likely in the future be aimed towards two of the six AC working groups: Sustainable Development Working Group and Emergency Preparedness, Prevention, and Response Working Group.

NARI.[4] An online database outlining past and present Arctic research projects in which NARI members are engaged was also created at this time.[5]

14.2.2 The NARI HSS Working Group: Reconceptualizing Arctic and Northern Studies in Ireland?

Currently, there is no discursive awareness in Irish academia of Northern studies; a Google search of 'Northern studies in Ireland' instead produces results pertaining to Northern Ireland, north-south relations, and cross-border studies. While these results are indicative of the ongoing focus on strengthening political and cultural relations between the Republic and Northern Ireland, it does call into question if both historical and contemporary research pertaining to neighbouring Arctic areas (i.e., northern periphery regions and islands) should be referred to as Arctic and Northern studies in Ireland.

The only existing publication that engages in interdisciplinary enquiry on Irish and Nordic connections is the edited volume by Barber et al. (2019) titled *Ireland and the North* that was produced as part of the Reimagining Ireland series. This book engaged with the relationship between Ireland and the Nordic countries, and more crucially, developed a 'double conceptualization of the North' to include Northern Ireland. In the following description of the book, the editors imply that they move beyond the nation-state as a key framework for analysis of human activity. Instead, this collection explores connections between Ireland and the Nordic countries in a variety of ways including "imaginary and material exchanges; as civic and personal linkages; as literary adaptation and appropriation; as transfers of cultural artefacts, political institutions, and ideas" (p. 7).

While the book falls under the category of cultural studies, chapter contributions within the edited volume come from authors exploring a wide range of multidisciplinary perspectives that include "art history, literary history and theory, archaeology, antiquarianism, media studies in addition to political analysis".[6] Collaboration for this edited volume began as a project within the Nordic Irish Studies Network (NISN),[7] demonstrating how formal and informal research collaboration with academics from Scottish, Northern English, and Scandinavian universities can lead to productive research outputs.

With the creation of NARI, there is a growing cognitive awareness among Irish researchers of the potential for linking existing Irish research with Nordic or Arctic

---

[4] NARI members elected to committees serve in the following positions: President, Vice-President, and Chair, one for each of the three working groups.

[5] The NARI project list is available at https://www.nari.ie/arctic-projects.

[6] See https://www.peterlang.com/document/1056779.

[7] The NISN appears to remain partially active via its Facebook group: https://www.facebook.com/groups/277449259523/.

together. Eventually, these links may lead to the development of an Arctic and Northern studies HSS research hub in a way that allows for greater multidisciplinary collaboration to strengthen research output by the production of published articles or books incorporating interdisciplinary approaches to the Arctic in a similar way as the *Ireland and the North* project. Furthermore, such collaboration could lead to the emergence of an Arctic and Northern studies research field within Irish academia.

In late 2020 and early 2021, discussions surrounding the organization activities of the NARI HSS Working Group, resulted in the subsequent creation of three research foci subgroups to represent the diversity of research interests in which members are currently engaged. The three groups are outlined in Table 14.1. The fruitfulness of this approach lies in the ability to cluster research projects of a multidisciplinary nature that would otherwise be scattered throughout the humanities

Table 14.1 Suggested research topics and sub-groupings within the Network of Arctic Researchers Ireland, Humanities and Social Science Working Group

1. Historical and cultural heritage of the Arctic and Northern regions	2. Climate change, sustainable development and society in Arctic and Northern communities	3. Politics, security and international relations of the Arctic
• Early Christian Ireland and the diaspora of Irish clergy • Ireland's Viking heritage • nineteenth and early twentieth century Irish Arctic explorers • Irish servicemen during the world wars whom were deployed to northern Europe and Arctic regions • Irish historical participation in economic activities in the north • The historical and contemporary Irish diaspora in northern regions • Cultural heritage research themes—including Irish music, dance, and storytelling. Irish craftsmanship, games, and traditional activities exported to northern regions • Cultural and anthropological studies of Arctic and northern peoples including indigenous studies	• Behaviour change • Perceptions of risk • Food economies and health • Participatory decision making • Diversity and inclusion • Digitalization and connectivity, including the space industry • Architecture and the built environment of the north	• Ireland's application for Arctic Council observer status • Politics and governance of the Arctic Council • Non-Arctic states and Arctic Council observers • Irish-Nordic relations • Arctic and North Atlantic security • Theories of international relations (IR) and the Arctic • The EU and the Arctic (may also include EU Arctic research strategy and funding programs such as the Interreg Northern Periphery and Arctic Programme (NPAP) or Horizon Europe)

Table credit: S. Milne and C. Slotten

and social sciences.[8] We hope that this clustering may promote the growth of new cross-disciplinary research projects between the three subgroups (i.e., intra-disciplinary HSS research). We consider this chapter to be an example of inter-disciplinary HSS research since it relates to both the first and the third of the three NARI HSS subgroups, namely, subgroup 1: Historical and Cultural Heritage of the Arctic and Northern Regions, and subgroup 3: Politics, Security, and International Relations of the Arctic. Arguably, a fourth subgroup within the NARI HSS Working Group could be created in the future for LIS since a primary focus of this chapter is to assess how appropriate LIS services may be developed to assist researchers in HSS, as well as the general public, in accessing Arctic and Northern resources more easily through new and comprehensive digital systems. Now, the chapter turns to outlining two key areas that relate to Irish-Arctic and Northern historical linkages, namely the early Christian era and the Viking Age in Ireland. We will include examples of past and current research projects in these areas to instil interest from both Irish and international researchers, librarians, and archivists on the potential for further exploring these areas and encouraging new research collaboration and international partnerships.

14.3 Part II: Ireland's Historical Ties to the Arctic: Outlining a Millennium-Old Northern Heritage

14.3.1 Overview

> The Irish Sea has long been considered not as a barrier between Ireland and the outside world, but rather as a highway. (Hegarty, 2011, p. 12)

Although Ireland is a small island nation located on the periphery of Europe in the northeast Atlantic, it has interacted with its northern neighbours for millennia through waves of inward and outward migration and trade, yet this has not always been fully acknowledged in historical narratives. Greater collective awareness of historical and genealogical research serves to lessen the negative effects of the pervasive myth that only a singular Irish identity exists, one that is polarized by the struggle over two forms: British colonialism and the unresolved political situation in Northern Ireland, and the much-romanticized ideals of Irish nationalism and the continuing quest for a united Ireland. Instead, as Grossberg (1996, p. 89) explains, the emphasis should be "on the multiplicity of identities and differences rather than on a singular identity and on the connections or articulations between the fragments and or differences." Exploring a broader connection to the North through Nordic

---

[8] It is beyond the scope of this paper to provide an in-depth discussion for all three research foci of the HSS Working Group, given that they cover such a broad range of themes. Also, because the HSS Working Group is still in its infancy, further involvement by NARI researchers specializing in key areas is required and we hope that this will take place over time.

and Arctic heritage allows for the emergence of less recognized yet deeply enriching multicultural influences within Irish identity from the time of the Vikings to the present day. This approach assists in the pursuit of exciting new research to visualize the multifaceted nature of Ireland's social, cultural, and national identity, and to illustrate how Ireland also influenced and shaped the history of other nations through the Irish diaspora.

With this aim in mind, Part II of this chapter demonstrates how Ireland's historical ties to the Arctic and Northern regions are stronger than would first appear, yet these ties must be brought to light and critically examined to identify gaps in the research that are overlooked. Focusing on a positive approach, Part II highlights some select examples of past and present research developments that would further enhance awareness on Ireland's Northern and Arctic connections. This section posits that Ireland can claim a Northern and near-Arctic heritage based on two of the six key historical themes identified within the NARI HSS Working Group as seen in the first column of Table 14.1. The two themes discussed here relate to Ireland's Northern and Arctic heritage in the following areas: (1) the migration of Irish missionaries to parts of Scandinavia (i.e., Norway, the Faroe Islands, and Iceland) in the early Christian Era (i.e., fifth through twelfth centuries); and (2) Ireland's strong Viking heritage owing to successive waves of incoming Nordic peoples during the early Middle Ages. Each theme is discussed to identify past and present research while also identifying research gaps and critical research areas, setting the stage for Part III of this chapter. Later, Part III suggests policy recommendations for the Irish Government including how LIS services could assist with digitally organizing this information in ways that would serve to further the development of Arctic and Northern studies research in Ireland.

14.3.2 The Migration of Irish Missionaries to Scandinavia in the Early Christian Era: Norway, the Faroe Islands, and Iceland

14.3.2.1 Introduction to the Early Christian Era

Ample archaeological evidence exists showing Irish-Nordic linkages that pre-date modern history; this has been covered in the literature pertaining to the early Christian Era, spanning the late Iron Age to the early medieval period. This period of approximately seven centuries is full of examples of how Irish monks and ecclesiastics set sail from Ireland to preach the gospel, establish monasteries in remote locations, and spread Christianity throughout Europe. In this section, the evidence of early Irish missionary activities within the three Scandinavian countries and territories of Norway, Iceland, and the Faroe Islands as part of the Kingdom of Denmark is discussed along with identification of research gaps that, if addressed, could enhance medieval studies on Irish, North Atlantic, and Arctic connections. Finally, two distinct past and present Irish research projects are outlined that focus on the early Christian Era: the *Brendan* project of 1978 and *Adapt Northern Heritage* project of 2017–2020, both of which demonstrate the rich potential that this era had for exciting contemporary research collaboration and promotion of Irish-Northern cultural heritage.

14.3.2.2 The Christianization of Norway

The Christianization of Scandinavia is an important research area that sheds greater insight into the role of Ireland with respect to the migrant flows of people and ideas throughout Northern Europe in medieval times. The Christianization of Norway in particular heralded major changes in Norwegian society, as cultural and religious practices were transferred from Ireland and Britain to Norway during this time; primitive stone crosses found in Western Norway serve as strong evidence of this. Birkelli (1971) explains that because the medieval Norwegians and Viking raiders likely saw several crosses in England, Scotland, and Ireland, they sought to make their own. In Western Norway, the presence of cross-worked runic stones and free-standing crosses dating from the tenth and eleventh centuries are conspicuous signs of missionary influence during that period (p. 35).

Evidence of further Irish Christian activity on the west coast of Norway centres around the tenth-century legend of St. Sunniva, patron saint of Bergen, virgin Irish princess, and early Christian martyr. O'Hara (2009) explains that it is not only that Sunniva is a woman and Irish that makes her unique, but the fact that the legend of St. Sunniva was preserved in written form in the *Acta Sanctorum in Selio*, one of the earliest surviving Latin manuscripts written in Norway dating from the early twelfth century. St. Sunniva was said to have been martyred on the island of Selja, which became an important monastic and episcopal centre during the eleventh century. Birkelli (1971, p. 27) considers that places such as Selje and Kinn on the Norwegian west coast were "ideal for Celtic and Irish missionaries" and much like Iona off the west coast of Scotland and Skellig Michael off the coast of Co. Kerry (p. 28). Later, in the twelfth century, St. Sunniva's relics were transferred to the city of Bergen by Bishop Paul and enshrined in a new cathedral there. O'Hara concludes that the account of St. Sunniva is a conversion narrative set during the transitional period in Norway between two religions:

> The figure of Sunniva and her unusual Anglo-Saxon name meaning 'sun-gift' could, if understood in such a way, personify the notion of Christianity's arrival in the country … and serve as the prelude to the Christianization of Norway under the aegis of Olaf Tryggson and his missionaries. (2009, p. 108)

In 2018, the National University of Ireland, Dublin City Council, Royal Norwegian Embassy, and University of Bergen held two events in association with the Dublin Festival of History (https://dublinfestivalofhistory.ie/). The events, celebrating Ireland and Norway's shared Viking heritage, also focused on St. Sunniva. Ambassador of the Kingdom of Norway to Ireland, Else Berit Eikeland, opened the one-day Viking symposium *Our Friends from the North? Irish and Norse in the*

Viking Age which took place on 4 October 2018 at the Wood Quay Venue, Dublin City Council Offices (National University of Ireland, 2018).[9] A second event held on 5 October 2018 at the Mansion House, Dublin included a lecture by Jan Erik Rekdal, a professor at the University of Oslo and member of the Norwegian Academy of Sciences, titled *The Legend of St. Sunniva and its Representation of Christianization of Norway* (National University of Ireland, 2018). The bishop of Bergen also visited Dublin and Waterford as part of the festival to thank Ireland for bringing Christianity to Norway.

14.3.2.3 The Faroe Islands

Turning north and westwards, it has been assumed that the Faroe Islands were the first steppingstone beyond Shetland for the North Atlantic Viking migrations, with ninth-century Viking settlements being the first major phase of human settlement in the Faroe Islands (Church et al., 2013). This idea was reinforced by the Faroese saga, dating the first settlement of the archipelago to approximately 825–875 AD (Als et al., 2006, p. 497). However, new archaeological evidence suggests that the settlement of the Faroes may have occurred possibly hundreds of years before the Vikings conquered the coastal regions of northwest Europe and beyond, from Scandinavia to Great Britain, Ireland, Iceland, Greenland, and as far as North America. Irish monks may have lived on the islands as early as 650 AD and later deserted them due to the appearance of the Vikings. Carbon dating of sediment layers containing the first appearance of barley-type pollen and peat ash mixed with small bits of burnt bone at sites such as Heimavatn in the north island chain and Hov in the south (Fig. 14.1) indicate that there must have been another, earlier group of sea-faring peoples who settled these islands some 300 to 500 years before the large-scale Viking colonization of the ninth century (Connor, 2013).

Other literary and paleoenvironmental evidence further support the idea that human settlement on the Faroes existed prior to the Vikings. The Latin manuscript *De Mesura Orbis Terrae*, written by the Irish monk Dícuil in 825 AD (see O'Driscoll & Färber, 2018) alludes to hermits from Ireland living in two sets of remote islands to the north of Britain. Although Dícuil does not refer to these places by name, it is plausible that these are the Shetland and Faroe Islands, respectively:

> [14] There are many other islands in the ocean to the north of Britain which can be reached from the northern islands of Britain in a direct voyage of two days and nights with sails filled with a continuously favourable wind. A devout priest told me that in two summer days and the intervening night he sailed in a two-benched boat and entered one of them. (p. 75)

> [15] There is another set of small islands, nearly all separated by narrow stretches of water; in these for nearly a hundred years hermits sailing from our country, Ireland, have lived. But just as they were always deserted from the beginning of the world, so now because of the Northman pirates they are emptied of anchorites and filled with countless sheep and very

---

[9] Papers explored the historical, archaeological, and literary connections between Ireland and western Scandinavia in the Viking Age.

14 The Irish Impact: Charting a Course for the Development of Historical Arctic...

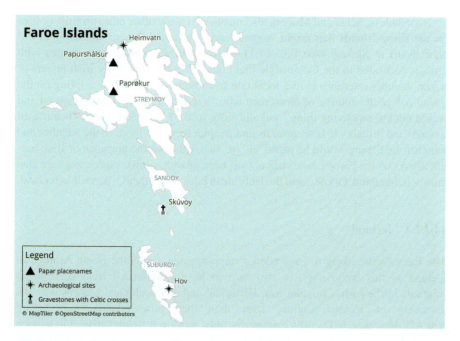

Fig. 14.1 Map of landmarks in the Faroe Islands with Irish connections. (Map credit: G. Taylor)

many diverse kinds of sea-birds. I have never found these islands mentioned in the authorities. (p. 77)

Schei and Moberg (2003, p. 67) suggest that a small group of Faroese placenames may be of Gaelic origin. Places such as Paprøkur near Vestmanna and Papurshálsur in Saksun (see Fig. 14.1) seem to refer to the Irish hermit monks, whom the Norsemen called *papar*. These holy men were said to have set sail from Ireland to the Scottish Hebrides and then onwards to other small islands in the North Atlantic "in small hide-covered boats called 'currachs' in search for new uninhabited places where they might settle and devote themselves to their faith" (Saga Museum, 2017, para. 2). However, placenames with the inclusion of the word *papar* must be considered with caution as they could also allude to the nesting places of the Atlantic puffin. The Latin name for this bird is *Fratercula Arctica* which translates to 'little brother' or 'little priest.' With its black and white feathers, this bird might have reminded early ornithologists of the monastic robes worn by the monks. Perhaps because they both favoured the same remote habitats, the Norse were said to have jokingly call the puffins *papi* as a deviation from the old Norse word for puffin, *lundi*.[10] Therefore, Schei and Moberg consider that placenames such as Paparøkur and Paparshálsur are more likely to allude to ledges and outcrops more suitable for puffins and other seabirds than for hermit monks (p. 67).

---

[10] Both the Faroese and Icelandic word for puffin is *lundi*, while the Danish and Norwegian word is *lunde*.

Nonetheless, Schei and Moberg also mentioned some other more promising sites on the Faroe Islands that might suggest early Celtic habitation, including an old churchyard in Skúvoy (see Fig. 14.1) where there are several gravestones with crosses decorated in the Celtic style that could have been made by Irish priests or papar. Another reference is to a local tale from Suduroy of holy men living on the island before the coming of Norsemen who "lived on milk, eggs and seaweed and would not kill any living thing" and allegedly worked "wonders such as healing all wounds and diseases in both animals and people; they also foretold the weather and whether the fishing would be plentiful" (p. 18). Although the presence of Irish hermit monks on the Faroe Islands has not yet been proven, similar placenames are also known in Shetland, Orkney, and the Hebridean Isles of Scotland,[11] as well as Iceland.

14.3.2.4 Iceland

The Faroes were likely to have been a steppingstone across the North Atlantic to Iceland as this archipelago is also said to have experienced Irish ecclesiastic migrants in the early Christian Era. Historical and archaeological records date the discovery of Iceland slightly later than the Faroe Islands, just before 870 AD. However, in Dícuil's manuscript holy men from Ireland arrived in a place called Thule, assumed to be Iceland, at the end of the eighth century and knew the route there before the Vikings (Sveinsson, 1957, p. 3). However, as with the Faroes, this claim has not yet been supported by archaeological or paleoenvironmental data. Nonetheless, traces were left behind on the Icelandic landscape and in Icelandic narrative culture within the early sagas. According to the Saga Museum's (2017, para. 1) exhibit *Papar: The First Inhabitants*, references to the papar were found within the *Landnámabók* [The Book of Settlements] and *Islendingabók* [The Book of Icelanders]. Written in 1122–1133 AD by Ari Þorgilsson, or Ari 'the Learned,' some 250 years after Iceland was settled by the Norsemen, *Íslendingabók* provides the oldest Icelandic record of the papar, serving as the basis for the acceptance that the papar were indeed the first settlers of Iceland:

> There were then Christians here, whom the Norsemen called the papar, but they later went away, because they did not wish to stay here with heathens; and they left behind them Irish books as well as crooks and bells from which it is possible to determine their origin. (Grønlie, 2006, p. 4)

According to *Landnámabók*, as described in the Saga Museum's exhibit (para. 4), Irish papar were living at Kirkjubær at Síða in Southern Iceland before the first Norse settlers arrived in the ninth century; this is why the 'Viking heathens' could not settle there.

Although no actual remains of the papar have been found in Iceland, references of them as written in the two aforementioned sagas are widely accepted in Iceland.

---

[11] For a study on the Hebrides, see Chapter 3: "Pabbays and Paibles: Pap-Names and Gaelic and Old Norse Speakers in Scotland's Hebridean Islands" in Ahronson (2015).

14 The Irish Impact: Charting a Course for the Development of Historical Arctic...

Like in the Faroes, there are several placenames in Iceland that allude to the presence of the papar and bear the 'papar' prefix. These are located mainly in the East Fjords (Fig. 14.2) and examples include Papey [Papar Island], Papýli [Papa farm], and Papafjörður [Papa fjord] in Lón (Saga Museum, 2017, para. 2). However, if placenames are not to be fully trusted, Ulff-Møller (2006) attests to how the oldest church designs in Iceland and Greenland show signs of Irish influence, not only in the churches themselves that are built as a shortened version of the Norse long house but also in their graveyards. Ulff-Møller claims that

> unlike early Norwegian graveyards, which have a square cemetery, the earliest churches in Iceland and Greenland have circular cemeteries which are also common for early churches in Ireland, Scotland and northern England. The Irish round enclosure may go back to prehistoric times as they can be found in the old royal seat of Tara where kings were elected within the round enclosure. (p. 985)

Further archaeological evidence in the form of stone crosses also exists in Iceland. As in the case of Norway and the Faroe Islands, stone crosses in Iceland may offer some answers to a Celtic connection in the Nordic countries. A good example can be found at Kverkarhellir cave in the south of Iceland (see Fig. 14.2). Within this cave, a cross was found etched on the wall in Gaelic style; however, it is dated to a later time of 800 AD. Having studied this cross and others, Ahronson (2000) produces new research findings that indicates Celtic explorers from Ireland, Scotland, and the west coast of the British Isles arrived in Iceland a century before Scandinavians appeared. Ahronson's study discovers over 100 simple crosses with

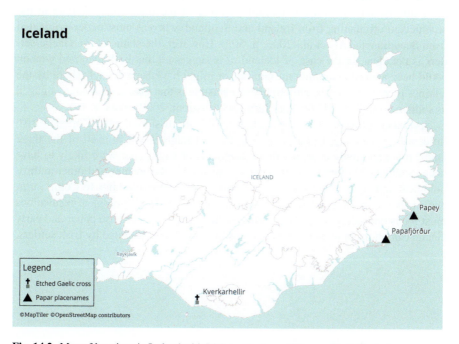

Fig. 14.2 Map of locations in Iceland with Irish connections. (Map credit: G. Taylor)

24 more elaborately carved or sculpted examples, all of which bear a striking resemblance to similar crosses found in Celtic regions of the British Isles, including the West Highlands and various Scottish islands (Fitch, 2015). From this evidence, Ahronson suggests that early Christian monks of the St. Columba sect were present in Southern Iceland prior to the Viking age.

While it is assumed that the papar did not contribute to the progeny of the Icelandic people, owing to their vows of celibacy, a genetic research project showed that Gaelic men of Irish and Scottish origins can be traced to the Icelandic gene pool. Agnar Helgason, an Icelander working at Oxford University in biological anthropology, carried out a genetic project that "included 181 Icelanders, 233 Scandinavians, and 283 'Gaels' from Ireland and Scotland" (Helgason et al., 2000). Dan Bradley, a lecturer in anthropology genetics at Trinity College Dublin, also participated on this project which sought out genetic markers in the Y chromosomes of men living in Iceland to determine if they had Scandinavian or Gaelic ancestry. Bradley said that "we agreed it might be great if we could add an Irish dimension to the story of Gaelic origins in Iceland" (Ahlstrom, 2000, para. 4). The data from the project suggests that "between 20–25% of Icelandic founding males had Gaelic ancestry, with the remainder having Norse ancestry" (Helgason et al., 2000, p. 697). A later study conducted by Helgason et al. (2001, p. 735) focuses on the mitochondrial DNA in women from Iceland, Orkney, the Western Isles and the Isle of Skye. Their findings show that "a sizeable portion of Icelandic [matrilineal] lines of decent are traced back 1100 years to females whose ancestry was firmly anchored in the British Isles." Similar findings are revealed in parallel studies on genetic ancestry in the Faroe Islands, with a considerable number of the first female settlers in the archipelago originating from Ireland and Scotland, whereas most males originated from Scandinavia (Als et al., 2006, p. 502). However, the status of the Gaelic settlers is not clear. In the case of Iceland, it is suggested that both men and women could have arrived as immigrant families or might have been brought there by the Vikings to work as slaves, although also plausible is that Gaelic men were engaged as soldiers to fight in ad hoc Norse armies (Ahlstrom, 2000, paras. 9, 12).

Several conclusions are to be made from this discussion of early Christian Irish influences in Norway, Iceland, and the Faroe Islands. First, in each of the three lands, it is commonly accepted that settlements of Irish papar were likely to have been established before the tenth century. Secondly, placenames and other anthropological and cultural markers such as stone crosses provide hints to Celtic influences in Nordic regions. Third, future research efforts and archaeological excavations must focus on finding tangible evidence such as grave sites of Irish papar and early Gaelic Christians in places that may plausibly have been inhabited by Irish settlers.

14.3.2.5 Two Notable Irish-Nordic Research Projects Focused on the Early Christian Era: The Brendan Voyage and Adapt Northern Heritage Project

With respect to Irish research projects focusing on Nordic regions during the early Christian Era, these fall into two key groups: finding evidence for the possibility that the Irish were present during this era in Nordic regions and preserving the archaeological heritage that was found in these places. The first project to discuss here is one that falls into the former category; although it stands outside of academia, it is nonetheless highly appraised for its boldness, rigour, and provision of new insight into the navigational and seafaring abilities of the medieval Irish ecclesiastic community. Perhaps best described as experiential archaeology, the *Brendan Voyage* project was an epic journey undertaken by the explorer, writer, and filmmaker Tim Severin (1940–2020) and crew to recreate the nautical voyage of the sixth-century Irish monk, St. Brendan (King, 2020). Severin (1978/2000) published the story of the remarkable adventure as *The Brendan Voyage*, a book that was translated into 16 languages and an international best seller. A documentary film directed by Severin and Scales (1978) about the voyage was released the same year as the book. The incentive for Severin's journey emerged from a debate surrounding content of the Latin manuscript *Navigatio sancti Brendani abbatis* [The Voyage of St. Brendan the Abbot] written by St. Brendan that describes this controversial sea voyage (circa 540 AD).[12] The manuscript relates the many adventures of Brendan and monks at sea before reaching a paradise-like 'promised land.' The text combines elements of a marvellous sea voyage and an allegorical journey through life that is closely connected with monastic culture.

Although some scholars interpret Brendan's manuscript metaphorically, others believe that the monk sailed to North America, as this could be interpreted as the promised land to which Brendan referred to in the manuscript (King, 2020). Severin wanted to find out if such a journey could have been completed and therefore sought to recreate the voyage in a boat made from the same materials as the monks would have used. On 17 May 1976, Severin and three fellow crew men, led by sailing master George Moloney, rowed out of Brandon Creek on the Dingle Peninsula, Co. Kerry, allegedly the same spot from where St. Brendan is reported to have departed almost 1500 years earlier (*The Irish Times*, 2021). Severin's re-enactment lasted 13 months to finish the 7200 km (4474 mi) journey from Ireland that led them on a steppingstone route across the North Atlantic (Fig. 14.3). From Brandon Creek, Co. Kerry, Severin and team first sailed to the Aran Islands off the west coast of Ireland, and from there north and east to Iona, and up through the Scottish Hebrides. Then

---

[12] Because of the popularity of this manuscript, many copies were created from the tenth to thirteenth centuries. According to the Collaborative Online Database and E-Resources for Celtic Studies (CODECS), over 140 copies of this text exist on the European continent (see https://codecs.vanhamel.nl/Navigatio_sancti_Brendani). Of these, there are five copies located within Irish university and ecclesiastical libraries.

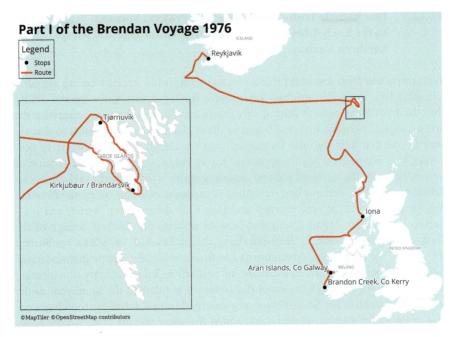

Fig. 14.3 Map of stage one of Tim Severin's journey to recreate the St. Brendan's voyage across the North Atlantic, beginning in Brandon Creek, Co. Kerry, Ireland. (Map credit: G. Taylor)

sailing northwest, the crew of the *Brendan* travelled to the Faroe Islands, landing in the harbour at Tjørnuvík (King, 2020).

In Sect. 14.3.2.1 of this chapter, we discuss papar placenames in the Faroe Islands. Interestingly, Severin, during his time in the Faroe Islands, spoke about this topic with the local Faroese people, discovering that there is another location on these islands that alludes to the historical presence of the early Irish monks. Severin recounts how

> Saint Brendan's name is familiar to every Faroese who learns in school that the Irish priests were the first people to settle in their remote islands. But no tangible remains of the Irish occupation have yet been found, presumably because the Papars, as the Irish priests were called, left too faint a mark on the islands before the Norsemen overprinted their massive stamp. Recently however, Faroese archaeologists working at Tjornuvik have dug up cereal grains which indicate that there was agriculture in the Faroes before any record of Viking settlement. And of course, there is the enduring literary and traditional evidence of the Papars in the islands. Nowhere is this tradition stronger than on the main island of Streymoy where, it is asserted, the Irish priests established themselves on a small, well-favoured creek on the southwestern corner of the island. To this day the creek still bears a significant name; it is called Brandarsvik – Brendan's Creek. (Severin, 1978/2000, p. 130)

Brandarsvik, more commonly known today as Kirkjubøur, is the southernmost village on the island of Stremoy. The name Brandarsvik [Brendan's Creek] suggests that this place was once associated with the Irish monk St. Brendan. The *Brendan* left the Faroe Islands on 3 July 1976, sailing for Iceland. After a stopover in

Reykjavík, the *Brendan* then continued to sail west, past the southern coast of Greenland, finally completing the journey in Newfoundland, Canada. While the *Brendan* voyage was a resounding success, there is still speculation as to whether St. Brendan ever reached North America a 1000 years before Columbus. Nonetheless, Severin's voyage showed that completion of such a journey was indeed possible (King, 2020). Today, the *Brendan*, a modern replica curragh that Severin used to sail from Ireland to North America, is now on permanent display in the archaeological open-air Celtic Museum Park as the *Craggaunowen* project, operated by Shannon Heritage and located in Co. Clare in the west of Ireland (https://www.craggaunowen.ie/living-past-experience/the-brendan-boat/).

The second research project to mention is the *Adapt Northern Heritage* project funded by the EU's Northern Periphery and Arctic Program, operational from June 2017 to May 2020. The project focused on assessing the risk for and vulnerabilities of historic places and produced adaptation plans for nine historical sites located in Iceland, Ireland, Norway, Russia, Sweden, and Scotland. The project's website outlines that

> due to the remoteness and geographical dispersedness, communities and authorities in Europe's Arctic area and northern periphery and other northern world regions are finding it particularly difficult to develop the required capacities, and allocate sufficient resources, to manage their cultural heritage in ways which actively take climate change into account. (n.d.-a, para. 3)

The project created a community network and held roundtable workshops and training events in support of collaboration and learning among partner countries involved in the project. The Irish case study focused on creating adaptation plans for Ballinkskelligs Abbey and Castle, an Augustinian priory situated on the Iveragh Peninsula in Co. Kerry dating from the twelfth century. Due to its exposed coastal location, the abbey and castle are threatened by rising sea levels and severe storms that sweep in from the Atlantic Ocean. The graveyard and church, as its centre point, was protected by a massive concrete sea wall, but this has been degraded under the forces of water and wind. Using the guide for risk management of historic places developed by the project, climate risk management plans (Adapt Northern Heritage, n.d.-b) were produced for each of the two historical structures at Ballinskelligs. The successful inclusion of the Ballinskelligs, Co. Kerry case study within project may encourage further Irish collaboration with Northern partners and sharing of risk management and preservation methods to ensure the archaeological and cultural conservation of historic sites.

14.3.3 Ireland's Viking Heritage

14.3.3.1 Tracing Ireland's Viking Heritage: New Genetic Research Uncovers Ancestral Diversity

Extensive textual and archaeological evidence exists attesting to the Viking presence in Ireland between the late eighth to twelfth centuries. The nature of the contact between Irish locals and Viking raiders and settlers has long been a topic of interest to scholars. Excavations in Dublin and other Irish towns and cities, mainly focused in the southern province of Munster, along with new developments in DNA methodologies, shed new light on both the fraught and friendly relationships between these two groups.

Isotopic and genetic work suggests free movement of people between Ireland and the rest of the North Atlantic and parts of the Arctic. In September 2020, the leading international journal *Nature* published the largest ever DNA analysis of Viking remains (Margaryan et al., 2020). Led by Eske Willerslev, a fellow at the University of Cambridge and director of the Lundbeck Foundation GeoGenetics Centre at the University of Copenhagen, the six-year project saw researchers from the National Museum of Ireland and Trinity College Dublin (TCD) become part of the international effort to decode the genetic make-up of the Viking world. Results contradict the modern image of the typical Viking as a blonde-haired Scandinavian warrior. Instead, the researchers uncovered ancestral diversity in Viking communities both within Scandinavia and across Europe, including Ireland.

Findings of the study show sharp ancestral differences between English and Irish Vikings. Irish Viking DNA showed evidence of a high degree of Norwegian ancestry, particularly from the north and west coasts of Norway whereas English Vikings had a stronger Danish influence (Gilbert et al., 2017). Interactions between Irish locals and Viking settlers would have also resulted in intermarriage between high-ranking members of Irish and Viking society (Downham, 2004). In defiance of the stereotypical Viking warrior depiction, many Vikings had brown hair, including the famous Eyrephort warrior from Co. Galway. Furthermore, Viking identity in Ireland was not limited to those of Norwegian ancestry. Smaller amounts of Danish and Swedish genetic ancestry were also seen within Irish Viking DNA. Comparable genetic ancestry was also found in Orkney and Scotland, and not found extensively in Wales and England; this makes sense given known Viking settlement patterns. Additionally, Irish, Scottish, and Orcadian genes were all found in modern Norwegian populations, suggesting the flow of genes was bidirectional (Gilbert et al., 2017; Margaryan et al., 2020). Similarly, genetic data on Irish populations found evidence of individuals who grew up in Ireland during the Viking Age who originated from Great Britain and Scandinavia (Montgomery et al., 2014). As previously mentioned, the genetic evidence from Iceland also showcases how Irish individuals were part of the exploration and original settlement groups. Mitochondrial DNA studies show that around 60% of matrilineal ancestry in Iceland derives from Irish and Scottish individuals, while 75% of patrilineal ancestry comes from

Scandinavia (Ebenesersdóttir et al., 2018). The modern samples show a higher percentage of Scandinavian ancestry than earlier historic samples, suggesting either a reproductive preference within the population or later immigration of other Scandinavian peoples (Ebenesersdóttir et al., 2018).

The genetic evidence shows that the influence of Scandinavian traders, raiders, and settlers spread to cover the entire Northern Atlantic. Ireland was originally an appealing target for raiding by the Norwegian Vikings, as the early Irish monastic settlements offered a large amount of portable wealth which was very tempting to the Viking raiders (Barrett, 2008).

14.3.3.2 Viking Settlement in Ireland

Although there were sporadic Viking raids in Britain and Ireland from the late eighth century, Lewis (2016, p. 9) attests that it was not until the following century that the Vikings began overwintering in Ireland, later establishing permanent bases. Early attempts at settlement were found along the west coast of Ireland in Co. Mayo and Galway from 812 AD where the Vikings used small islands for protection. However, the first permanent bases, called *longphuirt* (singular: *longphort*), or in English, 'longfort,' were initially mentioned in the records of 840 AD at Lough Neagh in Northern Ireland and in 841 AD at Dublin and Linn Duachaill near the village of Annagassan situated on Dundalk Bay, Co. Louth (p. 10) (Fig. 14.4).

Fig. 14.4 Map of potential longphuirt locations in Ireland. (Map credit: G. Taylor)

Irish coastal towns and settlements served a vital function for the Vikings as a connecting point between mainland Scandinavia and other northern peripheries such as the Scottish Hebrides, the Faroe Islands, and Iceland. From an archaeological perspective, Dublin serves as a model strategic Viking centre of trade and commerce. As Hurley (1995, p. 23) explains, the nineteenth century discovery of a Viking cemetery at Kilmainham and large-scale city excavations in the 1970s and 1980s at sites such as Wood Quay established Dublin as one of the foremost cities for Viking Age archaeology, research, and literature in Western Europe. Despite these large-scale excavations, no Viking style longhouses have been found in Dublin, or elsewhere in Ireland. Instead, Viking buildings from this time showcase a blend of Irish and Scandinavian building styles (Boyd, 2015, p. 345). Viking Dublin is now made more accessible to the public through the internationally acclaimed Dublinia Viking Museum (https://www.dublinia.ie/). Based in the heart of medieval Dublin in the historic Christchurch district, this museum is a major visitor attraction in Dublin. As a historical recreation museum, the Dublinia experience describes Dublin's Viking past and highlights the importance of Ireland's Viking heritage.

The portrayal of Vikings in Irish primary school textbooks underwent substantial change in the aftermath of these large-scale urban excavations as prior to this time the Vikings tended to be viewed primarily as enemy raiders who attacked and destroyed Irish monasteries and Christian sites. Nowadays, a far greater emphasis is placed on Viking roles as founders of Irish cities and traders active in the wider Viking world (Mary Immaculate College, 2013). For example, in October 2014, a new bilingual educational resource for primary school children titled *Viking Ireland: A New Voyage of Discovery* was launched by the Norwegian Deputy Head of Mission, Ms. Grete Odegaard, at Mary Immaculate College (MIC) in Limerick. Speaking about the importance of having an accurate resource of this nature, Eucharia McCarthy, Director of the Curriculum Development Unit, at MIC said:

> We have published 'Viking Ireland – A New Voyage of Discovery' to dispel some of the myths about the Vikings which permeate many of our primary school history textbooks. This new evidence-based resource provides accurate information about the Vikings and uses highly interactive teaching approaches that will bring history to life for our pupils. (Curriculum Development Unit, 2014, para. 3)

One of the most renowned discoveries to date demonstrating the trade links between Dublin and the Viking world occurred in Denmark in 1962 when five Viking ships were unearthed in the Roskilde Fjord. The largest of the five ships, a great longboat named *Skuldelev 2,* was constructed from Irish oak.[13] Extensive analysis of the ship was undertaken at the Vikingskibs Museet [Viking Ship Museum] (https://www.vikingeskibsmuseet.dk/) which was built on the banks of the Roskilde Fjord in the wake of this discovery (Killeen, 2004). Results from tree-ring dating of the timber

---

[13] It is believed that *Skuldelev 2* was intentionally sunk along with four other smaller Viking boats as part of a defensive barrier constructed to restrict access to Roskilde, the royal seat of Denmark at the time (MacGowan, 2015).

used for *Skuldelev 2* show that the ship was built of oak in the vicinity of Dublin around 1042 AD (Viking Ship Museum, n.d.). *Skuldelev 2* remains on permanent display, but the museum also built a replica that visited Dublin called the *Havhingsten af Glendalough* [Sea Stallion from Glendalough].[14] In 2004, the Irish Minister for Arts, Sport, and Tourism, John O'Donoghue, joined the Danish monarch Margrethe II Queen of Denmark in Copenhagen for the launch of *Sea Stallion* (Killeen, 2004). The inclusion of Irish dignitaries at the boat launch demonstrate how shared Viking heritage between Ireland and Scandinavia can facilitate cultural diplomacy. In 2007–2008, *Sea Stallion* completed a voyage from Roskilde to Dublin via the north of Scotland and back to Denmark through the English Channel and North Sea. A second voyage to Dublin took place in the summer of 2015.

Moving south from Dublin in a clockwise manner around the island of Ireland, other longphuirt flourished in Ireland during the Viking Age, including Wexford town and in areas adjacent to what would later become the cities of Waterford, Cork, and Limerick (Fig. 14.4). Sheehan (2008) proposes some additional potential longphuirt sites, although the current chapter focuses on those with the strongest evidence. Two excavated sites in Wexford town—Bride Street and 84–86 South Main Street—reveal evidence of Vikings from the eleventh century onwards. Excavations conducted in 1998 at Bride Street uncovered the remains of stratified houses dating from circa 1000 to 1300 AD, providing new information about the later Viking Age and daily medieval life in the town (Bourke, 1995). At 84–86 South Main Street, archaeological excavation uncovered part of the original shoreline revealing a steeply sloping area that was reclaimed at an early stage in the town's development by the dumping of domestic waste to provide a level surface for what would have then been a shoreside site. Excavations unearthed a hearth with charcoal remains surrounded by large clusters of stake-holes dating from the twelfth or thirteenth century, all of which suggest that this dwelling may have been set in an industrial area along the original shoreline (Buildings of Wexford, n.d.). Furthermore, a bank and ditch were uncovered at Barrack Street in 1995 which predates the Anglo-Norman occupation of the town and are likely to be part of Wexford's earlier Norse defences. The Irish National Heritage Park (https://www.irishheritage.ie/) located just outside Wexford town pays tribute to Wexford's Viking past with several Viking-themed tourist attractions including the immersive workshop *The Daily Life* in Viking Wexford where visitors can learn about and participate in activities related to the buildings, traditions, customs, and armaments of the Vikings. The park also offers the experience of staying overnight in a wooden Viking house on the shore of River Slaney where visitors can cook on an open fire and dress in costume. Special events honouring Wexford's Viking heritage include, for example, the Viking Fire Festival held in Wexford town in September 2019. For the festival, the Wexford

---

[14] The name of the replica ship attests to the *Skaldelev 2*'s Irish origins as Glendalough is the site of a large, early Christian monastery in Co. Wicklow that was raided by the Vikings in 836 AD.

quayside was transformed into a Viking village where re-enactors encouraged visitors to enjoy storytelling, fire events, a Viking market, and craft demonstrations.[15]

Many Viking-controlled ports in Ireland such as Wexford and Waterford became urban centres with modern port facilities, showing the continuing influence of Viking decisions on Ireland's contemporary settlement patterns and maritime infrastructure. In 2003 during construction of the Waterford bypass road, a previously unknown Viking settlement at Woodstown, Co. Waterford (see Fig. 14.4) was discovered. The route of the bypass, running along the southern bank of River Suir, reveals that this area was an attractive place for the Vikings to establish longphuirt settlements. The inland waterways provided widespread access to areas of land within the provinces of Munster and Leinster, thus facilitating easy raiding (Downham, 2004, p. 77). Archaeologist Neil Jackman explains that "the finds from Woodstown reflect the range of the Viking trading networks in the ninth century and include pieces of Irish-made jewellery, amber from the Baltic, and even silver coins minted in Iraq" (Daly, 2014, para. 4). However, one of the most important discoveries at Woodstown was of a richly furnished Viking warrior burial with grave goods including a sword, spear, axe, and shield. These objects are now on permanent display in the *Treasures of Viking Waterford* exhibition located at Reginald's Tower in Waterford city (https://www.waterfordtreasures.com/reginalds-tower). The Woodstown site was granted national monument status and plans are underway to ensure its development for tourism and educational purposes.[16] The Waterford Greenway cyclist route that runs adjacent to the site will also be incorporated into conservation plans to encourage alternative methods of transport in the area.

Unfortunately, the archaeological evidence of Vikings in the cities of Cork and Limerick is more elusive when compared with the finds from Dublin and Waterford. Hurley (1995, p. 25) suggests that the most likely site of the principal longphort of Viking Cork was probably on the South Island and may have been situated on the low lying, marshy ground adjacent to River Lee. Nonetheless, many elements such as the city layout, house form, and several Hiberno-Norse type artefacts clearly demonstrate a twelfth-century town existed around South Main Street. The term 'Hiberno-Norse' describes the culture of inhabitants from Viking towns in the eleventh to early twelfth centuries. Details on previous Viking excavations in Cork city are available in the book *Excavations in Cork City 1984–2000* (Cleary & Hurley, 2003).

Recent excavations undertaken in 2018 at the former Beamish and Crawford brewery in Cork city during major reconstruction of the area uncovered foundations

---

[15]Although the Wexford Viking Fire Festival appears to have been a one-off event rather than an annual festival, the popularity of the Vikings in Ireland has meant that other towns also launched Viking festivals. For example, Strangford in Northern Ireland held its first Viking festival in March 2022: https://www.tourismni.com/news/strangford-lough-viking-festival/.

[16]The conservation management plan for the Woodstown Viking site was commissioned by the Waterford City and County Council and funded through the Heritage Council's Heritage Plan Fund 2019 and 2020. The steering committee for the site included representatives from the Norwegian Embassy to Ireland, in addition to local and national stakeholders (Abarta Heritage, 2021).

of 19 wooden Viking Age houses from 1070 AD, the earliest in the city to date (Roche, 2018). Many of the artefacts found at the site are wooden, having been preserved in the acidic marshy ground settled by the Vikings. Among the other items found were a collection of spoons, ladles, and buckets as well as a wooden thread-winder with a carved design of two horse heads. The National Museum of Ireland loaned the newly discovered artefacts to the Cork Public Museum (https://www.corkcity.ie/en/cork-public-museum/), resulting in the Viking exhibition launched in May 2018 titled *Below Our Feet* in partnership with Cork City Council, Cork Public Museum, and University College Cork. In June 2021, a virtual conference organized by the Cork Historical and Archaeological Society (https://corkhist.ie/) was held to discuss Cork's Hiberno-Norse heritage for the first time and included a panel of Irish and international experts. University College Cork (UCC) archaeology lecturer Griffin Murray organized the conference, saying that the event would propose a new theory about where the first Hiberno-Norse settlement along River Lee was located (Browne, 2021). The conference showcased findings of the *World Tree Project* (http://www.worldtreeproject.org/) based at the School of English at UCC and funded by the Irish Research Council. The project is a digital collection on Old Norse-Icelandic and Viking studies that operated for a year from February 2016 to February 2017. The digital archive contains 12 exhibits on topics ranging from Old Norse poetry to Viking women and perceptions of Vikings in the twenty-first century. Materials for the exhibits were collected from members of the public, as well as institutions such as libraries and museums, other organizations, individual scholars, and interest groups.

Turning to Limerick, a city situated on the estuary of River Shannon in the southwest of Ireland, there are conflicting accounts of when the Viking raiders first appeared. Historical records suggest that a Norseman named Yorus established a raiding fort at Limerick in 861 AD (O'Donovan, 2003, p. 40). To date, an early Viking settlement within the vicinity of Limerick city has not been found. Therefore, the first identified Viking settlement in the region is further upstream in the townland of Athlunkard, Co. Clare (see Fig. 14.4) where a longphort is situated along the banks of River Shannon. Excavations conducted in the late 1990s at Athlunkard revealed iron objects dating from the ninth century, including an iron axe which still contains part of a wooden handle and a Viking silver weight was also found on the opposite riverbank at Corbally, Co. Limerick (Kelly & O'Donovan, 1998, p. 14). However, arguably the most impressive of the Viking artefacts found to date near Limerick are a pair of large, Viking-made silver 'kite-brooches,' named for the shape of the head of the brooch, which are now on display at the National Museum of Ireland in Dublin. The brooches were found in 1845 during the construction of the Limerick-Tipperary railway line. The style of the brooches indicates that they were made in Dublin, where several copper alloy examples were found and the size of the brooches demonstrates the large quantities of silver in Ireland during this period (Sikora, n.d.). Brian Hodkinson (2002, p. 1) of the Limerick Museum (https://www.limerick.ie/limerick-museum) mentions that the series of archaeological excavations within Limerick since the late 1980s throw little light on the Viking origins of Limerick city mostly because there were no deep excavations in the

Viking heart of the city, specifically beneath St. Mary's Cathedral, built in 1168 AD by Donal Mór O'Brien, King of Munster. The land on which the cathedral is built is said to have once been the site of a Viking *thingmote*, a raised mound used as a meeting place. Although sunken-featured buildings were uncovered in excavations at King John's Castle, they are dated to the later Hiberno-Norse period of the eleventh to twelfth centuries. As such, no true Viking Age deposits have yet been revealed.

Nonetheless, in recent years, Limerick began to capitalize on Viking tourism as it relates to the later Hiberno-Norse period. For example, since 2014, Red Viking Bus Tours operate within the city of Limerick taking visitors along a route to see sites relating to Viking Limerick, including St. Mary's Cathedral and King John's Castle. The growing interest in walking tours of Limerick city produced several maps and literary publications. A good example is O'Flaherty and Moore's (2010) pocket map *Limerick c.840 to c.1900: Viking Longphort to Victorian City* which captures 264 sites over 1000 years of the city's history.

A cross-disciplinary study called *Genes of the Gallgoídil* conducted from 2011 to 2013 by MIC (2013) at the University of Limerick in partnership with the University of Nottingham investigates the migration of Irish, Hiberno-Norse, and other Gaelic-speaking populations in the Viking Age. The project includes research contributions from individuals studying Celtic and Scandinavian languages; human genetics; literature, myth, and religion; material culture and archaeology; history; geography; and heritage management.

Irish coastal settlements and towns were increasingly relied upon by the Vikings for trading centres of raw materials during the Viking Age (Ashby et al., 2015; Wilson, 2014). However, important to note is that raw materials did not just flow from Irish outposts, but also to them. Ashby (2009) found that hair combs in Ireland and Scotland in the ninth century were made of reindeer antler, a material likely imported from Scandinavia, while other styles of comb originated in the British Isles before becoming popular in Scandinavia. The variety of goods used to buy or trade for these raw materials was in abundance around Viking settlements in Ireland. For instance, the early twentieth century find of the Knockmaon hoard in Co. Waterford included coins from Dublin, England, and France, as well as items produced in North Britain (Downham, 2004). However, it was not only materials that travelled throughout the interconnected parts of the Viking empire—ideas, objects, people, beliefs, and language flowed between Viking homelands and outposts just as easily.

The project on the sound of early Irish and Old Norse, *Augmented Vocality: Recomposing the Sounds of Early Irish and Old Norse* (Coccioli et al., 2020), was a two-year undertaking from 2020 to 2022 by Birmingham City University along with three European partners including Queen's University Belfast seeking to analyse and explore the sounds of early medieval languages. According to the project description, "combining linguistic expertise with sophisticated voice processing technologies, the project aims to give new life to early languages and help reclaim the oral quality at the heart of medieval literature" (Coccioli et al., 2021, para. 2). As part of the project, the researchers aimed to restore some of the performative power of the sounds of early Irish and Old Norse (O'Carroll, 2020). The multidisciplinary nature of the project stems from Coccioli's mixed academic background as the composer has a degree in linguistics and Anglo-Saxon literature. As such, Coccioli explains that the goal of the project was to produce musical compositions, public concerts, conference presentations, a digital audio database, and a sample library. All of these goals have been achieved. Coccioli also states that to reach these project goals, the research team collaborated with three European contemporary music ensembles. One of these, the Hard Rain Soloist Ensemble, is the ensemble-in-residence at Queen's University Belfast in Northern Ireland (O'Carroll, 2020). The uniqueness of the *Augmented Vocality* project is that it brings another dimension to the understanding of languages used in Ireland during the Viking Age while combining academic knowledge with artistic practice.

The aforementioned projects represent a new generation of Viking research that builds on the knowledge gained from earlier projects conducted in Ireland on the Viking Age. For example, the book *Viking Graves and Grave-Goods in Ireland* (Harrison & Floinn, 2015) is the result of a 15-year project to catalogue and discuss all Viking Age burials in Ireland uncovered until that point. Also, the genetic research by Margaryan et al. (2020) was undertaken by scholars from 64 different institutions across Europe, including Ireland and Scandinavia. These studies demonstrate the potential for international research collaboration on projects relating to the Viking Age in Ireland as they can draw immense interest from state institutions and scholars across time and geographical boundaries.

14.4 Part III: Policy Recommendations: Outlining Critical Research Areas and Potential Projects that Serve to Further the Development of Arctic and Northern Studies in Ireland

14.4.1 Recommendation No. 1

The first recommendation is that the Irish Government should continue to support existing political, cultural, and academic linkages in select Nordic cities and regions but also seek to strengthen connections in regions where Irish linkages exist but are less visible. The purpose of providing in-depth information on two key historical themes is to demonstrate that there is considerable scope for the further development of Irish historical research in Arctic and Northern studies, in addition to the creation of museum exhibits, tourist attractions, and heritage events. The Irish Government engages in cultural diplomacy as a method to advance not only its economic and trade interests in the Nordic region but also to avail new opportunities for research. Of course, successful bilateral relations in cultural diplomacy goes both ways and, in this regard, the Norwegian Embassy in Ireland (2017) and the Embassy of Denmark in Ireland (2017) respectively have each demonstrated that they are actively engaging in cultural diplomacy efforts to advance Irish-Norwegian and Irish-Danish bilateral relations. The current chapter demonstrates these relationships by highlighting some events that have taken place in the recent past including the 2018 St. Sunniva and Viking Dublin conference events, organized by a consortium of Irish and Norwegian partners, and the 2004 recreational voyage of the Danish-Irish *Sea Stallion* Viking longship launched by Irish and Danish dignitaries in Copenhagen.

However, much room exists for building on existing cultural ties with other Nordic countries that Ireland shares historical connections, including Iceland and the Faroe Islands. Less is known by us regarding present day Irish-Icelandic and Irish-Faroe political, cultural and historical relations, although we think that historical and cultural linkages can be easily uncovered as demonstrated in Part II of this chapter. From a diplomatic perspective, it must be noted that although Ireland has a consulate office in Reykjavík, there is not an Irish Ambassador in full-time residence.[17] Similarly, the Icelandic Government has a consulate office in Dublin, but this is listed under the Embassy of Iceland in London.[18] This structure may partially explain why less attention is paid to Irish-Icelandic cultural relations by both governments, and the absence of embassies may be indicative of there being only a small expat community in each country. Nonetheless, the DFA's (2021b, p. 17) Action Plan states that Ireland will seek to

> further develop its relationship with Iceland through an increased frequency of official and ministerial visits, reflecting our strong shared experience and cultural links, as well as a wide range of common interests, including on environment, maritime, social, and EU/ EEA topics.

Regarding the Faroes, Ireland does not have a consulate office in the Faroe Islands. However, this area is served by the Irish Embassy in Denmark because the islands are an autonomous self-governing region that forms part of the Kingdom of Denmark.[19] As an interesting suggestion for a future Irish-Faroe cultural event, we encourage the DFA to organize a celebration honouring the fiftieth anniversary of the *Brendan* voyage which would occur in 2026.

Cultural events to celebrate Irish-Icelandic linkages have taken place in Ireland. For example, in December 2018, a special event was held in Dublin to mark a century of Icelandic sovereignty. This event, "Celebrating a Century of Icelandic Sovereignty: History, Culture, and Irish Connections," was organized as part of the project *Cultural Memory and Contemporary Europe: Ireland, Iceland, and the Atlantic Periphery*, a collaboration between University College Dublin (UCD) (2021) and the University of Iceland. During this event, a roundtable discussion

---

[17] The Irish Ambassador for Norway (Keith Mc Bean, as of this writing) has a secondary accreditation as the Ambassador for Iceland. An honorary consulate (a position held by an Icelander) serves as a point of contact at the consular office in Reykjavik. See https://www.dfa.ie/embassies/irish-embassies-abroad/europe/iceland/.

[18] As shown on the Government of Iceland's webpage: https://www.government.is/diplomatic-missions/country/?itemid=3a7b5d51-f204-11e7-9423-005056bc530c.

[19] See https://www.dfa.ie/embassies/irish-embassies-abroad/europe/faroe-islands/.

titled "Iceland and Ireland Cultural Dialogues and Parallel Histories" was held and included a panel of Irish and Icelandic academics. Podcasts of the speakers were recorded by Real Smart Media and are available online from the UCD website.[20] Two of the academics who participated in the Dublin event—Fionnuala Dillane and Gunnþórunn Guðmundsdóttir—later published the book *Ireland—Iceland: Memory, Literature, Culture on the Atlantic Periphery* in 2022.

In addition to strengthening connections where Irish historical and cultural linkages exist but are less visible, as in the cases of Iceland and the Faroe Islands, we also believe it is important to foster new connections with Northern and Arctic Indigenous communities. Cultural exchanges and events could be co-organized in partnership with Irish universities or other relevant organizations on themes including but not limited to traditional music, folklore traditions, literature, and best practices in the preservation of minority languages and the arts. These connections would be mutually beneficial and culturally enriching for all partners involved, while at the same time could also assist creating new academic links with the aim of furthering a Northern and Arctic research agenda on the island of Ireland.

Current Irish-Canadian cultural relations serve here as an example of best practices owing to the leading role that the Canada-Ireland Foundation (https://www.canadairelandfoundation.com/) has played in promoting cross-cultural and multidisciplinary research. This organization supports academic exchanges and provides funding grants for Irish-Canadian research, although currently their emphasis is on promoting exchanges within a delineated geographic area akin to the eastern Canadian coastal provinces. In the future, the NARI could perform a similar role with respect to facilitating Irish-Nordic research via sharing information on upcoming funding grants and coordinating academic exchanges between Irish, Northern, and Arctic universities. In this way, the NARI could assist the Irish Government's political objectives of increasing academic collaboration, demonstrating that Ireland can make valuable contributions on Northern and Arctic issues.

14.4.2 Recommendation No. 2

The second recommendation is to construct LIS supports in Ireland for Arctic and Northern studies. Adequate LIS services are an essential component to this agenda for ensuring the advancement of NARI's HSS Working Group. Furthermore, constructing LIS supports in Ireland for Arctic and Northern studies would also contribute to the fulfilment of the Irish Government's policy objectives within its Nordic Strategy. As outlined in Part I of the chapter, the Irish Government intends to enhance cultural and heritage connections with Nordic countries. Objective III of the Nordic Strategy clearly states that the Government of Ireland (2021, p. 18) intends to

---

[20] Podcasts are available at https://cca.ucd.ie/icelandic-sovereignty-century-ria/.

encourage media collaboration focused on cultural, historical, and contemporary links between Ireland and the Nordic countries [in addition to] map business and cultural connections (on a phased basis) and develop links between regions and cities by facilitating collaboration between universities, Chambers of Commerce, city councils and businesses.

Unfortunately, neither the Nordic Strategy nor the Action Plan—which mainly focuses on Objective I and II—provides a clear roadmap for how this objective will be achieved. Thus, we believe that our recommendation to develop LIS supports serve as a concrete actionable step towards fulfilling this policy objective, and we offer this suggestion for inclusion in a future Action Plan. We also propose two further actions as contributions to the development of LIS supports for Arctic and Northern Studies in the HSS. First, we propose establishment of an Arctic and Northern studies digital archive to support media and cultural collaboration discussed in more detail in Sect. 14.4.3. Secondly, we endorse the creation of an Irish university consortium which we discuss in Sect. 14.4.4.

14.4.3 Recommendation No. 3

Our third recommendation is the creation of an Arctic digital archive to support Irish HSS research in Arctic and Northern studies. As demonstrated through the creation of the NARI, Ireland's political aspirations for attaining observer status in the AC is a driving factor behind the coordination of Irish Arctic research. These aspirations have invigorated efforts to coordinate Arctic research on the island of Ireland through the NARI, a key stakeholder organization within Ireland's Nordic Strategy. Going forward, the NARI's HSS Working Group should seek to organize the compilation of reading lists of literary and online sources on the research topics outlined in Table 14.1. This endeavour could be done in one of two ways: by updating the NARI website, or alternatively, becoming involved with the creation of an Irish digital archive. Such a collection might include both historical and contemporary material pertaining to the Arctic and Northern studies. This creation of a digital archive echoes a broader trend within Arctic research projects to preserve digital resources and databases online while also creating centralized platforms that provides information on Arctic issues and programs such as, for instance, the Arctic Portal gateway (https://arcticportal.org/) and EU-Polarnet (https://eu-polarnet.eu/). Such digital hubs also offer Arctic researchers a clearer picture of work that is being undertaken and gaps in the research that need to be filled. Regarding the preservation of Arctic cultural heritage, a good example is the University of Calgary's digital collections (https://digitalcollections.ucalgary.ca/).

Internationally, previous discussions took place on how a digital archive and library could materialize. For example, in 2016 and 2017, representatives from Canada, Finland, Sweden, and the United States participated in two workshops that focused on exploring the potential for creating an Arctic digital library (Fitzhugh & Nordlander, 2018). The aim was to discuss how to best integrate primary source material relating to the Arctic in one digital space. With the digital library, a user could access resources on a particular topic from multiple institutions located in different countries. This platform would help users connect disparate bits of data to create an interdisciplinary picture of a research question. Ultimately, the vision to develop truly international and collaborative Arctic research projects would benefit from an integrated digital research platform as doing so would greatly assist in transcending national boundaries and from which exciting new relationships and understandings of the Arctic could emerge. The NARI could assist in this endeavour by creating a single repository where Irish research projects relating to the Arctic are listed. An undertaking such as an Arctic digital library could either direct researchers to the external NARI site or incorporate that information into their repository to the benefit of Arctic scholars globally.

On a national scale, Ireland demonstrates considerable expertise in the building of digital repositories for the preservation of Irish culture and history. Such efforts began to emerge in the 2010s when the Digital Repository of Ireland (DRI) (https://www.dri.ie/) was founded in 2011. The mission of the DRI is to ensure the long-term digital preservation of Ireland's humanities, social science, and cultural heritage resources.[21] Sandra Collins, a member of the DRI Management Board, emphasized that "so much of our national memory is recorded in digital format and is gravely at risk right now. In 100 years from now, in 1000 years, what we collect, and curate now will shape the national memory in the future and tell the story of humanity" (DRI, 2023, para. 2). The DRI was originally built by a research consortium of six academic partners working together to deliver the repository, policies, guidelines, and training. Three core academic institutions continue to manage the repository: Trinity College Dublin (TCD), Royal Irish Academy, and Maynooth University (MU).

The Digital Preservation Coalition (2023, para. 1) describes the DRI as "a major initiative to safeguard Ireland's digital heritage...[that] stands as an exemplar of cooperation and best practice adoption in digital preservation because of its national cross-institutional structure, as well as its integration in the international network data repositories and e-infrastructures." Should an Irish-Arctic digital library be created or integrated into the DRI in the future, there exist two pathways that an organization may take to gain deposit authorization into the DRI repository: (1) an organization may decide to become an official DRI member, or (2) an organization may utilize the expertise and domain knowledge of one of the three existing DRI members. The first option allows for the possibility of the NARI becoming a DRI member. Alternatively, should the second option be pursued, a group of individual

---

[21] For example, the DRI coordinated projects such as *Inspiring Ireland* (https://www.inspiring-ireland.ie/), an ongoing initiative funded by the Irish Government's Department of Arts, Heritage, and the Gaeltacht. The pilot phase of the project was launched in 2014 with a collection of objects from eight of Ireland's national cultural institutions. These collections were organized into three broad but fundamental themes: sense of place, sense of identity, and sense of freedom, with the aim of providing a window into Ireland's rich social and cultural heritage. The second phase of the project, *Inspiring Ireland 1916*, focused on developing a series of exhibitions to mark the centenary of the 1916 Rising, a monumental event in Irish history that is viewed as the catalyst for Irish political independence from Great Britain.

NARI researchers could coordinate with one or both of the two existing Irish university partners, those being TCD and MU.

Another database deserves mention here: the *National Inventory of Intangible Cultural Heritage* (https://nationalinventoryich.chg.gov.ie/). As stated by the Department of Tourism, Culture, Arts, Gaeltacht, Sport, and Media (2023, para. 1):

> Intangible cultural heritage refers to the practices, representations, expressions, knowledge, skills – as well as the instruments, objects, artefacts, and cultural spaces associated therewith – that communities, groups and, in some cases, individuals recognize as part of their cultural heritage. This intangible cultural heritage, transmitted from generation to generation, is constantly recreated by communities and groups in response to their environment, their interaction with nature and their history, and provides them with a sense of identity and continuity, thus promoting respect for cultural diversity and human creativity.

This project can be traced back to 2015 when Ireland ratified UNESCO's (2003) *Convention for the Safeguarding of Intangible Cultural Heritage*. Ireland's obligations under the Convention included establishing a national inventory for intangible cultural heritage. Following the appointment of "an Expert Advisory Committee on Intangible Cultural Heritage, in July 2019 the Minister for Culture, Heritage, and the Gaeltacht approved the inscription of thirty cultural heritage elements on Ireland's permanent National Inventory" (Department of Tourism, Culture, Arts, Gaeltacht, Sport, and Media, 2023, para. 2).[22] Efforts to raise awareness on Ireland's Arctic and Northern heritage would benefit greatly from the organizational structure of the DRI and National Inventory and serve as templates for the potential development of new collections relating to historical Arctic and Northern topics of interest.

14.4.4   Recommendation No. 4

The fourth and final recommendation is the development of an Irish university consortium for Arctic and Northern studies, as well as a supporting Irish-Nordic university database. A key goal of the NARI is to promote education on the Arctic North within Ireland, yet it should be noted that cultural diplomacy can also make use of educational tools such as scholarship programs. For example, in recent years, the DFA in partnership with the Marine Institute, has offered a scholarship for an Irish Arctic researcher to attend the annual Arctic Frontiers Emerging Leaders program in northern Norway. The Emerging Leaders program is an opportunity for postgraduate students and early-career professionals to engage with their counterparts from Arctic and non-Arctic states.

Going forward, we believe it is essential to further promote Irish-Arctic linkages through establishing university partnerships and create opportunities for educational exchanges, scholarships, field-research trips, and conferences to strengthen

---

[22] Ireland was also successful in having three elements of living heritage inscribed on UNESCO's *Lists of Intangible Cultural Heritage* (https://ich.unesco.org/en/lists): Uilleann piping in 2017, Hurling in 2018, and Irish harping in 2019.

research collaboration. This activity coincides with the current Action Plan which identifies under objective II the goal of "encouraging Irish universities and relevant agencies to engage with their Nordic counterparts on promoting Irish expertise" and furthermore, to "establish new research partnerships with Nordic institutes and companies by 2025" (DFA, 2021b, pp. 12–13). Further action points relating to this goal include "consult with Irish universities to determine existing formal links with Nordic universities" and produce a "data-map showing Irish alumni in Nordic states" (DFA, 2021b, p. 18). In alignment with this specific action point, we propose that the creation of an Irish university consortium focused on multidisciplinary Northern and Arctic studies in HSS is beneficial to enable flexible learning opportunities that allow for the broadening of university curricula, and also to serve as a means for the sharing of knowledge and educational resources within HSS. In particular, courses offered online as distance learning will produce more opportunities for students and Arctic researchers to expand their knowledge on specific Northern and Arctic research areas within HSS. With the global COVID-19 pandemic, online teaching has become the new norm and technology allows greater flexibility with respect to the delivery of academic courses. The creation of new arts and humanities degrees at both undergraduate and postgraduate levels that include interdisciplinary studies will provide students with a deeper knowledge of the Arctic and Nordic countries, in addition to tailoring students' research and flexibility to remotely partake in elective classes offered at different institutions than their 'home' university.

In support of this consortium, we also envision the development of an information database of Irish and Nordic universities involved in HSS research that could be made available through the NARI website. Such a database could be created as either a standalone listing or integrated within a general university database for all academic disciplines relating to the Arctic and the North. However, we feel that with respect to Arctic and Northern studies within the HSS disciplines, such a database would be vital as HSS research is often less visible than the natural sciences, particularly when it comes to Arctic research. This database would provide specific details including the names and titles of university departments, contact personnel, and any existing academic exchange agreements or partnerships that Irish universities have with those in the Nordic countries. An Irish-Nordic university database would make it is easier to support existing partnerships, identify potential new connections, and reveal where gaps are present. Such gaps relate not only to research but also to university courses and curricula.

Two of the distinct historical periods on which Part II of this chapter focuses (i.e., early Christian Era and the Viking Age) demonstrate the important role that Irish and Celtic studies have in promoting Irish-Nordic historical connections. Students and academics involved in Irish-Nordic research on the island of Ireland currently participate in academic networks and international symposia such as the *Societas Celtologica Nordica*, a well-established Swedish symposium.[23] In contrast, however, the structur-

---

[23] Based within the Celtic Studies section in the Department of English at Uppsala University in Sweden, this symposium was created in 1990 by Irish Professor Ailbhe Ó Corráin, together with colleagues from Oslo and Helsinki, during the time that she was the Docent in Celtic Languages at

ing of Irish and Celtic studies degree programs offered within the Republic and north of Ireland[24] do not, at present, offer the possibility of studying Nordic culture or languages alongside Irish. Given the strong and evident historical ties between Ireland and the Nordic region, such degree courses should be developed in the future and modelled on Celtic-Nordic study programs that exist in neighbouring countries. For example, the University of Edinburgh in the UK offers a Master of Arts degree in Celtic and Scandinavian studies, combining literary studies in early Irish, medieval Welsh, and Scottish Gaelic with Scandinavian studies.[25] This degree could serve as a template for developing a similar program offered partially, or fully, online through one or more universities on the island of Ireland. In the Republic, the development of this type of degree could be a multidisciplinary educational initiative serving to promote Ireland's Nordic Strategy, especially if such a program could offer tuition in both the Irish and Nordic languages, thus providing ongoing opportunities for language exchange programs with Nordic partner universities.

Regarding development of international academic partnerships, new connections are already being established by Irish universities. On the same day that the NARI was officially launched (i.e., 20 February 2020), the Centre for the Environment at TCD announced that it had applied to the University of the Arctic (UArctic) (https://www.uarctic.org/) network and subsequently became the first UArctic member from Ireland. Endorsed by the Arctic Council, the UArctic network was launched in 2001 as an international association based in Finland. UArctic's activities are summarized as "a network of universities, colleges, research institutes, and other organizations concerned with education and research in and about the north" (UArctic, n.d., para. 1). The Halpin Centre for Research and Innovation, based in the National Maritime College of Ireland, a constituent college of MTU Cork, applied for UArctic status early in 2023, and was met with approval at the UArctic Assembly meeting in Québec in May 2023. It should be noted that the two above mentioned Irish UArctic members and their affiliated departments/research centres do not specialize in HSS research. However, expanding the number of Irish partners involved within the UArctic network is an important step in fostering international university collaboration between Ireland and Arctic partner universities and could also facilitate with the development of an Irish-Nordic university database.

Uppsala University. However, the Celtic Section can trace its Irish connections as far back as 1950, when Irishman James Carney founded the Celtic Section as a visiting professor from the Dublin Institute for Advanced Studies and was appointed Visiting Professor in Irish Studies. The Celtic Section proclaims that it is "the only one of its kind in Scandinavia and is solely dedicated to the study of Celtic languages and literature from the earliest times to the modern day" (Uppsala University, n.d., para. 1).

[24] There are six Irish higher educational institutions offering courses in Celtic and Irish. The four universities in the Republic are University College Dublin, University College Cork, Trinity College Dublin, and the National University of Ireland Galway. However, there also exists the School of Celtic Studies within the Dublin Institute for Advanced Studies, a research institute that employs academic staff and post-doctoral scholars. The two universities in Northern Ireland that offer Celtic Studies programs are Queen's University Belfast and Ulster University.

[25] The Scandinavian studies part of this MA degree includes classes on the languages, history, politics, and cultures of Scandinavian countries and their impact beyond the Nordic region.

14.5 Conclusion

This chapter began by framing Ireland's Northern and Arctic connections through a discussion on contemporary political developments, namely how Ireland's application for observer status in the AC provides a stimulus to organize and invigorate Northern and Arctic research in Ireland. Although it was a disappointing setback that Ireland did not achieve this status in 2021, there were many positive outcomes from the process of applying, including creation of the NARI and organization of events surrounding the launch of Ireland's AC application and release of its Nordic Strategy—these all helped raise the profile of Northern and Arctic research in Ireland. While these efforts may be perceived as largely government-led, academic researchers have an important contribution to make regarding how different Northern and Arctic identities, and especially Irish perceptions of these, are perceived and represented in the public domain. Through the creation of the NARI and subsequent HSS Working Group, this representation has a formal structure that could be utilized for future collaboration. Yet more work is needed particularly with respect to providing online resources and reading lists. The digitization of artefacts and documents relating to Northern and Arctic heritage as part of national digitalization projects, or an international Arctic digital library and archive, are reasonable next steps.

The present chapter adds to the literature and contributes to representation by raising important questions surrounding Ireland's newly emerging Northern and Arctic identities. By using the three categories of Arctic identities devised by Lanteigne, this chapter posits that Ireland potentially qualifies to claim all three. Furthermore, the chapter argues in support of Ireland being recognized as an Arctic-adjacent state that has political and economic interests in the Arctic region while also claiming rich and diverse historical linkages with the Nordic states. Through a brief analysis of Ireland's Nordic Strategy, the chapter points out that the Irish Government recognizes the value of utilizing historical and cultural connections with Nordic states to strengthen cultural diplomacy in the Nordic and Arctic region. The early Christian Era and Viking Age are successful themes for historical and cultural events while also proving popular with the public, in addition to strengthening Ireland's bilateral relations with Nordic states. However, for Ireland to fully achieve the objectives outlined in its Nordic Strategy, the Irish Government also must ensure a strong academic research base upon which to demonstrate regional expertise and scientific engagement.

Concerning input from the broader field of HSS, there will be challenges to this endeavour arising from ongoing funding and pedagogical issues that are not constrained to the Irish example alone (e.g., the structure and content of university courses, as well as the false divisions within and between academic fields). Although such influences do not lend well to the creation of a strong Irish interdisciplinary Arctic and Northern studies field in HSS, these challenges are not insurmountable. This process would require diligence and much work on behalf of Irish HSS researchers but could be achieved with the necessary funding supports. At the same time, this interdisciplinary field must be created with direct involvement of library and information science to help raise public awareness and provide both the necessary intellectual and networking supports for this endeavour.

References

Abarta Heritage. (2021). *Viking Woodstown conservation management plan*. https://bit.ly/4alby9B. Accessed 13 Dec 2023.

Adapt Northern Heritage. (n.d.-a). *About the project*. https://bit.ly/41iAdY6. Accessed 13 Dec 2023.

Adapt Northern Heritage. (n.d.-b). *Case studies and adaptation plans*. https://bit.ly/48dGI0F. Accessed 13 Dec 2023.

Ahlstrom, D. (2000, October 2). Why people in Iceland look just like us. *The Irish Times*. https://bit.ly/488OPMx. Accessed 13 Dec 2023.

Ahronson, K. (2000). Further evidence for a Columban Iceland: Preliminary results of recent work. *Norwegian Archaeological Review, 33*(2), 117–124. https://doi.org/cp3zpb

Ahronson, K. (2015). *Into the ocean: Vikings, Irish, and environmental change in Iceland and the North*. University of Toronto Press.

Als, T. D., Jorgensen, T. H., Børglum, A. D., Petersen, P. A., Mors, O., & Wang, A. G. (2006). Highly discrepant proportions of female and male Scandinavian and British Isles ancestry within the isolated population of the Faroe Islands. *European Journal of Human Genetics, 14*, 497–504. https://doi.org/dj98j2

Ashby, S. P. (2009). Combs, contact, and chronology: Reconsidering hair combs in early-historic and Viking-Age Atlantic Scotland. *Medieval Archaeology, 53*(1), 1–33. https://doi.org/d485nn

Ashby, S. P., Coutu, A. N., & Sindbæk, S. M. (2015). Urban networks and Arctic outlands: Craft specialists and reindeer antler in Viking towns. *European Journal of Archaeology, 18*(4), 679–704. https://doi.org/k8jk

Barber, F., Hansson, H., & McQuaid, S. D. (Eds.). (2019). *Ireland and the North*. Peter Lang.

Barrett, J. H. (2008). What caused the Viking Age? *Antiquity, 82*(317), 671–685. https://doi.org/gj5dgx

Birkelli, F. (1971). Earliest Christian missionary activities from England and Norway. *Nottingham Medieval Studies, 15*, 27–37.

Bourke, E. (1995). Life in the sunny south-east: Housing and domestic economy in Viking and medieval Wexford. *Archaeology Ireland, 9*(3), 33–36. https://bit.ly/46QdLa0. Accessed 13 Dec 2023.

Boyd, R. (2015). Where are the longhouses? Reviewing Ireland's Viking-Age buildings. In H. B. Clarke & R. Johnson (Eds.), *Before and after the Battle of Clontarf: The Vikings in Ireland and beyond* (pp. 325–345). Four Courts.

Browne, B. (2021, June 12). Conference to delve deep into Cork's Viking origins. *The Irish Independent*. https://bit.ly/3RFwS2g. Accessed 13 Dec 2023.

Buildings of Wexford. (n.d.). *Buildings of County Wexford—Built heritage of County Wexford: Town wall*. https://bit.ly/3uTv9xo. Accessed 13 Dec 2023.

Church, M. J., Arge, S. V., Edwards, K. J., Ascough, P. L., Bond, J. M., Cook, G. T., Dokrill, S. J., Dugmore, A. J., McGovern, T. H., Nesbitt, C., & Simpson, I. A. (2013). The Vikings were not the first colonizers of the Faroe Islands. *Quaternary Science Reviews, 77*, 228–232. https://doi.org/f5c2sj

Cleary, R. M., & Hurley, M. F. (Eds.). (2003). *Excavations in Cork city 1984–2000*. Cork City Council.

Coccioli, L., Hunt, E., Hall, S., Mhaonaigh, M. N., El-Idrissi, M., Wright, J., O'Malley, M., & Schorn, B. (2020). *Augmented vocality*. https://bit.ly/4afqaXU. Accessed 13 Dec 2023.

Coccioli, L., Mhaonaigh, M. N., Hall, S., & Hunt, E. (2021). *Augmented vocality: Recomposing the sounds of early Irish and Old Norse*. https://bit.ly/46TP908. Accessed 13 Dec 2023.

Connor, S. (2013, August 20). Did Irish monks find the Faroe Islands 400 years before the Vikings? *The Belfast Telegraph*. https://bit.ly/3NpNyrI. Accessed 13 Dec 2023.

Cunningham, P. (2020). Is it a stretch for Ireland to join the Arctic Council? *RTE*. https://bit.ly/3NrkgsV. Accessed 13 Dec 2023.

Curriculum Development Unit, Mary Immaculate College (MIC). (2014, October 17). *Viking Ireland: A new voyage of discovery*. https://bit.ly/3RmVprn. Accessed 13 Dec 2023.

Daly, S. (2014). Ancient Waterford site reveals Vikings moved from raiding to trading. *The Journal*. https://bit.ly/3RDS2NY. Accessed 13 Dec 2023.

Department of Foreign Affairs (DFA), Government of Ireland/An Roinn Gnóthaí Eachtracha, Rialtas na hÉireann. (2021a). *Ireland's bid to become an observer to the Arctic Council*. https://bit.ly/3Rk81PV. Accessed 13 Dec 2023.

Department of Foreign Affairs (DFA), Government of Ireland/An Roinn Gnóthaí Eachtracha, Rialtas na hÉireann. (2021b). *Global Ireland: Ireland's strategy for the Nordic region to 2025—Action Plan*. https://bit.ly/47W3c6A. Accessed 13 Dec 2023.

Department of Foreign Affairs (DFA), Government of Ireland/An Roinn Gnóthaí Eachtracha, Rialtas na hÉireann. (n.d.). *The Good Friday Agreement and today*. https://bit.ly/3REQJhU. Accessed 13 Dec 2023.

Department of Tourism, Culture, Arts, Gaeltacht, Sport, and Media, Government of Ireland/An Roinn Turasóireachta, Cultúir, Ealaíon, Gaeltachta, Spóirt agus Meán, Rialtas na hÉireann. (2023). *Intangible cultural heritage*. https://bit.ly/3uYtZAI. Accessed 13 Dec 2023.

Digital Preservation Coalition. (2023). *The digital repository of Ireland: Preserving Ireland's social and cultural record*. https://bit.ly/48fyghy. Accessed 13 Dec 2023.

Digital Repository of Ireland (DRI). (2023). *Introducing the IDCC20 keynotes—Dr. Sandra Collins*. https://bit.ly/41iFrDc. Accessed 13 Dec 2023.

Downham, C. (2004). The historical importance of Viking-Age Waterford. *Journal of Celtic Studies, 4*, 71–96.

Dybris McQuaid, S., Hansson, H., & Barber, F. (2019). Introduction: A new geography of reference. In F. Barber, H. Hansson, & S. Dybris McQuaid (Eds.), *Ireland and the North* (pp. 3–16). Peter Lang.

Ebenesersdóttir, S. S., Sandoval-Velasco, M., Gunnarsdóttir, E. D., Jagadeesan, A., Guðmundsdóttir, V. B., Thordardóttir, E. L., Einarsdóttir, M. S., Moore, K. H. S., Sigurðsson, Á., Magnúsdóttir, D. N., Jónsson, H., Snorradóttir, S., Hovig, E., Møller, P., Kockum, I., Olsson, T., Alfredsson, L., Hansen, T. F., Werge, T., Cavalleri, G. L., Gilbert, E., Lalueza-Fox, C., Walser, J. W., III, Kristjánsdóttir, S., et al. (2018). Ancient genomes from Iceland reveal the making of a human population. *Science, 360*(6392), 1028–1032. https://doi.org/gdpbqp

Embassy of Ireland in Denmark, Department of Foreign Affairs and Trade/Ambasáid na hÉireann An Danmhairg, An Roinn Gnóthaí Eachtracha agus Tradála. (2017). *Minister Humphreys trade and culture mission to Denmark*. https://bit.ly/41jZi4S. Accessed 13 Dec 2023.

Fitch, C. (2015). Unearthing Iceland's heritage. *Geographical*. https://bit.ly/472bNTY. Accessed 13 Dec 2023.

Fitzhugh, W. W., & Nordlander, D. (2018, May). Arctic digital library. *Arctic Studies Center Newsletter, 25*, 45. https://s.si.edu/3NpIJyE

Gilbert, E., O'Reilly, S., Merrigan, M., McGettigan, D., Molloy, A., Brody, L., Bodmer, W., Hutnik, K., Ennis, S., Lawson, D. J., Wilson, J. F., & Cavalleri, G. L. (2017). The Irish DNA atlas: Revealing fine-scale population structure and history within Ireland. *Scientific Reports, 7*(1), Article 17199, 1–11.

Government of Ireland/Rialtas na hÉireann. (2018). *Global Ireland 2025*. https://bit.ly/3NqpDse. Accessed 13 Dec 2023.

Government of Ireland/Rialtas na hÉireann. (2021). *Global Ireland: A strategy for the Nordic region: Delivering for Ireland in the Nordic region to 2025*. https://bit.ly/48cEcYC. Accessed 13 Dec 2023.

Grønlie, S. (Trans.). (2006). *Íslendingabok, Kristni saga* [The book of Icelanders, the story of the conversion]. Viking Society for Northern Research. https://bit.ly/3uXRfyN. Accessed 13 Dec 2023.

Grossberg, L. (1996). Identity and cultural studies: Is that all there is? In S. Hall & P. Du Gay (Eds.), *Questions of cultural identity* (pp. 87–107). Sage.

Harrison, S. J., & Floinn, R. Ó. (2015). *Viking graves and grave-goods in Ireland.* National Museum of Ireland.

Hegarty, N. (2011). *The story of Ireland: A history of the Irish people.* BBC Books.

Helgason, A., Sigurðardottir, S., Nicholson, J., Sykes, B., Hill, E. W., Bradley, D. G., Bosnes, V., Gulcher, J. R., Ward, R., & Stefánsson, K. (2000). Estimating Scandinavian and Gaelic ancestry in the male settlers of Iceland. *American Journal of Human Genetics, 67*(3), 697–717. https://doi.org/fcjm9g

Helgason, A., Hickey, E., Goodacre, S., Bosnes, V., Stefánsson, K., Ward, R., & Sykes, B. (2001). mtDNA and the islands of the North Atlantic: Estimating the proportions of Norse and Gaelic ancestry. *American Journal of Human Genetics, 68*(3), 723–737. https://doi.org/cd87ts

Hodkinson, B. (2002). The topography of pre-Norman Limerick. *North Munster Antiquarian Journal, 42,* 1–6. https://bit.ly/47TFkR4. Accessed 13 Dec 2023.

Houses of the Oireachtas/Tithe an Oireachtais. (2019, May 21). *International bodies—Dáil Eireann debate.* https://bit.ly/3RiWdxw. Accessed 13 Dec 2023.

Hurley, M. F. (1995). The Vikings in Munster: Evidence from Waterford and Cork. *Archaeology Ireland, 9*(3), 23–25. https://bit.ly/3RDNlUn. Accessed 13 Dec 2023.

Kelly, E. P., & O'Donovan, E. (1998). A Viking longphort near Athlunkard, Co. Clare. *Archaeology Ireland, 12*(4), 13–16. https://bit.ly/3tdQD7C. Accessed 13 Dec 2023.

Killeen, B. (2004, September 6). Ancient Irish-built Viking long boat lives again. *The Irish Times.* https://bit.ly/3RGoOyf. Accessed 13 Dec 2023.

King, S. (2020, July 24). The Brendan Voyage [blog]. *Looking North: Islands of the North Atlantic.* https://bit.ly/3NmFbNK. Accessed 13 Dec 2023.

Lanteigne, M. (2020). Inside, outside, upside down? Non-Arctic states in emerging Arctic security discourses. In K. Spohr, D. S. Hamilton, & J. C. Moyer (Eds.), *The Arctic and world order* (pp. 379–404). Brookings Institute Press. https://bit.ly/4afXMoz. Accessed 13 Dec 2023.

Lanteigne, M. (2021, February 11). *Near and (not) so far: How do non-Arctic states define themselves in the Arctic?* [Seminar]. NARI.

Lewis, S. M. (2016). Vikings on the Ribble: Their origin and longphuirt. *Northern History, 53*(1), 8–25. https://doi.org/k8mq

MacGowan, A. (2015, August 20). Let's go a Viking: Sailing on the Sea Stallion of Glendalough [Blog]. *Irish Archaeology.* https://bit.ly/3NnG48E. Accessed 13 Dec 2023.

Margaryan, A., Lawson, D. J., Sikora, M., Racimo, F., Rasmussen, S., Moltke, I., Cassidy, L. M., Jørsboe, E., Ingason, A., Pedersen, M. W., Korneliussen, T., Wilhelmson, H., Buś, M. M., de Barros Damgaard, P., Martiniano, R., Renaud, G., Bhérer, C., Moreno-Mayar, V., Fotakis, A. K., Allen, M., Allmäe, R., Molak, M., Cappellini, E., Scorrano, G., et al. (2020). Population genomics of the Viking world. *Nature, 585*(7825), 390–396. https://doi.org/ghcvxm

Mary Immaculate College (MIC), University of Limerick. (2013). *Genes of Gallgoídil.* https://bit.ly/3t87F7d. Accessed 13 Dec 2023.

Montgomery, J., Grimes, V., Buckberry, J., Evans, J. A., Richards, M. P. & Barrett, J. H. (2014). Finding Vikings with isotope analysis: The view from wet and windy islands. *Journal of the North Atlantic,* Special Volume, *7,* 54–70. https://bit.ly/3REXFeR. Accessed 13 Dec 2023.

National University of Ireland/Ollscoil na hÉireann. (2018). *Dublin festival of history: Viking symposium and lecture.* https://bit.ly/41kUJqZ. Accessed 13 Dec 2023.

O'Carroll, R. (2020, August 18). What did the early Irish sound like? Researchers hope to find out. *The Irish Times.* https://bit.ly/3RF7UzX. Accessed 13 Dec 2023.

O'Donovan, E. (2003). Limerick: New discoveries in an old city. *History Ireland, 11*(1), 39–43. https://bit.ly/3uXPRfp. Accessed 13 Dec 2023.

O'Driscoll, L. O., & Färber, B. (Comp.). (2018). *Liber de mesura orbis terrae* [Book of the measurement of the world]. Corpus of Electronic Texts. (Original work by Dícuil published in 825 AD). https://bit.ly/46YLcHB. Accessed 13 Dec 2023.

O'Flaherty, E., & Moore, J. (2010). *Limerick c. 840 to c. 1900: Viking longphort to Victorian City.* Royal Irish Academy.

O'Hara, A. (2009). Constructing a saint: The legend of Saint Sunniva in twelfth-century Norway. *Viking and Medieval Scandinavia, 5,* 105–121. https://bit.ly/3Nq6DKK. Accessed 13 Dec 2023.

Quinn, E. (2021). Lack of consensus punts Arctic Council observer applications to future ministerial. *Eye on the Arctic.* https://bit.ly/3GIioYW. Accessed 13 Dec 2023.

Roche, B. (2018, May 24). Viking houses from 1070 found in Cork dig at former Beamish and Crawford brewery. *The Irish Times.* https://bit.ly/3RlPMtF. Accessed 13 Dec 2023.

Ryniesjska-Kiełdanowicz, M. (n.d.). *Cultural diplomacy as a form of international communication.* https://bit.ly/47UPC3q. Accessed 13 Dec 2023.

Saga Museum. (2017). *Papar: The first inhabitants.* https://bit.ly/41sFah5. Accessed 13 Dec 2023.

Schei, L. K., & Moberg, G. (2003). *The Faroe Islands.* Birlinn.

Severin, T. (1978/2000). *The Brenden voyage: Sailing to America in a leather boat to prove the legend of the Irish sailor saints.* Modern Library.

Severin, T., & Scales, A. (Dirs.). (1978). *The Brenden voyage* [Film]. Barrow Hepburn.

Sheehan, J. (2008). The longphort in Viking Age Ireland. *Acta Archaelogica, 79,* 282–295. https://doi.org/ctbpn2

Sikora, M. (n.d.). *Limerick.* Viking Ship Museum/Vikingskibs Museet. https://bit.ly/41sq77e. Accessed 13 Dec 2023.

Sveinsson, E. Ó. (1957). Celtic elements in Icelandic tradition. *Béaloideas, 25,* 3–24.

The Irish Times. (2021, January 2). Tim Severin: Writer and explorer best known for the Brendan Voyage [Obituary]. https://bit.ly/3Nmx7N5. Accessed 13 Dec 2023.

Ulff-Møller, J. (2006). The Celtic impact on the Church in Iceland and Greenland. In J. McKinnell, D. Ashurst, & D. Kick (Eds.), *The fantastic in Old Norse/Icelandic literature: Preprint papers of the 13th international Saga conference, Durham and York, 6–12 August* (Vol. 2, pp. 978–987). Centre for Medieval and Renaissance Studies.. https://bit.ly/3TpOJLW. Accessed 13 Dec 2023.

UNESCO. (2003). *Convention for the safeguarding of intangible cultural heritage.* https://bit.ly/3ToRehw. Accessed 13 Dec 2023.

University College Dublin (UCD). (2021). *Celebrating a century of Icelandic sovereignty at the RIA.* https://bit.ly/46Y45Ks. Accessed 13 Dec 2023.

University of the Arctic. (n.d.). *About us.* https://bit.ly/3tfzQAW. Accessed 13 Dec 2023.

Uppsala University/Uppsala Universitet. (n.d.). *Department of English: Celtic studies.* https://bit.ly/3RqYfLQ

Viking Ship Museum/Vikingskibs Museet. (n.d.). *The five Viking ships—Skuldelev ships.* https://bit.ly/47WtLZe. Accessed 13 Dec 2023.

Wilson, A. (2014). The Vikings in Munster. In T. Birkett & C. Lee (Eds.), *The Vikings in Munster* (pp. 20–32). Centre for the Study of the Viking Age, University of Nottingham. https://bit.ly/4amcPgo. Accessed 13 Dec 2023.

Chapter 15
Part I: Library and Archives Engagement and Outreach Programs Using Sources from the Arctic and Northern Regions

Christena McKillop, Nadine Hoffman, and Regina Landwehr

Abstract Collaboration is important for flourishing engagement and outreach initiatives in archives, libraries, and special collections. By way of outreach events using primary sources from the Arctic and Northern regions of Canada, librarians and archivists can connect with interested students, faculty, and researchers and gain access to undergraduate classrooms for curriculum development, library instruction, archival literacy, and online tutorials. This chapter presents specific examples of how the authors engaged in outreach and marketing using library, archives, and special collections at the University of Calgary, including the Arctic Institute of North America (AINA) collections and the Glenbow Library and Archives collections. Digitization of these collections enabled greater support to online research throughout the COVID-19 pandemic when classes at the university went fully remote in March 2020. This chapter demonstrates that raising awareness of and facilitating engagement with unique and digital Arctic and Northern collections such as those of AINA and Glenbow can lead to new outreach opportunities with students, faculty, and researchers.

Keywords Archives · Arctic Institute of North America (AINA) · Canadian history · Glenbow · Libraries · Library & Archives Engagement · Library & Archives Outreach · Primary sources · Rare books

---

C. McKillop (✉) · N. Hoffman · R. Landwehr
University of Calgary, Calgary, AB, Canada
e-mail: christena.mckillop@ucalgary.ca; nadine.hoffman@ucalgary.ca; rlandweh@ucalgary.ca

© The Author(s), under exclusive license to Springer Nature
Switzerland AG 2024
S. Acadia (ed.), *Library and Information Sciences in Arctic and Northern Studies*, Springer Polar Sciences, https://doi.org/10.1007/978-3-031-54715-7_15

319

15.1 Introduction and Background

Collegial partnerships are important to effectively promote the use of primary and secondary sources by students, faculty, and researchers at the University of Calgary (https://www.ucalgary.ca/), a large degree-granting post-secondary institution located in Calgary, Alberta, Canada. The University of Calgary is recognized as a top Canadian research university. In this chapter, the first of two in this book, specific collaborations to be analysed are drawn from using the four distinct Arctic Institute of North America (AINA) collections of circulating library publications, circulating pipeline-specific grey literature (i.e., the AINA Pipeline Collection), non-circulating rare books, and archival material, as well as the Glenbow Library and Archives (i.e., the Glenbow collection). The first two of the AINA collections are part of the library's circulating collection while the other two collections are housed in the Archives and Special Collections (ASC) unit (https://asc.ucalgary.ca/). As of 2006, all these collections are part of the converged faculty of Libraries and Cultural Resources (LCR) (https://library.ucalgary.ca/) (Hinks, 2007, p. 27). The LCR is a "unique tapestry of libraries and archives, galleries and museums, the University of Calgary Press, the Copyright Office, and the Prairie Regional Research Data Centre. At the nexus of the LCR tapestry is the digital research library" (LCR, 2022, p. verso). As a brief history to this complex and diverse faculty at the University of Calgary, the University Library merged with the University Archives, University of Calgary Press, Communications Media unit, and Library Technology unit in Fall 1998 to form the larger Information Resources faculty (Hinks, 2007, p. 22). The Nickle Arts Museum, now the Nickle Galleries (https://nickle.ucalgary.ca/), and the Digitization unit were added in the 1999–2000 academic year (LCR fonds, 1998–2000) and the Founders' Gallery (https://founders.ucalgary.ca/) was added in 2009. The addition of the Glenbow collection was announced on 14 November 2018 (University Relations Staff, 2018) with the physical move completed in December 2020 (Beauline-Stuebing, 2020).

The university's mission and strategic plan, *Eyes High*, guides the direction of faculty and staff. As noted in the strategy statement, the University of Calgary (2017, p. 2) "is a global intellectual hub located in Canada's most enterprising city. In this spirited, high-quality learning environment, students will thrive in programs made rich by research, hands-on experiences, and entrepreneurial thinking." Importantly, the key directions of research, hands-on experiences, and community engagement are what connects our work as reflected in this chapter as well as the next one in Part II. Horowitz (2016, p. 10) notes that "collaboration does not just happen; it requires commitment and investment from all involved, and often, buy-in from supervisors and administrators." Alignment with strategic directions over time contributes to setting a solid foundation for collaborating on library and archival engagement and outreach programs. Scholarship of Teaching and Learning (SOTL) pedagogy also informs our professional practice. Malkmus (2010, p. 429) states that

> further research is needed to provide information about which outreach strategies are effective—emailing faculty to alert them of primary sources related to their courses, offering

15 Part I: Library and Archives Engagement and Outreach Programs Using Sources… 321

examples of how similar sources have been used by well-known professors, sending links to faculty of Scholarship of Teaching and Learning (SOTL)—based on reports and Websites, or having face-to-face discussions about using primary sources.

Furthermore, we draw upon current marketing theory, such as relationship marketing, as a good fit for promoting library collections and services. Broady-Preston (2013, p. 29), when commenting on contemporary marketing theories and paradigms, says that "in services marketing, the primary focus is on developing a relationship between the service provider and customer, to ensure the customer does not have a single transaction or encounter with the service, but returns on numerous occasions, thereby building a long term and loyal relationship with the provider." As well, a focus on the creation of integrated access systems for primary source collections can help different groups of information specialists provide streamlined and richer service to users (Timms, 2009). As shown in this chapter, the combination of committed collaboration, shared pedagogical understandings, and the employment of targeted marketing strategies resulted in several successful outreach events. The AINA and Glenbow collections opened new engagement and outreach opportunities and stimulated new research endeavours. These events offered opportunities to engage in other areas such as instruction and literacy opportunities and marketing primary source collections to students, faculty, and researchers.

The authors of the current chapter bring different professional backgrounds to their work and in their roles as archivist (Landwehr); history librarian (Hoffman); and engagement, learning, and outreach librarian (McKillop). Both the archivist and engagement, learning, and outreach librarian work in the ASC, while the history librarian reports to a library unit. Despite working in different units within LCR, all three share a common vision and pedagogical framework which contributes to successful collaborations across information disciplines.

15.2 Collaborations and Partnerships for Successful Engagement and Outreach

Collaborations create an environment for collections to be successfully incorporated into outreach partnerships and events, validating library and archival collections that can lead to research collaboration: "Collaboration is an educationally innovative process among academics, librarians, and other relevant parties who are working together to share knowledge and expertise to support the enhancement of teaching, learning, and research experiences for the university community" (Pham & Tanner, 2014, p. 23). When these elements are strategically combined and marketed, primary and secondary sources from content-rich collections can be incorporated to spark new understandings and incorporate research directions into learning opportunities and major research initiatives. Faculty-librarian collaboration can achieve "mutually beneficial goals or aspirations" and "can result in emergent (unexpected) outcomes or benefits" (Pham & Tanner, 2014, p. 22). Information professionals, particularly librarians and archivists, are well placed to collaborate with faculty and promote faculty partnerships. A study by Malkmus (2010) found that targeted outreach is an effective way for librarians and archivists to work together in creating effective outreach events. A similar conclusion reached by VanderBerg (2012, p. 136) states the demand for "digital access to information has reduced user tolerance for the boundaries that have traditionally defined libraries, archives and museums."

15.3 Definitions and Descriptions

This section defines and discusses terms necessary to understand our case studies.

15.3.1 Primary Sources

The definition of what constitutes a *primary* source is specific to individual disciplines. In addition to discipline-specific definitions, the *Oxford English Dictionary* (2022, entry 17) provides a general, interdisciplinary definition: "designating source material contemporary with the period or thing studied; designating an original document, source, or text rather than one of criticism, discussion, or summary." While scientific disciplines derive primary sources from lab work, quantitative research, or qualitative data, social science and humanities disciplines consider of paramount importance for determining what constitutes a primary source the period from which it was created, namely "material that contains first-hand accounts of events and that was created contemporaneous to those events or later recalled by an eyewitness" (Pearce-Moses, 2005, p. 309). According to the definition from the International Council of Archives (2016), *archives*, as one type of primary sources, are the documentary by-product of human activity retained for their long-term value in an archival repository; they are contemporary records created by individuals and organizations as they go about their business and provide a direct window on past events. Regardless of the specific definition, Pearce-Moses (2005, p. 309) emphasizes that "whether something is a primary or secondary source depends on how it is used, not some quality of the document or record itself." Primary sources come in a variety of formats, and they are "often mediated, making it almost impossible for course instructors wishing to use these sources to bypass collection or repository personnel. The partnership between them is therefore vital" (Djenno, 2019, p. 18).

15.3.2 Outreach

In considering the meaning of *outreach* in a library context, the American Library Association (ALA, 2022), in describing the work of outreach librarians, notes that it is "often described as services for those who are infrequent users or nonusers or as services for those who are traditionally underserved." Additionally, the Society of American Archivists (2022, entry 1) describes outreach in their *Dictionary of Archives Terminology* as "the process of identifying and providing services to constituencies with needs relevant to the repository's mission and tailoring services to meet those needs."

15.3.3 North-West Territories

As a historical term, the North-West Territories in Canada comprised the Arctic islands transferred from Great Britain to Canada in 1880 as well as the lands northwest of Central Canada. Prior to 1870, the North-West Territories was a large geographical area encompassing what is now known as Manitoba, Alberta, Saskatchewan, Yukon, Northwest Territories, and Nunavut as well as northern parts of Ontario and Québec (Nuttall, 2005a, p. 1498): "The Territories formerly known as 'Rupert's Land' Territories and the North-West Territory (with the exception of such defined, portion thereof as forms the Province of Manitoba and the District of Keewatin), shall continue to be styled and known as the North-West Territories" (*An Act to Amend and Consolidate the Several Acts Relating to the North-West Territories*, 1875). For this chapter, the term 'North-West' Territories is historically correct and, thus, used when referring to the geographical region; however, 'Northwest' Territories is the modern Canadian spelling used when referring to the region in the modern period. Figure 15.1 shows the vast geographical range of the North-West Territories as they were in 1882; Athabasca was later split into Alberta and the Yukon Territory (Nuttall, 2005a, p. 1498; 2005b, p. 2219).

Research interests for the North-West and Northwest Territories often relate to Inuit peoples, early explorers from Europe and the Franklin Expedition, colonial settlement, the Yukon Gold Rush, politics, sovereignty, climate change, geology, geography, and various industrial activities, such as fur trade, transportation, natural resource exploration, mining, and pipelines. Canadians using the collections described in this chapter likely have some basic understanding of the Canadian North and history of the North-West Territories. Education for young people in social studies units includes learning about the early history of Canada, including Northern and Arctic exploration and historically important explorers. Examples of social studies content delivered provincially may be found in the Alberta Education (2021) draft grade school curriculum and the Ontario Education (2018) curriculum.

Fig. 15.1 *General map of part of the North-West Territories including the province of Manitoba shewing Dominion land surveys to 31 December 1882.* Map created by J. Johnston (1883). (Figure credit: LCR Digital Collections, University of Calgary. https://bit.ly/3PkyPgx)

We leverage familiarity with media coverage of the Arctic region for Canadian audiences when using materials from the AINA and Glenbow collections for curiosity, excitement, questions, and commentary to generate audience interest in research and study with an interdisciplinary perspective.

15.3.4 Arctic Institute of North America (AINA) Collections

To gain a better understanding of collaboration for engagement and outreach activities using the AINA collections, an examination of its materials, including its background, is necessary. The AINA archival and rare book collections are mainly drawn from the North-West Territories, but the circulating materials are circumpolar in scope; this is important to consider because circumpolar historical and political forces have shaped and changed the historical North-West Territories into the contemporary Canadian Arctic. All AINA collections contain many rare and unique materials that are often overlooked and underused due to discoverability issues; there are at least four distinct physical locations and the collections originally used three different cataloguing systems with only a small selection of digitized content available.

15 Part I: Library and Archives Engagement and Outreach Programs Using Sources... 325

The history of the AINA and its collection of materials are recorded by MacDonald (2005) in the *Arctic* journal, tracing AINA's beginnings to Montréal, Québec in 1944. The parliamentary private act, *An Act to Incorporate the Arctic Institute of North America*, was passed to officially recognize the institute as of 18 December 1945. Originally located at McGill University in Montréal, MacDonald notes that part of AINA's stated mission was to collect and preserve records and materials pertinent to the Arctic, and make materials available to other researchers and governmental agencies. From its inception, the AINA was, and is, responsible for publishing reports, maps, charts, and other documentary material related to Arctic regions. An active acquisition program led to a diverse collection, organized and catalogued geographically. Materials in the historical library collection include items printed before 1800, early explorer correspondence (e.g., an 1825 letter written by Sir John Franklin (1786–1847) from Fort Franklin on Great Bear Lake), a small museum of artefacts, a photographic collection established in 1950, an art collection, and many publications from across all international Arctic regions in several languages. MacDonald comments that funding challenges in the 1970s in Montréal and new petroleum discoveries in Alberta contributed to the relocation of the AINA to Calgary in 1976.

Management of the AINA collections, originally called the AINA Library, were assumed by the University of Calgary Library on 1 April 1979, except for AINA's corporate archival records located at the national archives, Library and Archives Canada (https://library-archives.canada.ca/). The AINA collections are considered "one of the best libraries of historical records, research findings and other Arctic information in North America" (Freitag, 1979, p. 1). Beginning in 1980, the University of Calgary library split the AINA collections physically into the rare books and archival collections that moved into the Special Collections unit, maps moved to the Maps and Aerial photos unit, and the circulating library collection moved to the main library. As described by Maes (1980, p. 76),

> the valuable rare books collection of the Arctic Institute which, due to poor storage conditions while in Montreal and its subsequent relocation to the drier climate of Alberta, had suffered greatly, has been located in a separate collection in the Special Collections area of the University Library, where proper environmental conditions and care exist for its preservation.

The circulating library collection of publications became a distinct collection in the university library, was eventually added to the integrated catalogue, and acquisitions continue as part of the 'northern studies' subject area. To determine which items were moved to the non-circulating rare books collection, factors such as publication date, condition, and monetary value were considered.

The AINA Pipeline Collection is part of the circulating library collection. In a report prepared for the National Energy Board (NEB), who provided an initial grant to fund the cataloguing of unique materials for the AINA Pipeline Collection, the extent of the AINA's circulating library collection was described as

> one of the world's major collections of northern and other cold-temperature materials. The primary focus is the Canadian Arctic, but the collection holds extensive materials on other regions of the circumpolar Arctic as well as the Antarctic. Unique to the Arctic Institute

Collection is its large collection of documents dealing with northern Canadian oil and gas exploration, development, and transportation. (University of Calgary Library, 1997, p. 2)

Moreover, "this unique collection is a joint initiative between the library, Department of Geosciences, and AINA, including donated internal documents, government publications, and project reports since 1977 by more than 14 organizations" (Hinks, 2007, p. 9). These materials relate to northern pipelines running across Alaska, the Yukon Territory, Alberta, and the Northwest Territories. Among many others, the projects documented in the AINA Pipeline Collection include the Mackenzie Valley Pipeline Project, hearings under the NEB and Royal Commission chaired by Thomas Berger (1977), Alaska Highway Gas Pipeline Project, Interprovincial Pipe Line Norman Wells Project, Canadian Arctic Gas Pipeline, and Polar Gas Project. These materials are invaluable resources for researchers and scholars, and make the University of Calgary's collection the second-most complete, following the Canadian Energy Regulator's own library.[1]

The circulating library collection was physically integrated as part of the Gallagher Library in 2007 (Arctic Institute of North America, 2007; AINA News, 2007) and titles published prior to 2000 (i.e., about 75% of the AINA circulating library collection) were transferred to an offsite library storage centre in 2014 "to maintain the integrity of this important collection and to preserve this valuable research resource" (Cloutier, 2013, p. 14). The Gallagher Library, originally established for the geosciences collection, was chosen as the location for the AINA circulating library collection due to the AINA collection's interdisciplinary science focus. The circulating AINA collection is available for students, faculty, and researchers to borrow and most items are available to other libraries through regular interlibrary loan processes. How to make AINA's circulating library collection better known and used in student research has been grappled with for decades, but we are optimistic that this collection will be more frequently used following the final item from the cataloguing backlog added to the integrated library catalogue in 2020. Now that all items are discoverable, access to the entirety of this unique library collection is possible.

15.3.5   Glenbow Collection

A rich source of primary and secondary sources, the Glenbow collection is invaluable to researchers and scholars. This section focuses on describing the nature of the collection related to materials found in the AINA collections because both are often examined in conjunction with each other. The Glenbow collection focuses on the settlement and development of Western Canada from the 1800s through the late 1900s: "The most prized rare books are those in the field of exploration and

---

[1] The NEB is the predecessor to the Canadian Energy Regulator established by the Canadian Energy Regulator Act (2019).

discovery" with popular early explorers including Samuel Hearne (1745–1792), Sir Alexander Mackenzie (1764–1820), Captain George Vancouver (1757–1798), and Captain James Cooke (1728–1779) (Glenbow-Alberta Institute, n.d., p. 14). This collection moved from the Glenbow Museum in downtown Calgary to the University of Calgary's ASC over a two-year period from November 2018 to December 2020 (University Relations Staff, 2018). The Glenbow Foundation, the name of the museum, library, and archives at its inception in 1966, identified the institution's focus as "a major research centre for Western Canadian History" (Jameson, 1978, p. 72) to "document all aspects of life in a particular region—the Prairie West" (Rees, 1993, p. 175). Since the collection's move, the Glenbow collection continues to specialize in Western Canada, concentrating on Calgary and Southern Alberta.

While the collection has a strong focus on Western Canada, a region historically part of the North-West Territories, it also includes a wide array of Arctic and Northern primary and secondary sources, including corporate records and other materials of particular interest to the University of Calgary's Department of History: "In reaching out to faculty, it is useful to stress the complementarity of archival and online sources. Archival sources offer a physical connection with the past whereas online sources offer tremendous breadth and accessibility" (Malkmus, 2010, p. 429). Following Malkmus, we leveraged the unique aspects of the Glenbow collection to tie into the work of building connections and nurturing relationships within several departments to initiate successful outreach and engagement events based on the relationship marketing strategy described by Broady-Preston (2013).

The Glenbow collection doubled the holdings of the ASC from five linear shelf kilometres of archival holdings to approximately ten and added 125,000 published titles. Relocating the collection to the University of Calgary improves ease of accessibility for users who wish to consult both the Glenbow and AINA holdings simultaneously. Examples of the popularity of the relocation of the Glenbow collections include one history faculty member immediately recognizing the potential for graduate student recruitment, an emeritus faculty member historian promptly contacting us and others in LCR to determine when the new collection would be accessible before it even began to arrive, and several graduate students and faculty members expressing excitement in being able to use the collections on campus.

15.4 Events and Programs

We conducted a variety of events and programs where items from across the AINA and Glenbow collections were used. Three specific events and programs included: (1) *Nickle at Noon*, (2) *A Taste of the Archives and Special Collections,* and (3) *Glenbow Sneak Peek*, along with continued and new digital and physical curation activities. For these programs and events, we drew upon current trends in marketing for application in the library setting to achieve success in engagement and outreach. According to Dubicki (2007), understanding library user needs and interests can lead to successful outreach initiatives when these events are tailored to different categories of users by using the market segmentation strategy. Dubicki explains that "target marketing allows you to focus efforts on a group that is likely to be receptive to your message—similar to one-on-one marketing" (p. 10). In the engagement and outreach events and programs described in this section, the ASC staff participants provided positive feedback about their experience, audience engagement, promotion opportunities, and expressed a desire to participate in future programs. Additionally, these events increase staff familiarity with material housed in the collections.

15.4.1 Nickle at Noon

The *Nickle at Noon* community discussion series is hosted by the University of Calgary's Nickle Galleries as an ongoing program of talks, tours, workshops, performances, and more, designed to enhance understanding, appreciation, and enjoyment of current exhibitions and collections, as well as provide a forum for the discussion of broader issues in culture, heritage, and the arts. Previously featured speakers related to Arctic and Northern studies included George Colpitts, Canadian and Arctic historian at the University of Calgary, in 2022; Leslie Reid, Canadian artist, printmaker, and educator who described the *Mapping a Cold War* exhibition from a Northwest Passage expedition at the Founders' Gallery in 2016; and Alberta Rose Williams who spoke about an *Inuit Futures* residency installation in 2021.

When curators invite the ASC to lead presentations, discussions with one of this chapter's authors (McKillop) include topics or themes of interest to the audience with a wide range of ages and backgrounds. McKillop chooses a selection of primary and secondary materials from the collections that the ASC staff feel are interesting, unique, rare, or would pique audience curiosity, sometimes around a particular theme. Presentations include brief talks by ASC staff members about individual items, followed by question-and-answer segments. At the end of the hour, audiences are invited to view and examine materials more closely and ask questions. This part of the event tends to be popular as many members of the audience line up to get closer looks at the materials.

Prior to the COVID-19 pandemic, *Nickle at Noon* was held weekly in-person at the Taylor Family Digital Library (TFDL). Since before 2018, the ASC was regularly invited to deliver presentations and this successful partnership continued when the series moved online via Zoom in 2020 due to the pandemic. The new online format was well received by audiences and many email enquiries were received from audience members keen to view the recorded session, an unexpected positive outcome. With the audiovisual recordings available online, it is easy for ASC staff to track number of views, but the analytics are limited and do not have the capability to provide other data such as classification of viewer (e.g., student, faculty member, staff, or community user) or geographic location. In the community engagement pillar "Integrate the University with the Community" of the University of Calgary's strategic plan, programs such as *Nickle at Noon* help LCR demonstrate its value to the university and community as the ASC staff showcase unique and interesting primary and secondary materials from the AINA archival and rare books and Glenbow collections. The ASC presentations consistently have high attendance numbers as showcasing materials from the AINA archival and rare book collections in their original format proves popular with audiences. Audience feedback received is positive with many attendees expressing their appreciation for the depth and breadth of the primary and secondary source materials and high level of staff knowledge and passion for the collections. ASC staff presenters report a positive experience and desire to participate in future programs.

15.4.2 A Taste of the Archives and Special Collections

A Taste of the Archives and Special Collections is an engagement and outreach event used by McKillop to increase staff familiarity across LCR for special collections and archival material, reconnect the ASC with other units, and raise funds for a university-wide charity drive. Perkins Smith and McGillan (2019, p. 178) comment on a similar, successful approach "to reconnect Special Collections with other departments in the library and establish and strengthen relationships with library colleagues." In addition, when engagement and outreach events are hosted by special collections staff for faculty, it raises awareness about those collections by showcasing select materials. The event was launched by McKillop to introduce unknown materials from the vaults to LCR staff outside of the ASC unit and as a fundraising activity. This one-hour session included staff from ASC who selected materials and provided a brief talk followed by an opportunity to ask questions and closely examine materials. While this audience has a high level of library and university familiarity, attendees are not necessarily knowledgeable about specific collections of the ASC. AINA materials contribute to positive audience comments and reactions as those similarly described by Perkins Smith and McGillan.

Engagement and outreach programs are created with the principles of selecting materials from the ASC that are unique, disciplinary, relevant to departmental course offerings and faculty research interests, or of historical significance. According to Perkins Smith and McGillan's (2019, p. 178) study, success is based upon careful selection: "Materials were selected for inclusion in the workshop based on a combination of factors, including relevance to the discipline(s)." We find this strategy works well, contributes to building relationships with faculty members, and creates a firm foundation for engagement and outreach events. This strategy has been successful at LCR to build interest and pique curiosity for generating interest from the targeted audience. The thrill of discovery is also evident among engagement and outreach program audiences when materials are exhibited and discussed. As reported in the Malkmus (2010, p. 417) study, students experience this thrill when working with tangible, authentic primary sources. The event is a favourite for staff presenters and attendees as evidenced by the number of regular enquiries received regarding the specific date and content when offered. As we witness in our own work, the power of including primary sources from the AINA and Glenbow collections contributes to this positive reaction from users whether they are students, faculty, researchers, or members of the public community.

15.4.3 Glenbow Sneak Peek

The *Glenbow Sneak Peek* outreach program was an effective vehicle to launch the Glenbow collections and the newly opened Glenbow Western Research Centre (GWRC) reading room to the university community. Curated themed exhibits promoted the Glenbow collections to select departments and faculties via collaboration with key subject librarians. By understanding library users, librarians, archivists, and the ASC, staff are in a unique position to use marketing segmentation strategy. Dubicki (2007, p. 10) comments: "All library patrons do not have identical needs. Market segmentation is a process to divide the overall market into smaller, homogeneous groups within similar characteristics and needs." The success of this initiative hinged on working with specific subject librarians to identify potential faculties and departments interested in the collections. The subject librarians took the lead with departmental communication while working closely with McKillop and ASC staff to select and display materials for the event in the GWRC reading room. Departments originally identified included history, architecture, and English.

The GWRC opened in the TFDL, the main library at the centre of the University of Calgary's main campus, on 15 October 2019 (Sowa, 2019). The reading room occupies a prominent space on the second floor, featuring three sides of floor-to-ceiling glass. The selection of the GWRC as the location of the *Glenbow Sneak Peek* program strategically promoted the recently opened reading room while ensuring archival and special collections materials were safely and securely examined by the target audience of faculty, students, and researchers already familiar with proper handling of such materials. As Dubicki (2007, p. 10) notes, "in an academic library, one type of segmentation might be by academic major, another could be undergraduate, graduate, and doctoral students, and faculty and research groups." This marketing method was a useful strategy employed by McKillop and Hoffman who organized this event for the Department of History. The concept of a 'sneak peek' or special viewing of materials was scheduled outside of regular GWRC hours with subject-focused and themed displays curated with attendees in mind. This event was envisioned as a three-part pilot program, but due to scheduling conflicts and COVID-19 closures, only two parts occurred. Logistically, librarians and archival staff worked closely on many aspects of the event to draft and send targeted promotional emails to engage key faculty members and graduate students as well as ensure pertinent materials were selected. Glenbow collection materials intersecting with topics appropriate to the North-West Territories provided an opportunity to also promote the AINA archival and rare book collections.

Although the actual number of attendees to the *Glenbow Sneak Peek* program was small, there was a good range of enthusiastic faculty members, graduate students, and postdoctoral scholars. Feedback received from attendees indicate they learned about both the Glenbow collections, the AINA archival and rare books collections, and other relevant ASC materials pertinent to their discipline, especially for history related to the North-West Territories. Conversations about future course collaboration between librarians and archivists with faculty began at this event and continued during COVID-19 pandemic closures.

15.4.4 Digital and Physical Curation

As early as the mid-1990s, academic libraries realized the potential benefits of digitization as travel budgets for scholars were dwindling and collections were ageing (Pannekoek, 1998). Various digitization collection projects launched in October 2002 under the Canadian Initiative on Digital Libraries, a partnership of 20 libraries with initial funding from the Canadian Heritage Content Online Program over five years, and hosted by the Information Resources faculty at the University of Calgary and Laval University Library (Hinks, 2007; Westell, 2009). The first projects were *Our Roots* and *Our Future, Our Past: Alberta Heritage Digitization Project* and included the following: Alberta Law Collection, comprising primary legal materials for Alberta and the North-West Territories to 1992; Early Alberta Newspapers collection; Local Histories collection; Art collection from the Nickle Arts Museum; Medical History collection; and various oral histories, maps, and photographs. As of 2022, all digital collections except the institutional repository merged into the Cortex digital asset management system and individual collections were renamed. The move of the Glenbow collections included previously digitized photographs and secondary sources which also migrated as part of this process into the Glenbow Library and Archives Digital Collection (https://digitalcollections. ucalgary.ca/asset-management/2R340826N9XM).

A second digital initiative by the LCR created the PRISM institutional repository; it provides free digital access to open access publications, theses, preprints, conference presentations, and many other unpublished versions of research by those affiliated with the University of Calgary. Like Cortex, PRISM also provides added value in terms of metadata description, security features for embargoed titles due to copyright or graduation dates, analytical usage statistics for each item in the repository, and a permanent URL to reference.

Consequently, LCR and the AINA collaborated to digitize AINA's photographic archives, then consisting of over 4000 photographs dating from the late 1800s through the 1900s. Comprised of mostly black and white prints with some negatives and slides, the bulk of the collection dates to the first half of the twentieth century. The photos were taken on a variety of expeditions and patrols by scientists, mountaineers, police and military, and other Arctic explorers (MacDonald, 2005). As of 2022, the Arctic Institute of North America Photographic Archives Collection (https://digitalcollections.ucalgary.ca/Browse/Collections/Arctic-and-Northern-Studies/Arctic-Institute-of-North-America-Photographic-Archives) is maintained in Cortex.

Discovery of the HMS *Erebus* and HMS *Terror*, the two ships from Franklin's disastrous expedition of 1848, along Canada's Northern Arctic waters created renewed excitement about Franklin and Arctic history (CBC News, 2014; Davison, 2020; Hinchey, 2016). In the Canadian heritage community, these discoveries presented new opportunities to showcase collections relating to the Franklin Expedition and Arctic research. LCR created awareness about its own collections by launching the Arctic and Northern Studies Digital Collection (https://digitalcollections.ucalgary.ca/Browse/Collections/Arctic-and-Northern-Studies) using AINA archival and rare books collections. The University of Calgary media emphasized the significance of the AINA and LCR partnership in 2017 (Alexander, 2017) and this relationship was revived to resolve rights management issues and coordinate sharing with AINA's abstract and indexing database, ADA: Arctic Discovery & Access (https://ada.ucalgary.ca/) that began as an online service named ASTIS: Arctic Science and Technology Information System in 1981.

As a post-doctoral scholar and the AINA library manager re-familiarized themselves with the archival and rare book materials transferred from the AINA to LCR in 1979, discussions ensued to inventory AINA's research collections for future transfers to LCR. Moreover, the collaborative research between an AINA post-doctoral scholar and Landwehr regarding custody and ownership of the AINA archival and rare book collections uncovered early scholarly articles from AINA researchers that were published in the *Arctic* journal, resulting in the inclusion of selected Franklin correspondence transcriptions in the Arctic and Northern Studies digital collection. Landwehr collaborated with digitization specialists to determine which materials should appear in the Arctic and Northern Studies digital collection. Selection criteria included preservation concerns necessitating an alternative approach to physical handling, suitability for online research and teaching, genre of documents, legibility of texts, chronological scope for the history of Arctic discovery and exploration and the range of individuals involved. Virtual representations in the database strove to mitigate the perceived and real loss of connection when handling physical collections while using specialized tools for maximum resolution and enabling optical character recognition for full text searching of print text. Carefully prepared descriptive metadata further allows for rich and meaningful interactions with digitized materials, setting the stage for future expansion to include materials not yet digitized from the same collection. Metadata schema typical in libraries for published objects were reconciled with elements from archival description practice that aim to show the documents within their multi-level hierarchy of the collection of origin (VanderBerg, 2012).

Materials in this digitization initiative included correspondence between Sir John Franklin and officers of the Royal British Navy (Fig. 15.2), along with transcriptions; photographs of an expedition to Hudson Bay and Cumberland Gulf in the steamship *Diana* under the command of William Wakeham (1844–1915) in 1897 (Fig. 15.3); travel drawings and sketches in pencil and watercolour from Frederick William Beechey (1796–1856), rear-admiral of the British Navy from the early to mid-1800s who pioneered the field of scientific observations of the northern coast of America and the Arctic (Bershad, 1980) (Fig. 15.4); and early depictions of

15 Part I: Library and Archives Engagement and Outreach Programs Using Sources… 333

Fig. 15.2 Handwritten letter with red seal from Sir John Franklin to William Pryce Cumby dated 1 August 1832. (Figure credit: LCR Digital Collections, University of Calgary. https://bit.ly/3uB3le8)

the North Pole and the Canadian Arctic, including a 1595 reprint of *Septentrionalium Terrarum descriptio*, the first known map of the North Pole (Fig. 15.5). As of July 2022, the Arctic and Northern Studies digital collection comprise almost 600 rare published cartographic or unpublished archival documents and artworks dating from the 1600s to the 1900s.

The intentional inclusion also of students in digitization preparation work can aid future digitization projects and spark or enhance future student research projects. For example, a graduate history student was hired to assist in research and preparation of the physical exhibit to coincide with the official launch. Engagement with the wide-ranging materials led the student to discover records in the AINA collections of Harry Stallworthy (1895–1976), a member of the Royal Canadian Mounted Police and participant in the 1934–1935 Oxford University Ellesmere Land Expedition under Edward Shackleton (1911–1994). The student subsequently used this material in their master's thesis and the material was flagged for future digitization in the Arctic and Northern Studies digital collection.

Fig. 15.3 Four men on the expedition to Hudson Bay and Cumberland Gulf in the Steamship *Diana* in 1897 under the command of William Wakeham (shown here as the second person from the right). Photographer unknown. (Figure credit: LCR Digital Collections, University of Calgary. Arctic Institute of North America Collection. http://bit.ly/3ODBm6j)

Fig. 15.4 *H.M.S. Hecla in Winter Harbour*. Pencil and crayon drawing by Rear-Admiral Frederick William Beechey from the 1819–1820 Parry Expedition. (Figure credit: LCR Digital Collections, University of Calgary. https://bit.ly/3Rrb9sO)

15 Part I: Library and Archives Engagement and Outreach Programs Using Sources…

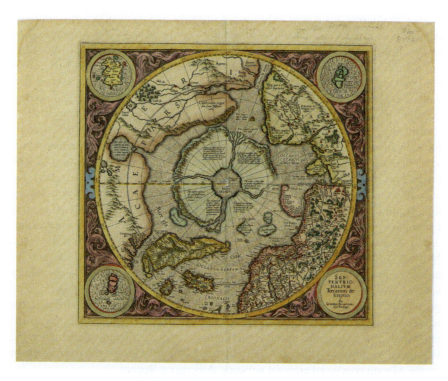

Fig. 15.5 *Septentrionalium Terrarum descriptio*, the first known map of the North Pole by cartographer Gerardus Mercator. This version is a hand-coloured eighteenth-century reprint of the original 1595 map. (Figure credit: LCR Digital Collections, University of Calgary. https://bit.ly/3yRpxmO)

The 2016 launch of the digital collection was accompanied by a physical exhibit in the TFDL foyer to bridge gaps between materiality and virtual representation (MacNeil & Mak, 2007). The physical exhibit also alerted users to more materials in the AINA archival and rare book collections by showing materials not yet included in the Arctic and Northern Studies digital collection. The launch of the digital collection and physical exhibit increased researcher requests to physically consult materials from the AINA collections. In addition, the work on the exhibit provided an educational opportunity to demonstrate current understandings and principles of curatorial ethics. Content was shown in one display case with additional label information to clarify historical context. One example where this was deemed appropriate was for a typed speech delivered by Harry Stallworthy (n.d.) in the 1930s to the Imperial Order Daughters of the Empire (n.d., para. 2), a Canadian organization founded in 1900 "to promote patriotism, loyalty, and service" regarding the Inuit peoples encountered during the 1934–1935 Oxford University Ellesmere Land Expedition.

Outdated terms and names in historic documents and publications are common. Audience sensitivity toward outdated terminology introduced and perpetuated by settlers is increasingly being addressed for primary source materials while recognizing that original sources themselves cannot be changed. Since the 2015 release of the Truth and Reconciliation Commission of Canada's *Calls to Action*, the Canadian galleries, libraries, archives, and museums (GLAM) sector recognizes the need to decolonize Canadian metadata as part of national solutions toward reconciliation, specifically harmful and inappropriate subject headings and resource descriptions for Indigenous peoples and communities who have been marginalized or missrepresented throughout Canada's history. Addressing colonial terminology across GLAM institutions in Canada through appropriate advisories prepares researchers for encountering inappropriate terminology in material descriptions, such as in legacy finding aids for archival materials or titles within digitized content (Canadian Federation of Library Associations, 2017; Truth and Reconciliation Commission, 2015). A notable announcement was made by the Canadian Research Knowledge Network (https://www.crkn-rcdr.ca/) in January 2022 to decolonize the subject headings in the Canadiana database of digitized historical Canadian primary sources. Much existing research examines subject headings related to Indigenous peoples in Canada (e.g., Hoffman (2021) concentrated on historical legal terms related to Inuit peoples in Canada). Many library and archival groups are now working to address Indigenous-specific terminology and classification, including the Provincial Archives of Alberta's (2020) updated subject headings and their adoption by the Alberta provincial archival network, Alberta on Record.

Further work includes the following: The National Indigenous Knowledge and Language Alliance (n.d., para. 1) began the *Respectful Terminology* project to "replace outdated and inappropriate terminologies" when classifying Indigenous materials; the Council of Prairie and Pacific University Libraries' (2022) Indigenous Knowledge Standing Committee have arranged decolonizing symposiums since 2017, with the 2022 Spring meeting including a panel with nine organizations discussing institutional initiatives; and both the Manitoba Archival Information Network's (n.d.) Subject Headings Working Group and the University of the Arctic's (https://www.uarctic.org/) thematic network on Decolonization of Arctic Library and Archives Metadata (2022, para. 1) were created to decolonize "metadata, descriptive cataloguing, archival description, classification systems, subject headings, and other terminology that is used by libraries and archives." Following these initiatives, LCR units at the University of Calgary are now collaborating on initiatives to decolonize all collections where possible, particularly across the Glenbow collections. According to the American Library Association's (ALA) Cataloging and Metadata Management Section's (CaMMS) Subject Analysis Committee (2022), the Library of Congress has created a plan to change its subject headings relating to Indigenous peoples, a welcome development to help address decolonization issues in North America.

15.5 COVID-19 and the Move Online

The global COVID-19 pandemic declared in 2020 by the World Health Organization caused profound changes around the world, including within the academy. As higher education institutions grappled with moving classes online, so too did university libraries and archives wrestle with how to best deliver services. At the University of Calgary, information and archival literacy instruction moved online like in most universities across Canada. LCR focused on digital services, finding new ways to support users remotely (Murphy et al., 2022, p. 83). While researchers experienced restrictions due to the pandemic, necessitating virtual consultations of primary source materials to conduct their research, usage of the Arctic and Northern Studies digital collection was high: annual data from September 2019 to September 2020 indicate that, while it was of comparatively small size, it was the highest accessed database of the 48 digital collections available from LCR.

While in-person access to collections was suspended, onsite LCR staff provided digital images of materials to fill patron requests related to the Glenbow collections. Although image requests were intended as one-time services, these images, once digitized, were treated with potential for repeat access. The increase in scanning materials contributed to the overall growth of available digital objects in Cortex, making material more accessible and readily used in online presentations, exhibits, instruction, and reference interactions.

LCR's forward-thinking digital initiatives provided the mechanism for staff to pivot faster during pandemic closures and provide services to faculty, students, and researchers. The pandemic accelerated the pace and timetable for content to move online in higher education, including the AINA and Glenbow collections: "Now, more than ever, the importance of adding content to the digital collections has taken on a new priority" (Murphy et al., 2021, p. 95). Furthermore, increased collaborations between the library and ASC units through Springshare's robust product suite, including creating LibGuides, enabling frequently asked questions, and deploying the LibAnswers online chat and ticketing system, allowed users to discover materials and get assistance more easily from across all LCR collections.

15.6 Conclusion and Future Considerations

Collaboration creates environments that can successfully incorporate library and archives collections into outreach partnerships and events. When collections are strategically marketed, incorporating primary and secondary sources can spark new learning opportunities and research directions. When pursuing the strategy of collaboration, we experienced first-hand Horowitz's claim described earlier by working together on several outreach and engagement projects, and partnering for class instruction, by successfully leveraging teaching and instruction contacts to build interest for outreach events and programs such as *Glenbow Sneak Peek*, *Nickle at Noon*, and *A Taste of the Archives and Special Collections*.

Probing successful collaborations relating to student learning and experience in higher education is another avenue for further exploration. Additionally, Horowitz (2016, p. 10), when reviewing librarian partnerships, asks: "What evidence do we have of the benefits students derive from these collaborations?" We have seen that master's theses can be enriched by the discovery of additional materials during digitization work. Considering how and what to assess in terms of outcomes will be important to determine strategies, programs, and events to pursue for future success.

In our own work, outreach opportunities can be expanded to include more Arctic- and Northern-specific examples in future outreach programs, in-person events, exhibits, and displays. Increasing digitized content enhances already robust holdings, adds records to LCR's discovery system, and can also be used for themed exhibits, social media, web promotion, and other special events to allow for collaboration across all LCR units: "Adding to the digital collection is a priority task, as it will provide enhanced online access to unique and rare items" (Murphy et al., 2022, p. 97). Drawing upon our combined expertise, shared interest, and enthusiasm, we welcome new venues for engagement and outreach activities such as the *Glenbow Sneak Peek* program as we consider these favourable opportunities to showcase rich collections and feature materials that are rare and unique such as those from the AINA and Glenbow collections. We anticipate further collaborations and programs in a post-pandemic world.

A solid foundation of collaborations contributed to successful engagement and outreach programs at the University of Calgary. By employing targeted marketing and finding colleagues with common visions and shared pedagogical frameworks, librarians, archivists, curators, and staff worked together to create engaging learning opportunities. ASC staff who participate in programs and events frequently report positive experiences and indicate a strong interest in playing an active role in future opportunities. By understanding faculty, students, and researchers conducting research on and off campus, the strategy of collaborative partnerships can be effectively applied. The outcome of strong collegial relationships can have many successes. When primary and secondary source materials such as those drawn from across the Glenbow and AINA collections are utilized in collaborative engagement and outreach activities, curiosity and new perspectives to investigate may result. We explore how utilizing Arctic and Northern materials for instruction can raise awareness about the Canadian North in the next chapter in this book, "Part II: Using Arctic and Northern Sources for Information and Archival Literacy and Research."

References

AINA News. (2007). *Arctic: Journal of the Arctic Institute of North America, 60*(4), 456–457. https://doi.org/h4k4

Alberta Education. (2021). *Draft social studies design blueprint.* https://bit.ly/3Rk7PPX. Accessed 11 Dec 2023.

Alexander, R. (2017, January 4). *History brought to life through a new digital collection.* http://bit.ly/3VrGqNj. Accessed 11 Dec 2023.

American Library Association (ALA). (2022). *Outreach librarian*. https://bit.ly/3uxqvll. Accessed 11 Dec 2023.

An Act to amend and consolidate the several Acts relating to the North-West Territories, 38 Vict, c 49, s 1. (1875). pp. 261–287.

An Act to incorporate the Arctic Institute of North America, SC 1945, c 45. (1945). pp. 35–37. http://bit.ly/3gBEDXg. Accessed 11 Dec 2023.

Arctic Institute of North America. (2007). *Community: Support, engage, build: Annual report 2007*. http://bit.ly/3gzmhGa. Accessed 11 Dec 2023.

Beauline-Stuebing, L. (2020, 26 October). U of Calgary offers a new state-of-the-art home for a massive collection of Western Canadian history. *University Affairs/Affaires universitaires*. https://bit.ly/3bQJile. Accessed 11 Dec 2023.

Berger, T. R. (1977). *Northern frontier, northern homeland: The report of the Mackenzie Valley pipeline inquiry* (Vol. 1). Minister of supply and services Canada / Ministre des Approvisionnements et services Canada. https://bit.ly/482Kaer. Accessed 11 Dec 2023.

Bershad, S. S. (1980). The drawings and watercolours by rear-admiral Frederick William Beechey, F.R.S., P.R.G.S. (1796–1856). *Arctic, 33*(1), 117–167. https://doi.org/h4k6

Broady-Preston, J. (2013). Changing marketing concepts: Contemporary theories and paradigms in services marketing. In D. K. Gupta, C. Koontz, & A. Massisimo (Eds.), *Marketing library and information services II: A global outlook* (pp. 23–42). de Gruyter. https://doi.org/h4k7

Canadian Energy Regulator Act, SC 2019, c 28, s 10. (2019). https://bit.ly/3PeA0hh. Accessed 11 Dec 2023.

Canadian Federation of Library Associations (CFLA)/Fédération canadienne des associations de bibliothèques (FCAB). (2017). *Truth and reconciliation report and recommendations*. https://bit.ly/3ysuJw2. Accessed 11 Dec 2023.

Canadian Research Knowledge Network (CRKN)/Réseau canadien de documentation pour la recherche (RCDR). (2022, January 25). *Decolonizing Canadiana metadata: An overdue step in removing harmful subject headings*. https://bit.ly/3PeACDB. Accessed 11 Dec 2023.

Cataloging and Metadata Management Section (CaMMS), Subject Analysis Committee. (2022, June 3). *SAC 2022 annual meeting LC_PTCP report*. http://bit.ly/3V5Vdh1. Accessed 11 Dec 2023.

CBC News. (2014, 1 October). *Franklin expedition ship found in Arctic ID'd as HMS Erebus*. https://bit.ly/3uBxNES. Accessed 11 Dec 2023.

Cloutier, C. (2013). AINA library. In *Arctic Institute of North America annual report 2013* (p. 14). https://bit.ly/3yodonQ. Accessed 11 Dec 2023.

Council of Prairie and Pacific University Libraries (COPPUL). (2022). *Decolonizing description*. https://bit.ly/3nQDF9r. Accessed 11 Dec 2023.

Davison, J. (2020, February 20). Artifacts recovered from HMS *Erebus* offer tantalizing links to sailors on doomed Franklin expedition. *CBC News*. https://bit.ly/3uwPoxN. Accessed 11 Dec 2023.

Decolonization of Arctic Library and Archives Metadata (DALAM). (2022). *Thematic network on decolonization of Arctic library and archives metadata*. University of the Arctic. https://bit.ly/3FZDKBw. Accessed 11 Dec 2023.

Djenno, M. (2019). Scaffolding the collection manager-instructor relationship: Partnerships for primary source instruction. *College and Research Library News, 80*(1), 18–21. https://doi.org/gfsv2f

Dubicki, E. (2007). Basic marketing and promotion concepts. *Serials Librarian, 53*(3), 5–15. https://doi.org/d53kt3

Freitag, M. (1979, February 2). Arctic institute may become U of C's baby. *The Gauntlet, 19*(29), 1. Accession 60.001, Archives and Special Collections, University of Calgary.

Glenbow-Alberta Institute. (n.d.). *Glenbow* [brochure].

Hinchey, G. (2016, September 12). Sir John Franklin's long-lost HMS *Terror* believed found. *CBC News*. https://bit.ly/3uCNsDM. Accessed 11 Dec 2023.

Hinks, Y. (2007). *A timeline of the history of the University of Calgary Libraries and Information Resources 1906–2007*. University of Calgary. https://bit.ly/3bQC4O6. Accessed 11 Dec 2023.

Hoffman, N. (2021). Controlled vocabulary and Indigenous terminology in Canadian Arctic legal research. In S. Acadia & M. T. Fjellestad (Eds.), *Library and information studies for Arctic social sciences and humanities* (pp. 110–132). Routledge.

Horowitz, S. M. (2016). Special collections and liaison librarian partnerships: A review of the literature. In K. Totleben & L. Birrell (Eds.), *Collaborating for impact: Special collections and liaison librarian partnerships* (pp. 2–16). Association of College and Research Libraries.

Imperial Order Daughters of the Empire (IODE) Canada. (n.d.). *Our history.* https://bit.ly/3auAwcn. Accessed 11 Dec 2023.

International Council of Archives (ICA). (2016). *What are archives?* https://bit.ly/3RmyOKM. Accessed 11 Dec 2023.

Jameson, S. S. (1978). The archives of the Glenbow-Alberta institute (Calgary). *Urban History Review, 6*(3/77), 69–79. https://doi.org/h4k8

Libraries and Cultural Resources (LCR) fonds. *Library council minutes*, UARC 2016.102, Box 5. Meeting #193 (8 October 1998), #204 (29 October 1999), and #210 (5 May 2000). *Archives and Special Collections*, University of Calgary.

Libraries and Cultural Resources (LCR). (2022). *Community report: 2019/2020/2021.* University of Calgary.

MacDonald, R. (2005). Challenges and accomplishments: A celebration of the Arctic Institute of North America. *Arctic, 58*(4), 440–451. https://doi.org/h4k9

MacNeil, H. M., & Mak, B. (2007). Constructions of authenticity. *Library Trends, 56*(1), 26–52. https://doi.org/h4mb

Maes, W. R. (1980, June 1–6). The library collection of the Arctic Institute of North America. In G. A. Cooke & G. Graham (Eds.), *Proceedings of the 8th Northern Libraries Colloquy* (pp. 75–80). Boreal Institute for Northern Studies.

Malkmus, D. (2010). "Old stuff" for new teaching methods: Outreach to history faculty teaching with primary sources. *Portal: Libraries and the Academy, 10*(4), 413–435. https://doi.org/fk7wz6

Manitoba Archival Information Network (MAIN). (n.d.). *Indigenous subject headings in MAIN.* https://bit.ly/3PhnGNy. Accessed 11 Dec 2023.

Murphy, J. E., Lewis, C. J., McKillop, C. A., & Stoeckle, M. (2022). Expanding digital academic library and archive services at the University of Calgary in response to the COVID-19 pandemic. *IFLA Journal, 48*(1), 83–98. https://doi.org/gmkc6q

National Indigenous Knowledge and Language Alliance (NIKLA)/Alliance nationale des connaissances et des langues autochtones (ANCLA). (n.d.). *Respectful terminology.* https://bit.ly/46SonoL. Accessed 11 Dec 2023.

Nuttall, M. (2005a). Northwest Territories. In *Encyclopedia of the Arctic* (p. 1498). Routledge.

Nuttall, M. (2005b). Yukon Territory. In *Encyclopedia of the Arctic* (p. 2219). Routledge.

Ontario Education. (2018). *The Ontario curriculum revised: Social studies grades 1–6, history and geography grades 7–8.* https://bit.ly/3OY0Zhr. Accessed 11 Dec 2023.

Oxford English Dictionary (OED) Online. (2022). *Primary, adj. and n.* Oxford University Press.

Pannekoek, F. (1998). *Canadian memory institutions and the digital revolution: The last five years.* https://bit.ly/3RCbZVr. Accessed 11 Dec 2023.

Pearce-Moses, R. (2005). A glossary of archival and records terminology. *Society of American Archivists.* https://bit.ly/3OUw8m7. Accessed 11 Dec 2023.

Perkins Smith, J., & McGillan, J. (2019). Towards a more collaborative experience: Connecting library and departmental faculty to improve and expand archival instruction. *Journal of Map and Geography Libraries, 15*(2/3), 173–186. https://doi.org/gpcc8g

Pham, H. T., & Tanner, K. (2014). Collaboration between academics and librarians: A literature review and framework for analysis. *Library Review, 63*(1/2), 15–45. https://doi.org/gqbmmc

Provincial Archives of Alberta. (2020). *Provincial Archives of Alberta Subject Headings* (PAASH). http://bit.ly/3u0akMR. Accessed 11 Dec 2023.

Rees, A. L. (1993). The Glenbow archives, 1966–2016: A history of design and circumstance. *Archivaria, 35* (Spring), 175–189. https://bit.ly/3uANwEj. Accessed 11 Dec 2023.

Society of American Archivists (SAA). (2022). Outreach. In *Dictionary of archives terminology*. https://bit.ly/3AUbgr1. Accessed 11 Dec 2023.

Sowa, J. (2019, October 15). Glenbow Western research Centre opens in Taylor family digital library. *UCalgary News*. https://bit.ly/3uAVvkD. Accessed 11 Dec 2023.

Stallworthy, H. (n.d.). *Speech to the Imperial order daughters of the empire*. Harry Stallworthy fonds, Acc 801/05.22, box 3.14, Archives and Special Collections, University of Calgary.

Timms, K. (2009). New partnerships for old sibling rivals: The development of integrated access systems for the holdings of archives, libraries, and museums. *Archiv, 68*(Fall), 69–95. https://bit.ly/3yRCsVE. Accessed 11 Dec 2023.

Truth and Reconciliation Commission of Canada/Commission de vérité et réconciliation du Canada. (2015). *Truth and Reconciliation Commission of Canada: Calls to action*. https://bit.ly/3nOLc8D. Accessed 11 Dec 2023.

University of Calgary. (2017). *Eyes high strategy 2017–22*. https://bit.ly/3aoXt0L. Accessed 11 Dec 2023.

University of Calgary Library. (1997, February 26). *Final report: Cataloguing of northern oil and gas industry reports into the Arctic Institute Collection of the University of Calgary Library*.

University Relations Staff. (2018, November 15). University of Calgary and Glenbow announce historic initiative. *UCalgary News*. https://bit.ly/3yvh5bf. Accessed 11 Dec 2023.

VanderBerg, R. (2012). Converging libraries, archives, and museums: Overcoming distinctions, but for what gain? *Archives and Manuscripts, 40*(3), 136–146. https://doi.org/h4mc

Westell, M. E. (2009, May 31). Bringing local history to life on the web*: Digital collections* [Conference presentation]. Alberta's cultural communities: A diverse history, Calgary, Alberta, Canada, University of Calgary. https://doi.org/h4md

Chapter 16
Part II: Using Arctic and Northern Sources for Information and Archival Literacy and Research

Nadine Hoffman, Christena McKillop, and Regina Landwehr

Abstract This chapter explains case studies that demonstrate successful collaboration between librarians, archivists, and faculty in the use of Canadian Arctic and sub-Arctic primary and secondary sources dating from the 1600s through the early 2020s in support of learning and research at a large Canadian post-secondary university. These library and archival resources provide windows into the past and present through which students, faculty, and researchers can look in their explorations and understandings of the North. Materials are strategically selected from the Arctic and Northern Studies collections, most notably library and archival materials from the Arctic Institute of North America and the Glenbow Library and Archives collections, with the goal of incorporating hands-on learning opportunities that raise awareness of Canada's North. Student information and archival literacy experiences become more meaningful when primary and secondary source materials are used. When teaching elements are effectively combined in information and archival literacy sessions, primary and secondary sources from content-rich collections spark new understandings and research directions for students, faculty, and researchers.

Keywords Archival literacy · Archives · Arctic Institute of North America (AINA) · Glenbow · Information literacy · Libraries · Primary sources

---

N. Hoffman (✉) · C. McKillop · R. Landwehr
University of Calgary, Calgary, AB, Canada
e-mail: nadine.hoffman@ucalgary.ca; christena.mckillop@ucalgary.ca;
rlandweh@ucalgary.ca

© The Author(s), under exclusive license to Springer Nature
Switzerland AG 2024
S. Acadia (ed.), *Library and Information Sciences in Arctic and Northern Studies*, Springer Polar Sciences, https://doi.org/10.1007/978-3-031-54715-7_16

343

16.1 Introduction and Background

The University of Calgary is home to an abundant Arctic and Northern studies collection, including vast special collections, archival materials, and published library materials, most notably from the Arctic Institute of North America (AINA) and the Glenbow Library and Archives (Glenbow collections). The authors of the present chapter bring different professional backgrounds to their work and in their roles as archivist (Landwehr), history librarian (Hoffman), and engagement, learning, and outreach librarian (McKillop). This chapter investigates the process of incorporating physical and digitized primary and secondary materials from the Arctic and Northern collections into library instruction, archival literacy, and research. In doing so, we reflect on how instruction and assessment contributes to student primary and secondary source literacy skills, especially during the move to online teaching in 2020 due to the global COVID-19 pandemic. Examples are drawn from assignments and worksheets used for in-class exercises and assessment as well as feedback from faculty and students.

Librarians and archivists are excellent partners when collaborating with each other and faculty in the use of different types of primary and secondary sources for teaching, instruction, and reference. In this chapter, specific collaborations analysed are drawn from various Arctic-related collections across the converged Libraries and Cultural Resources (LCR) faculty at the University of Calgary as described in the previous chapter of this book, "Part I: Library and Archival Engagement and Outreach Programs Using Sources from the Arctic and Northern Regions." These collections contain a wealth of primary sources of rare and unique materials from and about Canada's North. Collegial partnerships are a key component of promoting the use of primary and secondary sources by students, faculty, and researchers at the university. Librarians, archivists, and staff work closely with archival, rare book, and circulating library resources related to the Arctic, creating opportunities for collections to be successfully incorporated into learning and research partnerships. To effectively collaborate for instruction opportunities in classes, librarians and archivists must understand each other's disciplinary strengths in a practical manner as approaches may differ. As Rees (1993, p. 187) states, "libraries and archives handle their materials in different ways, each methodology being driven by the unique nature of the materials." The collaborative process as described by us adds unique insights and perspectives.

16.1.1 Literacy Concepts and Definitions for Teaching and Instruction

To better understand instructional intersections for collaboration across different types of information professionals in libraries and archives, some terms must be defined. This section outlines a series of definitions that shapes the framework for our work as librarians and archivists.

16.1.1.1 Examples of Primary Sources

Examples, but not an exhaustive list, of *primary sources* including archival sources in all formats such as diaries, maps, correspondence, manuscripts, corporate records, photographs, monographs, artefacts, coins, artwork, government sources, data sources, legal documents, oral histories, artwork, poems, speeches, personal narratives, interviews, and newspapers.

16.1.1.2 Archival Materials

According to the Society of American Archivists (SAA), *archival materials* are constituted in *fonds*, the entire body of records of an organization, family, or individual that are created and accumulated as the result of an organic process reflecting the functions of the creator (SAA, 2022). Examples of fonds are the manuscripts of an author, along with their correspondence and contracts with the publisher, or the records of an organization over the period of its existence.

16.1.1.3 Library Instruction and Literacy

Many terms are used for library and archival instruction sessions in post-secondary institutions including teaching, instruction, and literacy. Teaching collaboration in post-secondary education is often called *co-teaching* or *team teaching*: "Co-teaching is somewhat inconsistently defined in the literature and may often be referred to as team teaching, although team teaching may also be used to define an arrangement whereby multiple instructors collaborate on class design but deliver instruction separately" (Medaille & Shannon, 2012, p. 134).

The common definition for *information literacy* comes from the Association of College and Research Libraries (ACRL) (2015, p. 8) Framework: "Information literacy is the set of integrated abilities encompassing the reflective discovery of information, the understanding of how information is produced and valued, and the use of information in creating new knowledge and participating ethically in communities of learning." Specifically related to instruction, information literacy "empowers individuals and helps them to become self-reliant, effective, efficient, and ethical users of information" (Grassian & Kaplowitz, 2010, p. 2429). The SAA (2018, p. 11) defines *literacy* in their guidelines as "competency, knowledge, or skills in a specified area. Literacy is not a binary state, but rather a spectrum of competence within the area. Primary source literacy, information literacy, digital literacy, and visual literacy are all relevant to working with primary sources." While primary source literacy intersects with other literacies, it is "the ability to interrogate evidence (documents, images, objects) for credibility, trustworthiness, and accuracy using sourcing contextualization, and corroboration" (Yakel & Malkmus, 2016, p. 10).

In its shortest form, *archival literacy* is defined as competence in or knowledge of archival terminology, organization, and reference tools (SAA, 2020). More specifically, Yakel and Torres (2003, p. 51) posit that archival literacy requires archival intelligence which is

> a researcher's knowledge of archival principles, practices, and institutions, such as the reasons underlying archival rules and procedures, how to develop search strategies to explore research questions, and an understanding of the relationship between primary sources and their surrogates. Our contention is that a researcher's archival intelligence is separate from his or her domain or subject knowledge. Furthermore, we assert that archival intelligence is different from artifactual literacy, or the ability to interpret and analyze primary sources. While related to domain knowledge and artifactual literacy, archival intelligence refers to knowledge about the environment in which the search for primary sources is being conducted, in this case, the archives.

Furthermore, as Carini (2016, p. 195) concludes: "If a person cannot contextualize and understand the actual materials, then it does not matter if he or she can find them. This area of knowledge has received less discussion within the professional literature than it deserves."

Embeddedness is a relatively new term for an established practice by all information professionals, including archivists. An embedded librarian

> supports this idea of the librarian as a collaborator in a variety of co-teaching relationships, from course design to participation in online courses. In fact, collaboration lies at the very core of embedded librarianship through librarians' work with instruction, research, distance learning, and scholarly communications on a multitude of levels. (Medaille & Shannon, 2012, p. 136)

Information professionals can be embedded into courses, programs, and learning management systems.

16.1.2   Arctic-Related Collections: A Brief History

The University of Calgary's Arctic collections primarily include materials from the AINA and Glenbow collections. Both collections contain unique and rare primary materials related to Canada's North from the 1600s through the early 2020s. The AINA archival and rare book collections and Glenbow collections are co-located with other archival and rare book collections in the Archives and Special Collections (ASC) unit in the University of Calgary's LCR. Researchers can view and use these materials through the Glenbow Western Research Centre (GWRC), a secure and climate-controlled reading room located in the Taylor Family Digital Library (TFDL). The circulating AINA collection is international in scope and includes all Arctic and Antarctic regions, most Arctic languages, and an extensive collection of historical and contemporary North American pipeline materials.

16 Part II: Using Arctic and Northern Sources for Information and Archival Literacy...

16.1.2.1 Arctic Institute of North America (AINA) Collections

As of 2014, the AINA collections are in four distinct locations, with some materials digitally available and accessible through open access repositories. For more information about these collections and how they came about, see our previous chapter, Part I, in this book.

When the collection arrived at the University of Calgary in 1976, "to make the collection more accessible, in addition to providing staff with updates of books received, the Northern Studies/Arctic Institute librarian Eric Tull spoke to undergraduate classes about the collection and other aids to northern research" (MacDonald, 2005, p. 27). Following Tull's retirement, instruction related to the circulating library collection transferred to librarians on the science team then transitioned to one of the authors (Hoffman) between 2016 and 2020. This long transition was due to the collection's technical interdisciplinary focus and physical location. Hoffman's background in natural resources, energy, and the environment contributed to the decision to be assigned collection responsibilities for Northern studies. Using materials from the circulating library collections was more difficult due to staffing changes, but a more recent period of stability now allows Hoffman to use the circulating library collection in teaching activities on a regular basis. A similar scenario for integrating the AINA archival and rare book collections in archival literacy sessions exists because of staff changes and assignments in the ASC over time.

One of the attractions of the AINA collections is its age. University students, faculty, and researchers at the university can view and work with archival materials from the early era of Arctic discovery and exploration while attending campus, a rare opportunity for most without needing to travel. The expansion of the AINA collections to include the AINA Pipeline Collection strengthens the circulating library collection with a strong interdisciplinary collection of federal, provincial, and state government documents, non-governmental and industry reports, and corporate documents related to pipelines largely located in Western Canada and the North American Arctic and sub-Arctic regions. With all these materials catalogued and available in the library's discovery system as of 2020 (P. Johnson, personal communication, 3 March 2020), additional resources to include in library instruction can help students find more primary source materials. Instruction sessions making use of the circulating library collection address research topics on pipeline development, transportation, contracts, and transboundary issues across the North American Arctic, sub-Arctic, and North-West Territories geographical regions. Relevant definitions for primary sources and the North-West Territories are found in our previous chapter, Part I, in this book. Course subjects include area studies (e.g., Canadian studies, gender studies, Indigenous studies, Northern studies, and strategic studies), anthropology, archaeology, art and art history, business, economics, engineering, English, environmental science, geosciences, history, international relations, law, political science, public policy, religious studies, as well as interdisciplinary programs such as the Arts and Sciences Honours Academy, energy management, law and society, science and technology, and sustainable energy development.

16.1.2.2 Glenbow Collections

The Glenbow Library and Archives (Glenbow collections) focuses on Western Canada, including the historical North-West Territories. These extensive collections of primary and secondary materials, originally part of the Glenbow Foundation in 1966, moved to the University of Calgary beginning in 2018 (Beauline-Stuebing, 2020). The collections include archival materials with private corporate records, published library materials from the 1800s through 2018, news clippings files from the late 1960s through 2018, and microformat serials publications. More information about these collections can be found in our previous chapter, Part I, in this book. The Glenbow collections are often consulted alongside the AINA archival and rare book collections due to the related nature of their content. The authors, along with their colleagues, recognize the value of each collection in their instruction and, therefore, anticipate including more content from across the Glenbow and AINA collections.

16.2 Collaboration and Co-teaching

Undergraduate education increasingly makes mainstream use of primary source material using literacy guidelines such as those developed through the ACRL and SAA. According to Djenno (2019, p. 18), "instructors often see this as a way to increase student engagement, to enrich course content, and to distinguish their teaching by fostering the knowledge creation and originality associated with using primary source material." Although the literacy definitions are similar for both organizations, access to library primary sources may be curated more often, thus being more selective. Library primary sources are organized differently compared to archival materials. Library primary sources do not typically require as much mediation as archival materials because they are often reproduced in publications with context or in separately curated databases. Djenno (2019, pp. 19–20) asserts that student understanding of experienced professionals who work with these materials "can go a long way toward relieving this pressure" of working with primary sources. However, Wakimoto (2017, p. 3) argues the differences between library and archival information professionals: "If there is no consensus or understanding of the perspectives and values that are held by the different professions about archives, this can make collaboration difficult." We mitigated our own potential differences through exercising mutual respect for each other's background collection knowledge and professional expertise to ensure the best experience for students undertaking their individual research projects.

Strategic collaboration between faculty and information professionals such as librarians, archivists, and curators make student information and archival literacy learning more meaningful when tied directly to course assignments. Rockenbach (2011) saw opportunities for archivists and librarians to partner with faculty and integrate collections into curricula or take the charge on their own. Librarians are historically involved with a wider range of faculty collaborations, but "librarians may also find it useful to cultivate co-teaching relationships with other librarians and information professionals" (Medaille & Shannon, 2012, pp. 132–133). Librarian and archivist collaboration can help "break down some of the barriers that can exist within a library" (Victor Jr. et al., 2013, p. 170).

Library and archives teaching collaboration makes literacy instruction effective and meaningful by combining archival resources with items from across library collections as it can "showcase our resources and support in a creative and engaging manner; our approach does not dwell on the mechanics of searching as much as the experience of working with materials online and in print" (Cotton & Sharron, 2011, p. 42). Librarians endeavour to show formats beyond books and journal articles while reminding students how to effectively find resources using digital subscriptions and physical collections. From the archival perspective, "collections are viewed as records of importance, historical and primary sources in many different formats" (Wakimoto, 2017, p. 11). When working collaboratively, we bridge the gap between various collections and formats so that students have fewer information and resource barriers to conduct their research.

Although we focus on teaching to our individual strengths and collections, collaborating over multiple classes allows library and archival literacy to intentionally reinforce lessons through integrating hands-on activities and lectures. When collaborating with faculty members, integrating important skills into the wider course objectives can ensure students learn both library and archival skills in a complementary fashion. Moreover, "the librarians and archivist may benefit from learning and applying new techniques within their areas of expertise" (Victor Jr. et al., 2013, p. 154). Medaille and Shannon (2012, p. 138) describe other benefits of librarians and archivists as co-teachers; it is "the opportunity to leverage the different skills of the co-instructors ... to create a unique experience for student learners using a variety of collections and sources." We learn about each other's collections, reference practices for referral purposes, and details on what students learn from the other's perspective, allowing mutual respect for colleagues' areas of focus and broadening respective knowledge bases.

To best integrate library and archival instruction into an individual course, especially beginner courses, instructors should include library instruction prior to archival instruction, be it in the same class or at different classes throughout the term. This process allows library instruction to introduce tertiary, secondary, and primary resources, leading to archival instruction that is focused on primary sources from within university-owned collections: "Secondary and primary resources build upon each other, but faculty see that students struggle to integrate these two resources" (Viars & Pellerin, 2017, p. 238). Collaboration between librarians and archivists who teach students ensures information and archival literacy skills increase students' familiarity with all types of research materials as suggested by Viars and Pellerin (2017, p. 284): "Collaboration among librarians, archivists, and faculty ensures students increase their familiarity with archival materials and develop information literacy skills." Students apply the skills they learn through hands-on activities with physical archival primary sources in addition to working with digitized resources commonly used through academic libraries: "The hands-on nature of archival resources can help students to apply frames from the ACRL Information Literacy Framework, such as understanding the construction and context of information creation and use" (Viars & Pellerin, 2017, p. 290).

Archival-library strategic collaboration allows students to learn from both perspectives; this is particularly effective for history students. On co-teaching information literacy, the student experience should begin with tertiary and secondary sources that lead them to find primary sources using print resources; databases to find books, articles, and documents; microformat materials; and digitized primary source collections. These library sources help determine where pertinent archival primary sources and rare books are located. Archival literacy classes work with the available primary source collections preferably and conveniently located in and owned by the resident campus archives. Teaching collaborations through these relationships also provide insight into developing research interests. Librarians help students discover hard-to-find and hidden resources while

> archivists act as guides through the access and instruction process. Library-archives partnerships make these resources visible through the collaborative cycle, which provides students with an improved skill set for information finding, and the confidence to navigate an increasingly complex twenty-first century information environment. (Viars & Pellerin, 2017, p. 290)

Furthermore, working with and learning from archivists and librarians ensures the best student experience and fosters research interests when realizing how archival materials are experienced by students toward tailoring literacy sessions and programs to diverse researchers (Wakimoto, 2017). This view is in line with our own teaching practice and instruction philosophy.

16.3   Course Case Studies

The librarian-archivist collaborations for the course Historical Studies (HTST) 300: The Practice of History began formally in 2018. As each new faculty member is slated to teach the course, Hoffman arranges a meeting of relevant librarians and archivists with the instructor because "it is important to touch base in person when planning an instruction session in order to make certain that the planned session still makes sense within the current reality of the course" (Djenno, 2019, pp. 20–21). Hoffman, the library's history liaison, coordinates the process by contacting the course faculty member as soon as they are assigned the course. As Djenno (2019, p. 21) further asserts, "there is a distinct possibility that clarity and assertiveness on the part of librarians and archivists would be welcomed by our instructional partners, and could become a highly beneficial professional norm." At the time of writing, seven faculty members for the course include both librarians and archivists as guests to provide library and archival literacy. Instructor-specific approaches to HTST 300 means offering flexible modalities (i.e., online synchronous; online asynchronous; and hands-on, in-person). We anticipate this approach to continue for the foreseeable future. However, whether the hands-on archival and library instruction components are offered in the course is dependent on the individual course instructor; they are not required by the history department as part of this course's curriculum.

16.3.1 Courses Prior to HTST 300

Past collaborations with the history department led to strong partnerships for the HTST 300 course where librarians and archivists were firmly integrated into the syllabus, regardless of who was teaching the course. One history faculty member teaching courses in Canadian history and Canadian studies routinely included a hands-on assignment requiring student visits to various archival and library units to use primary sources. The same course instructor also requested one-time instruction in the classroom, also known as 'one shots,' led by archivists or librarians, albeit most without opportunity for hands-on activities or in-class exercises. These courses were the precursors to the current mandatory HTST 300 course for history majors.

In these two precursor courses, students chose their research topics from a list of over one hundred suggestions, then completed the "Research Assignment Template and Sample Arguments" document created by the professor. Arctic-related topics included: "The Yukon, North-West Territories, and Nunavut should (not) be granted full provincial status," "Aboriginals should (not) be given full self-governance as a founding nation," "Canada should (not) take greater measures to enforce its sovereignty over the Arctic Ocean," "Nunavut should (not) be accepted into the federation as a fully-realized province," and "Every high school student in Canada should (not) learn about Canadian history" (P. Stortz, personal communication, 13 July 2022). The instructor's pedagogical intent was for students to physically visit most service desks and library branches and reflect on the process in an assignment before writing their research paper on the topic. Students began with secondary and tertiary sources such as indexes, encyclopaedias, dictionaries, directories, book reviews, novels, almanacs, biographies, theses, monographs, journal articles, magazine articles, and newspaper articles before moving on to primary sources. Primary source examples included government documents, legislation, minutes, legislative debates, brochures, pamphlets, rare books, manuscripts, photographs, maps, films, diaries, oral histories, corporate records, interviews, statistics, artwork, posters, speeches, newspapers, press releases, annual reports, musical scores, plays, novels, census material, atlases, and raw data.

16.3.2 HTST 300 Case Study

HTST 300: The Practice of History, first taught in the Winter 2013 term, is offered to upper-year students and is a required research methods course for all history majors at the University of Calgary. The course is offered at least three times per year with an enrolment cap of 50–60 students. The designated supervised and controlled classroom space for the ASC is limited to 30 students, thus necessitating two sessions to be held for archival literacy instruction. More than any other undergraduate course, HTST 300 emphasizes the importance of working with primary source materials and involves collaboration between the faculty member, librarians, and archivists to ensure students understand how to find appropriate resources for their assignments. Primary source materials from the AINA rare books and archival collections are regularly examined by students in the archival literacy class and considered by them for further research.

Individual instructors have different ways of approaching the course. Prior to our coordinated involvement in HTST 300, some instructors contacted an archivist or librarian separately to provide one-shot literacy sessions with follow up for individual student consultations. Starting in 2014, Landwehr planned and carried out archival literacy sessions for HTST 300 regularly due to ongoing instructor relationships. Since 2016, Hoffman actively engages with the history department by holding weekly office hours and maintaining regular e-mail communication, allowing Hoffman to be embedded into the course. Since Hoffman is responsible for delivering library instruction, active collaboration occurs with Landwehr and McKillop who joined ASC in 2018 for archival instruction. Together, the collaboration between Hoffman, Landwehr and McKillop allows for a stronger presence of both LCR units in the HTST 300 course. Regular meetings are held, and frequent communication occurs, between all involved parties before, during, and after the course, resulting in strong partnerships for coordinating and delivering library and archival instruction while continuing to meet the learning objectives of the course and the teaching goals of faculty. A memo outlining archival protocols and rules for the archival classroom, including what to bring (e.g., pencils, paper, and electronic devices) and what not to bring (e.g., pens, bags, food, and drinks), is distributed to students by instructors prior to class and Hoffman reiterates this in the first information literacy class. Hoffman highlights digital primary source collections and skills to evaluate the origin of primary sources alongside the terminology needed to search primary source collections. Annotated screen captures are provided following the class as an additional learning tool with step-by-step instructions, allowing students to apply the skills they learn when conducting their own research. Plus, Hoffman includes several take-aways for students. In a semi-flipped class modality, students are asked to view YouTube video tutorials prior to the class related to evaluating sources and publication types. In addition to providing annotated PowerPoint slides after the lecture, a handout of library databases is distributed via the course management system. This database handout contains a brief list of secondary source databases and a primary source database chart by vendor. For in-person and synchronous classes, the database handout is available for in-class exercises.

McKillop and Landwehr work collaboratively with Hoffman and the instructor for the HTST 300 course to ensure that appropriate content is responsive to both special subject interests and course requirements. Students are surveyed at the beginning of each class to determine if any have used primary sources or previously visited archives. Students in the course typically indicate that they have very little or no previous archival research experience, consistent with Malkmus' (2008, p. 61) findings: "Most students graduate with very limited experience in searching for their own sources, and they have almost no familiarity with archives and archival practices."

For the hands-on archival literacy portion of the course, Landwehr and McKillop consider the number of students who will examine primary materials because it has a direct bearing on the type and quantity of materials selected and retrieved. Selected materials for the class may be grouped by topic or individually set out for students throughout the archival classroom. Figure 16.1 shows an example of AINA archival and rare book materials for students to examine. The format for the class includes an introduction to the ASC, a lecture with discussion on what are archives and special collections, and how archival materials are structured. This approach provides students with a clearer understanding of the differences and similarities of libraries and archives, including explaining archival concepts, finding aids, researcher agreements, and safe handling protocols. Throughout the lecture and slides, connections are made to the content of the course syllabus and assignments, and to the relevant content covered in the information literacy class. After the archival literacy classes, the lecture slides and handouts are uploaded to the course management system to be accessible for review as needed.

Fig. 16.1 Undergraduate students learn about the rare and unique materials in the University of Calgary's Archives and Special Collections through in-person opportunities to examine selected items. (Photo credit: D. Brown, University of Calgary)

Table 16.1 Document analysis worksheet used when teaching primary source and archival literacy

Analysis steps	Analysis prompts
1. Meet the document	Describe it as you were explaining it to someone who cannot see it.
2. Observe its parts	Who wrote it? Who received it (who was the intended audience)? When and where is it from?
3. Try to make sense of it	What is it talking about? Write a sentence summarizing this document. Quote evidence from the document that tells you about something that was happening at the time in history when this document was created.
4. Use it as historical evidence	What did you find out from this document that you might not learn anywhere else? Give an example of another document or piece of historical evidence that you will use to help you understand this event or topic.

Table credit: N. Hoffman, C. McKillop, and R. Landwehr

Worksheets with guiding questions are created by Landwehr and McKillop and routinely used to provide focus and reinforce concepts discussed in the lecture portion of the classes. Completed worksheets may be collected at the end of the session and reviewed to examine how well concepts from the lecture were understood as well as which materials were examined most frequently. Students are also invited to keep blank worksheet copies for their future use. Based on these student responses, changes may be made to the lecture content, materials, or worksheet for the next session. Smith and McGillan (2020, p. 182) comment on a similar strategy used in their teaching practice at Mississippi State University that "this method of review and assessment works well for us and sets the stage for continued teaching success."

Students are introduced to the concepts of primary source literacy and archival literacy based on the ACRL and SAA frameworks mentioned earlier. These concepts are reflected in the worksheets used. The "Document Analysis Worksheet" and "Example Study Questions Worksheet" are two worksheets we use in the classroom. Prior to consulting the archival materials during the hands-on archival literacy class, the "Document Analysis Worksheet" (Table 16.1) outlines a set of general questions for students to consider. These questions are based on content from the National Archives Educator Resources (2022) and modified to the HTST 300 course. The "Example Study Questions Worksheet" (Table 16.2) focuses on information about the archival materials in the finding aid for the individual fonds, how the item or file fits within the organization of the fonds, the physical condition and any access restrictions for the items, and questions specific to the item being analysed including suggested approaches to the archival materials and associated archival finding aids during consultation. Following the archival literacy portion of the class, students consider topics and ideas to pursue for their research, then complete the worksheet. Over time, the worksheets evolved and incorporated instructional practice and pedagogy in the archival literacy sessions. Use of the SAA and ACRL

16 Part II: Using Arctic and Northern Sources for Information and Archival Literacy... 355

Table 16.2 Example study questions used when teaching primary source and archival literacy

Topic 1: Sir John Franklin's letter to Commissioner Sir Robert Barrie (1821)
Between 1819 and 1822, Franklin led an overland expedition from Hudson Bay to chart the north coast of Canada eastwards from the mouth of the Coppermine River during which he exchanged letters with Sir Robert Barrie, commissioner of the dockyard at Kingston, Upper Canada, and senior naval officer in the Canadas.
What is the date of the letter? How does it relate to Franklin's voyages to discover the north-west passage? What else does the letter tell you, for example about letter writing, postage, mail service? Was anything attached to the letter? Where was Franklin going?
Topic 2: USS *Jeannette* witness report from the disastrous polar expedition (1881)
In 1879–1881, a US-led expedition attempted to follow a temperate current northward to find a gateway to the open polar sea. The ship was caught in ice and drifted for 2 years before sinking. Of the 33-member crew, 20 members including the captain died while attempting to navigate in small boats to the Siberian coast.
Would the unidentified author have been a regular member of the crew or one of the senior officers? Why was the report written? What could be the reasons for the sections glued over with paper patches?
Topic 3: Holographic report by Captain Sir Alfred Hastings Markham aboard the HMS *Alert* (1886)
The report details the voyage of the ship which left Halifax on June 22, 1886, giving descriptions of the conditions in Hudson's strait, including weather, ice flows and the navigability of the passage. Compare Markham's manuscript report with the government published report (sessional papers) of the commanding officer Lieutenant A.R. Gordon and the report Markham later gave to the Royal Geographic Society.
Who was the audience in each of the two cases? What position did Markam have/what role? Did the commanding structure impact on reporting? Why was the report on ice conditions so carefully scrutinized?
Topic 4: Medical reports by Lewis E.C. Davies (1956–1960)
A medical officer of the federal government of Canada, Dr. Davies assessed the health and living conditions of Inuit between 1956 and 1960 under the government's resettlement programs.
What is the tone of the captions of the photographs showing individuals being examined? What intentions were referenced in the medical report for the health assessment? What clothing types do you see and what would their purpose be?

Table credit: N. Hoffman, C. McKillop, and R. Landwehr

frameworks provides the basis for standardized understanding and adds authority and credibility to the exercises. As Roussain (2020, p. 90) states, "asking students to learn literacies through critical thinking requires a pedagogical approach suited to having students explore and interpret primary sources independently, ask questions, interact and play with archival theory, and formulate solutions to perceived problems."

Importantly, the *History Student's Handbook* (Department of History, 2022) and the HTST 300 course syllabus allow for the incorporation of several archival concepts into the worksheet. When combined with the archival literacy concepts discussed earlier, the worksheets are an effective learning tool. Malkmus (2008, p. 61) also notes that "archivists and faculty share the goal of helping students learn the next level of research skills—searching, selecting, and evaluating primary sources—whether online or onsite in a repository," and the Practice of History course stresses these skills and, thus, is an appropriate venue for incorporating information and archival literacy concepts in instruction. In some HTST 300 classes, instructors include the completion of a worksheet in their student assessment.

16.3.3 History of Energy Course Brief Case Example

The positive teaching partnership just described for the HTST 300 course provides the framework for collaborations between librarians and archivists in other courses at the University of Calgary. One such example was in the Fall 2021 term when Hoffman partnered with the Glenbow librarian and the Glenbow archivist to co-teach the History of Energy course following a specific instructor request. This partnership followed a typical one-shot library session to help students prepare for their digital group presentation. Student research projects were related to the 75th anniversary of the Leduc oil find on 13 February 1947 (Imperial Oil Company, 1948) in a geographic area adjacent to the sub-Arctic region in Alberta, Canada, marking the birth of the Alberta oil industry (Kerr, 1991). Because the Glenbow collections contain the Imperial Oil corporate fonds, this collaboration was a good match and also led to a physical display in the GWRC for the February 2022 anniversary, highlighting the Imperial Oil fonds from the Glenbow collections.

16.3.4 History Programs Brief Case Example

The above case studies relate to specific courses, but all the Glenbow and AINA collections are often used as examples by Hoffman to help student research in the history honours and history graduate programs at the University of Calgary. For example, Fig. 16.2 shows some students examining materials from the ASC collections. Sometimes, primary source research leads students into more substantial research projects and many individual students choose to research Canadian history relating to the North-West Territories for their thesis. Examples shared with us include two notable honours thesis research examples since 2016: the first relates to historical health services offered to Inuit peoples across the Yukon Territory, Western North-West Territories, and Alberta, and the second involves a case study of the federally protected spaces under the *Rocky Mountains Park of Canada Act* (1887) and *The National Parks Act* (1930) including a history of the Banff National Park's relation to tourism and economic development, Lake Louise, the Alpine Club of Canada and Canadian National Parks Association, and protection of bison herds in the Wood Buffalo National Park.

Fig. 16.2 Students in the Archives and Special Collections classroom examine a selection of items from the University of Calgary's Archives and Special Collections. (Photo credit: D. Brown, University of Calgary)

16.3.5 Law Programs Brief Case Example

Until 2020, all students in the law graduate programs focused on natural resources, energy, or environmental law. Many students made use of the AINA collections with more concentration on the circulating library materials related to Canadian natural resources industries (e.g., water, forestry, fisheries, mining, oil and gas, and public lands), pipeline regulation and development, sustainable development, climate change, and international law related to the geographic regions encompassing the regions of the Arctic, sub-Arctic, or North-West Territories. Students benefited from the scientific and energy focus of the historical AINA circulating library collection and the AINA Pipeline Collection materials, as well as ongoing collection development work to acquire new circulating library materials to support the Northern Studies program.

16.3.6 Feedback Following Teaching with Primary Sources

Students and faculty comment favourably on the content, as well as the range and scope, of materials selected for examination. As many students have not previously worked with primary sources, the HTST 300 library and archival classes are often their first experience with them. The age of the materials, fragility, and historical nature of the materials result in hesitancy by some students to begin the examination

Fig. 16.3 The steamship *Diana* under the command of William Wakeham in 1897. The ship was used in the expedition to Hudson Bay and Cumberland Gulf in northern Canada. (Photo credit: AINA collection, 32.85.M34, Archives and Special Collections, University of Calgary)

process as they feel overwhelmed and intimidated. This sentiment is in line with Mazak and Manista's (2008, p. 228) declaration that "some students (also) find intimidating the closed off rooms of an archives or special collections department and the rules and regulations within." Students also often comment on the original handwriting on documents as well as visible marks (e.g., ink blots and unidentifiable discolorations) they notice. These observations contribute to lively discussions among students, demonstrating active engagement with the materials. Depictions address changes in technology and equipment in various ways such as in old photographs; an example is the 1897 photograph of the steamship *Diana* under the command of William Wakeham (1844–1915) on his Arctic exploration (Fig. 16.3), depicting the transition from sail to steam-powered technology of vessel propulsion.

Anecdotal student feedback about the HTST 300 library and archival literacy classes provides commentary on the opportunity to examine materials, often ranging from being out of their comfort zone and invoking curiosity to describing the lectures as informative and insightful. The richness of the AINA collections make classes interesting to students while providing them a wide range of topics, formats, and time periods to investigate further. One history honours student decided to enrol in the program following their archival literacy session and research in the HTST 300 course in 2015. The student's thesis topic related to tuberculosis treatment of Inuit peoples in the Canadian Arctic and the student used primary sources from the AINA circulating collection, AINA archival and rare book collections, Glenbow collections, and various historical and contemporary provincial and federal government documents. This work led to one book chapter and at least three conference presentations (B. Sasges, personal communication, 30 May 2022). Also, following the History of Energy class assignment related to the Leduc oil find, one student received a Program for Undergraduate Research Experience (PURE) Award to research the history of hydropower in the city of Calgary. This student's work will contribute to an energy history map of Calgary as part of the *Calgary Atlas Project* (2022) of the Calgary Institute for the Humanities (P. Dolata, personal communication, 13 April 2022) anticipated in 2024.

Victor Jr. et al. (2013, p. 158) notes that "the archives and special collections is an important part of university libraries. However, they are often an underutilized resource because they tend to be isolated from the rest of the library." Yet, via these case studies, and despite Wakimoto's assertion that "archivists and librarians are seen to have different work" (Wakimoto, 2017, p. 11), the trio of Hoffman, Landwehr, and McKillop have been successful in increasing the visibility and use of primary source materials by students at the University of Calgary while at the same time bridging the gaps between 'library work' and 'archives work.'

16.4 The Move to Online Teaching During COVID-19

The March 2020 stay-at-home order declaration by the World Health Organization caused profound changes around the world and required classes at the University of Calgary to move online. Libraries and archives also changed their service delivery model. As a result, LCR moved information and archival literacy instruction services online to support students, faculty, and researchers remotely: "The University of Calgary rapidly expanded its digital teaching, learning, and research in the weeks and months" (Murphy et al., 2021, p. 1).

16.4.1 Using Existing Digitized Primary Source Collections and Databases

The University of Calgary is a leader in digitizing primary source collections (LCR, n.d.). Initial digitization collection projects launched in October 2002 under the Canadian Initiative on Digital Libraries, a partnership of 20 libraries with initial funding from the Canadian Heritage Content Online Program over five years and hosted in partnership by Information Resources, the predecessor to LCR, at the University of Calgary and Laval University Library to provide digital access to primary sources (Hinks, 2007; Westell, 2009). The project *Our Roots* and *Our Future, Our Past: Alberta Heritage Digitization Project* are the first digitization projects and include the following collections: Alberta Law Collection, comprising primary legal materials for Alberta and the North-West Territories to 1992; Early Alberta Newspapers; Local Histories; art from the Nickle Arts Museum, predecessor to the Nickle Galleries; Medical History; and various oral histories and photographs. These resources were readily available for online use prior to 2020.

Pivoting to the online instructional modality was faster for information literacy than for archival literacy sessions. Integrated library and discovery systems are, and have been, ubiquitous and prevalent for decades. Institution-specific, as well as networks of archival finding aid databases across Canada, the United States, and Europe have existed for a while, providing the use of digitized archival material for decades. Discovery systems now enable harvesting of metadata content from archival resource databases in addition to library and other electronic resources. Since 2021, enhancing the discoverability of ASC archival holdings in LCR's library discovery system is underway by addition of enhanced records. Additionally, for information literacy, many library database subscriptions, including for primary sources, already existed at the time of the mandated work-from-home order. As early as 2017, LCR's Collections unit began acquiring a significant number of online databases as additions to existing electronic holdings; prior to this time, many of our primary source collections existed only on microformats. This process began with 33 databases as part of Gale Primary Sources, later expanding to approximately 250 primary source databases from ProQuest through a multi-year arrangement in 2019. Search interfaces we use also include Adam Matthew, Alexander Street Press, ReadEx, HeinOnline, and EBSCOhost. At the start of the pandemic, the university library offered over 325 primary source database subscriptions with over 80 additional primary source databases purchased during the pandemic and in addition to published journal and back files of book titles (R. Tiessen & H. D'Amour, personal communication, 10 June 2022). Wakimoto (2017, p. 9) aptly describes the service potential for online resources: "Online venues also provide means of publicity and meeting people anytime as online collections are available even when physical reading rooms are closed. Librarians and archivists are seen as different, but related in providing access to information." Service pivots were different across LCR units as the TFDL remained open with reduced services while the GWRC and Nickle Galleries were forced to close temporarily, but continued offering some assistance by directing researchers to the existing digital collections created by the library and adding new digital copies of materials upon request by users.

Existing digital collections were key to the successful move to online teaching and research services during the COVID-19 pandemic as online resources were used throughout our information and archival literacy sessions. While researchers were experiencing restrictions due to COVID-19, necessitating virtual consultations of primary source materials to conduct their research, usage of the Arctic and Northern Studies digital collection was high. Of note is the annual reporting period for accessing digital collections: From September 2019 to September 2020, the Arctic and Northern Studies digital collection had the highest activity of access when compared to the 48 digital collections offered by the library; this is impressive due to the collection's relatively small size. At the same time, the inability to closely examine materials and engage with them physically was a limitation. Nonetheless, as Wakimoto (2017, p. 7) understands:

> digitization is viewed as a means of access, and possibly preservation, but researchers find physical objects to be superior to digital ones. However, online access points are seen as critical to archival effectiveness and to increasing visibility. Librarians and archivists are seen as having the same goals of helping people access information and increasing awareness of the archives.

Once the GWRC reopened its doors by appointment in Fall 2021, bookings for in-person access to archival and special collections were steady. Our collaborative practice during the turbulent and challenging period of constant class format changes during the 2021–2022 academic year enabled us to meet new challenges with positive outcomes throughout pandemic times.

16.4.2   Library and Archival Literacy

In the Winter 2020 semester, the HTST 300 course was the last in-person class to be taught in the TFDL classrooms prior to the campus-wide decision to move all classes online due to the pandemic. Hoffman and McKillop immediately pivoted to grade in-class exercises and provide virtual feedback to the instructor regarding student assessment. Our in-person information and archival literacy sessions included lectures, the slides of which were repurposed and edited to meet the needs of both synchronous and asynchronous online tutorials. The slides were also made available to students via the course management system.

As the pandemic continued, one instructor moved to a fully asynchronous modality and the University of Calgary continued with online learning for the Spring 2020 and Summer 2020 semesters. For the first time, HTST 300 was offered in both of those semesters as a fully asynchronous offering. The asynchronous option was challenging due to the recording technology as well as determining appropriate archival and library examples without completely recreating the literacy sessions. Hoffman and McKillop created narrated slides to be posted by the instructor in the course management system. Moreover, some of the slide content can be reused in future semesters without having to completely redo subsequent recordings. However, when the course is offered asynchronously, the structure of the course content results in minimal opportunities for students to interact with primary source materials; this means a diminished role for library and archival literacy, lack of opportunities for librarians and archivists to directly engage with students through hands-on, in-class exercises, and few students following up despite contact information included in the tutorials.

The COVID-19 pandemic continued in Canada through the Fall 2020 semester and the University of Calgary moved most classes online, including HTST 300. The faculty member teaching the course that semester was keen to deliver the course synchronously, inviting Hoffman and McKillop to discuss how literacy instruction with high student engagement could be delivered online to students. The instructor also incorporated library and archival in-class exercises into student assessment. We created a simple grading rubric with the categories of *unsatisfactory*, *satisfactory*, *good*, and *excellent* based on the quality and depth of student responses. We also created a spreadsheet to provide consistent feedback for the instructor when assigning student grades. The synchronous model, while not the same as the in-person instruction modality, worked well because student questions could be addressed, and discussion could occur, in real time.

In-person classes resumed at the end of February 2022, part-way through the Winter semester. Hoffman and Landwehr worked with a different HTST 300 instructor to offer in-person literacy sessions following the Reading Week term break; this was the first in-person class in the TFDL following the mandated work-from-home period. During this class, we intentionally incorporated the course's assigned teaching assistant (TA). TAs are graduate students who can be integrated into archival and information literacy classes by encouraging and offering opportunities for small group study outside regular class time. TAs have been present in earlier iterations of this course, but in this instance the graded assignment we created benefitted more directly from the TA who was grading the assignment. This TA also had knowledge of archival materials held in the ASC from their own research.

16.4.2.1 Online Library Literacy

Teaching how to effectively search library primary source databases must include a discussion about terminology and the need to strategically use the language of the corresponding time and place. Searching also must include concepts related to full text, as opposed to using an index. Hoffman's (2021) study, for instance, offers a useful Arctic-related example of the importance of terminology, especially as it involves searching for database content associated with Indigenous Arctic peoples. Students can easily fall into the 'primary sources trap' when beginning their research using primary source databases; this often occurs when instructors require using a minimum number of primary sources for a research assignment. Students often start looking for primary sources without knowing sufficient information about their research topic because they are more accustomed to finding and using secondary sources that provide scholarly analysis and do not realize the accompanying citations can lead them to locate appropriate primary sources more easily.

Throughout all information literacy sessions, Hoffman regularly reiterates the recommended practice of starting with secondary and tertiary sources to find the most relevant primary sources; however, when being exposed to primary sources during in-class literacy sessions, we provide students with background information for each item discussed or provided. For instance, students are encouraged through a literature search of secondary sources to study creator biographies of a given example, including from where it originates as well as the geographic association to historic events and other relevant individuals. A similar issue in using library primary source databases was discussed when Hoffman and Landwehr, along with the instructor, were preparing for the HTST 300 course in Winter 2022. The instructor specifically asserted that databases and websites containing digital versions of archival primary source documents are 'curated collections' and students must be made aware of potential pitfalls because these resources tend to have little context and often omit important related documents. Hoffman was specifically asked to address this potential discrepancy for student awareness during the second information literacy class. Similarly, Landwehr used this opportunity to draw comparisons between the university-owned digital collections of digitized archival materials from its own collections and commercial databases of primary sources to show how to evaluate and contextualize information associated with digital objects.

16.4.2.2 Online Archival Literacy

Archival arrangement concepts and descriptions can be taught through virtual treasure hunts that are part of synchronous online class delivery. At the University of Calgary, these hunts involve an archivist who provides a set of clues about a range of archival materials, including selections from the AINA archival and rare book collections, for students to find in both the university's archival access system of descriptions and the discovery system for university-owned digital collections. Students also answer specific questions from a worksheet aimed to build source evaluation skills. When classes were moved online, a shift from the in-person examination of materials to examining images from the digital collections was made. Five digital images were selected to represent different time periods in Canadian history, one of which was from the AINA archival and rare book collections: the Sir John Franklin holographic correspondence. Of the possible images for students to choose for their in-class exercise, the Franklin letters were the second most popular. Use of break-out rooms in the virtual classroom environment proved to be a fruitful opportunity to instruct small groups of students to virtually familiarize themselves with both the archival access and discovery systems. Overall, the students' experience was positive. Anecdotally, one student noted that the class was a window to learning something new about a perspective or topic in Canadian history, while many others commented they would consider consulting archival primary sources in the future. When McKillop and Landwehr included an assignment, student engagement with the materials increased as new archival literacy skills were put into practice, boosting the level of student satisfaction.

Demonstrating the use and purpose of metadata attached to each discrete digital object, pointing to the online archival finding aid for the fonds in which the object belongs, and emphasizing searchability are important learning objectives. In the context of the AINA archival and rare book collections, this learning goal is part of Landwehr's teaching pedagogy and practice. All digitized materials, from local archival or rare book collections or through library databases, represent a carefully curated selection that may create the false impression of completeness or comprehensiveness. An example of advantages to digitized primary sources include better full text searchability in textual documents using optical character recognition.

16.5 Reflections and Conclusion

Using Arctic and Northern primary sources for information and archival literacy instruction contributes to powerful learning experiences for students and creates opportunities for further research. The breadth and depth of all the unique and rich materials from the AINA and Glenbow collections are effectively used in the classroom and introduce new research opportunities. Strategic collaborations between librarians and archivists build strong relationships with faculty to become valued partners for delivery of course content to students, including student assessment via graded assignments.

Information and archival literacy can be successfully integrated into courses and align with the value and pedagogy of teaching research skills when librarians and archivists are invited to participate. Drawing from authoritative literacy frameworks, such as those developed by the ACRL and SAA, adds a formalized structure to learning research skills content. The HTST 300: Practice of History course, as well as the other courses and programs described in this chapter, describe real-life cases where Hoffman, McKillop, and Landwehr teach research and literacy skills. Indeed, the courses and programs mentioned in this chapter allow us to selectively draw upon AINA and Glenbow collections content. HTST 300 is especially suitable for providing important and rare opportunities for students to work closely with unique materials from these Arctic-related collections, and is a continued area for further investigation at the University of Calgary. When librarians and archivists create assignments and in-class exercises, whether graded or not, they can be valuable assessment tools to generate useful feedback from both students and faculty to improve information and archival literacy sessions. Not only have the students and faculty provided positive feedback after such literacy sessions, but new research has emerged from exposure to these Arctic-related primary source collections. The hands-on experience for students enrolled in the in-person classes is much different from those examining the digitized content in the online-only environment. Examining how instruction spaces and instructional design differ between in-person and online-only modalities for the most effective learning is an emerging area of investigation for us.

The COVID-19 pandemic forced instruction to move online, quickly resulting in new demands. However, many of LCR's services and resources were already in place to facilitate this transition. Additional digital content added during the pandemic contributed to a more robust online collection. However, challenges remain in the provision of instruction modalities for both in-person and online classes. Because faculty preference for course delivery modality directly impacts opportunities for librarian and archivist participation, it remains difficult to routinely plan for library and archival instruction for the HTST 300 course despite our positive collegial relationships with the Department of History.

Primary source materials are a boon for history students to learn and practice historical crafts. Arctic-related materials throughout LCR's collections lend themselves to be included in library and archival instruction. The wide range of primary and secondary sources from across these collections provide students and researchers with rare and unique materials to consult. When combined with faculty support, collaborative partnerships between librarians and archivists create meaningful connections to collections, expand access of those collections to students and researchers, and boost the visibility of these collections. We anticipate including all types and formats of these materials in future literacy sessions. Strategically selecting primary source materials to incorporate into class instruction, such as those from the AINA and Glenbow collections, are an effective way to raise awareness about Canada's North.

Finally, we hope other archivists and librarians working at universities with Arctic and Northern collections will be inspired by this chapter to embark on and publish results of similar case studies from their own institutions. More published examples are needed from librarians and archivists using Arctic and Northern materials in their information and archival literacy instruction.

References

Association of College and Research Libraries (ACRL). (2015). *Framework for information literacy for higher education*. https://bit.ly/3jo5vLf. Accessed 12 Dec 2023.

Beauline-Stuebing, L. (2020, October 26). U of Calgary offers a new state-of-the-art home for a massive collection of Western Canadian history. University Affairs/Affaires universitaires. https://bit.ly/3bQJile. Accessed 12 Dec 2023.

Calgary Atlas Project, Canadian Institute for the Humanities, University of Calgary. (2022). *About the Calgary Atlas Project*. https://bit.ly/3hU7LcP. Accessed 12 Dec 2023.

Carini, P. (2016). Information literacy for archives and special collections: Defining outcomes. *Portal: Libraries and the Academy, 16*(1), 191–206. https://doi.org/gq9wv5

Cotton, J., & Sharron, D. (2011). *Engaging students with archival and digital resources*. Chandos.

Department of History, University of Calgary. (2022). *History student's handbook*. https://bit.ly/3veDvMG. Accessed 12 Dec 2023.

Djenno, M. (2019). Scaffolding the collection manager-instructor relationship: Partnerships for primary source instruction. *College and Research Libraries News, 80*(1), 18–21. https://doi.org/gfsv2f

Grassian, E. S., & Kaplowitz, J. R. (2010). Information literacy instruction. In M. J. Bates & M. N. Maack (Eds.), *Encyclopedia of library and information sciences* (Vol. 3, 3rd ed., pp. 2429–2444). CRC.

Hinks, Y. (2007). *A timeline of the history of the University of Calgary library and information resources, 1906–2007*. https://doi.org/k8ht

Hoffman, N. (2021). Controlled vocabulary and Indigenous terminology in Canadian Arctic legal research. In S. Acadia & M. T. Fjellestad (Eds.), *Library and information studies for Arctic social sciences and humanities* (pp. 110–132). Routledge.

Imperial Oil Company. (1948). *A mile below the wheat* [Motion picture]. Crawley Films.

Kerr, A. (1991). *Leduc*. S. A. Kerr.

Libraries and Cultural Resources, University of Calgary. (n.d.). *Community report: 2019/2020/2021*. https://bit.ly/3GiNgQr. Accessed 12 Dec 2023.

MacDonald, R. (2005). Challenges and accomplishments: A celebration of the Arctic Institute of North America. *Arctic, 58*(4), 440–451. https://bit.ly/3jvUwzC. Accessed 12 Dec 2023.

Malkmus, D. J. (2008). Primary source research and the undergraduate: A transforming landscape. *Journal of Archival Organization, 6*(1/2), 47–70. https://doi.org/fwhhxs

Mazak, J., & Manista, F. (2008). Collaborative learning: University archives and freshman composition. *Reference Librarian, 32*(67/68), 225–242. https://doi.org/dp8k8d

Medaille, A., & Shannon, A. W. (2012). Co-teaching relationships among librarians and other information professionals. *Collaborative Librarianship, 4*(4), 132–148. https://doi.org/jq8f

Murphy, J. E., Lewis, C. J., McKillop, C. A., & Stoeckle, M. (2021). Expanding digital academic library and archive services at the University of Calgary in response to the COVID-19 pandemic. *IFLA Journal, 48*(1), 83–98. https://doi.org/gmkc6q

National Archives. (2022). *Educator resources: Document analysis.* https://bit.ly/3hP1kb3. Accessed 12 Dec 2023.

National Parks Act, SC 1930 (20–21 Geo 5), c 33. https://bit.ly/3BZZHhz. Accessed 12 Dec 2023.

Rees, A. L. (1993). Glenbow Archives, 1966–2016: A history of design and circumstance. *Archivaria, 35* (Spring), 175–189. https://bit.ly/3uANwEj. Accessed 12 Dec 2023.

Rockenbach, B. (2011). Archives, undergraduates, and inquiry-based learning: Case studies from Yale University library. *The American Archivist, 74*(1), 297–311. https://doi.org/gj77r6

Rocky Mountains Park of Canada Act, S Prov C 1887 (50–51 Vict), c 32. https://bit.ly/3jybcXi. Accessed 12 Dec 2023.

Roussain, J. (2020). Pedagogue in the archive: Reorienting the archivist as educator. *Archivaria, 90*, 70–111. https://bit.ly/3PTFJLh. Accessed 12 Dec 2023.

Smith, J. P., & McGillan, J. (2020). Towards a more collaborative experience: Connecting library and departmental faculty to improve and expand archival instruction. *Journal of Map and Geography Libraries, 15*(2/3), 173–186. https://doi.org/gpcc8g

Society of American Archivists (SAA). (2018). *Guidelines for primary source literacy.* https://bit.ly/3GiNIy7. Accessed 12 Dec 2023.

Society of American Archivists (SAA). (2022). *Fonds.* https://bit.ly/3veCNiv. Accessed 12 Dec 2023.

Viars, K. E., & Pellerin, A. G. (2017). Collaboration in the midst of change: Growing librarian-archivist partnerships for engaging new students and faculty. *Collaborative Librarianship, 9*(4), 281–292. https://bit.ly/3PTAV8n. Accessed 12 Dec 2023.

Victor, Jr., P., Otto, J., & Mutschler, C. (2013). Assessment of library instruction on undergraduate student success in a documents-based research course: The benefits of librarian, archivist, and faculty collaboration. *Collaborative Librarianship, 5*(3), 154–176. https://doi.org/jq8g

Wakimoto, D. K. (2017). Collections, connections, and change: Differences in experiencing archives. *Library Review, 66*(1/2), 2–15. https://doi.org/jq8h

Westell, M. E. (2009, May 31). Bringing local history to life on the web*: Digital collections* [Conference presentation]. Alberta's cultural communities: A diverse history, Calgary, Alberta, Canada. University of Calgary. https://doi.org/h4md

Yakel, E., & Malkmus, D. (2016). Module 9: Contextualizing archival literacy. In C. J. Prom & L. J. Hinchliffe (Eds.), *Teaching with primary sources* (pp. 5–67). Society of American Archivists.

Yakel, E., & Torres, D. (2003). AI: Archival intelligence and user expertise. *The American Archivist 66*(1), 51–78. https://doi.org/jq8j

Printed and bound by CPI Group (UK) Ltd, Croydon, CR0 4YY
03/12/2024
01799305-0010